D0341899

Strategies: Building on your Best for Career Success

Sixth Custom Edition

Taken from:

Go! with Microsoft® Office 2010, Volume 1, Second Edition
by Shelley Gaskin, Robert L. Ferrett, Alicia Vargas,
and Carolyn McLellan

Cornerstone: Building on Your Best for Career Success
by Robert M. Sherfield, Rhonda J. Montgomery,
and Patricia G. Moody

Cornerstone: Building on Your Best, Fourth Edition
by Robert M. Sherfield, Rhonda J. Montgomery,
and Patricia G. Moody

*Keys to Success: Building Successful Intelligence
for College, Career, and Life*, Brief Fourth Edition
by Carol Carter, Joyce Bishop,
and Sarah Lyman Kravits

Strategies for Active Citizenship
by Kateri M. Drexler and Gwen Garcelon

Cover Art: Courtesy of Fotolia.com/mipan

Taken from:

Go! with Microsoft® Office 2010, Volume 1, Second Edition
by Shelley Gaskin, Robert L. Ferrett, Alicia Vargas, and Carolyn McLellan
Copyright © 2013 by Pearson Education, Inc.
Published by Pearson Education, Inc.
Upper Saddle River, New Jersey 07458

Cornerstone: Building on Your Best for Career Success
by Robert M. Sherfield, Rhonda J. Montgomery, and Patricia G. Moody
Copyright © 2006 by Pearson Education, Inc.
Published by Prentice Hall

Cornerstone: Building on Your Best, Fourth Edition
by Robert M. Sherfield, Rhonda J. Montgomery, and Patricia G. Moody
Copyright © 2005, 2002, 2000, 1997 by Pearson Education, Inc.
Published by Prentice Hall

Keys to Success: Building Successful Intelligence for College, Career, and Life, Brief Fourth Edition
by Carol Carter, Joyce Bishop, and Sarah Lyman Kravits
Copyright © 2006, 2003, 2001, 1999 by Pearson Education, Inc.
Published by Prentice Hall

Strategies for Active Citizenship
by Kateri M. Drexler and Gwen Garcelon
Copyright © 2005 by Pearson Education
Published by Prentice Hall

Pearson Learning Solutions, 501 Boylston Street, Suite 900, Boston, MA 02116
A Pearson Education Company
www.pearsoned.com

Printed in the United States of America

1 2 3 4 5 6 7 8 9 10 V011 17 16 15 14 13

000200010271741359

JH/CM

ISBN 10: 1-256-99344-1
ISBN 13: 978-1-256-99344-5

Contents

PART 1
Strategies: Building on Your Best for Career Success

CHAPTER FOUR | Critical Thinking and Citing Sources 75

CHAPTER FIVE | Time Management and Teamwork 87

CHAPTER SIX | Managing Team Projects 111

CHAPTER SEVEN | Changes in the Workplace: Present and Future 119

INDEX 125

PART II

Taken from: *Go! with Microsoft® Office 2010, Volume 1*, Second Edition by Shelley Gaskin, Robert L. Ferrett, Alicia Vargas, and Carolyn McLellan

Common Features

CHAPTER ONE | Common Features of Microsoft Office 2010   135

Word

CHAPTER ONE | Creating Documents with Microsoft Word 2010   183

CHAPTER TWO | Using Tables and Templates to Create Resumes and Cover Letters   227

CHAPTER THREE | Creating Research Papers, Newsletters, and Merged Mailing Labels   271

Excel

CHAPTER ONE | Creating a Worksheet and Charting Data   311

Access

PowerPoint

CHAPTER ONE | Getting Started with Microsoft Office PowerPoint   521

CHAPTER TWO | Formatting PowerPoint Presentations   583

CHAPTER THREE | Enhancing a Presentation with Animation, Video, Tables, and Charts   643

Index   I-1

You can do it!

Portal to success

A portal is a grand and magnificent entrance into a new world. By becoming part of the ITT Technical Institute family, you have chosen to enter a portal that will lead you into a new career and different way of life. In your lifetime you will undoubtedly experience many events that can alter your views, personality, goals, and livelihood. Few decisions, however, will have as great an influence on the rest of your life as your decision to attend ITT Tech. This course, placed at the beginning of your educational journey, is the portal not only to your career but also to the rest of your life. Today you will begin preparing for the many opportunities that lie ahead. Regardless of what you might have experienced in the past—good or bad—you are entering a new era that will bring many exciting opportunities and challenges. Soon you will begin to understand yourself better and how you can realize your true potential.

Your golden potential

Have you ever thought of yourself as "golden"? More importantly, have you ever treated yourself as if you were "golden"? Consider the following true story as you begin your journey into your new career and life:

In 1957, a massive statue of Buddha was being moved from a temple in Thailand that had been abandoned in the early 1930's. The Buddha stands over 15 feet tall and measures over 12 feet in diameter. A crane had to be used to move the massive statue; but when the crane began to lift the Buddha, the weight was so great that the statue began to crack. To make matters worse, it began to rain. Concerned with the condition of the Buddha, the head monk decided to have the statue lowered so that it could be covered with a canvas until the rain stopped.

As nightfall came, the head monk took his flashlight outside to peer under the canvas to see whether the statue had begun to dry. As he moved the light from area to area, he noticed something shining in one of the cracks. He began to wonder whether something was under the clay. As he hammered and chiseled away at the crack, he found that the clay Buddha was NOT made of clay after all. The monk found that the 15-foot statue was really made of pure, 18-carat GOLD.

Many scholars and historians believe that the Buddha was cast sometime in the mid-1200's. According to one theory, in the 1700's the Siamese monks knew that the Burmese army planned to attack them and, hoping to protect their statue, they covered it in eight inches of clay, which dried and hardened like concrete. When the army attacked, all of the monks in the village were killed, leaving no one who knew the truth about the Buddha. The clay remained intact until the statue was moved on a rainy day in 1957.

Today, the Golden Buddha, which was once covered with clay and abandoned, is said to be valued at almost two hundred million dollars.

Excerpts taken from: *Cornerstone: Discovering Your Potential Learning Activity and Living Well,* Fourth Edition by Robert M. Sherfield, Rhonda J. Montgomery, and Patricia G. Moody.

YES You Can!

Your golden opportunity

We all have incredible talents, skills, and experiences that are all too often covered or underdeveloped. We move through life hiding our brightness—our golden self. As you begin to read and work through this text, think about the strengths and talents that you already have and how you can polish them and bring out their brilliance. Begin to chip away at the clay that may have been covering your true potential for years. Explore who you really are, what you have to offer to the world, and how best to live up to your golden potential. Think about the attitudes, beliefs, or behaviors that you may have to adjust to create your future success.

In discovering your potential, we also invite you to: Discover your open-mindedness

A truly educated person learns to consider a person's character rather than any one or set of factors like skin color and religion. As you become more open-minded, you will begin to understand the need to learn before judging, reason before reacting, and delve deeper before condemning. As you work to discover your potential, strive hard to develop a habit of practicing open-mindedness.

Discover your competence and ability to question

You have already established a certain level of competence or you wouldn't be here. Now is the time to push yourself to learn more than you ever have before. Your future depends on the knowledge you are gaining today. As you move through the coming months and years, don't be afraid to ask questions of others, especially your instructors. Questioning is the first step in becoming more competent and a more critical and logical thinker. Asking the right questions and listening will help you become a more active learner. You also have the opportunity to learn from your peers and their experiences.

Discover your need to be challenged

The "easy road" will never lead to greatness or help you discover your true potential. Winston Churchill said, "It is from adversity that we gain greatness." When you are struggling, remember that you are getting stronger. You are preparing for becoming the person you were meant to be. As you begin classes, talk to your instructors, and balance all the elements in your life, the experiences you have will make you stretch and ultimately lead you to another level in the search for your true potential.

Discover your ability to balance

No SINGLE thing will ever bring you joy, peace, or prosperity. Include family, friends, cultural events, social activities, work, and service to others in your daily life. Seek balance between work and play. You will endlessly search for happiness unless you have a sense of balance in your life. Harmony and balance help you reduce stress, have more time for what you love, and live well.

Discover your success and true potential

You need to define exactly what success means to you so you know where you are going. Whatever success is for you, pursue it with all of the passion and energy you have. Set your goals high and work hard to create a life that you can ultimately look back on with pride, satisfaction, and joy.

We recognize that, in order to take on your program of study, you are committing yourself to a greater amount of work than you have already been juggling. You would not commit to all of that work unless there was a major benefit when you finish. By putting in the effort now to complete your program and receive your degree, you will be in a position to realize your dreams. In your new career, you will find that your life has taken on a new meaning. Your degree will open up a new future for you that will undoubtedly lighten the load you are now carrying. Though you will find new challenges in your program and career, they will likely be interesting and exciting.

As you read about the concepts and challenges presented in this course, you will have many opportunities to personalize and mold the information to your needs. The more effort you put into doing the activities in this course and throughout your education, the more value you will gain. Our hope is that you will discover early in your education and career that the responsibility for your learning and development is primarily yours. We commend you for taking on the challenge ahead, and we are rooting for you! We'll be there along the way to help when we can, but we know the work ahead is mainly yours. The credit will be yours, as well, and we'll be there at the finish line to cheer you! You can do it, and ITT Tech can help!

and ITT Tech Can Help!

Preface

The purpose of this book and course is to help you enhance the quality of your career and life. Though the specialized skills that your future career requires will be presented throughout your education program at ITT Tech, this course is concerned with helping you build the essential skills needed for surviving and thriving in a continually changing world and workplace. Use this book to become a better student and learner, and those skills will carry into your future. By training yourself to become a more adept thinker, writer, speaker, and problem solver, you gather the tools you need to excel in many areas of your life.

Near the beginning of this text, you are asked to look within to determine your important values, because behaviors grow out of beliefs, and how we act shapes the quality of our lives. By becoming more self-aware, you can also learn more effectively and efficiently, understand your motivations and desires, and participate fully with others. Though individuals can accomplish great things, groups can usually accomplish more. This text also introduces the dynamics of working with others and how to build better working relationships.

It is our hope that this book will help you to see the possibilities of your future, anticipate and cope with new situations, guide you through difficult days, discover more about yourself and your unique gifts, develop study and learning habits that help you succeed, hone your creative and critical thinking skills, and be an effective problem solver.

CCO-STAR Goal Worksheet

Directions:
What is one goal you have for this Quarter?
State your initial goal on the line below:

_____

Review your goal, checking for the CCO-STAR characteristics below:

Challenging Congruous & Optimistic	Does this goal stretch my limits and help me to grow? How does this goal fit in to what I want to do, be, and have in my life? Why do I want to achieve this goal? Have I stated this goal in a positive, proactive way?
Specific	How will I know if I am making progress toward my goal? What measure will I use to check my progress on the way?
Time-sensitive	How long will it take me to reach this goal? By when do I expect to complete this goal successfully? Have I set a deadline for achievement?
Adaptable	What types of circumstances might cause me to have to modify my goal? How would I alter it? What would stay the same?
Realistic	What do I need to make it possible to reach this goal? What are my odds for success?

Now, make any necessary revisions in the way you stated your goal.
Re-state your goal below in CCO-STAR terms:

_____

PART 1

Strategies: Building on Your Best for Career Success

Excerpts taken from:

Cornerstone: Building on Your Best for Career Success
by Robert M. Sherfield, Rhonda J. Montgomery, and Patricia G. Moody

Cornerstone: Building on Your Best, Fourth Edition
by Robert M. Sherfield, Rhonda J. Montgomery, and Patricia G. Moody

Keys to Success: Building Successful Intelligence for College, Career, and Life,
Brief Fourth Edition
by Carol Carter, Joyce Bishop, Sarah Lyman Kravits

Strategies for Active Citizenship
by Kateri M. Drexler and Gwen Garcelon

chapter 1 | Getting Started at ITT Tech

Contents

What's in It for Me?
Your ITT Tech Experience

Regardless of your background or reasons for continuing your education, the experience of change is something you'll share with everyone. Will you be able to open yourself up to new people and new situations?

Welcome to the first day of the rest of your life! In your quest to realize your golden potential, you will undoubtedly find challenges ahead. Not only is the world changing rapidly, but now you will probably find that you will also begin to change. Your priorities and beliefs may be tested. In fact, you may find they are already different than they were even a few months ago. With everything in a state of flux, it becomes very important to *assess* who and where you are, *plan* for where you are going, and *apply* the plan to your life. The process of understanding and managing life change begins in this chapter. By looking at some of the elements of change, our values and how those impact motivation and self-esteem, we build a good foundation for everything that follows—in this course, in the rest of your program, and in your career.

Many students face challenges around balancing time commitments and pressures. Graduates find that their degrees have opened up a new future, the loads they were carrying before have been lightened, and in their new careers, their lives have taken on new meaning. By putting in the effort now to complete your program and receive your degree, you will be in a position to realize your dreams. Of course, the short-term process is not easy. If it were, everyone would do it. By taking on this challenge, you have put yourself into a unique category of people: career college student. It is our hope and strong belief that by investing yourself in this course, you will find the tools to make it a bit easier to be in a more unique category still: college graduate.

Before reading further, jot down some thoughts about what you want to achieve in college, what you value about being in college, what you expect from ITT Technical Institute, and what we expect from you.

So, What's This All About?

Why are you here? What is the driving force that brought you to the door of ITT Tech? Was it a desire to learn more about your field? Was it to fulfill a dream? Was it a need for a career shift? Did other major changes occur in your life? Do you need retraining for the world of work? Whatever the reason, you're here, and that is a positive and wonderful thing for you and your family.

Over 70% of entering students say that their primary reason for furthering their education is to be able to get a better job and make more money. Good news! According to the U.S. Census, people who further their education and training DO earn more than those with only a high school diploma or GED.

Beyond money, furthering your education can help you:

- Work in a career of your choosing (not just a job)
- Develop a healthier self-esteem
- Strengthen your confidence in many areas of your life
- Expand your independence (thus reducing your dependence)
- Become more knowledgeable about more things
- Increase your options for future employment
- Grow to be a role model and mentor for your family and friends

Education Level	Female	Male
less than 9th grade	$10,561	18,282
9th-12th grade	12,728	24,988
H.S. graduate (includes equivalency)	18,501	33,276
Some college, no degree	23,514	41,595
Associate degree	25,486	45,073
Bachelor's degree	34,757	64,923

1 unit = $10,000/year   female   male

Source: U.S. Census, Dept. of Commerce, 2001.

Figure 1.1 Annual Earnings by Education Level and Gender

Changes in the Days to Come

> You gain strength, experience, and confidence by every experience where you really stop to look fear in the face . . . You must do the thing you think you cannot.
>
> —Eleanor Roosevelt

One of the first changes you may notice about college is that you have to learn to juggle several things at once, including your course work, your finances, and perhaps job responsibilities. Learning how to set priorities for your time and resources is a critical step to successfully handling this challenge. Figure 1.2 offers a guide to understanding expectations.

Attitudes That Hinder Change

You can develop attitudes that hinder change and stop growth. Such attitudes are dangerous because they rob you of opportunity, happiness, growth, and goals. These attitudes include:

- The "I can't" syndrome
- Apathy, or the "I don't care" syndrome
- Closed-mindedness
- Unfounded anxiety
- Fear of taking chances
- Loss of motivation
- The "let someone else deal with it" syndrome

If you can learn to watch out for and control these negative attitudes, you will begin to view change as a wonderful and positive lifelong event.

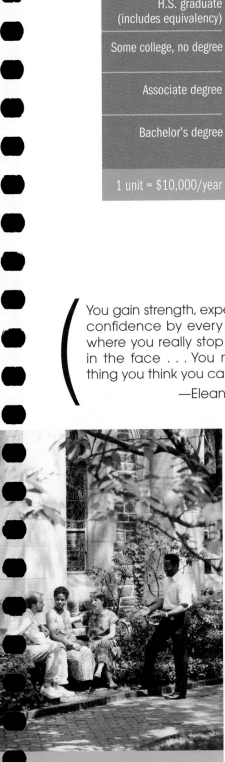

Change can introduce you to new people, ideas, cultures, and experiences.

	HIGH SCHOOL	POST SECONDARY	WORK
PUNCTUALITY AND ATTENDANCE	Expectations: • State law requires attendance • The hours in the day are managed for you • There may be some leeway in project dates Penalties: • You may get detention • You may not graduate • You may be considered truant • Your grades may suffer	Expectations: • Attendance and participation in class are enforced by some instructors • Some instructors will not give you an extension on due dates • You decide your own schedule and plan your own day Penalties: • You may not be admitted to class if you are late • You may fail the assignment if it is late • Repeated tardiness is sometimes counted as an absence • Most instructors do not take late assignments, especially if prior arrangements have not been made	Expectations: • You are expected to be at work and on time on a daily basis Penalties: • Your salary and promotions may depend on your daily attendance and punctuality • You will most likely be fired for abusing either
TEAMWORK AND PARTICIPATION	Expectations: • Most teamwork is assigned and carried out in class • You may be able to choose teams with your friends • Your grade reflects your participation Penalties: • If you don't participate, you may get a poor grade • You may jeopardize the grade of the entire team	Expectations: • Many instructors require group work • Your grade will depend on your participation • Your grade may depend on your entire team's performance • You may have to work on the project outside of class Penalties: • Lack of participation will probably lower your grade • Your team members will likely report you to the instructor if you do not participate and their grades suffer as a result	Expectations: • You will be expected to participate fully in any assigned task • You will be expected to rely on co-workers to help solve problems and increase profits • You will be required to attend and participate in meetings and sharing sessions • You will be required to participate in formal teams and possess the ability to work with a diverse workforce Penalties: • You will be "tagged" as non-team player • Your lack of participation and teamwork will cost you raises and promotions • You will most likely be terminated

Figure 1.2 A Guide to Understanding Expectations

	HIGH SCHOOL	POST SECONDARY	WORK
PERSONAL RESPONSIBILITY AND ATTITUDE	Expectations: • Teachers may coach you and try to motivate you • You are required to be in high school by law regardless of your attitude or responsibility level Penalties: • You may be reprimanded for certain attitudes • If your attitude prevents you from participating, you may fail the class	Expectations: • You are responsible for your own learning • Instructors will assist you, but there may be little "hand holding" or personal coaching for motivation • Continuing education did not choose you, you chose it, and you will be expected to hold this attitude toward your work Penalties: • You may fail the class if your attitude and motivation prevent you from participating	Expectations: • You are hired to do certain tasks and the company or institution fully expects this of you • You are expected to be positive and self-motivated • You are expected to model good behavior and uphold the company's work standards Penalties: • You will be passed over for promotions and raises • You may be reprimanded • You may be terminated
ETHICS AND CREDIBILITY	Expectations: • You are expected to turn in your own work • You are expected to avoid plagiarism • You are expected to write your own papers • Poor ethical decisions in high school may result in detention or suspension Penalties: • You may get detention or suspension • You will probably fail the project	Expectations: • You are expected to turn in your own work • You are expected to avoid plagiarism • You are expected to write your own papers • You are expected to conduct research and complete projects based on higher education and societal standards Penalties: • Poor ethical decisions may land you in front of a student ethics committee or a faculty ethics committee, or result in expulsion from the institution • You will fail the project • You may fail the class • You may face deportation if your visa is dependent on your student status	Expectations: • You will be required to carry out your job in accordance with company policies, laws, and moral standards • You will be expected to use adult vision and standards Penalties: • Poor ethical decisions may cause you to be severely reprimanded, terminated, or in some cases could even result in a prison sentence if your unethical behavior was also illegal.

Figure 1.2 A Guide to Understanding Expectations (*continued*)

So, I Want to Change
How Do I Do It?

After reading and reflecting thus far, you may have identified several changes that you need to make. Further, changes may have been thrust upon you by choices you or those around you have made. Although these and other events may happen to you, it's the choices that you make that will ultimately affect the outcomes in your life. The following model provides a method for dealing with and implementing change in your life and might be helpful in bringing about positive results.

The Need for Change

THE CHANGE IMPLEMENTATION MODEL

1 Determine what you need or want to change and why.

2 Research your options for making the desired changes and seek advice and assistance from a variety of sources.

3 Identify the obstacles to change and determine how to overcome them.

4 Establish a plan by outlining several positive steps to bring about the changes you identified.

5 Implement your plan for bringing about the desired change:

- Focus on the desired outcome.
- View problems as positive challenges.
- Turn your fears into energy by reducing anxiety through physical exercise, proper nutrition, and stress-management strategies.
- Associate with positive and motivated people.

For Change

1	Determine what you need or want to change and why.	You realize that you must change your study habits or fail the class. Your old study methods are not working.
2	Research your options for making the desired changes and seek advice and assistance from a variety of sources.	You look around campus to determine what services are available to you such as tutoring, learning centers, and learning communities. You also make an appointment to speak with the instructor. You talk to one of the members of a study group in class to see what benefits she is getting from the group.
3	Identify the obstacles to change and determine how to overcome them.	In the past, you have been afraid to get involved. You realize that you have never adjusted your time-management practices to post-secondary life; you are still studying on a "high school time frame." You realize that you have never reached out to classmates before. By listing the problems on paper, you see that you have to change your habits and take a risk by asking to join a study group.
4	Establish a plan by outlining several positive steps to bring about the changes you identified.	You spend a quiet evening thinking about steps that you can take to become a better student. You decide that you need to (1) approach members of the study group to ask permission to join, (2) make an appointment at the tutoring center, and (3) make a commitment to reading the assigned material every night.
5	Implement your plan for bringing about the desired change: • Focus on the desired outcome.	You know that you want and need to pass the class. This is the ultimate desired outcome, but you also know that you must change your study habits for other classes and this group may help you do so. You realize that if you can change your time and study practices, you will be successful in other areas.
	• View problems as positive challenges.	Instead of concentrating on the amount of time and energy required for the study group, you decide to look at it as a way to learn more, study better, and make new friends who have the same goals.
	• Turn your fears into energy by reducing anxiety through physical exercise, proper nutrition, and stress-management strategies.	You learn that two people from the study group also run every other morning. You decide to ask them if you can join them. You also decide that instead of going off campus to the Burger Hut, you will bring your own lunch and use this time to study for other classes.
	• Associate with positive and motivated people.	You notice that your attitude toward the class and life in general is improving because of the positive attitudes in the group. You can't believe how much you have changed in a few short weeks just by concentrating on the positive and associating with people who are motivated to succeed.

The Impact of Values
On Motivation, Goal Setting, and Self-Esteem

If you have been highly motivated to accomplish a goal in the past, this achievement was probably tied to something you valued a great deal. Most of what you do in life centers around what is truly important to you. You cannot get excited about achieving a goal or be disciplined enough to stick to it unless you definitely want to make it happen. If you really want to run a marathon, for example, you have to pay the price of long hours of practice, getting up early in the morning, and running when others are sleeping or playing. If you hate running, but you set a goal to complete a marathon in record time because your father was a champion runner and expects the same of you, you are not likely to achieve this goal. Your goals must relate to your personal value system.

Values, self-esteem, motivation, and goal setting are all mixed up together, making it difficult to separate one from the other. What you try to accomplish is directly connected to those things, ideas, and concepts that you value most. Values are central beliefs and attitudes that make you a unique person, while greatly impacting your choices and your personal lifestyle. If you cherish an attitude or belief, many of your actions will be centered around this ideal.

You were not born with your basic values. Your values were shaped to a great extent by your parents, the school you attended, the community where you grew up, and the culture that nourished you. Because of your personal background, you have developed a unique set of values. To make good decisions, set appropriate goals, and manage your priorities, you must identify those values that are central to who you are today. Until you clarify what you really value, you may try to accomplish what is important to someone else, and you will tend to wander around and become frustrated. Values, goals, and motivation bring direction to your life and help you get where you want to go.

As you become aware of and choose your values, they become an internal guidance system. To make good decisions, set appropriate goals, and manage priorities, it is important to identify the values that are central to who you are today and to who you want to become.

> (He who has a why to live can bear with almost any how.
> —Nietzsche)

Identify Your Values

Identifying and defining **values** is usually a work-in-progress that occurs throughout your life. Because our identities are constantly open to change and re-definition, the values that we hold are also as open to change. By practicing self-reflection, you can

Figure 1.3 Wheel of Life

learn how to be more intentional in your decisions and actions. You can learn to assess how your actions are expressing the things that are important to you.

The first step in assessing values is to examine how important the various aspects of work and life are to you. Look at the preceding Wheel of Life, and consider what areas of life might have a particular significance. We may find that some areas are more important than others at varying times in our lives; however, the wheel symbolizes our lives as a whole. Keeping the wheel segments balanced, as demonstrated in our lives, will help us proceed smoothly. Start to identify values in each of the areas. For each category, identify the importance by rating it from 1 to 10, with 10 being the most important.

Category	Importance
Personal Growth	
Money	
Relationships	
Education	
Community	
Play	
Family	
Spirituality	
Health	
Work	

Accountable
Being Accountable may include being:

Reliable	Trustworthy
Dependable	Responsible
Loyal	Secure

Committed
Committed may mean being:

Participative	Focused
Enthusiastic	Persistent
Energetic	Productive
Faithful	

Open
Openness may include being:

Fair	Unbiased
Patient	Open-minded
Tolerant	Joyful

Honest
Honesty may include being:

Authentic	Genuine
Outspoken	Sincere
Truthful	Frank
Balanced	

Responsible
Responsibility entails taking control of our own lives without blame or victimization

Giving
Giving may include being:

Dedicated	Compassionate
Accepting	Nurturing
Contributing	Helpful
Cooperative	Generous
Appreciative	Considerate
Forgiving	Respectful
Friendly	

The previous are some sample character traits and values that can be used as a starting point in developing a list of personal values. Consider how much you value the following traits. Use these traits to help you distinguish values. For instance, you may value being reliable to your family, or being committed to your education. What are traits and values that you would add to your list?

Plan to Act with Integrity

Webster's Dictionary defines integrity as *"the state of being whole or complete; acting with moral soundness."* When your actions are an honest expression of yourself, you have personal integrity. As you become more intentional about using your values to guide your actions, you develop greater personal integrity.

Among the widely accepted qualities of morality are fairness, honesty, service, excellence, patience, and treatment of others with dignity. Consider your own definition of moral soundness in order to assess the integrity of your actions.

Congruence

Becoming more self-aware allows you to become more intentional about your choices and how they affect the quality of your life and the lives of others. Congruence means *"to be in agreement or alignment"* and is another aspect of acting with integrity. In order to achieve true congruence in your life, what you think, say and do must be in alignment.

When actions are not in alignment with values, there is internal conflict, as well as conflict within relationships. The consequences of this conflict may include stress, depression, fatigue, anger, or anxiety. Conversely, when we act in accordance with what is true for us, we experience positive feelings. These may include happiness, satisfaction, passion, certainty, and abundance. Our feelings give us immediate feedback and are important guides for acting with integrity.

The Impact of Attitude
On Motivation, Goal Setting, and Self-Esteem

Have you ever met someone who turned you off immediately with a negative attitude? Some people whine about the weather or their parents; they verbally attack people who differ from them or degrade themselves with negative remarks. Listen for the negative comments people make, and the messages they send out about themselves. When people continually feed their brains negative messages, their bodies respond accordingly.

The impact of a bad attitude on your motivation and self-esteem is overpowering. On the other hand, focusing on the positive can bring dramatic changes in your life.

We all know that life sometimes deals bad blows, but your goal should be to be positive much more often than you are negative. Positive attitudes go hand-in-hand with energy, motivation, and friendliness. People with positive attitudes are more appealing; negative people drive others away.

Listen to yourself for a few days. Are you whining, complaining, griping, and finding fault with everything and everybody around you, including yourself? Is your bad grade the instructor's fault? Is your family responsible for everything bad that ever happened to you? If these kinds of thoughts are coming out of your mouth or are in your head, your first step toward improved motivation and self-esteem is to clean up your act.

How are the friends you are making in school influencing your decisions?

To be successful at anything, you have to develop a winning attitude. You have to eliminate negative thinking. Begin today: tell yourself only positive things about yourself; build on those positives; focus on the good things; work constantly to improve.

Winners get up early with an attitude of "I can't wait for this day to start so I can have another good day." OK, OK—so you may not get up early, but you can get up with a positive attitude. Tell yourself things that will put you in the right frame of mind to succeed. When you are talking to yourself—and everybody does—feed your brain positive thoughts. Think of your brain as a powerful computer; you program it with your words, and your body carries out the program.

Pay attention to the messages you send out to others as well. What kinds of remarks do you make about yourself and about others when you are with your friends? Do you sound positive or negative? Do you hear yourself saying positive things?

Stephen Covey, in his book *Seven Habits of Highly Effective People*, refers to the concept of the "inside-out" approach. Covey relates that if you want to create change in some area of your life, focus on what you think, say and how you act in that area. For instance, if you want to have better friendships, think about and practice being a more concerned and giving friend. If you want to be a better student, think about and practice taking sole responsibility for your learning.

Overcoming Doubts and Fears

Fear is a great motivator; it probably motivates more people than anything else. Unfortunately, it motivates most people to hold back, to doubt themselves, to accomplish much less than they could, and to hide the person they really are.

One of the biggest obstacles to reaching your potential may be your own personal fears. If you are afraid, you are not alone; everyone has fears. It is interesting to note that most of our fears are learned. As a baby, you had only two fears: a fear of falling and a fear of loud noises. As you got older, you added to your list of fears. And, if you are like most people, you let your fears dominate parts of your life, saying things to yourself like: "What if I try and fail?" "What if people laugh at me for thinking I can do this?" "What if someone finds out that this is my dream?"

(They who have conquered doubt and fear have conquered failure.
—James Allen)

You have two choices where fear is concerned. You can let fear dominate your life, or you can focus on those things you really want to accomplish, put your fears behind you, and go for it. The people most successful in their fields will tell you that they are afraid, but that they overcome their fear because their desire to achieve is greater. Barbra Streisand, recording artist and stage performer, becomes physically nauseated with stage fright when she performs, yet she faces these fears and retains her position as one of the most popular entertainers of our time.

Moving Out of Your Comfort Zone

Successful people face their fears because their motivation and ambition force them out of their "comfort zones." Your comfort zone is where you know you are good, you feel confident, and you don't have to stretch your talents far to be successful. If you stay in your comfort zone, you will never reach your potential and you will deny yourself the opportunity of knowing how it feels to overcome your fears.

Deciding to go to college probably caused you some level of discomfort and raised many fears: "What if I flunk out?" "What if I can't do my job, go to school, and manage a family at the same time?" The mere fact that you are here is a step outside your comfort zone—a very important step that can change your life dramatically.

Everyone has a comfort zone. When you are doing something that you do well, and you feel comfortable and confident, you are in your comfort zone. When you are nervous and afraid, you are stepping outside your comfort zone. When you realize you are outside your comfort zone, you should feel good about yourself because you are learning and growing and improving. You cannot progress unless you step outside your comfort zone.

Dealing With Hardship and Failure

To be motivated, you have to learn to deal with failure. Have you ever given up on something too quickly, or gotten discouraged and quit? Can you think of a time when you were unfair to yourself because you didn't stay with something long enough? Did you ever stop doing something you wanted to do because somebody laughed at you or teased you? Overcoming failure makes victory much more rewarding. Motivated people know that losing is a part of winning: the difference between being a winner and being a loser is the ability to try again. If you reflect on your life, you may well discover that you gained your greatest strengths through adversity. Difficult situations make you tougher and more capable of developing your potential. Overcoming adversity is an essential part of success in college and in life. Think of a time in your life when you faced difficulties but persisted and became stronger as a result.

Motivation
What is It and How Can I Get It?

Sometimes you might hear people talk about their lack of motivation or you hear someone else referred to as a "motivated person." You might wish you were more motivated but aren't sure how to get to that point. You see people who are highly self-disciplined and you would like to be more like them, but you don't have a clue how to get started. You've probably heard that old cliché, "A journey of a thousand miles begins with a single step." It may be old and sound a little corny, but actually, it's the truth.

Helen Keller

Though both blind and deaf, American lecturer and author Helen Keller (1880–1968) traveled the world over, fighting for improvement in the education and life of the physically handicapped.

Courtesy of Mary Evans Picture Library/ Alamy

Becoming motivated is a process—it's not one giant leap to becoming something you want to be. Motivation rarely comes overnight; rather, you become motivated by experiencing one small success after another as your confidence grows, and gradually, you try something bigger and more challenging. There are only two broad categories that will ever motivate you: a dream you have or a problem you are trying to overcome. Every goal and everything regarding motivation will fit into one of these two categories. Either dreaming of something or wanting to solve a problem is the first part of the formula for motivation. The other part is about making it happen—an action plan. Dreaming or wanting to solve a problem without action will get you nowhere. Nothing works unless you do! Motivation can be broken down into:

Desire + Courage + Goals + Discipline = Motivation

Understanding Motivation When you act from your own values and experience self-worth from within, you are said to be internally motivated. When you act to please others, or act in alignment with the values of others, you are externally motivated.

External Motivation Part of human nature is self-protection and the drive to sustain oneself. Many of us have learned to protect and nurture ourselves through gaining the approval of others. Children learn that they can gain love by pleasing others. The danger in **external motivation** is when we compromise our values and priorities in the pursuit of approval from others. This inevitably produces internal conflict, and the negative feelings that accompany it.

Internal Motivation Internally motivated people consult their own guidance in decision-making. Well-being and self-worth come from within and are not dependent on the validation of others.

When your self-worth comes from within, things may change in your life, but they cannot compromise your sense of value and empowerment. A study conducted by the University of Rochester's Human Motivation Research Group found, for example, that people whose motivation was internal exhibited more interest, confidence, excitement, persistence, creativity and performance than those who were motivated by external rewards.[1]

In order to stay motivated, you have to become committed to doing something. You need to face your fears and not let them become bigger than your dreams. You need to be willing to write your dream or desire down as a goal and say it out loud to your friends and family. You need to put those goals or commitments somewhere you can see them often in order to keep you on track. You need to take the initiative to get started. You have to be willing to form good habits and replace bad habits. For example, if you are a procrastinator, you have to work hard to change the habit that gets you in trouble over and over and over again. You need to be determined to take responsibility for yourself and your habits. In other words, you need to discipline yourself. If you can keep up a good practice for 21 days, it usually becomes a habit. Tell yourself, "I can do anything for 21 days."

No one can do any of this for you. The choice to be motivated, to be successful, to reach your potential is up to you. Blaming others, making excuses, using difficult circumstances as a crutch, or quitting will never get you anywhere. If you want to be motivated and successful, *get up and get started.*

When you are sure that you are becoming more disciplined, that your work habits are getting better, your grades are improving, and you are focused on success, reward yourself. Do something that you have really wanted to do for a long time. Share your successes with a few people who really care. Be careful not to boast. If you are good, people will know it. As you grow and become more successful, you will begin to make wiser choices; you will reach bigger goals; you will be on your way to accomplishing your dreams!

Your thoughts, words and actions are energy forces, and by focusing them toward specific and intentional points, you can intensify their strength. Choose goals that are in alignment with your values and personal integrity.

Becoming Who You Want to Be
The Goal-Setting Process

Goal setting itself is relatively easy. Many people make goals but fail to make the commitment to accomplish those goals. Instead of defining their goals in concrete, measurable terms, they think of them occasionally and have vague, unclear ideas about how to attain them. The first step toward reaching a goal is the commitment to pay the price to achieve it. Opportunities abound everywhere; commitment is a scarce commodity.

> There is only one definition of success: to be able to spend your life in your own way.
> —Christopher Morley

> All things are possible until they are proved impossible—and even the impossible may only be so, as of now.
> —Pearl S. Buck

Individual Goals Individual goals are goals that are set by you, and for which you alone develop and implement a strategy. They can be goals that you have for your own development and achievement. What makes them individual goals is that you alone are responsible for achieving them.

Collective Goals Collective goals are set, collectively, by members of a group. Necessarily, each member of the group has a role to play in the achieving the goal. In addition, all members will gain something in common by the achievement of the goal. Collective goals can be initiated by an individual, but if they are intended to benefit a group, they should be formulated and agreed upon by the group.

Short-Term and Long-Term Goals Having both short-term and long-term goals can be rewarding. Short-term goals are usually less complex and easier than long-term goals. We build momentum with each goal we complete, so setting short-term goals helps ensure that we'll have frequent victories.

Long-term goals (one year or longer) keep us headed in the right direction and can provide a sense of greater purpose. These goals may require a longer process in order to achieve their result, in which case it is helpful to break down the overarching, or long-term, goal into smaller goals that may be reachable in shorter periods of time. Breaking a long-term goal into smaller short-term goals can provide a sense of accomplishment if our ultimate goal requires patience and perseverance over a long period of time.

Prioritizing Goals

Most of us have several goals in different life areas that we would like to achieve. Prioritizing goals can be confusing if you think in terms of "which is more important?" Over the long term, all of your goals are probably important, or they wouldn't be goals. When prioritizing, think in terms of *timing*: "which will I focus on more right now?"

When deciding which goals to start with, consider the following:

- Will achieving certain goals first make others easier to achieve?
- Do any of your goals express values that are more important to you than others?
- Which goals will create the greatest impact on your solution with the fewest resources?
- Which goals will create long-term results?
- Which goals have the greatest chance of success?

Dealing with Conflicting Goals

Because the resources we have to spend on our goals—money, time, and energy—are limited, goals can often appear to be at odds with one another. Working on one can mean slipping on the other. Good management of your goals as a group is important for avoiding frustration.

Some suggestions for dealing with several goals at once include:

- **Stay focused.** Don't set too many goals at the same time, and make sure that your goals are in alignment with your most important values.

- **Have at least one simple goal and one difficult goal at any given time.** The simple goals motivate you as you accomplish them rapidly. The difficult goals keep you challenged and growing.

- **Have at least one short-term and one long-term goal at any given time.** As with simple goals, short-term goals help assure that you'll have frequent victories. Long-term goals keep you headed in the right direction.

- **Be flexible.** Decide which of your goals (and tasks) are most important, but be willing to change a goal or even put it on hold for a while, if necessary.

- **Look for ways to combine goals and tasks.** If you can work on two or more goals at once, you can consolidate your resources.

What Are Your Goals?

You can set many goals at this point without worrying about spreading yourself too thin because we make a distinction between setting a goal and managing a goal, or project. At this stage, think of many goals you'd like to shoot for even if you are focused on other things right now. However, also be mindful of the importance of balance. Make sure to set goals across different areas of your life: health, finance, family, relationships, personal growth, career, etc. The number of categories in which you should set goals depends on your particular situation. How well-balanced is your life right now? What are your priorities? Are you already strong in some areas, but weak in others? Answers to questions like these will give you a sense of where to focus your efforts. In general, expect to focus on a few goals in more than one category at a time. It's okay to set a lot of goals in multiple categories.

Plan for Attainable Goals

Typically, goal-setting theorists have suggested that goals have certain characteristics in order to be more easily attained. In general, goals should be:

Written

Research has shown that by simply writing down your goals, you will increase your odds of achieving them, on average, by 300 percent.[2]

A study was conducted by Yale University in 1953, and, though the study is older, it has some telling results about the importance of goals. A survey was given to the senior class, and they were asked several questions, three of which dealt with goals. The questions were:

- Have you set goals?

- Have you written them down?

- Do you have a plan to accomplish these goals?

Only three percent of the class answered "yes" to these questions. Twenty years later, the members of this class were surveyed again. The research showed that the three percent of the class who set goals were happier and more successful than those who did not have goals. In addition, the three percent who set goals had 97% of the wealth of the entire class. In other words, these three percent were wealthier than the entire rest of the class combined. This study illustrates that setting goals can lead to accomplishment and fulfillment.

Challenging

Although you will want to have some easier goals, some of your goals should also be challenging. Limit the number of challenging goals or tasks to avoid becoming overwhelmed or frustrated. When goals are so challenging that you wonder whether they are realistic, it might make sense to break the goals down into smaller, incremental goals. The challenging goals force you to grow.

Congruous

In order to be effective, your goals should conform to your value system and be internally motivated. If you set goals that will meet someone else's expectations or that do not fit within your values, you will find it more difficult to reach them. Your goals should fit into what you want to do, be, or have in your life. If you find it difficult to develop the motivation to achieve a goal, first look at where it fits into your value system and do some self-awareness work.

For example, someone might have the goal "to buy a bigger house than my brother's." Asking the question "why a bigger house?" could shed light on the fact that your friend wants to compete with his brother. Maybe there are other - issues to be addressed such as self-esteem and respect that owning a larger house will not solve. Perhaps a more congruous goal would be "to earn my brother's respect." Identifying the root goal could have a profound impact on this person's life that could not be achieved with a house of any size. Honest evaluation of why you want to achieve the goal can lead to insights and personal discovery.

Optimistic

Goals also have a greater ability to motivate us subconsciously if they are stated in an optimistic, proactive way. You may notice this in advertising messages. Nike says "Just Do It" instead of "Stop Sitting There." If your goal is to stop procrastinating, how can you state your ultimate goal, or what you really want, in an optimistic way? "I want to move with speed and direction in all my tasks and responsibilities" is more proactive. Negatively framed goals require not doing something, and thus focus our attention on what we don't want instead of on an optimistic vision. Optimistic goals keep us clear and focused on the images of what we want.

Specific and Measurable

Your goals should be specific and measurable enough for you to know definitively whether they have been completed. Though some goals are ongoing or will likely be works-in-progress throughout your life and may not in themselves be measurable, the individual tasks that you will later assign to these goals should be very specific and measurable.

Time-Sensitive

When we look at goals in terms of your group of goals, you'll want many of them to have a concrete deadline. However, there may be goals that you develop that are ongoing, such as attaining excellent health or contributing to world peace. Such goals will have no end date, though they should be tracked and monitored, and the individual tasks that comprise the goals should have deadlines.

Adaptable

The goals you set now may not be perfect, and even if they are, situations can change over time, making them imperfect. The reality is that most people's goals do change over time. In fact, goals usually should change, at least slightly, in response to things that change around you or new life events.

It's important to set goals, and to have something for which to strive, although once we set the goals, we need to detach from the outcome. You're not guaranteed specific results as you define them. But you gain the satisfaction of living your life for a higher purpose.

Realistic

Believing that your goals are at least possible for you to achieve will motivate you. More importantly, it is you who must believe, not anyone else. However, just because you should believe that the goal is possible does not mean that you must expect it to be easy.

A goal is realistic if you stand reasonably good odds of accomplishing it, given enough time and effort on your part. You must have some control over the effort in order for goals to be realistic. The majority of the goals you set should be very realistic or you risk becoming frustrated if you do not accomplish any of them.

Introducing the CCO-STAR Acronym

To help in ensuring that the goals you write are strong, sound, and attainable, use the acronym CCO-STAR. An acronym is a mnemonic device, a strategy to help you remember these important characteristics. Each letter of the CCO-STAR acronym is the first letter of one of the goal characteristics explained above (See page xvii for the CCO-STAR Goal Worksheet.):

Challenging
Congruous
Optimistic
Specific
Time-sensitive
Adaptable
Realistic

Determine the Values Behind Your Goals

Determining the Values Behind the Goal

For each of the goals you set, see if you can determine its underlying values.

For example:

Goal	Corresponding Value
Graduating in May	Being committed, perseverance, responsibility, patience

Goal	Corresponding Value
_____	_____
_____	_____
_____	_____
_____	_____
_____	_____

Loving Yourself More
Ten Ways to Increase Your Self-Esteem

If you were asked to name all the areas of your life that are impacted by self-esteem, what would you say? The correct answer is, "Everything." Self-esteem and self-understanding are two of the most important components of your personal makeup! In other words, you have got to know and love yourself! Did you know that your IQ score might not be as important as knowing your own talents and strengths and having healthy self-esteem? A student can be brilliant in terms of mental ability, but may perform at a very low capacity because of unhealthy self-esteem. Unhealthy self-esteem and a lack of self-understanding are also connected to loneliness and depression. "Self-esteem is the armor that protects kids from the dragons of life: drugs, alcohol, delinquency and unhealthy relationships" (McKay and Fanning, 2000).

- **Take control of your own life.** If you let other people rule your life, you will always have unhealthy self-esteem. You will feel helpless and out of control as long as someone else has power over your life. Part of growing up is taking control of your life and making your own decisions. Get involved in the decisions that shape your life. Seize control—don't let life happen to you!

- **Adopt the idea that "you are responsible for you."** The day you take responsibility for yourself and what happens to you is the day you start to develop your self-esteem. When you can admit your mistakes and celebrate your successes knowing you did it your way, you will learn to love yourself much better.

- **Refuse to allow friends and family to tear you down.** You may have family or friends who belittle you, criticize your decisions, and refuse to let you make your own decisions. Combat their negativity by admitting your mistakes and shortcomings to yourself and by making up your mind that you are going to overcome them. By doing this, you are taking their negative power away from them. Spend less time with people who make you feel small and insecure and more time with people who encourage you.

- **Control what you say to yourself.** "Self-talk" is important to your self-esteem and to your ability to motivate yourself positively. Your brain is like a powerful computer and it continually plays messages to you. If these self-talk messages are negative, they will have a detrimental impact on your self-esteem and on your ability to live up to your potential. Make a habit of saying positive things to yourself: "I will do well on this test because I am prepared." "I am a good and decent person, and I deserve to do well."

- **Take carefully assessed risks often.** Many people find risk taking very hard to do, but it is one of the very best ways to raise your self-esteem level. If you are going to grow to your fullest potential, you will have to learn to take some calculated risks. While you should never take foolhardy risks that might endanger your life, you must constantly be willing to push yourself out of your comfort zone. Every day, force yourself to take a little step outside your comfort zone.

- **Don't compare yourself to other people.** You may never be able to "beat" some people at certain things. But it really does not matter. You only have to beat yourself to get better. If you constantly tell yourself that you "are not as handsome as Bill" or "as smart as Mary" or "as athletic as Jack," your inner voice will begin to believe these statements, and your body will act accordingly. One of the best ways to improve self-esteem and to accomplish goals is simply to get a little better every day without thinking about what other people are doing. If you are always practicing at improving yourself, sooner or later you will become a person you can admire—and others will admire you, too!

- **Develop a victory wall or victory file.** Many times, you tend to take your accomplishments and hide them in a drawer or closet. Put your certificates, letters of praise, trophies, and awards out where you can see them on a daily basis. Keep a file of great cartoons, letters of support, or friendly cards so that you can refer to them from time to time.

- **Keep your promises and be loyal to friends, family, and yourself.** If you have ever had someone break a promise to you, you know how it feels to have your loyalty betrayed. The most outstanding feature of one's character is one's ability to be loyal, keep one's promises, and do what one has agreed to do. Few things can make you feel better about yourself than being loyal and keeping your word.

- **Win with grace—lose with class.** Everyone loves a winner, but everyone also loves a person who can lose with class and dignity. On the other hand, no one loves a bragging winner or a moaning loser. If you are engaged in sports, debate, acting, art shows, or math competitions, you will encounter winning and losing. Remember, whether you win or lose, if you're involved and active, you're already in the top 10 percent of the population.

- **Set goals and maintain a high level of motivation.** Find something that you can be passionate about; set a realistic goal to achieve this passion, and stay focused on this goal every day. By maintaining a high level of motivation, you will begin to see your goals come to fruition and feel your self-esteem soar. Setting a goal and achieving it is one of the most powerful ways to develop healthy self-esteem.

Endnotes

[1] Ryan, Richard M. and Edward L. Deci, "Self Determination Theroy and the Facilitation of Intrinsic Motivation, Social Development, and Well-Being," <u>American Psychologist</u> 55, 1 (January 2000) 68–78.

[2] Ziglar, Zig. <u>Sucess and the Self-Image</u>. New York: Simon & Schuster, 1995.

NOTES

chapter 2 | Strategies for Independent Learning

Contents

What's in It for Me?

To be successful, you have to last

Have you ever given up on something in the past and regretted it later? Do you ever think back and ask yourself, "What would my life be like if only I had done X or Y?" Have you ever made a decision or acted in a way that cost you dearly? If so, then you now know the value of persistence.

Persistence. The word itself means that you are going to stay—that you have found a way to stick it out, found a way to make it count, and found a way *not to give up*. That is what this chapter is all about—finding out how to make career college work for you. It is about giving you advice up front that can save your education and your future dreams.

Dropping out of school is not uncommon. As a matter of fact, *over 40 percent of the people who begin college never complete their programs.* Don't be mistaken in thinking that they dropped out because of their inability to learn. Many leave because they made serious and irreparable mistakes early.

> Before everything else, **getting ready** is the secret to success.
>
> —Henry Ford

Some students leave because they did not know how to manage their time. Some leave because they couldn't get along with an instructor. And still, some leave because they simply could not figure out how "the system" worked, and frustration, anger, disappointment, and fear got the better of them.

You do not have to be one of these students. This chapter and *indeed this book* are geared to help you AVOID those mistakes. They are geared to help you make the decisions that will lead to completion of your degree.

What You Need to Know Up Front

Policies and Procedures of ITT Tech

Familiarizing yourself with the policies and procedures of your college can save you a great deal of grief and frustration in the long run. Policies and procedures vary from institution to institution, but regardless, it is your responsibility to know what you can expect from your institution and what your institution expects from you. These policies can be found in the school catalog (traditional and online).

Though the ITT Tech campuses can vary in their rules, some universal policies include:

- Most colleges adhere to a strict drop/add date. Always check your schedule of classes for this information.
- Most colleges have an attendance policy for classroom instruction.
- Most colleges have a strict refund policy.
- Most colleges have an academic dishonesty policy.
- Most colleges have a standing drug and alcohol policy.
- Colleges do not put policies into place to hinder your degree completion; rather, the purpose is to ensure that all students are treated fairly and equitably.

The Golden Rule of Classroom Etiquette

You may be surprised, but the way you act in (and out of) class can mean as much to your success as what you know. No one can make you do anything or act in any way that you do not want. The following tips are provided from years of research and conversations with thousands of instructors teaching across America. Knowing this isn't enough, though. You have to be the one who chooses whether to use this advice.

- Bring your materials to class daily: texts, notebooks, pens, calculators, and syllabi.
- Come to class prepared: read your text and handouts, do the assigned work at home, bring questions to be discussed.
- Turn in papers, projects, and assignments on time. Many instructors do not accept late work.
- Participate in class. Ask questions, bring current events to the discussion, and contribute with personal experiences.
- Ask your instructor about the best time to come in for help. The time before and after class may not be the most appropriate time. Your instructor may have "back-to-back" classes and may be unable to assist you.
- If you are late for class, enter quietly. Do not walk in front of the instructor, don't let the door slam, don't talk on your way in, and take the seat nearest the door. Make every effort not to be late to class.
- Wait for the instructor to dismiss class before you begin to pack your bags to leave. You may miss important information or you may cause someone else to miss important information.
- Never carry on a conversation with another student while the instructor or another student is talking.
- Do not sleep in class.
- If for any reason you must leave during class, do so quietly and quickly. It is customary to inform the instructor that you will be leaving early before class begins.
- If you make an appointment with an instructor, keep it. If you must cancel, a courtesy call is in order.
- If you don't know how to address your instructor; that is, by Mr., Mrs., Miss, Ms., or Dr., ask them which they prefer.
- You should not wear sunglasses, oversized hats, strong cologne or perfume, skates, or earphones to class.
- Be respectful of other students. Treat diversity with dignity and respect.
- Mind your manners. Profanity and obscene language may offend some people. You can have strong, conflicting views without being offensive.
- Turn off your cell phone or beeper. If you have a home or work situation that requires that you "stay connected," put the device on vibrate.
- Remember that respect for others on your part will afford you the opportunity to establish relationships that otherwise you might never have had.
- Call your instructor or program chain to notify them if you are going to be late or absent. Remember that this is your job and you need to be accountable.
- Come dressed according to the dress code, if the school has one. Dress for success!

Some lecture classes have a lab component to provide students a hands-on learning experience.

Won't You Stay for a While?

Persisting in College

The age-old "scare tactic" for first-time students, "Look to your left, look to your right—one of those people will not graduate with you," is not far from the truth. But the good news (actually, the great news) is that you do not have to become a statistic. You can make it through your classes and graduate. You have the power to get through your program. Sure, you may have some catching up to do. You may have to work harder and longer, but the beauty of college is that if you want help, you can get help.

Below, you will find some powerful, helpful tips for persisting in college. Using only a few of them can increase your chances of graduating. Using all of them virtually assures it!

- **Visit your advisor or counselor** frequently and establish a relationship. Take his or her advice. Ask questions. Use your advisor or counselor as a mentor.

- **Make use of every academic service** that you need that the college offers, from tutoring sessions to writing centers; these are essential tools to your success.

- Work hard to **learn and understand your "learning style."** This can help you in every class in which you enroll.

- Work hard to **develop a sense of community.** Get to know a few people on campus such as a special faculty member, a secretary, another student, or anyone who you can turn to for help.

- **Join a club or organization.** Research proves that students who are connected to the campus through activities drop out less often.

- **Watch your finances carefully.** Don't get "credit-carditis." If you see yourself getting into financial trouble, seek counseling immediately! Poor financial management can cost you success as quickly as failing classes.

- Concentrate on setting realistic, achievable goals. **Visualize your goals.** Write them down. Find a picture that represents your goal and post it so that you can see your goal every day.

- Work hard to develop and **maintain a sense of self-esteem and self-respect.** The better you feel about yourself, the more likely you will reach your goals.

- **Learn to budget your time** as wisely as you budget your money. You've made a commitment to college and it will take a commitment of time to bring your dream to fruition.

- If you have trouble with an instructor, don't let it fester. Make an appointment to **speak with the instructor** and work through the problem.

Your Responsibility: Ask for Help

Many students find that they are afraid to ask for help when they don't understand something, whether it is information they learn in a class, general information about their program of study, or specific features of a new technology. When you do not understand something, there may be others who do not understand it as well. By asking questions, you may help other students. If fear keeps you from asking questions about something you don't fully comprehend, you may hinder your education and cheat yourself out of valuable information. You are investing your valuable resources in order to complete your program, and it is your right and your responsibility to find the information you need. Your instructors, deans, academic counselors and the entire administration are here to help you. They want to

Research suggests that stress can trigger chemical releases in the body that might cause forgetfulness. Learning to relax, breathe properly, and maintain perspective can help reduce stress during tests.

be helpful and are waiting for the opportunity. Even if you feel like you should already know the answer, if you don't know it-ask someone! If you don't get the answer you need, ask someone else.

What's in It for Me?

Technology is Your Friend

Technology enables adult learners to further their education using the convenience of the computer and the Internet. Motivated students can take courses, and sometimes complete programs online, interact with other students and their instructors via e-mail, and access an online library to help with research. Some courses are taught only in the classroom, some are taught only online, and others may use a combination of an online component and classroom time. The last kind of course is sometimes called "blended."

Many students like the idea of the convenience and easy access of online course offerings. Are you the type of student who likes the idea of going to class first thing while you're still in your pajamas, or late at night when everyone in your family has gone to bed? Online students appreciate that they don't have to be somewhere at any particular time and can go to class when, and where, they choose. The online class is always open. You can participate in online discussion forums; answer questions your instructor has posted; and turn in your assignments as you complete them.

In today's workplace, employees are often required to work with people from all over the country and world, virtually. Great online communication skills are assets you'll never regret developing.

NOTES

chapter 3 | Styles of Learning, Note and Test Taking Techniques

Contents

What's in It for Me?

Making the Most of Your Strengths

Many students, especially those who are returning to classes for the first time in years, often wonder if they know how to learn. You may be asking yourself, "Is there one 'best' way of learning?" The answer is no. It depends on so many variables. There are a number of theories about how learning styles, personal intelligences, personality typing, past experiences, and attitude affect how people process new information. Though not everyone agrees on every theory, there are some common elements among most of them.

The idea behind the study of learning styles, personal intelligences, and personality is something that educators have known for a very long time: students learn in different ways in different situations. While some students may not like the lecture format in class, for instance, others relish it. Some students learn best by touching and doing, while others learn best by listening and reflecting. Some students learn best with a group of people sitting outside under the trees, while others must be alone in the library. Other factors that determine how well students learn seem to include their motivation for learning, the physical setting they are in, their decision-making skills, and their commitment to their long-term goals.

What almost everyone agrees upon is that, in order to most effectively learn, students need a good reason for learning new material as well as a variety of methods, or styles, they can draw upon when needed. Many people have a predominant learning style that they favor and can use certain study techniques that accommodate this style. However, classes are taught in many different ways depending on the instructor. Some instructors lecture, others demonstrate or lead students to self-discovery; some focus on principles; some use applications; some emphasize memory and others understanding. When mismatches exist between a student's primary learning style and the teaching style of the instructor, the student may become bored and inattentive in class, do poorly on tests, get discouraged about the courses, the curriculum, and themselves, and in some cases drop out of school. In order to protect your future career and be in charge of your own learning, it will be helpful if you can use several styles of learning.

By understanding your primary learning style and developing additional ways to learn, evidence indicates that you will likely:

- Experience an increased comfort level and willingness to learn
- Practice different ways of thinking and solving problems, which will be quite useful as you move to become a fully effective professional
- Experience increased motivation and achievement in a whole range of activities
- Gain an understanding of how people differ, which will aid you in becoming a more effective team member
- Take control of your own learning and future

Discovering and Polishing Your Talents

In this section, we present three self-assessments to help you better understand your dominant intelligences, personality type, and learning style. This is not a hard science, and there are no right or wrong answers. It is possible that the conclusions you come to from doing these activities may not even be accurate. These assessments are just meant to be a guide—to give you something to think about regarding how you best learn and how others may best learn. These assessments are in no way intended to label you. They are not a measure of your intelligence. These are based on theories that have been both praised and criticized. They are also not meant to be used as a static indicator of who you are. Learning styles and personalities change over the years. They do not measure your worth or your capacities as a student. They are included so that you might gain a better understanding of your multiple intelligences and identify your learning styles and your personality type. Use them as tools to help you explore who you are and how you learn. We hope that by the end of this section, you will have experienced a "wow" or an "ah-ha!" moment as you explore and discover new and exciting possibilities for your education path.

Following each of the self-review activities, there are suggestions for how to use your strengths in different situations that we hope you will find informative and helpful. Many students have met with great success by identifying and molding their study environments and habits to reflect their primary learning styles and personality types. By recognizing and expanding their repertoire of learning techniques, many students have also been able to adapt more easily to different instructors.

Looking at Yourself in a New Way
Understanding Multiple Intelligences

There are many ways to learn how to ski. The learning technique that works best for you depends on many different factors, which may vary from situation to situation.

In 1983, Howard Gardner, a Harvard University professor, developed a theory called multiple intelligences. In his book *Frames of Mind*, he outlines seven intelligences that he feels are possessed by everyone:

• Visual/spatial
• Verbal/linguistic
• Musical/rhythm
• Logic/math
• Body/kinesthetic
• Interpersonal
• Intrapersonal

In 1996, he added an eighth intelligence: naturalistic. His conclusion, in short, is that when you have done things that have come easily for you, you are probably drawing on one of your intelligences that is well developed. On the other hand, if you have tried to do things that are very difficult to master or understand, you may be dealing with material that calls on one of your less-developed intelligences. If playing the piano by ear comes easily to you, your musical/rhythm intelligence may be very strong. If you have trouble writing or understanding poetry, your verbal/linguistic intelligence may not be as well developed. This does not mean that you will never be able to write poetry; it simply means that you have not fully developed your skills in this area.

ASSESS: YOUR MULTIPLE INTELLIGENCES

#1. Your Multiple Intelligences Survey (2005) by Robert M. Sherfield, Ph.D. Based, in part, on *Frames of Mind* by Howard Gardner, 1983. Read each statement carefully and thoroughly. After reading the statement, rate your response using the scale to the right. There are no right or wrong answers. This is not a timed survey.

Never or Almost never	Sometimes	Often
1	**2**	**3**

1. _____ When someone gives me directions, I have to visualize them in my mind in order to understand them.

2. _____ I know where everything is in my home such as supplies, gloves, flashlights, camera, and CDs.

3. _____ I like to draw pictures, graphs, or charts to better understand information.

4. _____ I enjoy working puzzles or mazes.

5. _____ I enjoy and learn more when seeing movies, slides, or videos in class.

_____ TOTAL for **VISUAL/SPATIAL**

1. _____ I enjoy crossword puzzles and games like Scrabble.

2. _____ I am a good speller.

3. _____ I have a good memory for names and dates.

4. _____ I am a good storyteller.

5. _____ I am a very good listener, and I enjoy listening to others' stories.

_____ TOTAL for **VERBAL/ LINGUISTIC**

1. _____ I enjoy dancing and can keep up with the beat of the music.

2. _____ I often sing or hum to myself in the shower or car, or while walking or just sitting.

3. _____ When I hear music, I "get into it" by moving, humming, tapping, or even singing.

4. _____ I can easily remember the words and melodies of songs.

5. _____ I need to study with music.

_____ TOTAL for **MUSICAL/RHYTHM**

1. _____ I like to repair things that are broken such as toasters, small engines, bicycles, and cars.

2. _____ I use a lot of gestures when I talk to people.

3. _____ I enjoy playing competitive sports.

4. _____ I usually touch people or pat them on the back when I talk to them.

5. _____ I enjoy physical activities such as bicycling, jogging, dancing, snowboarding, skateboarding, or swimming.

_____ TOTAL for **BODY/KINESTHETIC**

1. _____ I enjoy leadership activities.

2. _____ I can recognize and empathize with people's attitudes and emotions.

3. _____ I communicate very well with other people.

4. _____ I understand my family and friends better than most other people do.

5. _____ I am good at solving people's problems/conflicts.

_____ TOTAL for **INTERPERSONAL**

1. _____ I have the ability to get others to listen to me.

2. _____ I prefer to study alone.

3. _____ I know what I want, and I set goals to accomplish it.

4. _____ I don't always talk about my accomplishments with others.

5. _____ I have to have time alone to think about new information in order to remember it.

_____ TOTAL for **INTRAPERSONAL**

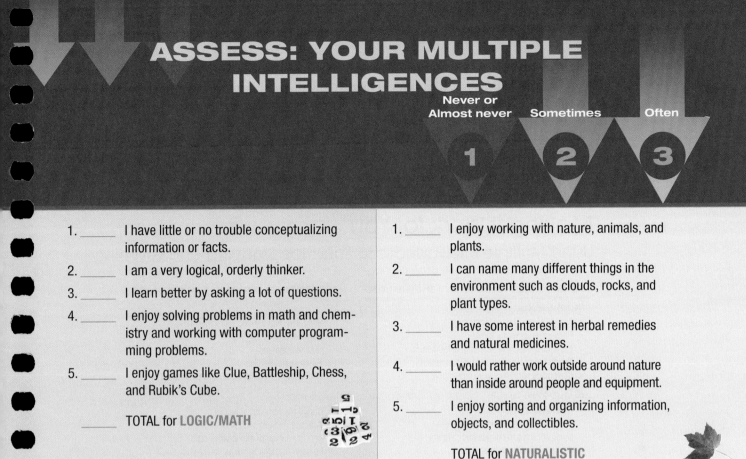

ASSESS: YOUR MULTIPLE INTELLIGENCES

Never or Almost never — 1
Sometimes — 2
Often — 3

1. _____ I have little or no trouble conceptualizing information or facts.

2. _____ I am a very logical, orderly thinker.

3. _____ I learn better by asking a lot of questions.

4. _____ I enjoy solving problems in math and chemistry and working with computer programming problems.

5. _____ I enjoy games like Clue, Battleship, Chess, and Rubik's Cube.

_____ TOTAL for LOGIC/MATH

1. _____ I enjoy working with nature, animals, and plants.

2. _____ I can name many different things in the environment such as clouds, rocks, and plant types.

3. _____ I have some interest in herbal remedies and natural medicines.

4. _____ I would rather work outside around nature than inside around people and equipment.

5. _____ I enjoy sorting and organizing information, objects, and collectibles.

_____ TOTAL for NATURALISTIC

Plan to Make the Most of the Eight Intelligences

The "Smart" descriptors were adapted from Thomas Armstrong (1994).

 Visual/Spatial (Picture Smart).   Thinks in pictures; knows where things are in the house; loves to create images and work with graphs, charts, pictures, and maps.

 Verbal/Linguistic (Word Smart).   Communicates well through language, likes to write, is good at spelling, great at telling stories, loves to read books.

 Musical/Rhythm (Music Smart).   Loves to sing, hum, and whistle; comprehends music; responds to music immediately; performs music.

 Logic/Math (Number Smart).   Can easily conceptualize and reason, uses logic, has good problem-solving skills, enjoys math and science.

 Body/Kinesthetic (Body Smart).   Learns through body sensation, moves around a lot, enjoys work involving the hands, is graced with some athletic ability.

 Interpersonal (People Smart).   Loves to communicate with other people, possesses great leadership skills, has lots of friends, is involved in extracurricular activities.

Intrapersonal *(Self-Smart).* Has a deep awareness of own feelings, is very reflective, requires time to be alone, does not get involved with group activities.

Naturalistic *(Environment Smart).* Has interest in the environment and in nature; can easily recognize plants, animals, rocks, and cloud formations; may like hiking, camping, and fishing.

Making It Work for You
Using Multiple Intelligences to Enhance Studying and Learning

ABILITIES AND SKILLS ASSOCIATED WITH EACH INTELLIGENCE	STUDY TECHNIQUES TO MAXIMIZE EACH INTELLIGENCE
Verbal–Linguistic	**Verbal–Linguistic**
• Analyzing own use of language • Remembering terms easily • Explaining, teaching, learning, using humor • Understanding syntax and word meaning • Convincing someone to do something	• Read text; highlight no more than 10% • Rewrite notes • Outline chapters • Teach someone else • Recite information or write scripts/debates
Musical–Rhythmic	**Musical–Rhythmic**
• Sensing tonal qualities • Creating/enjoying melodies, rhythms • Being sensitive to sounds and rhythms • Using "schemas" to hear music • Understanding the structure of music	• Create rhythms out of words • Beat out rhythms with hand or stick • Play instrumental music/write raps • Put new material to songs you already know • Take music breaks
Logical–Mathematical	**Logical–Mathematical**
• Recognizing abstract patterns • Reasoning inductively and deductively • Discerning relationships and connections • Performing complex calculations • Reasoning scientifically	• Organize material logically • Explain material sequentially to someone • Develop systems and find patterns • Write outlines and develop charts and graphs • Analyze information
Visual–Spatial	**Visual–Spatial**
• Perceiving and forming objects accurately • Recognizing relationships between objects • Representing something graphically • Manipulating images • Finding one's way in space	• Develop graphic organizers for new material • Draw mind maps • Develop charts and graphs • Use color in notes to organize • Visualize material (method of loci)
Bodily–Kinesthetic	**Bodily–Kinesthetic**
• Connecting mind and body • Controlling movement • Improving body functions • Expanding body awareness to all senses • Coordinating body movement	• Move or rap while you learn; pace and recite • Use "method of loci" or manipulatives • Move fingers under words while reading • Create "living sculptures" • Act out scripts of material, design games
Intrapersonal	**Intrapersonal**
• Evaluating own thinking • Being aware of and expressing feelings • Understanding self in relation to others • Thinking and reasoning on higher levels	• Reflect on personal meaning of information • Visualize information/keep a journal • Study in quiet settings • Imagine experiments
Interpersonal	**Interpersonal**
• Seeing things from others' perspectives • Cooperating within a group • Communicating verbally and nonverbally • Creating and maintaining relationships	• Study in a group • Discuss information • Use flash cards with others • Teach someone else
Naturalistic	**Naturalistic**
• Deep understanding of nature • Appreciation of the delicate balance in nature	• Connect with nature whenever possible • Form study groups of people with like interests

Adapted from Lazear, Seven Pathways of Learning, 1994

Figure 3.1 How to Put Your Multiple Intelligences to Work for You

Assess your personality with the Personality Spectrum

Personality assessments help you understand how you respond to the world around you—including information, thoughts, feelings, people, and events. The assessment used in this chapter is based on one of the most widely used personality inventories in the world—the Myers-Briggs Type Inventory, developed by Katharine Briggs and her daughter, Isabel Briggs Myers. It also relies upon the work of David Keirsey and Marilyn Bates, who combined the 16 Myers-Briggs types into four temperaments and developed an assessment called the Keirsey Sorter based on those temperaments.

The Personality Spectrum assessment adapts and simplifies their material into four personality types—Thinker, Organizer, Giver, and Adventurer—and was developed by Dr. Joyce Bishop. The Personality Spectrum helps you identify the kinds of interactions that are most, and least, comfortable for you. Figure 3.2, on page 38, shows techniques that improve performance, learning strategies, and ways of relating to others for each personality type.

PERSONALITY SPECTRUM

STEP 1. Rank order all 4 responses to each question from most like you (4) to least like you (1) so that for each question you use the numbers 1, 2, 3, and 4 one time each. Place numbers in the boxes next to the responses.

4 most like me **3** more like me **2** less like me **1** least like me

1. I like instructors who
   a. ☐ tell me exactly what is expected of me.
   b. ☐ make learning active and exciting.
   c. ☐ maintain a safe and supportive classroom.
   d. ☐ challenge me to think at higher levels.

2. I learn best when the material is
   a. ☐ well organized.
   b. ☐ something I can do hands-on.
   c. ☐ about understanding and improving the human condition.
   d. ☐ intellectually challenging.

3. A high priority in my life is to
   a. ☐ keep my commitments.
   b. ☐ experience as much of life as possible.
   c. ☐ make a difference in the lives of others.
   d. ☐ understand how things work.

4. Other people think of me as
   a. ☐ dependable and loyal.
   b. ☐ dynamic and creative.
   c. ☐ caring and honest.
   d. ☐ intelligent and inventive.

5. When I experience stress I would most likely
   a. ☐ do something to help me feel more in control of my life.
   b. ☐ do something physical and daring.
   c. ☐ talk with a friend.
   d. ☐ go off by myself and think about my situation.

6. I would probably not be close friends with someone who is
   a. ☐ irresponsible.
   b. ☐ unwilling to try new things.
   c. ☐ selfish and unkind to others.
   d. ☐ an illogical thinker.

7. My vacations could be described as
   a. ☐ traditional.
   b. ☐ adventuresome.
   c. ☐ pleasing to others.
   d. ☐ a new learning experience.

8. One word that best describes me is
   a. ☐ sensible.
   b. ☐ spontaneous.
   c. ☐ giving.
   d. ☐ analytical.

STEP 2. Add up the total points for each letter.

TOTAL FOR **a.** ☐ Organizer   **b.** ☐ Adventurer   **c.** ☐ Giver   **d.** ☐ Thinker

STEP 3. Plot these numbers on the brain diagram on page 51.

SCORING DIAGRAM FOR PERSONALITY SPECTRUM

Write your scores from p. 50 in the four squares just outside the brain diagram—Thinker score at top left, Giver score at top right, Organizer score at bottom left, and Adventurer score at bottom right.

Each square has a line of numbers that go from the square to the center of the diagram. For each of your four scores, place a dot on the appropriate number in the line near that square. For example, if you scored 15 in the Giver spectrum, you would place a dot between the 14 and 16 in the upper right-hand line of numbers. If you scored a 26 in the Organizer spectrum, you would place a dot on the 26 in the lower left-hand line of numbers.

Connect the four dots to make a four-sided shape. If you like, shade the four sections inside the shape using four different colors.

THINKER

Technical
Scientific
Mathematical
Dispassionate
Rational
Analytical
Logical
Problem Solving
Theoretical
Intellectual
Objective
Quantitative
Explicit
Realistic
Literal
Precise
Formal

GIVER

Interpersonal
Emotional
Caring
Sociable
Giving
Spiritual
Musical
Romantic
Feeling
Peacemaker
Trusting
Adaptable
Passionate
Harmonious
Idealistic
Talkative
Honest

ORGANIZER

Tactical
Planning
Detailed
Practical
Confident
Predictable
Controlled
Dependable
Systematic
Sequential
Structured
Administrative
Procedural
Organized
Conservative
Safekeeping
Disciplined

ADVENTURER

Active
Visual
Risking
Original
Artistic
Spatial
Skillful
Impulsive
Metaphoric
Experimental
Divergent
Fast-paced
Simultaneous
Competitive
Imaginative
Open-minded
Adventuresome

For the Personality Spectrum,
26–36 indicates a strong tendency in that dimension,
14–25 a moderate tendency,
and below 14 a minimal tendency.

Source for brain diagram: Understanding Psychology, 3/e, by Morris, © 1996.
Adapted by permission of Prentice-Hall, Inc., Upper Saddle River, NJ.

CHARACTERISTICS OF EACH PERSONALITY TYPE

Thinker

- Solving problems
- Developing models and systems
- Analytical and abstract thinking
- Exploring ideas and potentials
- Ingenuity
- Going beyond established boundaries
- Global thinking—seeking universal truth

Organizer

- Responsibility, reliability
- Operating successfully within social structures
- Sense of history, culture, and dignity
- Neatness and organization
- Loyalty
- Orientation to detail
- Comprehensive follow-through on tasks
- Efficiency
- Helping others

Giver

- Honesty, authenticity
- Successful, close relationships
- Making a difference in the world
- Cultivating potential of self and others
- Negotiation; promoting peace
- Openness
- Helping others

Adventurer

- High ability in a variety of fields
- Courage and daring
- Hands-on problem solving
- Living in the present
- Spontaneity and action
- Ability to negotiate
- Nontraditional style
- Flexibility
- Zest for life

STUDY TECHNIQUES TO MAXIMIZE PERSONALITY TYPES

Thinker

- Find time to reflect independently on new information
- Learn through problem solving
- Design new ways of approaching issues
- Convert material into logical charts
- Try to minimize repetitive tasks
- Look for opportunities to work independently

Organizer

- Try to have tasks defined in clear, concrete terms so that you know what is required
- Look for a well-structured, stable environment
- Request feedback
- Use a planner to schedule tasks and dates
- Organize material by rewriting and organizing class or text notes, making flash cards, or carefully highlighting

Giver

- Study with others
- Teach material to others
- Seek out tasks, groups, and subjects that involve helping people
- Find ways to express thoughts and feelings clearly and honestly
- Put energy into your most important relationships

Adventurer

- Look for environments that encourage nontraditional approaches
- Find hands-on ways to learn
- Seek people whom you find stimulating
- Use or develop games and puzzles to help memorize terms
- Fight boredom by asking to do something extra or perform a task in a more active way

Joyce Bishop, *Keys to Success,* © 2001

Figure 3.2 How to Put Your Personality Spectrum to Work for You

What Are the Benefits of Knowing How you Learn?

Generally, self-knowledge helps you make choices that boost your strong areas and help you to manage weaker ones. For example, understanding what you value can help you choose friends who cheer on your successes as well as friends who broaden your horizons with their different perspectives. Likewise for learning style: When you know your Multiple Intelligences and personality traits, you can choose strategies that will help you learn more, remember better, and use your knowledge more successfully—in any academic or workplace situation.

Study benefits

Knowing how you learn helps you choose study techniques that capitalize on your strengths. For example, if you learn successfully from a linear, logical presentation, you can look for order (for example, a chronology or a problem–solution structure) as you review notes. If you are a strong interpersonal learner, you can try to work in study groups whenever possible.

Learning style also points you toward strategies that help with tasks and topics that don't come so easily. An Adventurer who does *not* respond well to linear information, for example, has two choices when faced with logical presentations. She can apply her strengths to the material—for example, she might find a hands-on approach. Or she can work on her ability to handle the material by developing study skills that work well for linear learners.

When you study with others, understanding of diverse learning styles will help you assign tasks effectively and learn more comprehensively. An interpersonal learner might take the lead in teaching material to others; an Organizer might be the schedule coordinator for the group; a musical learner might present information in a new way that helps to solidify concepts.

Classroom benefits

Your college instructors will most likely have a range of teaching styles (an instructor's teaching style often reflects his or her dominant learning style). Your particular learning style may work well with some instructors and be a mismatch with others. After several class meetings, you should be able to assess an instructor's teaching styles (see Figure 3.3). Then you can use what you know to maximize styles that suit you and compensate for those that don't.

Although presentation styles vary, the standard lecture is still the norm in most classrooms. For this reason, the traditional college classroom is generally a happy home for the verbal or logical learner and the Thinker and Organizer. However, many students learn best when interacting more than a lecture allows. What can you do if your styles don't match up with those of your instructor?

Play to your strengths

For example, an Organizer with an instructor who delivers material in a random way might rewrite notes in an outline format to bring structure to concepts and insert facts where they fit best. Likewise, a Giver taking a straight lecture course with no student-to-student contact might meet with a study group to go over the details and fill in factual gaps.

Work to build weaker areas

> Learning is not attained by chance, it must be sought for with ardor and attended to with diligence.
> —Abigail Adams

As a visual learner reviews notes from a structured lecture course, he could outline them, allot extra time to master the material, and work with a study group. A Thinker, studying for a test from notes delivered by an Adventurer instructor, could find hands-on ways to review the material (for example, for a science course, working in the lab).

TEACHING STYLE	WHAT TO EXPECT IN CLASS
LECTURE, VERBAL FOCUS	Instructor speaks to the class for the entire period, with little class interaction. Lesson is taught primarily through words, either spoken or written on the board, overhead projector, handouts, or text.
GROUP DISCUSSION	Instructor presents material but encourages class discussion.
SMALL GROUPS	Instructor presents material and then breaks class into small groups for discussion or project work.
VISUAL FOCUS	Instructor uses visual elements such as diagrams, photographs, drawings, transparencies.
LOGICAL PRESENTATION	Instructor organizes material in a logical sequence, such as by time or importance.
RANDOM PRESENTATION	Instructor tackles topics in no particular order, and may jump around a lot or digress.

Figure 3.3 Instructors Often Rely On One or More Teaching Styles

Ask your instructor for additional help

If you are having trouble with coursework, communicate with your instructor through e-mail or face-to-face during office hours. This is especially important in large lectures where you are anonymous unless you speak up. The visual learner, for example, might ask the instructor to recommend graphs or figures that illustrate the lecture.

Instructors are unique. No instructor can give each of a diverse group of learners exactly what each one needs. The flexibility that you need to mesh your learning style with instructors' teaching styles is a tool for career and life success. Just as you can't hand-pick your instructors, you will rarely, if ever, be able to choose your supervisors or their work styles.

Workplace benefits

Knowing how you learn brings you these benefits in your career:

- **Better performance through self-awareness.** Since your learning styles are essentially the same as your working styles, knowing how you learn will help you identify career and work environments that suit you. Knowing your strengths will help you use and highlight them on the job. When a task involves one of your weaker skills, you can either take special care to accomplish it or suggest someone else who is a better fit.

- **Better teamwork.** The more attuned you are to abilities and personality traits, the better you will be at identifying the tasks you and others can best perform in team situations. For example, a Giver might enjoy helping new hires get used to the people and environment. Or a supervisor directing an intrapersonal learner might offer the chance to take material home to think about before a meeting.

ASSESS: WHAT CAN YOU LEARN ABOUT PERSONALITY

To begin, take the following PAP assessment.

#2. The Personality Assessment Profile (PAP) (2005) by Robert Sherfield, Ph.D. Based in part on the Myers Briggs Type Indicator (MBTI) by Katherine Briggs and Isabel Briggs-Myers. Read each statement carefully and thoroughly. After reading the statement, rate your response using the scale to the right. There are no right or wrong answers. This is not a timed survey.

Never or Almost never	Sometimes	Often
1	2	3

1. _____ I am a very talkative person.
2. _____ I am a very friendly and social person.
3. _____ I like to express my feelings and thoughts.
4. _____ I like to work with a group of people.
5. _____ I can be myself when I'm around others.

_____ TOTAL for **EXTROVERT**

1. _____ I am a more reflective person than a verbal person.
2. _____ I enjoy listening to others more than talking.
3. _____ I enjoy a great deal of tranquility and quiet time to myself.
4. _____ I would rather work independently.
5. _____ I can be myself when I am alone.

_____ TOTAL for **INTROVERT**

1. _____ I look to the future, and I can see possibilities.
2. _____ I enjoy being around and working with people who are dreamers and have a great deal of imagination.
3. _____ I like to create new ideas, methods, or ways of doing things.
4. _____ I learn best by relying on my gut feelings or intuition.
5. _____ I live in the future, planning and dreaming.

_____ TOTAL for **INTUITION**

1. _____ I am a very factual and literal person.
2. _____ I enjoy being around and working with people who have a great deal of common sense.
3. _____ I am a very pragmatic and realistic person.
4. _____ I learn best if I can see it, touch it, smell it, taste it, or hear it.
5. _____ I live in the here and now, in the present

_____ TOTAL for **SENSING**

1. _____ I value truth and justice over tact and emotion.
2. _____ One of my motivating forces is to do a job well.
3. _____ I make decisions with my brain.
4. _____ I am quick to criticize others.
5. _____ I think that if someone breaks the rules, the person should be punished.

_____ TOTAL for **THINKING**

1. _____ I find it easy to empathize with other people.
2. _____ I like to be recognized for, and I am motivated by, my accomplishments and awards.
3. _____ I make decisions with my heart.
4. _____ I compliment others very easily and quickly.
5. _____ I think that if someone breaks the rules, we should look at the person who broke the rules, examine the rules, and look at the situation at hand before a decision is made.

_____ TOTAL for **FEELING**

continued on next page

Never or Almost never — 1
Sometimes — 2
Often — 3

1. _____ I enjoy having freedom from control.
2. _____ I like to plan out my day before I go to bed.
3. _____ I am a very disciplined and orderly person.
4. _____ My life is systematic and organized.
5. _____ I do my work, then I play.

_____ TOTAL for JUDGING

1. _____ I enjoy having freedom from control.
2. _____ When I get up on a non-school or non-work day, I just like to let the day "plan itself."
3. _____ I don't make a lot of plans.
4. _____ I don't really pay attention to deadlines.
5. _____ I play, then do my work.

_____ TOTAL for PERCEIVING

Pap Scores

Personality Indicator

Look at the scores on your PAP. Is your score higher in the E or I line? Is your score higher in the S or N line? Is your score higher in the T or F line? Is your score higher in the J or P line? Write the code to the side of each section below.

Is your higher score	E or I	Code _____
Is your higher score	S or N	Code _____
Is your higher score	T or F	Code _____
Is your higher score	J or P	Code _____

Understanding Personality Typing (Typology)

The questions on the PAP helped you discover whether you are extroverted or introverted (E or I), sensing or intuitive (S or N), thinking or feeling (T or F), and judging or perceiving (J or P). These questions were based, in part, on work done by Carl Jung, Katharine Briggs, and Isabel Briggs-Myers. What personality typing can do is to "help us discover what best motivates and energizes each of us as individuals" (Tieger and Tieger, 2001).

Plan to Understand Personality Categories

Let's take a look at the four major categories of typing. Notice that the stronger your score in one area, the stronger your personality type is for that area. For instance, if you scored 15 on the E (extroversion) questions, this means that you are a strong extrovert. If you scored 15 on the I (introversion) questions, this means that you are a strong introvert. However, if you scored 7 on the E questions and 8 on the I questions, your score indicates that you possess almost the same amount of extroverted and introverted qualities. The same is true for every category on the PAP.

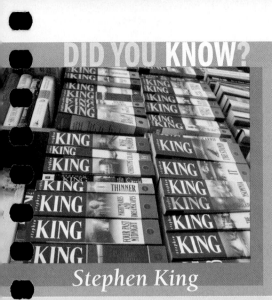
E Versus I (Extroversion/Introversion)

This category deals with the way we *interact with others and the world around us.*

Extroverts prefer to live in the outside world, drawing their strength from other people. They are outgoing and love interaction. They usually make decisions with others in mind. They enjoy being the center of attention. There are usually few secrets about extroverts.

Introverts draw their strength from the inner world. They need to spend time alone to think and ponder. They are usually quiet and make decisions alone.

S Versus N (Sensing/Intuition)

This category deals with the way we *learn and deal with information.*

Sensing types gather information through their five senses. They have a hard time believing something if it cannot be seen, touched, smelled, tasted, or heard. They like concrete facts and details. They do not rely on intuition or gut feelings. They usually have a great deal of common sense.

Intuitive types are not very detail-oriented. They can see possibilities, and they rely on their gut feelings. Usually, they are very innovative people. They tend to live in the future and often get bored once they have mastered a task.

T Versus F (Thinking/Feeling)

This category deals with the way we *make decisions.*

Thinkers are very logical people. They do not make decisions based on feelings or emotion. They are analytical and sometimes do not take others' values into consideration when making decisions. They can easily identify the flaws of others. They can be seen as insensitive and lacking compassion.

Feelers make decisions based on what they feel is right and just. They like to have harmony, and they value others' opinions and feelings. They are usually very tactful people who like to please others. They are very warm people.

J Versus P (Judging/Perceiving)

This category deals with the way we *live.*

Judgers are very orderly people. They must have a great deal of structure in their lives. They are good at setting goals and sticking to their goals. They are the type of people who would seldom, if ever, play before their work was completed.

Perceivers are just the opposite. They are less structured and more spontaneous. They do not like timelines. Unlike the judger, they will play before their work is done. They will take every chance to delay a decision or judgment.

With this information, you can make some decisions about your study habits and even your career choices. For instance, if you scored very strong in the extroversion section, it may not serve you well to pursue a career where you would be forced to work alone. It would probably be unwise to try to spend all of your time studying alone. If you are a strong extrovert, you would want to work and study around people.

Making It Work for You

Having identified your personality type, use the suggestions on the following pages to enhance studying using your present personality type, while improving your study skills using your less dominant type.

Type	Current Suggestions	Improvement
Extrovert	Study with groups of people in cooperative learning teams.	Work on listening skills.
	Seek help from others.	Be sure to let others contribute to the group.
	Discuss topics with friends.	Force yourself to develop solutions and answers before you go to the group.
	Establish debate or discussion groups.	Spend some time reflecting.
	Vary your study habits; meet in different places with different people.	Let others speak before you share your ideas and suggestions.
	Discuss new ideas and plans with your friends.	Work to be more patient.
		Think before acting or speaking.
Introvert	Study in a quiet place, undisturbed by others.	Get involved in a study group from time to time.
	When reading and studying, take time for reflection.	Allow others inside your world to offer advice and opinions.
	Use your time alone to read and study support and auxiliary materials.	Share your opinions and advice with others more often.
	Set aside large blocks of time for study and reflection.	Seek advice from others.
		Use mnemonics to increase your memory power.
		Instead of writing responses or questions, speak aloud to friends and peers.
Sensor	Observe the world around you.	Try to think about the information in an abstract form.
	Experience the information to the fullest degree; feel it and touch it.	Think "What would happen if . . ." Let your imagination run wild.
	Explain to your study group or partner the information in complete detail.	Think about the information in the future tense. Let your gut feelings take over from time to time.
	Apply the information to something in your life that is currently happening.	Take more chances with the unknown.
	Create a study schedule and stick to it.	Trust your feelings and inspirations.
	If your old study habits are not working, stop and invent new ways of studying. Explore what others are doing.	Think beyond reality. Don't oversimplify.
Intuitive	After studying the information or data, let your imagination apply this to something abstract.	Work on becoming more detail-oriented.
	Describe how the information could be used today, right now, in your life at the moment.	Look at information through the senses.
	Describe how this information could help others.	Verify your facts.
	View new information as a challenge.	Think in simple terms.
	Vary your study habits; don't do the same thing all the time.	Think about the information in a logical and analytical way.
	Rely on your gut feelings.	Try to explain new information in relation to the senses.

Continued

Type	Current Suggestions	Improvement
Thinker	Make logical connections between new information and what is already known.	Try to see information and data in more abstract terms.
	Remain focused.	Look for the "big picture."
	Explain the information in detailed terms to a study group.	Develop a passion for acquiring new information.
	Put things in order.	Think before you speak.
	Study with people who do their part for the group.	Strive to be more objective and open.
Feeler	Establish a supportive and open study group.	Strive to look at things more logically.
	Teach others the information.	Work to stay focused.
	Continue to be passionate about learning and exploring.	Praise yourself when others do not.
	Explain the information in a cause/effect scenario.	Try to be more organized.
	Focus on the "people" factor.	Work to stick to policies, rules, and guidelines.
		Don't give in to opposition just for the sake of harmony.
		Don't get caught up in the here and now; look ahead.
Judger	Set a schedule and stick to it.	Take your time in making decisions.
	Strive to complete projects.	Complete all tasks.
	Keep your study supplies in one place so that you can locate them easily.	Look at the entire situation before making a judgment.
	Prioritize tasks that need to be completed.	Don't act or make judgments too quickly.
	Create lists and agendas.	Don't beat yourself up if you miss a deadline.
Perceiver	Study in different places with different people.	Become more decisive.
	Since you see all sides of issues, share those with your study group for discussion.	Finish one project before you begin another.
	Obtain as much information as possible so that you can make solid decisions.	Don't put off the harder subjects until later; study them first.
	Create fun and exciting study groups with snacks and maybe music.	Learn to set deadlines.
	Be the leader of the study team.	Create lists and agendas to help you stay on target.
	Allow yourself a great deal of time for study so that you can take well-deserved breaks.	Do your work; then play.

ASSESS: HOW CAN YOU USE LEARNING STYLES?

To begin, take the following Learning Style Assessment # 3.
Learning Style Assessment (2006) by Kateri Drexler
Based in part on the Solomon and Felder's Index of Learning Styles
Read each statement carefully and thoroughly. After reading the statement, rate your response using the scale to the right. There are no right or wrong answers. This is not a timed survey.

Never or Almost never	Sometimes	Often
1	2	3

1. _____ I tend to understand details of a subject but may be fuzzy about its overall structure.

2. _____ Once I understand all the parts, I understand the whole thing.

3. _____ When I solve math problems I usually work my way to the solutions one step at a time.

4. _____ When I'm analyzing a story or a novel I think of the incidents and try to put them together to figure out the themes.

5. _____ It is more important to me that an instructor lay out the material in clear sequential steps.

_____ TOTAL for Sequential

1. _____ I understand something better after I try it out.

2. _____ When I am learning something new, it helps me to talk about it.

3. _____ In a group working on learning difficult material or a tough project, I am more likely to jump in and contribute ideas.

4. _____ In classes I have taken I have usually gotten to know many of the students.

5. _____ I would rather first try things out.

_____ TOTAL for Active

1. _____ I would rather be considered realistic.

2. _____ I find it easier to learn facts.

3. _____ If I were a teacher, I would rather teach a course that deals with facts and real life situations.

4. _____ In reading nonfiction, I prefer something that teaches me new facts or tells me how to do something.

5. _____ I prefer the idea of certainty.

_____ TOTAL for Sensing

1. _____ I tend to understand the overall structure but may be fuzzy about details.

2. _____ Once I understand the whole thing, I see how the parts fit.

3. _____ When I solve math problems I often just see the solutions but then have to struggle to figure out the steps to get to them.

4. _____ When I'm analyzing a story or a novel I just know what the themes are when I finish reading and then I have to go back and find the incidents that demonstrate them.

5. _____ It is more important to me that an instructor give me an overall picture and relate the material to other subjects.

_____ TOTAL for Global

1. _____ I understand something better after I think it through.

2. _____ When I am learning something new, it helps me to think about it.

3. _____ In a group working on learning difficult material or a tough project, I am more likely to sit back and listen.

4. _____ In classes I have taken I have rarely gotten to know many of the students.

5. _____ I would rather first think about how I'm going to do it.

_____ TOTAL for Reflective

1. _____ I would rather be considered innovative.

2. _____ I find it easier to learn concepts.

3. _____ If I were a teacher, I would rather teach a course that deals with ideas and theories.

4. _____ In reading nonfiction, I prefer something that gives me new ideas to think about.

5. _____ I prefer the idea of theory.

_____ TOTAL for Intuitive

ASSESS: HOW CAN YOU USE LEARNING STYLES?

1. _____ When I think about what I did yesterday, I am most likely to get a picture.	1. _____ When I think about what I did yesterday, I am most likely to get words.
2. _____ I prefer to get new information in pictures, diagrams, graphs, or maps.	2. _____ I prefer to get new information in written directions or verbal information.
3. _____ In a book with lots of pictures and charts, I am likely to look over the pictures and charts carefully.	3. _____ In a book with lots of pictures and charts, I am likely to focus on the written text.
4. _____ I like teachers who put a lot of diagrams on the board.	4. _____ I like teachers who spend a lot of time explaining.
5. _____ When I see a diagram or sketch in class, I am most likely to remember the picture.	5. _____ When I see a diagram or sketch in class, I am most likely to remember what the instructor said about it.
_____ TOTAL for Visual	_____ TOTAL for Verbal

Plan to Understand the Different Learning Styles

Sequential and Global Learners

This category deals with the way we *learn information as a whole*.

Sequential learners tend to gain understanding in linear steps, with each step following logically from the previous one. They follow logical pathways to find solutions. Sequential learners may not fully understand the material but they can nevertheless do something with it (like solve the homework problems or pass the test) because the pieces they have absorbed are logically connected. Sequential learners may know a lot about specific aspects of a subject but may have trouble relating them to different aspects of the same subject or to different subjects.

Global learners tend to learn in large jumps, absorbing material almost randomly without seeing connections, and then suddenly "getting it." They may be able to solve complex problems quickly or put things together in novel ways once they have grasped the big picture, but they may have difficulty explaining how they did it. What makes you global or not is what happens before the light bulb goes on. Strongly global learners who lack good sequential thinking abilities, on the other hand, may have serious difficulties until they have the big picture. Even after they have it, they may be fuzzy about the details of the subject.

Active and Reflective Learners

Active learners tend to retain and understand information best by doing something active with it—discussing or applying it or explaining it to others. "Let's try it out and see how it works" is an active learner's phrase. Active learners tend to like group work. Sitting through lectures without getting to do anything physical but take notes is hard for both learning types, but particularly hard for active learners.

Reflective learners prefer to think about it quietly first. "Let's think it through first" is the reflective learner's response. Reflective learners would rather avoid group work. They prefer working alone.

Sensing and Intuitive Learners

Sensing learners tend to like learning facts; intuitive learners often prefer discovering possibilities and relationships. Sensors often like solving problems by well-established methods and dislike complications and surprises. They are likely to resent being tested on material that has not been explicitly covered in class. Sensors tend to be patient with details and good at memorizing facts and doing hands-on (laboratory) work; Sensors tend to be practical and careful. Sensors don't like courses that have no apparent connection to the real world.

Intuitors like innovation and dislike repetition. Intuitive learners may be better at grasping new concepts and are often comfortable with abstractions and mathematical formulations. Intuitors tend to work faster and to be more innovative. They don't tend to like courses that involve a lot of memorization and routine calculations.

Visual and Verbal Learners

Visual learners remember best what they see—pictures, diagrams, flow charts, time lines, films, and demonstrations. In most college classes very little visual information is presented: students mainly listen to lectures and read material written on chalkboards and in textbooks and handouts. Unfortunately, most people are visual learners, which means that most students do not get nearly as much as they would if more visual presentation were used in class.

Verbal learners get more out of words—written and spoken explanations. Everyone learns more when information is presented both visually and verbally.

Making It Work for You
Using the Learning Styles to Learn More Effectively

Having identified your primary learning style, use the suggestions on the following pages to enhance studying using your present style, while improving your study skills using your less dominant type.

Type	Current Suggestions	Improvement
Sequential	Most college courses are taught in a sequential manner. If you are a sequential learner and you have an instructor who jumps around from topic to topic or skips steps, you can: Ask the instructor to fill in the skipped steps, or fill them in yourself by consulting references. Take the time to outline the lecture material for yourself in logical order, when you are studying.	Strengthen your global thinking skills by relating each new topic you study to things you already know. The more you can do so, the deeper your understanding of the topic is likely to be. Skim through the entire chapter of what you will be covering in class to get an overview.
Global	Realize that you need the big picture of a subject before you can master details. If your instructor plunges directly into new topics without explaining how they relate to what you already know, you can: Skim through the entire chapter of what you will be covering in class to get an overview. Immerse yourself in individual subjects for large blocks instead of spending a short time on every subject every night. Ask the instructor to help you see connections or consult additional resources to help you see them.	Prepare outlines of lecture material for yourself in logical order. Practice patience. Recognize that understanding of the big picture will come in time.
Active	If you are an active learner in a class that allows little or no class time for discussion or problem-solving activities, you should try to compensate for these lacks when you study by: Studying in a group in which the members take turns explaining different topics to each other. Work with others to guess what you will be asked on the next test and figure out how you will answer.	The next time you are about to take some action, try taking a minute to reflect on what you're going do.
Reflective	If you are a reflective learner in a class that allows little or no class time for thinking about new information, you should try to compensate for this lack when you study by: Stopping periodically during reading to review what you have read and to think of possible questions or applications. Writing short summaries of readings or class notes in your own words. Doing so may take extra time but will enable you to retain the material more effectively.	Get involved with a study group periodically. Actively participate in class discussions, recognizing that you reserve the right to change your mind about a topic later if you choose to.

Type	Current Suggestions	Improvement
Sequential	Sensors remember and understand information best if they can see how it connects to the real world. If you are in a class where most of the material is abstract and theoretical, you can: Ask your instructor for specific examples of concepts and procedures, and find out how the concepts apply in practice. Try to find some in your course text or other references or by brainstorming with friends or classmates.	If you overemphasize sensing, you may rely too much on memorization and familiar methods and not concentrate enough on understanding and innovative thinking. Ask your instructor for interpretations or theories that link the facts, or try to find the connections yourself.
Intuitive	Many college lecture classes are aimed at intuitors. However, if you are an intuitor and you happen to be in a class that deals primarily with memorization and rote substitution in formulas, you can: Ask your instructor for interpretations or theories that link the facts, or try to find the connections yourself. Be careful on tests and not get impatient with details. Take time to read the entire question before you start answering questions and be sure to check your results.	If you overemphasize intuition, you may miss important details or make careless mistakes in calculations or hands-on work. Think of exciting ways to memorize information that will be needed. Use mnemonic devices or flash cards.
Visual	If you are a visual learner, try to: Find diagrams, sketches, schematics, photographs, flow charts, or any other visual representation of course material that is predominantly verbal. Ask your instructor, consult reference books, and see whether any videotapes or CD-ROM displays of the course material are available. Prepare a mind map by listing key points, enclosing them in boxes or circles, and drawing lines with arrows between concepts to show connections. Color-code your notes with a highlighter so that everything relating to one topic is the same color.	Write summaries or outlines of course material in your own words.
Verbal	If you are a verbal learner, you can: Write summaries or outlines of course material in your own words. Work in groups and gain an understanding of material by hearing classmates' explanations. Summarize your understanding to your classmates.	Prepare a mind map by listing key points, enclosing them in boxes or circles, and drawing lines with arrows between concepts to show connections. Actively look for diagrams, sketches, schematics, photographs, flow charts, or any other visual representation of course material and seek to understand them

What Are Some Other Learning Styles?

There are many learning styles theories. The important thing to help you during your education is to recognize that you may have a dominant style. Fit your education around that when you can, and try to develop your other learning styles as much as possible. The following two theories may provide additional insight into how you process information.

Introduction to a Cognitive Learning Style

Kolb's Learning Style Inventory is one of the dominant approaches to categorizing cognitive styles. There are four basic learning styles: converger, diverger, assimilator, and accommodator. Their characteristics are described below:

Converger

The convergent learner uses active experimentation and abstract conceptualization. This style has great advantages in decision making, problem solving, traditional intelligent tests, and practical applications of theories. People with this style are typically superior in technical tasks and problems and inferior in social and interpersonal matters. They tend to choose to specialize in physical sciences.

Diverger

The divergent learning style has the opposite learning advantages over converger. This style depends mainly on concrete experience and reflective observation; it has great advantages in imaginative abilities and awareness of meaning and values. People with this tend to be imaginative, people- or feeling-oriented; they tend to choose to specialize in liberal arts and humanities.

Assimilator

People primarily using the assimilator learning style tend to focus more on the logical soundness and preciseness of ideas, rather than their practical values; they tend to choose to work in research and planning units.

Accommodator

The accommodative learning style has the opposite learning advantages over assimilation. These learners tend to intuitively solve problems in a trial-and-error manner, depending mainly on other people for information rather than on their own thinking. Therefore, persons with this style tend to deal with people easily and can excel in action-oriented jobs, such as marketing and sales.

Introduction to an Experiential Learning Style

Theorists in the experiential learning tradition identify four types of learning style: the activist learner, the reflective learner, the theorist learner and the pragmatic learner. The following table outlines those activities that will be most or least appropriate for each type of learner.

Activist style	
Learns best from activities where:	*Learns least from activities where:*
there are new experiences/problems, etc.;	learning involves a passive role, e.g. listening to lectures, reading, explanations;
they can become engrossed in short tasks, games, competitive teamwork tasks, etc.;	they are not directly involved;
there is excitement/drama/crisis and things chop and change with a range of diverse activities to tackle;	they are required to assimilate, analyze and interpret lots of data;
there is chance of limelight, e.g. leading discussions, giving presentations;	they are required to engage in solitary work, i.e. reading, writing, thinking on their own;
they are involved with other people, e.g. bouncing ideas off them, solving problems as part of a team.	they are asked to repeat the same activity over and over again.

Continued

Reflector style	
Learns best from activities where:	*Learns least from activities where:*
they are encouraged to watch/think/chew over activities;	they are forced into the limelight;
they are able to listen/observe a group;	they are worried by time pressures or rushed from one activity to another;
they can reach a decision in their own time without pressure and tight deadlines.	they are pitched into doing something without warning.

Theorist style	
Learns best from activities where:	*Learns least from activities where:*
they are in structured situations with a clear purpose;	they have to participate in situations that are unstructured, where ambiguity and uncertainty are high, e.g. open-ended problems;
they are required to understand and participate in complex situations;	they are faced with a hodgepodge of alternative/contradictory techniques without exploring any in depth;
they have time to explore the associations and interrelationships between ideas, events and situations.	they find the subject matter platitudinous, shallow or gimmicky.

Pragmatist style	
Learns best from activities where:	*Learns least from activities where:*
there is an obvious link between the subject matter and a problem set;	the learning is not related to an immediate need or relevance;
they are practicing techniques with coaching/feedback;	there is no practice or clear guidelines on how to do it;
they are given techniques that are applicable to the real world.	they cannot see sufficient reward from the learning activity.

Note-Taking Techniques
Tips for Effective Note-Taking During Reading

Taking notes is a useful way to organize your thoughts, focus on structure and key ideas, and help commit important information to memory. There are different reasons to take notes, and note-taking techniques may differ accordingly. We may take notes in order to:

- Brainstorm
- Explore ideas and gather more information
- Synthesize ideas
- Focus on a topic's details
- Present information

There are also different situations when we take notes, the most common being:

- Reading and researching
- Listening to a lecture or presentation

The note-taking techniques discussed later in this section include:

- Mapping
- T-format, or Cornell Method
- Outlining

Which method you use will depend on what works best for you. The following chart shows how the different techniques are best applied to the particular note-taking purpose.

Primary Note-Taking Purpose	Primary Note-Taking Techniques
Brainstorm	Mapping
Explore idea and gather more information	T-format
Synthesize ideas	T-format, Mapping
Focus on a topic's details	Outlining
Present information	Outlining

While taking notes during reading allows you the luxury of going back to passages for further understanding, you may have to do more synthesizing of multiple ideas and topics.

No matter which technique you use to take notes while reading, consider the following suggestions:

- Note any terms and definitions given. You can check the definitions of unfamiliar terms, as well as names, events, dates, steps, or directions.

- Wait until you read the document at least once before marking the text. If you mark text as you are reading you may tend to over-mark. Wait until you've finished a section, then go back and highlight the key points.

- Highlight key terms and concepts, if you own your text or are able to mark up a document. Mark the examples that explain and support the important ideas. You might try using more than one highlighter color to differentiate definitions or ideas from examples.

- Highlight figures and tables, if you own the text. Whatever information you need from the tables and figures should be highlighted along with any tables that summarize the concepts discussed in the text.

- Write notes in the margin, if you're able to mark the document. Comments such as "main point" or "important definition" will help you locate key sections later on. In addition, note any questions you may have about the document's validity in the margins.

- Review the highlights and organize into notes. Be an active reader. You will not necessarily learn from what you highlight unless you review it carefully.

Listening to people from different cultures, backgrounds, and religions can open many doors.

Now Hear This!
Tips for Effective Note-Taking in Class

It is important to develop several skills you will need to take notes. *First*, you need to cultivate and build your active listening skills. *Second*, you need to overcome obstacles to effective listening, such as prejudging, talking during a discussion, and bringing emotions to the table. *Finally*, you must scan, read, and use your textbook to understand the materials presented. Following are a few more important tips for taking notes.

Attend Class

This may sound like stating the obvious, but it is surprising how many college students feel they do not need to go to class. You may be able to copy notes from others, but you may very well miss the meaning behind them. To be an effective note taker, class attendance is crucial; there is no substitute for it.

Come to Class Prepared

Do you read your assignments nightly? Instructors are amazed at the number of students who come to class and then decide they should have read their homework. Doing your homework—reading your text, handouts, or workbooks or listening to tapes—is one of the most effective ways to become a better notetaker. It is always easier to take notes when you have a preliminary understanding of what is being said. As a student, you will find fewer tasks more difficult than trying to take notes on material that you have never seen or heard before. Coming to class prepared means doing your homework and coming to class ready to listen.

Coming to class prepared also means bringing the proper materials for taking notes: your textbook or lab manual, at least two pens, enough sharpened pencils to make it through the lecture, a notebook, and a highlighter. Some students also use a tape recorder. If you choose to use a tape recorder, be sure to get permission from the instructor before recording.

Bring Your Textbook to Class

Although many students think they do not need to bring their textbook to class if they have read the homework, you will find that many instructors repeatedly refer to the text while lecturing. Always bring your textbook to class with you. The instructor may ask you to highlight, underline, or refer to the text in class, and following along in the text as the instructor lectures may also help you organize your notes.

Ask Questions and Participate in Class

Two of the most critical actions you can perform in class are to ask questions and to participate in the class discussion. If you do not understand a concept or theory, ask questions.

Don't leave class without understanding what has happened and assume you'll pick it up on your own. Many instructors use students' questions as a way of teaching and reviewing materials. Your questions and participation will definitely help you, but they could also help others who did not understand something!

Listen Up!
Building Listening Skills

Listening is one of the most important and useful skills human beings possess. For all animals, listening is a survival skill needed for hunting and obtaining food; for humans, listening is necessary for establishing relationships, growth, survival, knowledge, entertainment, and even health. It is one of our most widely used tools. How much time do you think you spend listening every day? Research suggests that we spend almost 70% of our waking time communicating, and 53% of that time is spent in listening situations (Adler, Rosenfeld, and Towne, 2001). Effective listening skills can mean the difference between success and failure, A's and F's, relationships and loneliness.

For students, good listening skills are critical. Over the course of your program, you will be given a lot of information in lectures. Cultivating and improving your active listening skills will help you to understand the lecture material, take accurate notes, participate in class discussions, and communicate with your peers.

The Difference between Listening and Hearing

We usually do not think much about listening until a misunderstanding occurs. You've no doubt been misunderstood or misunderstood someone yourself. Misunderstandings arise because we tend to view listening as an automatic response when it is instead a learned, voluntary activity, like driving a car, painting a picture, or playing the piano. Having ears does not make you a good listener.

After all, having hands does not mean you are capable of painting the *Mona Lisa*. You may be able to paint the *Mona Lisa*, but only with practice and guidance. Listening, too, takes practice and guidance. Becoming an active listener requires practice, time, mistakes, guidance, and active participation.

Hearing, however, is not learned; it is automatic and involuntary. If you are within range of a sound, you will probably hear it although you may not be listening to it. Hearing a sound does not guarantee that you know what it is or what made it. Listening actively, though, means making a conscious effort to focus on the sound and to determine what it is.

Listening Defined

According to Ronald Adler (Adler, Rosenfeld, and Towne, 2001), the drawing of the Chinese verb "to listen" provides a comprehensive and practical definition of listening (see Figure 3.4). To the Chinese, listening involves the ears, the eyes, undivided attention, and the heart. Do you make it a habit to listen with more than your ears? The Chinese view listening as a whole-body experience. People from Western cultures seem to have lost the ability to involve their whole body in the listening process. We tend to use only our ears, and sometimes we don't even use them. At its

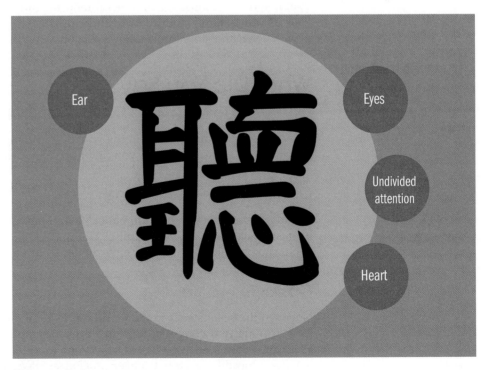

Figure 3.4 The Chinese Pictograph for "Listen"

College classes demand active critical listening skills.

core, listening is "the ability to hear, understand, analyze, respect, and appropriately respond to the meaning of another person's spoken and nonverbal messages" (Daly and Engleberg, 2002, p. 270). Although this definition involves the word "hear," listening goes far beyond just the physical ability to catch sound waves.

The first step in listening *is* hearing, but true listening involves one's full attention and the ability to filter out distractions, emotional barriers, cultural differences, and religious biases. Listening means that you are making a conscious decision to understand and show reverence for the other person's communication efforts.

Listening needs to be personalized and internalized. To understand listening as a whole-body experience, we can define it on three levels:

1. Listening with a purpose
2. Listening objectively
3. Listening constructively

Listening with a purpose suggests a need to recognize different types of listening situations—for example, class, worship, entertainment, and relationships. People do not listen the same way in every situation.

Listening objectively means listening with an open mind. You will give yourself few greater gifts than the gift of knowing how to listen without bias and prejudice. This is perhaps the most difficult aspect of listening. If you have been cut off in mid-conversation or mid-sentence by someone who disagreed with you, or if someone has left the room while you were giving your opinion of a situation, you have had the experience of talking to people who do not know how to listen objectively.

Listening constructively means listening with the attitude of "How can this be helpful to my life or my education?" This type of listening involves evaluating the information you are hearing and determining whether it has meaning to your life. Sound easy? It is more difficult than it sounds because, again, we all tend to shut out information that we do not view as immediately helpful or useful. To listen constructively, you need to know how to listen and store information for later.

What Did You Say?
Obstacles to Listening

Several major obstacles stand in the way of becoming an effective listener. To begin building active listening skills, you first have to remove some barriers.

Obstacle One: Prejudging

Prejudging means that you automatically shut out what is being said; it is one of the biggest obstacles to active listening. You may prejudge because of the content; the person communicating; or your environment, culture, social status, or attitude.

Obstacle Two: Talking

Not even the best listener in the world can listen while he or she is talking. The next time you are in a conversation with a friend, try speaking while your friend is speaking—then see if you know what your friend said. To become an effective listener, you need to learn the power of silence. Silence gives you the opportunity to think about what is being said before you respond.

TIP — Tips for Overcoming Prejudging

1. Listen for information that may be valuable to you as a student. Some material may not be pleasant to hear but may be useful to you later on.

2. Listen to the message, not the messenger. If you do not like the speaker, try to go beyond personality and listen to what is being said, without regard to the person saying it. Conversely, you may like the speaker so much that you automatically accept the material or answers without listening objectively to what is being said.

3. Try to remove cultural, racial, gender, social, and environmental barriers. Just because a person is different from you or holds a different point of view does not make that person wrong; and just because a person is like you and holds a similar point of view does not make that person right. Sometimes, you have to cross cultural and environmental barriers to learn new material and see with brighter eyes.

TIP — Tips for Overcoming the Urge to Talk Too Much

1. Force yourself to be silent at parties, family gatherings, and friendly get-togethers. We're not saying you should be unsociable, but force yourself to be silent for 10 minutes. You'll be surprised at what you hear. You may also be surprised how hard it is to do this. Test yourself.

2. Ask someone a question and then allow that person to answer the question. Too often we ask questions and answer them ourselves. Force yourself to wait until the person has formulated a response. If you ask questions and wait for answers, you will force yourself to listen.

Obstacle Three: Bringing Your Emotions to the Table

Emotions can form a strong barrier to active listening. Worries, problems, fears, and anger can keep you from listening to the greatest advantage. Have you ever sat in a lecture, and before you knew what was happening your mind was a million miles away because you were angry or worried about something? If you have, you know what it's like to bring your emotions to the table.

TIP — Tips for Overcoming Emotions

1. Know how you feel before you begin the listening experience. Take stock of your emotions and feelings ahead of time.

2. Focus on the message; determine how to use the information.

3. Create a positive image about the message you are hearing.

Listening for Key Words, Phrases, and Hints

Learning how to listen for key words, phrases, and hints can help you become an active listener and an effective note taker. For example, if an auto mechanics instructor began a lecture saying, "There are ten basic elements to engine maintenance," you might jot down the number 10 under the heading "Maintenance" or put the numbers 1 through 10 on sequential lines of your notebook page, leaving space for notes. If by the end of class you had listed only six elements, you would know that you had missed a part of the lecture. At that point, you would need to ask the instructor some questions.

Here are some key phrases and words to listen for:

- in addition
- most important
- you'll see this again
- for example
- in contrast
- the characteristics of
- on the other hand

- another way
- such as
- therefore
- to illustrate
- in comparison
- the main issue is
- as a result of

- above all
- specifically
- finally
- as stated earlier
- nevertheless
- moreover
- because

Listening When English Is Your Second Language
Suggestions for ESL Students

For students whose first language is not English, the college classroom can present some uniquely challenging situations. One of the most pressing and important challenges is the ability to listen, translate, understand, and capture the message on paper in a quick and continuous manner. According to Lynn Forkos, Professor and Coordinator of the Conversation Center for International Students at the Community College of Southern Nevada, the following tips can be beneficial:

- Don't be afraid to **stop the instructor** to ask for clarification. Asking questions allows you to take an active part in the listening process. If the instructor doesn't answer your questions sufficiently, be certain to make an appointment to speak with him or her during his or her office hours.

- If you are in a situation in which the instructor can't stop or you're watching a movie or video in class, listen for words that you do understand and try to **figure out unfamiliar words in the context** of the sentence.

- **Enhance your vocabulary** by watching and listening to TV programs such as *Dateline, 20/20, Primetime Live, 60 Minutes,* and the evening news. You might also try listening to radio programming such as National Public Radio as you walk or drive.

- Be certain that you **write down everything** that the instructor puts on the board, overhead, or PowerPoint. You may not need every piece of this information, but this technique gives you (and hopefully your study group) the ability to sift through the information outside of class. It gives you a visual history of what the instructor said.

- Finally, if there is a conversation group or club that meets on campus, take the opportunity to join. **By practicing language,** you become more attuned to common words and phrases. If a conversation group is not available, consider starting one of your own.

Plan to Write It Right
Methods for Effective Note-Taking

Good note-taking skills help you do more than simply record what you're taught in class or read in a book so that you can recall it. These skills can also help to reinforce that information so that you actually know it.

There are three common note-taking systems: (1) the **outline** technique; (2) the **Cornell**, or split-page technique (also called the **T** system); and (3) the **mapping** technique.

No matter which method you use, the L-STAR system can help you improve your note-taking skills, enhance your ability to participate in class, help other students, study more effectively, and perform well on exams and quizzes.

The L-Star System

One of the most effective ways to take notes begins with the **L-STAR** system.

L	Listening
S	Setting It Down
T	Translating
A	Analyzing
R	Remembering

This five-step program will enable you to compile complete, accurate, and visual notes for future reference.

L—Listening

One of the best ways to become an effective note-taker is to become an active listener. A concrete step you can take toward becoming an active listener in class is to sit near the front of the room where you can hear the instructor and see the board and overheads. Choose a spot that allows you to see the instructor's mouth and facial expressions. If you see that the instructor's face has become animated or expressive, you can bet that you are hearing important information. Write it down. If you sit in the back of the room, you may miss out on these important clues.

S—Setting It Down

The actual writing of notes can be a difficult task. Some instructors are organized in their delivery of information; others are not. Your listening skills, once again, are going to play an important role in determining what needs to be written down. In most cases, you will not have time to take notes word for word. You will have to be selective about the information you choose to set down. One of the best ways to keep up with the information being presented is to develop a shorthand system of your own. Many of the symbols you use will be universal, but you may use some symbols, pictures, and markings that are uniquely your own.

Some of the more common symbols are:

w/	with	w/o	without
=	equals	≠	does not equal
<	less than	>	greater than
%	percentage	#	number
&	and	^	increase
+	plus or addition	−	minus or subtraction
*	important	etc	and so on
eg	for example	vs	against
esp	especially	"	quote
?	question	. . .	and so on

These symbols can save you valuable time when taking notes. Because you will use them frequently, it might be a good idea to memorize them. As you become more adept at note-taking, you will quickly learn how to abbreviate words, phrases, and names.

T—Translating

One of the most valuable activities you can undertake as a student is to translate your notes immediately after each class. Doing so can save you hours of work when you begin to prepare for exams. Many students feel that this step is not important, or too time-consuming, and leave it out. Don't. Often, students take notes so quickly that they make mistakes or use abbreviations that they may not be able to decipher later. After each class, go to the library or some other quiet place and review your notes. You don't have to do this immediately after class, but before the end of the day, you will need to rewrite and translate your classroom notes. This process gives you the opportunity to put the notes in your own words and to incorporate your text notes into your classroom notes. You can correct spelling, reword key phrases, write out abbreviations, and prepare questions for the next class. Sounds like a lot of work, doesn't it? It is a great deal of work, but if you try this technique for one week, you should see a vast improvement in your comprehension of material. Eventually, you should see an improvement in your grades. Translating your notes helps you to make connections among previous material and will prove a valuable gift to yourself when exam time comes.

A—Analyzing

This step takes place while you translate your notes from class. When you analyze your notes, you are asking two basic questions: (1) What does this mean? and (2) Why is it important? If you can answer these two questions about your material, you have almost mastered the information. Though some instructors will want you to spit back the exact same information you were given, others will ask you for a more detailed understanding and a synthesis of the material. When you are translating your notes, begin to answer these two questions using your notes, textbook, supple-mental materials, and information gathered from outside research. Once again, this process is not simple or quick, but testing your understanding of the material is important. Remember that many lectures are built on past lectures.

R—Remembering

Once you have listened to the lecture, set your notes on paper, and trans-lated and analyzed the material, it is time to study, or remember, the infor-mation. Some effective ways to remember information include creating a visual picture, speaking the notes out loud, using mnemonic devices, and finding a study partner.

DID YOU KNOW?

Ludwig van Beethoven

Born in 1770, Beethoven composed many concertos and symphonies, totaling more than 850 pages. At age 32, he began to lose his hearing and fell into deep depression that would haunt him until his death. *While completely deaf* and in poverty, he composed *The Ninth Symphony*, considered to be his most beautiful and impressive work.

It's as Simple as A, B, C—1, 2, 3
The Outline Technique

The outline system uses a series of major headings and multiple subhead-ings formatted in hierarchical order. The outline technique is one of the most commonly used note-taking systems, yet it is also one of the most mis-used systems. It can be difficult to outline notes in class, especially if your instructor does not follow an outline while lecturing.

When using the outline system, it is best to get all the information from the lecture and afterward to combine your lecture notes and text notes to create an outline. Most instructors would advise against using the outline system of note-taking in class, although you may be able to use a modified version. The most important thing to remember is not to get bogged down in a system during class; what is critical is getting the ideas down on paper. You can always go back after class and rearrange your notes as needed.

If you are going to use a modified or informal outline while taking notes in class, you may want to consider grouping information together under a heading as a means of outlining. It is easier to remember information that is logically grouped than to remember information that is scattered across several pages. If your study skills lecture is on listening, you might outline your notes using the headings "The Process of Listening" and "Definitions of Listening (see Figure 3.5 on next page).

It's a Split Decision
The Cornell (Modified Cornell, Split Page, or T) System

The basic principle of the Cornell system, developed by Dr. Walter Pauk of Cornell University, is to split the page into two sections, each section to be used for different information. Section A is used for questions that summarize information found in Section B; Section B is used for the actual notes from class. The blank note-taking page should be divided as shown in Figure 3.6.

Sometimes the basic Cornell layout is modified to include a third section at the bottom of the page for additional or summary comments. In such cases the layout is referred to as a "T system" for its resemblance to an upside-down T. To implement the Cornell system, you will want to choose the technique that is most comfortable and beneficial for you; you might use mapping (discussed next) or outlining on a Cornell page (see Figure 3.7).

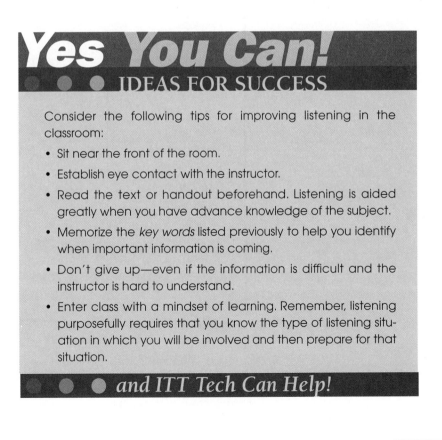

Yes You Can!
● ● ● IDEAS FOR SUCCESS

Consider the following tips for improving listening in the classroom:

- Sit near the front of the room.
- Establish eye contact with the instructor.
- Read the text or handout beforehand. Listening is aided greatly when you have advance knowledge of the subject.
- Memorize the *key words* listed previously to help you identify when important information is coming.
- Don't give up—even if the information is difficult and the instructor is hard to understand.
- Enter class with a mindset of learning. Remember, listening purposefully requires that you know the type of listening situation in which you will be involved and then prepare for that situation.

● ● ● *and ITT Tech Can Help!*

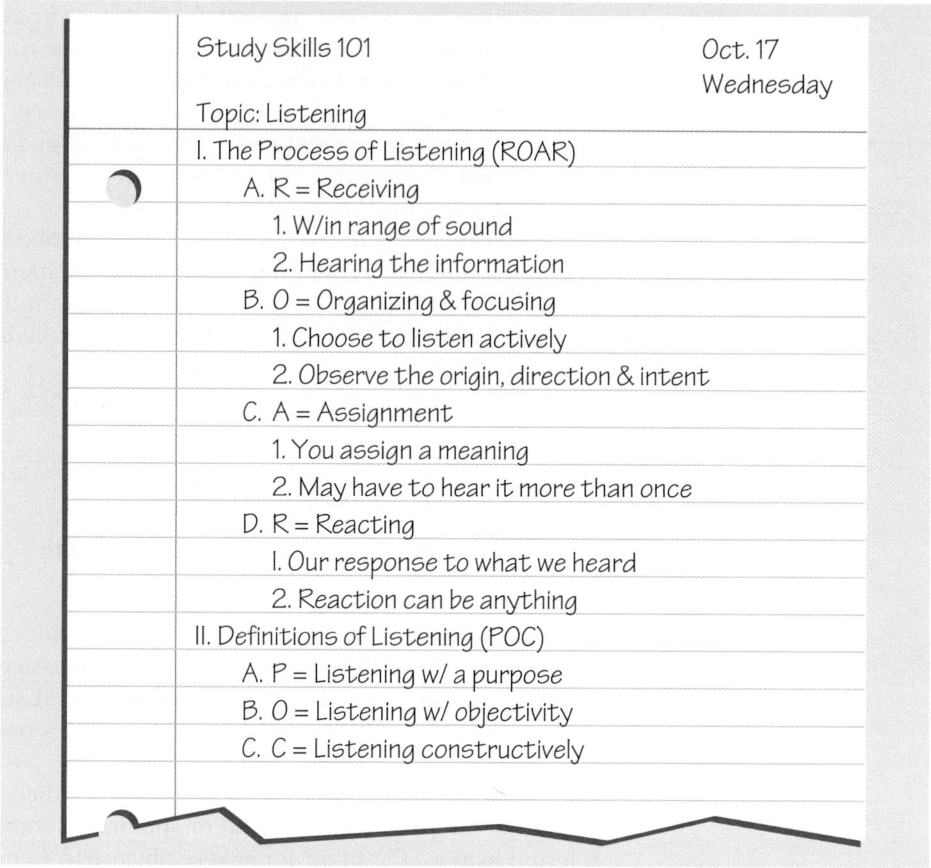

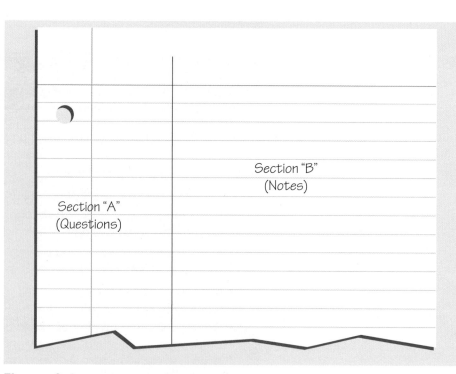

Study Skills 101   Oct. 17
                                          Wednesday
Topic: Listening

I. The Process of Listening (ROAR)
   A. R = Receiving
      1. W/in range of sound
      2. Hearing the information
   B. O = Organizing & focusing
      1. Choose to listen actively
      2. Observe the origin, direction & intent
   C. A = Assignment
      1. You assign a meaning
      2. May have to hear it more than once
   D. R = Reacting
      I. Our response to what we heard
      2. Reaction can be anything
II. Definitions of Listening (POC)
   A. P = Listening w/ a purpose
   B. O = Listening w/ objectivity
   C. C = Listening constructively

Figure 3.5 The Outline Technique

Section "B"
(Notes)

Section "A"
(Questions)

Figure 3.6 A Blank Cornell Frame

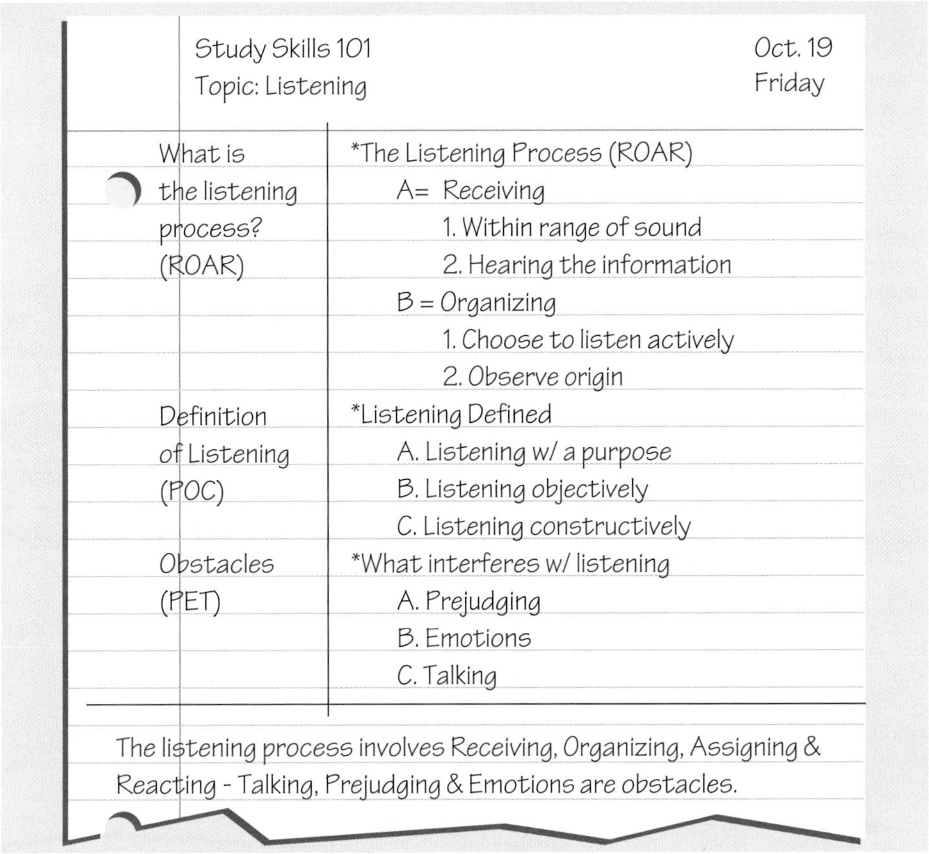

Figure 3.7 Outline Using a Cornell Frame

The Cornell frame contains the following notes:

Study Skills 101 — Oct. 19
Topic: Listening — Friday

What is the listening process? (ROAR)	*The Listening Process (ROAR)
	A= Receiving
	1. Within range of sound
	2. Hearing the information
	B = Organizing
	1. Choose to listen actively
	2. Observe origin
Definition of Listening (POC)	*Listening Defined
	A. Listening w/ a purpose
	B. Listening objectively
	C. Listening constructively
Obstacles (PET)	*What interferes w/ listening
	A. Prejudging
	B. Emotions
	C. Talking

The listening process involves Receiving, Organizing, Assigning & Reacting - Talking, Prejudging & Emotions are obstacles.

Going Around in Circles
The Mapping System

If you are a visual learner, this system may be especially useful for you. The mapping system of note-taking generates a picture of information (see Figure 3.8). The mapping system creates a map, or web, of information that allows you to see the relationships among facts or ideas. (See Figure 3.9 for an example of mapping using a Cornell frame.) The most important thing to remember about each note-taking system is that it must work for you. Do not use a system because your friends use it or because you feel that you should use it. Experiment with each system or combination to determine which is best for you. Always remember to keep your notes organized, dated, and neat. Notes that cannot be read are no good to you or to anyone else.

What to Do When You Get Lost

Have you ever been in a classroom trying to take notes and the instructor is speaking so rapidly that you cannot possibly get all of the information? Just when you think you're caught up, you realize that he or she has made an important statement and you missed it. What do you do? How can you handle, or avoid, this difficult note-taking situation? Here are several hints:

- Raise your hand and ask the instructor to repeat the information.

- Ask your instructor to slow down.

- If he or she will do neither, leave a blank space with a question mark at the side margin. You can get this information after class. This can be a difficult task to master. The key is to focus on the information at hand. Focus on what is being said at the exact moment.

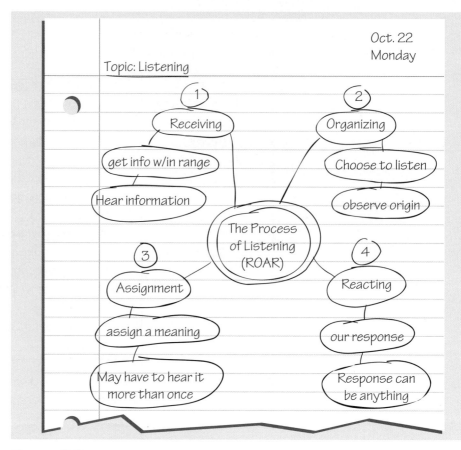

Figure 3.8 The Mapping System

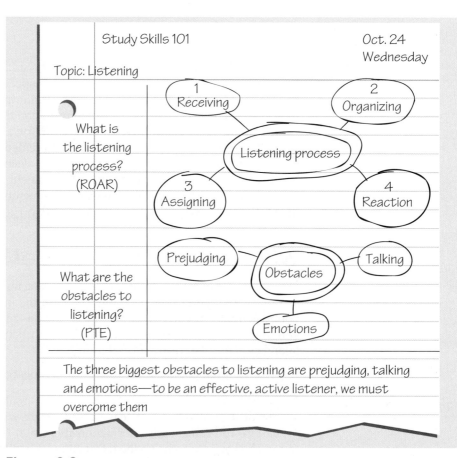

Figure 3.9 Mapping Using a Cornell Frame

- Meet with your instructor during break or immediately after class, or at the earliest time convenient for both of you.
- Form a note-taking group that meets after each class. This serves two purposes: (1) you can discuss and review the lecture, and (2) you will be able to get the notes from one of your note-taking buddies.
- Never lean over and ask questions of another student during the lecture. This will cause them to lose the information as well.
- Rehearse your note-taking skills at home by taking notes from TV news magazines or channels like the History Channel.
- Ask the instructor's permission to use a tape recorder during the lecture. Do not record a lecture without permission.

We suggest that you try to use other avenues, such as the ones listed above, instead of taping your notes. It is a time-consuming task to listen to the lecture for a second time. However, if this system works for you, use it.

Adapting Note-Taking to Different Instructor Styles

You can adjust your note-taking techniques according to the varying styles and personalities of lecturers. If your lecturer can be characterized as using primarily one of the following, use the associated tips for taking notes.

Lecturer Style	Tips for Note-Taking
Organized Lecturer	Copy all material from the board or slide.
	Understand the definition of all key words and phrases.
	Be prepared by doing background reading.
Entertaining Lecturers	Predict what an outline of the topic would look like and write this down before the lecture.
	As you listen to the lecture, remind yourself to ask "What is the point?" or "What am I learning?" "What is this story an illustration of?" "What is this example demonstrating?"
	Ask questions to clarify.
Questioning Lecturer	Record your own responses to the instructor's questions, even if you don't voice your response.
	Note when the lecturer affirms an idea ("Yes, that's right" or "Exactly, that's an important point").
	Note when the lecturer summarizes or paraphrases an idea.

What's in It for Me? Test Taking

How do you really feel about tests? Successful students realize that testing is necessary and even useful, that it has several positive purposes. Testing provides motivation for learning, offers feedback to the student and to the instructor, and determines mastery of material.

Successful people accept testing as a fact of life. You have to be tested to drive a car; to continue in school; to join the armed services; to become a teacher, a lawyer, a doctor, or a nurse; and often to be promoted at work. To pretend that testing is not always going to be a part of your life is to deny yourself many opportunities. Testing now prepares you for the world of work.

You may dread tests for a variety of reasons and may be afraid of the test itself and the questions it may pose. Test anxiety can be overcome, however, and this chapter presents several ways you can become a more confident test taker and get started on the path to success. Remember, too, some test anxiety is normal and can help you do your best!

Controlling Test Anxiety

Some students have physical reactions to testing, including nausea, headaches, and blackouts. Such physical reactions may be a result of being underprepared or not knowing how to take an exam. You reduce anxiety when you are in control of the situation, and you gain control by convincing yourself that you will be successful. If you honestly tell yourself that you have done everything possible to prepare for a test, then the results are going to be positive. Tests are a "mind game" and you can win!

It is important to realize that a test is not an indication of who you are as a person or a mark of your worth as a human being. Not everyone can be good at all things. You will have areas of strength and of weakness. You will spare yourself a great deal of anxiety and frustration if you understand from the start that you may not score 100 on every test. If you expect absolute perfection on everything, you are setting yourself up to fail. Think positively, prepare well, and do your best, but also be prepared to receive less than a perfect score on occasion.

Predicting Exam Questions

You can also reduce test anxiety by trying to predict what types of test questions the instructor will give. Instructors frequently give clues ahead of time about what they will be asking and what types of questions will be given. Several classes before the test is scheduled, find out from your instructor what type of test you can expect. Some questions you might ask are:

1. What type of questions will be on the test?
2. How long is the test?
3. Is there a time limit on the test?
4. Will there be any special instructions, such as use pen only or use a number 2 pencil?
5. Is there a study sheet?
6. Will there be a review session?
7. What is the grade value of the test?

Asking these simple questions will help you know what type of test will be administered, how you should prepare for it, and what supplies you will need. You will want to begin predicting questions early. Listen to the instructor intently. Instructors use cue phrases, such as, "You will see this again," and "If I were to ask you this question on the test." Pay close attention to what is written on the board, what questions are asked in class, and what areas the instructor seems to be concentrating on more than others. You will begin to get a feel for what types of questions the instructor might ask on the test.

It may also be beneficial for you to keep a running page of test questions that you have predicted. As you read through a chapter, ask yourself many questions at the end of each section. When it is time to study for the test, you may have already predicted many of the questions your instructor will ask.

Save all quizzes and exams that you are allowed to keep. These are a wonderful resource for studying for the next exam or for predicting questions for the course final.

Most test anxiety can be reduced by studying, predicting questions, reviewing, and relaxing.

Helpful Reminders for Reducing Test Anxiety

- Approach the test with an "I can" attitude.
- Prepare yourself emotionally for the test, control your self-talk, and be positive.
- Remind yourself that you studied and that you know the material.
- Overlearn the material—you can't study too much.
- Chew gum or eat hard candy during the test if allowed; it may help you relax.
- Go to bed early. Do not pull an all-nighter before the test.
- Eat a healthy meal before the test.
- Arrive early for the test (at least 15 minutes early).
- Sit back, relax, breathe, and clear your mind if you become nervous.
- Come to the test with everything you need: pencils, calculator, and other supplies.
- Read over the entire test first; read all the directions; highlight the directions.
- Listen to the instructor before the test begins.
- Keep an eye on the clock.

- Answer what you know first, the questions that are easiest for you.
- Check your answers, but remember, your first response is usually correct.
- Find out about the test before it is given; ask the instructor what types of questions will be on the test.
- Find out exactly what the test will cover ahead of time.
- Ask the instructor for a study sheet; you may not get one, but it does not hurt to ask!
- Know the rules of the test and of the instructor.
- Attend the review session if one is offered.
- Know what grade value the test holds.
- Ask about extra credit or bonus questions on the test.
- When you get the test, jot down any mnemonic you might have developed on the back or at the top of a page.
- Never look at another student's test or let anyone see your test.

Three Types of Responses to Test Questions

Almost every test question will elicit one of three types of responses from you as the test taker:

- Quick-time response
- Lag-time response
- No response

Your response is a *quick-time response* when you read a question and know the answer immediately. You may need to read only one key word in the test question to know the correct response. Even if you have a quick-time response, however, always read the entire question before answering. The question may be worded in such a way that the correct response is not what you originally expected. By reading the entire question before answering, you can avoid losing points to careless error.

You have a *lag-time response* when you read a question and the answer does not come to you immediately. You may have to read the question several times or even move on to another question before you think of the correct response. Information in another question will sometimes trigger the response you need. Don't get nervous if you have a lag-time response. Once you've begun to answer other questions, you usually begin to remember more, and the response may come to you. You do not have to answer questions in order on most tests.

No response is the least desirable situation when you are taking a test. You may read a question two or three times and still have no response. At this point, you should move on to another question to try to find some related information. When this happens, you have some options:

1. Leave this question until the very end of the test.
2. Make an intelligent guess.
3. Try to eliminate all unreasonable answers.
4. Watch for modifiers within the question.
5. See if one question answers another.
6. Look for hints throughout the test.
7. Don't panic . . . simply move on.

Test-Taking Strategies and Hints for Success

The most common types of questions are:

- Matching
- True–false
- Multiple-choice
- Short answer
- Essay

Before you read about the strategies for answering these different types of questions, think about this: There is no substitute for studying! You can know all the tips, but if you have not studied, they will be of little help to you.

Strategies for Matching Questions

Matching questions frequently involve knowledge of people, dates, places, or vocabulary. When answering matching questions, you should:

- Read the directions carefully.
- Read each column before you answer.
- Determine whether there is an equal number of items in each column.
- Match what you know first.
- Cross off information that is already used.
- Use the process of elimination for answers you might not know.
- Look for logical clues.
- Use the longer statement as a question; use the shorter statement as an answer.
- Answer all the questions.

What's Sleep Got to Do with It?

You've heard the old saying, "You are what you eat." This may be true, but many sleep experts would say, "You are how you sleep." Sleep deprivation is one of the leading causes of poor productivity and academic performance, workplace and auto accidents, lack of concentration, diminished immune systems, decreased metabolism, cardiovascular problems, and even poor communication efforts.

The National Traffic Safety Administration estimates that 100,000 crashes each year are the result of sleepy drivers. These crashes cause nearly 1,600 deaths, 71,000 injuries, and $12.5 billion in property loss and diminished activity (Hidden Menace, 2003).

Mark Rosekind, Ph. D., an expert on fatigue and performance issues and a member of the board of directors for the National Sleep Foundation, states, "Without sufficient sleep it is more difficult to concentrate, make careful decisions, and follow instructions; we are more likely to make mistakes or errors, and are more prone to being impatient and lethargic. Our attention, memory, and reaction time are all affected" (Cardinal, 2003).

According to the National Sleep Foundation, the following symptoms can signal inadequate sleep:

- Dozing off while engaged in an activity such as reading, watching TV, sitting in meetings, or sitting in traffic.
- Slowed thinking and reacting.
- Difficulty listening to what is said or understanding directions.
- Difficulty remembering or retaining information.
- Frequent errors or mistakes.
- Narrowing of attention, missing important changes in a situation.
- Depression or negative mood.
- Impatience or being quick to anger.
- Frequent blinking, difficulty focusing eyes, or heavy eyelids.

Indeed, lack of sleep can decrease your ability to study, recall information, and perform well on tests and assignments. This can be especially true during midterm and final exam periods. Those late or all-night cram sessions can actually be more detrimental to your academic success than helpful. By including your study sessions in your time-management plan, you can avoid having to spend your sleep time studying.

Different people need different amounts of sleep within a 24-hour period. Some people absolutely need 8–10 hours of sleep, while others can function well on 4–6 hours. If you are not sleeping enough to rest and revive your body, you will experience sleep deprivation.

Researchers suggest that missing as little as 2 hours of sleep for one night can take as long as 6 days to recover—if it is recovered at all (Moss, 1990). It is generally estimated that 8–9 hours of good, solid, restful sleep per night can decrease your chances of sleep deprivation.

Below, you will find some helpful hints for getting a good night's rest:

- Avoid alcohol and caffeine (yes, alcohol is a depressant, but it interrupts both REM and slow-wave sleep, and caffeine can stay in your system for as long as 12 hours).
- Exercise during the day (but not within four hours of your sleep time).
- Regulate the temperature in your bedroom to a comfortable setting for you.
- Wind down before trying to sleep. Complete all tasks at least one hour prior to your bedtime. This gives you time to relax and prepare for rest.
- Avoid taking naps during the day.
- Have a set bedtime and try to stick to it.
- Take a warm bath before bedtime.
- Go to bed only when you are tired. If you are not asleep within 15–30 minutes, get up and do something restful like reading or listening to soft music.
- Use relaxation techniques such as visualization and mind travel.
- Avoid taking sleeping aids. This can cause more long-term problems than sleep deprivation.

Sample Test #1: Matching

Directions: Match the information in column A with the correct information in column B. Use uppercase letters.

LISTENING SKILLS

A

____ They can be long or short, social, academic, religious, or financial

____ A step in the change process

____ Studying cooperatively

____ Your "true self"

____ Listening with an open mind

B

A. Child within

B. Objectivity

C. Letting go

D. Group or teamwork

E. Goals

(You are fast becoming that you are going to be.

—Anonymous)

Strategies for True–False Questions

True–false tests ask if a statement is true or not. True–false questions can be some of the most challenging questions you will encounter on tests. Some students like them; some hate them. There is a 50/50 chance of answering correctly, but you can use the following strategies to increase your odds on true–false tests:

- Read each statement carefully.
- Watch for key words in each statement, for example, negatives.
- Read each statement for double negatives, such as "not untruthful."

Sample Test #2: True–False

Directions: Place "T" for true or "F" for false beside each statement.

NOTE-TAKING SKILLS

1. _____ Note taking creates a history of your course content.

2. _____ "Most importantly" is not a key phrase.

3. _____ You should always write down everything the instructor says.

4. _____ You should never ask questions in class.

5. _____ The L-STAR system is a way of studying.

6. _____ W/O is not a piece of shorthand.

7. _____ You should use 4-by-6-inch paper to take classroom notes.

8. _____ The outline technique is best used with lecture notes.

9. _____ The Cornell method should never be used with textbook notes.

10. _____ The mapping system is done with a series of circles.

- Pay attention to words that may indicate that a statement is true, such as "some," "few," "many," and "often."

- Pay attention to words that may indicate that a statement is false, such as "never," "all," "every," and "only."

- Remember that if any part of a statement is false, the entire statement is false.

- Answer every question unless there is a penalty for guessing.

Strategies for Multiple-Choice Questions

Many instructors give multiple-choice tests because they are easy to grade and provide quick, precise responses. A multiple-choice question asks you to choose from among usually two to five answers to complete a sentence. Some strategies for increasing your success in answering multiple-choice questions are the following:

- Read the question and try to answer it before you read the answers provided.

- Look for similar answers; one of them is usually the correct response.

- Recognize that answers containing extreme modifiers, such as *always*, *every*, and *never*, are usually wrong.

- Cross off answers that you know are incorrect.

- Read all the options before selecting your answer. Even if you believe that A is the correct response, read them all.

Sample Test #3: Multiple Choice

Directions: Read each statement and select the best response from the answers given below.

STUDY SKILLS

1. When reading your text, you should have

   A. an open mind.

   B. a dictionary.

   C. a highlighter.

   D. all of the above.

2. There are three types of memory; they are:

   A. short-term, sensory, computer.

   B. computer, long-term, perfect.

   C. perfect, short-term, long-term.

   D. sensory, short-term, long-term.

3. To be an effective priority manager, you have to:

   A. be very structured and organized.

   B. be very unstructured and disorganized.

   C. be mildly structured and organized.

   D. be sometimes a little of both.

   E. know what type of person you are and work from that point.

- Recognize that when the answers are all numbers, the highest and lowest numbers are usually incorrect.
- Recognize that a joke is usually wrong.
- Understand that the most inclusive answer is often correct.
- Understand that the longest answer is often correct.
- If you cannot answer a question, move on to the next one and continue through the test; another question may trigger the answer you missed.
- Make an educated guess if you must.
- Answer every question unless there is a penalty for guessing.

Strategies for Short-Answer Questions

Short-answer questions, also called fill-in-the-blanks, ask you to supply the answer yourself, not to select it from a list. Although "short answer" sounds easy, these questions are often very difficult. Short-answer questions require you to draw from your long-term memory. The following hints can help you answer this type of question successfully:

- Read each question and be sure that you know what is being asked.
- Be brief in your response.
- Give the same number of answers as there are blanks; for example, _____ and _____ would require two answers.
- Never assume that the length of the blank has anything to do with the length of the answer.
- Remember that your initial response is usually correct.
- Pay close attention to the word immediately preceding the blank; if the word is "an," give a response that begins with a vowel (a, e, i, o, u).
- Look for key words in the sentence that may trigger a response.
- Answer all the questions.

Sample Test #4: Short Answer

Directions: Fill in the blanks with the correct response. Write clearly.

LISTENING SKILLS

1. Listening is a _____ act. We choose to do it.

2. The listening process involves receiving, organizing, _____, and reacting.

3. _____ is the same as listening with an open mind.

4. Prejudging is an _____ to listening.

5. Leaning forward, giving eye contact, being patient, and leaving your emotions at home are characteristics of _____ listeners.

Strategies for Essay Questions

Most students look at essay questions with dismay because they take more time. Yet essay tests can be among the easiest tests to take because they give you a chance to show what you really know. An essay question requires you to supply the information. If you have studied, you will find that once you begin to answer an essay question, your answer will flow easily. Some tips for answering essay questions are the following:

- More is not always better; sometimes more is just more. Try to be as concise and informative as possible. An instructor would rather see one page of excellent material than five pages of fluff.

Sample Test #5: Essay

Directions: Answer each question completely. Use a separate paper if you wish.

STUDY SKILLS

1. Identify and discuss two examples of mnemonics.

_____

_____

_____

2. Discuss why it is important to use the SQ3R method.

_____

_____

_____

3. Justify your chosen notebook and study system.

_____

_____

_____

4. Compare an effective study environment with an ineffective study environment.

_____

_____

_____

_____

- Pay close attention to the action word used in the question and respond with the appropriate type of answer. Key words used in questions include the following:

discuss	illustrate	enumerate	describe
compare	define	relate	list
contrast	summarize	analyze	explain
trace	evaluate	critique	interpret
diagram	argue	justify	prove

- Write a thesis statement for each answer.

- Outline your thoughts before you begin to write.

- Watch your spelling, grammar, and punctuation.

- Use details, such as times, dates, places, and proper names, where appropriate.

- Be sure to answer all parts of the question; some discussion questions have more than one part.

- Summarize your main ideas toward the end of your answer.

- Write neatly.

- Proofread your answer.

Learning how to take a test and learning how to reduce your anxiety are two of the most important gifts you can give yourself as a student. Although tips and hints may help you, don't forget that there is no substitute for studying and knowing the material.

Contents

Almost any profession you choose to go into will require the ability to think through problems, make decisions, and apply other critical-thinking skills.

What's in It for Me?
Thinking about Thinking

Thinking is defined, according the American Heritage Dictionary, as "to reason about or reflect on; to ponder." Although critical thinking involves thinking more analytically and reflectively about an issue or problem, knowing facts and figures is also essential for clear thinking.

Benjamin Bloom created a taxonomy, or classification, for categorizing levels of thinking. At the first level, we observe and recall information. At the next level of thinking, we move into understanding meaning. The third level involves applying the information in some way. At the fourth level of thinking, we recognize patterns and can analyze information, and the fifth and sixth levels involve combining old ideas to create new ideas and recommending action. The lower levels of thinking are the foundation of critical thinking, which takes place at the higher levels in this categorization. Reflective thought must be grounded in factual knowledge. Critical thinking entails seeking to understand different aspects of an issue, and in deciding what to believe, looking not only at truths and untruths, but also at stories that display bias or are incomplete.

Bloom's Taxonomy

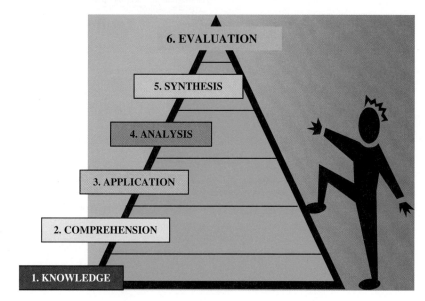

6. EVALUATION
5. SYNTHESIS
4. ANALYSIS
3. APPLICATION
2. COMPREHENSION
1. KNOWLEDGE

Steps in Critical Thinking

To think critically using the higher levels, we might:

- Evaluate sources of information
- Explore different points of view
- Question opinions and assumptions
- Evaluate the context
- Look for false logic and bias

Step One: Evaluate Sources of Information

Considering the source of the information is crucial to weighing the potential bias of its content. Information can be embedded in a context that manipulates the conclusion in order to serve the interests of a particular group. The higher your level of interest in an issue, the more effort you might want to expend in assessing the source.

Level of Competence	Skills Demonstrated
1. Knowledge	Observation and recall of information Knowledge of dates, events Able to: list, define, tell, describe, identify, show, label, collect, examine, quote, name
2. Comprehension	Grasp meaning Translate knowledge into new context Interpret facts Predict consequences Able to: summarize, describe, interpret, contrast, predict, associate, distinguish, estimate, differentiate
3. Application	Use information Use methods, concepts, theories Solve problems Able to: apply, demonstrate, calculate, solve, complete, relate, discover
4. Analysis	See patterns Organize parts Recognize hidden meanings Able to: analyze, separate, order, explain, connect, classify, arrange, divide, compare, infer
5. Synthesis	Use old ideas to create new ones Relate knowledge from several areas Predict Draw conclusions Able to: combine, integrate, modify, rearrange, substitute, plan, create, design, invent, compose, formulate
6. Evaluation	Compare and discriminate between ideas Assess value of theories, presentations Make choices based on reasoned argument Verify value of evidence Recognize subjectivity Able to: assess, decide, rank, grade, test, measure, recommend, convince, select, judge, discriminate, support, conclude, compare, summarize

Internet Reference materials need to be analyzed with a critical eye. The Internet is a reference that especially warrants the use of critical thinking. Information today is readily available. By using search engines on the Internet, we can retrieve vast amounts of information on many subjects quickly and easily. However, determining the accuracy and reliability of the information is another matter. It may take less time to find information, but we must spend more time verifying the information.

Traditional newspapers rely on editors to determine the accuracy and overall quality of their articles. Many journals also rely on the peer-review process. But a great deal of online information does not go through these traditional filters.

When critically evaluating Web sites and their information, consider scrutinizing:

Accuracy

- Has the page been rated or evaluated in some manner? If so, who did the evaluation?
- Is the author's point of view clear and sound?
- Is there a bias—political, ideological, or cultural? Does the author hope to persuade you in some way?
- When was the site produced and last updated?

Authority

- Are the qualifications of the site's author or producer indicated on the page?
- Who sponsors the site? Is it a commercial or educational site, or does it appear to be created by an individual?

Completeness

- How well and thoroughly is the subject covered?
- Are the links appropriate, relevant, and comprehensive?

Content

- How many items are included on the page?
- Is a copyright notice indicated on the page?
- Does the site include a bibliography?
- Is the level of detail appropriate for the subject?

Propaganda

- Does the author present accurate descriptions of alternative views?
- Does the author attack other perspectives?
- Is the writing overly emotional?

Step Two: Maintain Objectivity

Emotions are an inescapable part of our human experience. Our feelings of happiness, excitement, surprise, anger, fear, sadness, and frustration give us the ability to relate to others' experiences. Emotions may compel us to feel compassion and reach out in times of need *or* to turn away, ignore, and stop listening to others. We may find that our own emotions, although very important in motivating us to act, can negatively affect our ability to think critically if they are so strongly felt that we lose objectivity. If we have an extreme reaction to an issue or topic, we can take that as a clue that our ability to think objectively may be compromised. In this case, it is helpful to identify our emotions and the personal issues that may be triggering them. Ultimately, knowing our *own* emotions helps us understand issues from *different* perspectives.

> Nothing in this world is bad or good but thinking makes it so.
> —William Shakespeare

Candid discussions, and sometimes brutal honesty, are useful and necessary when you are addressing complex or difficult issues. However, be careful not to let emotions take over your objectivity.

Step Three: Separate Facts and Opinions

A factual statement offers proof from a source that can be verified. Assumptions, or opinions, are more often based on emotion and myth.

If a statement is based on facts, it will likely pass one or more of the following three tests:

1. Can it be observed?
2. Has it been established over the years?
3. Can it be tested?

If a statement is an opinion, it will probably meet one or more of the following criteria:

1. Others may not agree with it.
2. Superlatives like "best," "tremendous," and "outstanding" are used.
3. Opinion keywords such as "think," "believe," "assume," "imagine," "feel," "surmise," "may," or "suppose" are used.
4. It implies that the statement is true for everyone through words like "all," "none," "every," "no," "only," "nobody," "everybody," "always," and "never."

Step Four: Evaluate the Context

When people are trying to mislead or influence others toward their point of view, they may exaggerate a story or take it out of context. Question the stories you hear. Are they representative of the problem or are they exceptions? Finding out as much information about the topic as possible will help you put the issue into a proper context.

Step Five: Recognize False Logic and Bias

By learning to recognize faulty arguments and deceptive logic, you can improve your ability to think critically about issues. The following are some common faulty persuasion techniques:

Glittering Generalities say little specifically but convey emotion. "Jim has made this country a better place."

Hasty Generalizations are conclusions based on insufficient evidence. "Windows has some serious problems—I saw an article about that."

False Dilemma poses only two choices when there are a variety of possibilities and perspectives to consider. "Get an "A" in that course and you'll be set; anything less and you won't get a good job."

Card Stacking involves presenting evidence in a partial or skewed way to promote the interests of a particular group. Saying that "the average income is rising" may be accurate when only the income level of the top ten percent of the population is considered.

Bandwagon is an approach that encourages people to do something because it is the popular thing to do. "Everybody is doing it!"(This is what your mother was referring to when she said, "If everyone jumped off a bridge would you, too?!")

Appeals to Emotion summons anger, pity or fear, including alienation, disapproval and violence, to entice support. A scare tactic is one use of an appeal to emotion. "If you don't use that minty mouthwash, you'll have bad breath and no one will like you."

Ad verecundiam is used when people invoke quotes and phrases from popular or famous people, or from those in an authoritative position, in order to support their views.

False Cause and Effect is used to insist that an event is caused by another event just because it took place afterwards.

Straw arguments are used when people attack their opponent's argument in the hopes that this will make their own arguments stronger (as opposed to focusing on the strengths of their own argument.)

Ad hominem is a persuasive technique that involves attacking the person and not the ideas. This is also called slander or name-calling.

Appeals to Tradition look at the past and suggest because things have always been done one way, they should continue to be done that way.

Step Six: Use Your Values

What you know to be true can help to guide you no matter how persuasive an argument is to the contrary. In analyzing arguments, we use more than just our intellect. Critical thinking involves tapping into our intuition and values, as well. It is important to access your core values when a good argument attempts to sway you or when you may feel intimidated without the facts and figures in front of you.

Yes You Can!
IDEAS FOR SUCCESS

Put into action the following tips for critical thinking:

- Don't let your emotions cloud the truth about a situation or problem.
- Keep an open mind about people and don't stereotype them.
- Remember that negative attitudes about people, places, and situations can get in the way of critical thinking.
- If you have difficulty thinking through a situation, use the analysis technique with an A and B column.
- Be certain to listen to all sides of the argument before making up your mind.
- Try to stay away from the "I'm right, you're wrong" mentality.
- When faced with a new situation, try to look at it differently, as you did with the penny exercise.
- Don't just accept information as real or factual. Do your homework.

and ITT Tech Can Help!

Your Role	Situation	Noncritical Thinking Response	Critical Thinker's Response
Student	Instructor is lecturing on the rising use of a particular operating system in companies.	You assume that everything your instructor tells you is true and you concentrate solely on learning the new operating system.	You consider what the instructor says; write down questions; initiate discussion with the professor, other classmates, and the IT departments where you would like to work; and you read professional journals.
Student	You read that companies are having a hard time finding technical employees.	You assume that you won't have to do any work to find a job and will be able to set your terms of employment.	You prepare yourself for what companies need; ask questions about whether this situation will always be the case; read several journals and pay particular attention to what seems standard in the industry.
Citizen	You encounter a homeless person.	You avoid the person and the issue.	You examine whether the community has a responsibility to the homeless, and if you find that it does, you explore how to fulfill that responsibility.
Consumer	You want to buy a car.	You decide on a brand-new car without thinking about how you will handle the payments.	You consider the different effects of buying a new car vs. buying a used car; you examine your money situation to see what kind of payment you can handle each month.
Employee	You hear rumors of an impending lay-off.	You become depressed and stop doing your best work.	You ask people in the industry what companies need; you determine what skills you may need; you read publications about growth sectors; you consider all options recognizing that you have the ability to adjust to change.

You may find that you silence yourself or change your opinions, sometimes, in the face of arguments over issues because you're not prepared. Trust your values to guide you in these instances, and research the needed information.

Critical thinking can be used in all areas of your life. Consider the following roles you might play and how you can more critically think about issues. The table (opposite) compares how a noncritical thinker and a critical thinker might respond to particular situations.

Creative Thinking

The best problem solvers are also creative. Creativity is the ability to create anything new, whether it is a solution, a tangible product, a work of art, an idea, a system, a program, or a format—anything at all. Everyone is creative in some way. Some people assume that the word *creative* refers primarily to visual and performing artists, writers, designers, musicians, and other who work in fields whose creative bents are obvious. However, creativity is inside everyone and exists in every field.

Creativity means thinking in fresh new ways. It requires that you loosen up your brain and be more flexible in your approaches and tactics. These are some of the characteristics that creative thinkers have in common. Everyone has the capacity to be creative, though this skill takes courage.

Plan to Be Creative

Creativity is likely the most exciting trait you can develop. It can also be the most frustrating because it can be difficult to nurture. Learn to use your imagination and not be constrained by what others think. The following techniques can help you improve your creative thinking ability:

1. **Learn to brainstorm.** Some schools reinforce rigid thinking. We take multiple-choice tests, which reinforce the idea that there are only right and wrong answers. However, in life, there can be dozens of ways to solve a problem or answer a question. Brainstorming, the art of considering numerous possibilities from the silly to the practical, allows people to explore a problem or an issue from many different angles. Get in the habit of making brainstorming lists when you are trying to solve a problem. Brainstorming will give you practice at keeping your mind open to new possibilities.

2. **Think through ideas with others.** Once you've become comfortable with the process of brainstorming, learn to discuss your ideas with other people. Encourage them to open their minds, to develop their own ideas, and to help you critique and develop yours. This is an enjoyable part of teamwork and it yields the best ideas.

3. **Look for the possibilities.** See situations in terms of what they can become, not what they are at first glance. In order to go in new and different directions, you have to visualize how things could be. Don't be afraid to come up with fresh ideas.

4. **Make connections.** Creative people are good at seeing patterns in seemingly unrelated things. They perceive both similarities and differences and frequently come up with ingenious ways of capitalizing on a trend, a set of circumstances, or existing need. This is how inventions come to be.

What Problem? No Problem Here!
Steps in Problem Solving

Managing the myriad problems that arise throughout your lifetime takes skill and careful consideration. Every day you are called to make numerous decisions, for school (how to juggle your schedule to accommodate all your coursework), work (how to deal with a difficult colleague or boss), or your personal life (how to increase your income or deal with a medical problem). Being a skilled and thoughtful problem solver can help you succeed at whatever you do.

Solving problems is not always easy. Some people try to solve their problems by making a snap decision and not thinking things through. They may also do what someone else tells them without making their own judgment about what is best. They may even try to avoid the problem altogether by doing nothing and waiting for the problem to sort itself out. While these are common approaches to problem solving, they rarely lead to good results.

> The significant problems we face cannot be solved at the same level of thinking we were at when we created them.
> —Albert Einstein

In order to be a good problem solver, you must first be a critical thinker. We have already looked at how to become a critical thinker. Now let's apply that knowledge to the problem-solving process. To solve a problem using critical thinking, you might engage in the following activities of critical thinking:

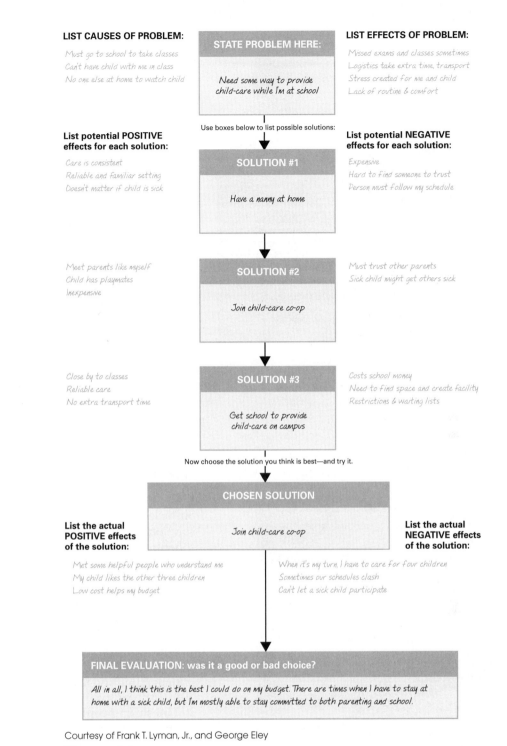

LIST CAUSES OF PROBLEM:

Must go to school to take classes
Can't have child with me in class
No one else at home to watch child

STATE PROBLEM HERE:

Need some way to provide child-care while I'm at school

LIST EFFECTS OF PROBLEM:

Missed exams and classes sometimes
Logistics take extra time, transport
Stress created for me and child
Lack of routine & comfort

Use boxes below to list possible solutions:

List potential POSITIVE effects for each solution:

Care is consistent
Reliable and familiar setting
Doesn't matter if child is sick

SOLUTION #1

Have a nanny at home

List potential NEGATIVE effects for each solution:

Expensive
Hard to find someone to trust
Person must follow my schedule

Meet parents like myself
Child has playmates
Inexpensive

SOLUTION #2

Join child-care co-op

Must trust other parents
Sick child might get others sick

Close by to classes
Reliable care
No extra transport time

SOLUTION #3

Get school to provide child-care on campus

Costs school money
Need to find space and create facility
Restrictions & waiting lists

Now choose the solution you think is best—and try it.

CHOSEN SOLUTION

Join child-care co-op

List the actual POSITIVE effects of the solution:

Met some helpful people who understand me
My child likes the other three children
Low cost helps my budget

List the actual NEGATIVE effects of the solution:

When it's my turn, I have to care for four children
Sometimes our schedules clash
Can't let a sick child participate

FINAL EVALUATION: was it a good or bad choice?

All in all, I think this is the best I could do on my budget. There are times when I have to stay at home with a sick child, but I'm mostly able to stay committed to both parenting and school.

Courtesy of Frank T. Lyman, Jr., and George Eley

Figure 4.1 Sample Problem and Solution

1. **State the problem clearly.** What are the facts of the situation? Name the problem specifically without focusing on causes or effects.

2. **Analyze the problem.** What is happening that needs to change? What are the causes and effects of the problem?

3. **Brainstorm possible solutions.** Brainstorming will help you think of similar problems and how you solved them. When brainstorming, generate possible solutions spontaneously and rapidly without immediately analyzing whether those solutions will work. During brainstorming, no idea is a bad idea! The more ideas, the better.

When solving a problem, it is helpful to look at all possible alternatives and decide on the best one. Sometimes there is one right answer, but often you'll have to settle for the best answer.

4. **Determine the criteria for your solution.** How are you going to determine which solution to choose? Are there any constraints, such as time or money, that must be overcome? Establishing criteria that the solution must meet will help you narrow down your choices and pick the best solution for the given situation.

5. **Explore each solution.** Determine how and why each possible solution would or would not work. Evaluate the negative and positive effects of each solution by applying the standards (criteria) that you previously established.

6. **Choose and execute the solution you decide is best.** Decide how you will put your solution to work.

7. **Evaluate the solution.** Look at how well your solution worked. What are the positive and negative effects of what you did? Was it a useful solution?

8. **Continue to refine the solution.** Problem solving is a process, and you may need to refine your solution to solve any remaining problems that arise.

Obstacles to Problem Solving

Problem solving isn't always easy. There are many obstacles that can hinder the process of finding good solutions. Here are some common stumbling blocks to solving problems. Watch for these pitfalls as you work to solve the problems that come your way.

1. **The perfect solution.** Believing that every problem has one perfect solution can intimidate you. If you can come up with fifty ideas, but none seems exactly right, you may want to give up. Try to refrain from looking for the perfect solution. Instead, look for the best solution, using whatever time frame you have.

2. **The smart-people complex.** If you run into a snag while trying to solve a problem, you might get yourself off the hook by deciding that only a much smarter person could solve the problem. This excuse leads to both an unsolved problem and a negative assessment of your abilities. Think positively. Believe that any person, thinking critically and carefully, can solve this problem.

3. **The first choice is the best.** If you come up with a good idea right away, it is tempting to go with it. Be sure to give each of your ideas equal time, even if the first one is good. Evaluate each so you can be sure you have covered every angle. The more solutions you generate, the better chance you have of finding the absolute best one.

4. **Focusing on the "easier" cause.** If you are not doing very well in a course, you may want to believe it is because your instructor is incompetent. It is easier to blame someone—anyone—else for the cause of a problem. However, look for the true causes. In this case, it might be because you're not studying effectively or enough. Blaming the instructor won't solve your difficulties if the true cause lies elsewhere. It also may add to the problems you are already experiencing.1

Making important decisions about what you will do to solve a problem can take time. Think through your decisions thoroughly, considering your own ideas as well as those of others you trust, but don't hesitate to act once you have your plan. You cannot benefit from your decision until you act upon it and follow through.

Citation and Plagiarism

When you get excited about writing something, it can be easy to overlook the obvious: you must give credit to the resources where you found your material. If you don't, that's called *plagiarism* and it is a very serious academic offense, sometimes resulting in expulsion from school.

It's increasingly easy to forget to cite sources with advancing technology, and with so much information and the easy cut-and-paste feature of most word processing programs.

Picture this scenario: You are reading from a Web site and you see a great quote that you'd like to use. You quickly cut and paste it into your notes. Then . . . the tea kettle starts whistling, the dog starts barking . . . you get up to get your tea . . . Once you return to your computer, you have forgotten that you needed to copy the name of the author, too. This scenario is innocent enough, but the risk of plagiarism is high. If you use the quote without including a citation, that's plagiarism.

Using some old-fashioned practices of annotating your sources or keeping note cards is a way to make sure you keep your sources straight.

The Index Card Method

Index cards can be used for detailed information that comes from specific sources. The information noted on these cards is readily accessible, easily organized, and can be used when preparing presentations and reports. Keeping a stack by your computer is handy. Simply write down quotes and the authors' names along with the source, publication dates, and any other pertinent information. Later, you can use the cards to compile your source list.

Number of Source or Author's Last Name and Date	Rating System for Value of Information	Key Word for Subtopic or Question
Most important facts:		
Paraphrased specific information:		
Summary:		
Direct quote:		
Primary source of info:		

You may not like this particular method of keeping track of sources; but however you do it, you must not forget to cite a source and commit plagiarism. You can also use a Notes program, either in Microsoft Outlook or Notepad, to keep track of citations.

If something is "common knowledge," you don't have to cite it. If the information is indisputable, such as the signing date of the Declaration of Independence, which has been recorded in many, many places, it is common knowledge.

Paraphrasing

You can also *paraphrase* a source and not cite it. Paraphrasing means you express content from a source in your own words. Alternating between direct quotes and paraphrasing is an effective writing tool to lend some variety to your writing. But, be careful to paraphrase accurately. Altering the spirit of a quote or its context is a misuse of the source.

To paraphrase, try the following steps:

- Skim the material to get the overall meaning.
- Read the material thoroughly.
- List the main ideas.
- Review the selection.
- Write your paraphrase restating the author's ideas in your own words. Stick to the basics. Don't insert your own ideas or opinions.
- Put quotations around important words taken directly from the source.
- Check your paraphrase for accuracy—could someone understand the author's meaning just from reading your paraphrase?

chapter 5 | Time Management and Teamwork

Contents

What's in It for Me?
Putting Time on Your Side

Have you ever tried to define time? This is an interesting exercise. If you stop now and try to define exactly what time is, you will probably find it difficult. Time is elusive and flexible and also restrictive and binding. Time is an unusual and puzzling resource. You can't save it in a box until you need it. You don't feel it passing by like wind in your face. It has no color. If you are in a hurry or if you are pressured to reach a deadline, time seems to fly. If you are bored or have nothing to do, it seems to creep at a very slow pace. You can't get your arms around it; yet, you know it exists. Though time is an invisible commodity, it is one of our most important resources. We all know how much trouble we can bring down on our heads when we use it poorly or waste it. The truth is, many students' worst problems start with poor use of time. Staying power actually begins with how you manage your time and get control of your life.

Some people seem to be born with the ability to get so much more done than most other people. They appear to always be calm and collected, to have it together, to reach lofty goals. Many people from this group work long hours in addition to going to school. They never appear to be stressed out, and they seem to attend all the social functions.

You are probably aware of others who are always late with assignments, never finish their projects on time, rarely seem to have time to study, and appear to have no concrete goals for their lives. Many people from this second group never make it past their first class of continuing education.

Sometimes, we get the idea that one group of people accomplishes more because they have more time or because they don't have to work or they don't have children or they are smarter or wealthier. While in some cases, this may be true, it doesn't change the fact that we all have the same amount of time each week, and we decide how to spend most of it. Even if you are rich, you can't buy more time than the allotted 10,080 minutes that each of us is given every week. So, while everyone has the same amount of time in their days and nights, the secret is that one group organizes for success, whereas the other never knows what happened to them.

Corporate managers realize the value of time because they pay consultants millions of dollars to teach their employees how to use their time more wisely. *Time is money in the business world;* employees who can produce excellent work by established deadlines are highly valued.

There is no guarantee that someone will finish an educational program just because he has enrolled. Some students lack staying power because they don't know how to manage themselves. Time must be considered one of your most valuable resources while you are in school and after you complete your program. Time management is actually about managing YOU, taking control. The sooner you get control of how you use your time, the quicker you will be on your way to becoming successful in your program and at work. Learning to manage your time is a lesson that you will use throughout your learning endeavors and beyond. It is really about self-management. Time management is paying attention to how you are spending your most valuable resource and then devising a plan to use it more effectively.

You Have All the Time There Is
Taking Control of Time and Yourself

With all the advances in technology that have given us time-saving devices, how is it that many of us feel that we have less time than ever? We may find ourselves engaged in activities that aren't totally satisfying or are in conflict with our values. As a result, we have less time to accomplish the important goals, and many of us feel overextended. Defining values and setting goals are important to managing resources, but we can lose sight of those on a daily basis when deadlines loom, urgent family needs interrupt us, and we are forced to respond to one crisis after the next. At times, there may

Staying power begins with how you manage your time. Strive to build on your best in all areas of your life—school, work, family, and friends.

seem to be too much distraction at the day-to-day, hour-to-hour level to even think about the more important goals.

We can find our lives reduced to blocks of allocated time, week after week. Recognizing that time management is about managing our actions and our energy, David Allen, author of *Getting Things Done: The Art of Stress-Free Productivity*, asserts that, "it's possible for a person to have an overwhelming number of things to do and still function productively with a clear head and a positive sense of relaxed control." The key to achieving high levels of effectiveness and efficiency is to recognize that our ability to be productive is directly proportional to our ability to relax. When our actions are congruent with our values and goals, our minds become clear and we can relax with what we are doing in the moment. In this state of clarity we access the energy to get a lot done.

Have you ever done something that you love and noticed that time seemed to "stand still," or even expand? When you engage fully and consciously in the important activities of your life, you may notice this sense of relaxation, and heightened efficiency and productivity.

Plan to Get the Important Things Done

(Lost time is never found again.
—Benjamin Franklin)

Steps in Time Management   Time continues on no matter what we do and is a cultural concept that has no absolute meaning on its own. Westerners, for example, think in terms of twenty-four hours in a day, seven days in a week. Those divisions, however, are arbitrary. The real issue in time management is how to make appropriate choices about what action to take at any point in time. When we are making choices that help us to move toward greater long-term fulfillment, we will naturally use our resources in the best way for us.

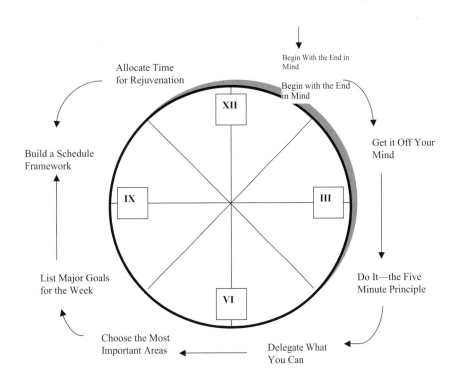

Begin With the End in Mind

Allocate Time for Rejuvenation

Begin with the End in Mind

Build a Schedule Framework

Get it Off Your Mind

List Major Goals for the Week

Do It—the Five Minute Principle

Choose the Most Important Areas

Delegate What You Can

Begin with the End in Mind

Outcome thinking, or thinking to define desired results, is one of the most effective means available for turning goals into reality. After going through the goal-setting process, focusing on those goals can have a dramatically beneficial effect. Management expert Peter Drucker has written, "There is usually no right answer. Rather, there are choices, and results have to be clearly specified if productivity is to be achieved."

Getting It Off Your Mind

Write down what is most on your mind at this moment. What most bothers you, distracts you, interests you, or in some other way consumes a large part of your attention? It may be a project or problem that you are being pressed to handle, or a situation you feel you must deal with soon.

Next describe, in a single written sentence, your intended successful outcome for this problem or situation.

Finally, write down the very next physical action required to move the situation forward. If you had nothing else to do in your life, what visible action would you take?

What did you gain from going through this thinking exercise? You may be feeling a bit more in control, more relaxed, and focused. Nothing has changed in the physical realm, but your feelings about the problems may have changed by writing them down and getting them off your mind.

Get It Done; Get It Off Your Mind

There is usually an inverse proportion between how much something is on your mind and how much is getting done. If you're thinking about doing something too much, chances are that you're probably not doing it. These are open items that pull at your attention and can include everything from "get that promotion" to the more modest "complete assignment" to the smallest task such as "get gas." These open items can take up a lot of attention, adding to the anxious feeling that there is too much to do. Writing down everything you need to do will move it from your mind and make it more likely that you'll get it done.

Follow the "Five-Minute Principle"

Discipline yourself to make decisions immediately about all of the tasks you take on so you will always have a plan for actions that you can implement.

If there's anything you absolutely must do that you can do in five minutes or less, do it now.

Delegate What You Can

If there's anything that absolutely must get done soon, and you have others who are willing to help, delegate. Delegating is entrusting tasks to others. It is hard to give up control sometimes, but if you delegate properly, it can dramatically increase your overall effectiveness. Effective delegation is a three-step process:

a. Decide what you want to give to others

b. Select people with the proper skills

c. Design a plan for review of the work

Choose the Most Important Areas

Vilfredo Pareto, a nineteenth-century Italian economist and sociologist, developed a principle that has been used frequently since termed. Pareto's 80/20 Principle implies that about 20% of what we do in any given area delivers 80% of the results. Going after the "right" 20% will get you 80% of the results. This is how *to work smarter and not harder.*

	MAJOR GOALS FOR WEEK
LIFE CATEGORY 1:	1.
LIFE CATEGORY 2:	2.
LIFE CATEGORY 3:	3.
LIFE CATEGORY 4:	4.

Build a Schedule Framework

Steps six and seven in a strategic time management process include listing the major goals for the week and building out a schedule framework by day and hour. First, include the top four goals you need to accomplish this week. List those in the template. Don't worry for now about the days of the week or the time blocks. On the left hand side, incorporate the goals you have for the week by life category.

Using the following template, you can now map out what you know you need to do during the week. Include activities such as work hours, classes, study time, and all other scheduled activities.

How does your schedule match your major life goals at this moment? Are there things you can change in your schedule to better meet your main goals? It's important to know how you spend your time, but some people don't have a clue how they spend their time. That puts them at a serious disadvantage in meeting their important goals. Another pitfall in time management for students is that they sometimes are quite unprepared for the fact that their programs will probably require a lot of time outside of class. Experts advise students to count on spending at least three hours outside of class for every hour spent in class.

TIME	MONDAY	TUESDAY	WEDNESDAY	THURSDAY	FRIDAY	SATURDAY	SUNDAY
6:00AM							
7:00AM							
8:00AM							
9:00AM							
10:00AM							
11:00AM							
12:00AM							
1:00PM							
2:00PM							
3:00PM							
4:00PM							
5:00PM							
6:00PM							
7:00PM							
8:00PM							
9:00PM							
10:00PM							
11:00PM							

Some other people actually do work hard, but their work habits are so poor that they still don't produce very much. Others try to work while they are simultaneously entertaining themselves. For example, they watch TV while they read. This doesn't work! Consider first working in a quiet place where you can concentrate. Then, reward yourself with 30 minutes to watch your program or record it to watch when you know that you have a predictable dip in energy.

Allocate Time for Rejuvenation

While committing ourselves to our goals is important, if we spend too much time "on task" and not enough time just "being," we may become drained and lose motivation. We need periods of structure as well as unstructured time for rejuvenation. Build into your schedule a time where you can relax, reflect, and discover who you are.

In the *Dance of Life: the Other Dimensions of Time*, Edward T. Hall contrasts the way people of American-European heritage think about time with time concepts in other cultures. In summarizing the differences between the Hopi Indians, who "live in the eternal present," and American-European people, Hall writes: ". . . one feels that [for the Hopi] time is not a harsh taskmaster nor is it equated with money and progress as it is with [American-European people] . . . who tend to think that because nothing overt is happening, nothing is going on. With many cultures there are long periods during which people are making up their minds or waiting for a consensus to be achieved."

Julie Cameron, in her book *The Artist's Way,* describes a useful tool for tapping into the creativity available in times that we allow ourselves for rejuvenation. She suggests scheduling an *"artist date"* once a week when you spend time by yourself doing something creative, interesting, or fun.

The "P" Word: Procrastination
How to Quit Avoiding the Hard Jobs and Get Your Priorities in Order

Even with the best plan in place, we may find ourselves procrastinating. Everyone does it. Then, we worry and promise we'll never do it again if we can just get through this day. We say things to ourselves like, "If I can just live through this test, I will never wait until the last minute again." But something else comes along and we put off our school work again. Why do we do this? Why do we procrastinate when we all know how unpleasant the results can be? Why aren't we disciplined and organized and controlled so we can reap the rewards that come from being prepared?

People procrastinate for different reasons. Common reasons that students procrastinate include:

- **Superhuman expectations.** You simply overdo and put more on your calendar than Superman or Superwoman could accomplish. Many of these to-do items might not relate to your major goals. Think about the 80/20 rule.

- **Fear of failing.** You have failed a difficult subject in the past, and you are afraid it is going to happen again, so you do the natural thing and avoid unpleasant experiences. Think about how much you have already accomplished getting to this place. You have already succeeded in being here. Know that you are wiser now and that any goal can be accomplished if you approach it one step at a time.

- **Emotional blocks.** It is time to get started and you have no routine and no past regimen to get you started. You are already feeling guilty because you have wasted so much time. You feel tired, depressed, and beaten. You may feel like the job ahead is so big that you cannot get it done. The thing to do in these situations is to make yourself spend ten minutes on the task. You can do ten minutes, and at the end of that time, the job may look more approachable. You might even be able to put a game plan together for attacking the problem. If not, take a break and spend another ten minutes on it later.

- **Fear of being unworthy.** You may be telling yourself that smart people don't have to study, and everybody is smart but you. Recognize that smart people are studying or they have studied in the past and have already mastered the material you are struggling with now. Sooner or later, you must pay the price to gain knowledge. We all have different strengths. Recognize that this education is for you. If you aren't picking up a subject as well as you had hoped, study hardier. Another subject may come much easier for you than for others.

> We have only this moment, sparkling like a star in our hand . . . and melting like a snowflake. Let us use it before it is too late.
>
> —Marie Ray

Plan to Beat Procrastination

Not only is it important that you overcome procrastination for the sake of your education, but it is also equally crucial to your success at work. Procrastination is a bad habit that will haunt you until you make up your mind to overcome it. In other words, don't procrastinate in beating procrastination!

The chart on the following pages offers 25 tips that might help.

25 Ways to Beat Procrastination

- **Face up to the results of procrastination.** What will happen if you procrastinate? How will you feel if you fail the test? How miserable will you be over the weekend if you have to write a last-minute paper while your family and friends get to go see a movie?

- **Concentrate on the rewards of managing yourself and your time.** Think about the rewards that you will get when you finish a difficult task. You can go to a movie or relax or spend time with your children. You can get a good grade. Think about how good you will feel when the weekend comes and your paper is finished and you don't have to spend all your time working on a project. Focus on how good you will feel when you did well on a project. While you are working, stop periodically and focus on the rewards.

- **Break up big tasks into small ones.** If you have to write a paper, can you work on one segment tonight and another one tomorrow? If you start early and finish a small segment each day, a big paper is just a series of small tasks.

- **Give yourself a time limit to accomplish a task.** Work will expand to take up as much time as we allow it to. Push yourself to work faster and more efficiently.

- **Set a regular time for study, and do not vary from it.** Determine your personal "best time" and "best place."

- **Start studying with positive, realistic thoughts.** Push negative thoughts out of your mind. Tell yourself that you are growing and becoming more competent. Remember, "You can do this."

- **Establish good study habits.**

- **Set reasonable, concrete goals that you can reach in about 20 to 25 minutes.** Then, set others for the next block of time.

- **Face fear; look it right in the face.** Make up your mind you are going to overcome fear by studying and preparing every day.

(continued)

- **Get help from your instructor.** Show the instructor what you have done and ask whether you are on the right track.

- **Avoid whining and people who whine and complain.** You have this job to do, and it is not going away.

- **Allow yourself more time than you think you need to complete an assignment or to study for a test.**

- **Practice your new study habits for 21 days.** By then, you will have gone a long way toward getting rid of your procrastination habits.

- **Actually reward yourself when you have accomplished an important body of work.** Perhaps you spent two hours looking for research articles on the Internet. Now, you deserve a reward. Watch a TV program; visit a friend for a few minutes; talk on the phone; answer your e-mail; read a book to a child. If you have not finished your work, push yourself to go back to work for a few more minutes. When you do this, you are building your discipline and staying power. Ask yourself: "Can I work just 15 more minutes?"

- **Look at this task in terms of your long-range goals.** Where does it fit in your plans of getting what you want? Does passing this test get you admitted to the job you want? Does making a B1 on this test take you one step closer to your career? Does making a good grade on this speech move you toward overcoming your fear of public speaking?

- **Avoid getting involved in too many organizations, accepting too many commitments, or overextending yourself.** Stop and think about how much you really want to do something before you accept. How much time will it take? Does it help you grow and learn? Does it fit with your goals? It's better to say "no" than to accept something that will make you miserable before you finish. "NO!" is a powerful word—use it! Weed out activities that take too much of your time and provide you very little personal reward. You only have so much personal time. Fill that time with activities that give you pleasure and energy.

- **Force yourself to jump in.** Even if your initial work is not satisfactory, you have made a start, and chances are you will get focused as you progress. Sometimes, you just have to plunge in. You can't jump off the high dive in small steps. Just do it!

- **Start on the difficult, most boring tasks first.** Sometimes, it is effective to do these difficult tasks early in the morning before breakfast. This depends on your personal "best time" to work.

- **Practice "do it now."** Do simple tasks as you get them. Practice multitasking. What things can you do at the same time? For example, you can read a chapter while the clothes are washing. You can take your children on a walk and get your own exercise at the same time.

- **Find a quiet place to study and concentrate.** Small children might not understand that Mommy or Daddy needs to study very badly. You may need to make regular visits to the library or to a computer laboratory so you can focus on your work.

- **Gain the support of your family and/or friends.** Talk to the important people in your life and let them know how important your education is to you. Ask them to help and support you.

- **Weed out your personal belongings and living space.** Clean out and organize your closets and drawer space. Give things you no longer wear to charity. Buy fewer things that require waxing, polishing, recharging, cleaning, or storing. Things become monsters that take up your valuable time. Live a simpler life.

- **Prepare to be successful by getting ready the evening before.** Be sure your car has gas; select and press your clothes; put all your materials in order; check to see if the children's necessities and clothes have been organized. Often, the first few minutes of every day determine if you are going to have a good day. Program yourself for success!

- **Take time to smell the roses.** Part of every day should belong to you to do what you want. We all need to find time for regular exercise; we need to spend quality time with people we love and enjoy; we need to pay attention to

25 Ways to Beat Procrastination

friends and relationships; we need time to focus on spiritual development. Don't overmanage yourself to the point that you lose sight of what is really important—friends and family and self!

- **Balance your load.** If you are working full-time and paying for all of your expenses, you may need to take a lighter load so you can have a life. If you are a nontraditional student who is working and has small children and a home to take care of, you might need to rethink your schedule. Very few people will ever lament that they didn't do more work. But many will be sorry they didn't spend quality time with their parents, grandparents, or small children when they could have. It is true that you can do it all, but most of us can't do it all at one time. This race is just yours. You are not racing everyone else around you—just yourself.

Tools of Time Management

Having some type of scheduling system or calendar is important when managing activities. "ABC" priority codes and daily "to-do" lists have been key techniques to help sort through choices in some meaningful way. What you may have already discovered, however, is that a calendar, though important, can really effectively help you manage only a small portion of what you need to organize and is inadequate to deal with the volume of things to do and the variable nature of priorities.

E-mail, personal digital assistants (PDAs), scheduling software, and other digital data are becoming increasingly viable means of keeping track of our actions. If you've tried to use any of these processes or tools, however, you may have found them also unable to accommodate the complexity and changing priority factors. The ability to be successful, relaxed, and in control requires that we use these tools only to help us, not limit us. They cannot prioritize for us. They cannot advise us when we need to change our plans due to unforeseen opportunities or responsibilities. They can't remember to add new activities, or develop strategies for specific goals. In other words, they can't think for us. However, they can be extremely useful in organizing much of what we need to accomplish.

Time Bandits
Watch the Number of Commitments

Much of the stress people experience comes from inappropriately managed commitments they make or accept. When we intend to do something, or commit to doing something for others and are not able to follow through, we experience conflict. We run the risk of damaging trust with ourselves and with others. Most of us are almost always juggling commitments in several different areas of our lives. A good way to estimate if you have too many commitments is to write them all down and estimate how many hours you'll be spending on them during a week's time.

Saying "no" is something many of us have a hard time doing. We want to do it all, and we don't want to disappoint others or miss out on opportunities. Check in with what is most important, and be aware of what will be compromised when you agree to something. When you are clear about who you are and what you are creating in your life, "no" becomes "yes," because you are ultimately saying "yes" to what you know will be most satisfying to you in the long term. If priorities grow out of a profound sense of values, according to management expert Stephen Covey, we will enjoy a relaxed approach to dealing with important tasks. "Only when you have the self-awareness to examine your values and create a value-centered purpose, will you have the power to say no with a genuine smile to the unimportant."

Develop Good Habits

Good habits replenish energy. These good habits are the activities that are most meaningful to you and help you accomplish your goals. One way to develop good habits is to establish rituals. Jim Lohr and Tony Schwartz write in their book *The Power of Full Engagement,* "The bigger the storm, the more inclined we are to revert to our survival habits, and the more important positive rituals become."

Avoid Crisis Management

There's a certain frenetic energy around managing a crisis that causes an illusion of importance. With this feverish pace of activity, we release stress hormones such as adrenaline, noradrenaline, and cortisol that may actually be addictive.

Stephen Covey, time-management expert, relates that if we are *overly* externally motivated, we will tend to prioritize the needs of others over our own goals and needs. If you do this, you will find yourself continually dealing with crises and interruptions and not using your time for what is most important. When you live in crisis mode, you attempt to get relief from pressing problems by becoming busy with seemingly urgent but unimportant tasks. However, if you spend your time building relationships, recognizing new opportunities, and planning and preventing crises, you will be more effective at achieving goals.

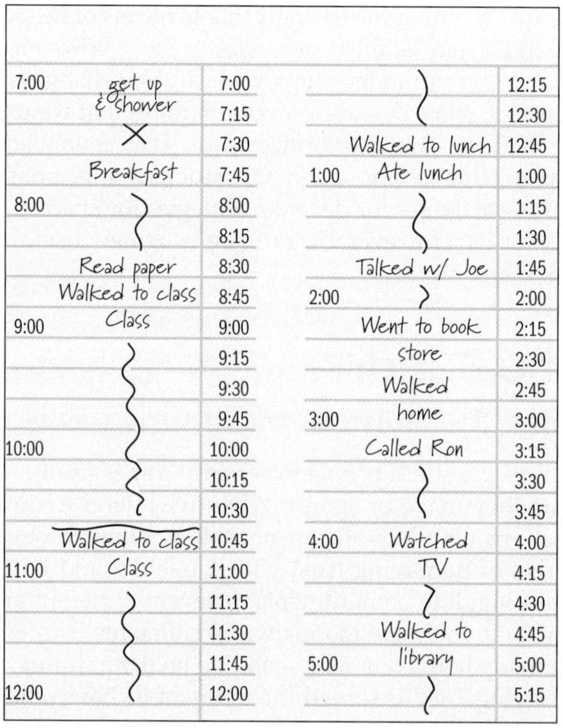

Figure 5.1 Evaluating How You Really Spend Your Time

Planning and Organizing for School

Each evening, you should take a few minutes (and literally, that is all it will take) and sit in a quiet place and make a list of all that needs to be done tomorrow.

Successful time management comes from planning the NIGHT BEFORE! Let's say your list includes the following:

Research project

Study, test on Friday

Read Chapter 13

Meet with study group

Attend class, 8:00

Attend class, 10:00

Help child with school project

Exercise

Buy birthday card for mom

Wash the car

Wash clothes

Buy groceries

Call Janice about weekend

Now, you have created a list of tasks that you will face tomorrow. Next, separate this list into three categories: **MUST** *Do, Would* **LIKE** *to Do,* and **FUN** *Breaks*.

MUST DO

Read Chapter 13

Meet with study group

Study, test on Friday

Exercise

Help child with school project

Attend class, 8:00

Attend class, 10:00

WOULD LIKE TO DO

Research project

Buy birthday card for Mom

Wash clothes

Buy groceries

FUN BREAKS

Wash the car

Call Janice

Don't get too excited yet. Your time-management plan is not finished. You have not done the most important part yet. Now, you will need to rank the items in order of their importance. You put a 1 by the most important, a 2 by the next most important, and so forth in each category. It may look something like this:

MUST DO

1 Read Chapter 13

1 Meet with study group

1 Study, test on Friday

2 Attend class, 8:00

2 Attend class, 10:00

2-Help child with school project

3 Exercise

WOULD LIKE TO DO

1 Research project

2 Buy birthday card for Mom

3 Wash clothes

2 Buy groceries

FUN BREAKS

2 Wash the car

1 Call Janice

Planning and Organizing for Work

Some supermen and superwomen work full-time and go to school full-time while they juggle families and other responsibilities. If kept up for a long period, you can burn out from the stress that such a pace imposes on your mind and body; and if you have children, they may be adversely affected in the short run by your overfull schedule. If you can work less or experience less stress at work, it can take away some of the pain.

Important Principles for Priority Management at Work

- Organize your materials at work as they are organized at home. If you have a desk in both places, keep your supplies in the same place in both desks. Simplify your life by following similar patterns at work and at home. Make your office or work space inviting, attractive, and stimulating. If you are a

> The more time we spend . . . on planning . . . a project, the less total time is required for it. Don't let today's busy work crowd planning time out of your schedule.
>
> —Edwin C. Bliss

visual thinker and need to see different assignments, be considerate of others who may work close to you. Use clear plastic boxes, colored file folders, and colored file boxes to organize your projects.

- Write directions down! Keep a notebook for repetitive tasks. Keep a calendar, and be on time to meetings.
- Learn to do paperwork immediately rather than let it build up. File—don't pile!
- Never let your work responsibilities slide because you are studying on the job. Employers always notice.
- Leave the office for lunch, breaks, and short walks.
- When you are given projects that require working with others, plan carefully to do your work well and on time.
- Keep an address book (electronic or paper) handy with important phone numbers and addresses that you use frequently.
- Perform difficult, unpleasant tasks as soon as you can so you don't have them hanging over your head.
- When you plan your work schedule, allow for unexpected problems that might interfere with the schedule.
- Practice detached concern—care about your work but don't take it home with you.

Planning and Organizing at Home

Some people organize effectively at work and school but allow things to fall apart at home. Your home should be a place where you can study, relax, laugh, invite your friends, and find solitude. The following ideas about home organization will help you maximize your time.

Important Principles for Priority Management at Home

- Organize as effectively at home as you do at work.
- If applicable, divide the chores. Insist on everyone doing his or her share.
  - Plan a rotation schedule for major household chores and stick to it—do laundry on Mondays and Thursdays; clean bathrooms on Saturdays; iron on Wednesdays; and so on.
  - Organize your closet and your dresser drawers. Get rid of clothes you don't wear. Put a sign by your telephone that reads "TIME" to remind yourself not to waste it on the phone. If you can't study at home because of drop-in visitors or other housemates, go to the library.
  - Pay bills twice monthly. Pay them on time so you don't ruin your credit rating.
  - Manage your money wisely so you are not stressed by too many bills and too little money.
  - If you drive to class or work, fill up your tank ahead of time so you won't be late.
  - Keep yourself physically fit with a regular exercise plan and nutritious meals.
  - Get out of the house. Take a walk. Visit a friend.
  - If you have children, teach them to be organized so they don't waste your time searching for their shoes, books, and assignments. Help family members take responsibility!
  - You can't work, go to school, and hold everybody's hand all the time. Give each of your children a drawer in a filing cabinet. Show them how to organize their work. You will be preparing them to be successful.

DID YOU KNOW?

Jeffrey Katzenberg

Walt Disney fired Jeffrey Katzenberg in 1994. He went on to co-create DreamWorks Studio. DreamWorks now produces movies such as *Shrek Forever After, How to Train Your Dragon, Monsters vs. Aliens,* and *Madagascar 3.*

- If you are a perfectionist and want everything in your home to be perfect, get over it!
- Get rid of the clutter in your home or apartment, basement, and closets.
- Establish a time for study hall in your home. Children do their homework, and you do yours.
- If you have a family, insist that all of you organize clothes in advance for school or work for several days.
- Put a message board in a convenient place for everyone to use.
- If your children are old enough to drive, have them run errands at the post office and grocery store.
- Carpool with other parents in your neighborhood.
- Delegate, delegate, delegate! You are not superwoman or superman. Tell your family you need help. Children can feed pets, make their own beds, fold clothes, vacuum, sweep, and cut the grass if they are old enough.
- Schedule at least one hour alone with each of your children each week. Make this a happy, special time—a fun break!
- Make meals happy, relaxed times when each person's successes are shared and celebrated. Discuss current events.
- Plan special times with your spouse or partner if you have one so that he or she does not get fed up with your going to school.
- Tell your family and friends when you have to study; ask them to respect you by not calling or dropping by at this time.
- Post a family calendar where everyone can see it. Put all special events on it—for example, Janie's recital, Mike's baseball game, Jasmine's company party.
- Put sacred days on this calendar so that your entire family has something to look forward to.

Yes You Can!
IDEAS FOR SUCCESS

Consider the following tips for managing your time and money:
- Push yourself to use your time more wisely. Can you get more done in less time by focusing on what you have learned?
- Use your time-management practices at work and for school.
- Focus on doing hard, unpleasant jobs first, then reward yourself.
- Analyze how you are actually spending your time.
- Practice the strategies you have learned for avoiding procrastination.
- Map out your activities and tasks for a week and a month at a time.

and ITT Tech Can Help!

What's in It for Me?
Becoming a Team Player

What kind of team player are you? Do you support others? Are you competitive? Do you like to work in teams?

In today's world, it is very likely that, no matter what your job, you will work on teams during your career. Teamwork is one of the business strategies of the 21st century.

Employers are looking for people who excel as team members.

Organizations are always changing the way they do business on every level. Recently, efficiency and creativity have been emphasized, particularly in how resources and outcomes are linked. Employees are directly impacted by this focus because they are expected to help achieve these shared goals.

Communication skills can prove to be very important to groups' efforts. Several researchers have found that the way team members communicate with each other is critical to the overall effectiveness of the team. The good news is that team and communication skills *can be learned and improved.*

Understanding the Types of Teams

Understanding how teams function and how you can best interact in a team is very important to your career success. A **team** is a unit of two or more people who interact and coordinate their work to accomplish a specific goal. Although they can be quite large, most teams have fewer than 15 people.

There are many types of teams:

- *Formal teams* are formed by the organization as part of the organizational structure.

- *Special purpose teams* are formed to take on a temporary project, such as solving a problem or developing a new process or system.

- *Self-directed teams* rotate jobs to produce a product or service.

- *Virtual teams* use technology to collaborate on projects.

Regardless of the type of team, effectiveness depends on the quality of team members' interactions. The teams you work on will likely be diverse, including people from different ethnic groups, education levels, and professional fields. The more you understand individual roles and the dynamics of group interaction, the more valuable and effective you can be as a team member.

What's Your Role?
Understanding Team Structure and Roles

Teams come in many shapes and sizes. They may be highly structured, which means that everyone's role on the team is predetermined and clearly defined; or they may be unstructured, which means that roles emerge as the team members begin to interact.

There are numerous roles that individuals can play as part of a team. Formal or assigned roles can include team leader, note taker, or scheduler. Informal roles develop during group interactions and generally fall into two categories: roles that focus on the accomplishment of tasks (the **task specialist role**) and roles that focus on the social and emotional needs of the group or the team's working relationships (the **socioemotional role**). The most effective teams have members who fulfill roles in both of these areas and not exclusively in one or the other.

Team members in the **task specialist** role frequently engage in the following behaviors:

Initiator: proposing solutions and opinions to team members

Information seeker: asking for task-relevant facts

Summarizer: pulling ideas together

Energizer: stimulating a team into action when interest falls

Team members in the **socioemotional role** frequently perform the following functions:

Encourager: praising others; encouraging others' ideas

Harmonizer: reconciles group conflicts; reduces tension

Compromiser: compromises opinions to go along with the group

Task Specialist Role	**Socioemotional Role**
Focuses on task accomplishment over members' needs	Focuses on people's needs over task accomplishment

You will likely play different roles in different groups. No matter what role you play, your participation as well as that of each other member is valuable and important to the success of the overall team. The potential of the team lies in the combination of talents, knowledge, and insights that each person brings.

Look over the different roles played by the task specialist and the socioemotional team member. Which roles do you tend to play?

Let's Work Together
Team Development Stages

After a team has been created, the team members navigate through a set of stages as they learn to become a productive unit. These stages are normal, and every team must go through them. The stages may last a short time, depending on the team members and task deadline. In the worst case, a team may never move into the performance stage. Understanding this process will help the team members move more quickly through the stages and complete their tasks.

When a team is formed, the team members must get to know each other, establish their roles and norms, divide up the work, and understand their task in order to achieve their goal(s). The following stages generally occur in sequence:

Forming   In the forming stage, the members break the ice and test one another for friendship opportunities and task orientation. They determine whether each other's behaviors are acceptable. Uncertainty runs high during this stage as members wonder what the ground rules are, what their duties will be, and whether they will fit in. Social discussions should be encouraged during this stage.

Storming   During this stage individual personalities emerge and people become more assertive in clarifying their roles and what is expected of them. There is conflict and disagreement, possibly over the team's tasks and goals or individual positions within the team. People may jockey for the leadership role. This stage is unavoidable, though if a team stays here for long, it may never achieve its goals. Members should propose ideas, disagree with one another, and work through the uncertainties. During this stage the members should concentrate on defining the group's goals. If people allow their egos to intrude too much, the group will be held back. On the other hand, if members do not speak their opinions about the group's mission because they are afraid of confrontation, the group could lose the benefit of stimulating ideas. Pick your battles and know why you are fighting them.

Norming   During this stage, conflict is resolved. A consensus develops concerning who is the leader and members' roles. Members develop a sense of cohesion and belonging. This stage typically lasts a short time.

Performing   During this stage, members focus on accomplishing the assigned tasks. Problems are solved and most discussion is based around the team goal(s). Members who have mainly played the socioemotional role will now contribute to the task. Everything is focused on getting the job done.

FORMING

Getting to know each other

↓

STORMING

Conflict over goals and positions

↓

NORMING

Team cohesion is established

↓

PERFORMING

Team goals are accomplished

> No member of a crew is praised for the rugged individuality of his rowing.
>
> —Ralph Waldo Emerson

Understanding these stages of team development will help you deal with the inevitable challenges that arise in group situations. By recognizing these stages, you can see that becoming an effective team is a process of working out relationships and is not a given. Work and thought are required from the participants so they understand their roles in relation to each other and learn how to manage interaction.

Talk Among Yourselves
Team Communication

Successful interaction between team members is the key to effective teams. This successful interaction begins with communication. How effectively we communicate with those around us can make a huge difference in our success. Like learning skills, communication skills can be developed and are critical to success as a technology professional.

The word "communication" is derived from the same Latin root, *communis*, as the word "communion," which implies mutual participation. For communication to take place, whereby information is shared, the mutual participation of two or more parties is necessary. Even with active, mutual participation, however, there may at times be a gap in the communication process between what someone intends to communicate and what is actually heard.

To understand this principle, think about the telephone game in which a child whispers a message to the next child in the line, who then whispers the message to the next child, and so on down the line. The last child in line receives the message and announces it. Invariably, the message received by the last child is different from the one whispered by the first child in line. Because each of us hears and considers information through our own set of intellectual, emotional and physical filters, we may interpret messages in ways that were not intended by the people communicating the messages.

Types of Team Communication

Verbal Communication   Verbal communication is the expression of something in words or language, whether spoken, written, or thought.

Virtual Communication   Virtual communication is a form of verbal communication that is prevalent in our society today.

The two categories of virtual communication are:

Synchronous communication, which takes place at the same time—real-time interaction. This could include telephone and video conferencing, electronic display (whiteboard), and chatting.

Asynchronous communication, which takes place at different times—delayed interaction. This could include e-mail, voice-mail, group calendars and schedules, bulletin boards and Web pages, and file sharing.

Researchers have investigated how much and how quickly people reveal information about themselves and the overall impressions they make when using the computer to communicate. Many studies have found that people reveal much more information online than they would in a face-to-face interaction and even developed more socially rich relationships than people who interacted face-to-face. Developing relationships with others may take longer using virtual communication, but it does occur.

Using e-mail for messages, however, can hinder understanding. It may contribute to greater polarization of opinions; group members may take more extreme positions when putting information in writing than when communicating orally.

Nonverbal Communication Have you ever watched comedians' faces? Sometimes their faces are reflecting something entirely different from what's actually happening. The difference between the two messages can create very funny results. Nonverbal communication works hand in hand with verbal communication to send a message. If you speak the same sentence three times—once in a loud voice while standing up, once quietly while sitting with arms and legs crossed, and once while maintaining eye contact and taking the receiver's hand—you are sending three entirely different messages.

Nonverbal communication is communication that does not rely on written or spoken words. Body posture and movement, eye contact, facial expression, seating arrangement, spatial relationships, personal appearance, response time, and tone of voice all communicate nonverbal messages. When body language contradicts verbal language, the message conveyed by the body is dominant. Consider, for example, if someone asks you how you feel, and you say "fine" even though you don't feel fine at all. In such a case, your posture, eye contact, and other body language may convey the real message loud and clear.

We also send messages with our actions. For instance, the people with whom we spend time, what we spend our money on, how we care for our health, and how we care for others are all ways in which we communicate nonverbally.

Nonverbal communication also includes internal conversations and thoughts. Our internal thought processes create emotion and energy. Even when we don't give voice to these feelings, they may influence others around us.

To improve your nonverbal communication:

- Pay attention to what other people communicate nonverbally.

- Note when someone misinterprets what you have said.

- Look for ways in which your nonverbal communication affects your message.

- Be aware of saying things with your body that contradict what you are saying; you will confuse your listeners.

- Notice the distance between you and others when you're speaking. In some cultures, casual acquaintances stand very close to one another when speaking; in others, only very intimate, personal conversations are carried out while standing close together.

- Notice your eye contact when talking and listening. American culture encourages eye contact, interpreting it as honesty and openness; other cultures frown on it, interpreting it as a sign of disrespect.

Nonverbal communication takes practice. If you have a VCR at home, put on a video and turn off the sound. Look at the nonverbal messages the actors are conveying. Another way to improve your nonverbal awareness is to play charades. Or, go to the mall and watch people as they go past. What are their mannerisms saying? Do you think you're reading them accurately? You might even want to observe yourself if you have the chance. Look at old video tapes or pictures. What are you conveying with your nonverbal signs? Remember to practice. Communication takes effort.

> As I grow older, I pay less attention to what people say: I just watch what they do.
> —Andrew Carnegie

Communication Styles

The first step in developing communication skills for teams is to become aware of yourself and your communication style. Self-awareness encompasses knowing your personal capabilities and your weaknesses. You have already begun this process by learning about your personality type, your intelligences, and your learning styles. The following chart will help you understand different styles of communication and suggested strategies for using them in a group.

MULTIPLE INTELLIGENCE STRATEGIES FOR

Communication ←

Using techniques corresponding to your stronger intelligences boosts your communication skills both as a speaker and as a listener.

INTELLIGENCE	SUGGESTED STRATEGIES	WHAT WORKS FOR YOU? WRITE NEW IDEAS HERE
Verbal–Linguistic	• Find opportunities to express your thoughts and feelings to others—either in writing or in person. • Remind yourself that you have two ears and only one mouth. Listening is more important than talking.	
Logical–Mathematical	• Allow yourself time to think through solutions before discussing them—try writing out a logical argument on paper and then rehearsing it orally. • Accept the fact that others may have communication styles that vary from yours and that may not seem logical.	
Bodily–Kinesthetic	• Have an important talk while walking or performing a task that does not involve concentration. • Work out physically to burn off excess energy before having an important discussion.	
Visual–Spatial	• Make a drawing or diagram of points you want to communicate during an important discussion. • If your communication is in a formal classroom or work setting, use visual aids to explain your main points.	
Interpersonal	• Observe how you communicate with friends. If you tend to dominate the conversation, brainstorm ideas about how to communicate more effectively. • Remember to balance speaking with listening.	
Intrapersonal	• When you have a difficult encounter, take time alone to evaluate what happened and to decide how you can communicate more effectively next time. • Remember that, in order for others to understand clearly, you may need to communicate more than you expect to.	
Musical	• Play soft music during an important discussion if it helps you, making sure it isn't distracting to the others involved.	
Naturalistic	• Communicate outdoors if that is agreeable to all parties. • If you have a difficult exchange, imagine how you might have responded differently had it taken place outdoors.	

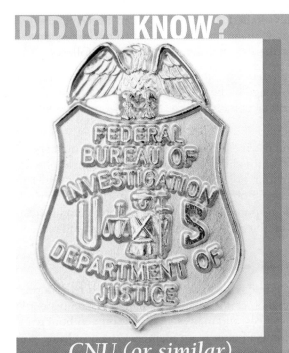

CNU (or similar)

The unit (Crisis Negotiation Unit), a major component of our Critical Incident Response Group, which was formed in 1994 in response to the Waco siege a year earlier, is dedicated to resolving hostage, barricade, attempted suicide, and kidnapping cases throughout the world.

Our agents, meanwhile, have to pass a rigorous two-week National Crisis Negotiation Course, held a few times a year at the FBI Academy in Virginia, to become negotiators. The course puts students in real-life scenarios and tests their mettle, because there are no second chances when called to help.

Courtesy of Stephen Mulcahey / Alamy

Keeping the Peace
How to Have Difficult Conversations

Have you ever been involved in a heated conversation when you notice that you're sweating or that your stomach is tightening and you think you can feel your blood starting to boil? Kerry Patterson et al., in their book *Crucial Conversations*, call conversations that are challenging, frustrating, frightening or annoying, and, at the same time, could have an impact on the quality of your life or work **crucial conversations.** These conversations are usually about tough issues. You may experience physical responses during these conversations, such as tightening of the stomach. Look for clues that you are involved in a crucial conversation.

While it's common to want to back away from such situations, if you know how to master these types of conversations, you can engage in ways that create beneficial outcomes for all the participants. Leadership expert Stephen Covey believes that, by employing several critical communication skills, it is possible to create a level of "mutual understanding and creative synergy"[3] that moves people to agree and act on effective solutions.

Make People Feel Safe   People feel safe to share creative ideas or confrontational information when they trust that they won't be attacked or humiliated. When people feel unsafe, they generally either attack defensively or withdraw into silence. A common response is to react in kind, and the communication continues in a downward spiral.

Many times, people can receive tough feedback without becoming defensive if they believe that the giver of the feedback is trying to help or support. We can look for opportunities in such challenging conversations for greater awareness and movement toward our goals.

Ways to create or restore safety:

- Notice when others are withdrawing or attacking.
- Watch the impact you are having on others, and how you are feeling in response to others.
- Make others feel respected by recognizing your own weaknesses.
- Consider others' points of view and look for common interests.

Take Responsibility for Feelings   We all choose our response to the actions and words of others. No one can "make" us feel a certain way. How we feel is always our choice.

In responding to the actions and words of others, use "I" statements as opposed to "you" statements.

- **"I" statement:** "I feel stressed out and rushed when you give me a deadline for tasks to accomplish without checking with me about my schedule."
- **"You" statement:** "You make me feel stressed out and rushed when you give me a deadline for tasks to accomplish without checking with me about my schedule."

Accept Criticism   Understanding what criticism is and is not can help us avoid getting caught in the downward spiral of communication gone awry. Too often we take critiques personally, assuming the criticism is about us as people rather than about what we've done. You are not your project or your grade. Getting well-intentioned criticism does not mean that you have failed. It means you can do things better. Sometimes, however, people are not well meaning. They intend to put others down. Psychologist Lonnie Barbach describes these "put down" individuals as follows:

> "People who feel insecure and inadequate often get into the right/wrong battle. They try to raise their self-image by being "right." One way of proving oneself right is to make the other person wrong. Making someone feel wrong has an alienating effect."

Critically evaluate the criticism you receive. Is it from a source whom you respect? Is the criticism itself valid? Is any part of it valid? Can you use the feedback to make changes for the better? If so, then set an intention to do that. If not, then let the criticism go. In the midst of an adversarial conversation, know that you can evaluate the feedback at a later time; you do not have to respond immediately. Be aware of your physical responses, and remember to focus on the general context of the conversation.

How to Give a Useful Group Peer Review

At times in your courses and in some groups at work, you will be asked to do a peer review—to rate your team members on their contribution to the group. Usually people are quite easy on each other in these instances, and many leave the group without gaining any knowledge about how to become a better team member. The best thing you can do for each other, especially during your peer reviews in your classes, is to be honest and helpful. Use the principles of good communication to explain what you really feel about how your teammates have contributed and how they could better contribute in the future. Likewise, as you receive feedback, recognize that any criticism can ultimately help you far more than positive feedback. Practice accepting, and even welcoming, honest feedback.

Giving useful feedback requires empathy, sensitivity, and self-awareness. We can never know what is most beneficial for someone else, though we can share what works and what doesn't work for us.

Some tips for giving and receiving feedback include:

Giving Feedback to Others

- Ask whether they want feedback before offering any.
- Be mindful of the timing and environment. Avoid emotional situations and giving feedback in public settings.
- Find something positive about their performance, and comment on it.
- Give others a chance to give feedback to themselves.
- Be specific—refer to specific scenarios or situations.
- Give a suggestion for how you believe they could be more effective.

Receiving Feedback from Others

- Let others know if the timing or location doesn't work for you.
- Assume the givers have your best interests at heart.
- Be open and nondefensive.
- Ask questions if you are unclear. Strive for understanding.
- Ask how you could have done things differently.

Getting More of What You Want
The Art of Negotiation

Negotiations occur in many areas of life. We may negotiate a job offer, a relationship, or a treaty among nations. Usually in negotiation, each side takes a position, argues for it, and makes concessions to reach a compromise.

Evaluate What You Want   To negotiate, begin with understanding what you want. Negotiation leads back to our values and our understanding of those values. In the heat of a discussion about an important issue, you may feel intense emotions welling, and you may be tempted to give in or act in a way that is uncharacteristic. You may feel the need to avoid embarrassment, win, be right, or punish others. As you make an effort to discover the underlying motive, you may conclude that you're pushing harder to win an argument than it merits.

To allow for healthy dialogue to occur in these instances, step away from the interaction and look at your desires in light of the following questions. Alternatively, you can frame your desires in advance before you enter into a conversation that is likely to require negotiation. Ask yourself:

1. What do I really want for myself?

2. What do I really want for others?

Based on those answers, ask yourself how you would behave if you wanted those outcomes.

Also evaluate what you don't want to occur for yourself, others, or the relationship. Put this into the following framework:

I want _____ AND I don't want _____.

Then, you have a foundation for discovering a solution.

Foster Cooperation and Dialogue   You can think of negotiation as a compromise: the parties each have their desires and meet as close to the middle as they can get. Negotiation can also involve a synergistic process through which parties achieve the optimum solution for both.

Typical Compromise

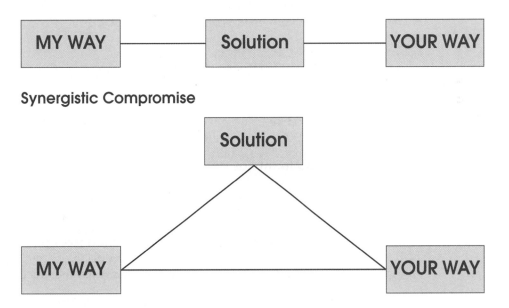

Synergistic Compromise

Synergistic compromise involves an understanding that our thoughts are interconnected, and, through an intentional dialogue, we can collaborate toward greater understanding and levels of creativity than we could access alone. A group may explore complex issues by involving people with many different points of view. But in order for dialogue to occur, the participants must agree to share their points of view while suspending their assumption that their viewpoint is correct. Participants must agree that the possibility exists for an "alternate way" that none of them had previously considered.

You are not trying to win in a dialogue. Everyone wins if you're doing it right. This type of communication is as much about a collective learning process as it is about the sharing of information.

The basic conditions necessary for effective compromise are:

- All participants suspend assumptions. Participants are aware of their programming and opinions and agree to be open to other ways of thinking.
- All participants regard each other as colleagues, peers, or equals. Every participant's input is considered equally.
- There must be a facilitator who makes sure the process is maintained and respected.

> He that complies against his will is of his own opinion still.
>
> —Samuel Butler

Conflict Is Inevitable
How Do You Deal with It?

Many people intensely dislike conflict and will go to extreme measures to avoid it. On the other hand, some people seem to thrive on conflict and enjoy creating situations that put people at odds with each other. While in college, you certainly will not be sheltered from conflicts. In fact, on a college campus where a very diverse population lives and learns together, conflict is likely to arise on a regular basis. The simple truth is, conflict is pervasive throughout our culture, and you simply cannot avoid having some confrontations with other people. Therefore, you should not try to avoid conflict; rather, you can use it to create better relationships by exploring workable solutions.

You may experience conflict in a classroom when another student takes issue with your opinions and continues to harass you about your ideas after the class is over. You could be placed on a team where conflicts arise among the members. A major conflict could erupt in the parking lot if someone thoughtlessly pulls into a parking space that you have been waiting for. You could even experience conflict with a faculty member because you intensely disagree with the grade he or she assigned you on a project. Conflict can occur in any relationship, whether it is your parents, your girlfriend or boyfriend, your best friend, a roommate, a spouse or partner, your children, or a total stranger.

Plan to Build Effective Teams
Characteristics of an Effective Team

Effective teams get results and provide satisfaction and meaning to their members. Characteristics of effective teams include:

The team has developed well-defined, elevating goals.   The team goals of effective teams are usually very specific and measurable. They are also larger goals than any individual could accomplish alone and are considered by the group to be elevating and important.

Team members have clearly defined roles and responsibilities.   Research has shown that people who belong to an effective team usually have a clear sense of their particular role or function on the team and the function of other members.

Team members share leadership.   All members of the team are encouraged to take responsibility and give input into decision making and direction of the team. There is open exchange between members as equal colleagues or peers.

Team members prioritize collaboration and partnership.   The team develops a collective vision and strategies and methods, rather than carrying out directives or acting on preformed opinions. Team members are encouraged to express their own ideas. Mutual inspiration is valued above competition.

Disorder is considered as a source of creativity. Effective teams look for opportunities in fluctuations, chaos and disturbances and use these opportunities for growth and learning.

> All for one and one for all!
> —Alexander Dumas

Team members are competent. Team members need to know not only what their assignment is but also how to perform their job. Members need adequate training in teamwork, problem-solving, and job skills in addition to being open, straightforward, supportive, action-oriented and friendly.

The team applies standards of excellence. A team is more likely to achieve its potential if it establishes high standards.

Team members give each other useful feedback. One of the ways that team members support each other in developing excellent performance is to effectively give and receive feedback. Studies show that when people are deprived of information regarding their performance, their self-confidence suffers as much as when they are given criticism. Constructive feedback, on the other hand, is an effective way to support positive growth.

Yes You Can!

Consider the following strategies when trying to resolve a conflict:

- Control yourself. Keep your words, actions, tone of voice, and body language respectful. Resist the urge to use name calling, hurtful words, and interruptions. Remember, you can't control or change anyone else.

- Establish an environment where people feel safe. This is not the time for intimidating body language, yelling, or obscenities. If you are going to resolve a conflict, you must keep your anger under control.

- Listen to what the other person has to say first. Let the other person know that you respect his or her opinions and rights.

- Avoid "gunnysacking," which is the practice of suppressing a long list of complaints and bringing them up all at one time. Sometimes, this suppressed hostility explodes and escalates.

- Try to reach some common ground. Focus your conversations on finding solutions instead of placing blame.

- Think of ways you can arrive at a "win–win" solution by first looking for common ground and things that you do agree on. Be sure you are considering the other person's needs as well as your own. Taking care of your needs and leaving the other person unhappy will only result in future conflicts that may be even worse.

and ITT Tech Can Help!

NOTES

chapter 6 | **Managing Team Projects**

Contents

Managing Team Projects

Understanding how teams function and how to communicate within them is just the beginning of building your team skills. Teams must also produce. They are formed to complete some type of project, utilizing the skills of the team members. Projects are the means to achieve business objectives. Project management is the process of planning, organizing and managing all the people and activities involved in a project from the project's concept to its completion. All organizations have projects. A project may be a large task or a complex activity, in fact, any work that is done to achieve an objective on time and within budget. Projects are ideas in motion. Examples of projects include efforts to: move an office to another location; put on an event; merge two organizations; institute a new training program; put together a budget; create a new product; change or produce a Web site, or put a new process into place. More and more people recognize that their ability to effectively manage projects is now key to their success within the organization. To successfully complete a project, teams must be well organized.

When you start a new project, you probably have many things going on in your mind. How long will it take? Are there enough people to do the work? How will you get it done on time?

In this section we will take a brief look at how projects can be organized and managed.

Project Phases

Well-organized projects generally involve the following steps or phases:

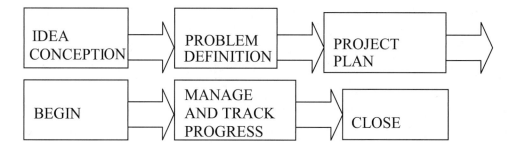

In the **conception** phase, the idea for the project comes about. What do you want to get done? Every person and every department affected by the project are also identified.

The **definition** phase includes a detailed description of the problem and the results to be produced.

The **project plan** includes a list of all the work that needs to be performed and the roles that everyone working on the project will perform. Budgets should also be established during this phase, as well as a detailed project schedule.

Once the project plan is in place, the project can **begin.**

The progress of the project is **managed and tracked** throughout the process.

The **close** of the project includes preparing any final reports as well as a post-project evaluation.

Project Planning

Perhaps the most important work in project management is done during the early phases of a project, before the actual project begins. Although many people try to shortcut these phases by moving directly into the project, experts have found that projects that are not well thought-out and planned at the beginning almost always take longer that those that are. Taking extra time at the beginning to plan saves much more time over the course of the entire project. Because of the great importance of good planning, in this section we will look in more detail at the problem definition and project plan development phases of a project.

Project management software packages that are on the market today can make the planning process easier. However, never underestimate the critical thinking that is involved with project management. As with all other forms of technology, the software can be used as a tool to help in the work, as a hammer aids in the building of a house. But, the software can no more manage the project than the hammer can design the house.

Before you can develop the project plan, you must have a clear project definition. The project definition should include the following information:

- Who is affected by the project?
- How important is this project to the company?
- What is the project trying to achieve and how will these results be measured?
- Are the objectives clear and specific? Are they "'CCO-STAR goals" (see the following box)?
- What are the limitations of the project in terms of time and resources?
- Will the benefits of the project be worth the costs of doing the project?

"CCO-STAR" goals have the following characteristics:

Challenging: Although you will want to have some easier goals, some of your goals should also be challenging.

Congruous: Your goals should conform to your value system and be internally motivated.

Optimistic: Goals have a greater ability to motivate us subconsciously if they are stated in an optimistic, proactive way.

Specific and Measurable: Each goal should be defined clearly, in detail. They should also have indicators that you can use to determine whether you met them.

Time-Sensitive: Each goal should have a set end date.

Adaptable: Goals usually should change, at least slightly, in response to things that change around you or new life events.

Realistic: Goals should be attainable. Excessively aggressive goals that cannot be reached, realistically, will not motivate people working on the project.

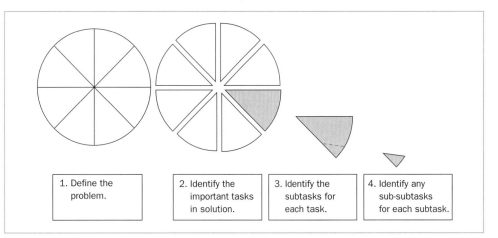

| 1. Define the problem. | 2. Identify the important tasks in solution. | 3. Identify the subtasks for each task. | 4. Identify any sub-subtasks for each subtask. |

With the project clearly defined, you can now develop your project plan. Developing the project plan means thinking about the "big picture" of the entire project as well as thinking about all the details. It involves identifying each big goal of the project and breaking it down into specific tasks. The figure on the previous page illustrates this process.

Let's look at a hypothetical team project.

Scenario   It has come to the attention of the management that there are some serious problems in communicating across departments in the company. The production department is not communicating with the marketing department, and this is hurting customer relations. The IT department is unable to process everyone's requests because there are too many requests and too few IT people. In order to stimulate more company cohesion and get everyone talking to each other, your boss has requested that you and three co-workers put on a day-long conference on best practices for working together. She would like you to have presenters from every department give an overview of what they are working on, what problems they have, and how other departments can help them. Your boss would like the conference to take place as soon as possible, ideally in the next two weeks. You quickly realize that in order to make this happen, you will have to get busy immediately.

Identify Important Tasks

After defining the problem, identify the important tasks. In our conference example, these might be:

1. Decide on a location and date for the event.
2. Find the speakers.
3. Invite attendees and advertise internally.

Identify Subtasks

Identify the steps that will make up each of your important tasks. In our example, these might include:

1. **Decide on a location and date for the event.**
   1.1 Call event center to determine open dates.
   1.2 Check with department heads on scheduling conflicts.
   1.3 Arrange teleconferencing equipment so remote employees can participate.
2. **Find speakers.**
   2.1 Work on vision and goals for the event.
   2.2 Have president of company send global e-mail outlining conference goals.
   2.3 Call departments for speaker nominations and topics.
   2.4 Write short descriptions for internal advertisements and send back to departments for approval.
3. **Invite attendees and advertise internally.**
   3.1 Finalize schedule.
   3.2 Develop flyer.
   3.3 E-mail flyer to all employees.
   3.4 Leave global voice mail.
   3.5 Publish on internal Web site.
4. **Plan for day of event.**
   4.1 Determine equipment and room needs.
   4.2 Finalize with events center.
   4.3 Develop survey.
   4.4 Put together packets.

Identify the Sub-Subtasks

If there are additional steps for each of the subtasks, identify those. In the conference example, these might include:

2.1 Work on vision and goals for the event.

    2.11 Schedule brainstorming session with group.

    2.22 Finalize list of vision and goals.

    2.23 Present to president of company for approval.

3.2 Develop flyer.

    3.21 Write content.

    3.22 Place order with graphics department.

    3.23 Get approval.

After you have identified all of the tasks, subtasks, and sub-subtasks, you can assign time estimates for each. Project management software allows you to do this easily. You can also assign task dependencies (or predecessors) in the software, or tasks that must be completed before another task can begin. You can automatically enter this information as you go, and the software will keep track of the total time. The following figure shows how the time estimates might look for the project.

Task	Estimated Time	Predecessors
1. Decide on a location and date for the event.		
1.1 Call event center to determine open dates.	1 day	
1.2 Check with department heads on scheduling conflicts.	2 days	1.1
1.3 Arrange teleconferencing equipment so remote employees can participate.	1 day	1.2
2. Find speakers.		
2.1 Work on vision and goals for the event.		
2.11 Schedule brainstorming session with group.	1 day	
2.12 Finalize list of vision and goals.	1 day	2.11
2.13 Present to president of company for approval.	1 day	2.12
2.2 Have president of company send global e-mail outlining conference goals.	1 day	2.1
2.3 Call departments for speaker nominations and topics.	2 days	2.2
2.4 Write short descriptions for internal advertisements and send back to departments for approval.	3 days	2.3
3. Invite attendees and advertise internally.		
3.1 Finalize schedule.	2 days	2.4
3.2 Develop flyer.		
3.21 Write content.	1 day	3.1
3.22 Place order with graphics department.	1 day	3.21
3.23 Get approval.	1 day	3.22
3.3 E-mail flyer to all employees.	1 day	3.23
3.4 Leave global voice mail.	1 day	3.1
3.5 Publish on internal Web site.	1 day	3.23
4. Plan day of event.		
4.1 Determine equipment needs.	1 day	
4.2 Finalize with events center.	1 day	3.1
4.3 Develop survey.	1 day	
4.4 Put together packets.	2 days	3.23

Tasks can also be displayed as a diagram. A typical diagram might look as follows for this project:

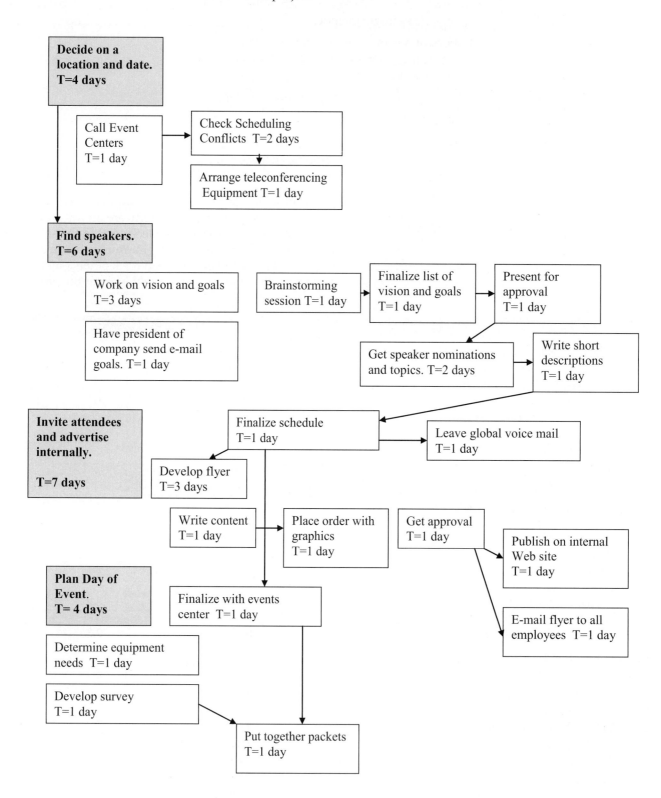

To complete a chart such as the one above, sometimes referred to as a pert chart, begin with all activities that have no predecessors. These can be started at the same time as soon as the project begins. Then continue filling in boxes with the activities that follow those you have already filled in. You can also write the time it takes to complete each of the activities within the boxes. Some will take longer than others.

If you are using project management software, these categories are built in, and you can fill them in as you go. Project management software also allows you to input all the resources you will need to complete a project, assign tasks to different people, and will visually show you how long each task will take in terms of the total project.

Yes You Can!

As organizations continue to adapt to technological changes, the nature of the organization itself is dramatically changing. Organizations are moving into more team-based, project-oriented structures where employees direct and discipline their own activities. Employees who are self-directed and who have project management skills are now in high demand. Developing these skills further, in addition to communication skills and knowledge of team dynamics, can greatly enhance your success as a technology professional.

● ● ●   *and ITT Tech Can Help!*

	❶	Task Name	Duration	Start	Finish	Predecessors
1		⊟ **Decide on location an ddate**	**4 days**	**Mon 9/24/07**	**Thu 9/27/07**	
2		Call events center	1 day	Mon 9/24/07	Mon 9/24/07	
3		Check with department he	2 days	Tue 9/25/07	Wed 9/26/07	2
4		Arrange teleconferencing	1 day	Thu 9/27/07	Thu 9/27/07	3
5		⊟ **Find speakers**	**6 days**	**Mon 9/24/07**	**Mon 10/1/07**	
6		⊟ **Work on vision and go**	**3 days**	**Tue 9/25/07**	**Thu 9/27/07**	10
7		Schedule brainstormi	1 day	Tue 9/25/07	Tue 9/25/07	
8		Finalize list of vision i	1 day	Wed 9/26/07	Wed 9/26/07	7
9		Present to president	1 day	Thu 9/27/07	Thu 9/27/07	8
10		Have president send glob	1 day	Mon 9/24/07	Mon 9/24/07	
11		Get speaker nominations	2 days	Tue 9/25/07	Wed 9/26/07	10
12		Write short descriptions	3 days	Thu 9/27/07	Mon 10/1/07	11,14
13		⊟ **Invite attendees and adver**	**3 days**	**Mon 9/24/07**	**Wed 9/26/07**	
14		Finalize schedule	1 day	Tue 9/25/07	Tue 9/25/07	16,20,24
15		⊟ **Develop flyer**	**3 days**	**Mon 9/24/07**	**Wed 9/26/07**	
16		Write content	1 day	Mon 9/24/07	Mon 9/24/07	
17		Place order with grap	1 day	Tue 9/25/07	Tue 9/25/07	16
18		Get approval	1 day	Wed 9/26/07	Wed 9/26/07	17,19,21,26
19		Email flyer to all employee	1 day	Mon 9/24/07	Mon 9/24/07	
20		Leave global voice mail	1 day	Mon 9/24/07	Mon 9/24/07	
21		Publish on internal websit	1 day	Mon 9/24/07	Mon 9/24/07	
22		⊟ **Hold event**	**2 days**	**Mon 9/24/07**	**Tue 9/25/07**	
23		Determine equipment nee	1 day	Mon 9/24/07	Mon 9/24/07	
24		Finalize with events cente	1 day	Mon 9/24/07	Mon 9/24/07	
25		Develop survey	1 day	Mon 9/24/07	Mon 9/24/07	
26		Put together packets	2 days	Mon 9/24/07	Tue 9/25/07	

NOTES

chapter 7 | Changes in the Workplace: Present and Future

 Contents

Suggestions for video conferences include:

- Monitor your gestures and facial expressions.
- Don't interrupt.
- Dress for the camera. Don't wear white; avoid patterns, shiny jewelry, or other fashion accents.
- Become familiar with the technology beforehand.

Studies suggest that the benefit of video conferencing is not in the outcome of the immediate conversation but instead in the building of relationships.

What's Changing in the Workplace of the 21st Century

As the world changes we have to adjust, technologically as well as in other ways. Some of the changes that are likely to occur in this century are technical, of course. We'll see new technologies emerge and old ones subside. The nature of work is also going to change. Where the jobs are will change. Manufacturing used to be the mainstay of the U.S. economy, but we are increasingly becoming a service-based economy, in which the majority of workers provide services instead of commodities.

Manufacturing jobs are moving overseas to countries such as China and India. This trend is call *off-shoring* if a whole company is moved to another country and *out-sourcing* if only part of the firm's work—for example, the accounting—is sent to workers in another country. One important reason that companies are hiring abroad is that is where the fastest-growing markets exist. Companies such as Procter & Gamble, IBM, Caterpillar, and Coca-Cola get more than half of their sales and income from markets outside of the United States.

Due to the globalization of the workplace, many workers will find that they need to work shifts other than 8 A.M. to 5 P.M in order to reach and collaborate with coworkers in other countries at times when they are on duty. Global workplaces are made easier by the computer, which enables us to keep in touch with coworkers at all times of day and night. When someone sells an item in Detroit, for example, that order can be immediately transmitted to China, where the item is produced and then shipped to the buyer. This is called *supply-chaining*.

The United States has remained a powerful and strong economy due to constant innovation in products, services, and companies. Now we are competing with other nations that also are very good at innovating. Product innovation depends largely on engineers. Both China and India are graduating more engineers than is the United States. In fact, China and India together are graduating approximately three times more engineers than the United States does per year.

However, we shouldn't worry about change. Many of today's jobs did not exist 15 years ago. There are now more options for ways to perform your work, such as telecommuting or starting your own business. Today's worker faces fewer stigmas associated with changing jobs or changing careers. In fact, most workers will change their jobs up to 12 times in their careers and will make three to five career changes in their lifetime.

More job opportunities will be available at all hours of the day or night, any day of the week. Many workers will be required to use and adapt to new technology. Many will start as temporary employees and will need to prove their skills in order to be considered for long-term positions. More job opportunities will be available in the expanding service and information systems sectors. This is an exciting time to be entering into a new career, but it certainly requires that you understand the key trends that are shaping the workplace.

DID YOU KNOW?

Total employment is projected to increase by 15.3 million, or 10.1 percent, during the 2008-18 period, the U.S. Bureau of Labor Statistics reported. The projected growth for 2008-18 period is larger than the increase of 10.4 million over the 1998-2008 period, or 7.4 percent. The relatively slow growth rate for the earlier 10 year period was affected by the recession, which began in December 2007, and the projected growth rate is higher than would otherwise be expected because the 2008 starting point is a recession year.

How could a student assistant position with a professor help your career?

The Need for Knowledge Workers

An employee becomes more valuable as he or she accumulates new skills. The challenge is to remain an outstanding contributor on the job while learning new skills. As organizations downsize or flatten, employees must possess multiple skills, such as the ability to learn, use new technology, or sell a product. These people have an edge. They may, for example, be able to transfer from the training division, if it is reduced in size, to the sales division and therefore remain employed.

There is good opportunity to move up within a company these days, though. A generation ago, the country shifted to a service-based economy in which fewer people produced industrial goods. Instead, more people provided services such as advertising or accounting or sold retail or wholesale products. Now we are in the midst of another shift, toward a knowledge-based economy in which employees will be expected to manage technology and information itself. The Bureau of Labor Statistics predicts in its occupational forecast for the year 2014 that the fastest-growing careers are in highly skilled professional, managerial, and technical areas. The fastest job growth will be in areas that involve the management and production of specialized knowledge.

Sometimes it is necessary to spend time after work taking classes and studying job-related materials to keep learning new skills. In years past, some employers took an active role in guiding employees toward new skills and often paid for training. In the current workplace, however, this responsibility almost entirely belongs to employees, who are expected to be proactive in learning new skills. Seek out training opportunities inside and outside of work and make sure your employer knows that you are interested in putting in the effort to learn.

The Importance of New Technology

Technology is so much a part of everyday life that most of us don't stop to think about how much we depend on it. Think about what you did today since you woke up. You will probably be able to name many activities that depend on technology. Just as it has affected our personal life, technology has revolutionized the kind of work we do, where we work, and how we complete our work. One in eight jobs is directly related to the field of high technology. Software engineer, CAD operator, computer programmer, and network administrator are some of these job titles. However, technology is used in almost all of today's jobs to some extent.

Technology has affected where and how we work. Thanks to telecommuting, some workers can work from a home office rather than a company site, using phones, fax machines, modems, e-mail, and other communication tools to stay in touch with coworkers and clients. Small businesses are being created and operated from home as well, with the aid of technology.

Think about technology and careers on a continuum. On one end are jobs that are directly related to technology such as computer programmer. These are the jobs that produce the technology we use daily. These are the jobs of the new economy. The fastest-expanding industries are those for which the main product or service is information. As you move along the continuum, jobs are less directly tied to technology. Somewhere in the middle of the continuum are the jobs of administrative assistants who use software packages for work processing as well as jobs that are influenced by technology. For example, teachers have vast amounts of information available for research over the Internet. Distance education technology teachers will be in increased demand as more people try to learn at any time and any place. Such a teacher must be able to adapt to the changes in teaching that require the use of technology. Many jobs will be affected by advances in technology, and those persons who are comfortable with and knowledgeable about computers may be the best job candidates regardless of where their jobs fall on the continuum.

At the opposite end of the continuum are the jobs that are least influenced by technology. These are the jobs of the old economy. Workers in construction, transportation, general manufacturing, and retail stores are furthest from the technology end of the job continuum and must deal with real-time issues that affect the bottom line. These industries take longer to lower costs, develop new products, and increase profits. In manufacturing, new technology that reduces costs may also reduce the need for some employees, resulting in layoffs. Furthermore, wages in these industries tend to rise with cost-of-living adjustments rather than through company profits.

The contrast between the new and old economy can be seen in the salaries offered to new college graduates. According to a report by the Office of Policy Development, Economics and Statistics Administration, average wages per worker in information technology industries are twice the national average. Information technology employment also provides self-employed and independent contractors the flexibility and mobility to work outside of a traditional organization. Although these temporary workers often earn less in wages and benefits and have less security than permanent workers, many prefer to be independent because they can command comparably high salaries and move from one employment situation to another with relative ease.

The Global Economy and the Changing Corporate Structure

A decade ago the United States was generating most of the world's technology; today that figure has diminished. The United States is striving to develop a more global economy by establishing trade agreements with other countries, such as the North American Free Trade Agreement (NAFTA). Global competition and multinational corporations will continue to influence the business world and our economy. Today it is not just the Fortune 500 companies, such as General Electric, IBM, and AT&T, that conduct business and have offices throughout the world. Employees wishing to advance in this new international economy must have the ability to speak more than one language and understand the cultural customs of other countries.

In today's global economy, NAFTA has created a need for multilingual talents, and Asian investments in Latin America and Mexico are expanding. Many of the border factories—in Tijuana, for example—are run by Japanese, Chinese, and Korean corporations. The ability to converse in two or more languages is an asset in the workplace.

Success in the global economy requires innovative, high-quality, timely, customized and efficiently produced products and flatter, leaner organizations. Successful companies these days tend to have the following traits:

- They have a flat management structure that has shifted away from management-directed systems toward team-directed systems that require knowledge workers on each team.

- They utilize a virtual corporation by spreading out their functions across the globe.

- They create production efficiencies through the use of technology.

- They move manufacturing plants to locations that offer good educational institutions and low labor costs.

- They recruit highly skilled workers.
- They are able to evolve and adapt as a company.
- They pursue e-commerce opportunities and customization of products to consumer demand.

In a global economy, an employee who helps the company remain competitive by being informed about technology, competition, and alternative ways to complete job requirements more effectively and efficiently will be recognized as extremely important to the company. Such employees will have the core jobs, whereas others will be hired as temporary employees. The more skills that you can demonstrate to an employer, the more valuable you will be. For example, a network technician who can communicate effectively with the various departments within a company and displays an aptitude for helping customers will be able to evolve with the expansions and changes that occur within the industry.

Lifelong Learning

The ability to adapt to the changing world of work is of the utmost importance. An estimated 40 percent of the jobs that will be available in 2010 have yet to be created. It is also possible that, due to advancing technology and other factors, you may advance in your career or change careers later in life. No matter how your career evolves, the need to continue educating yourself to keep up with technological change will be ever-present.

The Internet is bringing such education to people whenever they have time for it. Just 23 million Americans were enrolled in continuing education programs in 1984. That figure is predicted to be over 100 million by 2007, according to the National Center for Educational Statistics. There are also now over 2,000 corporate universities. More and more college classes are combining class attendance and Web-based instruction to maximize use of the research that can be found on the Internet.

To maintain currency in your career, you must get updated training throughout your life. To be able to do this, though, you must have good time-management skills and self-discipline.

As it gets easier to study anytime and anywhere, more people are earning college degrees, which is making the job market more competitive. Many of the best job opportunities during the next decade will demand that applicants have cross-functional training to broaden their qualifications. Today's career college graduates are finding that, to compete for the best jobs, they must commit to lifelong continuing education to bolster their job skills and prepare for career changes.

NOTES

Index

Internet resources. *See also* Technology
evaluation of, 78

J

.jpeg. *See* Joint Photograph Experts Group format
.jpg. *See* Joint Photograph Experts Group format
Judging vs. perceiving, 45

K

Katzenberg, Jeffrey, 98
Keirsey Sorter, 35
Keirsey, David, 35
Key words and phrases, listening for, 57–58
Knowledge workers, demand for, 121

L

Lag-time response, 67
Learning Style Assessment, 47
Learning styles, 30
  active vs. reflective, 47, 48, 50, 52
  cognitive, 51
  effective learning and, 48–50
  intuition vs. sensing, 43–44, 48, 50
  job performance and, 41
  self-assessment for, 47
  sensing vs. intuitive, 47–48
  sequential vs. global, 47, 49
  study methods and, 34
  teaching styles and, 40–41
  theorist, 51, 52
  visual vs. verbal, 48, 50
Learning, 31
  accommodative, 51
  assimilation, 51

convergent, 51
divergent, 51
experiential, 51
individual differences in, 30
lifelong, 123
multiple intelligences and, 31–34
personality traits and, 35–39
pragmatic, 51, 52
Lectures
  note-taking during, 59–65
  See also Note-taking
  taping of, 63–65
Lifelong learning, 123
Lincoln, Abraham, 15
Listening, 54–58
  constructive, 63
  cultural aspects of, 55, 56
  definition of, 55
  effective, 54–55
  emotions and, 57
  for key words and phrases, 57–58
  in L-STAR system, 59
  objective, 56
  obstacles to, 56–57
  prejudging and, 56
  with purpose, 56
  talking and, 56–57
  vs. hearing, 55
  as whole-body experience, 55–56
Logic, false, 79–80
Lohr, Jim, 96
L-STAR system, 59–60

M

Mapping system, 63–66
Matching questions, 68, 70
Mission statement, 12, 13
.mov. *See* Apple QuickTime movies
Modern Language Association style. *See* MLA style

Motivation, 14–16
  attitude and, 12–13
  external, 15
  fear and, 13–14
  internal, 15–16
  sources of, 15
  values and, 10
Multiculturalism. *See* Cultural diversity
Multinational corporations, 122–123
Multiple intelligences, 30, 31–34
  communication and, 104
  self-assessment for, 32–33
  skills associated with, 34
  Smart descriptors for, 34
  study techniques and, 34
Multiple-choice questions, 71–72
Musical Instrument Digital Interface files. *See* MIDI files
Myers, Isabel Briggs, 35, 42
Myers-Briggs Type Inventory, 35, 42

N

NAFTA, 122
New Presentations dialog box, 187
Nonverbal communication, 103
North American Free Trade Agreement (NAFTA), 122
Note-taking, 59–65
  in class, 53–54
  Cornell system for, 61–62, 63
  L-STAR system for, 59–60
  mapping system for, 63–65
  missed information in, 63
  outline technique for, 60–61
  during reading, 52–53
  symbols for, 60
  teaching styles and, 65
  vs. taping, 63–65

PART II

Taken from: *Go! with Microsoft® Office 2010, Volume 1*, Second Edition
by Shelley Gaskin, Robert L. Ferrett, Alicia Vargas, and Carolyn McLellan

The *GO!* System: Designed for student success!

The goal of the *GO! Series* is to provide you with the skills to solve business problems using the computer as a tool, for both yourself and the organization for which you might be employed. When you use the *GO! Series* in one of your courses, you use a "system" that includes a textbook with integrated multimedia tools.

Student **textbook**

- **Project-based** so you learn by creating real-world projects, not by reading long pages of text or simply practicing features of an application.

- **Very clear instruction** directs you first where to go, then what to do, when completing steps of the projects to help ensure you don't get lost.

- **Visual Summary** shows you up front what your completed project will look like, and a **File Guide** clearly shows you which files are needed for each project and how to save the document.

- **Lots of large screen shots** allow you to check your work and make sure you are on the right track at numerous points in the project.

Student **Companion Web Site**: www.pearsonhighered.com/go

An interactive web site featuring self-study tools to help you succeed in this course!

- **Online Study Guide** provides practice of the chapter material by answering auto-graded objective questions.

- **Glossary** of key terms reinforces terminology as you learn the language of computing.

- **Student Data Files** needed to complete the projects in the book are downloadable from this site.

- **Student Videos** help you visually learn the skills in each chapter, and **Podcasts** allow you to listen to instruction.

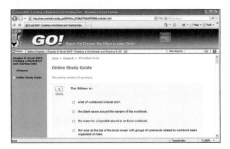

Students

How to Find the Student Data Files to Complete the Projects in This Book

Projects in this book begin either with a new blank file or from a student data file that has already been started for you.

The student data files can be accessed from the *GO!* web site.

1. Decide where you want to store your student data files.

   - If you are storing on the hard drive of your computer or on a network drive, you may want to create a folder with an appropriate name on that drive.

   - If you are storing on a removable storage device such as a USB flash drive or Zip disk, insert the device now.

2. From your web browser, go to *www.pearsonhighered.com/go*

3. From the list of books provided, point to the title of this book, click the active link and then follow the instructions as specified on the web site.

Common Features of Microsoft Office 2010

OUTCOMES

At the end of this chapter you will be able to:

OBJECTIVES

Mastering these objectives will enable you to:

PROJECT 1A

Create, save, and print a Microsoft Office 2010 file.

1. Use Windows Explorer to Locate Files and Folders (p. 137)
2. Locate and Start a Microsoft Office 2010 Program (p. 140)
3. Enter and Edit Text in an Office 2010 Program (p. 143)
4. Perform Commands from a Dialog Box (p. 145)
5. Create a Folder, Save a File, and Close a Program (p. 147)
6. Add Document Properties and Print a File (p. 152)

PROJECT 1B

Use the Ribbon and dialog boxes to perform common commands in a Microsoft Office 2010 file.

7. Open an Existing File and Save It with a New Name (p. 156)
8. Explore Options for an Application (p. 159)
9. Perform Commands from the Ribbon (p. 160)
10. Apply Formatting in Office Programs (p. 166)
11. Use the Microsoft Office 2010 Help System (p. 177)
12. Compress Files (p. 178)

Christy Thompson/Shutterstock

In This Chapter

In this chapter, you will use Windows Explorer to navigate the Windows folder structure, create a folder, and save files in Microsoft Office 2010 programs. You will also practice using the features of Microsoft Office 2010 that are common across the major programs that comprise the Microsoft Office 2010 suite. These common features include creating, saving, and printing files.

Common features also include the new Paste Preview and Microsoft Office Backstage view. You will apply formatting, perform commands, and compress files. You will see that creating professional-quality documents is easy and quick in Microsoft Office 2010, and that finding your way around is fast and efficient.

The projects in this chapter relate to **Oceana Palm Grill**, which is a chain of 25 casual, full-service restaurants based in Austin, Texas. The Oceana Palm Grill owners plan an aggressive expansion program. To expand by 15 additional restaurants in North Carolina and Florida by 2018, the company must attract new investors, develop new menus, and recruit new employees, all while adhering to the company's quality guidelines and maintaining its reputation for excellent service. To succeed, the company plans to build on its past success and maintain its quality elements.

Project 1A PowerPoint File

Project Activities

In Activities 1.01 through 1.06, you will create a PowerPoint file, save it in a folder that you create by using Windows Explorer, and then print the file or submit it electronically as directed by your instructor. Your completed PowerPoint slide will look similar to Figure 1.1.

Project Files

For Project 1A, you will need the following file:

New blank PowerPoint presentation

You will save your file as:

Lastname_Firstname_1A_Menu_Plan

Project Results

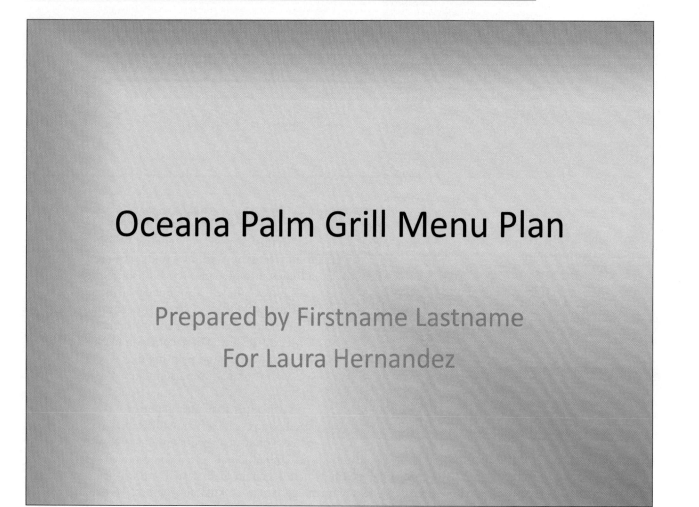

Figure 1.1
Project 1A Menu Plan

Objective 1 | Use Windows Explorer to Locate Files and Folders

A *file* is a collection of information stored on a computer under a single name, for example, a Word document or a PowerPoint presentation. Every file is stored in a *folder*—a container in which you store files—or a *subfolder*, which is a folder within a folder. Your Windows operating system stores and organizes your files and folders, which is a primary task of an operating system.

You *navigate*—explore within the organizing structure of Windows—to create, save, and find your files and folders by using the *Windows Explorer* program. Windows Explorer displays the files and folders on your computer, and is at work anytime you are viewing the contents of files and folders in a *window*. A window is a rectangular area on a computer screen in which programs and content appear; a window can be moved, resized, minimized, or closed.

Activity 1.01 | Using Windows Explorer to Locate Files and Folders

1 Turn on your computer and display the Windows *desktop*—the opening screen in Windows that simulates your work area.

> **Note | Comparing Your Screen with the Figures in This Textbook**
>
> Your screen will match the figures shown in this textbook if you set your screen resolution to 1024 × 768. At other resolutions, your screen will closely resemble, but not match, the figures shown. To view your screen's resolution, on the Windows 7 desktop, right-click in a blank area, and then click Screen resolution. In Windows Vista, right-click a blank area, click Personalize, and then click Display Settings. In Windows XP, right-click the desktop, click Properties, and then click the Settings tab.

2 In your CD/DVD tray, insert the **Student CD** that accompanies this textbook. Wait a few moments for an **AutoPlay** window to display. Compare your screen with Figure 1.2.

> *AutoPlay* is a Windows feature that lets you choose which program to use to start different kinds of media, such as music CDs, or CDs and DVDs containing photos; it displays when you plug in or insert media or storage devices.

> **Note | If You Do Not Have the Student CD**
>
> If you do not have the Student CD, consult the inside back flap of this textbook for instructions on how to download the files from the Pearson Web site.

Figure 1.2

AutoPlay window ⎯
Close button ⎯
Windows desktop (yours may vary in color and arrangement) ⎯

3 In the upper right corner of the **AutoPlay** window, move your mouse over—*point* to—the **Close** button ![Close button], and then *click*—press the left button on your mouse pointing device one time.

4 On the left side of the **Windows taskbar**, click the **Start** button 🪟 to display the **Start menu**. Compare your screen with Figure 1.3.

> The *Windows taskbar* is the area along the lower edge of the desktop that contains the *Start button* and an area to display buttons for open programs. The Start button displays the *Start menu*, which provides a list of choices and is the main gateway to your computer's programs, folders, and settings.

Figure 1.3

Computer on Start menu

Start menu (your array of programs may vary)

Windows 7 taskbar

Start button

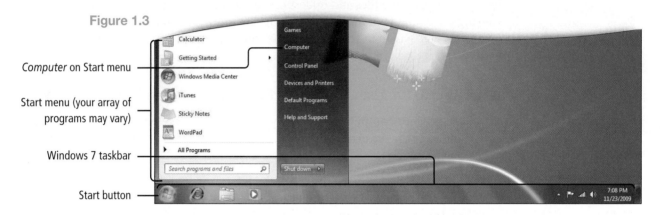

5 On the right side of the **Start menu**, click **Computer** to see the disk drives and other hardware connected to your computer. Compare your screen with Figure 1.4, and then take a moment to study the table in Figure 1.5.

> The *folder window* for *Computer* displays. A folder window displays the contents of the current folder, *library*, or device, and contains helpful parts so that you can navigate within Windows.

> In Windows 7, a library is a collection of items, such as files and folders, assembled from *various locations*; the locations might be on your computer, an external hard drive, removable media, or someone else's computer.

> The difference between a folder and a library is that a library can include files stored in *different locations*—any disk drive, folder, or other place that you can store files and folders.

Figure 1.4

Back and Forward

Address bar

File list

Navigation pane

Folder window toolbar

Views button

Search box

Preview pane button

Details pane

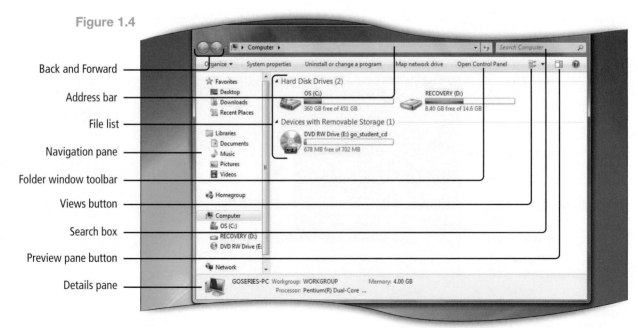

Window Part	Use to:
Address bar	Navigate to a different folder or library, or go back to a previous one.
Back and Forward buttons	Navigate to other folders or libraries you have already opened without closing the current window. These buttons work in conjunction with the address bar; that is, after you use the address bar to change folders, you can use the Back button to return to the previous folder.
Details pane	Display the most common file properties—information about a file, such as the author, the date you last changed the file, and any descriptive *tags*, which are custom file properties that you create to help find and organize your files.
File list	Display the contents of the current folder or library. In Computer, the file list displays the disk drives.
Folder window for *Computer*	Display the contents of the current folder, library, or device. The Folder window contains helpful features so that you can navigate within Windows.
Folder window toolbar	Perform common tasks, such as changing the view of your files and folders or burning files to a CD. The buttons available change to display only relevant tasks.
Navigation pane	Navigate to, open, and display favorites, libraries, folders, saved searches, and an expandable list of drives.
Preview pane button	Display (if you have chosen to open this pane) the contents of most files without opening them in a program. To open the preview pane, click the Preview pane button on the toolbar to turn it on and off.
Search box	Look for an item in the current folder or library by typing a word or phrase in the search box.
Views button	Choose how to view the contents of the current location.

Figure 1.5

6   On the toolbar of the **Computer** folder window, click the **Views button arrow** 📇 ▾ —the small arrow to the right of the Views button—to display a list of views that you can apply to the file list. If necessary, on the list, click **Tiles**.

> The Views button is a *split button*; clicking the main part of the button performs a *command* and clicking the arrow opens a menu or list. A command is an instruction to a computer program that causes an action to be carried out.

> When you open a folder or a library, you can change how the files display in the file list. For example, you might prefer to see large or small *icons*—pictures that represent a program, a file, a folder, or some other object—or an arrangement that lets you see various types of information about each file. Each time you click the Views button, the window changes, cycling through several views—additional view options are available by clicking the Views button arrow.

Another Way
Point to the CD/DVD drive, right-click, and then click Open.

7   In the **file list**, under **Devices with Removable Storage**, point to your **CD/DVD Drive**, and then *double-click*—click the left mouse button two times in rapid succession—to display the list of folders on the CD. Compare your screen with Figure 1.6.

> When double-clicking, keep your hand steady between clicks; this is more important than the speed of the two clicks.

Figure 1.6

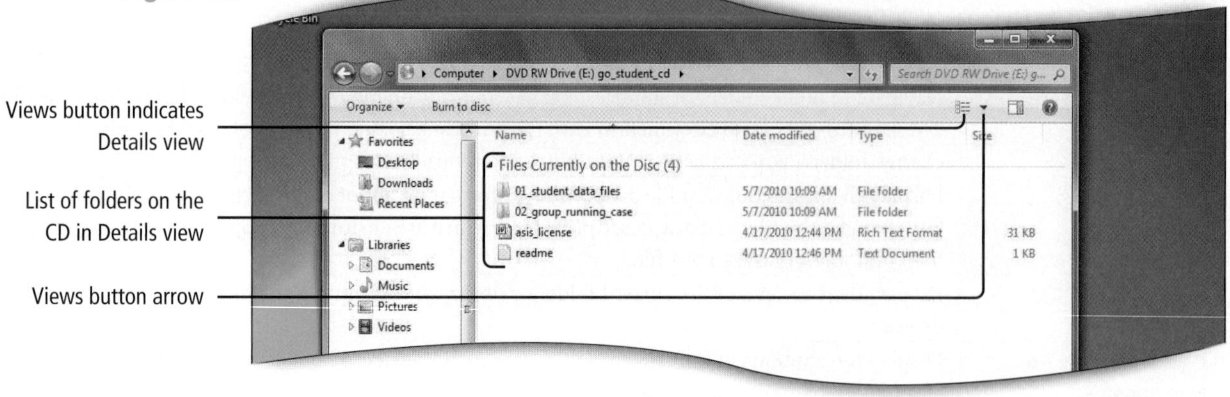

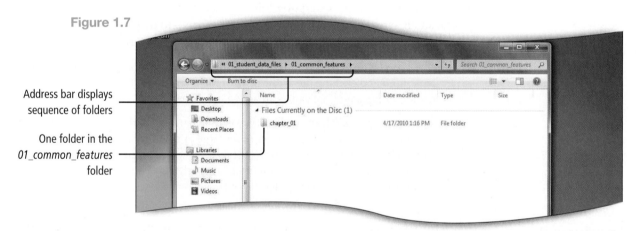

Views button indicates Details view

List of folders on the CD in Details view

Views button arrow

8 In the **file list**, point to the folder **01_student_data_files** and double-click to display the list of subfolders in the folder. Double-click to open the folder **01_common_features**. Compare your screen with Figure 1.7.

The Student Resource CD includes files that you will use to complete the projects in this textbook. If you prefer, you can also copy the **01_student_data_files** folder to a location on your computer's hard drive or to a removable device such as a *USB flash drive*, which is a small storage device that plugs into a computer USB port. Your instructor might direct you to other locations where these files are located; for example, on your learning management system.

Figure 1.7

Address bar displays sequence of folders

One folder in the *01_common_features* folder

9 In the upper right corner of the **Computer** window, click the **Close** button to redisplay your desktop.

Objective 2 | Locate and Start a Microsoft Office 2010 Program

Microsoft Office 2010 includes programs, servers, and services for individuals, small organizations, and large enterprises. A *program*, also referred to as an *application*, is a set of instructions used by a computer to perform a task, such as word processing or accounting.

Activity 1.02 | Locating and Starting a Microsoft Office 2010 Program

1 On the **Windows taskbar**, click the **Start** button 🏁 to display the **Start** menu.

2 From the displayed **Start** menu, locate the group of **Microsoft Office 2010** programs on your computer—the Office program icons from which you can start the program may be located on your Start menu, in a Microsoft Office folder on the **All Programs** list, on your desktop, or any combination of these locations; the location will vary depending on how your computer is configured.

All Programs is an area of the Start menu that displays all the available programs on your computer system.

3 Examine Figure 1.8, and notice the programs that are included in the Microsoft Office Professional Plus 2010 group of programs. (Your group of programs may vary.)

Microsoft Word is a word processing program, with which you create and share documents by using its writing tools.

Microsoft Excel is a spreadsheet program, with which you calculate and analyze numbers and create charts.

Microsoft Access is a database program, with which you can collect, track, and report data.

Microsoft PowerPoint is a presentation program, with which you can communicate information with high-impact graphics and video.

Additional popular Office programs include *Microsoft Outlook* to manage e-mail and organizational activities, *Microsoft Publisher* to create desktop publishing documents such as brochures, and *Microsoft OneNote* to manage notes that you make at meetings or in classes and to share notes with others on the Web.

The Professional Plus version of Office 2010 also includes *Microsoft SharePoint Workspace* to share information with others in a team environment and *Microsoft InfoPath Designer and Filler* to create forms and gather data.

Figure 1.8

All Programs menu

Microsoft Office folder

Programs in Microsoft Office (your list may vary)

4 Click to open the program **Microsoft PowerPoint 2010**. Compare your screen with Figure 1.9, and then take a moment to study the description of these screen elements in the table in Figure 1.10.

Figure 1.9

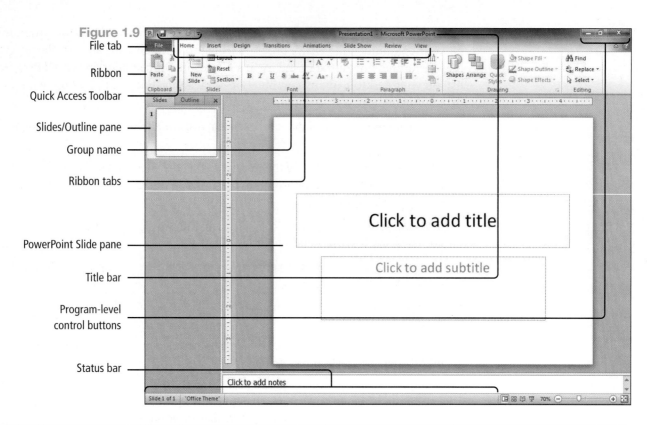

File tab

Ribbon

Quick Access Toolbar

Slides/Outline pane

Group name

Ribbon tabs

PowerPoint Slide pane

Title bar

Program-level control buttons

Status bar

Screen Element	Description
File tab	Displays Microsoft Office Backstage view, which is a centralized space for all of your file management tasks such as opening, saving, printing, publishing, or sharing a file—all the things you can do *with* a file.
Group names	Indicate the name of the groups of related commands on the displayed tab.
PowerPoint Slide pane	Displays a large image of the active slide in the PowerPoint program.
Program-level control buttons	Minimizes, restores, or closes the program window.
Quick Access Toolbar	Displays buttons to perform frequently used commands and resources with a single click. The default commands include Save, Undo, and Redo. You can add and delete buttons to customize the Quick Access Toolbar for your convenience.
Ribbon	Displays a group of task-oriented tabs that contain the commands, styles, and resources you need to work in an Office 2010 program. The look of your Ribbon depends on your screen resolution. A high resolution will display more individual items and button names on the Ribbon.
Ribbon tabs	Display the names of the task-oriented tabs relevant to the open program.
Slides/Outline pane	Displays either thumbnails of the slides in a PowerPoint presentation (Slides tab) or the outline of the presentation's content (Outline tab). In each Office 2010 program, different panes display in different ways to assist you.
Status bar	Displays file information on the left and View and Zoom on the right.
Title bar	Displays the name of the file and the name of the program. The program window control buttons—Minimize, Maximize/Restore Down, and Close—are grouped on the right side of the title bar.

Figure 1.10

Objective 3 | Enter and Edit Text in an Office 2010 Program

All of the programs in Office 2010 require some typed text. Your keyboard is still the primary method of entering information into your computer. Techniques to *edit*—make changes to—text are similar among all of the Office 2010 programs.

Activity 1.03 | Entering and Editing Text in an Office 2010 Program

1 In the middle of the PowerPoint Slide pane, point to the text *Click to add title* to display the I pointer, and then click one time.

> The *insertion point*—a blinking vertical line that indicates where text or graphics will be inserted—displays.
>
> In Office 2010 programs, the mouse *pointer*—any symbol that displays on your screen in response to moving your mouse device—displays in different shapes depending on the task you are performing and the area of the screen to which you are pointing.

2 Type **Oceana Grille Info** and notice how the insertion point moves to the right as you type. Point slightly to the right of the letter *e* in *Grille* and click to place the insertion point there. Compare your screen with Figure 1.11.

Figure 1.11

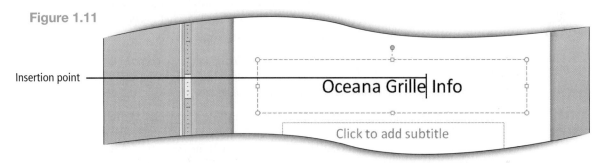

Insertion point

Oceana Grille Info

Click to add subtitle

3 On your keyboard, locate and press the [Backspace] key to delete the letter *e*.

> Pressing [Backspace] removes a character to the left of the insertion point.

4 Point slightly to the left of the *I* in *Info* and click one time to place the insertion point there. Type **Menu** and then press [Spacebar] one time. Compare your screen with Figure 1.12.

> By *default*, when you type text in an Office program, existing text moves to the right to make space for new typing. Default refers to the current selection or setting that is automatically used by a program unless you specify otherwise.

Figure 1.12

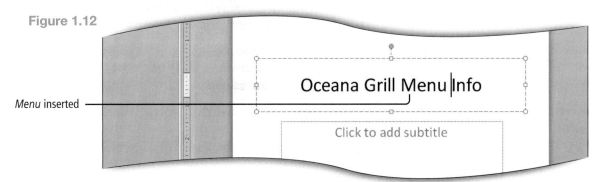

Menu inserted

Oceana Grill Menu Info

Click to add subtitle

5 Press ⌨Del four times to delete *Info* and then type **Plan**

> Pressing ⌨Del removes—deletes—a character to the right of the insertion point.

6 With your insertion point blinking after the word *Plan*, on your keyboard, hold down the ⌨Ctrl key. While holding down ⌨Ctrl, press ⬅ three times to move the insertion point to the beginning of the word *Grill*.

> This is a **keyboard shortcut**—a key or combination of keys that performs a task that would otherwise require a mouse. This keyboard shortcut moves the insertion point to the beginning of the previous word.
>
> A keyboard shortcut is commonly indicated as ⌨Ctrl + ⬅ (or some other combination of keys) to indicate that you hold down the first key while pressing the second key. A keyboard shortcut can also include three keys, in which case you hold down the first two and then press the third. For example, ⌨Ctrl + ⌨Shift + ⬅ selects one word to the left.

7 With the insertion point blinking at the beginning of the word *Grill*, type **Palm** and press ⌨Spacebar.

8 Click anywhere in the text *Click to add subtitle*. With the insertion point blinking, type the following and include the spelling error: **Prepered by Annabel Dunham**

9 With your mouse, point slightly to the left of the *A* in *Annabel*, hold down the left mouse button, and then **drag**—hold down the left mouse button while moving your mouse—to the right to select the text *Annabel Dunham*, and then release the mouse button. Compare your screen with Figure 1.13.

> The **Mini toolbar** displays commands that are commonly used with the selected object, which places common commands close to your pointer. When you move the pointer away from the Mini toolbar, it fades from view.
>
> To **select** refers to highlighting, by dragging with your mouse, areas of text or data or graphics so that the selection can be edited, formatted, copied, or moved. The action of dragging includes releasing the left mouse button at the end of the area you want to select. The Office programs recognize a selected area as one unit, to which you can make changes. Selecting text may require some practice. If you are not satisfied with your result, click anywhere outside of the selection, and then begin again.

Figure 1.13

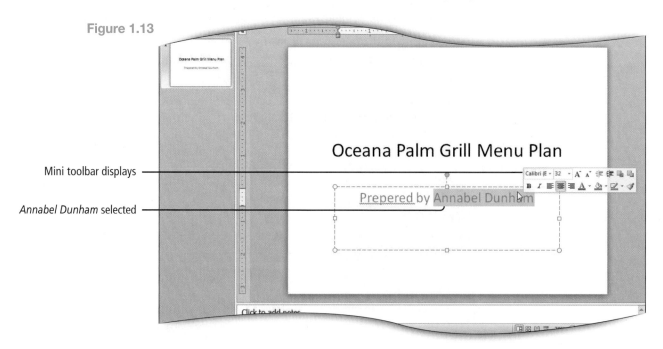

Mini toolbar displays

Annabel Dunham selected

Oceana Palm Grill Menu Plan

Prepered by Annabel Dunham

10 With the text *Annabel Dunham* selected, type your own firstname and lastname.

In any Windows-based program, such as the Microsoft Office 2010 programs, selected text is deleted and then replaced when you begin to type new text. You will save time by developing good techniques to select and then edit or replace selected text, which is easier than pressing the [Del] key numerous times to delete text that you do not want.

11 Notice that the misspelled word *Prepered* displays with a wavy red underline; additionally, all or part of your name might display with a wavy red underline.

Office 2010 has a dictionary of words against which all entered text is checked. In Word and PowerPoint, words that are *not* in the dictionary display a wavy red line, indicating a possible misspelled word or a proper name or an unusual word—none of which are in the Office 2010 dictionary.

In Excel and Access, you can initiate a check of the spelling, but wavy red underlines do not display.

12 Point to *Prepered* and then ***right-click***—click your right mouse button one time.

The Mini toolbar and a ***shortcut menu*** display. A shortcut menu displays commands and options relevant to the selected text or object—known as ***context-sensitive commands*** because they relate to the item you right-clicked.

Here, the shortcut menu displays commands related to the misspelled word. You can click the suggested correct spelling *Prepared*, click Ignore All to ignore the misspelling, add the word to the Office dictionary, or click Spelling to display a ***dialog box***. A dialog box is a small window that contains options for completing a task. Whenever you see a command followed by an ***ellipsis*** (…), which is a set of three dots indicating incompleteness, clicking the command will always display a dialog box.

13 On the displayed shortcut menu, click **Prepared** to correct the misspelled word. If necessary, point to any parts of your name that display a wavy red underline, right-click, and then on the shortcut menu, click Ignore All so that Office will no longer mark your name with a wavy underline in this file.

More Knowledge | **Adding to the Office Dictionary**

The main dictionary contains the most common words, but does not include all proper names, technical terms, or acronyms. You can add words, acronyms, and proper names to the Office dictionary by clicking Add to Dictionary when they are flagged, and you might want to do so for your own name and other proper names and terms that you type often.

Objective 4 | Perform Commands from a Dialog Box

In a dialog box, you make decisions about an individual object or topic. A dialog box also offers a way to adjust a number of settings at one time.

Activity 1.04 | Performing Commands from a Dialog Box

1 Point anywhere in the blank area above the title *Oceana Palm Grill Menu Plan* to display the ☐ pointer.

2 Right-click to display a shortcut menu. Notice the command *Format Background* followed by an ellipsis (…). Compare your screen with Figure 1.14.

> Recall that a command followed by an ellipsis indicates that a dialog box will display if you click the command.

Figure 1.14

Shortcut menu ————

Ellipsis following command ————

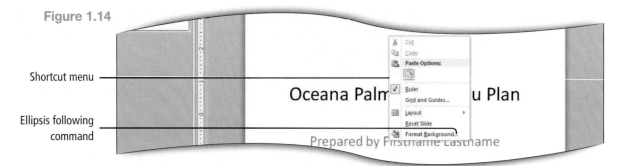

3 Click **Format Background** to display the **Format Background** dialog box, and then compare your screen with Figure 1.15.

Figure 1.15

Fill selected ————

Format Background dialog box ————

Options related to the background fill ————

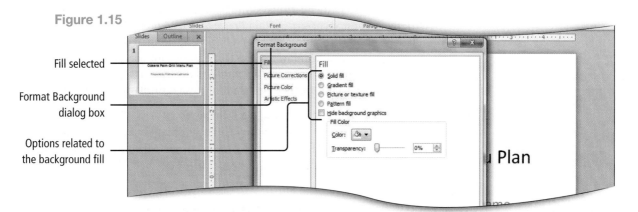

4 On the left, if necessary, click **Fill** to display the **Fill** options.

> *Fill* is the inside color of an object. Here, the dialog box displays the option group names on the left; some dialog boxes provide a set of tabs across the top from which you can display different sets of options.

5 On the right, under **Fill**, click the **Gradient fill** option button.

> The dialog box displays additional settings related to the gradient fill option. An *option button* is a round button that enables you to make one choice among two or more options. In a gradient fill, one color fades into another.

6 Click the **Preset colors arrow**—the arrow in the box to the right of the text *Preset colors*—and then in the gallery, in the second row, point to the fifth fill color to display the ScreenTip *Fog*.

> A *gallery* is an Office feature that displays a list of potential results. A *ScreenTip* displays useful information about mouse actions, such as pointing to screen elements or dragging.

7 Click **Fog**, and then notice that the fill color is applied to your slide. Click the **Type arrow**, and then click **Rectangular** to change the pattern of the fill color. Compare your screen with Figure 1.16.

Figure 1.16

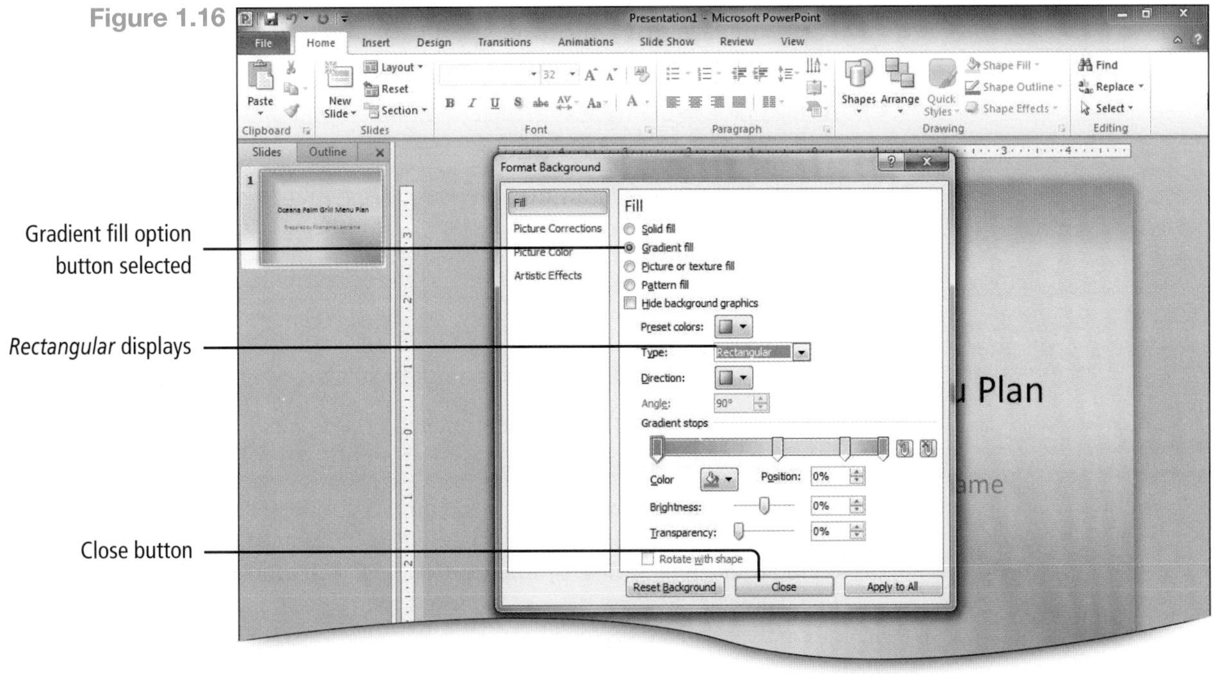

Gradient fill option
button selected

Rectangular displays

Close button

8 At the bottom of the dialog box, click **Close**.

> As you progress in your study of Microsoft Office, you will practice using many dialog boxes and applying dramatic effects such as this to your Word documents, Excel spreadsheets, Access databases, and PowerPoint slides.

Objective 5 | Create a Folder, Save a File, and Close a Program

A *location* is any disk drive, folder, or other place in which you can store files and folders. Where you store your files depends on how and where you use your data. For example, for your classes, you might decide to store primarily on a removable USB flash drive so that you can carry your files to different locations and access your files on different computers.

If you do most of your work on a single computer, for example your home desktop system or your laptop computer that you take with you to school or work, store your files in one of the Libraries—Documents, Music, Pictures, or Videos—provided by your Windows operating system.

Although the Windows operating system helps you to create and maintain a logical folder structure, take the time to name your files and folders in a consistent manner.

Activity 1.05 | Creating a Folder, Saving a File, and Closing a Program

A PowerPoint presentation is an example of a file. Office 2010 programs use a common dialog box provided by the Windows operating system to assist you in saving files. In this activity, you will create a folder on a USB flash drive in which to store files. If you prefer to store on your hard drive, you can use similar steps to store files in your My Documents folder in your Documents library.

1 Insert a USB flash drive into your computer, and if necessary, **Close** [X] the **AutoPlay** dialog box. If you are not using a USB flash drive, go to Step 2.

As the first step in saving a file, determine where you want to save the file, and if necessary, insert a storage device.

2 At the top of your screen, in the title bar, notice that *Presentation1 – Microsoft PowerPoint* displays.

Most Office 2010 programs open with a new unsaved file with a default name—*Presentation1*, *Document1*, and so on. As you create your file, your work is temporarily stored in the computer's memory until you initiate a Save command, at which time you must choose a file name and location in which to save your file.

3 In the upper left corner of your screen, click the **File tab** to display **Microsoft Office Backstage** view. Compare your screen with Figure 1.17.

Microsoft Office *Backstage view* is a centralized space for tasks related to *file management*; that is why the tab is labeled *File*. File management tasks include, for example, opening, saving, printing, publishing, or sharing a file. The *Backstage tabs*—*Info*, *Recent*, *New*, *Print*, *Save & Send*, and *Help*—display along the left side. The tabs group file-related tasks together.

Above the Backstage tabs, *Quick Commands*—*Save*, *Save As*, *Open*, and *Close*—display for quick access to these commands. When you click any of these commands, Backstage view closes and either a dialog box displays or the active file closes.

Here, the *Info tab* displays information—*info*—about the current file. In the center panel, various file management tasks are available in groups. For example, if you click the Protect Presentation button, a list of options that you can set for this file that relate to who can open or edit the presentation displays.

On the Info tab, in the right panel, you can also examine the *document properties*. Document properties, also known as *metadata*, are details about a file that describe or identify it, such as the title, author name, subject, and keywords that identify the document's topic or contents. On the Info page, a thumbnail image of the current file displays in the upper right corner, which you can click to close Backstage view and return to the document.

More Knowledge | Deciding Where to Store Your Files

Where should you store your files? In the libraries created by Windows 7 (Documents, Pictures, and so on)? On a removable device like a flash drive or external hard drive? In Windows 7, it is easy to find your files, especially if you use the libraries. Regardless of where you save a file, Windows 7 will make it easy to find the file again, even if you are not certain where it might be.

In Windows 7, storing all of your files within a library makes sense. If you perform most of your work on your desktop system or your laptop that travels with you, you can store your files in the libraries created by Windows 7 for your user account—Documents, Pictures, Music, and so on. Within these libraries, you can create folders and subfolders to organize your data. These libraries are a good choice for storing your files because:

- From the Windows Explorer button on the taskbar, your libraries are always just one click away.
- The libraries are designed for their contents; for example, the Pictures folder displays small images of your digital photos.
- You can add new locations to a library; for example, an external hard drive, or a network drive. Locations added to a library behave just like they are on your hard drive.
- Other users of your computer cannot access your libraries.
- The libraries are the default location for opening and saving files within an application, so you will find that you can open and save files with fewer navigation clicks.

Figure 1.17

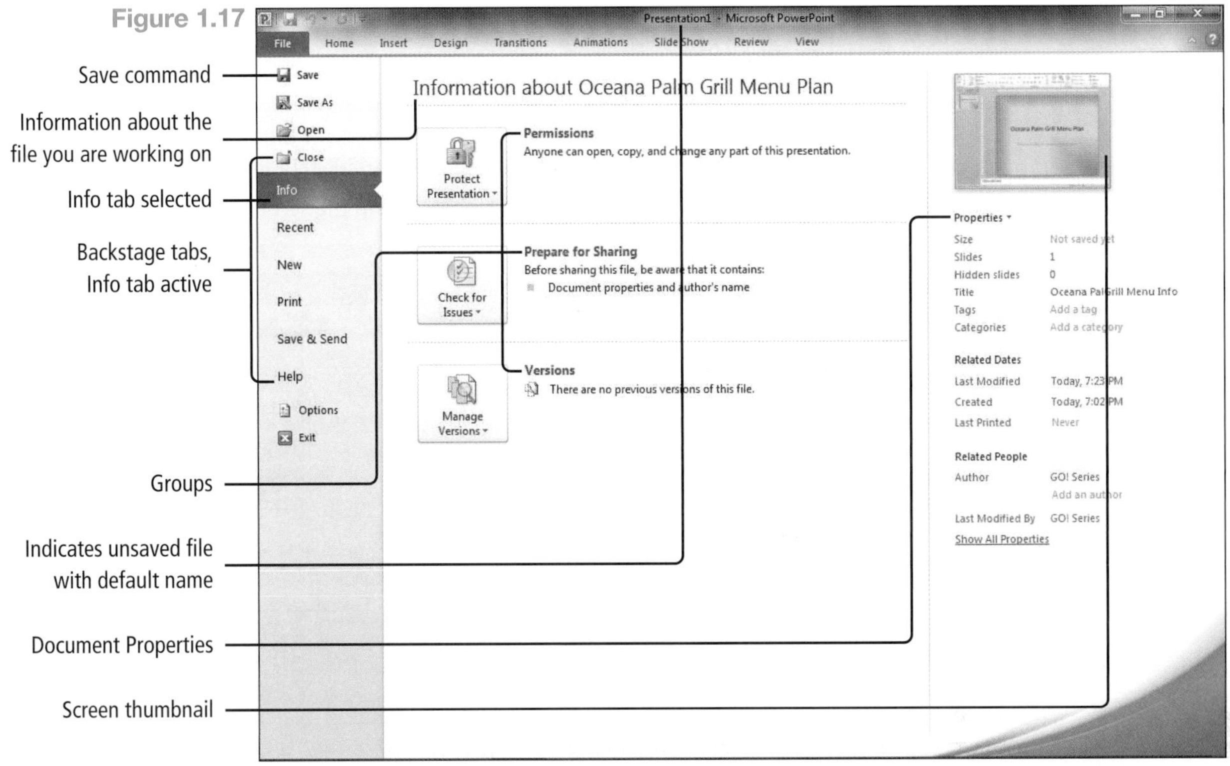

Save command

Information about the
file you are working on

Info tab selected

Backstage tabs,
Info tab active

Groups

Indicates unsaved file
with default name

Document Properties

Screen thumbnail

4 Above the **Backstage tabs**, click **Save** to display the **Save As** dialog box.

Backstage view closes and the Save As dialog box, which includes a folder window and an area at the bottom to name the file and set the file type, displays.

When you are saving something for the first time, for example a new PowerPoint presentation, the Save and Save As commands are identical. That is, the Save As dialog box will display if you click Save or if you click Save As.

Note | Saving Your File

After you have named a file and saved it in your desired location, the Save command saves any changes you make to the file without displaying any dialog box. The Save As command will display the Save As dialog box and let you name and save a new file based on the current one—in a location that you choose. After you name and save the new document, the original document closes, and the new document—based on the original one—displays.

---

5 In the **Save As** dialog box, on the left, locate the **navigation pane**; compare your screen with Figure 1.18.

By default, the Save command opens the Documents library unless your default file location has been changed.

Figure 1.18

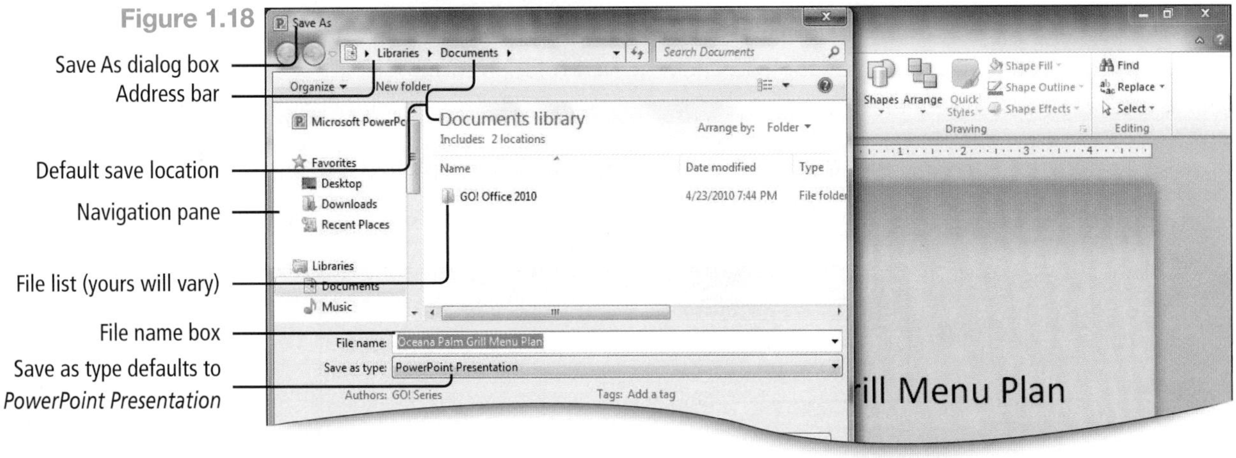

Save As dialog box
Address bar

Default save location

Navigation pane

File list (yours will vary)

File name box
Save as type defaults to
PowerPoint Presentation

6 On the right side of the **navigation pane**, point to the **scroll bar**. Compare your screen with Figure 1.19.

> A *scroll bar* displays when a window, or a pane within a window, has information that is not in view. You can click the up or down scroll arrows—or the left and right scroll arrows in a horizontal scroll bar—to scroll the contents up or down or left and right in small increments.
>
> You can also drag the *scroll box*—the box within the scroll bar—to scroll the window in either direction.

Figure 1.19

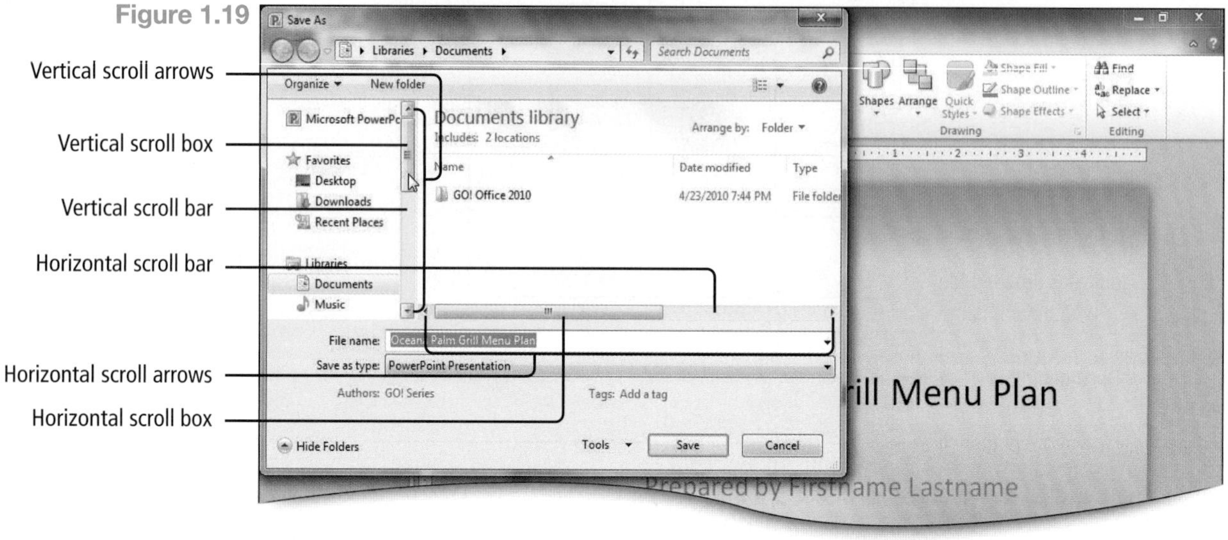

Vertical scroll arrows

Vertical scroll box

Vertical scroll bar

Horizontal scroll bar

Horizontal scroll arrows

Horizontal scroll box

7 Click the **down scroll arrow** as necessary so that you can view the lower portion of the **navigation pane**, and then click the icon for your USB flash drive. Compare your screen with Figure 1.20. (If you prefer to store on your computer's hard drive instead of a USB flash drive, in the navigation pane, click Documents.)

Figure 1.20

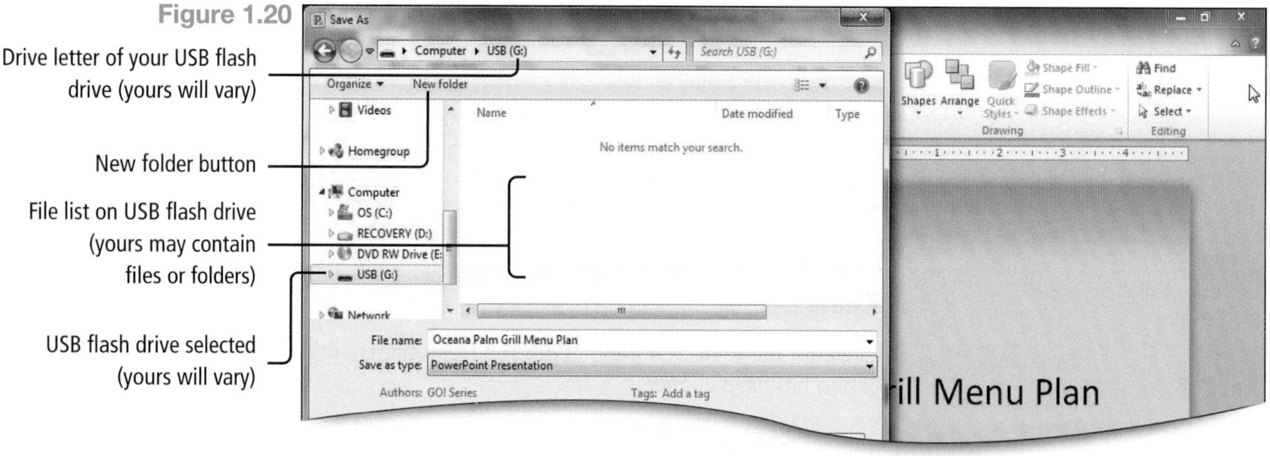

Drive letter of your USB flash drive (yours will vary)

New folder button

File list on USB flash drive (yours may contain files or folders)

USB flash drive selected (yours will vary)

8 On the toolbar, click the **New folder** button.

> In the file list, a new folder is created, and the text *New folder* is selected.

9 Type **Common Features Chapter 1** and press Enter. Compare your screen with Figure 1.21.

> In Windows-based programs, the Enter key confirms an action.

Figure 1.21

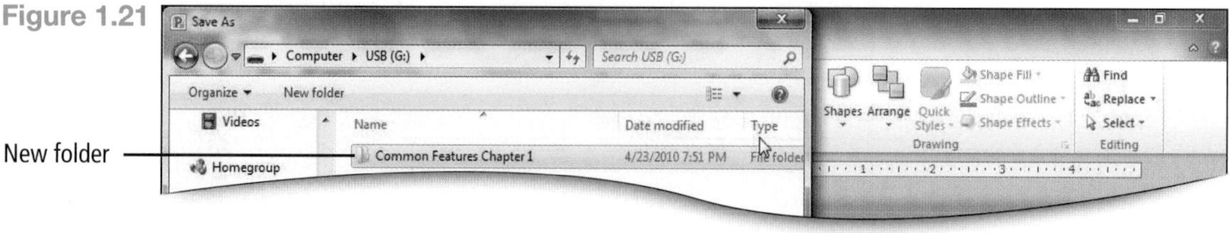

New folder

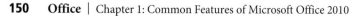

10 In the **file list**, double-click the name of your new folder to open it and display its name in the **address bar**.

11 In the lower portion of the dialog box, click in the **File name** box to select the existing text. Notice that Office inserts the text at the beginning of the presentation as a suggested file name.

12 On your keyboard, locate the ⎤ key. Notice that the Shift of this key produces the underscore character. With the text still selected, type **Lastname_Firstname_1A_ Menu_Plan** Compare your screen with Figure 1.22.

> You can use spaces in file names, however some individuals prefer not to use spaces. Some programs, especially when transferring files over the Internet, may not work well with spaces in file names. In general, however, unless you encounter a problem, it is OK to use spaces. In this textbook, underscores are used instead of spaces in file names.

Figure 1.22

File name box indicates
your file name

Save as type box indicates
PowerPoint Presentation

Save button

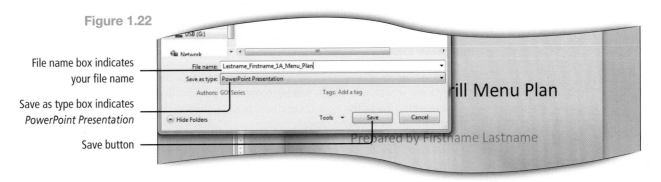

13 In the lower right corner, click **Save**; or press Enter. See Figure 1.23.

> Your new file name displays in the title bar, indicating that the file has been saved to a location that you have specified.

Figure 1.23

File name in title bar

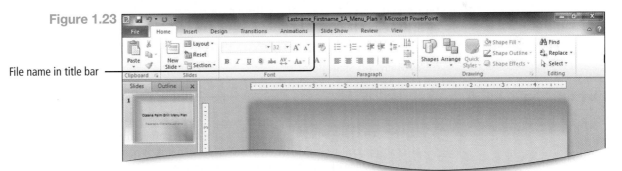

14 In the text that begins *Prepared by*, click to position the insertion point at the end of your name, and then press Enter to move to a new line. Type **For Laura Hernandez**

15 Click the **File tab** to display **Backstage** view. At the top of the center panel, notice that the path where your file is stored displays. Above the Backstage tabs, click **Close** to close the file. In the message box, click **Save** to save the changes you made and close the file. Leave PowerPoint open.

> PowerPoint displays a message asking if you want to save the changes you have made. Because you have made additional changes to the file since your last Save operation, an Office program will always prompt you to save so that you do not lose any new data.

Objective 6 | Add Document Properties and Print a File

The process of printing a file is similar in all of the Office applications. There are differences in the types of options you can select. For example, in PowerPoint, you have the option of printing the full slide, with each slide printing on a full sheet of paper, or of printing handouts with small pictures of slides on a page.

Activity 1.06 | Adding Document Properties and Printing a File

> **Alert! | Are You Printing or Submitting Your Files Electronically?**
>
> If you are submitting your files electronically only, or have no printer attached, you can still complete this activity. Complete Steps 1-9, and then submit your file electronically as directed by your instructor.

1 In the upper left corner, click the **File tab** to display **Backstage** view. Notice that the **Recent tab** displays.

Because no file was open in PowerPoint, Office applies predictive logic to determine that your most likely action will be to open a PowerPoint presentation that you worked on recently. Thus, the Recent tab displays a list of PowerPoint presentations that were recently open on your system.

2 At the top of the **Recent Presentations** list, click your **Lastname_Firstname_1A_ Menu_ Plan** file to open it.

3 Click the **File tab** to redisplay **Backstage** view. On the right, under the screen thumbnail, click **Properties**, and then click **Show Document Panel**. In the **Author** box, delete the existing text, and then type your firstname and lastname. Notice that in PowerPoint, some variation of the slide title is automatically inserted in the Title box. In the **Subject** box, type your Course name and section number. In the **Keywords** box, type **menu plan** and then in the upper right corner of the **Document Properties** panel, click the **Close the Document Information Panel** button ✕.

Adding properties to your documents will make them easier to search for in systems such as Microsoft SharePoint.

> **Another Way**
> Press Ctrl + P or Ctrl + F2 to display the Print tab in Backstage view.

4 Redisplay **Backstage** view, and then click the **Print tab**. Compare your screen with Figure 1.24.

On the Print tab in Backstage view, in the center panel, three groups of printing-related tasks display—Print, Printer, and Settings. In the right panel, the *Print Preview* displays, which is a view of a document as it will appear on the paper when you print it.

At the bottom of the Print Preview area, on the left, the number of pages and arrows with which you can move among the pages in Print Preview display. On the right, *Zoom* settings enable you to shrink or enlarge the Print Preview. Zoom is the action of increasing or decreasing the viewing area of the screen.

Figure 1.24

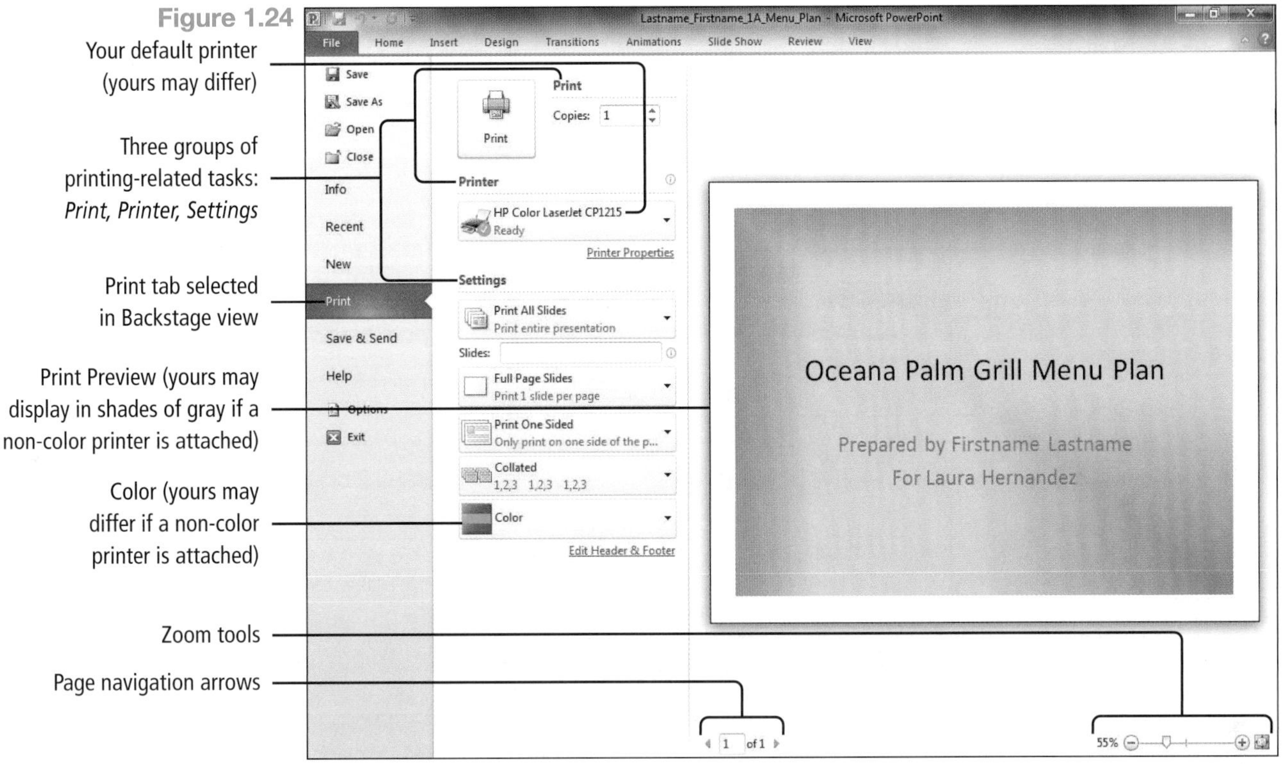

Your default printer
(yours may differ)

Three groups of
printing-related tasks:
Print, Printer, Settings

Print tab selected
in Backstage view

Print Preview (yours may
display in shades of gray if a
non-color printer is attached)

Color (yours may
differ if a non-color
printer is attached)

Zoom tools

Page navigation arrows

5 Locate the **Settings group**, and notice that the default setting is to **Print All Slides** and to print **Full Page Slides**—each slide on a full sheet of paper.

6 Point to **Full Page Slides**, notice that the button glows orange, and then click the button to display a gallery of print arrangements. Compare your screen with Figure 1.25.

Figure 1.25

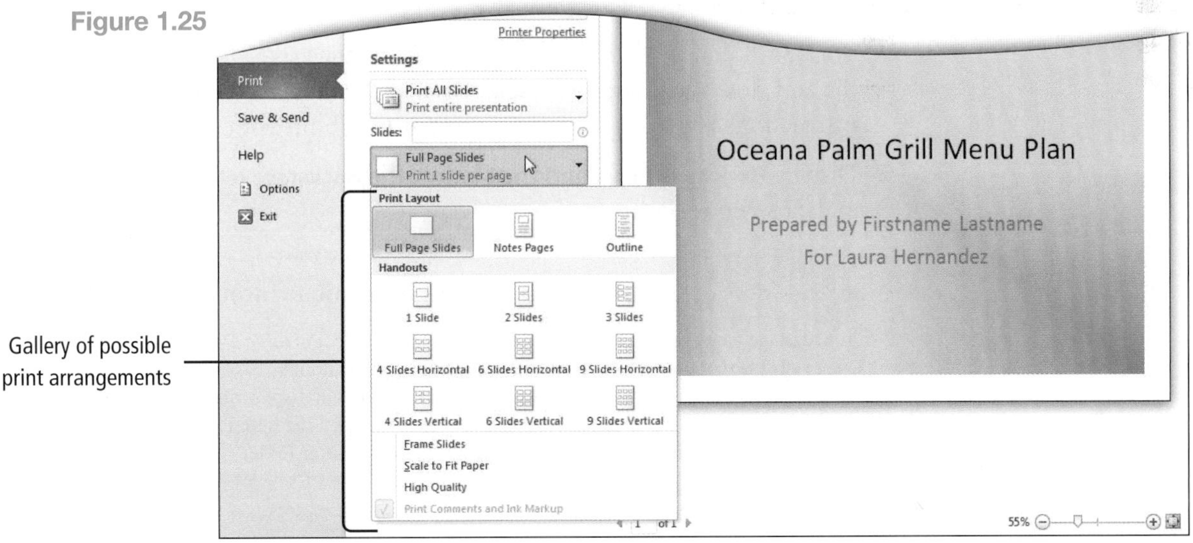

Gallery of possible
print arrangements

7 In the displayed gallery, under **Handouts**, click **1 Slide**, and then compare your screen with Figure 1.26.

The Print Preview changes to show how your slide will print on the paper in this arrangement.

Figure 1.26

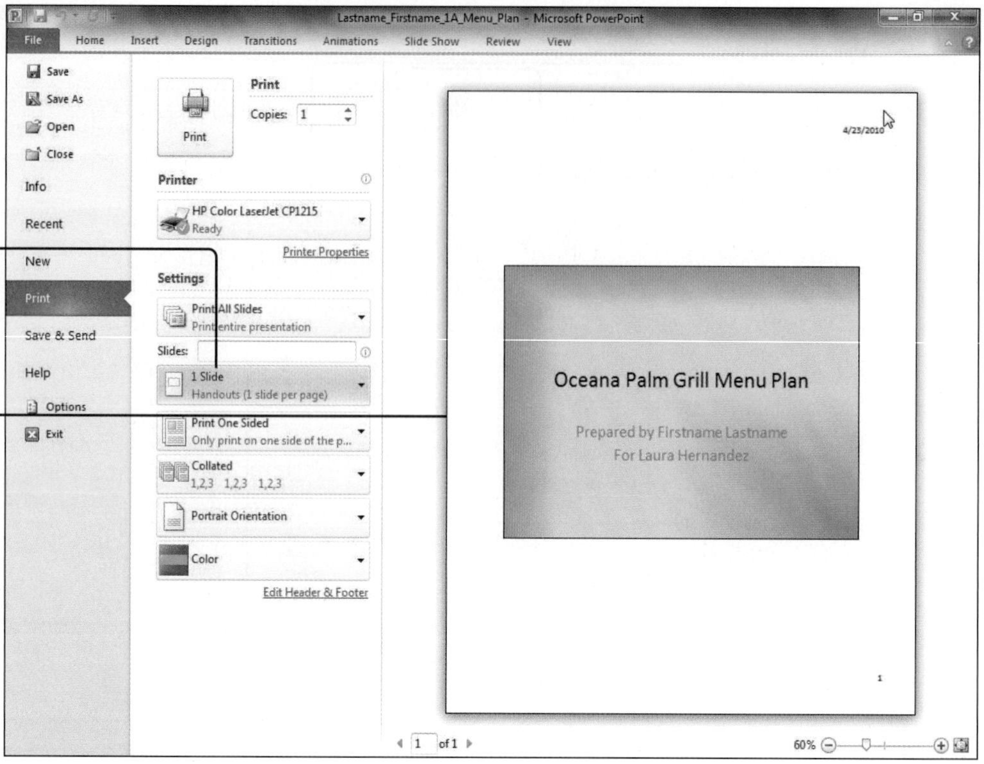

Handouts selected

Print Preview displays
the 1 slide printed as
handouts setting

8 To submit your file electronically, skip this step and move to Step 9. To print your slide, be sure your system is connected to a printer, and then in the **Print group**, click the **Print** button. On the Quick Access Toolbar, click **Save** 🖫, and then move to Step 10.

> The handout will print on your default printer—on a black and white printer, the colors will print in shades of gray. Backstage view closes and your file redisplays in the PowerPoint window.

9 To submit your file electronically, above the **Backstage tabs**, click **Close** to close the file and close **Backstage** view, click **Save** in the displayed message, and then follow the instructions provided by your instructor to submit your file electronically.

Another Way

In the upper right corner of your PowerPoint window, click the red Close button.

10 Display **Backstage** view, and then below the **Backstage tabs**, click **Exit** to close your file and close PowerPoint.

More Knowledge | Creating a PDF as an Electronic Printout

From Backstage view, you can save an Office file as a *PDF file*. *Portable Document Format* (PDF) creates an image of your file that preserves the look of your file, but that cannot be easily changed. This is a popular format for sending documents electronically, because the document will display on most computers. From Backstage view, click Save & Send, and then in the File Types group, click Create PDF/XPS Document. Then in the third panel, click the Create PDF/XPS button, navigate to your chapter folder, and then in the lower right corner, click Publish.

End **You have completed Project 1A**

Project 1B Word File

Project Activities

In Activities 1.07 through 1.16, you will open, edit, save, and then compress a Word file. Your completed document will look similar to Figure 1.27.

Project Files

For Project 1B, you will need the following file:

> cf01B_Cheese_Promotion

You will save your Word document as:

> Lastname_Firstname_1B_Cheese_Promotion

Project Results

Memo

TO: Laura Mabry Hernandez, General Manager

FROM: Donna Jackson, Executive Chef

DATE: December 17, 2014

SUBJECT: Cheese Specials on Tuesdays

To increase restaurant traffic between 4:00 p.m. and 6:00 p.m., I am proposing a trial cheese event in one of the restaurants, probably Orlando. I would like to try a weekly event on Tuesday evenings where the focus is on a good selection of cheese.

I envision two possibilities: a selection of cheese plates or a cheese bar—or both. The cheeses would have to be matched with compatible fruit and bread or crackers. They could be used as appetizers, or for desserts, as is common in Europe. The cheese plates should be varied and diverse, using a mixture of hard and soft, sharp and mild, unusual and familiar.

I am excited about this new promotion. If done properly, I think it could increase restaurant traffic in the hours when individuals want to relax with a small snack instead of a heavy dinner.

The promotion will require that our employees become familiar with the types and characteristics of both foreign and domestic cheeses. Let's meet to discuss the details and the training requirements, and to create a flyer that begins something like this:

Oceana Palm Grill Tuesday Cheese Tastings

Lastname_Firstname_1B_Cheese_Promotion

Figure 1.27
Project 1B Cheese Promotion

Objective 7 | Open an Existing File and Save It with a New Name

In any Office program, use the Open command to display the ***Open dialog box***, from which you can navigate to and then open an existing file that was created in that same program.

The Open dialog box, along with the Save and Save As dialog boxes, are referred to as ***common dialog boxes***. These dialog boxes, which are provided by the Windows programming interface, display in all of the Office programs in the same manner. Thus, the Open, Save, and Save As dialog boxes will all look and perform the same in each Office program.

Activity 1.07 | Opening an Existing File and Saving it with a New Name

In this activity, you will display the Open dialog box, open an existing Word document, and then save it in your storage location with a new name.

1 Determine the location of the student data files that accompany this textbook, and be sure you can access these files.

> For example:
>
> If you are accessing the files from the Student CD that came with this textbook, insert the CD now.
>
> If you copied the files from the Student CD or from the Pearson Web site to a USB flash drive that you are using for this course, insert the flash drive in your computer now.
>
> If you copied the files to the hard drive of your computer, for example in your Documents library, be sure you can locate the files on the hard drive.

2 Determine the location of your **Common Features Chapter 1** folder you created in Activity 1.05, in which you will store your work from this chapter, and then be sure you can access that folder.

> For example:
>
> If you created your chapter folder on a USB flash drive, insert the flash drive in your computer now. This can be the same flash drive where you have stored the student data files; just be sure to use the chapter folder you created.
>
> If you created your chapter folder in the Documents library on your computer, be sure you can locate the folder. Otherwise, create a new folder at the computer at which you are working, or on a USB flash drive.

3 Using the technique you practiced in Activity 1.02, locate and then start the **Microsoft Word 2010** program on your system.

<table>
<tr><td>

Another Way

In the Word (or other program) window, press Ctrl + F12 to display the Open dialog box.

</td><td>

4 On the Ribbon, click the **File tab** to display **Backstage** view, and then click **Open** to display the **Open** dialog box.

5 In the **navigation pane** on the left, use the scroll bar to scroll as necessary, and then click the location of your student data files to display the location's contents in the **file list**. Compare your screen with Figure 1.28.

</td></tr>
</table>

> For example:
>
> If you are accessing the files from the Student CD that came with your book, under Computer, click the CD/DVD.
>
> If you are accessing the files from a USB flash drive, under Computer, click the flash drive name.
>
> If you are accessing the files from the Documents library of your computer, under Libraries, click Documents.

Figure 1.28

Open dialog box

Scroll bar in navigation pane

Navigation pane

CD/DVD selected (or location of your student files)

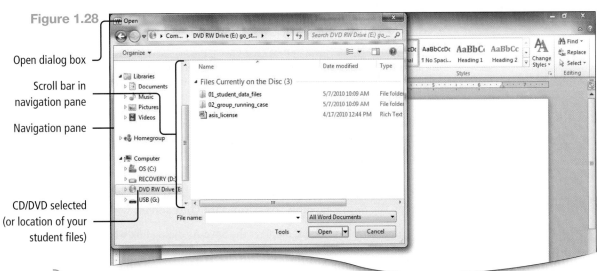

Another Way

Point to a folder name, right-click, and then from the shortcut menu, click Open.

6 Point to the folder **01_student_data_files** and double-click to open the folder. Point to the subfolder **01_common_features**, double-click, and then compare your screen with Figure 1.29.

Figure 1.29

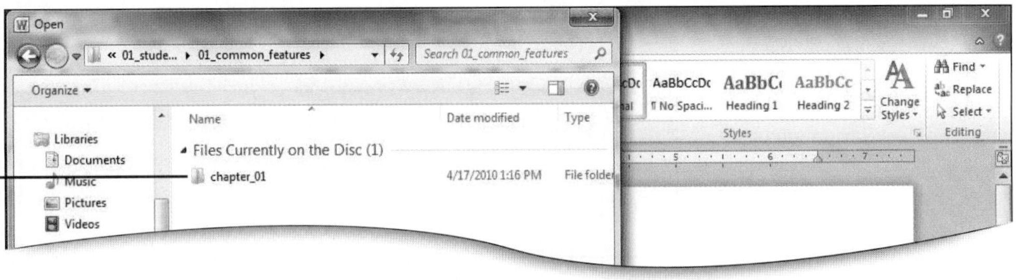

File list displays the contents of the *01_common_features* folder

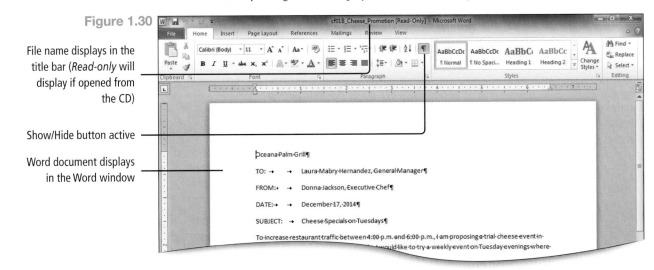

Another Way

Click one time to select the file, and then press Enter or click the Open button in the lower right corner of the dialog box.

7 In the **file list**, point to the **chapter_01** subfolder and double-click to open it. In the **file list**, point to Word file **cf01B_Cheese_Promotion** and then double-click to open and display the file in the Word window. On the Ribbon, on the **Home tab**, in the **Paragraph group**, if necessary, click the **Show/Hide** button ¶ so that it is active—glowing orange. Compare your screen with Figure 1.30.

On the title bar at the top of the screen, the file name displays. If you opened the document from the Student CD, (*Read-Only*) will display. If you opened the document from another source to which the files were copied, (*Read-Only*) might not display. *Read-Only* is a property assigned to a file that prevents the file from being modified or deleted; it indicates that you cannot save any changes to the displayed document unless you first save it with a new name.

Figure 1.30

File name displays in the title bar (*Read-only* will display if opened from the CD)

Show/Hide button active

Word document displays in the Word window

Another Way
Press F12 to display the Save As dialog box.

8 Click the **File tab** to display **Backstage** view, and then click the **Save As** command to display the **Save As** dialog box. Compare your screen with Figure 1.31.

> The Save As command displays the Save As dialog box where you can name and save a *new* document based on the currently displayed document. After you name and save the new document, the original document closes, and the new document—based on the original one—displays.

Figure 1.31

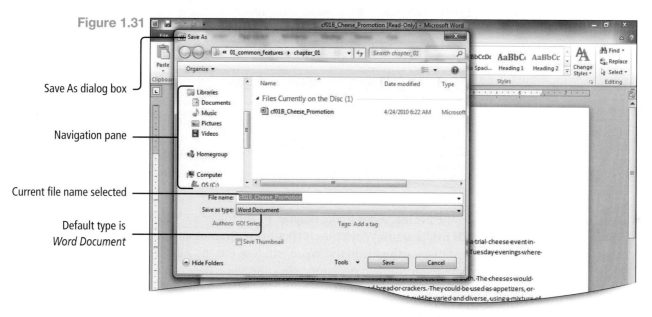

Save As dialog box

Navigation pane

Current file name selected

Default type is *Word Document*

9 In the **navigation pane**, click the location in which you are storing your projects for this chapter—the location where you created your **Common Features Chapter 1** folder; for example, your USB flash drive or the Documents library.

10 In the **file list**, double-click the necessary folders and subfolders until your **Common Features Chapter 1** folder displays in the **address bar**.

11 Click in the **File name** box to select the existing file name, or drag to select the existing text, and then using your own name, type **Lastname_Firstname_1B_Cheese_Promotion** Compare your screen with Figure 1.32.

> As you type, the file name from your 1A project might display briefly. Because your 1A project file is stored in this location and you began the new file name with the same text, Office predicts that you might want the same or similar file name. As you type new characters, the suggestion is removed.

Figure 1.32

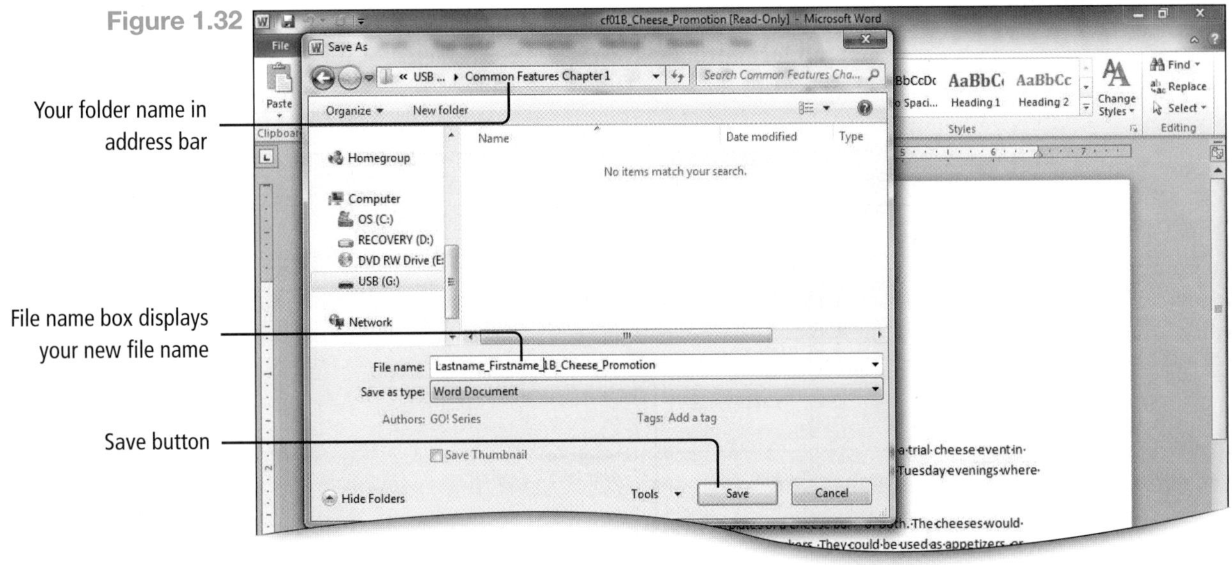

Your folder name in
address bar

File name box displays
your new file name

Save button

12 In the lower right corner of the **Save As** dialog box, click **Save**; or press Enter. Compare your screen with Figure 1.33.

The original document closes, and your new document, based on the original, displays with the name in the title bar.

Figure 1.33

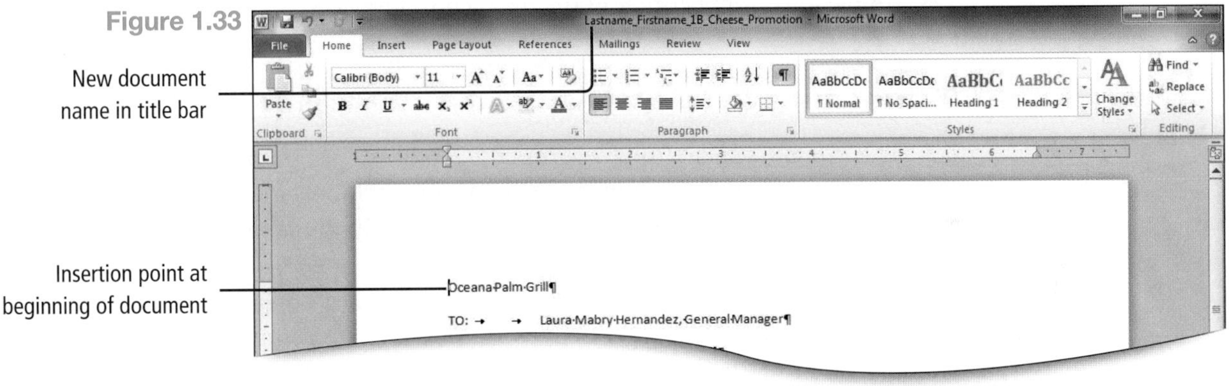

New document
name in title bar

Insertion point at
beginning of document

Objective 8 | Explore Options for an Application

Within each Office application, you can open an *Options dialog box* where you can select program settings and other options and preferences. For example, you can set preferences for viewing and editing files.

Activity 1.08 | Viewing Application Options

1 Click the **File tab** to display **Backstage** view. Under the **Help tab**, click **Options**.

2 In the displayed **Word Options** dialog box, on the left, click **Display**, and then on the right, locate the information under **Always show these formatting marks on the screen**.

When you press Enter, Spacebar, or Tab on your keyboard, characters display to represent these keystrokes. These screen characters do not print, and are referred to as *formatting marks* or *nonprinting characters*.

3 Under **Always show these formatting marks on the screen**, be sure the last check box, **Show all formatting marks**, is selected—select it if necessary. Compare your screen with Figure 1.34.

Figure 1.34

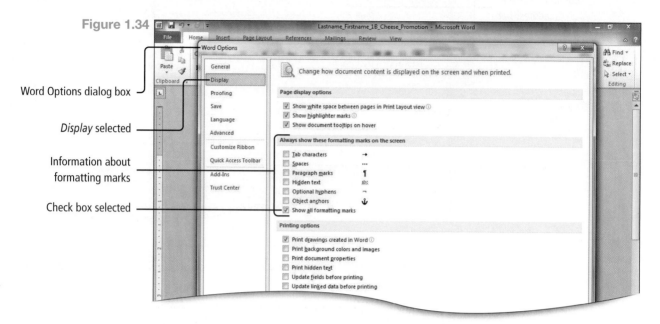

Word Options dialog box

Display selected

Information about formatting marks

Check box selected

4 In the lower right corner of the dialog box, click **OK**.

Objective 9 | Perform Commands from the Ribbon

The **Ribbon**, which displays across the top of the program window, groups commands and features in a manner that you would most logically use them. Each Office program's Ribbon is slightly different, but all contain the same three elements: **tabs**, **groups**, and commands.

Tabs display across the top of the Ribbon, and each tab relates to a type of activity; for example, laying out a page. Groups are sets of related commands for specific tasks. Commands—instructions to computer programs—are arranged in groups, and might display as a button, a menu, or a box in which you type information.

You can also minimize the Ribbon so only the tab names display. In the minimized Ribbon view, when you click a tab the Ribbon expands to show the groups and commands, and then when you click a command, the Ribbon returns to its minimized view. Most Office users, however, prefer to leave the complete Ribbon in view at all times.

Activity 1.09 | Performing Commands from the Ribbon

1 Take a moment to examine the document on your screen.

This document is a memo from the Executive Chef to the General Manager regarding a new restaurant promotion.

2 On the Ribbon, click the **View tab**. In the **Show group**, if necessary, click to place a check mark in the **Ruler** check box, and then compare your screen with Figure 1.35.

> When working in Word, display the rulers so that you can see how margin settings affect your document and how text aligns. Additionally, if you set a tab stop or an indent, its location is visible on the ruler.

Figure 1.35
Quick Access Toolbar
Ruler selected
Button to minimize Ribbon
Rulers

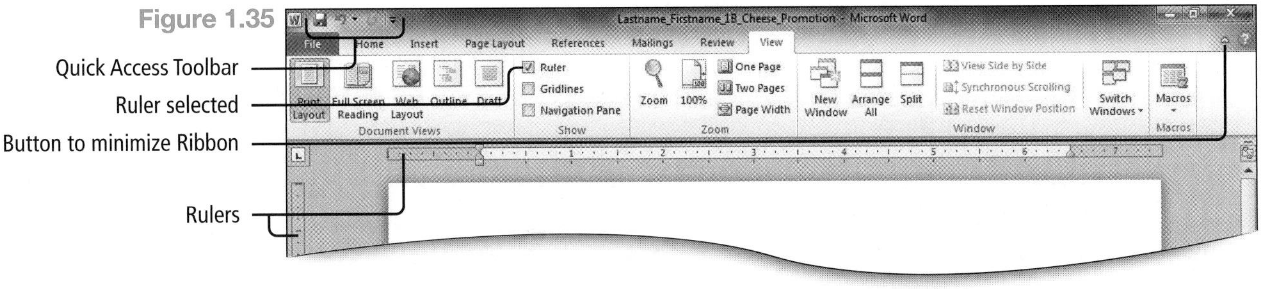

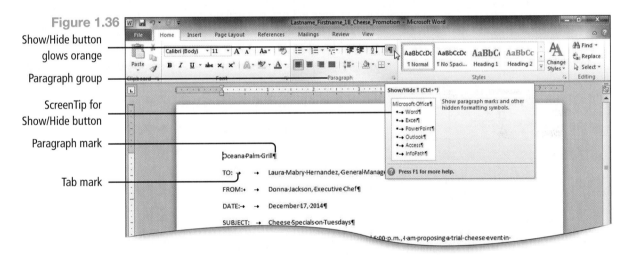

3 On the Ribbon, click the **Home tab**. In the **Paragraph group**, if necessary, click the **Show/Hide** button ¶ so that it glows orange and formatting marks display in your document. Point to the button to display information about the button, and then compare your screen with Figure 1.36.

> When the Show/Hide button is active—glowing orange—formatting marks display. Because formatting marks guide your eye in a document—like a map and road signs guide you along a highway—these marks will display throughout this instruction. Many expert Word users keep these marks displayed while creating documents.

Figure 1.36
Show/Hide button glows orange
Paragraph group
ScreenTip for Show/Hide button
Paragraph mark
Tab mark

4 In the upper left corner of your screen, above the Ribbon, locate the **Quick Access Toolbar**.

> The *Quick Access Toolbar* contains commands that you use frequently. By default, only the commands Save, Undo, and Redo display, but you can add and delete commands to suit your needs. Possibly the computer at which you are working already has additional commands added to the Quick Access Toolbar.

5 At the end of the Quick Access Toolbar, click the **Customize Quick Access Toolbar** button ▾.

6 Compare your screen with Figure 1.37.

A list of commands that Office users commonly add to their Quick Access Toolbar displays, including *Open*, *E-mail*, and *Print Preview and Print.* Commands already on the Quick Access Toolbar display a check mark. Commands that you add to the Quick Access Toolbar are always just one click away.

Here you can also display the More Commands dialog box, from which you can select any command from any tab to add to the Quick Access Toolbar.

Figure 1.37

Customize Quick
Access Toolbar

Popular commands to add

Existing commands
checked

Displays *More
Commands* dialog box

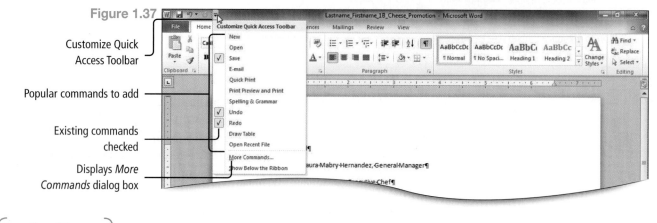

Another Way

Right-click any
command on the
Ribbon, and then on
the shortcut menu,
click Add to Quick
Access Toolbar.

7 On the displayed list, click **Print Preview and Print**, and then notice that the icon is added to the **Quick Access Toolbar**. Compare your screen with Figure 1.38.

The icon that represents the Print Preview command displays on the Quick Access Toolbar. Because this is a command that you will use frequently while building Office documents, you might decide to have this command remain on your Quick Access Toolbar.

Figure 1.38

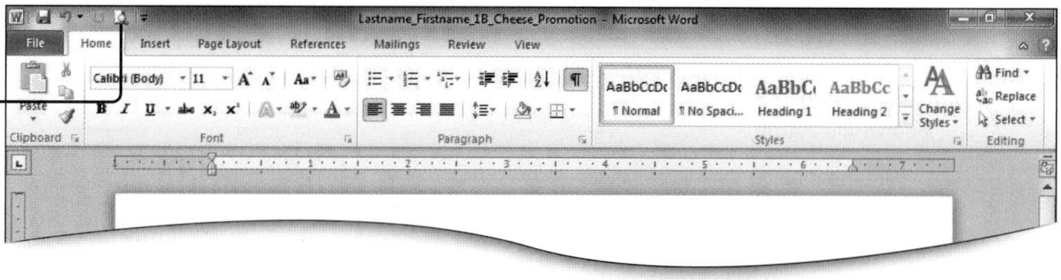

Icon for Print Preview
command added to
Quick Access Toolbar

8 In the first line of the document, be sure your insertion point is blinking to the left of the *O* in *Oceana.* Press Enter one time to insert a blank paragraph, and then click to the left of the new paragraph mark (¶) in the new line.

The ***paragraph symbol*** is a formatting mark that displays each time you press Enter.

9 On the Ribbon, click the **Insert tab**. In the **Illustrations group**, point to the **Clip Art** button to display its ScreenTip.

Many buttons on the Ribbon have this type of ***enhanced ScreenTip***, which displays more descriptive text than a normal ScreenTip.

10 Click the **Clip Art** button.

The Clip Art ***task pane*** displays. A task pane is a window within a Microsoft Office application that enables you to enter options for completing a command.

11 In the **Clip Art** task pane, click in the **Search for** box, delete any existing text, and then type **cheese grapes** Under **Results should be:**, click the arrow at the right, if necessary click to *clear* the check mark for **All media types** so that no check boxes are selected, and then click the check box for **Illustrations**. Compare your screen with Figure 1.39.

Figure 1.39

Search term

Blank paragraph

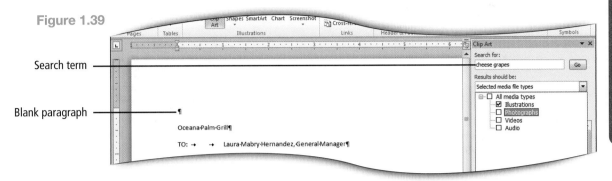

12 Click the **Results should be arrow** again to close the list, and then if necessary, click to place a check mark in the **Include Office.com content** check box.

> By selecting this check box, the search for clip art images will include those from Microsoft's online collections of clip art at www.office.com.

13 At the top of the **Clip Art** task pane, click **Go**. Wait a moment for clips to display, and then locate the clip indicated in Figure 1.40.

Figure 1.40

Check box selected

Locate this image

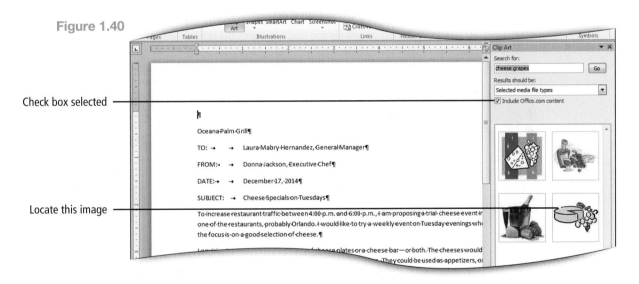

14 Click the image indicated in Figure 1.40 one time to insert it at the insertion point, and then in the upper right corner of the **Clip Art** task pane, click the **Close** ☒ button.

Alert! | If You Cannot Locate the Image

If the image shown in Figure 1.40 is unavailable, select a different cheese image that is appropriate.

---

15 With the image selected—surrounded by a border—on the Ribbon, click the **Home tab**, and then in the **Paragraph group**, click the **Center** button ☰. Click anywhere outside of the bordered picture to *deselect*—cancel the selection. Compare your screen with Figure 1.41.

Figure 1.41

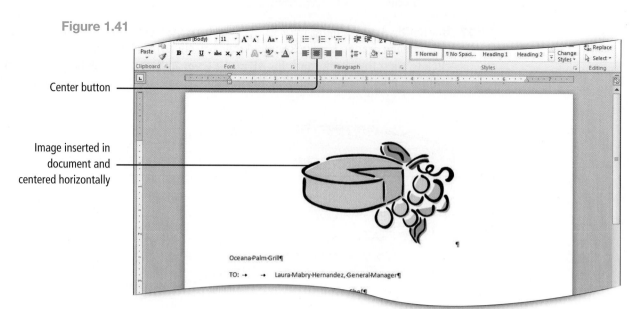

Center button

Image inserted in document and centered horizontally

16 Point to the inserted clip art image, and then watch the last tab of the Ribbon as you click the image one time to select it.

> The *Picture Tools* display and an additional tab—the *Format* tab—is added to the Ribbon. The Ribbon adapts to your work and will display additional tabs—referred to as ***contextual tabs***—when you need them.

17 On the Ribbon, under **Picture Tools**, click the **Format tab**.

Alert! | The Size of Groups on the Ribbon Varies with Screen Resolution

Your monitor's screen resolution might be set higher than the resolution used to capture the figures in this book. In Figure 1.42 below, the resolution is set to 1024 × 768, which is used for all of the figures in this book. Compare that with Figure 1.43 below, where the screen resolution is set to 1280 × 1024.

At a higher resolution, the Ribbon expands some groups to show more commands than are available with a single click, such as those in the Picture Styles group. Or, the group expands to add descriptive text to some buttons, such as those in the Arrange group. Regardless of your screen resolution, all Office commands are available to you. In higher resolutions, you will have a more robust view of the commands.

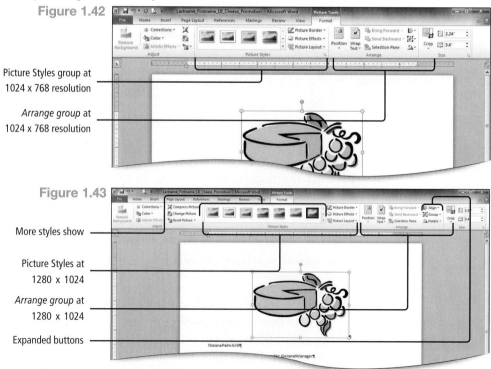

Figure 1.42

Picture Styles group at 1024 x 768 resolution

Arrange group at 1024 x 768 resolution

Figure 1.43

More styles show

Picture Styles at 1280 x 1024

Arrange group at 1280 x 1024

Expanded buttons

---

18 In the **Picture Styles group**, point to the first style to display the ScreenTip *Simple Frame, White*, and notice that the image displays with a white frame.

19 Watch the image as you point to the second picture style, and then to the third, and then to the fourth.

This is *Live Preview*, a technology that shows the result of applying an editing or formatting change as you point to possible results—*before* you actually apply it.

20 In the **Picture Styles group**, click the fourth style—**Drop Shadow Rectangle**—and then click anywhere outside of the image to deselect it. Notice that the Picture Tools no longer display on the Ribbon. Compare your screen with Figure 1.44.

Contextual tabs display only when you need them.

Figure 1.44

Picture Tools no longer display on the Ribbon

Drop Shadow Rectangle picture style applied to image

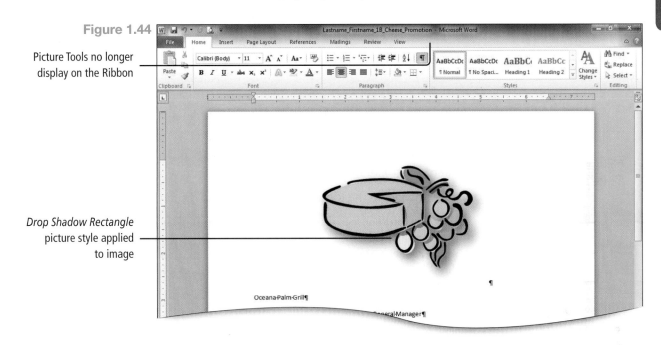

21 In the upper left corner of your screen, on the Quick Access Toolbar, click the **Save** button 🖫 to save the changes you have made.

Activity 1.10 | Minimizing and Using the Keyboard to Control the Ribbon

Instead of a mouse, some individuals prefer to navigate the Ribbon by using keys on the keyboard. You can activate keyboard control of the Ribbon by pressing the Alt key. You can also minimize the Ribbon to maximize your available screen space.

1 On your keyboard, press the Alt key, and then on the Ribbon, notice that small labels display. Press N to activate the commands on the **Insert tab**, and then compare your screen with Figure 1.45.

Each label represents a *KeyTip*—an indication of the key that you can press to activate the command. For example, on the Insert tab, you can press F to activate the Clip Art task pane.

Figure 1.45

KeyTips indicate that
keyboard control
of the Ribbon is active

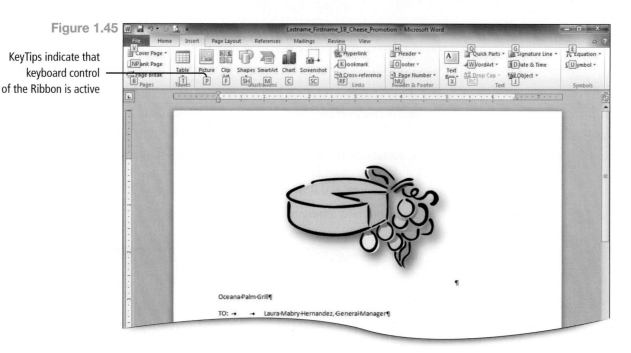

2 Press Esc to redisplay the KeyTips for the tabs. Then, press Alt again to turn off keyboard control of the Ribbon.

3 Point to any tab on the Ribbon and right-click to display a shortcut menu.

> Here you can choose to display the Quick Access Toolbar below the Ribbon or minimize the Ribbon to maximize screen space. You can also customize the Ribbon by adding, removing, renaming, or reordering tabs, groups, and commands on the Ribbon, although this is not recommended until you become an expert Office user.

Another Way

Double-click the active tab; or, click the Minimize the Ribbon button at the right end of the Ribbon.

4 Click **Minimize the Ribbon**. Notice that only the Ribbon tabs display. Click the **Home tab** to display the commands. Click anywhere in the document, and notice that the Ribbon reverts to its minimized view.

Another Way

Double-click any tab to redisplay the full Ribbon.

5 Right-click any Ribbon tab, and then click **Minimize the Ribbon** again to turn the minimize feature off.

> Most expert Office users prefer to have the full Ribbon display at all times.

6 Point to any tab on the Ribbon, and then on your mouse device, roll the mouse wheel. Notice that different tabs become active as your roll the mouse wheel.

> You can make a tab active by using this technique, instead of clicking the tab.

Objective 10 | Apply Formatting in Office Programs

Formatting is the process of establishing the overall appearance of text, graphics, and pages in an Office file—for example, in a Word document.

Activity 1.11 | Formatting and Viewing Pages

In this activity, you will practice common formatting techniques used in Office applications.

1 On the Ribbon, click the **Insert tab**, and then in the **Header & Footer group**, click the **Footer** button.

Another Way

On the Design tab, in the Insert group, click Quick Parts, click Field, and then under Field names, click FileName.

2 At the top of the displayed gallery, under **Built-In**, click **Blank**. At the bottom of your document, with *Type text* highlighted in blue, using your own name type the file name of this document **Lastname_Firstname_1B_Cheese_Promotion** and then compare your screen with Figure 1.46.

Header & Footer Tools are added to the Ribbon. A *footer* is a reserved area for text or graphics that displays at the bottom of each page in a document. Likewise, a *header* is a reserved area for text or graphics that displays at the top of each page in a document. When the footer (or header) area is active, the document area is inactive (dimmed).

Figure 1.46

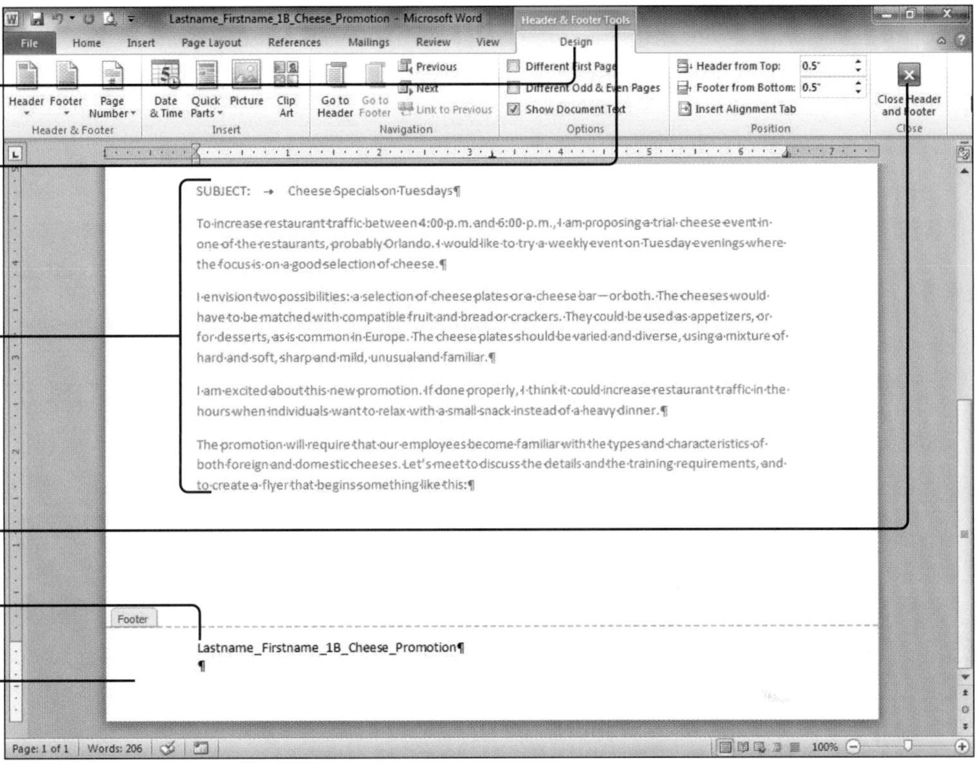

Design tab added

Header & Footer Tools active

Document area inactive (dimmed) when footer area is active

Close Header and Footer button

Your file name

Footer area displays

3 On the Ribbon, on the **Design tab**, in the **Close group**, click the **Close Header and Footer** button.

4 On the Ribbon, click the **Page Layout tab**. In the **Page Setup group**, click the **Orientation** button, and notice that two orientations display—*Portrait* and *Landscape*. Click **Landscape**.

In *portrait orientation*, the paper is taller than it is wide. In *landscape orientation*, the paper is wider than it is tall.

5 In the lower right corner of the screen, locate the **Zoom control** buttons.

To zoom means to increase or decrease the viewing area. You can zoom in to look closely at a section of a document, and then zoom out to see an entire page on the screen. You can also zoom to view multiple pages on the screen.

6 Drag the **Zoom slider**  to the left until you have zoomed to approximately *60%*. Compare your screen with Figure 1.47.

Figure 1.47

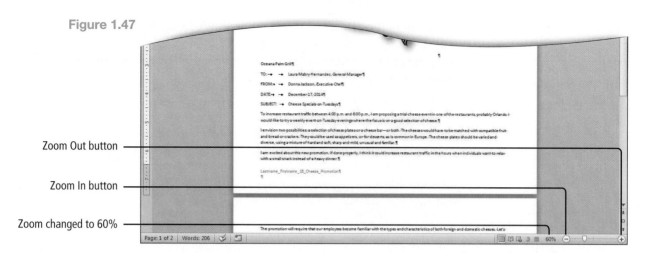

Zoom Out button

Zoom In button

Zoom changed to 60%

7 On the **Page Layout tab**, in the **Page Setup group**, click the **Orientation** button, and then click **Portrait**.

> Portrait orientation is commonly used for business documents such as letters and memos.

8 In the lower right corner of your screen, click the **Zoom In** button ⊕ as many times as necessary to return to the **100%** zoom setting.

> Use the zoom feature to adjust the view of your document for editing and for your viewing comfort.

9 On the Quick Access Toolbar, click the **Save** button 🖫 to save the changes you have made to your document.

Activity 1.12 | Formatting Text

1 To the left of *Oceana Palm Grill*, point in the margin area to display the 🖈 pointer and click one time to select the entire paragraph. Compare your screen with Figure 1.48.

> Use this technique to select complete paragraphs from the margin area. Additionally, with this technique you can drag downward to select multiple-line paragraphs—which is faster and more efficient than dragging through text.

Figure 1.48

Paragraph selected

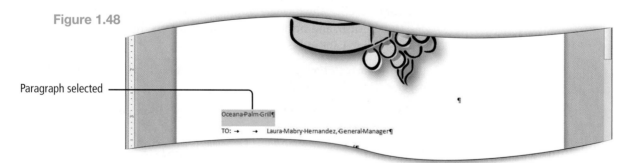

2 On the Ribbon, click the **Home tab**, and then in the **Paragraph group**, click the **Center** button ≣ to center the paragraph.

> *Alignment* refers to the placement of paragraph text relative to the left and right margins. *Center alignment* refers to text that is centered horizontally between the left and right margins. You can also align text at the left margin, which is the default alignment for text in Word, or at the right margin.

3 On the **Home tab**, in the **Font group**, click the **Font button arrow** `Calibri (Body)  ▾`. At the top of the list, point to **Cambria**, and as you do so, notice that the selected text previews in the Cambria font.

> A *font* is a set of characters with the same design and shape. The default font in a Word document is Calibri, which is a *sans serif* font—a font design with no lines or extensions on the ends of characters.

> The Cambria font is a *serif* font—a font design that includes small line extensions on the ends of the letters to guide the eye in reading from left to right.

> The list of fonts displays as a gallery showing potential results. For example, in the Font gallery, you can see the actual design and format of each font as it would look if applied to text.

4 Point to several other fonts and observe the effect on the selected text. Then, at the top of the **Font** gallery, under **Theme Fonts**, click **Cambria**.

> A *theme* is a predesigned set of colors, fonts, lines, and fill effects that look good together and that can be applied to your entire document or to specific items.

> A theme combines two sets of fonts—one for text and one for headings. In the default Office theme, Cambria is the suggested font for headings.

5 With the paragraph *Oceana Palm Grill* still selected, on the **Home tab**, in the **Font group**, click the **Font Size button arrow** `11 ▾`, point to **36**, and then notice how Live Preview displays the text in the font size to which you are pointing. Compare your screen with Figure 1.49.

Figure 1.49

Font Size button

Font button

Font Size list

Pointing to 36 pt font size

Oceana Palm Grill centered,
Cambria font applied

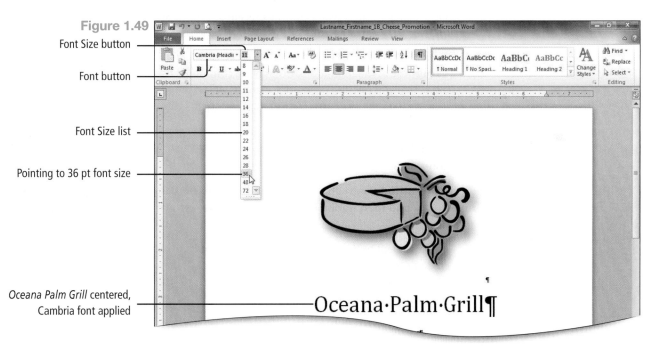

6 On the displayed list of font sizes, click **20**.

> Fonts are measured in *points*, with one point equal to 1/72 of an inch. A higher point size indicates a larger font size. Headings and titles are often formatted by using a larger font size. The word *point* is abbreviated as *pt*.

7 With *Oceana Palm Grill* still selected, on the **Home tab**, in the **Font group**, click the **Font Color button arrow** `A ▾`. Under **Theme Colors**, in the seventh column, click the last color—**Olive Green, Accent 3, Darker 50%**. Click anywhere to deselect the text.

8 To the left of *TO:*, point in the left margin area to display the 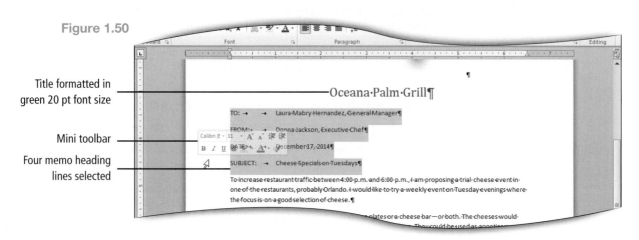 pointer, hold down the left mouse button, and then drag down to select the four memo headings. Compare your screen with Figure 1.50.

> Use this technique to select complete paragraphs from the margin area—dragging downward to select multiple-line paragraphs—which is faster and more efficient than dragging through text.

Figure 1.50

Title formatted in green 20 pt font size

Mini toolbar

Four memo heading lines selected

9 With the four paragraphs selected, on the Mini toolbar, click the **Font Color** button , which now displays a dark green bar instead of a red bar.

> The font color button retains its most recently used color—Olive Green, Accent 3, Darker 50%. As you progress in your study of Microsoft Office, you will use other buttons that behave in this manner; that is, they retain their most recently used format.

> The purpose of the Mini toolbar is to place commonly used commands close to text or objects that you select. By selecting a command on the Mini toolbar, you reduce the distance that you must move your mouse to access a command.

10 Click anywhere in the paragraph that begins *To increase*, and then **triple-click**—click the left mouse button three times—to select the entire paragraph. If the entire paragraph is not selected, click in the paragraph and begin again.

11 With the entire paragraph selected, on the Mini toolbar, click the **Font Color button arrow** , and then under **Theme Colors**, in the sixth column, click the first color— **Red, Accent 2**.

> It is convenient to have commonly used commands display on the Mini toolbar so that you do not have to move your mouse to the top of the screen to access the command from the Ribbon.

12 Select the text *TO:* and then on the displayed Mini toolbar, click the **Bold** button and the **Italic** button .

> *Font styles* include bold, italic, and underline. Font styles emphasize text and are a visual cue to draw the reader's eye to important text.

13 On the displayed Mini toolbar, click the **Italic** button again to turn off the Italic formatting. Notice that the Italic button no longer glows orange.

> A button that behaves in this manner is referred to as a **toggle button**, which means it can be turned on by clicking it once, and then turned off by clicking it again.

14 With *TO:* still selected, on the Mini toolbar, click the **Format Painter** button [image]. Then, move your mouse under the word *Laura*, and notice the [image] mouse pointer. Compare your screen with Figure 1.51.

> You can use the ***Format Painter*** to copy the formatting of specific text or of a paragraph and then apply it in other locations in your document.

> The pointer takes the shape of a paintbrush, and contains the formatting information from the paragraph where the insertion point is positioned. Information about the Format Painter and how to turn it off displays in the status bar.

Figure 1.51

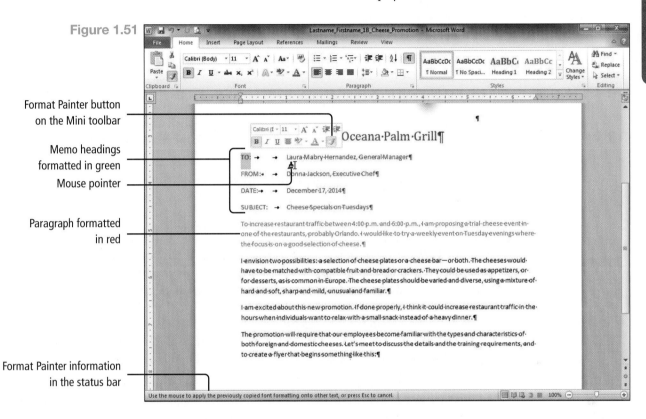

Format Painter button on the Mini toolbar

Memo headings formatted in green

Mouse pointer

Paragraph formatted in red

Format Painter information in the status bar

15 With the [image] pointer, drag to select the text *FROM:* and notice that the Bold formatting is applied. Then, point to the selected text *FROM:* and on the Mini toolbar, *double-click* the **Format Painter** button [image].

16 Select the text *DATE:* to copy the Bold formatting, and notice that the pointer retains the [image] shape.

> When you *double-click* the Format Painter button, the Format Painter feature remains active until you either click the Format Painter button again, or press (Esc) to cancel it—as indicated on the status bar.

17 With Format Painter still active, select the text *SUBJECT:*, and then on the Ribbon, on the **Home tab**, in the **Clipboard group**, notice that the **Format Painter** button [image] is glowing orange, indicating that it is active. Compare your screen with Figure 1.52.

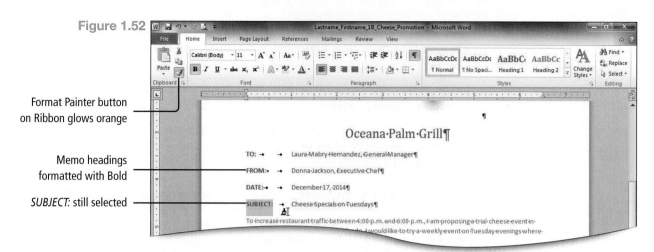

Figure 1.52

Format Painter button on Ribbon glows orange

Memo headings formatted with Bold

SUBJECT: still selected

18 Click the **Format Painter** button on the Ribbon to turn the command off.

19 In the paragraph that begins *To increase*, triple-click again to select the entire paragraph. On the displayed Mini toolbar, click the **Bold** button **B** and the **Italic** button *I*. Click anywhere to deselect.

20 On the Quick Access Toolbar, click the **Save** button to save the changes you have made to your document.

Activity 1.13 | Using the Office Clipboard to Cut, Copy, and Paste

The **Office Clipboard** is a temporary storage area that holds text or graphics that you select and then cut or copy. When you *copy* text or graphics, a copy is placed on the Office Clipboard and the original text or graphic remains in place. When you *cut* text or graphics, a copy is placed on the Office Clipboard, and the original text or graphic is removed—cut—from the document.

After cutting or copying, the contents of the Office Clipboard are available for you to *paste*—insert—in a new location in the current document, or into another Office file.

1 Hold down Ctrl and press Home to move to the beginning of your document, and then take a moment to study the table in Figure 1.53, which describes similar keyboard shortcuts with which you can navigate quickly in a document.

To Move	Press
To the beginning of a document	Ctrl + Home
To the end of a document	Ctrl + End
To the beginning of a line	Home
To the end of a line	End
To the beginning of the previous word	Ctrl + ←
To the beginning of the next word	Ctrl + →
To the beginning of the current word (if insertion point is in the middle of a word)	Ctrl + ←
To the beginning of a paragraph	Ctrl + ↑
To the beginning of the next paragraph	Ctrl + ↓
To the beginning of the current paragraph (if insertion point is in the middle of a paragraph)	Ctrl + ↑
Up one screen	PgUp
Down one screen	PageDown

Figure 1.53

2 To the left of *Oceana Palm Grill*, point in the left margin area to display the 🔏
pointer, and then click one time to select the entire paragraph. On the **Home tab**, in
the **Clipboard group**, click the **Copy** button 📋.

Because anything that you select and then copy—or cut—is placed on the Office
Clipboard, the Copy command and the Cut command display in the Clipboard group of
commands on the Ribbon.

There is no visible indication that your copied selection has been placed on the Office
Clipboard.

3 On the **Home tab**, in the **Clipboard group**, to the right of the group name
Clipboard, click the **Dialog Box Launcher** button 🔲, and then compare your
screen with Figure 1.54.

The Clipboard task pane displays with your copied text. In any Ribbon group, the
Dialog Box Launcher displays either a dialog box or a task pane related to the group of
commands.

It is not necessary to display the Office Clipboard in this manner, although sometimes it
is useful to do so. The Office Clipboard can hold 24 items.

Figure 1.54

Copy button

Dialog Box Launcher
in Clipboard group

Clipboard task
pane displays

Selected text on the
Office Clipboard

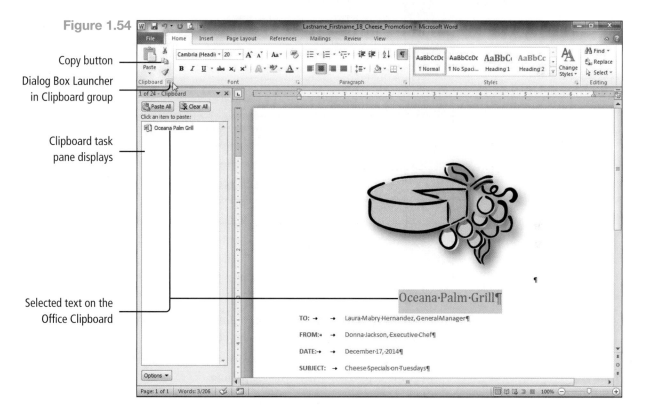

4 In the upper right corner of the **Clipboard** task pane, click the **Close** button ✕.

5 Press Ctrl + End to move to the end of your document. Press Enter one time to create
a new blank paragraph. On the **Home tab**, in the **Clipboard group**, point to the **Paste**
button, and then click the *upper* portion of this split button.

The Paste command pastes the most recently copied item on the Office Clipboard at the
insertion point location. If you click the lower portion of the Paste button, a gallery of
Paste Options displays.

6 Click the **Paste Options** button 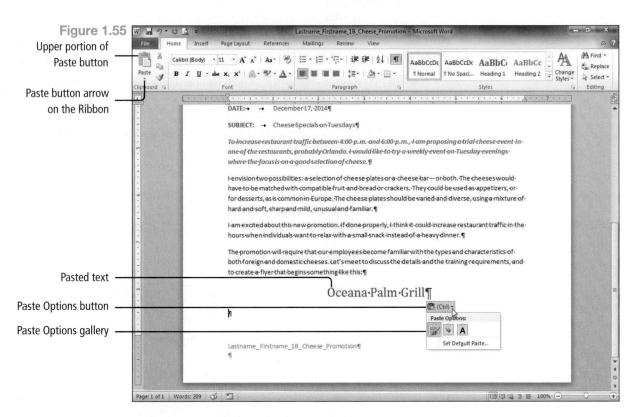 that displays below the pasted text as shown in Figure 1.55.

> Here you can view and apply various formatting options for pasting your copied or cut text. Typically you will click Paste on the Ribbon and paste the item in its original format. If you want some other format for the pasted item, you can do so from the ***Paste Options gallery***.

> The Paste Options gallery provides a Live Preview of the various options for changing the format of the pasted item with a single click. The Paste Options gallery is available in three places: on the Ribbon by clicking the lower portion of the Paste button—the Paste button arrow; from the Paste Options button that displays below the pasted item following the paste operation; or, on the shortcut menu if you right-click the pasted item.

Figure 1.55
Upper portion of Paste button
Paste button arrow on the Ribbon
Pasted text
Paste Options button
Paste Options gallery

7 In the displayed **Paste Options** gallery, *point* to each option to see the Live Preview of the format that would be applied if you clicked the button.

> The contents of the Paste Options gallery are contextual; that is, they change based on what you copied and where you are pasting.

8 Press Esc to close the gallery; the button will remain displayed until you take some other screen action.

9 Press Ctrl + Home to move to the top of the document, and then click the **cheese image** one time to select it. While pointing to the selected image, right-click, and then on the shortcut menu, click **Cut**.

> Recall that the Cut command cuts—removes—the selection from the document and places it on the Office Clipboard.

Another Way

On the Home tab, in the Clipboard group, click the Cut button; or, use the keyboard shortcut Ctrl + X.

10 Press [Del] one time to remove the blank paragraph from the top of the document, and then press [Ctrl] + [End] to move to the end of the document.

11 With the insertion point blinking in the blank paragraph at the end of the document, right-click, and notice that the **Paste Options** gallery displays on the shortcut menu. Compare your screen with Figure 1.56.

Figure 1.56

Paste Options on
shortcut menu

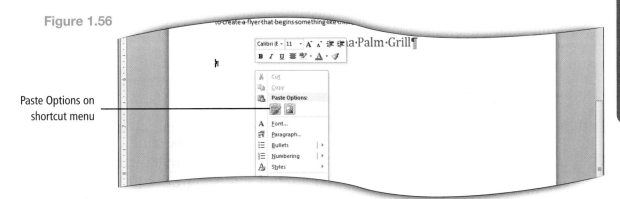

12 On the shortcut menu, under **Paste Options**, click the first button—**Keep Source Formatting** .

13 Click the picture to select it. On the **Home tab**, in the **Paragraph group**, click the **Center** button .

14 Above the cheese picture, click to position the insertion point at the end of the word *Grill*, press [Spacebar] one time, and then type **Tuesday Cheese Tastings** Compare your screen with Figure 1.57.

Figure 1.57

Heading

Picture inserted
and centered

Activity 1.14 | Viewing Print Preview and Printing a Word Document

1 Press [Ctrl] + [Home] to move to the top of your document. Select the text *Oceana Palm Grill*, and then replace the selected text by typing **Memo**

2 Display **Backstage** view, on the right, click **Properties**, and then click **Show Document Panel**. Replace the existing author name with your first and last name. In the **Subject** box, type your course name and section number, and then in the **Keywords** box, type **cheese promotion** and then **Close** the **Document Information Panel**.

Another Way

Press Ctrl + F2 to display Print Preview.

3 On the Quick Access Toolbar, click **Save** 🖫 to save the changes you have made to your document.

4 On the Quick Access Toolbar, click the **Print Preview** button 🔍 that you added. Compare your screen with Figure 1.58.

Figure 1.58

Memo typed

If no printer is attached to your system, OneNote is the default printer

Print tab active in Backstage view

Print Preview (if you have a non-color printer as your default printer, the preview may display in shades of gray)

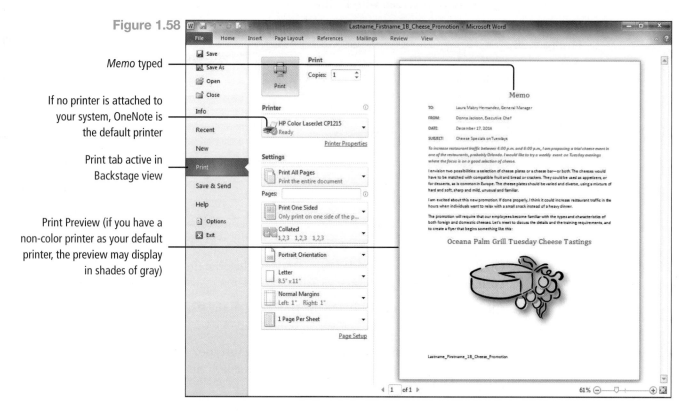

5 Examine the **Print Preview**. Under **Settings**, notice that in **Backstage** view, several of the same commands that are available on the Page Layout tab of the Ribbon also display.

For convenience, common adjustments to Page Layout display here, so that you can make last-minute adjustments without closing Backstage view.

6 If you need to make any corrections, click the Home tab to return to the document and make any necessary changes.

It is good practice to examine the Print Preview before printing or submitting your work electronically. Then, make any necessary corrections, re-save, and redisplay Print Preview.

7 If you are directed to do so, click Print to print the document; or, above the Info tab, click Close, and then submit your file electronically according to the directions provided by your instructor.

If you click the Print button, Backstage view closes and the Word window redisplays.

8 On the Quick Access Toolbar, point to the **Print Preview icon** 🔍 you placed there, right-click, and then click **Remove from Quick Access Toolbar**.

If you are working on your own computer and you want to do so, you can leave the icon on the toolbar; in a lab setting, you should return the software to its original settings.

9 At the right end of the title bar, click the program **Close** button [×].

10 If a message displays asking if you want the text on the Clipboard to be available after you quit Word, click **No**.

> This message most often displays if you have copied some type of image to the Clipboard. If you click Yes, the items on the Clipboard will remain for you to use.

Objective 11 | Use the Microsoft Office 2010 Help System

Within each Office program, the Help feature provides information about all of the program's features and displays step-by-step instructions for performing many tasks.

Activity 1.15 | Using the Microsoft Office 2010 Help System in Excel

In this activity, you will use the Microsoft Help feature to find information about formatting numbers in Excel.

> **Another Way**
>
> Press [F1] to display Help.

1 **Start** the **Microsoft Excel 2010** program. In the upper right corner of your screen, click the **Microsoft Excel Help** button [?].

2 In the **Excel Help** window, click in the white box in upper left corner, type **formatting numbers** and then click **Search** or press [Enter].

3 On the list of results, click **Display numbers as currency**. Compare your screen with Figure 1.59.

Figure 1.59

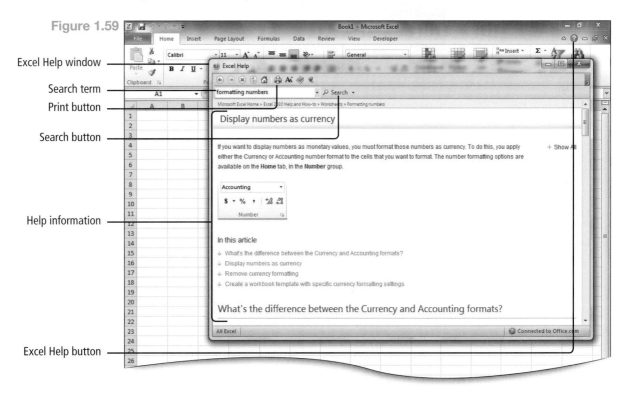

Excel Help window

Search term

Print button

Search button

Help information

Excel Help button

4 If you want to do so, on the toolbar at the top of the **Excel Help** window, click the **Print** [🖨] button to print a copy of this information for your reference.

5 On the title bar of the Excel Help window, click the **Close** button ![x]. On the right side of the Microsoft Excel title bar, click the **Close** button ![x] to close Excel.

Objective 12 | Compress Files

A ***compressed file*** is a file that has been reduced in size. Compressed files take up less storage space and can be transferred to other computers faster than uncompressed files. You can also combine a group of files into one compressed folder, which makes it easier to share a group of files.

Activity 1.16 | Compressing Files

In this activity, you will combine the two files you created in this chapter into one compressed file.

1 On the Windows taskbar, click the **Start** button ![start], and then on the right, click **Computer**.

2 On the left, in the **navigation pane**, click the location of your two files from this chapter—your USB flash drive or other location—and display the folder window for your **Common Features Chapter 1** folder. Compare your screen with Figure 1.60.

Figure 1.60

Address bar displays path —

Your chapter files in file list (your name displays) —

Folder window for your chapter folder —

Location selected in navigation pane (your location may vary) —

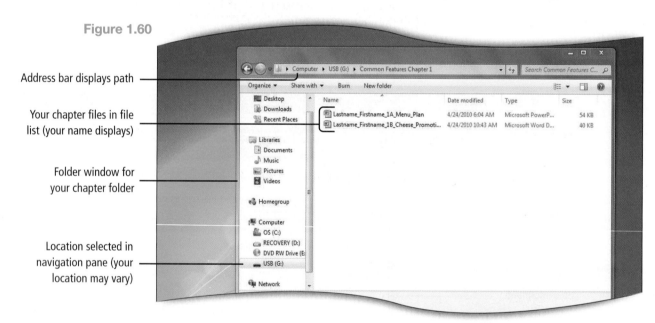

3 In the **file list**, click your **Lastname_Firstname_1A_Menu_Plan** file one time to select it.

4 Hold down Ctrl, and then click your **Lastname_Firstname_1B_Cheese_Promotion** file to select both files. Release Ctrl.

In any Windows-based program, holding down Ctrl while selecting enables you to select multiple items.

5 Point anywhere over the two selected files and right-click. On the shortcut menu, point to **Send to**, and then compare your screen with Figure 1.61.

Figure 1.61

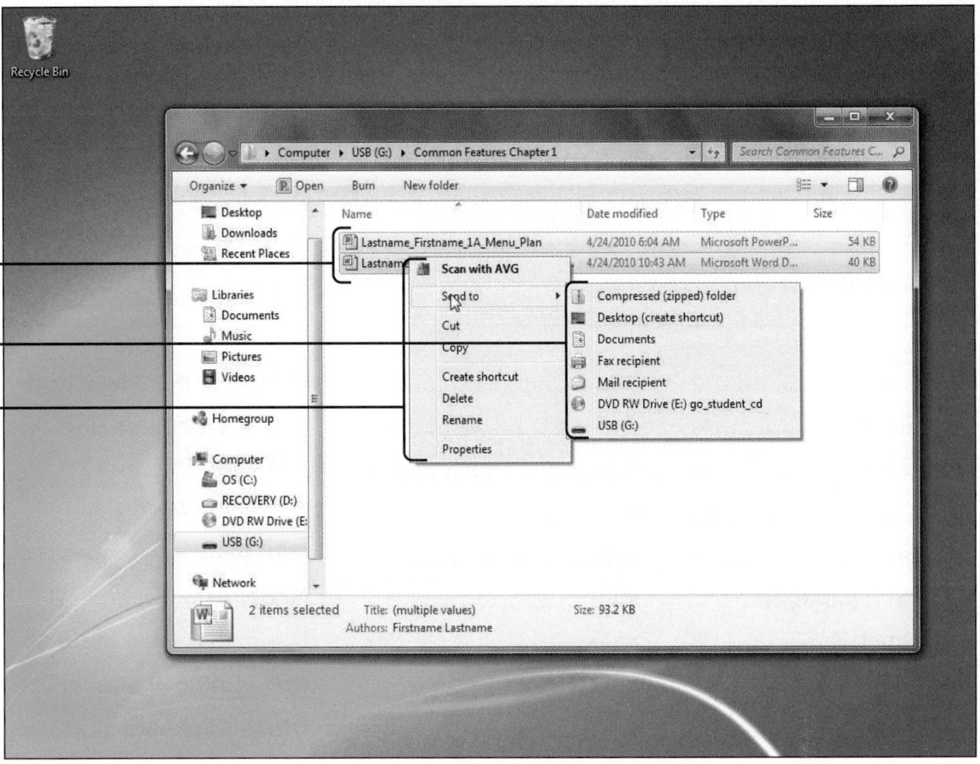

Two files selected

Send to submenu

Shortcut menu
(yours may vary)

6 On the shortcut submenu, click **Compressed (zipped) folder**.

Windows creates a compressed folder containing a *copy* of each of the selected files. The folder name is the name of the file or folder to which you were pointing, and is selected—highlighted in blue—so that you can rename it.

7 Using your own name, type **Lastname_Firstname_Common_Features_Ch1** and press Enter.

The compressed folder is now ready to attach to an e-mail or share in some other electronic format.

8 **Close** ✕ the folder window. If directed to do so by your instructor, submit your compressed folder electronically.

More Knowledge | Extracting Compressed Files

Extract means to decompress, or pull out, files from a compressed form. When you extract a file, an uncompressed copy is placed in the folder that you specify. The original file remains in the compressed folder.

End **You have completed Project 1B** ──────────────

Content-Based Assessments

Summary

In this chapter, you used Windows Explorer to navigate the Windows file structure. You also used features that are common across the Microsoft Office 2010 programs.

Key Terms

Content-Based Assessments

Matching

Match each term in the second column with its correct definition in the first column by writing the letter of the term on the blank line in front of the correct definition.

_____ 1. A collection of information stored on a computer under a single name.

_____ 2. A container in which you store files.

_____ 3. A folder within a folder.

_____ 4. The program that displays the files and folders on your computer.

_____ 5. The Windows menu that is the main gateway to your computer.

_____ 6. In Windows 7, a window that displays the contents of the current folder, library, or device, and contains helpful parts so that you can navigate.

_____ 7. In Windows, a collection of items, such as files and folders, assembled from various locations that might be on your computer.

_____ 8. The bar at the top of a folder window with which you can navigate to a different folder or library, or go back to a previous one.

_____ 9. An instruction to a computer program that carries out an action.

_____ 10. Small pictures that represent a program, a file, a folder, or an object.

_____ 11. A set of instructions that a computer uses to perform a specific task.

_____ 12. A spreadsheet program used to calculate numbers and create charts.

_____ 13. The user interface that groups commands on tabs at the top of the program window.

_____ 14. A bar at the top of the program window displaying the current file and program name.

_____ 15. One or more keys pressed to perform a task that would otherwise require a mouse.

A Address bar

B Command

C File

D Folder

E Folder window

F Icons

G Keyboard shortcut

H Library

I Microsoft Excel

J Program

K Ribbon

L Start menu

M Subfolder

N Title bar

O Windows Explorer

Multiple Choice

Circle the correct answer.

1. A small toolbar with frequently used commands that displays when selecting text or objects is the:
   A. Quick Access Toolbar
   B. Mini toolbar
   C. Document toolbar

2. In Office 2010, a centralized space for file management tasks is:
   A. a task pane
   B. a dialog box
   C. Backstage view

3. The commands Save, Save As, Open, and Close in Backstage view are located:
   A. above the Backstage tabs
   B. below the Backstage tabs
   C. under the screen thumbnail

4. The tab in Backstage view that displays information about the current file is the:
   A. Recent tab
   B. Info tab
   C. Options tab

5. Details about a file, including the title, author name, subject, and keywords are known as:
   A. document properties
   B. formatting marks
   C. KeyTips

6. An Office feature that displays a list of potential results is:
   A. Live Preview
   B. a contextual tab
   C. a gallery

7. A type of formatting emphasis applied to text such as bold, italic, and underline, is called:

   A. a font style   **B.** a KeyTip   **C.** a tag

8. A technology showing the result of applying formatting as you point to possible results is called:

   A. Live Preview   **B.** Backstage view   **C.** gallery view

9. A temporary storage area that holds text or graphics that you select and then cut or copy is the:

   A. paste options gallery   **B.** ribbon   **C.** Office clipboard

10. A file that has been reduced in size is:

    A. a compressed file   **B.** an extracted file   **C.** a PDF file

Creating Documents with Microsoft Word 2010

OUTCOMES

At the end of this chapter you will be able to:

OBJECTIVES

Mastering these objectives will enable you to:

PROJECT 1A
Create a flyer with a picture.

1. Create a New Document and Insert Text (p. 185)
2. Insert and Format Graphics (p. 187)
3. Insert and Modify Text Boxes and Shapes (p. 192)
4. Preview and Print a Document (p. 196)

PROJECT 1B
Format text, paragraphs, and documents.

5. Change Document and Paragraph Layout (p. 203)
6. Create and Modify Lists (p. 209)
7. Set and Modify Tab Stops (p. 214)
8. Insert a SmartArt Graphic (p. 216)

Pattie Steib/Shutterstock

In This Chapter

In this chapter, you will use Microsoft Word, which is one of the most common programs found on computers and one that almost everyone has a reason to use. You will use many of the new tools found in Word 2010. When you learn word processing, you are also learning skills and techniques that you need to work efficiently on a computer. You can use Microsoft Word to perform basic word processing tasks such as writing a memo, a report, or a letter. You can also use Word to complete complex word processing tasks, such as creating sophisticated tables, embedding graphics, writing blogs, creating publications, and inserting links into other documents and the Internet. Word is a program that you can learn gradually, and then add more advanced skills one at a time.

The projects in this chapter relate to **Laurel College**. The college offers this diverse geographic area a wide range of academic and career programs, including associate degrees, certificate programs, and non-credit continuing education and personal development courses. The college makes positive contributions to the community through cultural and athletic programs and partnerships with businesses and nonprofit organizations. The college also provides industry-specific training programs for local businesses through its growing Economic Development Center.

Project 1A Flyer

my**i**tlab
Project 1A Training

In Activities 1.01 through 1.12, you will create a flyer announcing a new rock climbing class offered by the Physical Education Department at Laurel College. Your completed document will look similar to Figure 1.1.

Project Files

For Project 1A, you will need the following files:

New blank Word document
w01A_Fitness_Flyer
w01A_Rock_Climber

You will save your document as:

Lastname_Firstname_1A_Fitness_Flyer

Project Results

Figure 1.1
Project 1A Fitness Flyer

Objective 1 | Create a New Document and Insert Text

When you create a new document, you can type all of the text, or you can type some of the text and then insert additional text from another source.

Activity 1.01 | Starting a New Word Document and Inserting Text

1 **Start** Word and display a new blank document. On the **Home tab**, in the **Paragraph group**, if necessary click the Show/Hide button ¶ so that it is active (glows orange) to display the formatting marks. If the rulers do not display, click the View tab, and then in the Show group, select the Ruler check box.

2 Type **Rock Climbing 101** and then press Enter two times. As you type the following text, press the Spacebar only one time at the end of a sentence: **Increase your fitness level by learning basic rock climbing using the new Laurel College Gymnasium rock climbing wall. The Physical Education Department is offering Rock Climbing 101 as part of its Recreational Fitness Program.**

As you type, the insertion point moves to the right, and when it approaches the right margin, Word determines whether the next word in the line will fit within the established right margin. If the word does not fit, Word moves the entire word down to the next line. This feature is called *wordwrap* and means that you press Enter *only* when you reach the end of a paragraph—it is not necessary to press Enter at the end of each line of text.

> **Note | Spacing Between Sentences**
>
> Although you might have learned to add two spaces following end-of-sentence punctuation, the common practice now is to space only one time at the end of a sentence.

3 Press Enter one time. Take a moment to study the table in Figure 1.2 to become familiar with the default document settings in Microsoft Word, and then compare your screen with Figure 1.3.

When you press Enter, Spacebar, or Tab on your keyboard, characters display in your document to represent these keystrokes. These characters do not print and are referred to as *formatting marks* or *nonprinting characters*. These marks will display throughout this instruction.

Default Document Settings in a New Word Document

Setting	Default format
Font and font size	The default font is Calibri and the default font size is 11.
Margins	The default left, right, top, and bottom page margins are 1 inch.
Line spacing	The default line spacing is 1.15, which provides slightly more space between lines than single spacing does—an extra 1/6 of a line added between lines than single spacing.
Paragraph spacing	The default spacing after a paragraph is 10 points, which is slightly less than the height of one blank line of text.
View	The default view is Print Layout view, which displays the page borders and displays the document as it will appear when printed.

Figure 1.2

Figure 1.3

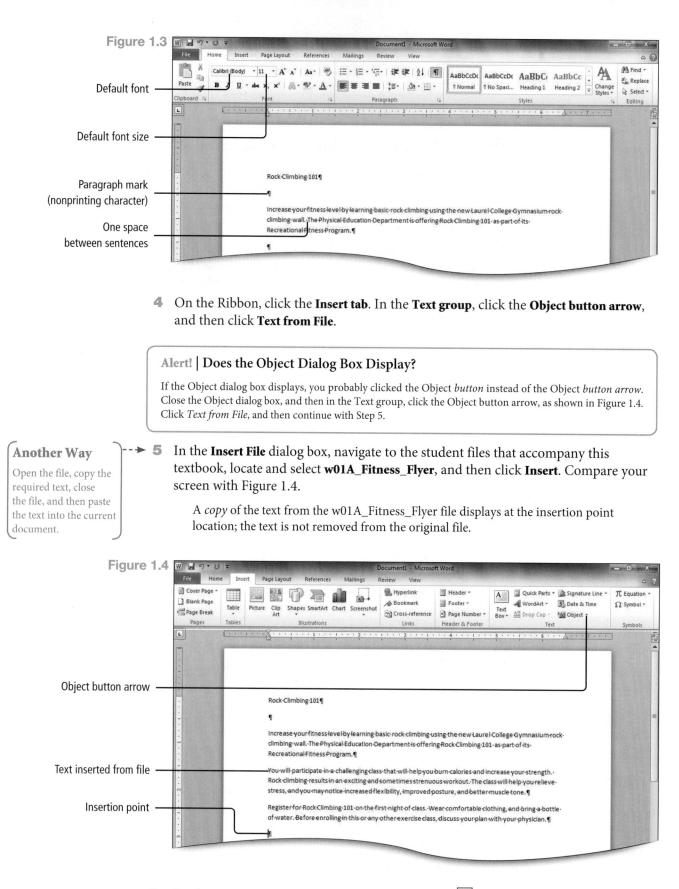

Default font

Default font size

Paragraph mark
(nonprinting character)

One space
between sentences

4　On the Ribbon, click the **Insert tab**. In the **Text group**, click the **Object button arrow**, and then click **Text from File**.

> **Alert!** | **Does the Object Dialog Box Display?**
>
> If the Object dialog box displays, you probably clicked the Object *button* instead of the Object *button arrow*. Close the Object dialog box, and then in the Text group, click the Object button arrow, as shown in Figure 1.4. Click *Text from File*, and then continue with Step 5.

Another Way

Open the file, copy the required text, close the file, and then paste the text into the current document.

5　In the **Insert File** dialog box, navigate to the student files that accompany this textbook, locate and select **w01A_Fitness_Flyer**, and then click **Insert**. Compare your screen with Figure 1.4.

A *copy* of the text from the w01A_Fitness_Flyer file displays at the insertion point location; the text is not removed from the original file.

Figure 1.4

Object button arrow

Text inserted from file

Insertion point

6　On the **Quick Access Toolbar**, click the **Save** button 🖫. In the **Save As** dialog box, navigate to the location where you are saving your files for this chapter, and then create and open a new folder named **Word Chapter 1** In the **File name** box, replace the existing text with **Lastname_Firstname_1A_Fitness_Flyer** and then click **Save**.

> **More Knowledge | Word's Default Settings Are Easier to Read Online**
>
> Until just a few years ago, word processing programs used single spacing, an extra blank paragraph to separate paragraphs, and 12 pt Times New Roman as the default formats. Now, studies show that individuals find the Word default formats described in Figure 1.2 to be easier to read online, where many documents are now viewed and read.

Objective 2 | Insert and Format Graphics

To add visual interest to a document, insert **graphics**. Graphics include pictures, clip art, charts, and **drawing objects**—shapes, diagrams, lines, and so on. For additional visual interest, you can convert text to an attractive graphic format; add, resize, move, and format pictures; and add an attractive page border.

Activity 1.02 | Formatting Text Using Text Effects

Text effects are decorative formats, such as shadowed or mirrored text, text glow, 3-D effects, and colors that make text stand out.

1   Including the paragraph mark, select the first paragraph of text—*Rock Climbing 101.* On the **Home tab**, in the **Font group**, click the **Text Effects** button.

2   In the displayed **Text Effects** gallery, in the first row, point to the second effect to display the ScreenTip *Fill - None, Outline - Accent 2* and then click this effect.

3   With the text still selected, in the **Font group**, click in the **Font Size** box to select the existing font size. Type **60** and then press Enter.

> When you want to change the font size of selected text to a size that does not display in the Font Size list, type the number in the Font Size button box and press Enter to confirm the new font size.

4   With the text still selected, in the **Paragraph group**, click the **Center** button to center the text. Compare your screen with Figure 1.5.

Figure 1.5

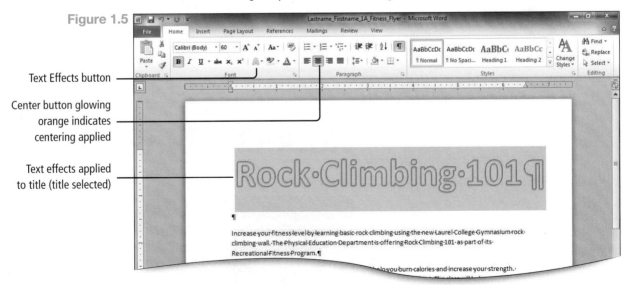

Text Effects button

Center button glowing orange indicates centering applied

Text effects applied to title (title selected)

5   With the text still selected, in the **Font group**, click the **Text Effects** button. Point to **Shadow**, and then under **Outer**, in the second row, click the third style—**Offset Left**.

6   With the text still selected, in the **Font group**, click the **Font Color button arrow**. Under **Theme Colors**, in the fourth column, click the first color—**Dark Blue, Text 2**.

7 Click anywhere in the document to deselect the text, and then compare your screen with Figure 1.6.

Figure 1.6

Title color changed
and shadow added

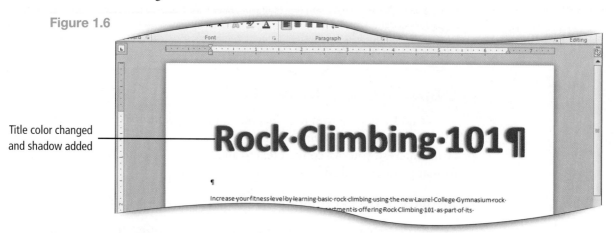

Rock·Climbing·101¶

¶

Increase·your·fitness·level·by·learning·basic·rock·climbing·using·the·new·Laurel·College·Gymnasium·rock·
...rtment·is·offering·Rock·Climbing·101·as·part·of·its·

8 Save 💾 your document.

Activity 1.03 | Inserting and Resizing Pictures

1 In the paragraph that begins *Increase your fitness*, click to position the insertion point at the beginning of the paragraph.

2 On the **Insert tab**, in the **Illustrations group**, click the **Picture** button. In the **Insert Picture** dialog box, navigate to your student data files, locate and click **w01A_Rock_Climber**, and then click **Insert**.

> Word inserts the picture as an ***inline object***; that is, the picture is positioned directly in the text at the insertion point, just like a character in a sentence. Sizing handles surround the picture indicating it is selected.

3 If necessary, scroll to view the entire picture. Notice the round and square sizing handles around the border of the selected picture, as shown in Figure 1.7.

> The round corner sizing handles resize the graphic proportionally. The square sizing handles resize a graphic vertically or horizontally only; however, sizing with these will distort the graphic. A green rotate handle, with which you can rotate the graphic to any angle, displays above the top center sizing handle.

Figure 1.7

Center sizing handle

Rotate handle

Corner sizing handles

Rock·Climbing·101¶

Increase·your·fitness·level·by·learning·basic·rock·climbing·
using·the·new·Laurel·College·Gymnasium·rock·climbing·wall.·The·Physical·Education·Department·is·

4　At the lower right corner of the picture, point to the round sizing handle until the ⤡ pointer displays. Drag upward and to the left until the bottom of the graphic is aligned at approximately **4 inches on the vertical ruler**. Compare your screen with Figure 1.8. Notice that the graphic is proportionally resized.

Figure 1.8

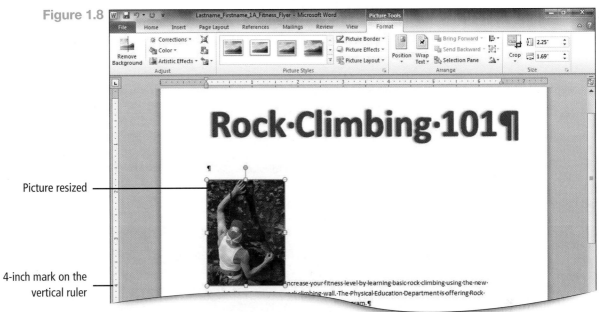

Picture resized

4-inch mark on the vertical ruler

Another Way

Click the Undo button to undo the change.

5　On the **Format tab**, in the **Adjust group**, click the **Reset Picture button arrow** 🖼, and then click **Reset Picture & Size**.

6　In the **Size group**, click the **Shape Height spin box up arrow** as necessary to change the height of the picture to **4.5″**. Scroll down to view the entire picture on your screen, compare your screen with Figure 1.9, and then **Save** 💾 your document.

When you use the Height and Width **spin boxes** to change the size of a graphic, the graphic will always resize proportionally; that is, the width adjusts as you change the height and vice versa.

Figure 1.9

Picture height increased to 4.5 inches

Activity 1.04 | Wrapping Text Around a Picture

Graphics inserted as inline objects are treated like characters in a sentence, which can result in unattractive spacing. You can change an inline object to a *floating object*—a graphic that can be moved independently of the surrounding text characters.

1 Be sure the picture is selected—you know it is selected if the sizing handles display.

2 On the **Format tab**, in the **Arrange group**, click the **Wrap Text** button to display a gallery of text wrapping arrangements.

Text wrapping refers to the manner in which text displays around an object.

3 From the gallery, click **Square** to wrap the text around the graphic, and then notice the *anchor* symbol to the left of the first line of the paragraph. Compare your screen with Figure 1.10.

Select square text wrapping when you want to wrap the text to the left or right of the image. When you apply text wrapping, the object is always associated with—anchored to—a specific paragraph.

Figure 1.10

Wrap Text button

Anchor symbol

Text wrapped around picture

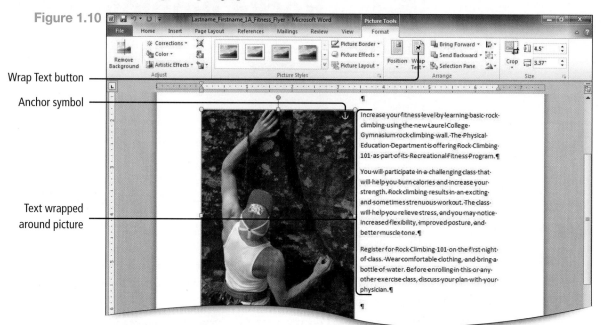

4 **Save** your document.

Activity 1.05 | Moving a Picture

1 Point to the rock climber picture to display the pointer.

2 Hold down Shift and drag the picture to the right until the right edge of the picture aligns at approximately **6.5 inches on the horizontal ruler**. Notice that the picture moves in a straight line when you hold down Shift. Compare your screen with Figure 1.11.

Figure 1.11

Right edge aligned with right margin

Top edge aligned with top of paragraph

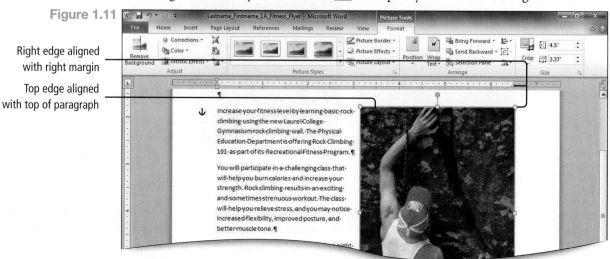

3 If necessary, press any of the arrow keys on your keyboard to *nudge*—move in small increments—the picture in any direction so that the text wraps to match Figure 1.11. **Save** 🖫 your document.

Activity 1.06 | Applying Picture Styles and Artistic Effects

Picture styles include shapes, shadows, frames, borders, and other special effects with which you can stylize an image. *Artistic effects* are formats that make pictures look more like sketches or paintings.

1 Be sure the rock climber picture is selected. On the **Format tab**, in the **Picture Styles group**, click the **Picture Effects** button. Point to **Soft Edges**, and then click **5 Point**.

> The Soft Edges feature fades the edges of the picture. The number of points you choose determines how far the fade goes inward from the edges of the picture.

2 On the **Format tab**, in the **Adjust group**, click the **Artistic Effects** button. In the first row of the gallery, point to, but do not click, the third effect—**Pencil Grayscale**.

> Live Preview displays the picture with the *Pencil Grayscale* effect added.

3 In the second row of the gallery, click the third effect—**Paint Brush**. Notice that the picture looks like a painting, rather than a photograph, as shown in Figure 1.12. **Save** 🖫 your document.

Figure 1.12

Paint Brush artistic effect applied to picture

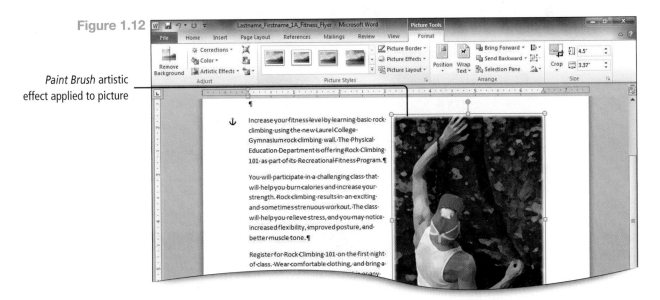

Activity 1.07 | Adding a Page Border

Page borders frame a page and help to focus the information on the page.

1 Click anywhere outside the picture to deselect it. On the **Page Layout tab**, in the **Page Background group**, click the **Page Borders** button.

2 In the **Borders and Shading** dialog box, under **Setting**, click **Box**. Under **Style**, scroll down the list about a third of the way and click the heavy top line with the thin bottom line—check the **Preview** area to be sure the heavier line is the nearest to the edges of the page.

3 Click the **Color arrow**, and then in the fourth column, click the first color—**Dark Blue, Text 2**.

4 Under **Apply to**, be sure *Whole document* is selected, and then compare your screen with Figure 1.13.

Figure 1.13

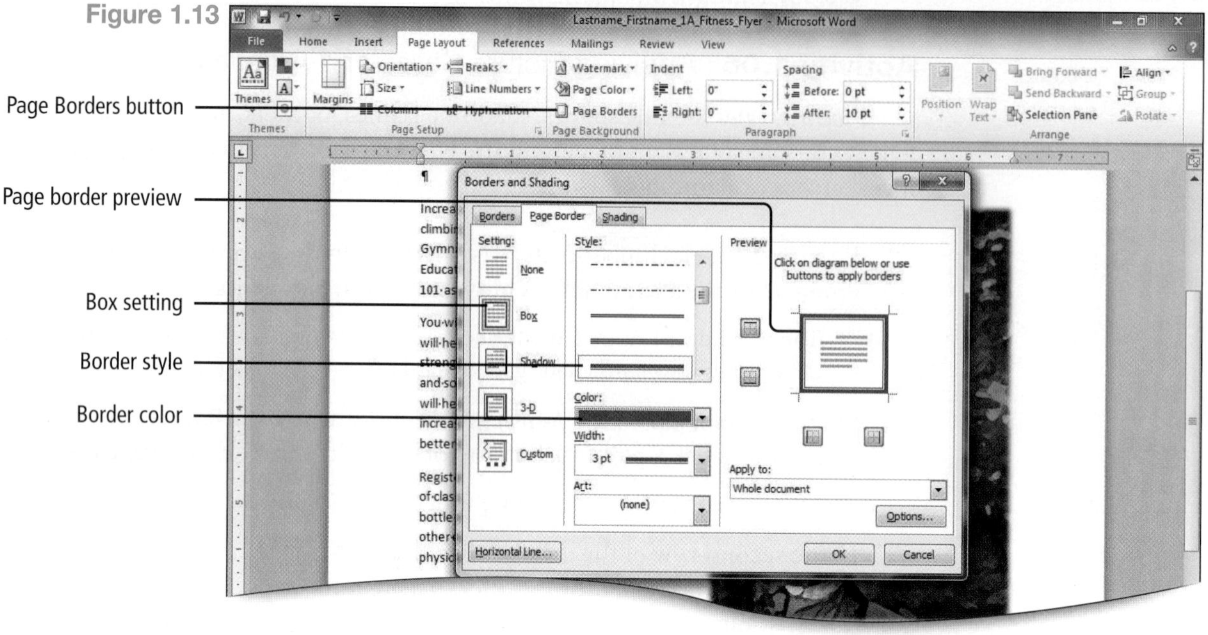

Page Borders button

Page border preview

Box setting

Border style

Border color

5 At the bottom of the **Borders and Shading** dialog box, click **OK**.

6 Press [Ctrl] + [Home] to move to the top of the document, and then compare your page border with Figure 1.14. **Save** [img] your document.

Figure 1.14

Page Border
added to document

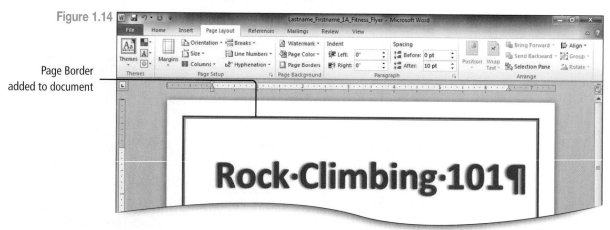

Rock·Climbing·101¶

Objective 3 | Insert and Modify Text Boxes and Shapes

Word provides predefined *shapes* and *text boxes* that you can add to your documents. A shape is an object such as a line, arrow, box, callout, or banner. A text box is a movable, resizable container for text or graphics. Use these objects to add visual interest to your document.

Activity 1.08 | Inserting a Shape

1 Press [↓] one time to move to the blank paragraph below the title. Press [Enter] four times to make space for a text box, and notice that the picture anchored to the paragraph moves with the text.

2 Press [Ctrl] + [End] to move to the bottom of the document, and notice that your insertion point is positioned in the empty paragraph at the end of the document.

3 Click the **Insert tab**, and then in the **Illustrations group**, click the **Shapes** button to display the gallery. Compare your screen with Figure 1.15.

Figure 1.15

Shapes button

Rounded Rectangle shape

Shapes gallery

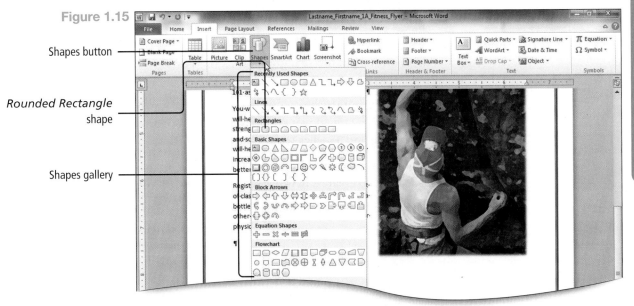

4 Under **Rectangles**, click the second shape—**Rounded Rectangle**, and then move your pointer. Notice that the ⊞ pointer displays.

5 Position the ⊞ pointer just under the lower left corner of the picture, and then drag down approximately **1 inch** and to the right edge of the picture.

6 Point to the shape and right-click, and then from the shortcut menu, click **Add Text**.

7 With the insertion point blinking inside the shape, point inside the shape and right-click, and then on the Mini toolbar, change the **Font Size** to **16**, and be sure **Center** ≡ alignment is selected.

8 Click inside the shape again, and then type **Improve your strength, balance, and coordination** If necessary, use the lower middle sizing handle to enlarge the shape to view your text. Compare your screen with Figure 1.16. **Save** 🖫 your document.

Figure 1.16

Rounded Rectangle shape inserted and formatted, text added

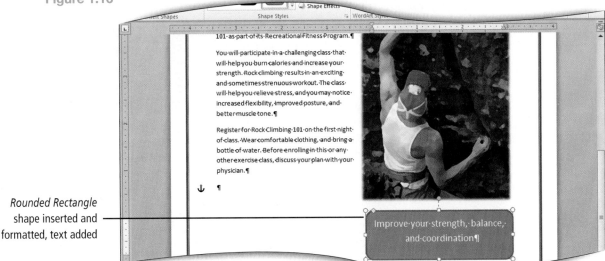

Activity 1.09 | Inserting a Text Box

A text box is useful to differentiate portions of text from other text on the page. You can move a text box anywhere on the page.

1 Press **Ctrl** + **Home** to move to the top of the document.

2 On the **Insert tab**, in the **Text group**, click the **Text Box** button. At the bottom of the gallery, click **Draw Text Box**.

3 Position the ⊞ pointer below the letter *k* in *Rock*—at approximately **1.5 inches on the vertical ruler**. Drag down and to the right to create a text box approximately **1.5 inches** high and **3 inches** wide—the exact size and location need not be precise.

4 With the insertion point blinking in the text box, type the following, pressing **Enter** after each line to create a new paragraph:

> **Meets Tuesdays and Thursdays, 7-9 p.m.**
>
> **Begins September 13, ends December 16**
>
> **College Gymnasium, Room 104**

5 Compare your screen with Figure 1.17.

Figure 1.17

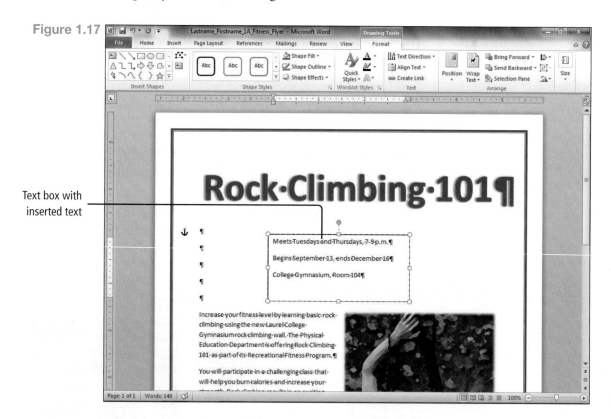

Text box with inserted text

6 **Save** 🖫 your document.

Activity 1.10 | Moving, Resizing, and Formatting Shapes and Text Boxes

1 In the text box you just created in the upper portion of the flyer, select all of the text. From the Mini toolbar, change the **Font Size** to **14**, apply **Bold** **B**, and then **Center** ≡ the text.

2 On the **Format tab**, in the **Size group**, if necessary, click the **Size** button. Click the **Shape Height spin arrows** as necessary to set the height of the text box to **1.2″**. Click the **Shape Width spin arrows** as necessary to set the width of the text box to **4″**.

3 In the **Shape Styles group**, click the **Shape Effects** button. Point to **Shadow**, and then under **Outer**, in the first row, click the first style—**Offset Diagonal Bottom Right**.

4 In the **Shape Styles group**, click the **Shape Outline button arrow**. In the fourth column, click the first color—**Dark Blue, Text 2** to change the color of the text box border.

5 Click the **Shape Outline button arrow** again, point to **Weight**, and then click **3 pt**.

6 Click anywhere in the document to deselect the text box. Notice that with the text box deselected, you can see all the measurements on the horizontal ruler.

7 Click anywhere in the text box and point to the text box border to display the pointer. By dragging, visually center the text box vertically and horizontally in the space below the *Rock Climbing 101* title. Then, if necessary, press any of the arrow keys on your keyboard to nudge the text box in precise increments to match Figure 1.18.

Figure 1.18

Text formatted and centered in text box, shadow added, border color and weight changed

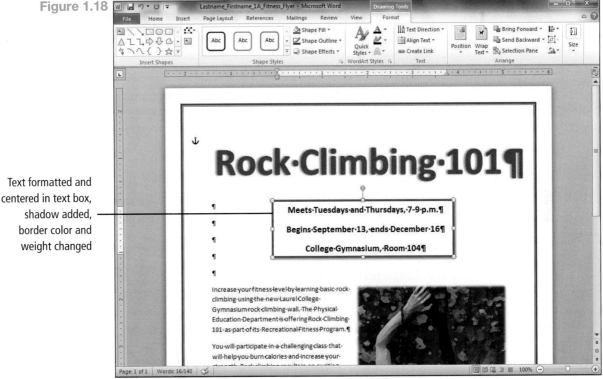

8 Press Ctrl + End to move to the bottom of the document. Click on the border of the rounded rectangular shape to select it.

9 On the **Format tab**, in the **Size group**, if necessary, click the **Size** button. Click the **Shape Height spin arrows** as necessary to change the height of the shape to **0.8″**.

10 In the **Shape Styles group**, click the **Shape Fill button arrow**, and then at the bottom of the gallery, point to **Gradient**. Under **Dark Variations**, in the third row click the first gradient—**Linear Diagonal - Bottom Left to Top Right**.

11 In the **Shape Styles group**, click the **Shape Outline button arrow**. In the sixth column, click the first color—**Red, Accent 2**.

12 Click the **Shape Outline button arrow** again, point to **Weight**, and then click **1 1/2 pt**. Click anywhere in the document to deselect the shape. Compare your screen with Figure 1.19, and then **Save** 🖫 your document.

Figure 1.19

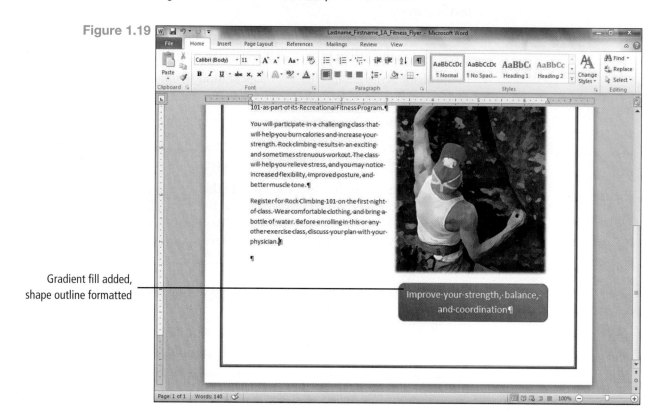

Gradient fill added, shape outline formatted

Objective 4 | Preview and Print a Document

While you are creating your document, it is useful to preview your document periodically to be sure that you are getting the result you want. Then, before printing, make a final preview to be sure the document layout is what you intended.

Activity 1.11 | Adding a File Name to the Footer

Information in headers and footers helps to identify a document when it is printed or displayed electronically. Recall that a header is information that prints at the top of every page; a footer is information that prints at the bottom of every page. In this textbook, you will insert the file name in the footer of every Word document.

Another Way

At the bottom edge of the page, right-click; from the shortcut menu, click Edit Footer.

1 Click the **Insert tab**, and then, in the **Header & Footer group**, click the **Footer** button.

2 At the bottom of the **Footer** gallery, click **Edit Footer**.

The footer area displays with the insertion point blinking at the left edge, and on the Ribbon, the Header & Footer Tools display and add the Design tab.

3 On the **Design tab**, in the **Insert group**, click the **Quick Parts** button, and then click **Field**. In the **Field** dialog box, under **Field names**, use the vertical scroll bar to examine the items that you can insert in a header or footer.

A *field* is a placeholder that displays preset content such as the current date, the file name, a page number, or other stored information.

4 In the **Field names** list, scroll as necessary to locate and then click **FileName**. Compare your screen with Figure 1.20.

Figure 1.20

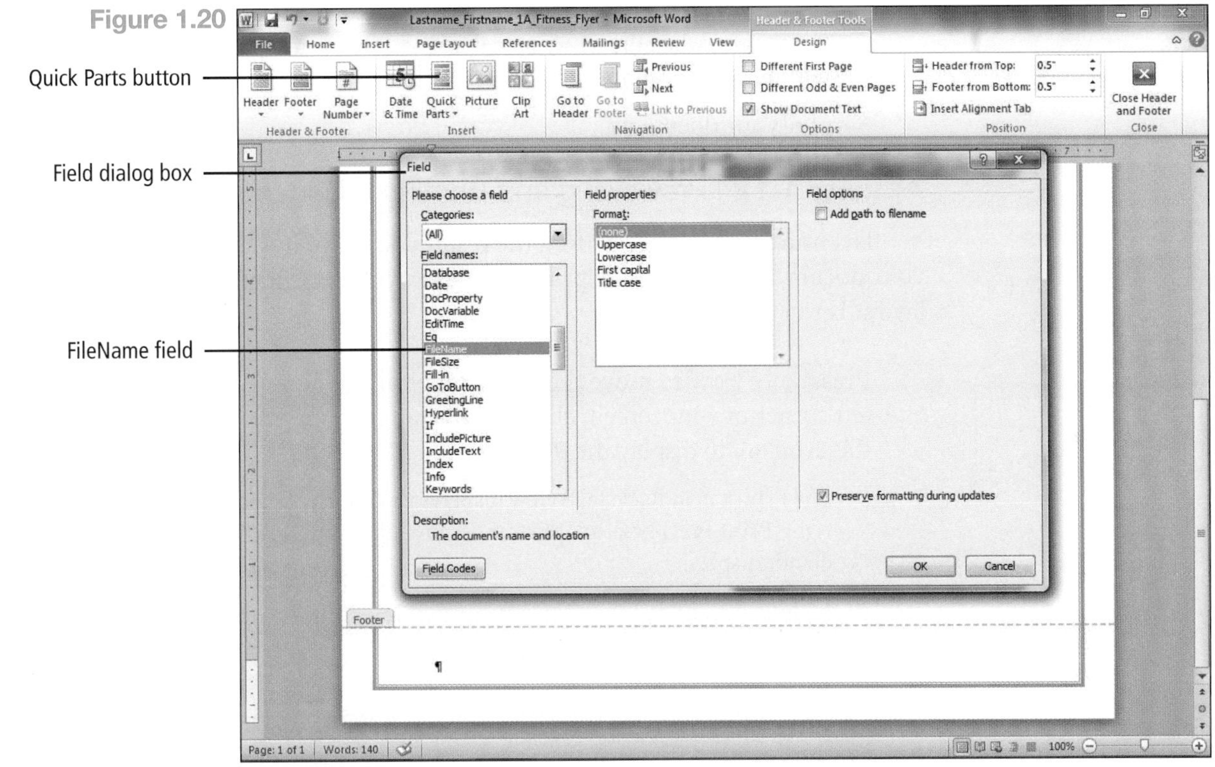

Quick Parts button

Field dialog box

FileName field

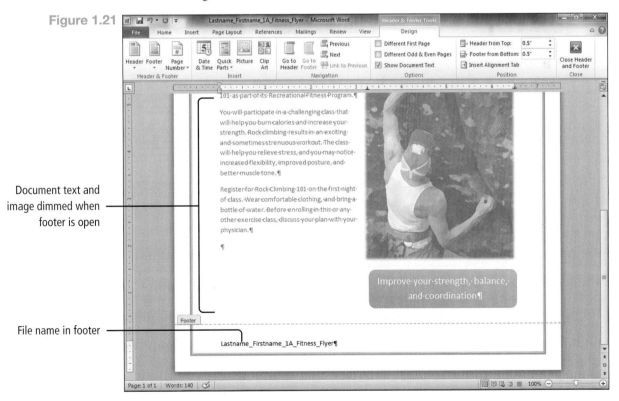

5 In the lower right corner of the **Field** dialog box, click **OK**, and then compare your screen with Figure 1.21.

Figure 1.21

Document text and image dimmed when footer is open

File name in footer

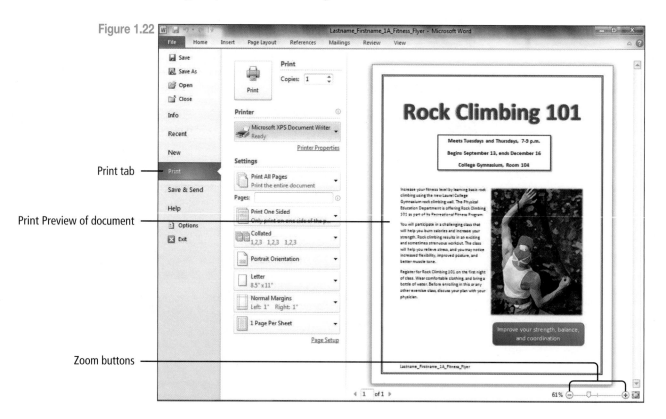

Another Way
Double-click anywhere in the document to close the footer area.

6 On the **Design tab**, at the far right in the **Close group**, click the **Close Header and Footer** button.

> When the body of the document is active, the footer text is dimmed—displays in gray. Conversely, when the footer area is active, the footer text is not dimmed; instead, the document text is dimmed.

7 **Save** 📄 your document.

Activity 1.12 | Previewing and Printing a Document

To ensure that you are getting the result you want, it is useful to periodically preview your document. Then, before printing, make a final preview to be sure the document layout is what you intended.

Another Way
Press Ctrl + F2 to display Print Preview.

1 Press Ctrl + Home to move the insertion point to the top of the document. In the upper left corner of your screen, click the **File tab** to display **Backstage** view, and then click the **Print tab** to display the **Print Preview**.

> The Print tab in Backstage view displays the tools you need to select your settings. On the right, Print Preview displays your document exactly as it will print; the formatting marks do not display.

2 In the lower right corner of the **Print Preview**, notice the zoom buttons that display. Compare your screen with Figure 1.22.

Figure 1.22

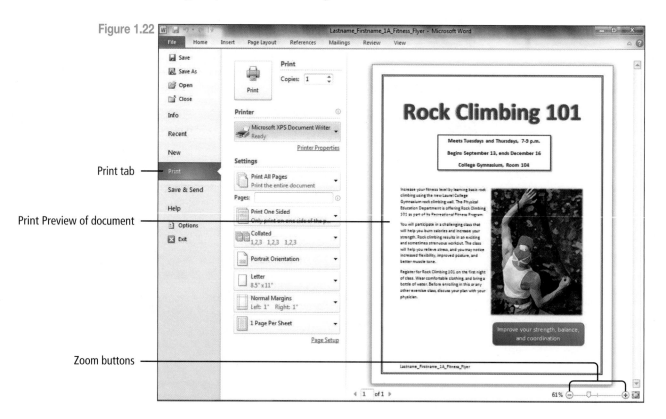

Print tab

Print Preview of document

Zoom buttons

3 Click the **Zoom In** button ⊕ to view the document at full size, and notice that a larger preview is easier to read. Click the **Zoom Out** button ⊖ to view the entire page.

4   Click the **Info tab**. On the right, under the screen thumbnail, click **Properties**, and then click **Show Document Panel**.

> Here you can adjust the document properties.

5   In the **Author** box, delete any text and then type your firstname and lastname. In the **Subject** box type your course name and section number, and in the **Keywords** box type **fitness, rock climbing Close** ☒ the Document Panel.

6   **Save** 🖫 your document. To print, display **Backstage** view, and then on the **navigation bar**, click **Print**. In the **Settings group**, be sure the correct printer is selected, and then in the **Print group**, click the **Print** button. Or, submit your document electronically as directed by your instructor.

7   In **Backstage** view, click **Exit** to close the document and exit Word.

End **You have completed Project 1A** —————————————————————

GO! Beyond Office

Objective | Create a Windows Live Account and Save a Document on Your SkyDrive

> **Alert! | Working with Web-Based Applications and Services**
>
> Computer programs and services on the Web receive continuous updates and improvements. Thus, the steps to complete this Web-based Activity may differ from the ones shown. You can often look at the screens and the information presented to determine how to complete the Activity.

Windows Live SkyDrive is a free file storage and file sharing service provided by *Windows Live*—a collection of programs and services for individuals. The programs include Hotmail e-mail, Live Messenger instant messaging, Photo Gallery, Movie Maker, the Office Web Apps, and mobile phone applications. Think about the Windows Live technologies as they relate to the *platform*—the underlying hardware or software for a system—on which you might use them; for example, on the Web, on your PC, or on your smartphone.

Activity | Creating a Windows Live Account and Saving a Document on Your SkyDrive

In this activity, you will create a Windows Live account if you do not already have one. Then you will create a folder on your Windows Live SkyDrive and upload your completed Lastname_Firstname_1A_Fitness_Flyer document into the folder. From SkyDrive, you can view and edit the file online, and also share the file with others if you want to do so.

1 Launch your Web browser, and navigate to **http://explore.live.com** View information about the various services within Windows Live.

2 If you already have a Windows Live account, go to Step 6. In the Windows Live window, point to **Home**, and then click **Get started**. Click **Sign up now**, click in the **Hotmail address** box, and then type the name you want to use as your Windows Live ID, for example **Firstname_Lastname** using the underscore instead of spaces. In the second box, click the arrow, and then click **live.com**.

The live.com designation is considered more current than the hotmail.com designation, although you can use either. The system will check the availability of your selected address. If the name that you typed is not available, experiment with variations using your middle initial, last name first, inserting an underscore, inserting a number, and so on, until you have a logical address that includes your name.

3 Create a password, and then type an alternate e-mail address or choose a security question for password reset.

4 Fill in the remainder of the form and the CAPTCHA, and then compare your screen with Figure A.

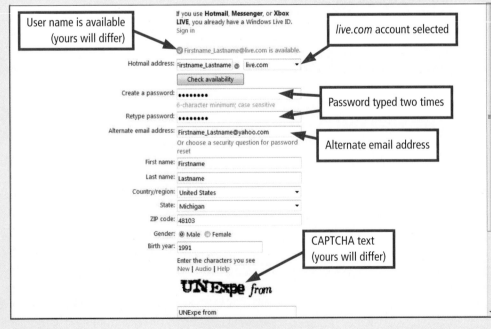

Figure A

GO! Beyond Office

A **CAPTCHA**, which is an acronym for Completely Automated Public Turing Test To Tell Computers and Humans Apart, is a program that protects Web sites against *bots* by generating and grading tests that humans can pass but current computer programs cannot. A bot—also known as an **Internet bot** or a **Web robot**—is a program that can run automated tasks over the Internet typically at a higher rate than would be possible for a human alone. Humans can read distorted text, like the text shown in Figure A, but current computers cannot.

5   At the bottom of the screen, click **I accept**.

Your new Windows Live site displays with your name in the upper right corner. The amount of storage space reserved for you displays below your name. Because this is a free set of applications, some advertising may display.

6   At the top of the screen, point to **SkyDrive**, and then click **Documents**.

A new SkyDrive has a single folder—My Documents—which is shared only with yourself until you indicate some other sharing arrangement.

7   Near the top of the screen, locate the icons for Word, Excel, PowerPoint, and OneNote. To the right of the OneNote icon, point to the **Folder** icon to display the ScreenTip *Create folder*, and then click one time. In the **Name** box, type **GO! Beyond Office-Word** and then click **Next**.

This action creates a new folder on your SkyDrive and opens the folder to enable you to add files. You can browse to locate files on your storage devices to add files to your SkyDrive, or you can upload a file to your SkyDrive from within a Microsoft application.

8   In the upper right corner of the Windows Live window, under your name, click **sign out**, and then **Close** your browser window.

If you are working at a public computer, for example in a classroom or lab, sign out of your Windows Live account. At your own computer, you can stay signed in.

9   From Windows Explorer, locate and open your completed **Lastname_Firstname_1A_Fitness_Flyer** document in Word. On the Ribbon, click the **File tab**, and then on the left, click **Save & Send**. Under **Save & Send**, click **Save to Web**. Notice that in the third panel, the **Save to Windows Live SkyDrive** section displays. Click the **Sign In** button, enter your Windows Live e-mail address and password in the **Connecting to docs.live.net** dialog box, and then click **OK**.

10   Double-click the **GO! Beyond Office-Word** folder. Wait a moment for the **Save As** dialog box to display, and then click **Save. Close** Word, go to **live.com**, sign in and display your **SkyDrive**, and then click the **GO! Beyond Office-Word** folder. Compare your screen with Figure B.

11   Display the **Start** menu, and then click **All Programs**. On the list of programs, click the **Accessories** folder, and then click **Snipping Tool**. In the **Snipping Tool** dialog box, click the **New arrow**. On the displayed list, click **Full-screen Snip**.

12   On the **Snipping Tool** markup window toolbar, click the **Save Snip** button. In the **Save As** dialog box, navigate to your USB drive and open the **Word Chapter 1** folder. Be sure the **Save as type** box displays **JPEG file**. In the **File name** box, using your own name, type **Lastname_Firstname_1A_SkyDrive_Snip** and then click **Save**. Close all open windows, and then submit the file as directed.

Figure B

Project 1B Information Handout

Project Activities

In Activities 1.13 through 1.23, you will format and add lists to an information handout that describes student activities at Laurel College. Your completed document will look similar to Figure 1.23.

Project Files

For Project 1B, you will need the following file:

w01B_Student_Activities

You will save your document as:

Lastname_Firstname_1B_Student_Activities

Project Results

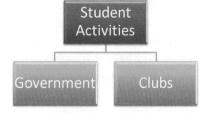

Every spring, students vote for the President, Vice President, Treasurer, Secretary, and Student Trustee for the following year. Executive Officers work with the college administration to manage campus activities and to make changes to policies and procedures. For example, the Student Trustee is a

...h consists of elected members from the
...college budget, and employee hiring.
...the Board to vote for a proposal to
...ocations in Laurelton and outlying areas.

...clubs and academic organizations vote for
...on information and applications on the
...mpus and in the student newspaper.

...f interests, including academic, political,
...currently in existence at Laurel College. A
...oin a club, you may enjoy being a member
...or you may decide to take a leadership role

...fice in the Campus Center, Room CC208, or
...d complete the form online. Clubs accept
...e following are the first meeting dates and

...October 8, 2:00 p.m., Room CC214
...ctober 5, 5:00 p.m., Computer Café
...7, 3:00 p.m., Field House, Room 2A
...October 6, 2:00 p.m., Room CC212
...6, 4:00 p.m., Math Tutoring Lab, L35
...October 8, 3:00 p.m., Room CC214
...4, 5:30 p.m., Photo Lab, Foster Hall
...........October 8, 5:00 p.m., Room L24
...October 7, 4:30 p.m., Room CC214
...October 4, 3:00 p.m., Little Theater

...listed here, are great, but your goals are
...ing a degree or certificate. Maybe you want
...ou leave Laurel College. Whatever your
...ur education, work experience, and
...lly ones in which you had a leadership role,

Associated Students of Laurel College

Get Involved in Student Activities

Your experience at Laurel College will be richer and more memorable if you get involved in activities that take you beyond the classroom. You will have the opportunity to meet other students, faculty, and staff members and will participate in organizations that make valuable contributions to your college and to the community.

Consider becoming involved in student government or joining a club. You might take part in activities such as these:

✓ Volunteering to help with a blood drive
✓ Traveling to a foreign country to learn about other cultures
✓ Volunteering to assist at graduation
✓ Helping to organize a community picnic
✓ Planning and implementing advertising for a student event
✓ Meeting with members of the state legislature to discuss issues that affect college students—for example, tuition costs and financial aid

Student Government

As a registered student, you are eligible to attend meetings of the Executive Officers of the Associated Students of Laurel College. At the meetings, you will have the opportunity to learn about college issues that affect students. At the conclusion of each meeting, the Officers invite students to voice their opinions. Eventually, you might decide to run for an office yourself. Running for office is a three-step process:

1. Pick up petitions at the Student Government office.
2. Obtain 100 signatures from current students.
3. Turn in petitions and start campaigning.

Lastname_Firstname_1B_Student_Activities

Figure 1.23
Project 1B Student Activities

Objective 5 | Change Document and Paragraph Layout

Document layout includes *margins*—the space between the text and the top, bottom, left, and right edges of the paper. Paragraph layout includes line spacing, indents, and tabs. In Word, the information about paragraph formats is stored in the paragraph mark at the end of a paragraph. When you press the Enter, the new paragraph mark contains the formatting of the previous paragraph, unless you take steps to change it.

Activity 1.13 | Setting Margins

1   **Start** Word. From **Backstage** view, display the **Open** dialog box. From your student files, locate and open the document **w01B_Student_Activities**. On the **Home tab**, in the **Paragraph group**, be sure the **Show/Hide** button ¶ is active—glows orange—so that you can view the formatting marks.

2   From **Backstage** view, display the **Save As** dialog box. Navigate to your **Word Chapter 1** folder, and then **Save** the document as **Lastname_Firstname_1B_Student_Activities**

3   Click the **Page Layout tab**. In the **Page Setup group**, click the **Margins** button, and then take a moment to study the buttons in the Margins gallery.

>   The top button displays the most recent custom margin settings, while the other buttons display commonly used margin settings.

4   At the bottom of the **Margins** gallery, click **Custom Margins**.

5   In the **Page Setup** dialog box, press Tab as necessary to select the value in the **Left** box, and then, with *1.25"* selected, type **1**

>   This action will change the left margin to 1 inch on all pages of the document. You do not need to type the inch (") mark.

6   Press Tab to select the margin in the **Right** box, and then type **1** At the bottom of the dialog box, notice that the new margins will apply to the **Whole document**. Compare your screen with Figure 1.24.

Figure 1.24

Margins button ——

Left and Right margins changed ——

Changes applied to entire document ——

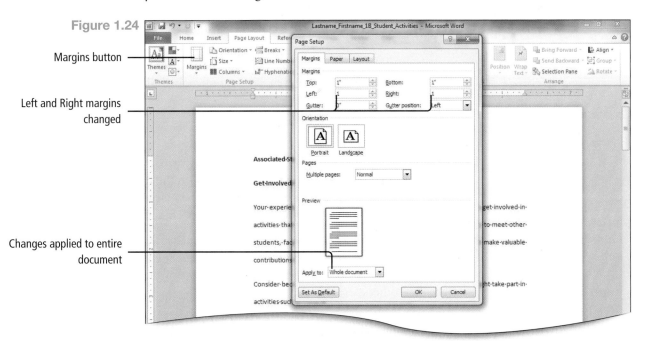

7 Click **OK** to apply the new margins and close the dialog box. If the ruler below the Ribbon is not displayed, at the top of the vertical scroll bar, click the View Ruler button ⌧.

8 Scroll to view the bottom of **Page 1** and the top of **Page 2**. Notice that the page edges display, and the page number and total number of pages display on the left side of the status bar.

9 Near the bottom edge of **Page 1**, point anywhere in the margin area, right-click, and then click **Edit Footer** to display the footer area.

10 On the **Design tab**, in the **Insert group**, click the **Quick Parts** button, and then click **Field**. In the **Field** dialog box, under **Field names**, locate and click **FileName**, and then click **OK**.

11 Double-click anywhere in the document to close the footer area, and then **Save** ⊟ your document.

Activity 1.14 | Aligning Text

Alignment refers to the placement of paragraph text relative to the left and right margins. Most paragraph text uses *left alignment*—aligned at the left margin, leaving the right margin uneven. Three other types of paragraph alignment are: *center alignment*—centered between the left and right margins; *right alignment*—aligned at the right margin with an uneven left margin; and *justified alignment*—text aligned evenly at both the left and right margins. See the table in Figure 1.25.

Paragraph Alignment Options		
Alignment	**Button**	**Description and Example**
Align Text Left	▤	Align Text Left is the default paragraph alignment in Word. Text in the paragraph aligns at the left margin, and the right margin is uneven.
Center	▤	Center alignment aligns text in the paragraph so that it is centered between the left and right margins.
Align Text Right	▤	Align Text Right aligns text at the right margin. Using Align Text Right, the left margin, which is normally even, is uneven.
Justify	▤	The Justify alignment option adds additional space between words so that both the left and right margins are even. Justify is often used when formatting newspaper-style columns.

Figure 1.25

1 Scroll to position the middle of **Page 2** on your screen, look at the left and right margins, and notice that the text is justified—both the right and left margins of multiple-line paragraphs are aligned evenly at the margins. On the **Home tab**, in the **Paragraph group**, notice that the **Justify** button ▤ is active.

2 In the paragraph that begins *Every spring, students vote*, in the first line, look at the space following the word *Every*, and then compare it with the space following the word *Trustee* in the second line. Notice how some of the spaces between words are larger than others.

> To achieve a justified right margin, Word adjusts the size of spaces between words in this manner, which can result in unattractive spacing in a document that spans the width of a page. Many individuals find such spacing difficult to read.

Another Way

On the Home tab, in the Editing group, click the Select button, and then click Select All.

3 Press Ctrl + A to select all of the text in the document, and then on the **Home tab**, in the **Paragraph group**, click the **Align Text Left** button ▤.

4 Press Ctrl + Home. At the top of the document, in the left margin area, point to the left of the first paragraph—*Associated Students of Laurel College*—until the ⌐⊿ pointer displays, and then click one time to select the paragraph. On the Mini toolbar, change the **Font Size** to **26**.

Use this technique to select entire lines of text.

5 Point to the left of the first paragraph—*Associated Students of Laurel College*—to display the ⌐⊿ pointer again, and then drag down to select the first two paragraphs, which form the title and subtitle of the document.

6 On the Mini toolbar, click the **Center** button ▤ to center the title and subtitle between the left and right margins, and then compare your screen with Figure 1.26.

Figure 1.26

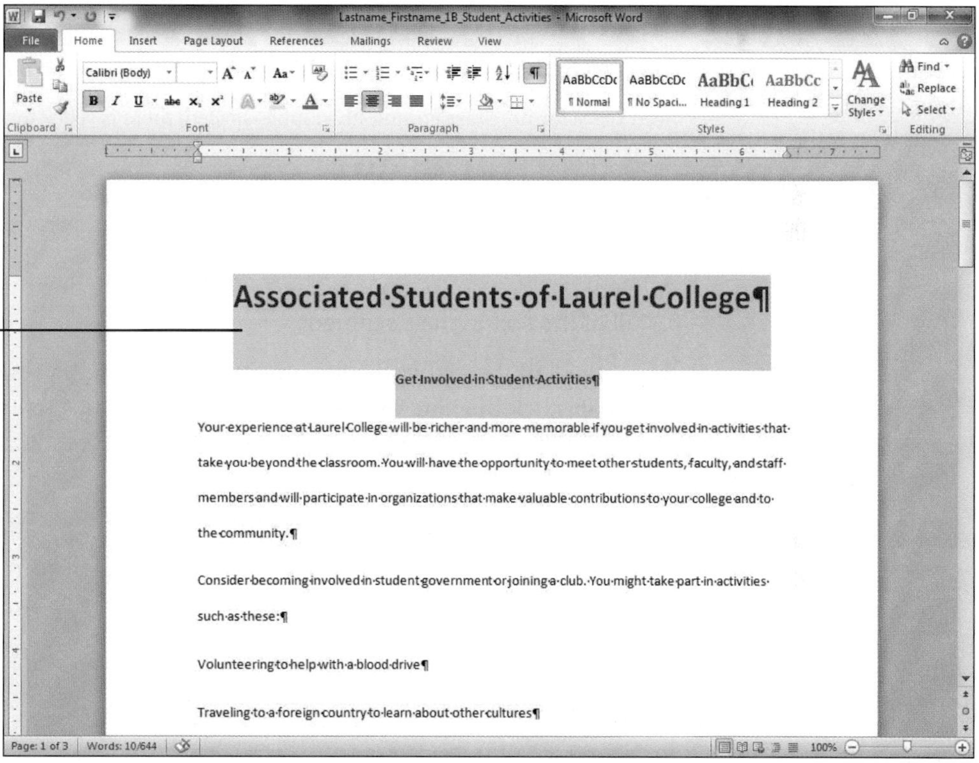

Title centered and font size set to 26

7 Scroll down to view the bottom of **Page 1**, and then locate the first bold subheading—*Student Government*. Point to the left of the paragraph to display the ⌐⊿ pointer, and then click one time.

8 With *Student Government* selected, use your mouse wheel or the vertical scroll bar to bring the lower portion of **Page 2** into view. Locate the subheading *Clubs*. Move the pointer to the left of the paragraph to display the ⌐⊿ pointer, hold down Ctrl, and then click one time.

Two subheadings are selected; in Windows-based programs, you can hold down Ctrl to select multiple items.

9 On the Mini toolbar, click the **Center** button ▤ to center both subheadings, and then click **Save** 🖫.

Activity 1.15 | Changing Line Spacing

Line spacing is the distance between lines of text in a paragraph. Three of the most commonly used line spacing options are shown in the table in Figure 1.27.

Line Spacing Options	
Alignment	**Description, Example, and Information**
Single spacing	**This text in this example uses single spacing**. Single spacing was once the most commonly used spacing in business documents. Now, because so many documents are read on a computer screen rather than on paper, single spacing is becoming less popular.
Multiple 1.15 spacing	**This text in this example uses multiple 1.15 spacing**. The default line spacing in Microsoft Word 2010 is 1.15, which is equivalent to single spacing with an extra 1/6 line added between lines to make the text easier to read on a computer screen. Many individuals now prefer this spacing, even on paper, because the lines of text appear less crowded.
Double spacing	**This text in this example uses double spacing**. College research papers and draft documents that need space for notes are commonly double-spaced; there is space for a full line of text between each document line.

Figure 1.27

1 Press [Ctrl] + [Home] to move to the beginning of the document. Press [Ctrl] + [A] to select all of the text in the document.

2 With all of the text in the document selected, on the **Home tab**, in the **Paragraph group**, click the **Line Spacing** button, and notice that the text in the document is double spaced—**2.0** is checked. Compare your screen with Figure 1.28.

Figure 1.28

Document text double-spaced

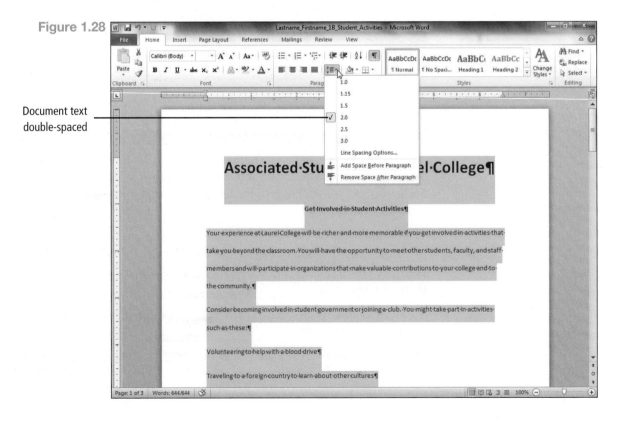

3 On the **Line Spacing** menu, click the *second* setting—**1.15**—and then click anywhere in the document. Compare your screen with Figure 1.29, and then **Save** 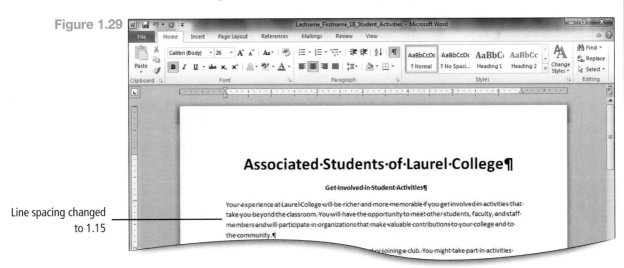 your document.

> Double spacing is most commonly used in research papers and rough draft documents. Recall that 1.15 is the default line spacing for new Word documents. Line spacing of 1.15 has slightly more space between the lines than single spacing. On a computer screen, spacing of 1.15 is easier to read than single spacing. Because a large percentage of Word documents are read on a computer screen, 1.15 is the default spacing for a new Word document.

Figure 1.29

Line spacing changed to 1.15

Activity 1.16 | Indenting Text and Adding Space After Paragraphs

Common techniques to distinguish paragraphs include adding space after each paragraph, indenting the first line of each paragraph, or both.

1 Below the title and subtitle of the document, click anywhere in the paragraph that begins *Your experience*.

2 On the **Home tab**, in the **Paragraph group**, click the **Dialog Box Launcher** .

3 In the **Paragraph** dialog box, on the **Indents and Spacing tab**, under **Indentation**, click the **Special arrow**, and then click **First line** to indent the first line by 0.5″, which is the default indent setting. Compare your screen with Figure 1.30.

Figure 1.30

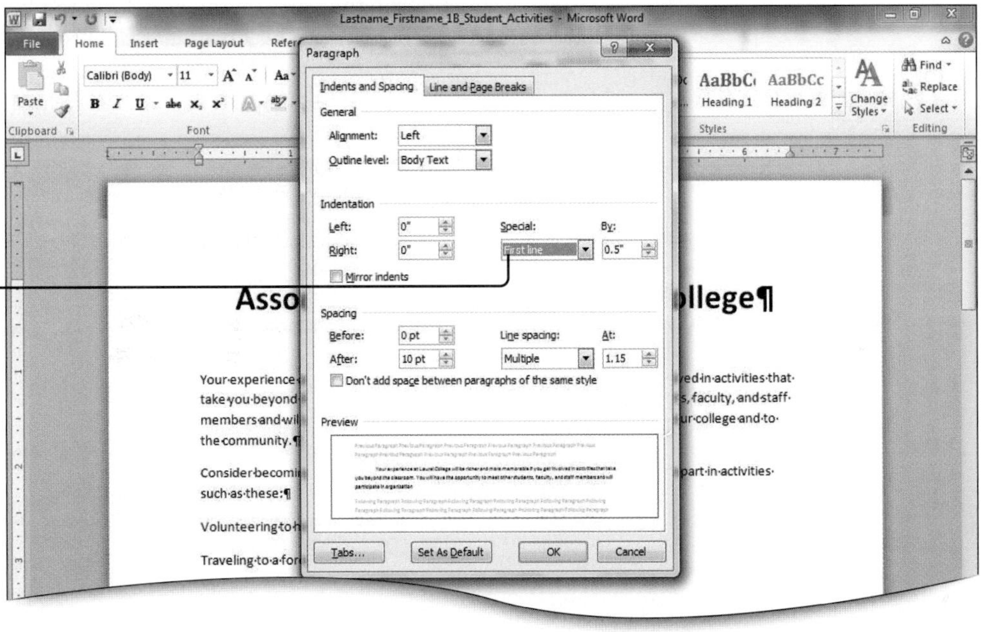

First line indent applied

4 Click **OK**, and then click anywhere in the next paragraph, which begins *Consider becoming*. On the ruler under the Ribbon, drag the **First Line Indent** button ▽ to **0.5 inches on the horizontal ruler**, and then compare your screen with Figure 1.31.

Figure 1.31

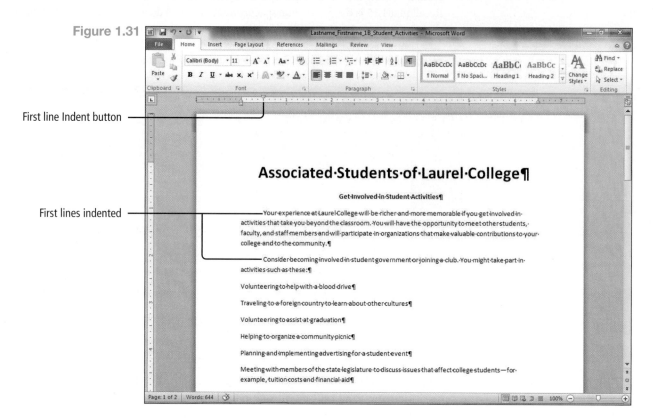

First line Indent button

First lines indented

5 By using either of the techniques you just practiced, or by using the Format Painter, apply a first line indent of **0.5"** in the paragraph that begins *As a registered* to match the indent of the remaining paragraphs in the document.

Another Way

On either the Home tab or the Page Layout tab, display the Paragraph dialog box from the Paragraph group, and then under Spacing, click the spin box arrows as necessary.

6 Press Ctrl + A to select all of the text in the document. Click the **Page Layout tab**, and then in the **Paragraph group**, under **Spacing**, click the **After spin box down arrow** one time to change the value to **6 pt**.

> To change the value in the box, you can also select the existing number, type a new number, and then press Enter. This document will use 6 pt spacing after paragraphs.

7 Press Ctrl + Home, and then compare your screen with Figure 1.32.

Figure 1.32

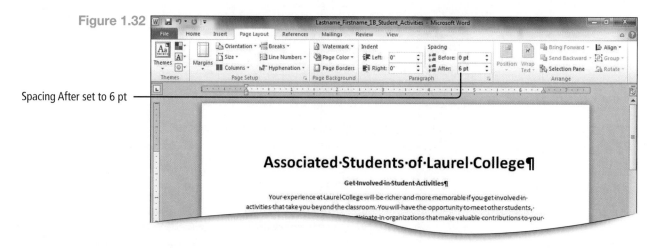

Spacing After set to 6 pt

8   Scroll to view the lower portion of **Page 1**. Select the subheading *Student Government*, including the paragraph mark following it, hold down Ctrl, and then select the subheading *Clubs*.

9   With both subheadings selected, in the **Paragraph group**, under **Spacing**, click the **Before up spin box arrow** two times to set the **Spacing Before** to **12 pt**. Compare your screen with Figure 1.33, and then **Save** 🖫 your document.

> This action increases the amount of space above each of the two subheadings, which will make them easy to distinguish in the document. The formatting is applied only to the two selected paragraphs.

Figure 1.33

Spacing before set to 12 pt.

12-point spacing before paragraphs

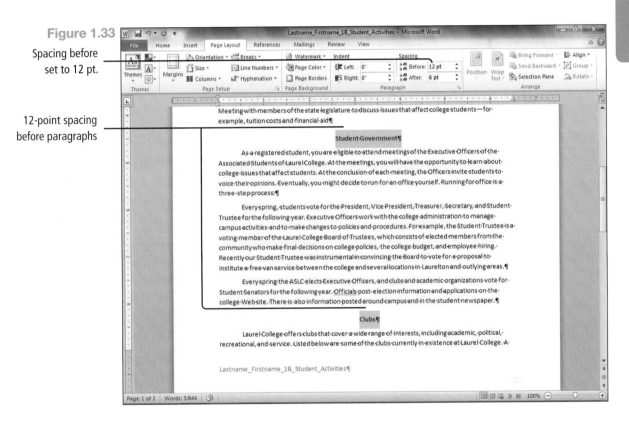

Objective 6 | Create and Modify Lists

To display a list of information, you can choose a ***bulleted list***, which uses ***bullets***—text symbols such as small circles or check marks—to introduce each item in a list. You can also choose a ***numbered list***, which uses consecutive numbers or letters to introduce each item in a list.

Use a bulleted list if the items in the list can be introduced in any order; use a numbered list for items that have definite steps, a sequence of actions, or are in chronological order.

Activity 1.17 | Creating a Bulleted List

1   In the upper portion of **Page 1**, locate the paragraph that begins *Volunteering to help*, and then point to this paragraph from the left margin area to display the 🔏 pointer. Drag down to select this paragraph and the next five paragraphs.

2 On the **Home tab**, in the **Paragraph group**, click the **Bullets** button ⊞▾ to change the selected text to a bulleted list.

> The spacing between each of the bulleted points changes to the spacing between lines in a paragraph—in this instance, 1.15 line spacing. The spacing after the last item in the list is the same as the spacing after each paragraph—in this instance, 6 pt. Each bulleted item is automatically indented.

3 On the ruler, point to the **First Line Indent** button ▽ and read the ScreenTip, and then point to the **Hanging Indent** button ▽. Compare your screen with Figure 1.34.

> By default, Word formats bulleted items with a first line indent of 0.25″ and adds a Hanging Indent at 0.5″. The hanging indent maintains the alignment of text when a bulleted item is more than one line, for example, the last bulleted item in this list.

Figure 1.34

Hanging Indent button on ruler

Bulleted list

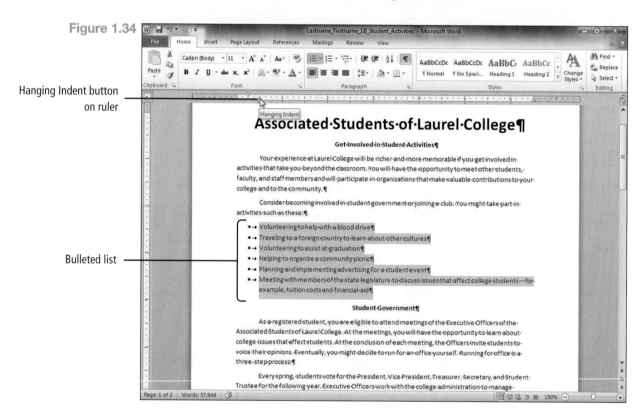

4 Scroll down to view **Page 2**. By using the 🖉 pointer from the left margin area, select all of the paragraphs that indicate the club names and meeting dates, beginning with *Chess Club* and ending with *Theater Club*.

5 In the **Paragraph group**, click the **Bullets** button ⊞▾, and then **Save** 🖫 your document.

Activity 1.18 | Creating a Numbered List

1 Scroll to view **Page 1**, and then under the subheading *Student Government*, in the paragraph that begins *As a registered student*, click to position the insertion point at the *end* of the paragraph following the colon. Press Enter to create a blank paragraph.

2 Notice that the paragraph is indented, because the First Line Indent from the previous paragraph carried over to the new paragraph.

3 To change the indent formatting for this paragraph, on the ruler, drag the **First Line Indent** button to the left so that it is positioned directly above the lower button. Compare your screen with Figure 1.35.

Figure 1.35

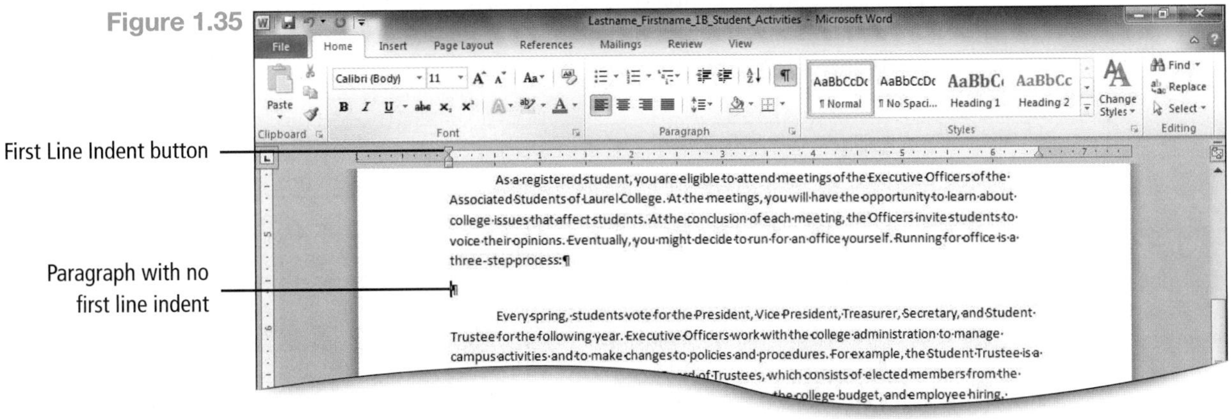

First Line Indent button

Paragraph with no first line indent

4 Being sure to include the period, type **1.** and press Spacebar.

Word determines that this paragraph is the first item in a numbered list and formats the new paragraph accordingly, indenting the list in the same manner as the bulleted list. The space after the number changes to a tab, and the AutoCorrect Options button displays to the left of the list item. The tab is indicated by a right arrow formatting mark.

Alert! | Activating Automatic Numbered Lists

If a numbered list does not begin automatically, display Backstage view, and then click the Options tab. On the left side of the Word Options dialog box, click Proofing. Under AutoCorrect options, click the AutoCorrect Options button. In the AutoCorrect dialog box, click the AutoFormat As You Type tab. Under *Apply as you type*, select the *Automatic numbered lists* check box, and then click OK two times to close both dialog boxes.

---

5 Click the **AutoCorrect Options** button, and then compare your screen with Figure 1.36.

From the displayed list, you can remove the automatic formatting here, or stop using the automatic numbered lists option in this document. You also have the option to open the AutoCorrect dialog box to *Control AutoFormat Options*.

Figure 1.36

AutoCorrect Options button

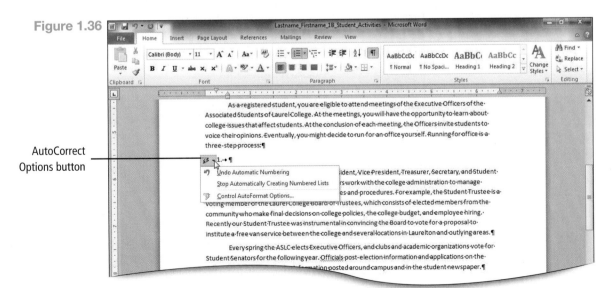

6 Click the **AutoCorrect Options** button again to close the menu without selecting any of the commands. Type **Pick up petitions at the Student Government office.** and press Enter. Notice that the second number and a tab are added to the next line.

7 Type **Obtain 100 signatures from current students.** and press Enter. Type **Turn in petitions and start campaigning.** and press Enter. Compare your screen with Figure 1.37.

Figure 1.37

Numbered list

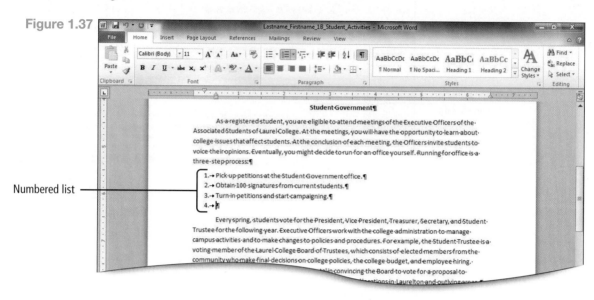

8 Press ←Bksp to turn off the list numbering. Then, press ←Bksp three more times to remove the blank paragraph. Compare your screen with Figure 1.38.

Figure 1.38

Three items in the list, item 4 deleted

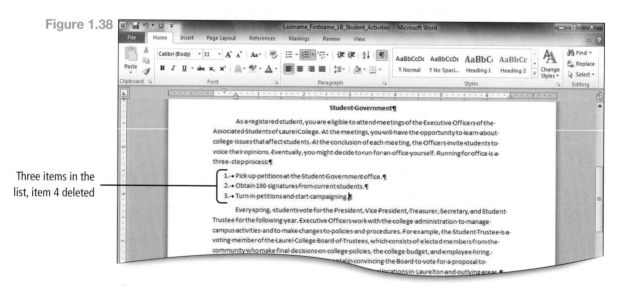

9 **Save** your document.

More Knowledge | **To End a List**

To turn a list off, you can press ←Bksp, click the Numbering or Bullets button, or press Enter a second time. Both list buttons—Numbering and Bullets—act as *toggle buttons*; that is, clicking the button one time turns the feature on, and clicking the button again turns the feature off.

Activity 1.19 | Customizing Bullets

1 Press Ctrl + End to move to the end of the document, and then scroll up as necessary to display the bulleted list containing the list of clubs.

2 Point to the left of the first list item to display the ⬚ pointer, and then drag down to select all the clubs in the list—the bullet symbols are not highlighted.

3 Point to the selected list and right-click. From the shortcut menu, point to **Bullets**, and then compare your screen with Figure 1.39.

Figure 1.39

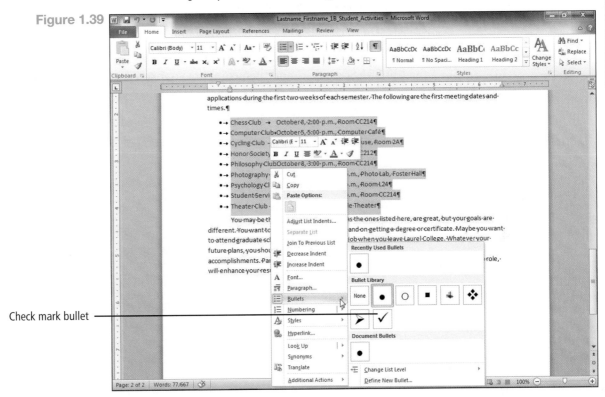

Check mark bullet

4 Under **Bullet Library**, click the **check mark** symbol. If the check mark is not available, choose another bullet symbol.

5 With the bulleted list still selected, right-click over the list, and then on the Mini toolbar, click the **Format Painter** button ⬚.

6 Use the vertical scroll bar or your mouse wheel to scroll to view **Page 1**. Move the pointer to the left of the first item in the bulleted list to display the ⬚ pointer, and then drag down to select all of the items in the list and to apply the format of the second bulleted list to this list. Compare your screen with Figure 1.40, and then **Save** ⬚ your document.

Figure 1.40

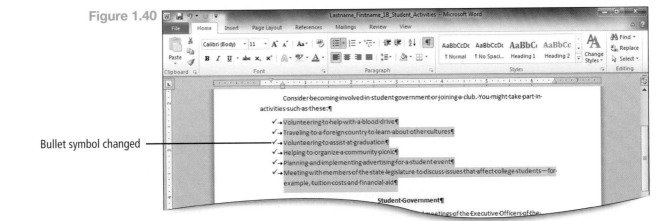

Bullet symbol changed

Objective 7 | Set and Modify Tab Stops

Tab stops mark specific locations on a line of text. Use tab stops to indent and align text, and use the Tab key to move to tab stops.

Activity 1.20 | Setting Tab Stops

1 Scroll to view the middle of **Page 2**, and then by using the ⟦☝⟧ pointer at the left of the first item, select all of the items in the bulleted list. Notice that there is a tab mark between the name of the club and the date.

> The arrow that indicates a tab is a nonprinting formatting mark.

2 To the left of the horizontal ruler, point to the **Tab Alignment** button ⟦L⟧ to display the *Left Tab* ScreenTip, and then compare your screen with Figure 1.41.

Figure 1.41

Tab Alignment button —
Left Tab ScreenTip —

Tab mark —

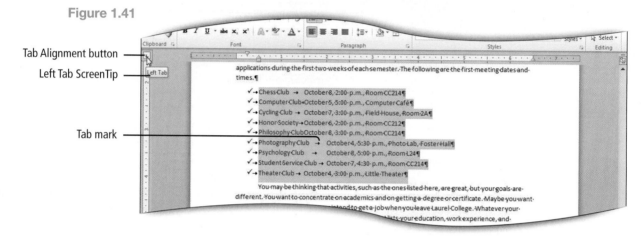

3 Click the **Tab Alignment** button ⟦L⟧ several times to view the tab alignment options shown in the table in Figure 1.42.

Tab Alignment Options

Type	Tab Alignment Button Displays This Marker	Description
Left	⟦L⟧	Text is left aligned at the tab stop and extends to the right.
Center	⟦⊥⟧	Text is centered around the tab stop.
Right	⟦⅃⟧	Text is right aligned at the tab stop and extends to the left.
Decimal	⟦⊥⟧	The decimal point aligns at the tab stop.
Bar	⟦|⟧	A vertical bar displays at the tab stop.
First Line Indent	⟦▽⟧	Text in the first line of a paragraph indents.
Hanging Indent	⟦△⟧	Text in all lines except the first line in the paragraph indents.
Left Indent	⟦⊔⟧	Moves both the First Line Indent and Hanging Indent buttons.

Figure 1.42

4 Display the **Left Tab** button ⟦L⟧. Along the lower edge of the horizontal ruler, point to and then click at **3 inches on the horizontal ruler**. Notice that all of the dates left align at the new tab stop location, and the right edge of the column is uneven.

5 Compare your screen with Figure 1.43, and then **Save** 🖫 your document.

Figure 1.43

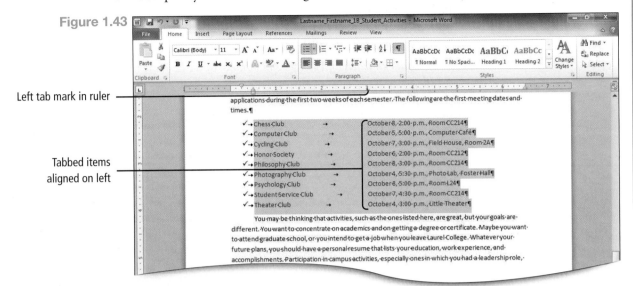

Left tab mark in ruler

Tabbed items aligned on left

Activity 1.21 | Modifying Tab Stops

Tab stops are a form of paragraph formatting, and thus, the information about tab stops is stored in the paragraph mark in the paragraphs to which they were applied.

1 With the bulleted list still selected, on the ruler, point to the new tab marker, and then when the *Left Tab* ScreenTip displays, drag the tab marker to **3.5 inches on the horizontal ruler**.

In all of the selected lines, the text at the tab stop left aligns at 3.5 inches.

> **Another Way**
>
> On the Home tab, in the Paragraph group, click the Dialog Box Launcher. At the bottom of the Paragraph dialog box, click the Tabs button.

2 On the ruler, point to the tab marker to display the ScreenTip, and then double-click to display the **Tabs** dialog box.

3 In the **Tabs** dialog box, under **Tab stop position**, if necessary select *3.5″* and then type **6**

4 Under **Alignment**, click the **Right** option button. Under **Leader**, click the **2** option button. Near the bottom of the **Tabs** dialog box, click **Set**.

Because the Right tab will be used to align the items in the list, the tab stop at 3.5″ is no longer necessary.

5 In the **Tabs** dialog box, in the **Tab stop position** box, click **3.5″** to select this tab stop, and then in the lower portion of the **Tabs** dialog box, click the **Clear** button to delete this tab stop, which is no longer necessary. Compare your screen with Figure 1.44.

Figure 1.44

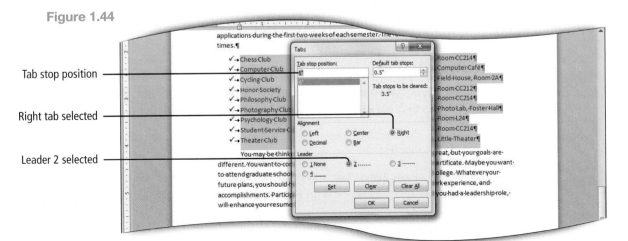

Tab stop position

Right tab selected

Leader 2 selected

6 Click **OK**. On the ruler, notice that the left tab marker at *3.5″* no longer displays, a right tab marker displays at *6″*, and a series of dots—a **dot leader**—displays between the columns of the list. Notice also that the right edge of the column is even. Compare your screen with Figure 1.45.

> A **leader character** creates a solid, dotted, or dashed line that fills the space to the left of a tab character and draws the reader's eyes across the page from one item to the next. When the character used for the leader is a dot, it is commonly referred to as a dot leader.

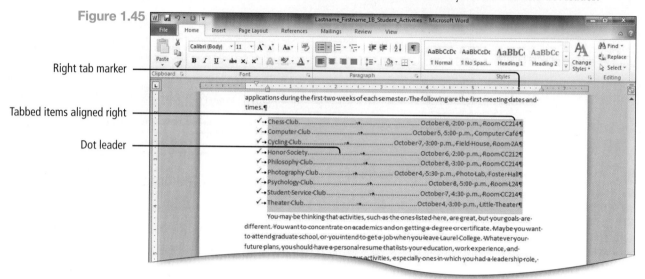

Figure 1.45

Right tab marker

Tabbed items aligned right

Dot leader

7 In the bulleted list that uses dot leaders, locate the *Honor Society* item, and then click to position the insertion point at the end of that line. Press [Enter] to create a new blank bullet item.

8 Type **Math Club** and press [Tab]. Notice that a dot leader fills the space to the tab marker location.

9 Type **October 6, 4:00 p.m., Math Tutoring Lab, L35** and notice that the text moves to the left to maintain the right alignment of the tab stop.

10 Save [💾] your document.

Objective 8 | Insert a SmartArt Graphic

SmartArt graphics are designer-quality visual representations of information, and Word provides many different layouts from which you can choose. A SmartArt graphic can communicate your messages or ideas more effectively than plain text and adds visual interest to a document or Web page.

Activity 1.22 | Inserting a SmartArt Graphic

1 Press [Ctrl] + [Home] to move to the top of the document. Press [End] to move to the end of the first paragraph—the title—and then press [Enter] to create a blank paragraph.

> Because the paragraph above is 26 pt font size, the new paragraph mark displays in that size.

2 Click the **Insert tab**, and then in the **Illustrations group**, point to the **SmartArt** button to display its ScreenTip. Read the ScreenTip, and then click the button.

3 In the center portion of the **Choose a SmartArt Graphic** dialog box, scroll down and examine the numerous types of SmartArt graphics available.

4 On the left, click **Hierarchy**, and then in the first row, click the first graphic— **Organization Chart**.

> At the right of the dialog box, a preview and description of the graphic displays.

5 Compare your screen with Figure 1.46.

Figure 1.46

SmartArt button

Preview of selected SmartArt

Hierarchy category

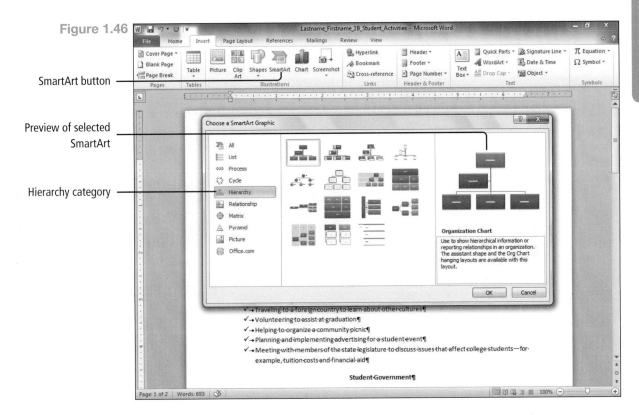

6 Click **OK**. If the pane indicating *Type your text here* does not display on the left side of the graphic, on the Design tab, in the Create Graphic group, click the Text Pane button. **Save** your document.

> The SmartArt graphic displays at the insertion point location and consists of two parts— the graphic itself, and the Text Pane. On the Ribbon, the SmartArt Tools add the Design tab and the Format tab. You can type directly into the graphics, or type in the Text Pane. By typing in the Text Pane, you might find it easier to organize your layout.

Activity 1.23 | Modifying a SmartArt Graphic

1 In the SmartArt graphic, in the second row, click the border of the *[Text]* box to display a *solid* border and sizing handles, and then press Del. Repeat this procedure in the bottom row to delete the middle *[Text]* box.

Another Way

Close the Text Pane and type the text directly in the SmartArt boxes.

2 In the **Text Pane**, click in the top bulleted point, and then type **Student Activities** Notice that the first bulleted point aligns further to the left than the other points.

> The *top-level points* are the main points in a SmartArt graphic. *Subpoints* are indented second-level bullet points.

3 Press ⬇. Type **Government** and then press ⬇ again. Type **Clubs** and then compare your screen with Figure 1.47.

Figure 1.47

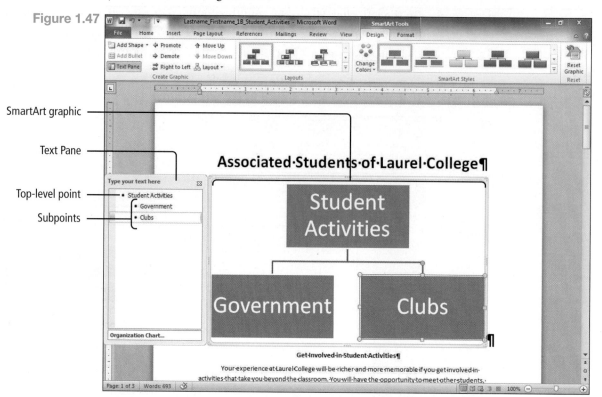

SmartArt graphic

Text Pane

Top-level point

Subpoints

4 In the upper right corner of the **Text Pane**, click the **Close** button 🗙.

5 Click the border of the SmartArt graphic—a pale border surrounds it. Click the **Format tab**, and then in the **Size group**, if necessary, click the **Size** button to display the **Shape Height** and **Shape Width** boxes.

6 Set the **Height** to **2.5″** and the **Width** to **4.2″**, and then compare your screen with Figure 1.48.

Figure 1.48

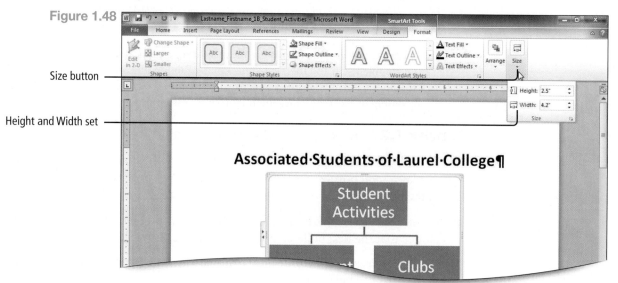

Size button

Height and Width set

7 With the SmartArt graphic still selected, click the **Design tab**, and then in the **SmartArt Styles group**, click the **Change Colors** button. Under **Colorful**, click the second style—**Colorful Range - Accent Colors 2 to 3**.

8 On the **Design tab**, in the **SmartArt Styles group**, click the **More** button ⬇. Under **3-D**, click the first style—**Polished**. Compare your screen with Figure 1.49.

Figure 1.49

Polished style selected ——

SmartArt color and style changed ——

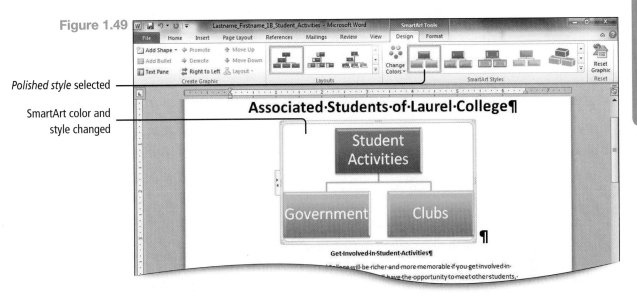

9 Click outside of the graphic to deselect it. Display **Backstage** view. On the right, under the screen thumbnail, click **Properties**, and then click **Show Document Panel**. In the **Author** box, delete any text and then type your firstname and lastname. In the **Subject** box, type your course name and section number, and in the **Keywords** box type **Student Activities, Associated Students Close** ☒ the Document Panel and **Save** 💾 your document.

10 Display **Backstage** view, and then click **Print** to display **Print Preview**. At the bottom of the preview, click the **Next Page** ▶ and **Previous Page** ◀ buttons to move between pages. If necessary, return to the document and make any necessary changes.

11 As directed by your instructor, print your document or submit it electronically. **Close** ☒ Word.

More Knowledge | Changing the Bullet Level in a SmartArt Graphic

To increase or decrease the level of an item, on the Design tab, in the Create Graphic group, click either the Promote or the Demote button.

End **You have completed Project 1B**

GO! Beyond Office

Objective | Download Windows Live Essentials Programs and Post a Document to a Blog

Windows Live Essentials is a set of free programs available on the Microsoft Web site, including programs that enable you to organize and edit photos, edit and publish videos, stay in touch with your friends, create an e-mail account, publish a document to a blog, and customize your Web browser. You can download all of the programs at one time, or download the programs one at a time as you need them.

> **Alert!** | **Working with Web-Based Applications and Services**
>
> Computer programs and services on the Web receive continuous updates and improvements. Thus, the steps to complete this Web-based Activity may differ from the ones shown. You can often look at the screens and the information presented to determine how to complete the Activity.

Activity | Downloading Windows Live Essentials Programs and Posting a Document to a Blog

In this activity, you will download several Windows Live Essentials programs, and then you will use Windows Live Writer to create a blog entry using the WordPress blog service.

1 From the **Start** menu 🌐, click **All Programs**, click the **Accessories** folder, and then click **Getting Started**. In the **Getting Started** dialog box, double-click **Go online to get Windows Live Essentials**. Scroll down to view the list of available programs.

2 Scroll to the top of the window, and then click the **Download now** button. In the displayed message box, click **Run**. If a User Account Control dialog box displays, click Yes. Wait a moment, and then in the **Windows Live Essentials** dialog box, under **What do you want to install?**, click **Choose the programs you want to install**.

3 Click to *clear* all of the check boxes *except* **Photo Gallery** and **Movie Maker** and **Writer**, and then compare your screen with Figure A.

4 Click **Install**. If other programs are open, a message box may ask you to close them; follow the instructions to close the programs. Wait for the program installation to complete. **Close** ✖ all open dialog boxes and windows.

5 From the **Start** menu 🌐, click **All Programs**. Notice that two of the three programs you downloaded— Photo Gallery and Movie Maker—display in the list of programs.

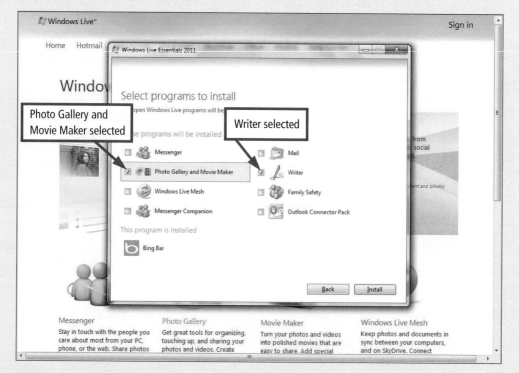

Figure A

The new programs display with a shaded background, indicating that they are recently installed and have not yet been used.

6 Click **Windows Live Photo Gallery** to open the program.

The Windows Live Photo Gallery program—like Microsoft Word that you used in this chapter—includes a Ribbon, tabs, and groups of commands on each tab. The navigation pane on the left side of the screen displays the folders in your Pictures and Videos libraries. The pictures that display on the right will depend on the pictures stored in those libraries.

7 **Close** 🖼 Photo Gallery. From the **Start** menu 🪟, click **All Programs**. Scroll to the bottom of the list, click the **Windows Live** folder, and then click **Windows Live Writer**.

Windows Live Writer is a simple word processor. Its only function is to create blog entries that you can post on blog services. A *blog* is a web log to express your opinions, show pictures and videos, keep an ongoing diary, or post links to sites that you find interesting. Friends, colleagues, coworkers, and others can read your blog and comment on your postings. A *blog service* is a Web site that provides space to which you can post your blogs.

8 In the **Windows Live Writer** dialog box, read the text, and then click **Next**.

Before you can use Windows Live Writer, you must set up the program, which includes designating a blog service that you can use to post your blogs. In this project, you will set up an account with WordPress. If you already

subscribe to a blog service, you can use that instead; in that case, follow the instructions from your blog service.

9 In the **Windows Live Writer** dialog box, be sure the **Create a new blog** option button is selected, and then click **Next**.

10 In the **Windows Live Writer** dialog box, click the **www.WordPress.com** link.

11 Under **Step 1**, click the **Connect** button. In the **Connect to Messenger** dialog box, click **No thanks**.

If you have a Windows Live Messenger account, you can link that account to WordPress, which makes it easy to communicate and share information with your friends and colleagues.

12 In the **Create your WordPress.com account** window, enter the required information. When you have finished, be sure to select the **Legal Flotsam** check box—you cannot proceed without agreeing to the WordPress terms of service—and then, take a moment to read the terms by clicking on the *fascinating terms of service* link. Compare your screen with Figure B.

Be sure you use only lowercase letters for your username.

13 In the **Create your WordPress.com account** window, click **Next**.

All of the information you need to run your blog displays, including the Web address your friends can use to access your blog.

14 Write down your new username, Web address, and password. Then, near the bottom of the **Create your**

Figure B

GO! Beyond Office

WordPress.com account window, under **Privacy**, click the **Private: My blog should be visible only to users I choose** option button. Compare your screen with Figure C.

WordPress gives you several privacy options. You can make your blog public, which will enable anyone to search for text in your blog or to search for your blog name. You can choose to prohibit the use of search engines to find your blog, or you can restrict access to your blog to those people you choose, although this means that each user will have to log in using a user name and password.

15 At the bottom of the **Create your WordPress.com account** window, click **Signup**.

A *Check Your E-mail to Complete Registration* window displays. In order to complete the sign-up procedure you must check your e-mail, and then activate your account. It may take up to 30 minutes for the e-mail to reach your inbox, although the e-mail typically arrives within a minute after you click the activation link. If you do not activate the account within two days, the account will be removed and you will have to start the procedure over again.

16 Open your e-mail account, and in the inbox, locate and click the message from **WordPress**. Click the link in the message to activate the account.

Your account is activated, and the WordPress dashboard opens. You can write your blogs using either the WordPress dashboard or using Windows Live Writer.

You can update your profile information if you want to do so, although it is good practice not to put too much personal information in your profile.

17 **Close** your browser and close any other open windows. From the **Start** menu, locate and click **Windows Live Writer**, and then click **Next**.

The final setup procedure links Windows Live Writer and the blog service of your choice—in this instance, WordPress.

18 In the **Windows Live Writer** dialog box, click the **WordPress** option button, and then click **Next**. Under **Add a blog account**, fill out the **Web address**, **User name**, and **Password** of your new account, and then click **Next**.

19 If necessary, click the *Type of blog that you are using* arrow and select WordPress.com. Then, replace *<blogname>* with the blog name you chose when you set up your account—be sure to delete < and >.

20 In the **Download Blog Theme** dialog box, click **No**. When the blog is set up, make a note of your blog nickname, and then click **Finish** to open Windows Live Writer.

21 Click in the **Enter a post title** box, type **New Student Activities Flyer** and then click below the text you just typed.

22 From Windows Explorer, navigate to and open your completed **Lastname_Firstname_1B_Student_Activities** document. Press [Ctrl] + [A] to select the entire document.

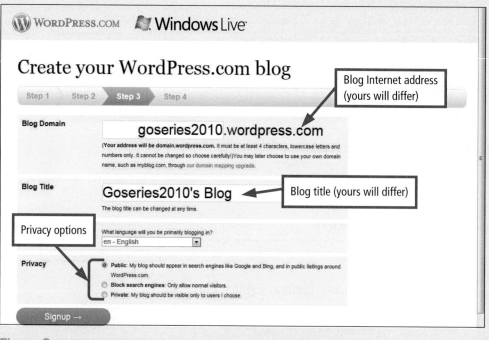

Figure C

GO! Beyond Office

On the **Home tab**, in the **Clipboard group**, click the **Copy** button—*do not use the keyboard shortcut to copy the text.*

23 Switch to **Windows Live Writer**, and then on the **Home tab**, click the **Clipboard** button. Click the **Paste** button, and then click **Paste special**. Click the **Keep Formatting** option button, and then click **OK**.

24 On the **Home tab**, in the **Publish group**, click the **Publish** button. Type your WordPress password, and then click **OK**. Because the blog is private, you will have to log in to see the post. Compare your screen with Figure D.

25 Display the **Start** menu ☺, and then click **All Programs**. On the list of programs, click the **Accessories** folder, and then click **Snipping Tool**. In the **Snipping Tool** dialog box, click the **New arrow**. On the displayed list, click **Full-screen Snip**.

26 On the **Snipping Tool** markup window toolbar, click the **Save Snip** button 🖫. In the **Save As** dialog box, navigate to your **Word Chapter 1** folder. Be sure the **Save as type** box displays **JPEG file**. In the **File name** box, type **Lastname_Firstname_1A_Blog_snip** and then click **Save. Close** all open windows, and then submit the file as directed.

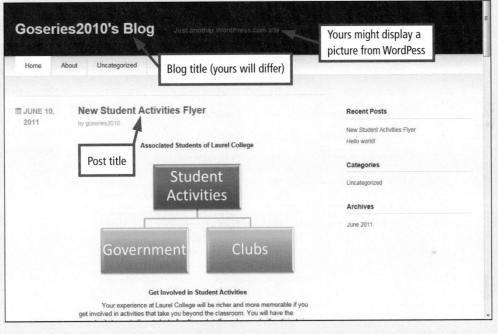

Figure D

Content-Based Assessments

Summary

In this chapter, you created and formatted documents using Microsoft Word 2010. You inserted and formatted graphics, created and formatted bulleted and numbered lists, and created and formatted text boxes. You also created lists using tab stops with dot leaders, and created and modified a SmartArt graphic.

Key Terms

Matching

Match each term in the second column with its correct definition in the first column by writing the letter of the term on the blank line in front of the correct definition.

_____ 1. Formats that make pictures look more like sketches or paintings.

_____ 2. A small box with an upward- and downward-pointing arrow that enables you to move rapidly through a set of values by clicking.

_____ 3. Small circles in the corners of a selected graphic with which you can resize the graphic proportionally.

_____ 4. The manner in which text displays around an object.

_____ 5. An object or graphic that can be moved independently of the surrounding text.

_____ 6. The process of using the arrow keys to move an object in small precise increments.

_____ 7. An object or graphic inserted in a document that acts like a character in a sentence.

_____ 8. Frames, shapes, shadows, borders, and other special effects that can be added to an image to create an overall visual style for the image.

_____ 9. Predefined drawing objects, such as stars, banners, arrows, and callouts, included with Microsoft Office, and that can be inserted into documents.

A Artistic effects

B Bullets

C Floating object

D Inline object

E Justified alignment

F Left alignment

G Line spacing

H Nudge

I Picture styles

J Shapes

K Sizing handles

L SmartArt

M Spin box

N Tab stop

O Text wrapping

_____ 10. A commonly used alignment of text in which text is aligned at the left margin, leaving the right margin uneven.

_____ 11. An alignment of text in which the text is evenly aligned on both the left and right margins.

_____ 12. The distance between lines of text in a paragraph.

_____ 13. Text symbols such as small circles or check marks that introduce items in a list.

_____ 14. A mark on the ruler that indicates the location where the insertion point will be placed when you press the Tab key.

_____ 15. A designer-quality graphic used to create a visual representation of information.

Multiple Choice

Circle the correct answer.

1. Characters that display on the screen to show the location of paragraphs, tabs, and spaces, but that do not print, are called:
   A. text effects   B. bullets   C. formatting marks

2. The placement of paragraph text relative to the left and right margins is referred to as:
   A. alignment   B. spacing   C. indents

3. The symbol that indicates to which paragraph an image is attached is:
   A. a small arrow   B. an anchor   C. a paragraph mark

4. A movable, resizable container for text or graphics is a:
   A. text box   B. dialog box   C. SmartArt graphic

5. A banner is an example of a predefined:
   A. paragraph   B. format   C. shape

6. A placeholder that displays preset content, such as the current date, the file name, a page number, or other stored information is:
   A. a leader   B. a field   C. a tab

7. The space between the text and the top, bottom, left, and right edges of the paper are referred to as:
   A. alignment   B. margins   C. spacing

8. A group of items in which items are displayed in order to indicate definite steps, a sequence of actions, or chronological order is a:
   A. numbered list   B. bulleted list   C. outline list

9. A series of dots following a tab that serve to guide the reader's eye is a:
   A. leader   B. field   C. shape

10. Tab stops are a form of:
    A. line formatting   B. document formatting   C. paragraph formatting

NOTES

Using Tables and Templates to Create Resumes and Cover Letters

OUTCOMES
At the end of this chapter you will be able to:

OBJECTIVES
Mastering these objectives will enable you to:

PROJECT 2A
Create a resume by using a Word table.

1. Create a Table (p. 229)
2. Add Text to a Table (p. 230)
3. Format a Table (p. 233)

PROJECT 2B
Create a cover letter and resume by using a template.

4. Create a New Document from an Existing Document (p. 245)
5. Change and Reorganize Text (p. 248)
6. Use the Proofing Options (p. 255)
7. Create a Document Using a Template (p. 259)

Michael D Brown/Shutterstock

In This Chapter

Tables are useful for organizing and presenting data. Because a table is so easy to use, many individuals prefer to arrange tabular information in a Word table rather than setting a series of tabs. Use a table when you want to present rows and columns of information or to create a structure for a document such as a resume.

When using Word to write business or personal letters, use a commonly approved letter format. You will make a good impression on prospective employers if you use a standard business letter style when you are writing a cover letter for a resume. You can create a resume using one of the Microsoft resume templates included with Microsoft Office or available online.

The projects in this chapter relate to **Madison Staffing Services**. Many companies prefer to hire employees through a staffing service, so that both the employer and the employee can determine if the match is a good fit. Madison Staffing Services takes care of the details of recruiting, testing, hiring, and paying the employee. At the end of the employment assignment, neither the employer nor the employee is required to make a permanent commitment. Many individuals find full-time jobs with an employer for whom they initially worked through a staffing agency.

Project 2A Resume

myitlab
Project 2A Training

Project Activities

In Activities 2.01 through 2.09, you will create a table to use as the structure for a resume for one of Madison Staffing Services' clients. Your completed document will look similar to Figure 2.1.

Project Files

For Project 2A, you will need the following file:

w02A_Experience

You will save your document as:

Lastname_Firstname_2A_Resume

Project Results

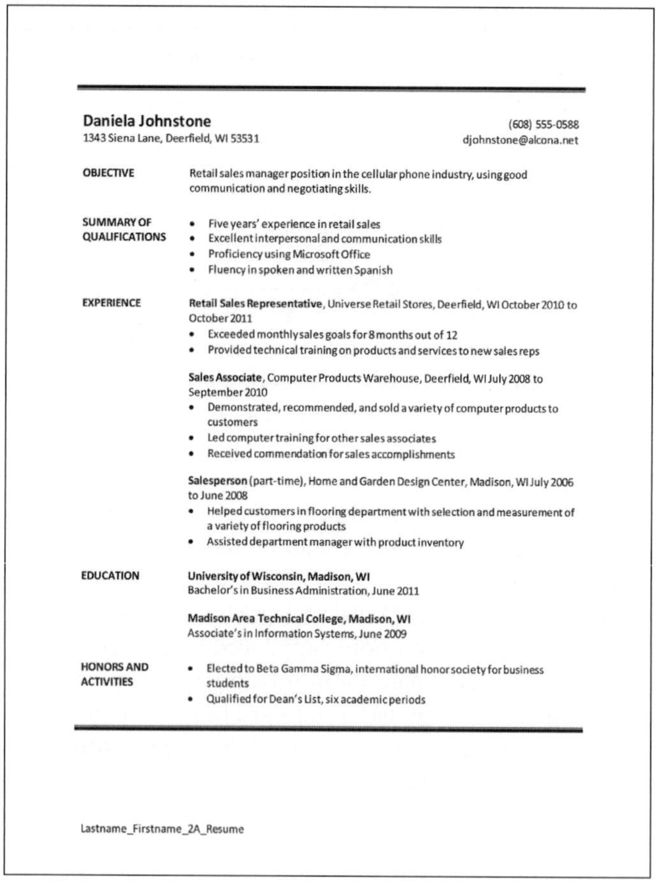

Daniela Johnstone
1343 Siena Lane, Deerfield, WI 53531

(608) 555-0588
djohnstone@alcona.net

OBJECTIVE
Retail sales manager position in the cellular phone industry, using good communication and negotiating skills.

SUMMARY OF QUALIFICATIONS
- Five years' experience in retail sales
- Excellent interpersonal and communication skills
- Proficiency using Microsoft Office
- Fluency in spoken and written Spanish

EXPERIENCE
Retail Sales Representative, Universe Retail Stores, Deerfield, WI October 2010 to October 2011
- Exceeded monthly sales goals for 8 months out of 12
- Provided technical training on products and services to new sales reps

Sales Associate, Computer Products Warehouse, Deerfield, WI July 2008 to September 2010
- Demonstrated, recommended, and sold a variety of computer products to customers
- Led computer training for other sales associates
- Received commendation for sales accomplishments

Salesperson (part-time), Home and Garden Design Center, Madison, WI July 2006 to June 2008
- Helped customers in flooring department with selection and measurement of a variety of flooring products
- Assisted department manager with product inventory

EDUCATION
University of Wisconsin, Madison, WI
Bachelor's in Business Administration, June 2011

Madison Area Technical College, Madison, WI
Associate's in Information Systems, June 2009

HONORS AND ACTIVITIES
- Elected to Beta Gamma Sigma, international honor society for business students
- Qualified for Dean's List, six academic periods

Lastname_Firstname_2A_Resume

Figure 2.1
Project 2A Resume

Objective 1 | Create a Table

A **table** is an arrangement of information organized into rows and columns. The intersection of a row and a column in a table creates a box called a **cell** into which you can type. Tables are useful to present information in a logical and orderly manner.

Activity 2.01 | Creating a Table

1 **Start** Word, and in the new blank document, display formatting marks and rulers.

2 Click the **File tab**, and then in **Backstage** view, click **Save As**. In the **Save As** dialog box, navigate to the location where you are storing your projects for this chapter. Create a new folder named **Word Chapter 2**

3 **Save** the file in the **Word Chapter 2** folder as **Lastname_Firstname_2A_Resume**

4 Scroll to the end of the document, right-click near the bottom of the page, and then click **Edit Footer**. On the **Design tab**, in the **Insert group**, click the **Quick Parts** button, and then click **Field**.

5 Under **Field names**, scroll down, click **FileName**, and then click **OK**. **Close** the footer area.

6 On the **Insert tab**, in the **Tables group**, click the **Table** button. In the **Table** grid, in the fourth row, point to the second square, and notice that the cells display in orange and *2 × 4 Table* displays at the top of the grid. Compare your screen with Figure 2.2.

Figure 2.2

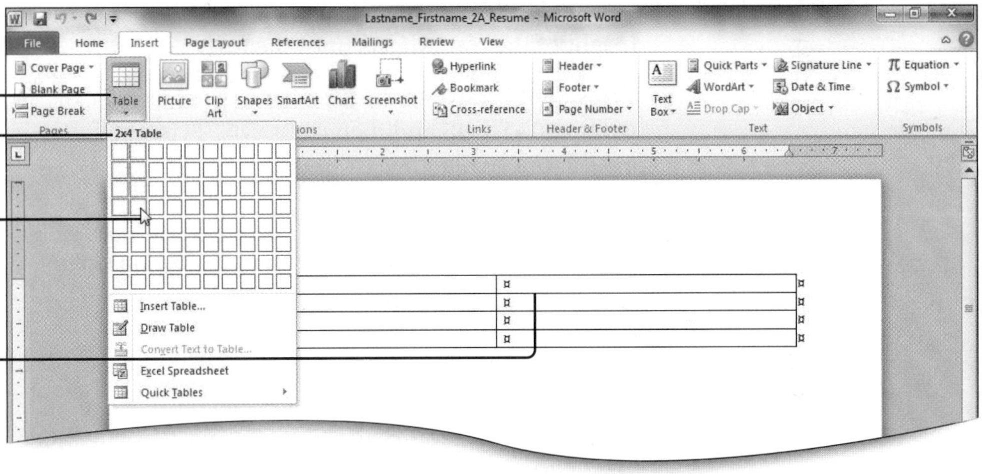

- Table button
- Table size
- Pointer indicates table size
- Preview of table

7 Click one time to create the table. Notice that formatting marks in each cell indicate the end of the contents of each cell and the mark to the right of each *row* indicates the row end. **Save** your document, and then compare your screen with Figure 2.3.

A table with four rows and two columns displays at the insertion point location, and the insertion point displays in the upper left cell. The table fills the width of the page, from the left margin to the right margin. On the Ribbon, Table Tools display and add two tabs—*Design* and *Layout*. Borders display around each cell in the table.

Figure 2.3

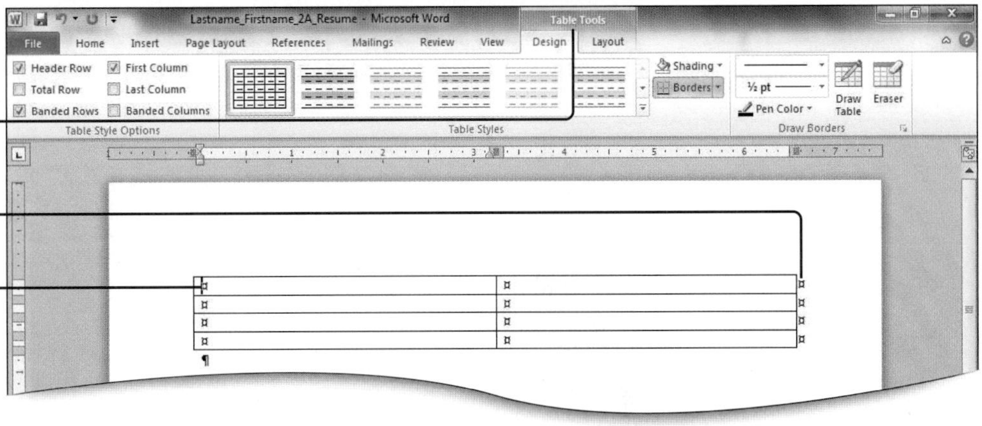

- Table Tools
- Indicates the end of a row
- Indicates the end of cell contents

Objective 2 | Add Text to a Table

In a Word table, each cell behaves similarly to a document. For example, as you type in a cell, when you reach the right border of the cell, wordwrap moves the text to the next line. When you press Enter, the insertion point moves down to a new paragraph in the same cell. You can also insert text from another document into a table cell.

Activity 2.02 | Adding Text to a Table

There are numerous acceptable formats for resumes, many of which can be found in Business Communications textbooks. The layout used in this project is suitable for a recent college graduate and places topics in the left column and details in the right column.

1 Scroll up to view the top of the document. With the insertion point blinking in the first cell in the first row, type **OBJECTIVE** and then press Tab.

Pressing Tab moves the insertion point to the next cell in the row, or, if the insertion point is already in the last cell in the row, pressing Tab moves the insertion point to the first cell in the following row.

2 Type **Retail sales manager position in the cellular phone industry, using good communication and negotiating skills.** Notice that the text wraps in the cell and the height of the row adjusts to fit the text.

3 Press Tab to move to the first cell in the second row. Type **SUMMARY OF QUALIFICATIONS** and then press Tab. Type the following, pressing Enter at the end of each line *except* the last line:

Five years' experience in retail sales

Excellent interpersonal and communication skills

Proficiency using Microsoft Office

Fluency in spoken and written Spanish

The default font and font size in a table are the same as for a document—Calibri 11 pt. The default line spacing in a table is single spacing with no space before or after paragraphs, which differs from the defaults for a document.

4 **Save** your document, and then compare your screen with Figure 2.4.

Figure 2.4

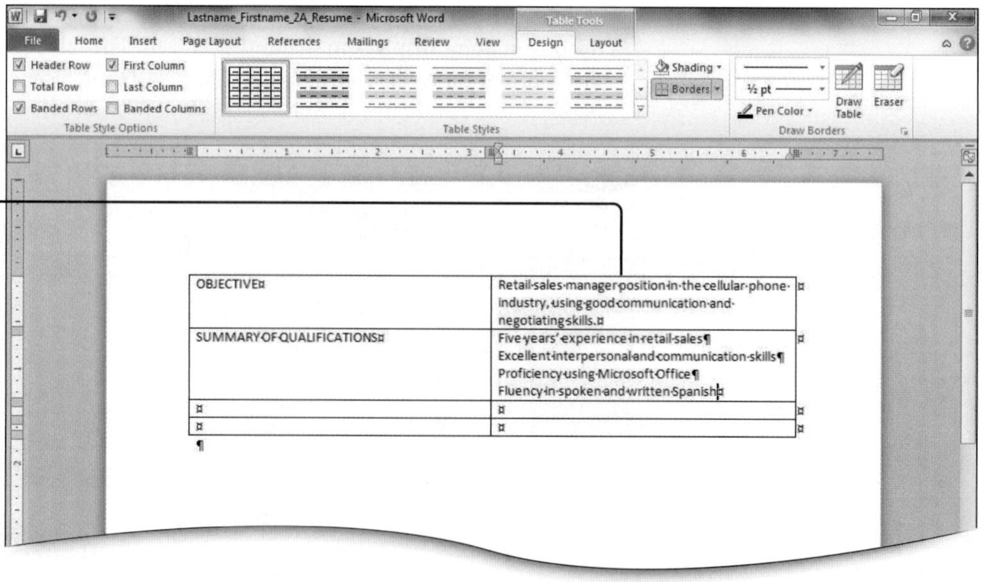

Text typed in cells

Activity 2.03 | Inserting Existing Text into a Table Cell

1 Press Tab to move to the first cell in the third row. Type **EXPERIENCE** and then press Tab.

2 Type the following, pressing Enter after each line:

> **Retail Sales Representative, Universe Retail Stores, Deerfield, WI October 2010 to October 2011**
>
> **Exceeded monthly sales goals for 8 months out of 12**
>
> **Provided technical training on products and services to new sales reps**

3 Be sure your insertion point is positioned in the second column to the left of the cell marker below *sales reps*. Compare your screen with Figure 2.5.

Figure 2.5

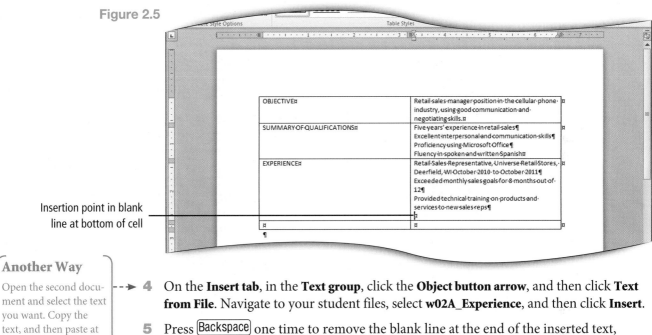

Insertion point in blank line at bottom of cell

> **Another Way**
>
> Open the second document and select the text you want. Copy the text, and then paste at the desired location.

4 On the **Insert tab**, in the **Text group**, click the **Object button arrow**, and then click **Text from File**. Navigate to your student files, select **w02A_Experience**, and then click **Insert**.

5 Press Backspace one time to remove the blank line at the end of the inserted text, and then compare your screen with Figure 2.6.

Figure 2.6

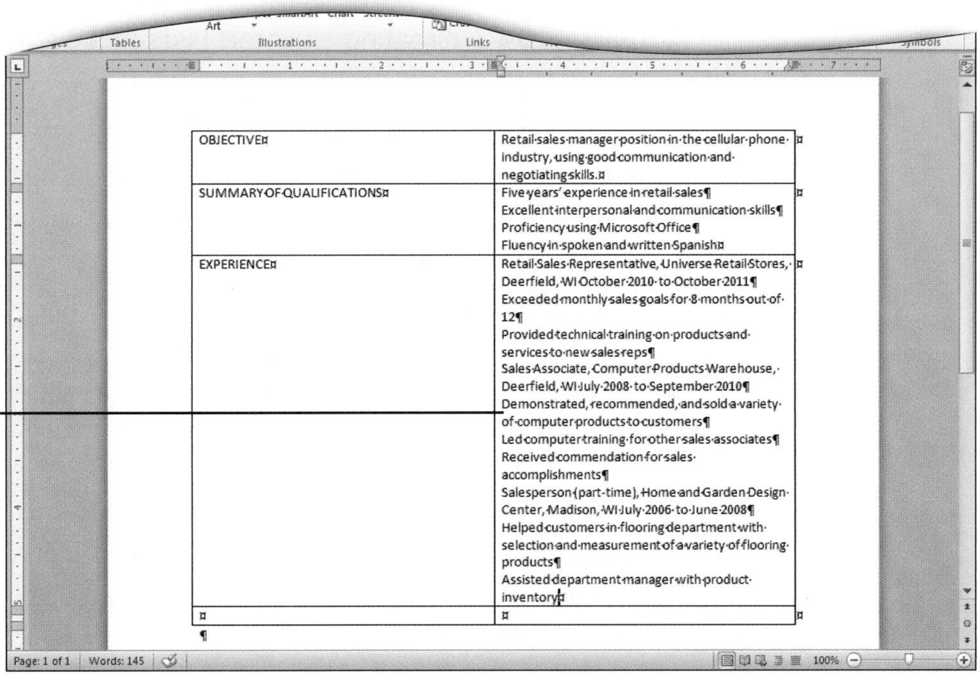

Text inserted from file

6 Press `Tab` to move to the first cell in the fourth row. Type **EDUCATION** and then press `Tab`.

7 Type the following, pressing `Enter` at the end of each item *except* the last one:

> **University of Wisconsin, Madison, WI**
>
> **Bachelor's in Business Administration, June 2011**
>
> **Madison Area Technical College, Madison, WI**
>
> **Associate's in Information Systems, June 2009**

8 Compare your screen with Figure 2.7.

Figure 2.7

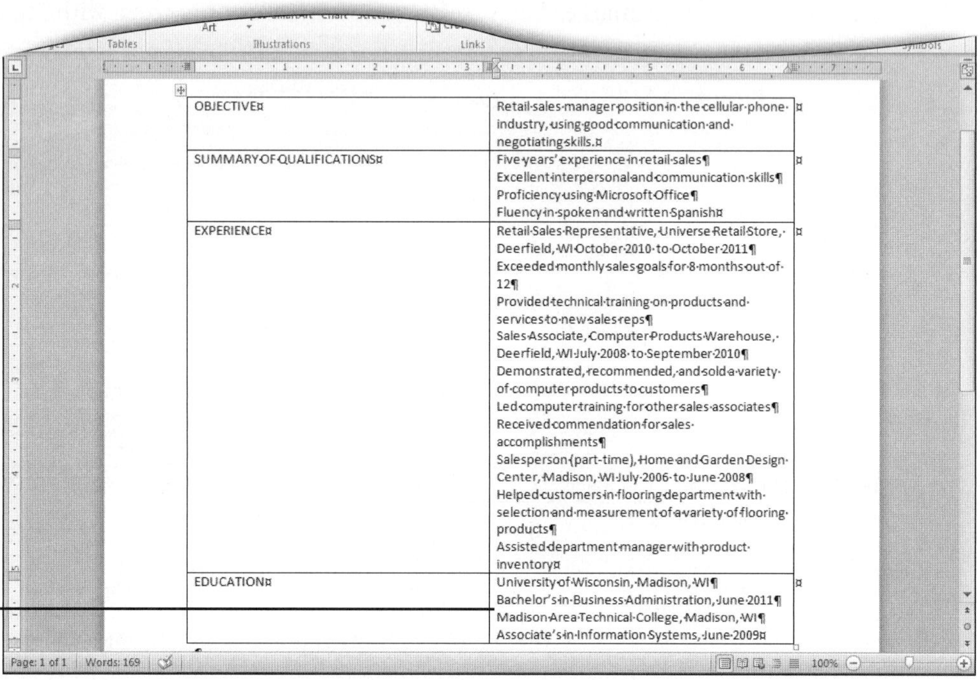

Text entered in new cell ————

OBJECTIVE¤	Retail·sales·manager·position·in·the·cellular·phone·industry,·using·good·communication·and·negotiating·skills.¤
SUMMARY·OF·QUALIFICATIONS¤	Five·years'·experience·in·retail·sales¶ Excellent·interpersonal·and·communication·skills¶ Proficiency·using·Microsoft·Office¶ Fluency·in·spoken·and·written·Spanish¤
EXPERIENCE¤	Retail·Sales·Representative,·Universe·Retail·Store,·Deerfield,·WI·October·2010·to·October·2011¶ Exceeded·monthly·sales·goals·for·8·months·out·of·12¶ Provided·technical·training·on·products·and·services·to·new·sales·reps¶ Sales·Associate,·Computer·Products·Warehouse,·Deerfield,·WI·July·2008·to·September·2010¶ Demonstrated,·recommended,·and·sold·a·variety·of·computer·products·to·customers¶ Led·computer·training·for·other·sales·associates¶ Received·commendation·for·sales·accomplishments¶ Salesperson·(part-time),·Home·and·Garden·Design·Center,·Madison,·WI·July·2006·to·June·2008¶ Helped·customers·in·flooring·department·with·selection·and·measurement·of·a·variety·of·flooring·products¶ Assisted·department·manager·with·product·inventory¤
EDUCATION¤	University·of·Wisconsin,·Madison,·WI¶ Bachelor's·in·Business·Administration,·June·2011¶ Madison·Area·Technical·College,·Madison,·WI¶ Associate's·in·Information·Systems,·June·2009¤

Page: 1 of 1   Words: 169   100%

9 **Save** your document.

Activity 2.04 | Creating Bulleted Lists in a Table

1 Scroll to view the top of your document, and then in the cell to the right of *SUMMARY OF QUALIFICATIONS*, select all of the text.

2 On the **Home tab**, in the **Paragraph group**, click the **Bullets** button .

> The selected text displays as a bulleted list. Using a bulleted list in this manner makes each qualification more distinctive.

3 In the **Paragraph group**, click the **Decrease Indent** button one time to align the bullets at the left edge of the cell.

4 In the **Clipboard group**, double-click the **Format Painter** button. In the cell to the right of *EXPERIENCE*, select the second and third paragraphs—beginning *Exceeded* and *Provided*—to create the same style of bulleted list as you did in the previous step.

> When you double-click the Format Painter button, it remains active until you turn it off.

5 In the same cell, under *Sales Associate*, select the three paragraphs that begin *Demonstrated* and *Led* and *Received* to create another bulleted list aligned at the left edge of the cell.

Another Way

Click the Format Painter again.

6 With the Format Painter pointer still active, in the same cell, select the paragraphs that begin *Helped* and *Assisted* to create the same type of bulleted list.

7 Press [Esc] to turn off the Format Painter. Click anywhere in the table to deselect the text, and then compare your screen with Figure 2.8.

Figure 2.8

Bullets added to text ————

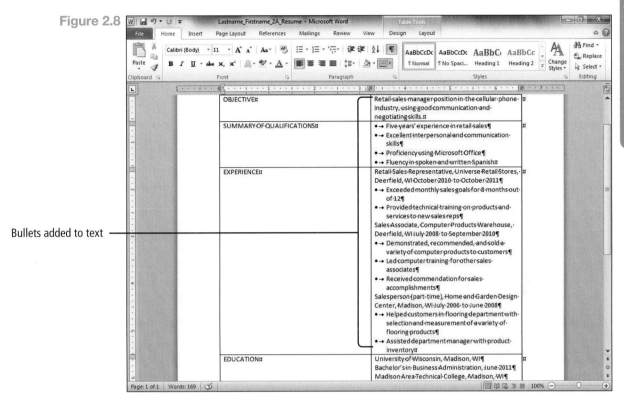

8 **Save** 📄 your document.

Objective 3 | Format a Table

Use Word's formatting tools to make your tables attractive and easy to read. Types of formatting you can add to a table include changing the row height and the column width, removing or adding borders, increasing or decreasing the paragraph or line spacing, or enhancing the text.

Activity 2.05 | Changing the Width of Table Columns

When you create a table, all of the columns are of equal width. In this activity, you will change the width of the columns.

1 In any row, point to the vertical border between the two columns to display the ⇔ pointer.

2 Drag the column border to the left to approximately **1.25 inches on the horizontal ruler**.

3 Scroll to the top of the document. Notice that in the second row, the text *SUMMARY OF QUALIFICATIONS* wraps to two lines to accommodate the new column width.

4 If necessary, in the left column, click in any cell. On the Ribbon, under **Table Tools**, click the **Layout tab**.

5 In the **Cell Size group**, click the **Table Column Width button spin arrows** [⊞ 1.37″ ⇕] as necessary to change the width of the first column to **1.4″**. Compare your screen with Figure 2.9.

> After dragging a border with your mouse, use the Width button to set a precise measurement if necessary.

Figure 2.9

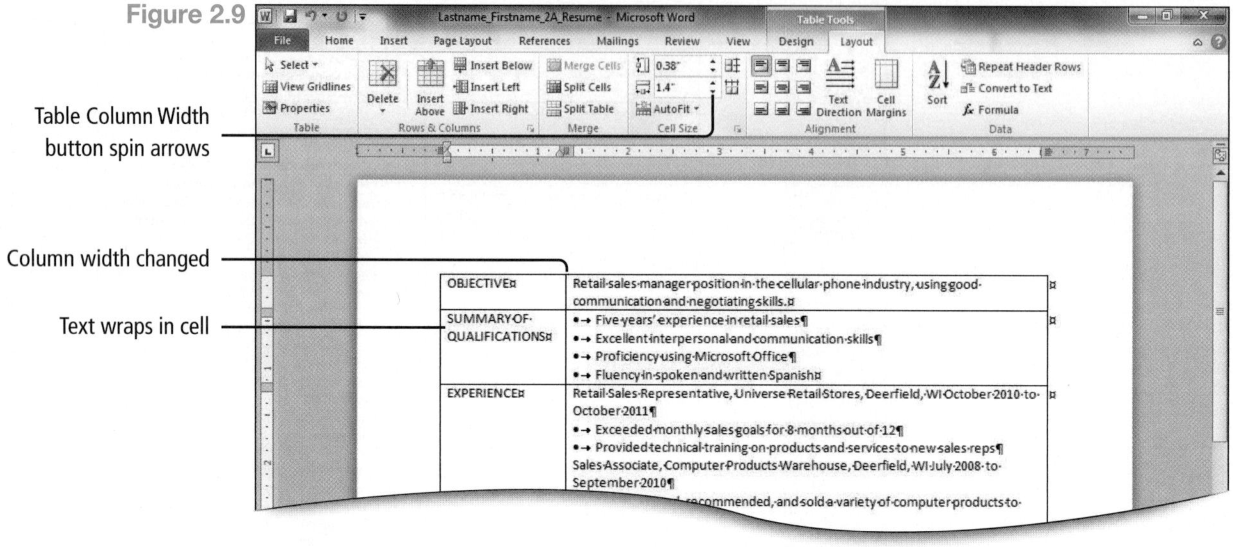

Table Column Width button spin arrows

Column width changed

Text wraps in cell

6 Save [💾] your document.

More Knowledge | Changing Column Widths

You will typically get the best results if you change the column widths starting at the left side of the table, especially in tables with three or more columns. Word can also calculate the best column widths for you. To do this, select the table. Then, on the Layout tab, in the Cell Size group, click the AutoFit button and click AutoFit Contents.

Activity 2.06 | Adding Rows to a Table

You can add rows or columns anywhere in a table.

1 Scroll to view the lower portion of the table. In the last row of the table, click anywhere in the *second* cell that contains the educational information, and then press Tab.

> A new row displays at the bottom of the table. When the insertion point is in the last cell in the bottom row of a table, you can add a row by pressing the Tab key; the insertion point will display in the first cell of the new row.

2 Type **HONORS AND ACTIVITIES** and then press Tab.

3 Type the following, pressing Enter after the first item but not the second item:

Elected to Beta Gamma Sigma, international honor society for business students

Qualified for Dean's List, six academic periods

4 Select the text you typed in the last cell of the bottom row. On the **Home tab**, in the **Paragraph group**, click the **Bullets** button [≣ ▾], and then click the **Decrease Indent** button [⇤] one time to align the bullets at the left edge of the cell.

5 Scroll up to view the entire table, click anywhere in the table to deselect the text, and then compare your screen with Figure 2.10.

Figure 2.10

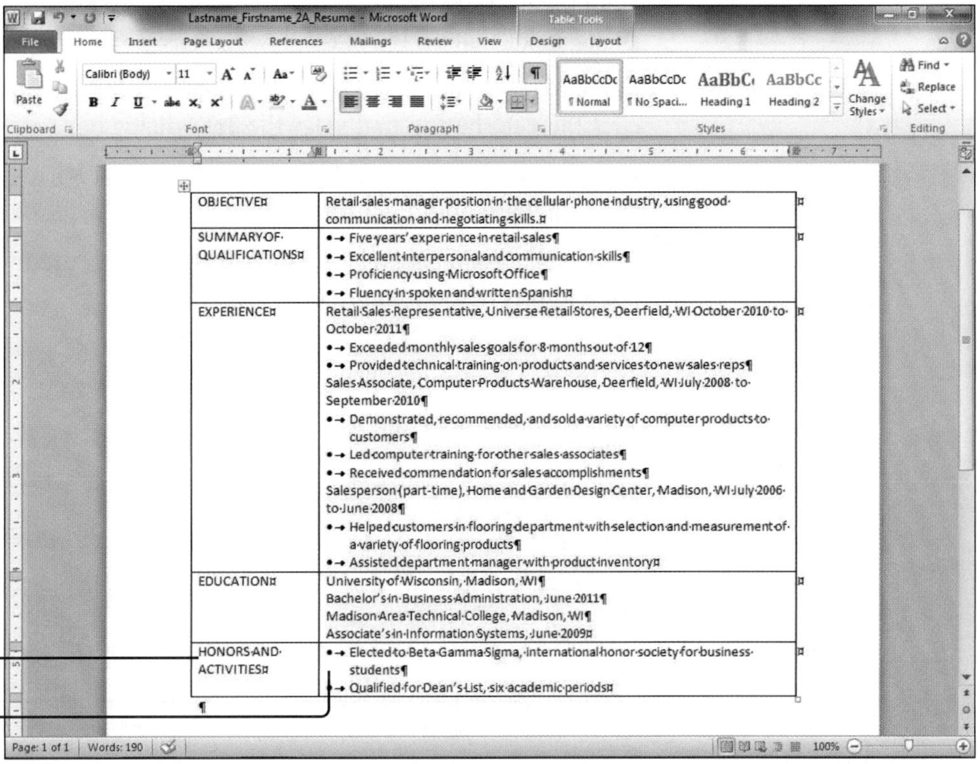

Row added to table ─────

Bullets added to text ─────

6 Click anywhere in the top row of the table.

Another Way

Right-click in the top row, point to Insert, and then click Insert Rows Above.

7 On the **Layout tab**, in the **Rows & Columns group**, click the **Insert Above** button. Compare your screen with Figure 2.11.

A new row displays above the row that contained the insertion point, and the new row is selected.

Figure 2.11

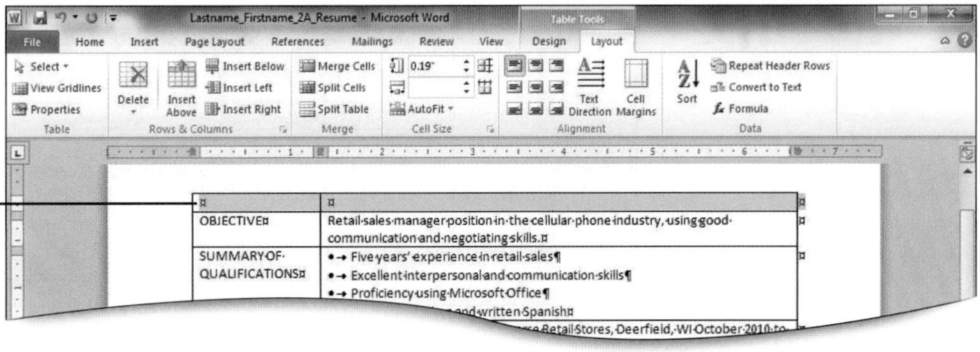

Row inserted at top of table ─────

8 **Save** 🖫 your document.

Activity 2.07 | Merging Cells

The title of a table typically spans all of the columns. In this activity, you will merge cells so that you can position the personal information across both columns.

1 Be sure the two cells in the top row are selected; if necessary, drag across both cells to select them.

2 On the **Layout tab**, in the **Merge group**, click the **Merge Cells** button.

> The cell border between the two cells no longer displays.

3 With the merged cell still selected, on the **Home tab**, in the **Paragraph group**, click the **Dialog Box Launcher** 🔲 to display the **Paragraph** dialog box.

4 In the **Paragraph** dialog box, on the **Indents and Spacing tab**, in the lower left corner, click the **Tabs** button to display the **Tabs** dialog box.

5 In the **Tabs** dialog box, under **Tab stop position**, type **6.5** and then under **Alignment**, click the **Right** option button. Click **Set**, and then click **OK** to close the dialog box.

6 Type **Daniela Johnstone** Hold down Ctrl and then press Tab. Notice that the insertion point moves to the right-aligned tab stop at 6.5".

> In a Word table, you must use Ctrl + Tab to move to a tab stop, because pressing Tab is reserved for moving the insertion point from cell to cell.

7 Type **(608) 555-0588** and then press Enter.

8 Type **1343 Siena Lane, Deerfield, WI 53531** Hold down Ctrl and then press Tab.

9 Type **djohnstone@alcona.net** and then compare your screen with Figure 2.12.

Figure 2.12

Right tab stop added to ruler

Cells merged in top row

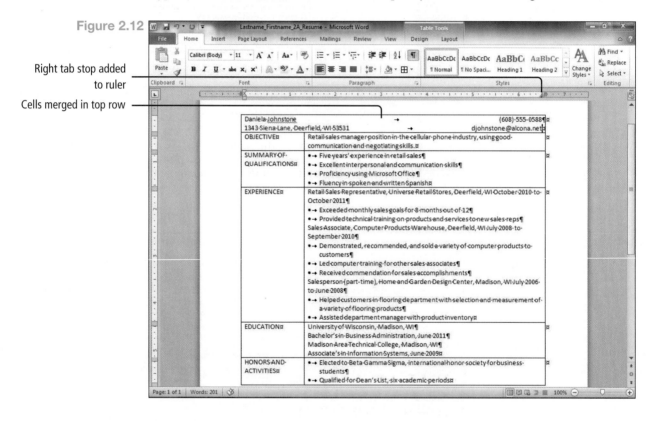

10 **Save** 🔲 your document.

Activity 2.08 | Formatting Text in Cells

1 In the first row of the table, select the name *Daniela Johnstone*, and then on the Mini toolbar, apply **Bold** B and change the **Font Size** to **16**.

2 Under *Daniela Johnstone*, click anywhere in the second line of text, which contains the address and e-mail address.

3 On the **Page Layout tab**, in the **Paragraph group**, click the **Spacing After up spin arrow** three times to add **18 pt** spacing between the first row of the table and the second row. Compare your screen with Figure 2.13.

These actions separate the personal information from the body of the resume and add focus to the applicant's name.

Figure 2.13

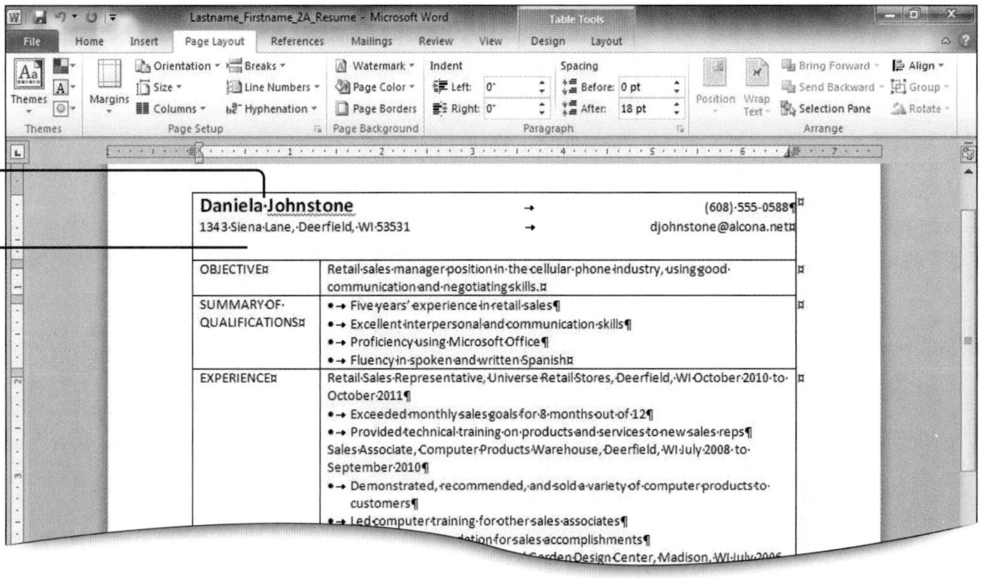

Text formatted

18 pt space added after paragraph

4 Using the technique you just practiced, in the second column, click in the last paragraph of every cell and add **18 pt Spacing After** the last paragraph of all rows including the last row; a border will be added to the bottom of the table, and spacing will be needed between the last row and the border.

5 In the second row, point to the word *OBJECTIVE*, hold down the left mouse button, and then drag downward in the first column only to select all the headings in uppercase letters. On the Mini toolbar, click the **Bold** button **B**.

Note | Selecting Only One Column

When you drag downward to select the first column, a fast mouse might also begin to select the second column when you reach the bottom. If this happens, drag upward slightly to deselect the second column and select only the first column.

---

6 In the cell to the right of *EXPERIENCE*, without selecting the following comma, select *Retail Sales Representative* and then on the Mini toolbar, click the **Bold** button **B**.

7 In the same cell, apply **Bold** **B** to the other job titles—*Sales Associate* and *Salesperson*—but do not bold *(part time)*.

8 In the cell to the right of *EDUCATION*, apply **Bold** **B** to *University of Wisconsin, Madison, WI* and *Madison Area Technical College, Madison, WI.*

9 In the same cell, click anywhere in the line beginning *Bachelor's*. On the **Page Layout tab**, in the **Paragraph group**, click the **Spacing After up spin arrow** two times to add **12 pt** spacing after the paragraph.

10 In the cell to the right of *EXPERIENCE*, under *Retail Sales Representative*, click anywhere in the second bulleted item, and then add **12 pt Spacing After** the item.

11 In the same cell, repeat this process for the last bulleted item under *Sales Associate*.

12 Scroll to the top of the screen, and then compare your screen with Figure 2.14.

Figure 2.14

Bold emphasis added to first column

Space added after paragraphs in second column

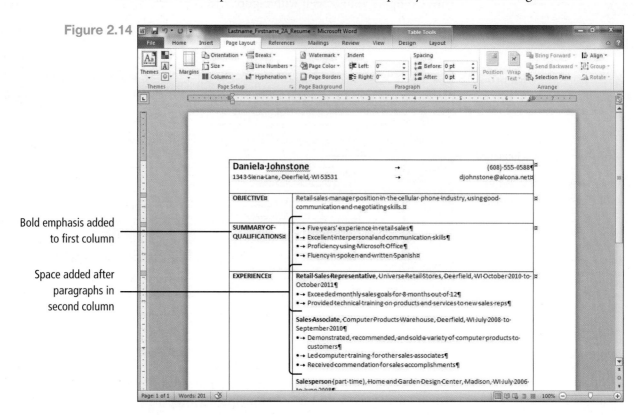

13 **Save** 💾 your document.

Activity 2.09 | Changing the Table Borders

When you create a table, all of the cells have black borders. Most resumes do not display any cell borders. A border at the top and bottom of the resume, however, is attractive and adds a professional look to the document.

1 If necessary, press [Ctrl] + [Home] to move the insertion point to the top of the table, and then point slightly outside of the upper left corner of the table to display the **table move handle** 🔲.

2 With the 🔯 pointer, click one time to select the entire table, and notice that the row markers at the end of each row are also selected.

Shaded row markers indicate that the entire row is selected.

3 Click the **Design tab**. In the **Table Styles group**, click the **Borders button arrow**, and then click **No Border**.

The black borders no longer display; instead, depending on your setup, either no borders—the default setting—or nonprinting blue dashed borders display.

4 Click the **File tab** to display **Backstage** view, and then click the **Print tab** to preview the table. Notice that no borders display in the preview, as shown in Figure 2.15.

Figure 2.15

Document preview

All table borders removed

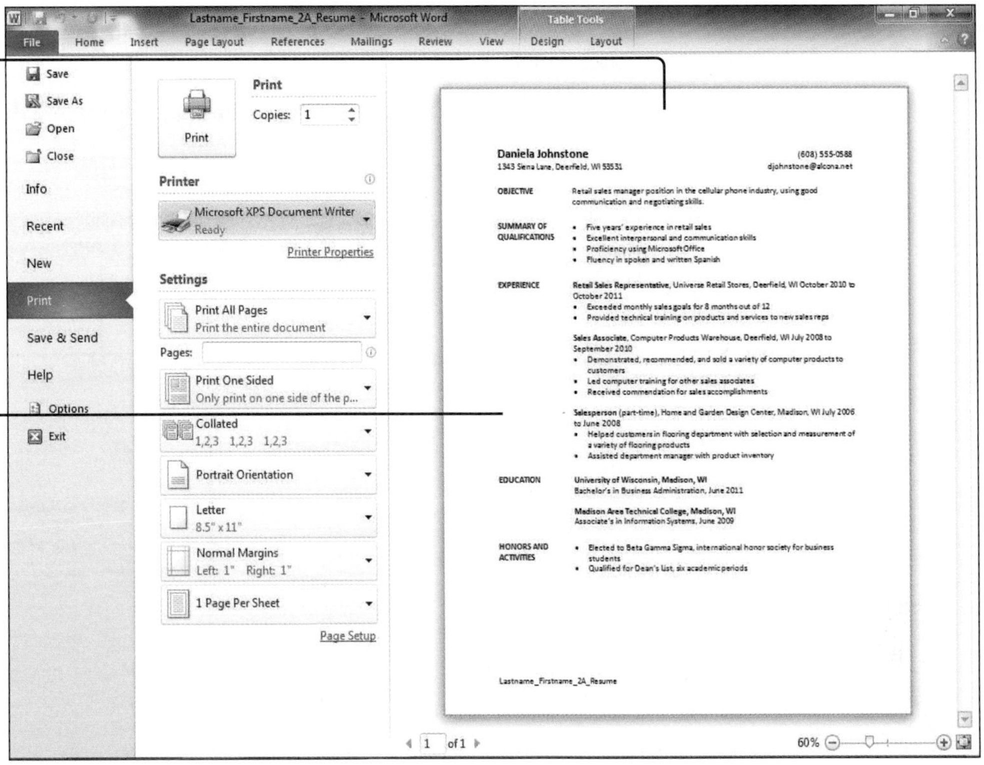

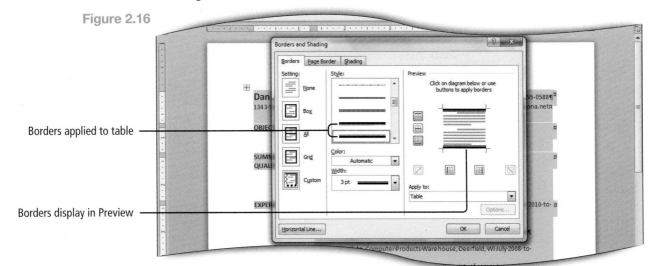

Another Way

Right-click the selected table, click Borders and Shading, and then click the Borders tab.

Another Way

Click the top border button, which is one of the buttons that surround the Preview.

5 Click the **Design tab**; be sure the table is still selected. In the **Table Styles group**, click the **Borders button arrow**, and then at the bottom of the **Borders** gallery, click **Borders and Shading**.

6 Under **Setting**, click the **Custom** button. Under **Style**, scroll down about a third of the way and click the style with the thick upper line and the thin lower line.

7 In the **Preview** box at the right, point to the *top* border of the small preview and click one time.

8 Under **Style**, click the style with the thin upper line and the thick lower line, and then in the **Preview** box, click the *bottom* border of the preview. Compare your screen with Figure 2.16.

Figure 2.16

Borders applied to table

Borders display in Preview

9 Click **OK**, click anywhere to cancel the selection, and then notice that there is only a small amount of space between the upper border and the first line of text.

10 Click anywhere in the text *Daniela Johnstone*, and then on the **Page Layout tab**, in the **Paragraph group**, click the **Spacing Before up spin arrow** as necessary to add **18 pt** spacing before the first paragraph.

11 Display **Backstage** view. Click the **Print tab** to preview the table. Compare your screen with Figure 2.17.

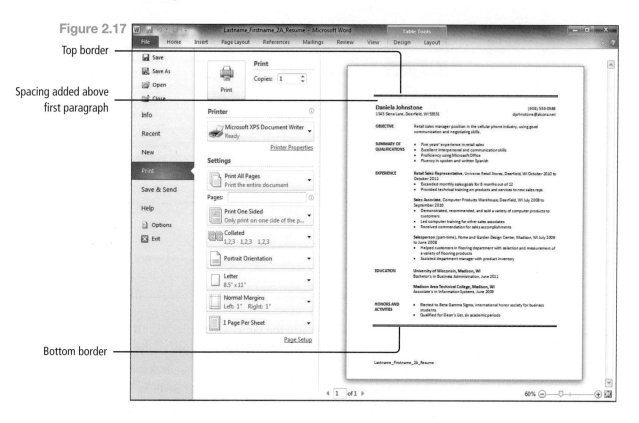

Figure 2.17

Top border

Spacing added above first paragraph

Bottom border

12 In **Backstage** view, click the **Info tab**. On the right, under the document thumbnail, click **Properties**, and then click **Show Document Panel**. In the **Author** box, delete any text and then type your firstname and lastname. In the **Subject** box, type your course name and section number, and in the **Keywords** box, type **resume, Word table**

13 **Close** ☒ the **Document Panel**. **Save** 🖫 and then print your document, or submit it electronically, as directed by your instructor. **Exit** Word.

End **You have completed Project 2A** ————————————

NOTES

GO! Beyond Office

Objective | Upload a Professional-Level Resume to the Web

After you graduate from college and begin your career, it is a good idea to network with others in your profession. There are some networking sites specifically geared toward professionals. One of these is LinkedIn.com—a professional network with more than 100,000,000 members—that enables you to post your personal and professional information, network with colleagues and friends, join groups of people with similar interests, and post your resume. By posting your resume and identifying your area of expertise and your skills, employers who are searching for people with your qualifications can find you on LinkedIn.

> **Alert!** | **Working with Web-Based Applications and Services**
>
> Computer programs and services on the Web receive continuous updates and improvements. Thus, the steps to complete this Web-based Activity may differ from the ones shown. You can often look at the screens and the information presented to determine how to complete the Activity.

Activity | Uploading a Professional Resume to the Web

In this activity, you will open the 2A_Resume document and change the information to match your own personal experience, education, skills, and goals. Then you will create a LinkedIn account and post information from your resume to your LinkedIn account.

1 Locate and open the **Lastname_Firstname_2A_ Resume** document that you created in Project 2A. On the **File tab**, click **Save As**. In the **Save As** dialog box, navigate to your **Word Chapter 2** folder or create a folder with this name and open it. In the **File name** box, type **Lastname_Firstname_2A_LinkedIn_Resume** Click the **Save as type arrow**, click **Word 97-2003 document**, and then click **Save**.

2 Substitute your name in place of *Daniela Johnstone*. If you wish, substitute your address, telephone number, and e-mail address. Personalize the remainder of the information in the resume. If you choose not to change the information, delete the second and third parts of the EXPERIENCE section—*Sales Associate* and *Salesperson*—including the bulleted lists. If a blank bullet point

displays, press Backspace as necessary to remove the blank line.

3 **Save** the document, and then **Exit** Word.

4 Open your browser, and then go to www.linkedin.com If you do not have a LinkedIn account, in the **Join LinkedIn Today** box, type your first and last name, your live.com e-mail address, and a password of six or more characters. Click the **Join Now** button, and then compare your screen with Figure A.

5 Fill out the professional profile information page— the fields with asterisks are required. If you are not currently employed, use your school as the Company, select *Higher Education* as the Industry, and then type *Student* as your Job Title. Click **Create my profile**.

Figure A

6 In the **See Who You Already Know on LinkedIn** dialog box, unless you want to use the LinkedIn site to make professional contacts, click **Skip this step**; otherwise, click **Continue** and follow the onscreen instructions.

If you skip the e-mail search at this point, you can perform the search once you finish creating your account.

7 If you clicked *Continue*, finish filling out the required information; otherwise, click **Confirm my Windows Live Hotmail Account**. In the **Windows Live** window, click **Allow access**. If a message displays indicating that your e-mail cannot be confirmed, follow the instructions to try again. When you see the *LinkedIn Email Confirmation* message, click the **Click here** link and follow the instructions to complete the process.

8 In the **Connect to more people you know and trust** box, add any e-mail addresses you wish to include—separated by commas—or click **Skip this step**.

9 In the **Your Account is Set Up—Choose Your Plan Level** window, under **Basic (Free)**, click **Choose Basic**.

10 On the **LinkedIn** menu, point to **Profile**, and then click **Edit Profile**. Take a moment to see what types of information you can add to your LinkedIn site.

11 Near the top of the right column, under **Add another position**, click **Import your resume**. In the **Import your resume** box, click the **Browse** button. You can upload Word, PDF, or HTML files.

12 Locate and select your **2A_LinkedIn_Resume** file—be sure you select the file saved as a Microsoft Word

97-2003 Document. Click the **Open** button. In the **Import your resume** box, click the **Upload Resume** button. Compare your screen with Figure B. Under **Experience**, clear the **Time Period** check box. In the **from** and **to** boxes, enter the dates of employment as **October 2009** to **October 2010** In the time period for the current job, enter the starting date of employment as **October 2010**

When you import a resume, experience and education information are extracted from the resume and added to your profile.

13 Scroll to the bottom of the page and notice that the Education information has been extracted from the resume. When you are finished, click the **Save Changes** button.

14 Scroll down the profile page to display the **Education** and **Experience** sections. Display the **Start** menu ⊕, and then click **All Programs**. On the list of programs, click the **Accessories** folder, and then click **Snipping Tool**. In the **Snipping Tool** dialog box, click the **New arrow**. On the displayed list, click **Full-screen Snip**.

15 On the **Snipping Tool** markup window toolbar, click the **Save Snip** button 💾. In the **Save As** dialog box, navigate to your USB drive and open the **Word Chapter 2** folder. Be sure the **Save as type** box displays **JPEG file**. In the **File name** box, type **Lastname_Firstname_2A_LinkedIn_Resume_Snip** and then click **Save**. **Close** the Snipping Tool markup window.

16 **Close** ⊞ all open windows. Submit the Word 97-2003 version of the resume and the snip file as directed.

GO! Beyond Office

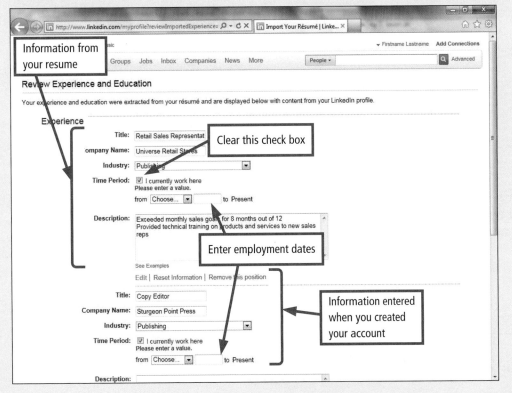

Figure B

Project 2B Cover Letter and Resume

Project Activities

In Activities 2.10 through 2.22, you will create a letterhead, and then use the letterhead to create a cover letter. You will also create a short resume using a Microsoft template and save it as a Web page. Your completed documents will look similar to Figure 2.18.

Project Files

For Project 2B, you will need the following file:

w02B_Cover_Letter_Text

You will save your documents as:

Lastname_Firstname_2B_Letterhead
Lastname_Firstname_2B_Cover_Letter
Lastname_Firstname_2B_Brief_Resume
Lastname_Firstname_2B_HTML_Resume

Project Results

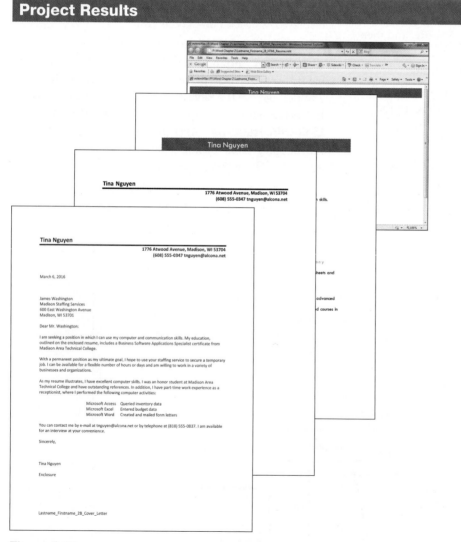

Figure 2.18
Project 2B Cover Letter and Resume

Objective 4 | Create a New Document from an Existing Document

A *template* is an *existing* document that you use as a starting point for a *new* document. The template document opens a copy of itself, unnamed, and then you use the structure—and possibly some content, such as headings—as the starting point for a new document.

All documents are based on a template. When you create a new blank document, it is based on Word's *Normal template*, which serves as the starting point for all new Word documents.

Activity 2.10 | Creating a Letterhead

A *letterhead* is the personal or company information that displays at the top of a letter, and which commonly includes a name, address, and contact information. The term also refers to a piece of paper imprinted with such information at the top.

1 **Start** Word, and in the new blank document, be sure that formatting marks and rulers display.

2 On the **Home tab**, in the **Styles group**, click the **More** button ▾. In the displayed gallery, click the **No Spacing** button.

> Recall that the default spacing for a new Word document is 10 points of blank space following a paragraph and line spacing of 1.15. The *No Spacing style* inserts *no* extra space following a paragraph and uses single spacing.
>
> By using the No Spacing style, you will be able to follow the prescribed format of a letter, which Business Communications texts commonly describe in terms of single spacing.

3 Type **Tina Nguyen** and then press Enter.

4 Type **1776 Atwood Avenue, Madison, WI 53704** and then press Enter.

5 Type **(608) 555-0347 tnguyen@alcona.net** and then press Enter. If the e-mail address changes to blue text, right-click the e-mail address, and then from the shortcut menu, click **Remove Hyperlink**. Compare your screen with Figure 2.19.

Figure 2.19

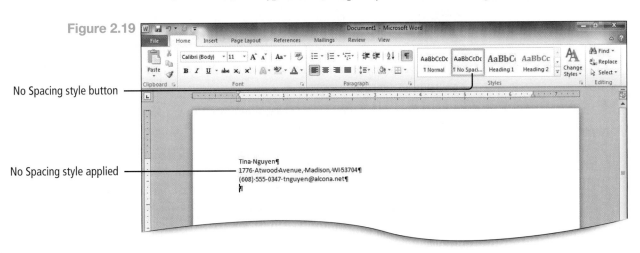

No Spacing style button

No Spacing style applied

6 Select the first paragraph—*Tina Nguyen*—and then on the Mini toolbar, apply **Bold** **B** and change the **Font Size** to **16**.

7 Select the second and third paragraphs. On the Mini toolbar, apply **Bold** B and change the **Font Size** to **12**.

Another Way

Press Ctrl + R to align text to the right.

8 With the two paragraphs still selected, on the **Home tab**, in the **Paragraph group**, click the **Align Text Right** button ▤.

9 Click anywhere in the first paragraph—*Tina Nguyen*. In the **Paragraph group**, click the **Borders button arrow** ▦▾, and then at the bottom, click **Borders and Shading**.

10 In the **Borders and Shading** dialog box, under **Style**, be sure the first style—a single solid line—is selected.

Another Way

Alternatively, click the bottom border button ▦.

11 Click the **Width arrow**, and then click **3 pt**. To the right, under **Preview**, click the bottom border of the diagram. Under **Apply to**, be sure *Paragraph* displays. Compare your screen with Figure 2.20.

Figure 2.20

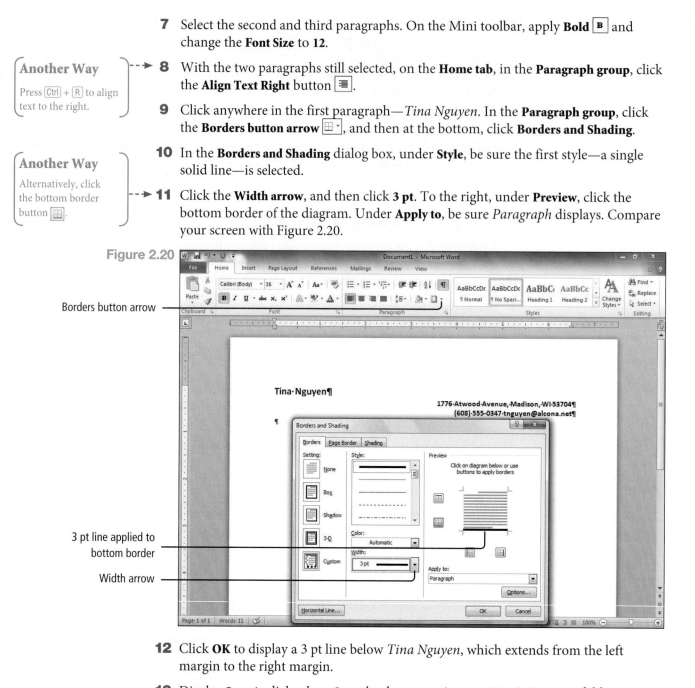

Borders button arrow

3 pt line applied to bottom border

Width arrow

12 Click **OK** to display a 3 pt line below *Tina Nguyen*, which extends from the left margin to the right margin.

13 Display **Save As** dialog box, **Save** the document in your **Word Chapter 2** folder as **Lastname_Firstname_2B_Letterhead** and then add the file name to the footer.

14 Display **Backstage** view, click the **Info tab**, and then on the right, under the document thumbnail, click **Properties**. Click **Show Document Panel**. In the **Author** box, delete any text and then type your firstname and lastname. In the **Subject** box, type your course name and section number, and in the **Keywords** box type **personal letterhead**

15 **Close** ✕ the **Document Panel**.

16 **Save** 🖫 your document. Display **Backstage** view, and then click **Close** to close the document but leave Word open. Hold this file until you complete this project.

Activity 2.11 | Creating a Document from an Existing Document

To use an existing document as the starting point for a new document, Word provides the ***New from existing*** command.

1 Click the **File tab** to display **Backstage** view, and then click **New** to display the new document options. Compare your screen with Figure 2.21.

Here you can create a new document in a variety of ways, including from an existing document.

Figure 2.21

New from Existing template

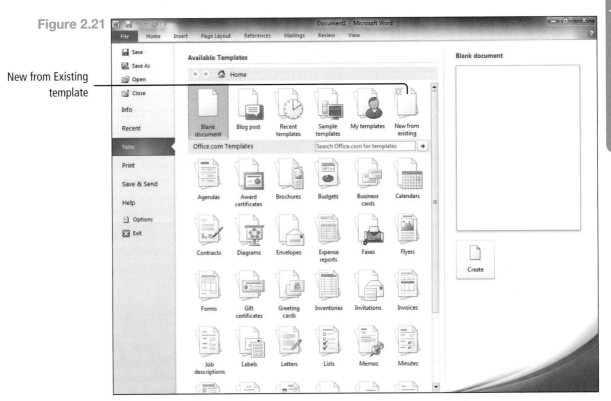

2 Under **Available Templates**, click the **New from existing** button. In the displayed **New from Existing Document** dialog box, if necessary, navigate to your **Word Chapter 2** folder, click your **Lastname_Firstname_2B_Letterhead** document to select it, and then in the lower right corner, click **Create New**. Compare your screen with Figure 2.22.

Word opens a copy of your 2B_Letterhead document in the form of a new Word document—the title bar indicates *Document* followed by a number. You are not opening the original document, and changes that you make to this new document will not affect the contents of your 2B_Letterhead document.

Figure 2.22

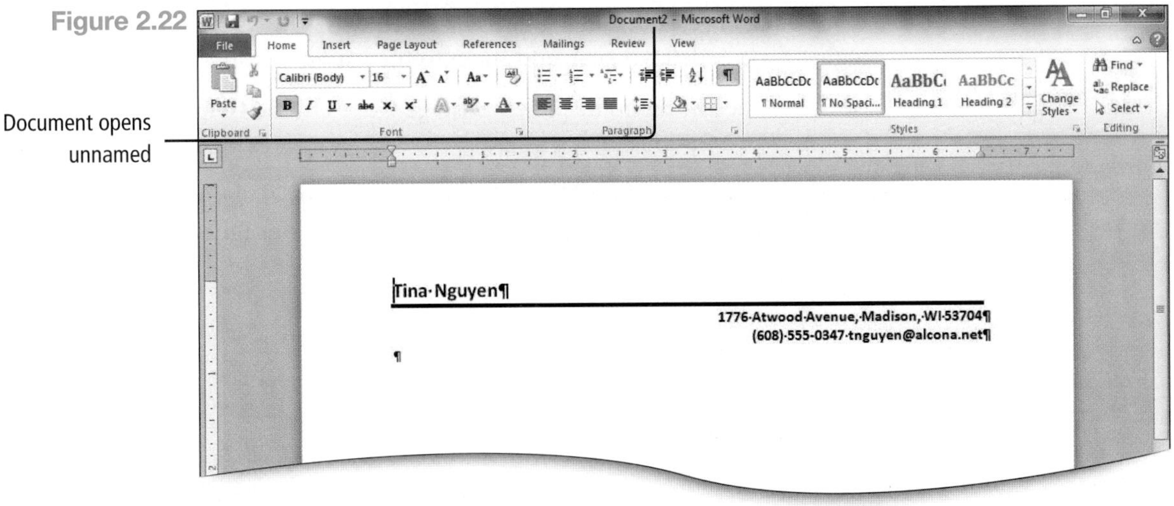

Document opens unnamed

3 Display the **Save As** dialog box, and then navigate to your **Word Chapter 2** folder. **Save** the file as **Lastname_Firstname_2B_Cover_Letter**

> The personal information that you typed in the 2B_Letterhead Document Panel remains in the new document.

4 Scroll down to view the footer area, and notice that a footer displays.

> The footer displays because it was included in the document that you saved as a template. The *FileName* field does not automatically update to the new file name.

5 Point to the footer and right-click, and then click **Edit Footer**. Point to the highlighted footer text, right-click, and then from the shortcut menu, click **Update Field**. At the far right end of the Ribbon, click the **Close Header and Footer** button.

6 Save ▣ your document.

More Knowledge | Creating a Template File

You can also identify an original document so that your Windows operating system always knows that you want to create a new unnamed copy. To do so, save your document as a template file instead of a document. Word will then attach the dotx extension to the file, instead of the docx extension that is applied for a document, and will store the template file in a special location with other templates. Then, you can open the template from the New Document dialog box by clicking *My templates*.

Objective 5 | Change and Reorganize Text

Business letters follow a standard format and contain the following parts: the current date, referred to as the *date line*; the name and address of the person receiving the letter, referred to as the *inside address*; a greeting, referred to as the *salutation*; the text of the letter, usually referred to as the *body* of the letter; a closing line, referred to as the *complimentary closing*; and the *writer's identification*, which includes the name or job title (or both) of the writer, and which is also referred to as the *writer's signature block*.

Some letters also include the initials of the person who prepared the letter, an optional *subject line* that describes the purpose of the letter, or a list of *enclosures*—documents included with the letter.

Activity 2.12 | Recording AutoCorrect Entries

You can correct commonly misspelled words automatically by using Word's *AutoCorrect* feature. Commonly misspelled words—such as *teh* instead of *the*—are corrected using a built-in list that is installed with Office. If you have words that you frequently misspell, you can add them to the list for automatic correction.

1 Click the **File tab** to display **Backstage** view. On the **Help tab**, click **Options** to display the **Word Options** dialog box.

2 On the left side of the **Word Options** dialog box, click **Proofing**, and then under **AutoCorrect options**, click the **AutoCorrect Options** button.

3 In the **AutoCorrect** dialog box, click the **AutoCorrect tab**. Under **Replace**, type **resumee** and under **With**, type **resume**

> If another student has already added this AutoCorrect entry, a Replace button will display.

4 Click **Add**. If the entry already exists, click Replace instead, and then click Yes.

5 In the **AutoCorrect** dialog box, under **Replace**, type **computr** and under **With**, type **computer** and then compare your screen with Figure 2.23.

Figure 2.23

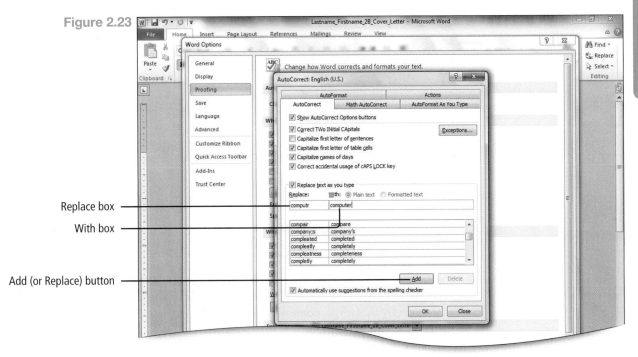

Replace box

With box

Add (or Replace) button

6 Click **Add** (or Replace) and then click **OK** two times to close the dialog boxes.

Activity 2.13 | Creating a Cover Letter

There are a variety of accepted letter formats that you will see in reference manuals and Business Communication texts. The one used in this chapter is a block style cover letter taken from *Business Communication Today*.

1 Press Ctrl + Esc to move the insertion point to the blank line below the letterhead. Press Enter three times, and then type **March 16, 2016** to create the dateline.

> Most Business Communication texts recommend that the dateline be positioned at least 0.5 inch (3 blank lines) below the letterhead; or, position the dateline approximately 2 inches from the top edge of the paper.

2 Press Enter four times, which leaves three blank lines. Type the following inside address on four lines, but do not press Enter following the last line:

James Washington

Madison Staffing Services

600 East Washington Avenue

Madison, WI 53701

> The recommended space between the dateline and inside address varies slightly among Business Communication texts and office reference manuals. However, all indicate that the space can be from one to 10 blank lines depending on the length of your letter.

3 Press [Enter] two times to leave one blank line. Compare your screen with Figure 2.24.

Figure 2.24

Three blank lines between letterhead and dateline

Dateline

Three blank lines between dateline and inside address

Inside address

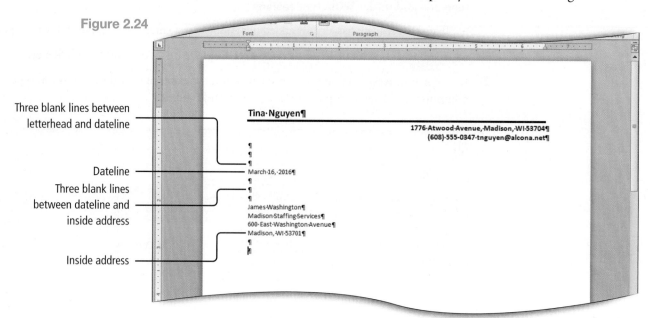

4 Type the salutation **Dear Mr. Washington:** and then press [Enter] two times.

Always leave one blank line above and below the salutation.

5 Type, exactly as shown, the following opening paragraph that includes an intentional word usage error: **I am seeking a position in witch I can use my** and press [Spacebar]. Type, exactly as shown, **computr** and then watch *computr* as you press [Spacebar].

The AutoCorrect feature recognizes the misspelled word, and then changes *computr* to *computer* when you press [Spacebar], [Enter], or a punctuation mark.

6 Type the following, including the misspelled last word: **and communication skills. My education, outlined on the enclosed resumee** and then type **,** (a comma). Notice that when you type the comma, AutoCorrect replaces *resumee* with *resume*.

7 Press [Spacebar]. Complete the paragraph by typing **includes a Business Software Applications Specialist certificate from MATC.** Compare your screen with Figure 2.25.

Figure 2.25

Paragraphs are single spaced

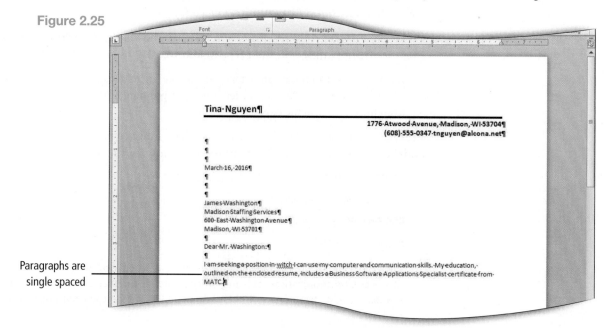

8 Press [Enter] two times. On the **Insert tab**, in the **Text group**, click the **Object button arrow**, and then click **Text from File**. From your student files, locate and **Insert** the file **w02B_Cover_Letter_Text**.

Some of the words in the cover letter text display red, green, or blue wavy underlines. These indicate potential spelling, grammar, or word usage errors, and you will correct them before the end of this project.

9 Scroll as necessary to display the lower half of the letter on your screen, and be sure your insertion point is positioned in the blank paragraph at the end of the document.

10 Press [Enter] one time to leave one blank line between the last paragraph of the letter and the complimentary closing.

11 Type **Sincerely,** as the complimentary closing, and then press [Enter] four times to leave three blank lines between the complimentary closing and the writer's identification.

12 Type **Tina Nguyen** as the writer's identification, and then press [Enter] two times.

13 Type **Enclosure** to indicate that a document is included with the letter. **Save** 🖫 your document, and then compare your screen with Figure 2.26.

Figure 2.26

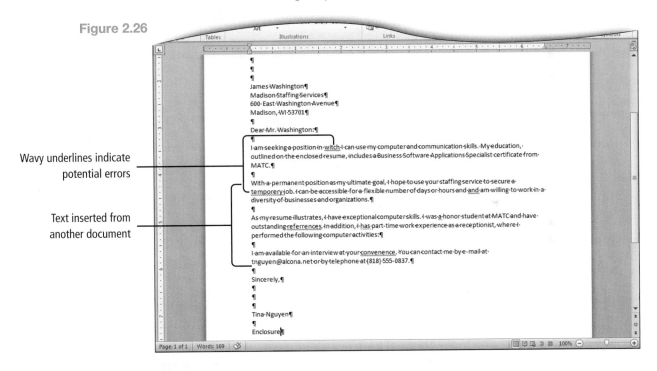

Wavy underlines indicate potential errors

Text inserted from another document

Activity 2.14 | Finding and Replacing Text

Use the Find command to locate text in a document quickly. Use the Find and Replace command to make the same change, or to make more than one change at a time, in a document.

1 Press [Ctrl] + [Home] to position the insertion point at the beginning of the document.

Because a find operation—or a find and replace operation—begins from the location of the insertion point and proceeds to the end of the document, it is good practice to position the insertion point at the beginning of the document before initiating the command.

Another Way

Hold down [Ctrl] and press [F].

2 On the **Home tab**, in the **Editing group**, click the **Find** button.

The Navigation Pane displays on the left side of the screen, with a search box at the top of the pane.

3 In the search box, type **ac** If necessary, scroll down slightly in your document to view the entire body text of the letter, and then compare your screen with Figure 2.27.

In the document, the search letters *ac* are selected and highlighted in yellow for all three words that contain the letters *ac* together. In the Navigation Pane, the three instances are shown in context—*ac* displays in bold.

Figure 2.27

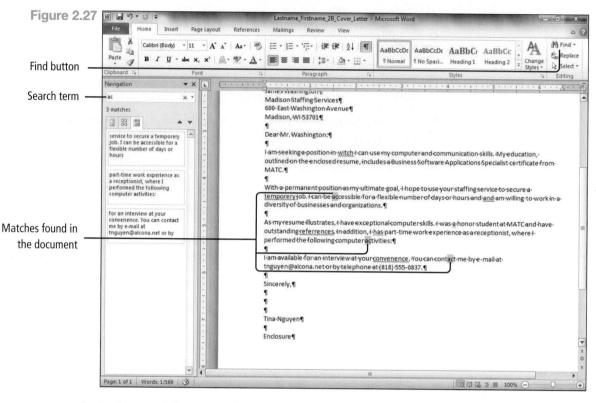

Find button

Search term

Matches found in
the document

4 In the search box, complete the word **accessible**

One match for the search term displays in context in the Navigation Pane and is highlighted in the document.

5 In the document, point to the yellow highlighted word *accessible*, double-click, and then type **available** to replace the word. Notice that the list of results is now empty.

6 Close ☒ the **Navigation Pane**, and then on the **Home tab**, in the **Editing group**, click the **Replace** button.

7 In the **Find and Replace** dialog box, in the **Find what** box, replace the existing text by typing **MATC** In the **Replace with** box, type **Madison Area Technical College** and then compare your screen with Figure 2.28

Figure 2.28

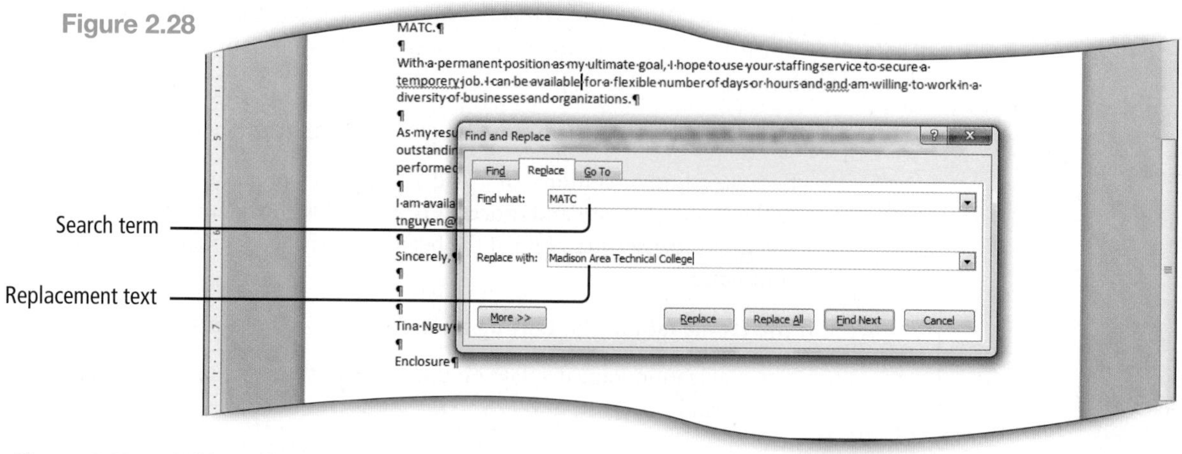

Search term

Replacement text

8 In the lower left corner of the dialog box, click the **More** button to expand the dialog box, and then under **Search Options**, select the **Match case** check box.

> The acronym *MATC* appears in the document two times. In a formal letter, the reader may not know what the acronym means, so you should include the full text instead of an acronym. In this instance, you must select the *Match case* check box so that the replaced text will match the case you typed in the Replace with box, and *not* display in all uppercase letters in the manner of *MATC*.

9 In the **Find and Replace** dialog box, click the **Replace All** button to replace both instances of *MATC*. Click **OK** to close the message box.

10 In the **Find and Replace** dialog box, clear the **Match case** check box, click the **Less** button, and then **Close** the dialog box.

> The Find and Replace dialog box opens with the settings used the last time it was open. Thus, it is good practice to reset this dialog box to its default settings each time you use it.

11 Save 🖫 your document.

Activity 2.15 | Selecting and Moving Text to a New Location

By using Word's ***drag-and-drop*** feature, you can use the mouse to drag selected text from one location to another. Drag-and-drop is most effective when the text to be moved and the destination are on the same screen.

1 Take a moment to study the table in Figure 2.29 to become familiar with the techniques you can use to select text in a document quickly.

Selecting Text in a Document

To Select	Do This
A portion of text	Click to position the insertion point at the beginning of the text you want to select, hold down Shift, and then click at the end of the text you want to select. Alternatively, hold down the left mouse button and drag from the beginning to the end of the text you want to select.
A word	Double-click the word.
A sentence	Hold down Ctrl and click anywhere in the sentence.
A paragraph	Triple-click anywhere in the paragraph; or, move the pointer to the left of the line, into the margin area. When the 🔏 pointer displays, double-click.
A line	Move the pointer to the left of the line. When the 🔏 pointer displays, click one time.
One character at a time	Position the insertion point to the left of the first character, hold down Shift, and press ← or → as many times as desired.
A string of words	Position the insertion point to the left of the first word, hold down Shift and Ctrl, and then press ← or → as many times as desired.
Consecutive lines	Position the insertion point to the left of the first word, hold down Shift and press ↑ or ↓.
Consecutive paragraphs	Position the insertion point to the left of the first word, hold down Shift and Ctrl and press ↑ or ↓.
The entire document	Hold down Ctrl and press A. Alternatively, move the pointer to the left of any line in the document. When the 🔏 pointer displays, triple-click.

Figure 2.29

2 Be sure you can view the entire body of the letter on your screen. In the paragraph that begins *With a permanent position*, in the second line, locate and double-click *days*.

3 Point to the selected word to display the ⬚ pointer.

4 Drag to the right until the dotted vertical line that floats next to the pointer is positioned to the right of the word *hours* in the same line, as shown in Figure 2.30.

Figure 2.30

Word will be dragged to new location

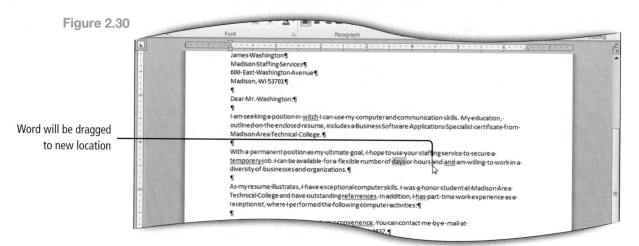

5 Release the mouse button to move the text. Select the word *hours* and drag it to the left of the word *or*—the previous location of the word *days*. Click anywhere in the document to deselect the text.

6 Examine the text that you moved, and add or remove spaces as necessary.

7 Hold down Ctrl, and then in the paragraph that begins *I am available*, click anywhere in the first sentence to select the entire sentence.

8 Drag the selected sentence to the end of the paragraph by positioning the small vertical line that floats with the pointer to the left of the paragraph mark. Compare your screen with Figure 2.31.

Figure 2.31

Sentence moved to end of paragraph

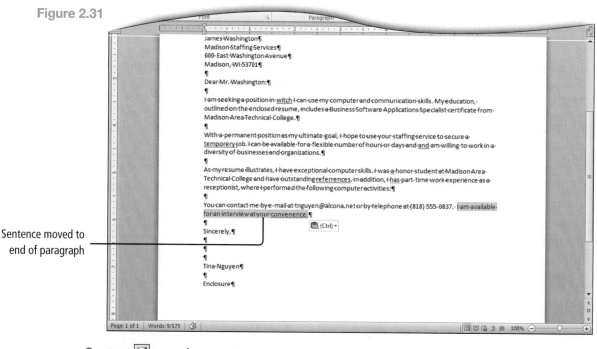

9 **Save** 🖫 your document.

Activity 2.16 | Inserting and Formatting a Table in a Document

1 Locate the paragraph that begins *As my resume*, and then click to position the insertion point in the blank line below that paragraph. Press [Enter] one time.

2 On the **Insert tab**, in the **Tables group**, click the **Table** button. In the **Table** grid, in the third row, click the second square to insert a 2 × 3 table.

3 In the first cell of the table, type **Microsoft Access** and then press [Tab]. Type **Queried inventory data** and then press [Tab]. Complete the table using the following information:

Microsoft Excel	**Entered budget data**
Microsoft Word	**Created and mailed form letters**

4 Point slightly outside of the upper left corner of the table to display the **table move handle** button 田. With the ⃗ pointer, click one time to select the entire table.

5 On the **Layout tab**, in the **Cell Size group**, click the **AutoFit** button, and then click **AutoFit Contents** to have Word choose the best column widths for the two columns based on the text you entered.

6 On the **Home tab**, in the **Paragraph group**, click the **Center** button ≡ to center the table between the left and right margins.

7 On the **Design tab**, in the **Table Styles group**, click the **Borders button arrow**, and then click **No Border**. Click anywhere to cancel the selection of the table, and then compare your screen with Figure 2.32.

> A light dashed line may display in place of the original table borders if your default settings have been changed.

Figure 2.32

Table inserted in letter ———

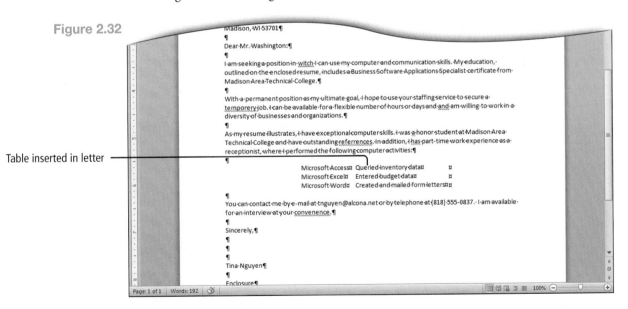

8 **Save** 🖫 your document.

Objective 6 | Use the Proofing Options

Word compares your typing to words in the Office dictionary and compares your phrases and punctuation to a list of grammar rules. This automatic proofing is set by default. Words that are not in the dictionary are marked with a wavy red underline. Phrases and punctuation that differ from the grammar rules are marked with a wavy green underline.

Word also compares commonly misused words with a set of word usage rules, and marks misused words with a wavy blue underline; for example the misuse of *their*, *there*, and *they're*. However, Word will not flag the word *sign* as misspelled even though you intended to type *sing a song* rather than *sign a song*, because both are words contained within Word's dictionary. Your own knowledge and proofreading skills are still required, even when using a sophisticated Word processing program like Word.

Activity 2.17 | Checking Spelling and Grammar Errors

There are two ways to respond to spelling and grammar errors flagged by Word. You can right-click a flagged word or phrase, and then from the shortcut menu choose a correction or action. Or, you can initiate the Spelling and Grammar command to display the Spelling and Grammar dialog box, which provides more options than the shortcut menus.

> **Alert! | Spelling and Grammar Checking**
>
> If you do not see any wavy red, green, or blue lines under words, the automatic spelling and/or grammar checking has been turned off on your system. To activate the spelling and grammar checking, display Backstage view, on the Help tab, click Options, click Proofing, and then under *When correcting spelling in Microsoft Office programs*, select the first four check boxes. Under *When correcting spelling and grammar in Word*, select the first four check boxes, and then click the Writing Style arrow and click Grammar Only. Under *Exceptions for*, clear both check boxes. To display the flagged spelling and grammar errors, click the Recheck Document button, and then close the dialog box.

1 Position the body of the letter on your screen, and then examine the text to locate green, red, and blue wavy underlines. Compare your screen with Figure 2.33.

> A list of grammar rules applied by a computer program like Word can never be exact, and a computer dictionary cannot contain all known words and proper names. Thus, you will need to check any words flagged by Word with wavy underlines, and you will also need to proofread for content errors.

Figure 2.33

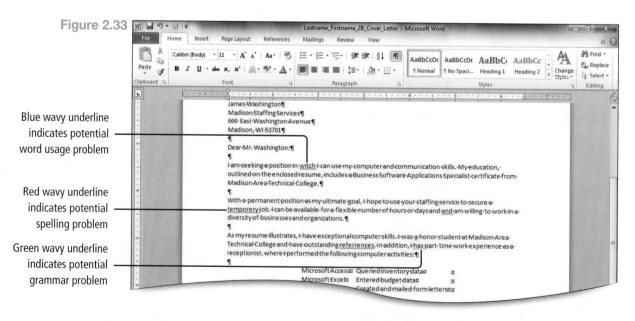

Blue wavy underline indicates potential word usage problem

Red wavy underline indicates potential spelling problem

Green wavy underline indicates potential grammar problem

2 In the lower left corner of your screen, in the status bar, locate and point to the 🕮 icon to display the ScreenTip *Proofing errors were found. Click to correct.*

> If this button displays, you know there are potential errors identified in the document.

3 In the paragraph that begins *With a permanent*, locate the word *temporery* with the wavy red underline. Point to the word and right-click to display the shortcut menu, and then compare your screen with Figure 2.34.

Figure 2.34

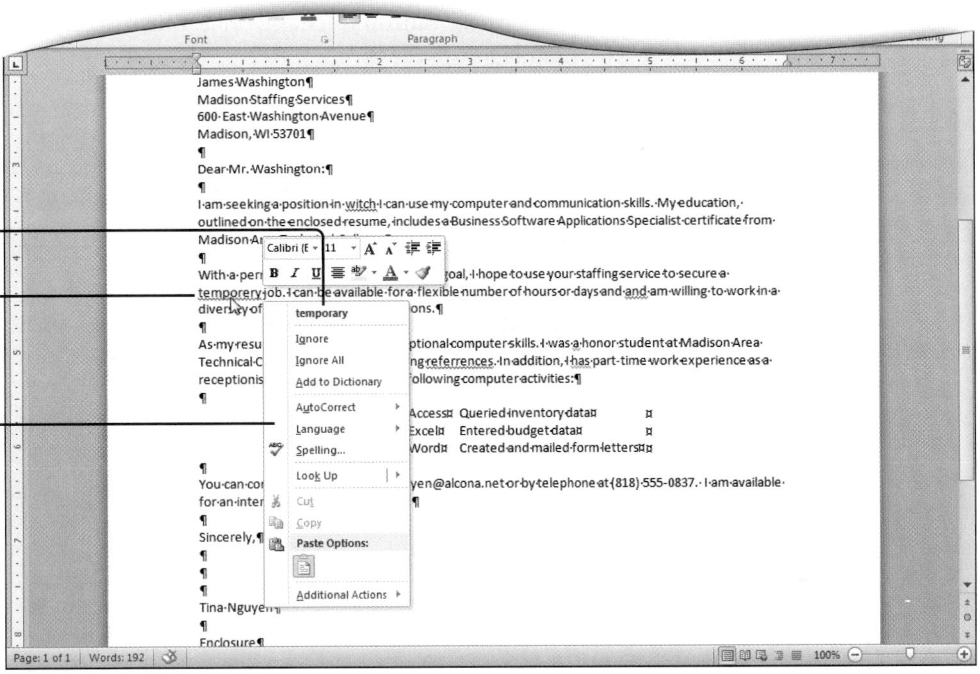

Suggested spelling correction

Misspelled word

Shortcut menu

4 On the shortcut menu, click **temporary** to correct the spelling error.

5 In the next line, locate the word *and* that displays with a wavy red underline, point to word and right-click, and then from the shortcut menu, click **Delete Repeated Word** to delete the duplicate word.

> **Another Way**
>
> Press F7 to start the Spelling & Grammar command.

- - → **6** Press Ctrl + Home to move the insertion point to the beginning of the document. Click the **Review tab**, and then in the **Proofing group**, click the **Spelling & Grammar** button to check the spelling and grammar of the text in the document. Compare your screen with Figure 2.35.

The word *witch* is highlighted—a *Possible Word Choice Error*—and the sentence containing the potential error displays in the dialog box. A suggested change also displays.

Figure 2.35

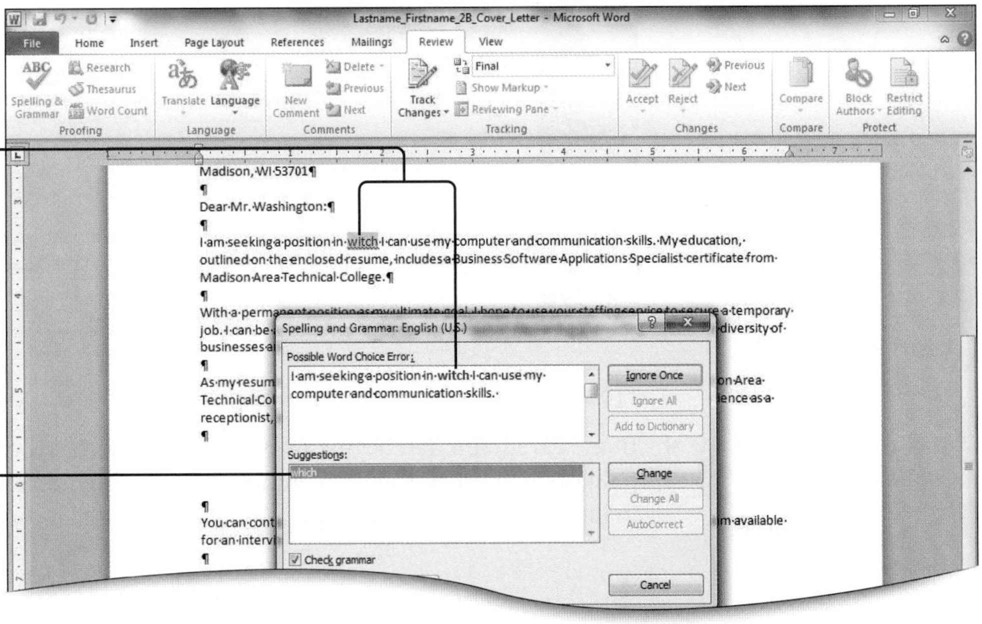

Word usage error

Suggested correction

7 In the **Spelling and Grammar** dialog box, click the **Change** button to change to the correct usage *which*.

> The next marked word—a possible spelling error—displays.

8 Click the **Change** button to change *referrences* to *references*. Notice that the next error is a possible grammar error.

9 Click the **Change** button to change *a* to *an*. Continue the spelling and grammar check and change *has* to *have* and correct the spelling of *convenence*.

10 When Word indicates *The spelling and grammar check is complete*, click **OK**.

11 **Save** 🖫 your document.

Activity 2.18 | Using the Thesaurus

A *thesaurus* is a research tool that lists *synonyms*—words that have the same or similar meaning to the word you selected.

1 Scroll so that you can view the body of the letter. In the paragraph that begins *With a permanent*, at the end of the second line, locate and right-click the word *diversity*.

2 On the shortcut menu, point to **Synonyms**, and then compare your screen with Figure 2.36.

> A list of synonyms displays; the list will vary in length depending on the selected word.

Figure 2.36

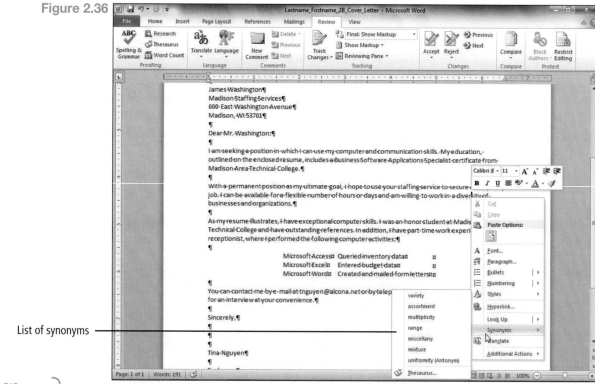

List of synonyms

3 From the list of synonyms, click **variety** to replace *diversity* with *variety*.

4 In the paragraph that begins *As my resume*, point to the word *exceptional*, right-click, point to **Synonyms**, and then at the bottom of the shortcut menu, click **Thesaurus** to display the **Research** task pane.

5 In the **Research** task pane, under **Thesaurus**, point to the non-bold word *excellent*, and then click the **arrow**. Compare your screen with Figure 2.37.

Figure 2.37

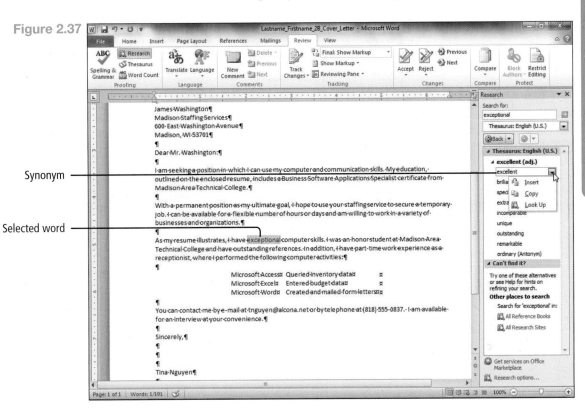

Synonym

Selected word

6 On the menu, click **Insert**, and then **Close** ☒ the **Research** task pane.

excellent replaces the word *exceptional*.

7 Display **Backstage** view and click the **Info tab**. On the right, under the document thumbnail, click **Properties**, and then click **Show Document Panel**. In the **Author** box, type your firstname and lastname. Be sure your course name and section number display in the **Subject** box, and as the **Keywords**, replace any existing text with **cover letter**

8 **Close** ☒ the **Document Panel**.

9 **Save** 🖫, and then display **Backstage** view. Click **Close** to close the document but leave Word open. Hold this file until you complete this project.

Objective 7 | Create a Document Using a Template

Microsoft provides pre-designed templates for letters, resumes, invoices, and other types of documents. Recall that when you open a template, it opens unnamed so that you can reuse it as often as you need to do so.

Activity 2.19 | Locating and Opening a Template

If you need to create a short resume quickly, or if you need ideas about how to format your resume, Microsoft Word provides pre-designed resume templates. Some templates are available on your computer; many more are available online. After opening a template, you can add text as indicated, modify the layout and design, and add or remove resume elements.

1 Close any open documents, and then from **Backstage** view, click **New**.

2 Under **Available Templates**, click **Sample templates**.

3 Under **Available Templates**, scroll toward the bottom of the window, and then click **Median Resume**. Notice that a preview of the *Median Resume* template displays on the right. Compare your screen with Figure 2.38.

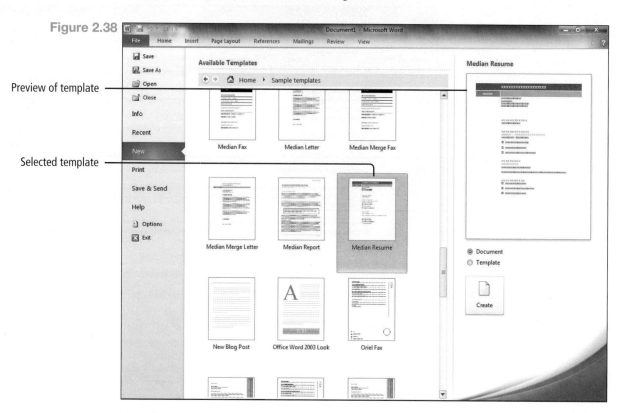

Figure 2.38

Preview of template

Selected template

4 In the lower right corner, click the **Create** button.

The template opens a copy of itself in the form of a new Word document—the title bar indicates *Document* followed by a number. Recall that you are not opening the template itself, and that changes you make to this new document will not affect the contents of the template file.

5 Display the **Save As** dialog box. **Save** the document in your **Word Chapter 2** folder as **Lastname_Firstname_2B_Brief_Resume** and then add the file name to the footer— called the *First Page Footer* in this template.

6 Save 🖬 your document.

Activity 2.20 | Replacing Template Placeholder Text

After you save the template file as a Word document, you can begin to substitute your own information in the indicated locations. You can also remove unneeded resume elements that are included with the template.

1 Click on the picture, and notice that a Picture Tool tab is added to the Ribbon.

2 Click the **Layout tab**, and then in the **Table group**, click the **View Gridlines** button to display non-printing table borders.

This template consists of two Word tables, and the name in the first row of the upper table displays either the user name or the text *[Type your name]* in square brackets.

3 At the top of the upper table, click the **Resume Name tab arrow**, and then compare your screen with Figure 2.39.

> There are two styles available with the Median template—with or without a photo. You should not include a picture on a resume unless physical appearance is directly related to the job for which you are applying—for example, for a job as an actor or a model.

Figure 2.39

Resume Name tab arrow

Two styles available

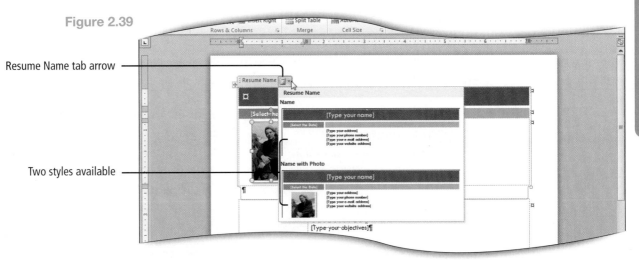

4 In the **Resume Name** gallery, click the first style—**Name**—to switch to the style with no picture.

5 In the first row of the table, select the displayed text—typically the name of your computer as indicated in your Windows operating system—and replace the text by typing **Tina Nguyen**

Another Way

Select the entire row, right-click, and then from the shortcut menu, click Delete Rows.

6 In the second row, click anywhere in the date control *[Select the Date]*. On the Ribbon, click the **Layout tab**. In the **Rows & Columns group**, click the **Delete** button, and then click **Delete Rows**.

> Text surrounded by brackets is called a ***content control***. There are several different types of content controls, including date, picture, and ***text controls***. Most of the controls in this template are text controls. Because resumes do not typically include a date, you can delete this row.

7 Click anywhere in the content control *[Type your address]*. Compare your screen with Figure 2.40.

> For the name and address at the top of the document, all of the text controls are grouped together. Each control has ***placeholder text***, text that indicates the type of information to be entered. The name in the first row may also be a content control with placeholder text.

Figure 2.40

Placeholder text replaced

Date removed

Picture removed

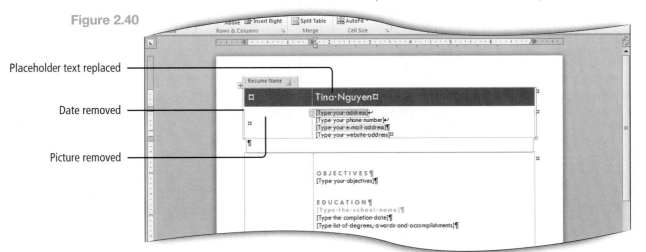

8 Complete the personal information by using the following information:

[Type your address]	**1776 Atwood Avenue, Madison, WI 53704**
[Type your phone number]	**(608) 555-0347**
[Type your e-mail address]	**tnguyen@alcona.net**
[Type your website address]	(leave this blank)

9 In the lower table, click in the *[Type your objectives]* control, and then type **To obtain a position using my computer and communications skills.**

10 Complete the **Education** section by using the following information:

[Type the school name]	**Madison Area Technical College**
[Type the completion date]	**June 2015**
[Type list of degrees, awards and accomplishments] *(type three separate lines)*	**Business Computing Specialist certificate** **Dean's List, four semesters** **President, Community Service Club**

11 Complete the **Experience** section by using the following information:

[Type the job title]	**Office Assistant (part-time)**
[Type the company name]	**The Robinson Company**
[Type the start date]	**September 2014**
[Type the end date]	**present**
[Type list of job responsibilities]	**Data entry and report generation using company spreadsheets and databases.**

12 Click in the *[Type list of skills]* control, type **Proficiency using Word, Excel, and Access (completed advanced courses in Microsoft Office programs)** and then press Enter.

13 As the second bulleted point, type **Excellent written and verbal communications (completed courses in Business Communications, PowerPoint, and Speech)** and then compare your screen with Figure 2.41. **Save** 🖫 your document.

Figure 2.41

Placeholder text replaced ———

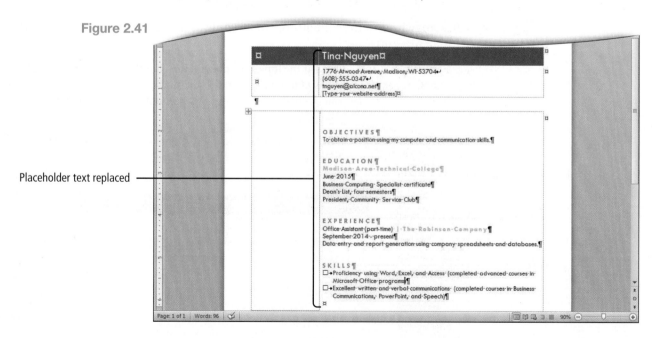

Activity 2.21 | Removing Template Controls and Formatting the Resume

1 Near the top of the document, point to the text control that you did not use—*[Type your website address]*. Right-click the control, and then from the shortcut menu, click **Remove Content Control**. Press ⌊Backspace⌋ as necessary to position the insertion point at the end of the e-mail address. Select the three lines with the address, phone, and e-mail information. On the Mini toolbar, notice that the text size is *11.5*. Click the **Font Size button arrow**, and then click **12**.

2 Click anywhere in lower table—the table with the *Objectives* row at the top—and then point to the upper left corner of the active table to display the **move table handle**. Click one time to select the lower table.

3 On the Mini toolbar, change the **Font Size** to **12** to match the table above.

4 Click anywhere to cancel the selection. On the **Page Layout tab**, in the **Page Setup group**, click the **Margins** button, and then click **Custom Margins**. Change the **Top** margin to **1.5** and the **Left** and **Right** margins to **1** to make this short resume better fill the page. Compare your screen with Figure 2.42.

Figure 2.42

New margins

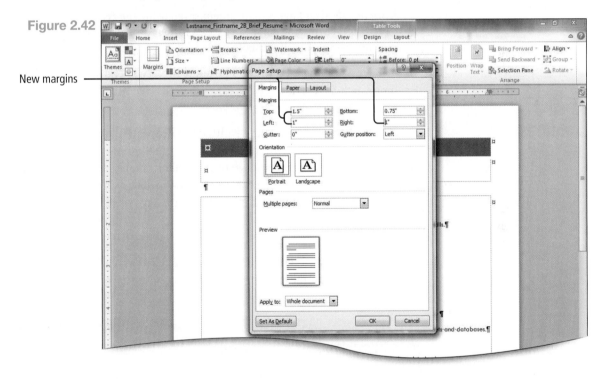

5 Click **OK** to close the **Page Setup** dialog box and apply the new margins. If the name at the top of the document changes back to a placeholder, click the control and type **Tina Nguyen**

6 Right-click the name at the top of the document—*Tina Nguyen*—and then from the shortcut menu, click **Remove Content Control**.

This action will leave the name but remove the control. Remove the control if the Document Properties will have an author other than the name in this control. If you do *not* remove the content control, when you add document properties, the name will change to the name you type in the Author box.

7 Press `Ctrl` + `F2` to display the Print Preview in **Backstage** view. Click the **Info tab**. On the right, under the document thumbnail, click **Properties**, and then click **Show Document Panel**. In the **Author** box, delete any text and then type your firstname and lastname. In the **Subject** box, type your course name and section number, and in the **Keywords** box, type **short resume, template**

8 **Close** ☒ the **Document Panel**. **Save** 🖫 your document, and then hold this file until you complete this project. Leave the resume displayed on your screen.

Activity 2.22 | Saving a Resume as a Web Page

You can save your resume as a Web page. This enables you to post the Web page on your own Web site or on Web space provided by your college. It also enables you to send the resume as an e-mail attachment that can be opened using any Web browser.

1 With your **2B_Brief_Resume** still open on your screen, click **Save** 🖫 to be sure the current version of the document is saved.

2 Display the **Save As** dialog box. In the lower portion of the **Save As** dialog box, click the **Save as type arrow**, and then click **Single File Web Page**.

> A *Single File Web Page* is a document saved using the *Hypertext Markup Language (HTML)*. HTML is the language used to format documents that can be opened using a Web browser such as Internet Explorer.

3 In the **Save As** dialog box, in the **File name** box, type **Lastname_Firstname_2B_HTML_ Resume** Click **Save**, and then click **Yes** if a message box displays. Notice that the Web page displays in Word.

4 Display **Backstage** view. On the right, click **Properties**, and then click **Advanced Properties**. In the **Properties** dialog box, on the **Summary tab**, in the **Subject** box, be sure your course name and section number display. In the **Author** box, be sure your first and last names display. In the **Keywords** box, replace the existing text with **HTML** Click **OK**, and then click the **Home tab**. **Save** 🖫 the document; print or submit electronically as directed.

5 **Exit** Word. From the **Start** menu 🟢, click **Computer**. Navigate to your **Word Chapter 2** folder, and then double-click your **Lastname_Firstname_2B_HTML_Resume** file to open the resume in your Web browser. Compare your screen with Figure 2.43.

Figure 2.43

Resume displayed in a Web browser

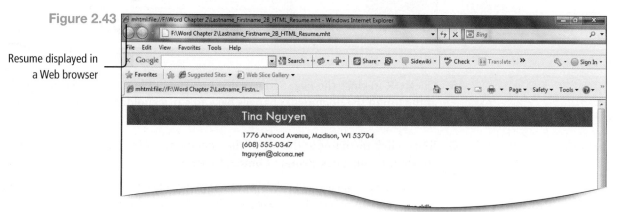

6 **Close** your Web browser. As directed by your instructor, print or submit electronically the four files from this project—2B_Letterhead, 2B_Cover_Letter, 2B_Brief_Resume, and 2B_HTML_Resume.

End **You have completed Project 2B** ————————————————

GO! Beyond Office

Objective | Post an Entry-Level Resume to the Web

Creating a resume is the first step to finding a job; getting the resume in front of prospective employers is the second step. You can hand deliver your resume or mail it to employers. You can also post your resume on the Internet at an employment site. The largest of these is Monster.com, which has over a million job postings a month and tens of millions of resumes on file. Employers can search the site for keywords and locate resumes of people with the skills they need. Monster.com also offers a great deal of support for job seekers—resume and cover letter tips and samples, interviewing tips, and methods to get your resume noticed—even for those looking for their first job. After you sign up for this service, you can upload your resume and add information to your profile that will help prospective employers find you.

> **Alert! | Working with Web-Based Applications and Services**
>
> Computer programs and services on the Web receive continuous updates and improvements. Thus, the steps to complete this Web-based Activity may differ from the ones shown. You can often look at the screens and the information presented to determine how to complete the Activity.

Activity | Posting an Entry-Level Resume to the Web

In this activity, you will modify the 2B_Brief_Resume that you created from a template, create a Monster.com account, fill in your profile, and then upload the resume.

1 Locate and open the **Lastname_Firstname_2B_Brief_Resume** document that you created in Project 2B. In the first line of text, replace *Tina Nguyen* with your name. Replace the address and telephone number with your information.

2 Revise the Objectives, Education, Experience, and Skills sections of the resume to reflect your information.

When you post a resume to Monster.com, you can update it as often as necessary to reflect changes in your resume information. If you decide you do not want to keep a resume on Monster.com, you can remove the resume and any information you have included in your profile.

3 On the **File tab**, click **Save As**. **Save** the document in your **Word Chapter 2** folder as **Lastname_Firstname_2B_Online_Resume** Double-click in the footer area, right-click the file name, and then click **Update Field**.

4 **Save** 🔳, and then **Close** ✖ the document.

5 Open your browser, and then go to **www.monster.com** If an *Are You An Employer* banner displays at the top of the window, on the right side of the banner click *Don't show me this again*.

6 At the top of the window, click **Join Us**. In the **Become a Member** window, fill in the information, and then compare your screen with Figure A.

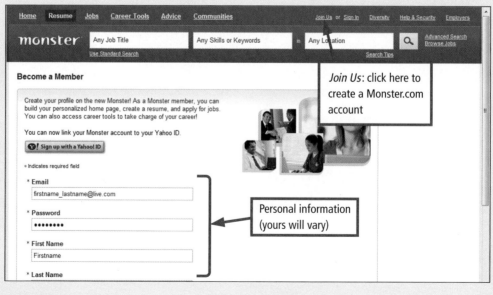

Figure A

7 In the **Become a Member** window, click the **Join** button. If an advertisement displays, in the upper right corner of the window, click *Skip this Offer*—do this whenever an ad window displays. In the **Stay Informed** window, scroll down the page and select e-mails you would like to receive or online communities you would like to join. At the bottom of the page, click **Continue**.

8 Enter any other Profile information you would like to add. From the menu, point to **My Profile**, and then click **Post a Resume**. In the **Create Resume** window, click the **Create Resume** button. In the **Create Resume** dialog box, click the **What type of resume** box, and then click **Upload**.

9 Under **Select the resume**, click the **Browse** button. In the **Choose File to Upload** dialog box, locate and select your **2B_Online_Resume** document, and then click **Open**. Fill in the rest of the information in the dialog box, and then decide if you want to have your resume searchable by employers—if not, clear the check box.

10 At the bottom of the **Create Resume** dialog box, click the **Create** button. In the **Resume Visibility** window, add any other information you would like an employer to see, such as the locations in which you would like to work and what industries you would like to work in. When you are finished, near the top of the window click the **Save** button.

11 In the menu, point to **My Profile**, and then on the right of the list, click your resume name. Compare your screen with Figure B.

12 Display the **Start** menu ⊕, and then click **All Programs**. On the list of programs, click the **Accessories** folder, and then click **Snipping Tool**. In the **Snipping Tool** dialog box, click the **New arrow**. On the displayed list, click **Full-screen Snip**.

13 On the **Snipping Tool** markup window toolbar, click the **Save Snip** button 🖫. In the **Save As** dialog box, navigate to your USB drive and open the **Word Chapter 2** folder. Be sure the **Save as type** box displays **JPEG file**. In the **File name** box, type **Lastname_Firstname_2B_Online_Resume_Snip** and then click **Save**. Close all open windows, and then submit the Word file and the snip as directed.

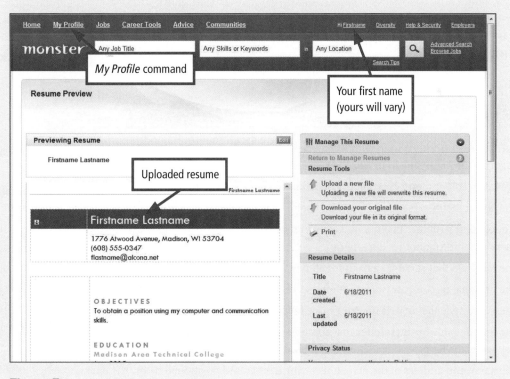

Figure B

Content-Based Assessments

Summary

In this chapter, you created a table, and then used the table to create a resume. You created a letterhead template, and then created a document using a copy of the letterhead template. You created a cover letter for the resume, moved text, corrected spelling and grammar, and used the built-in thesaurus. Finally, you created a short resume using a template, and also saved the resume as a Web page.

Key Terms

AutoCorrect..............248	**Inside address**...........248	**Table** 229
Body..........................248	**Letterhead**.................245	**Template** 245
Cell 229	**New from existing** 246	**Text control**...............261
Complimentary	**No Spacing style**........245	**Thesaurus** 258
closing 248	**Normal template**........245	**Writer's**
Content control 261	**Placeholder text** 261	identification...........248
Date line....................248	**Salutation**..................248	**Writer's signature**
Drag-and-drop...........253	**Single File Web**	block 248
Enclosures 248	Page.......................264	
HTML..........................264	**Subject line** 248	
Hypertext Markup	**Synonyms**..................258	
Language (HTML) ...264		

Matching

Match each term in the second column with its correct definition in the first column by writing the letter of the term on the blank line in front of the correct definition.

_____ 1. An arrangement of information organized into rows and columns.

_____ 2. The box at the intersection of a row and column in a table.

_____ 3. A document structure that opens a copy of itself, opens unnamed, and is used as the starting point for another document.

_____ 4. The template that serves as a basis for all new Word documents.

_____ 5. The personal or company information that displays at the top of a letter.

_____ 6. The Word style that inserts no extra space following a paragraph and uses single spacing.

_____ 7. The first line in a business letter that contains the current date and that is positioned just below the letterhead if a letterhead is used.

_____ 8. The name and address of the person receiving a letter and positioned below the date line.

_____ 9. The greeting line of a letter.

_____ 10. A parting farewell in a letter.

_____ 11. The name and title of the author of a letter, placed near the bottom of the letter under the complimentary closing.

A AutoCorrect

B Cell

C Complimentary closing

D Date line

E Drag and drop

F Enclosures

G Inside address

H Letterhead

I No Spacing

J Normal template

K Salutation

L Subject line

M Table

N Template

O Writer's identification

_____ 12. The optional line following the inside address in a business letter that states the purpose of the letter.

_____ 13. Additional documents included with a business letter.

_____ 14. A Word feature that corrects common spelling errors as you type, for example changing *teh* to *the*.

_____ 15. A technique by which you can move, by dragging, selected text from one location in a document to another.

Multiple Choice

Circle the correct answer.

1. When you create a table, the width of all of cells in the table is:
   A. equal   B. proportional   C. 1 inch

2. To indicate words that might be misspelled because they are not in Word's dictionary, Word flags text with:
   A. blue wavy underlines   B. green wavy underlines   C. red wavy underlines

3. To indicate possible grammar errors, Word flags text with:
   A. blue wavy underlines   B. green wavy underlines   C. red wavy underlines

4. To indicate possible errors in word usage, Word flags text with:
   A. blue wavy underlines   B. green wavy underlines   C. red wavy underlines

5. A research tool that provides a list of words with similar meanings is:
   A. a thesaurus   B. a dictionary   C. an encyclopedia

6. A word with the same or similar meaning as another word is:
   A. an acronym   B. a search term   C. a synonym

7. In a template, an area indicated by placeholder text into which you can add text, pictures, dates, or lists is a:
   A. text control   B. content control   C. quick control

8. A document saved in HTML, which can be opened using a Web browser, is a:
   A. Web page   B. template   C. resume

9. Using drag-and-drop to move text is most useful when both the text and the destination are on the same:
   A. document   B. section   C. screen

10. To locate specific text in a document quickly, use the:
    A. Find command   B. Replace command   C. Locate command

NOTES

Creating Research Papers, Newsletters, and Merged Mailing Labels

OUTCOMES

At the end of this chapter you will be able to::

PROJECT 3A
Create a research paper that includes citations and a bibliography.

OBJECTIVES

Mastering these objectives will enable you to:

1. Create a Research Paper (p. 273)
2. Insert Footnotes in a Research Paper (p. 275)
3. Create Citations and a Bibliography in a Research Paper (p. 280)

PROJECT 3B
Create a multiple-column newsletter and merged mailing labels.

4. Format a Multiple-Column Newsletter (p. 291)
5. Use Special Character and Paragraph Formatting (p. 296)
6. Create Mailing Labels Using Mail Merge (p. 299)

In This Chapter

Microsoft Word provides many tools for creating complex documents. For example, Word has tools that enable you to create a research paper that includes citations, footnotes, and a bibliography. You can also create multiple-column newsletters, format the nameplate at the top of the newsletter, use special character formatting to create distinctive title text, and add borders and shading to paragraphs to highlight important information.

In this chapter, you will edit and format a research paper, create a two-column newsletter, and then create a set of mailing labels to mail the newsletter to multiple recipients.

wawritto/Shutterstock

The projects in this chapter relate to **Memphis Primary Materials** located in the Memphis area. In addition to collecting common recyclable materials, the company collects and recycles computers, monitors, copiers and fax machines, cell phones, wood pallets, and compostable materials. The company's name comes from the process of capturing the "primary materials" of used items for reuse. Memphis Primary Materials ensures that its clients comply with all state and local regulations. They also provide training to clients on the process and benefits of recycling.

Project 3A Research Paper

myitlab
Project 3A Training

Project Activities

In Activities 3.01 through 3.07, you will edit and format a research paper that contains an overview of recycling activities in which businesses can engage. This paper was created by Elizabeth Freeman, a student intern working for Memphis Primary Metals, and will be included in a customer information packet. Your completed document will look similar to Figure 3.1.

Project Files

For Project 3A, you will need the following file:

w03A_Green_Business

You will save your document as:

Lastname_Firstname_3A_Green_Business

Project Results

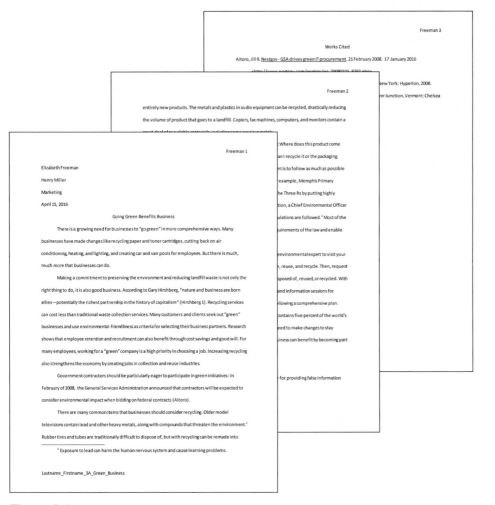

Figure 3.1
Project 3A Green Business

Objective 1 | Create a Research Paper

When you write a research paper or a report for college or business, follow a format prescribed by one of the standard *style guides*—a manual that contains standards for the design and writing of documents. The two most commonly used styles for research papers are those created by the *Modern Language Association (MLA)* and the *American Psychological Association (APA)*; there are several others.

Activity 3.01 | Formatting Text and Page Numbers in a Research Paper

When formatting the text for your research paper, refer to the standards for the style guide that you have chosen. In this activity, you will create a research paper using the MLA style. The MLA style uses 1-inch margins, a 0.5" first line indent, and double spacing throughout the body of the document, with no extra space above or below paragraphs.

1 **Start** Word. From your student files, locate and open the document **w03A_Green_Business**. If necessary, display the formatting marks and rulers. In the location where you are storing your projects for this chapter, create a new folder named **Word Chapter 3** and then **Save** the file in the folder as **Lastname_Firstname_3A_Green_Business**

2 Press Ctrl + A to select the entire document. On the **Home tab**, in the **Paragraph group**, click the **Line and Paragraph Spacing** button, and then change the line spacing to **2.0**. On the **Page Layout tab**, in the **Paragraph group**, change the **Spacing After** to **0 pt**.

3 Press Ctrl + Home to deselect and move to the top of the document. Press Enter one time to create a blank line at the top of the document, and then click to position the insertion point in the blank line. Type **Elizabeth Freeman** and press Enter.

4 Type **Henry Miller** and press Enter. Type **Marketing** and press Enter. Type **April 15, 2016** and press Enter. Type **Going Green Benefits Business** Right-click anywhere in the line you just typed, and then on the Mini toolbar, click the **Center** button. Compare your screen with Figure 3.2.

Figure 3.2

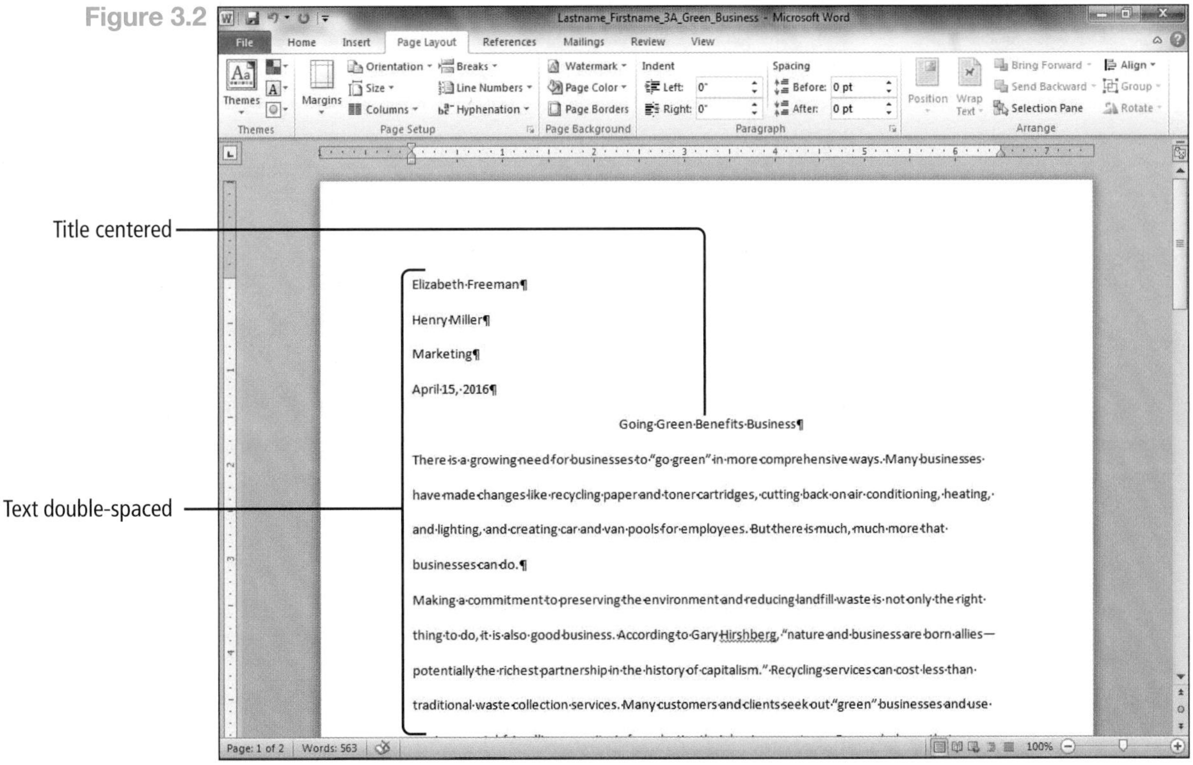

Title centered

Text double-spaced

5 At the top of the **Page 1**, point anywhere in the white top margin area, right-click, and then click **Edit Header**. In the header area, type **Freeman** and then press Spacebar.

> Recall that the text you insert into a header or footer displays on every page of a document. Within a header or footer, you can insert many different types of information; for example, automatic page numbers, the date, the time, the file name, or pictures.

6 On the **Design tab**, in the **Header & Footer group**, click the **Page Number** button, and then point to **Current Position**. In the displayed gallery, under **Simple**, click **Plain Number**. Compare your screen with Figure 3.3.

> Word will automatically number the pages using this number format.

Figure 3.3

Page number field added to header

Last name in header

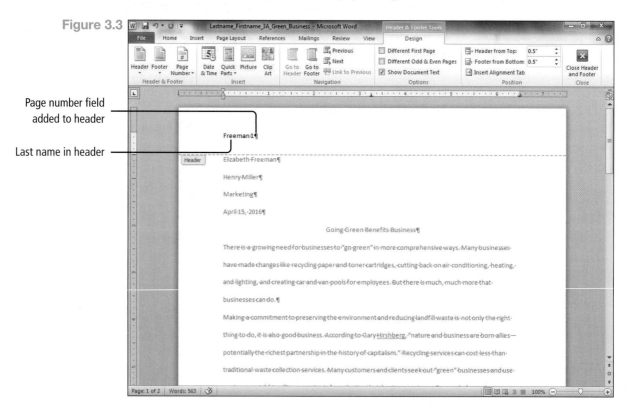

7 On the **Home tab**, in the **Paragraph group**, click the **Align Text Right** button [≡]. Double-click anywhere in the document to close the header area.

8 Near the top of **Page 1**, locate the paragraph beginning *There is a growing*, and then click to position the insertion point at the beginning of the paragraph. By moving the vertical scroll bar, scroll to the end of the document, hold down Shift, and then click to right of the last paragraph mark to select all of the text from the insertion point to the end of the document. Release Shift.

Another Way

Right-click the selected text, click Paragraph, on the Indents and Spacing tab, under Indentation, click the Special arrow, and then click First line. Under Indentation, in the By box, be sure 0.5" displays.

9 With the text selected, on the ruler, point to the **First Line Indent** button, and then drag the button to **0.5" on the horizontal ruler**. Compare your screen with Figure 3.4.

The MLA style uses 0.5-inch indents at the beginning of the first line of every paragraph. Indenting—moving the beginning of the first line of a paragraph to the right or left of the rest of the paragraph—provides visual cues to the reader to help divide the document text and make it easier to read.

Figure 3.4

First Line Indent button moved to 0.5" on the ruler

First line indented 0.5 inch

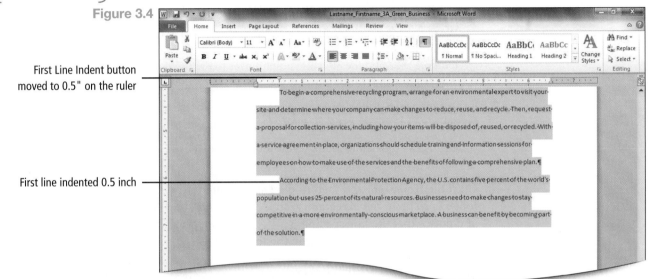

10 Click anywhere to deselect the text. Scroll to view the bottom of **Page 1**, point anywhere in the bottom white margin area, right-click, and then click **Edit Footer**. On the **Design tab**, in the **Insert group**, click the **Quick Parts** button, and then click **Field**. In the **Field** dialog box, under **Field names**, locate and click **FileName**, and then click **OK**.

The file name in the footer is *not* part of the research report format, but it is included in projects in this textbook so that you and your instructor can identify your work.

11 Double-click anywhere in the document to close the Footer area, and then **Save** your document.

More Knowledge | Suppressing the Page Number on the First Page

Some style guidelines require that the page number and other header and footer information on the first page be hidden from view—*suppressed*. To hide the information contained in the header and footer areas on Page 1 of a document, double-click in the header or footer area. Then, on the Design tab, in the Options group, select the Different First Page check box.

Objective 2 | Insert Footnotes in a Research Paper

Reports and research papers typically include information that you find in other sources, and these must be credited. Within report text, numbers mark the location of **notes**—information that expands on the topic being discussed but that does not fit well in the document text. The numbers refer to **footnotes**—notes placed at the bottom of the page containing the note, or to **endnotes**—notes placed at the end of a document or chapter.

Activity 3.02 | Inserting Footnotes

Footnotes can be added as you type the document or after the document is complete. Word renumbers the footnotes automatically, so footnotes do not need to be entered in order, and if one footnote is removed, the remaining footnotes renumber automatically.

1. Scroll to view the top of **Page 2**. Locate the paragraph that begins *Consumers and businesses*. In the seventh line of text, toward the end of the line, click to position the insertion point to the right of the period after *followed*.

2. On the **References tab**, in the **Footnotes group**, click the **Insert Footnote** button.

> Word creates space for a footnote in the footnote area at the bottom of the page and adds a footnote number to the text at the insertion point location. Footnote *1* displays in the footnote area, and the insertion point moves to the right of the number. A short black line is added just above the footnote area. You do not need to type the footnote number.

3. Type **Tennessee, for example, imposes penalties of up to $10,000 for providing false information regarding the recycling of hazardous waste.**

> This is an explanatory footnote; the footnote provides additional information that does not fit well in the body of the report.

4. Click the **Home tab**, and then in the **Font group**, notice that the font size of the footer is *10 pt*. In the **Paragraph group**, click the **Line and Paragraph Spacing** button, and notice that the line spacing is *1.0*—single-spaced—even though the font size of the document text is 11 pt and the text is double-spaced, as shown in Figure 3.5.

Figure 3.5

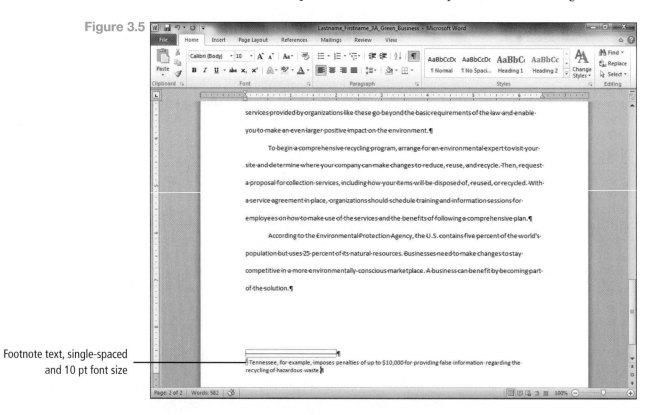

Footnote text, single-spaced and 10 pt font size

5. Scroll to view the bottom of **Page 1**, and then locate the paragraph that begins *There are many common*. At the end of the second line of text, click to position the insertion point to the right of the period following *environment*.

6 On the **References tab**, in the **Footnotes group**, click the **Insert Footnote** button. Type **Exposure to lead can harm the human nervous system and cause learning problems.** Notice that the footnote you just added becomes the new footnote *1*, as shown in Figure 3.6.

> The first footnote is renumbered as footnote *2*.

Figure 3.6

Footnote number in text ——

New footnote ——

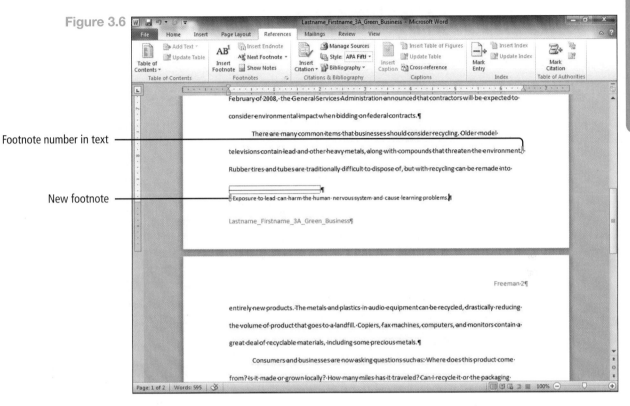

7 **Save** your document.

More Knowledge | **Using Symbols Rather Than Numbers for Notes**

Instead of using numbers to designate footnotes, you can use standard footnote symbols. The seven traditional symbols, available from the Footnote and Endnote dialog box, in order, are * (asterisk), † (dagger), ‡ (double dagger), § (section mark), || (parallels), ¶ (paragraph mark), and # (number or pound sign). This sequence can be continuous (this is the default setting), or can begin anew with each page.

Activity 3.03 | Modifying a Footnote Style

Microsoft Word contains built-in paragraph formats called *styles*—groups of formatting commands, such as font, font size, font color, paragraph alignment, and line spacing—which can be applied to a paragraph with one command.

The default style for footnote text is a single-spaced paragraph that uses a 10-point Calibri font and no paragraph indents. MLA style specifies double-spaced text in all areas of a research paper—including footnotes. According to the MLA style, first lines of footnotes must also be indented 0.5 inch and use the same font size as the report text.

1 Scroll to view the bottom of **Page 2**. Point anywhere in the footnote text and right-click, and then from the shortcut menu, click **Style**. Compare your screen with Figure 3.7.

The Style dialog box displays, listing the styles currently in use in the document, in addition to some of the word processing elements that come with special built-in styles. Because you right-clicked on the footnote text, the selected style is the Footnote Text style.

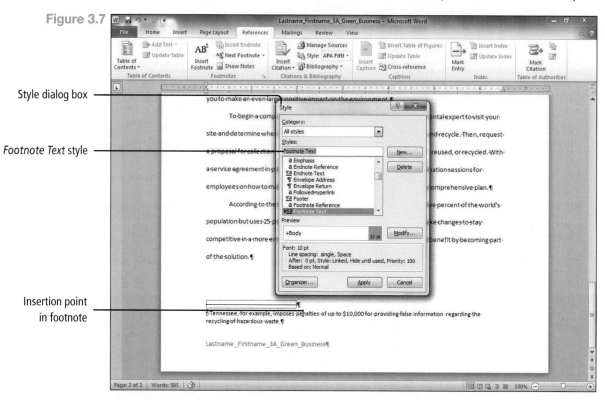

Figure 3.7

Style dialog box

Footnote Text style

Insertion point in footnote

2 In the **Style** dialog box, click the **Modify** button to display the **Modify Style** dialog box.

3 In the **Modify Style** dialog box, locate the small **Formatting** toolbar in the center of the dialog box, click the **Font Size button arrow**, click **11**, and then compare your screen with Figure 3.8.

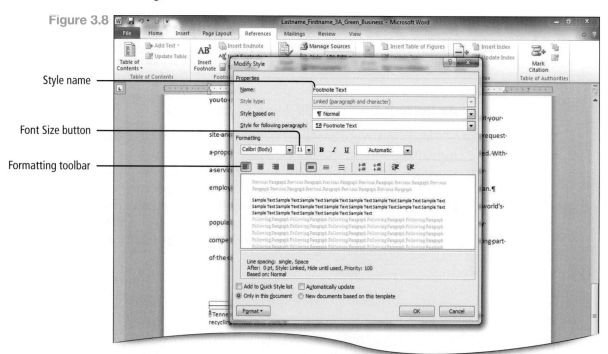

Figure 3.8

Style name

Font Size button

Formatting toolbar

4 In the lower left corner of the dialog box, click the **Format** button, and then click **Paragraph**. In the **Paragraph** dialog box, under **Indentation**, click the **Special arrow**, and then click **First line**.

5 Under **Spacing**, click the **Line spacing button arrow**, and then click **Double**. Compare your dialog box with Figure 3.9.

Figure 3.9

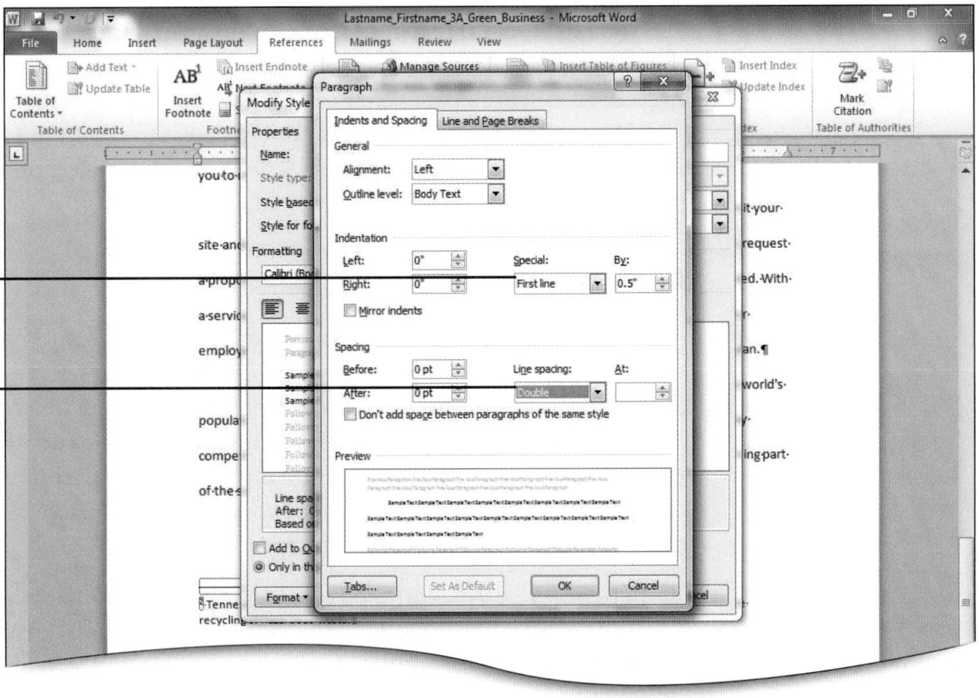

First line indent selected

Line spacing set to *Double*

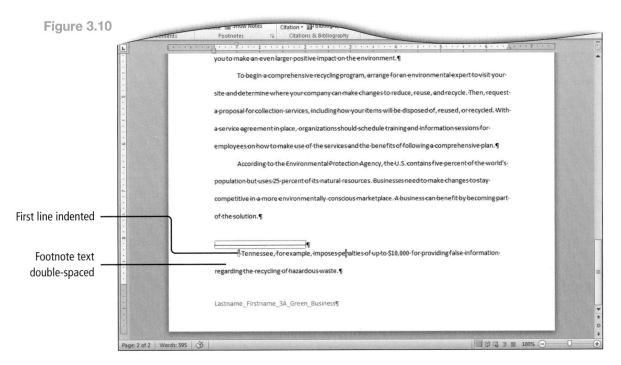

6 Click **OK** to close the **Paragraph** dialog box, click **OK** to close the **Modify Style** dialog box, and then click **Apply** to apply the new style. Notice that when you click Apply, the Style dialog box closes. Compare your screen with Figure 3.10.

Your inserted footnotes are formatted with the new Footnote Text paragraph style; any new footnotes that you insert will also use this format.

Figure 3.10

First line indented

Footnote text double-spaced

you·to·make·an·even·larger·positive·impact·on·the·environment.¶

To·begin·a·comprehensive·recycling·program,·arrange·for·an·environmental·expert·to·visit·your·site·and·determine·where·your·company·can·make·changes·to·reduce,·reuse,·and·recycle.·Then,·request·a·proposal·for·collection·services,·including·how·your·items·will·be·disposed·of,·reused,·or·recycled.·With·a·service·agreement·in·place,·organizations·should·schedule·training·and·information·sessions·for·employees·on·how·to·make·use·of·the·services·and·the·benefits·of·following·a·comprehensive·plan.¶

According·to·the·Environmental·Protection·Agency,·the·U.S.·contains·five·percent·of·the·world's·population·but·uses·25·percent·of·its·natural·resources.·Businesses·need·to·make·changes·to·stay·competitive·in·a·more·environmentally-conscious·marketplace.·A·business·can·benefit·by·becoming·part·of·the·solution.¶

⁰Tennessee,·for·example,·imposes·penalties·of·up·to·$10,000·for·providing·false·information·regarding·the·recycling·of·hazardous·waste.¶

Lastname_Firstname_3A_Green_Business¶

7 Scroll to view the bottom of **Page 1** to confirm that the new format was also applied to the first footnote, and then **Save** 🔲 your document.

Objective 3 | Create Citations and a Bibliography in a Research Paper

When you use quotations from, or detailed summaries of, other people's work, you must specify the source of the information. A ***citation*** is a note inserted into the text of a report or research paper that refers the reader to a source in the bibliography. Create a ***bibliography*** at the end of a document to list the sources referred to in the document. Such a list is typically titled ***Works Cited*** (in MLA style), *Bibliography*, *Sources*, or *References*.

Activity 3.04 | Adding Citations

When writing a long research paper, you will likely reference numerous books, articles, and Web sites. Some of your research sources may be referenced many times, others only one time. References to sources within the text of your research paper are indicated in an *abbreviated* manner. However, as you enter a citation for the first time, you can also enter the *complete* information about the source. Then, when you have finished your paper, you will be able to automatically generate the list of sources that must be included at the end of your research paper.

1 Press Ctrl + Home, and then locate the paragraph that begins *Making a commitment*. In the third line, following the word *capitalism*, click to position the insertion point to the right of the quotation mark.

> The citation in the document points to the full source information in the bibliography, which typically includes the name of the author, the full title of the work, the year of publication, and other publication information.

2 On the **References tab**, in the **Citations & Bibliography group**, click the **Style button arrow**, and then click **MLA Sixth Edition** (or the latest edition) to insert a reference using MLA style.

3 Click the **Insert Citation** button, and then click **Add New Source**. Be sure *Book* is selected as the **Type of Source**. Add the following information, and then compare your screen with Figure 3.11:

Author:	**Hirshberg, Gary**
Title:	**Stirring it Up: How to Make Money and Save the World**
Year:	**2008**
City:	**New York**
Publisher:	**Hyperion**

> In the MLA style, citations that refer to items on the *Works Cited* page are placed in parentheses and are referred to as ***parenthetical references***—references that include the last name of the author or authors and the page number in the referenced source, which you add to the reference. No year is indicated, and there is no comma between the name and the page number.

Figure 3.11

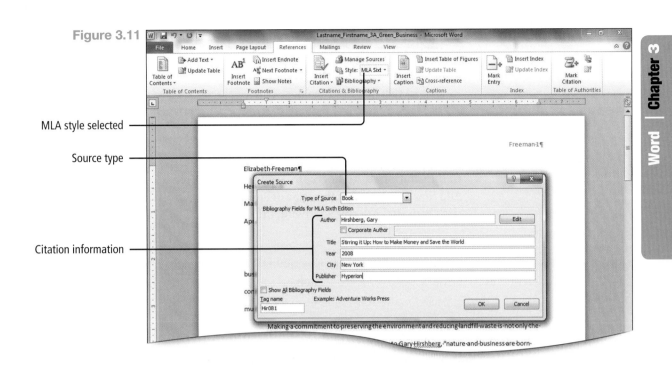

MLA style selected

Source type

Citation information

Note | Citing Corporate Authors

If the author of a document is identified as the name of an organization only, select the Corporate Author check box and type the name of the organization in the Corporate Author box.

---

4 Click **OK** to insert the citation. In the paragraph, point to *(Hirshberg)* and click one time to select the citation.

5 In the lower right corner of the box that surrounds the reference, point to the small arrow to display the ScreenTip *Citation Options*. Click this **Citation Options arrow**, and then from the list of options, click **Edit Citation**.

6 In the **Edit Citation** dialog box, under **Add**, in the **Pages** box, type **1** to indicate that you are citing from Page 1 of this source. Compare your screen with Figure 3.12.

Figure 3.12

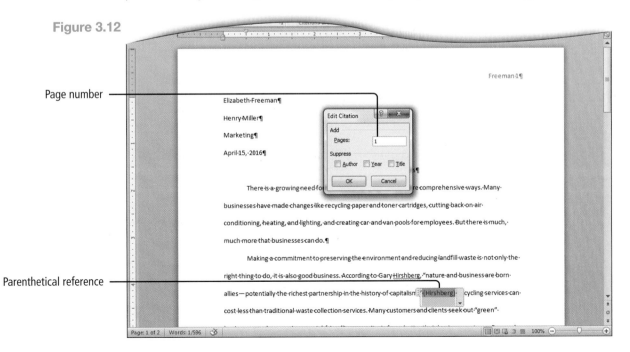

Page number

Parenthetical reference

7 Click **OK** to display the page number of the citation. Click outside of the citation box to deselect it. Then type a period to the right of the citation, and delete the period to the left of the quotation mark.

> In the MLA style, if the reference occurs at the end of a sentence, the parenthetical reference always displays to the left of the punctuation mark that ends the sentence.

8 In the next paragraph, which begins *Government contractors*, click to position the insertion point at the end of the paragraph, but before the period.

9 In the **Citations & Bibliography group**, click the **Insert Citation** button, and then click **Add New Source**. Click the **Type of Source arrow**, scroll down as necessary, and then click **Web site**. Add the following information:

Author:	**Aitoro, Jill R.**
Name of Web Page:	**Nextgov - GSA drives green IT procurement**
Year:	**2008**
Month:	**February**
Day:	**21**
Year Accessed:	**2016**
Month Accessed:	**January**
Day Accessed:	**17**
URL:	**http://www.nextgov.com/nextgov/ng_20080221_8792.php**

10 Compare your screen with Figure 3.13, and then click **OK** to close the **Create Source** dialog box and add the citation.

> A parenthetical reference is added. Because the cited Web page has no page numbers, only the author name is used in the parenthetical reference.

Figure 3.13

Web site citation

Insertion point indicates location of parenthetical reference

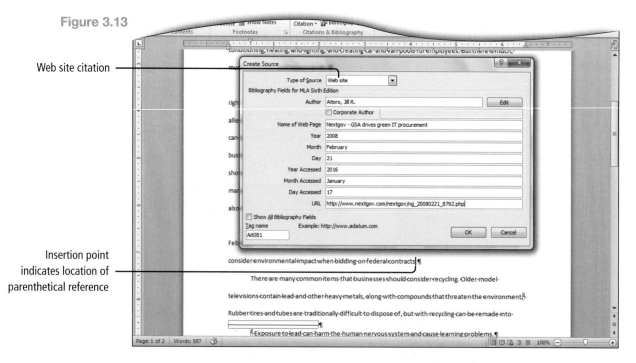

11 Near the top of **Page 2**, in the paragraph that begins *Consumers and businesses*, in the third line, click to position the insertion point following the word *toxic* to the left of the question mark.

12 In the **Citations & Bibliography group**, click the **Insert Citation** button, and then click **Add New Source**. Click the **Type of Source arrow**, if necessary scroll to the top of the list, click **Book**, and then add the following information:

Author:	**Scott, Nicky**
Title:	**Reduce, Reuse, Recycle: An Easy Household Guide**
Year:	**2007**
City:	**White River Junction, Vermont**
Publisher:	**Chelsea Green Publishing**

13 Click **OK**. Click the inserted citation to select it, click the **Citation Options arrow**, and then click **Edit Citation**.

14 In the **Edit Citation** dialog box, under **Add**, in the **Pages** box, type **7** to indicate that you are citing from page 7 of this source. Click **OK**.

15 On the **References tab**, in the **Citations & Bibliography group**, click the **Manage Sources** button. In the **Source Manager** dialog box, under **Current List**, click the third source and then compare your screen with Figure 3.14.

> The Source Manager dialog box displays. Other citations on your computer display in the Master List box. The citations for the current document display in the Current List box. Word maintains the Master List so that if you use the same sources regularly, you can copy sources from your Master List to the current document. A preview of the selected bibliography entry also displays at the bottom of the dialog box.

Figure 3.14

Sources used in this document

Other available sources (yours will vary)

Preview of selected citation

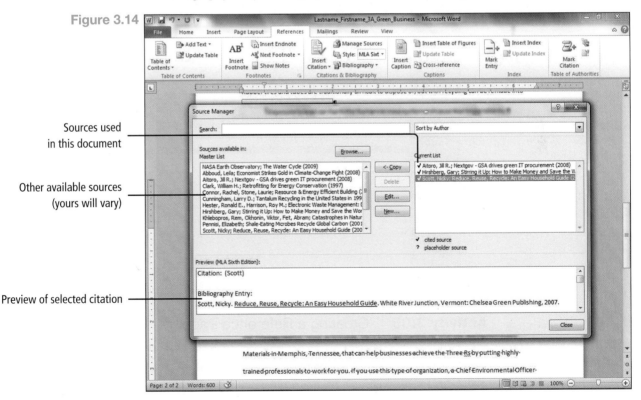

16 At the bottom of the **Source Manager** dialog box, click **Close**. Click anywhere in the document to deselect the parenthetical reference, and then **Save** 🖫 your document.

Activity 3.05 | Inserting Page Breaks

In this activity you will insert a manual page break so that you can begin your bibliography on a new page.

1 Press Ctrl + End to move the insertion point to the end of the document. Notice that the insertion point displays at the end of the final paragraph, but above the footnote—the footnote is always associated with the page that contains the citation.

2 Press Ctrl + Enter to insert a manual page break.

A ***manual page break*** forces a page to end at the insertion point location, and then places any subsequent text at the top of the next page. Recall that the new paragraph retains the formatting of the previous paragraph, so the first line is indented.

3 On the ruler, point to the **First Line Indent** button ▽, and then drag the **First Line Indent** button to the left to **0 inches on the horizontal ruler**.

4 Scroll as necessary to position the bottom of **Page 2** and the top of **Page 3** on your screen.

5 Compare your screen with Figure 3.15, and then **Save** 🖫 your document.

A ***page break indicator***, which shows where a manual page break was inserted, displays at the bottom of the Page 2, and the footnote remains on the page that contains the citation, even though it displays below the page break indicator.

Figure 3.15

First Line Indent button at 0 inches

Page Break indicator shows manual page break inserted

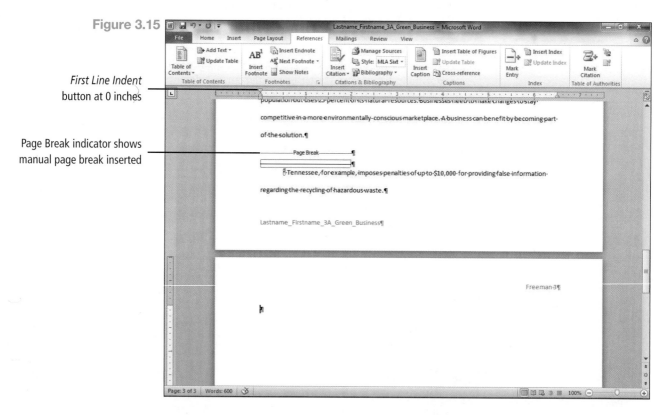

Activity 3.06 │ Creating a Reference Page

At the end of a report or research paper, include a list of each source referenced. *Works Cited* is the reference page heading used in the MLA style guidelines. Other styles may refer to this page as a *Bibliography* (Business Style) or *References* (APA Style). This information is always displayed on a separate page.

1 With the insertion point blinking in the first line of **Page 3**, type **Works Cited** and then press Enter. On the **References tab**, in the **Citations & Bibliography group**, in the **Style** box, be sure *MLA* displays.

2 In the **Citations & Bibliography group**, click the **Bibliography** button, and then near the bottom of the list, click **Insert Bibliography**.

3 Scroll as necessary to view the entire list of three references, and then click anywhere in the inserted text.

> The bibliography entries that you created display as a field, which is indicated by the gray shading when you click in the text. The field links to the Source Manager for the citations. The references display alphabetically by the author's last name.

4 In the bibliography, point to the left of the first entry—beginning *Aitoro, Jill*—to display the 🔏 pointer. Drag down to select all three references.

Another Way

Display the Paragraph dialog box. Under Spacing, click the Line spacing arrow, and then click Double. Under Spacing, in the After box, type 0.

5 On the **Home tab**, in the **Paragraph group**, change the **Line spacing** to **2.0**, and then on the **Page Layout tab**, in the **Paragraph group**, change the **Spacing After** to **0 pt**.

> The entries display according to MLA guidelines; the text is double-spaced, the extra space between paragraphs is removed, and each entry uses a *hanging indent*—the first line of each entry extends 0.5 inch to the left of the remaining lines of the entry.

6 At the top of **Page 3**, right-click the *Works Cited* title, and then click the **Center** button ▤. Compare your screen with Figure 3.16, and then **Save** 🖫 your document.

> In MLA style, the *Works Cited* title is centered.

Figure 3.16

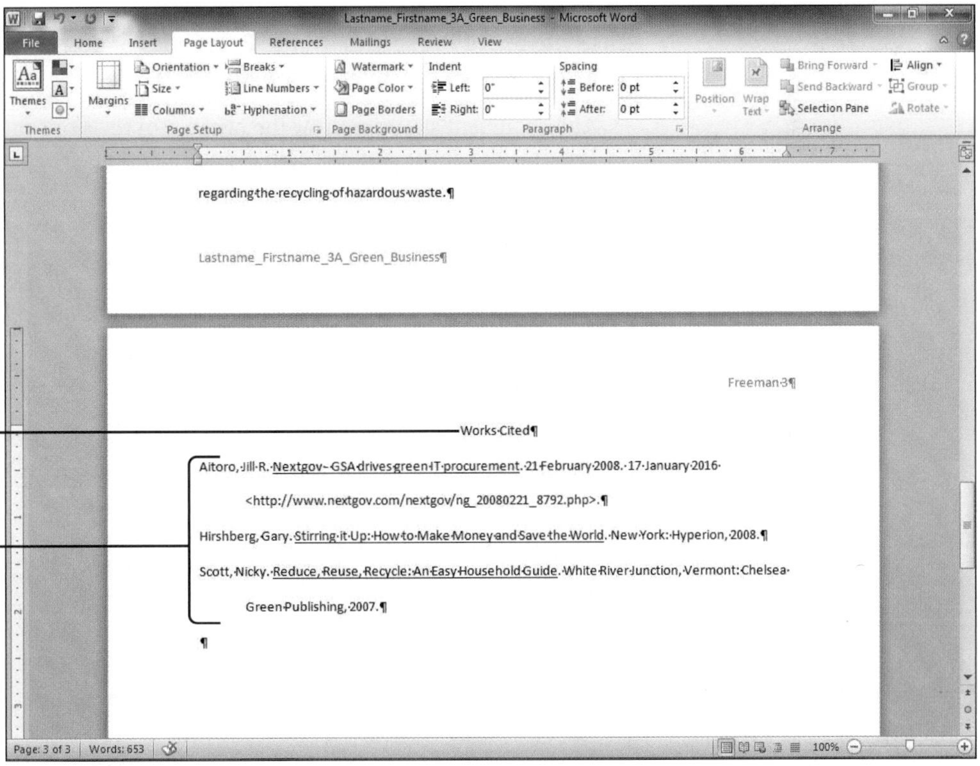

Works Cited title centered

Bibliography inserted, double-spaced, and hanging indent applied

Activity 3.07 | Managing Document Properties

Recall that document property information is stored in the Document Panel. An additional group of property categories is also available.

1 Display **Backstage** view. On the right, under the document thumbnail, click **Properties**, and then click **Show Document Panel** to display the **Document Panel**.

2 Type your name and course information, and then add the keywords **green business, research paper**

3 In the upper left corner of the **Document Panel**, click the **Document Properties** button, and then compare your screen with Figure 3.17.

Figure 3.17

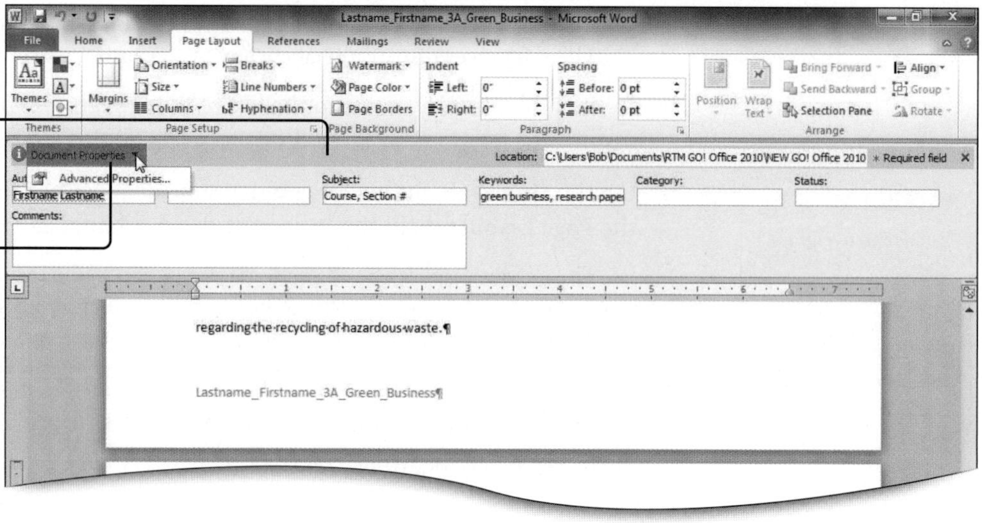

Document Panel

Document Properties button

4 Click **Advanced Properties**. In the **Properties** dialog box, click the **Statistics tab**, and then compare your screen with Figure 3.18.

The document statistics show the number of revisions made to the document, the last time the document was edited, and the number of paragraphs, lines, words, and characters in the document.

Figure 3.18

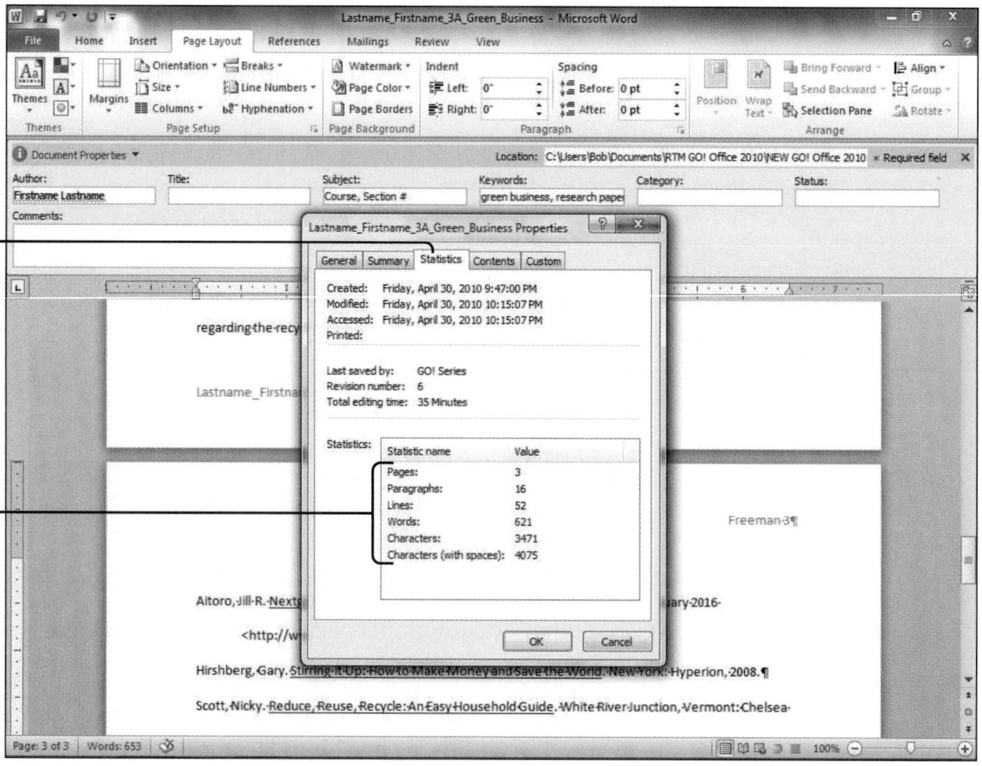

Statistics tab

Document statistics (yours may vary)

5 In the **Properties** dialog box, click the **Summary tab**. Notice that not all of the categories are filled in, and also notice that there are categories on this tab that are not found in the Document Panel.

Some of the boxes may contain information from your computer system.

6 In the **Properties** dialog box, click in the **Title** box and type **Going Green Benefits Business**

7 Click in the **Manager** box and type **Henry Miller**

8 In the **Company** box, select and delete any existing text, and then type **Memphis Primary Materials**

9 Click in the **Category** box and type **Marketing Documents**

10 Click in the **Comments** box and type **Draft copy of a research report that will be included in the marketing materials packet**

Additional information categories are available by clicking the Custom tab.

11 Compare your screen with Figure 3.19, and then at the bottom of the **Properties** dialog box, click **OK**.

Figure 3.19

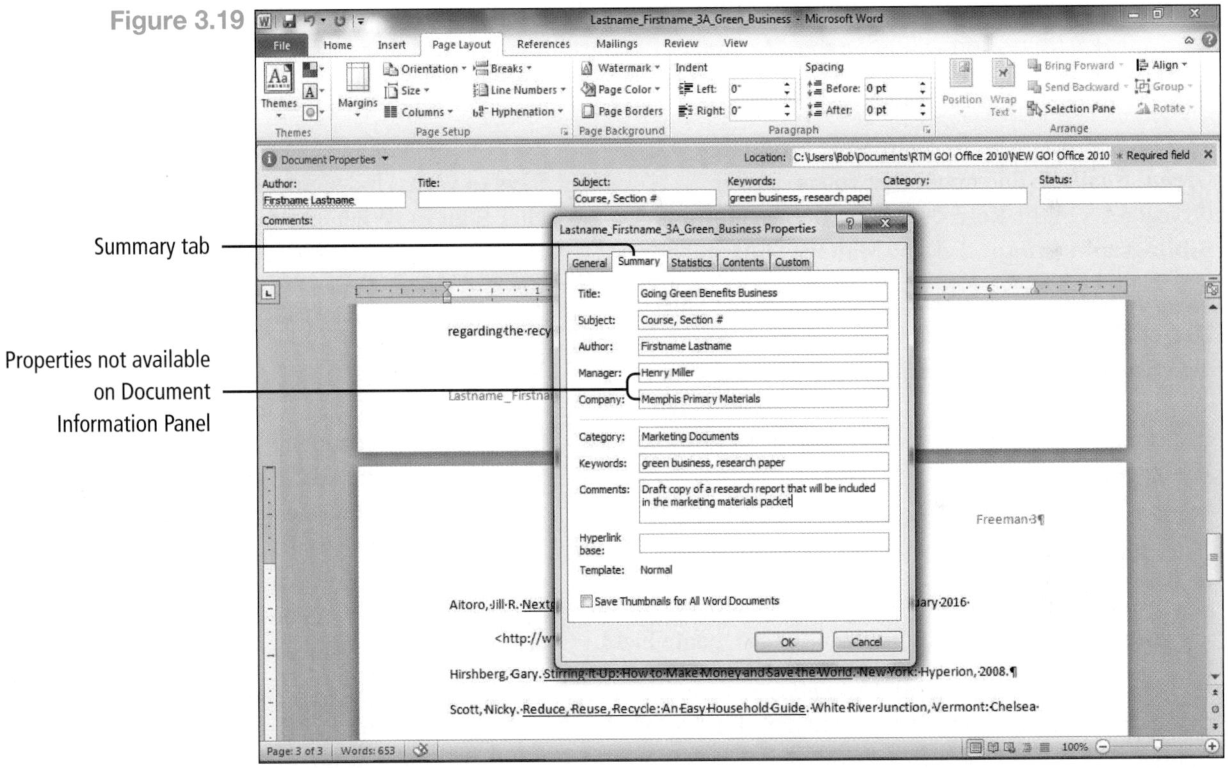

Summary tab

Properties not available on Document Information Panel

12 **Close** ✕ the **Document Panel**. Press Ctrl + F2, and then examine the three pages of your document in **Print Preview**. Redisplay your document.

If necessary, make any corrections or adjustments.

13 **Save** 🖫 your document, and then print or submit electronically as directed by your instructor. **Exit** Word.

End **You have completed Project 3A**

Objective | Edit and Share a Word Document Using the Word Web App

The Word Web App—part of the Windows Live Essentials Office Web Apps package—enables you to create documents online, share the documents with others for collaborative writing, and edit the same document in either the Word Web App or Microsoft Word. The Word Web App has a limited feature set, so if you want to use some of the advanced tools, you will need to use Microsoft Office. The file format is the same for both versions of Word.

> **Alert!** | **Working with Web-Based Applications and Services**
>
> Computer programs and services on the Web receive continuous updates and improvements. Thus, the steps to complete this Web-based Activity may differ from the ones shown. You can often look at the screens and the information presented to determine how to complete the Activity.

Activity | Editing and Sharing a Word Document Using the Word Web App

In this activity, you will open the 3A_Green_Business document, change the document name, and then edit the document in the Word Web App. You will save the document on both your SkyDrive and on your USB drive.

1 Locate and open the **Lastname_Firstname_3A_Green_Business** document that you created in Project 3A. On the **References tab**, in the **Citations & Bibliography group**, click the **Manage Sources** button.

2 In the **Source Manager** dialog box, under **Current List**, click the first cited source that begins *Aitoro*. Click the **Edit** button. In the **Edit Source** dialog box, change the **Month Accessed** from *January* to **May** and then click **OK**. If a message displays, click Yes. **Close** the **Source Manager** dialog box.

Editing references in the Source Manager is one of the features that is not available in the Word Web.

3 Move to the end of the document. Right-click anywhere in the bibliography, and then click **Update Field**.

4 On the **File tab**, click **Save As**, and then **Save** the document as **Lastname_Firstname_3A_Recycle** Double-click in the footer area, right-click the file name, and then click **Update Field**.

5 On the **File tab**, click **Save & Send**, and then click **Save to Web**. Under **Save to Windows Live SkyDrive**, click **Sign In**. When prompted, enter your Windows Live ID and password. Under **Personal Folders**, click the **GO! Beyond Office-Word** folder that you created previously, and then click **Save As**. Wait a moment for the **Save As** dialog box; click **Save**.

6 **Exit** Word. Open your browser and go to **live.com**. Log in to your account, at the top of the screen click **SkyDrive**. Click the **GO! Beyond Office-Word** folder, point to the **3A_Recycle** document that you just created, and then at the right end of the row, point to the Show information button 🛈, and then click the button one time to display a menu on the right. On the menu, click **Edit in browser**. Compare your screen with Figure A.

The citation references and the footnote references in the document display highlighted in gray, indicating that these features cannot be edited in the Word Web App.

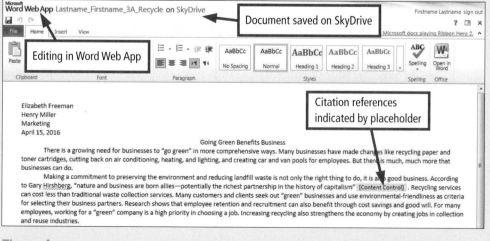

Figure A

Objective 4 | Format a Multiple-Column Newsletter

All newspapers and most magazines and newsletters use multiple columns for articles because text in narrower columns is easier to read than text that stretches across a page. Word has a tool with which you can change a single column of text into two or more columns, and then format the columns. If a column does not end where you want it to, you can end the column at a location of your choice by inserting a *manual column break*.

Activity 3.08 | Changing One Column of Text to Two Columns

Newsletters are usually two or three columns wide. When using 8.5 × 11-inch paper in portrait orientation, avoid creating four or more columns because they are so narrow that word spacing looks awkward, often resulting in one long word on a line by itself.

1 **Start** Word. From your student files, locate and open the document **w03B_Memphis_ Newsletter**. If necessary, display the formatting marks and rulers. **Save** the file in your **Word Chapter 3** folder as **Lastname_Firstname_3B_Memphis_Newsletter** and then add the file name to the footer.

2 Select the first paragraph of text—*Memphis Primary Materials*. From the Mini toolbar, change the **Font** to **Arial Black** and the **Font Size** to **24**.

3 Select the first two paragraphs—the title and the Volume information and date. From the Mini toolbar, click the **Font Color button arrow** A, and then under **Theme Colors**, in the fifth column, click the last color—**Blue, Accent 1, Darker 50%**.

4 With the text still selected, on the **Home tab**, in the **Paragraph group**, click the **Borders button arrow**, and then at the bottom, click **Borders and Shading**.

5 In the **Borders and Shading** dialog box, on the **Borders tab**, click the **Color arrow**, and then under **Theme Colors**, in the fifth column, click the last color—**Blue, Accent 1, Darker 50%**.

> **Another Way**
>
> In the Preview area, click the Bottom Border button.

6 Click the **Width arrow**, and then click **3 pt**. In the **Preview** box at the right, point to the *bottom* border of the small preview and click one time. Compare your screen with Figure 3.21.

Figure 3.21

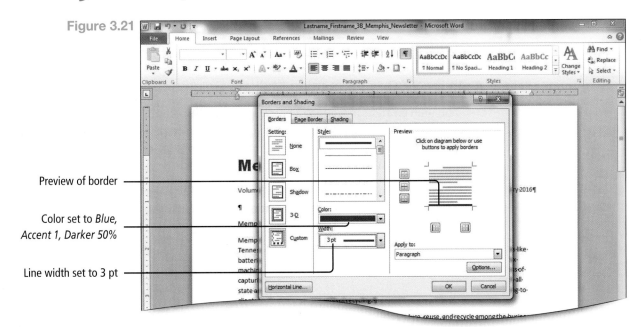

Preview of border

Color set to *Blue, Accent 1, Darker 50%*

Line width set to 3 pt

7 In the **Borders and Shading** dialog box, click **OK**.

> The line visually defines the newsletter *nameplate*—the banner on the front page of a newsletter that identifies the publication.

8 Below the nameplate, beginning with the paragraph *Memphis Primary Materials: An Introduction*, select all of the text to the end of the document, which extends to two pages.

9 On the **Page Layout tab**, in the **Page Setup group**, click the **Columns** button. From the **Columns** gallery, click **Two**.

10 Scroll up to view the top of **Page 1**, and then compare your screen with Figure 3.22, and then **Save** 🔲 the document.

> Word divides the text into two columns, and inserts a *section break* below the nameplate, dividing the one-column section of the document from the two-column section of the document. A *section* is a portion of a document that can be formatted differently from the rest of the document. A section break marks the end of one section and the beginning of another section. Do not be concerned if your columns do not break at the same line as shown in the figure.

Figure 3.22

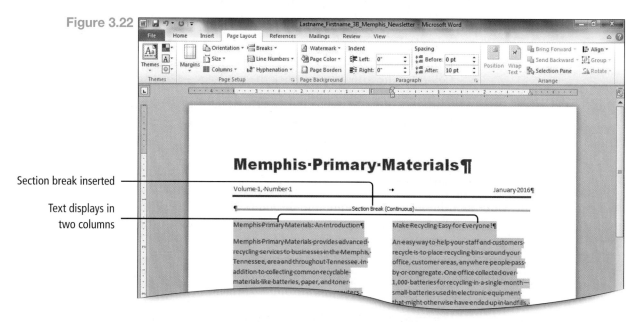

Section break inserted

Text displays in two columns

Activity 3.09 | Formatting Multiple Columns

The uneven right margin of a single page-width column is easy to read. When you create narrow columns, justified text is sometimes preferable. Depending on the design and layout of your newsletter, you might decide to reduce extra space between paragraphs and between columns to improve the readability of the document.

1 With the two columns of text still selected, on the **Page Layout tab**, in the **Paragraph group**, click the **Spacing After down spin arrow** one time to change the spacing after to **6 pt**.

2 On the **Home tab**, in the **Paragraph group**, click the **Justify** button 🔲.

3 Click anywhere in the document to deselect the text, and then compare your screen with Figure 3.23. **Save** 🖫 the document.

Figure 3.23

Column text justified

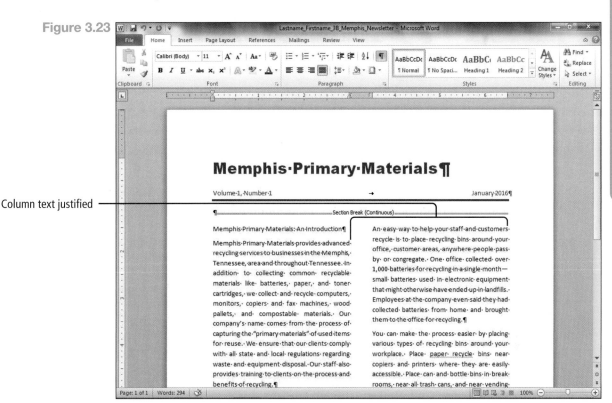

More Knowledge | Justifying Column Text

Although many magazines and newspapers still justify text in columns, there are a variety of opinions about whether to justify the columns, or to use left alignment and leave the right edge uneven. Justified text tends to look more formal and cleaner, but in a word processing document, it also results in uneven spacing between words. It is the opinion of some authorities that justified text is more difficult to read, especially in a page-width document. Let the overall look and feel of your newsletter be your guide.

Activity 3.10 | Inserting a Column Break

1 Scroll down to view the lower portion of the page. In the first column, locate the company address that begins with the paragraph *Memphis Primary Materials*, and then select that paragraph and the three following paragraphs, ending with the telephone number.

2 On the **Page Layout tab**, in the **Paragraph group**, click the **Spacing After down spin arrow** one time to change the spacing after to **0 pt**.

3 Select the three paragraphs that begin with *CEO* and end with *CFO*, and then in the **Paragraph group**, change the **Spacing After** to **0 pt**.

4 Near the bottom of the first column, click to position the insertion point at the beginning of the line that begins *Make Recycling*.

5 On the **Page Layout tab**, in the **Page Setup group**, click the **Breaks** button to display the gallery of Page Breaks and Section Breaks. Compare your screen with Figure 3.24.

Figure 3.24

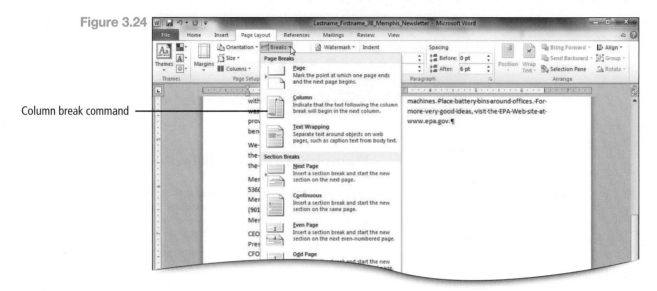

Column break command

6 Under **Page Breaks**, click **Column**. Scroll to view the bottom of the first column.

A column break displays at the insertion point; text to the right of the insertion point moves to the top of the next column.

7 Compare your screen with Figure 3.25, and then **Save** 💾 the document.

A *column break indicator*—a dotted line containing the words *Column Break*—displays at the bottom of the column.

Figure 3.25

Manual column break inserted

Activity 3.11 | Inserting a ClipArt Image

Clip art images—predefined graphics included with Microsoft Office or downloaded from the Web—can make your document visually appealing and more interesting.

1 Press Ctrl + Home. On the **Insert tab**, in the **Illustrations group**, click the **Clip Art** button to display the **Clip Art** task pane on the right of your screen.

2 In the **Clip Art** task pane, click in the **Search for** box, and then replace any existing text with **environmental awareness** so that Word can search for images that contain the keywords *environmental* and *awareness*.

3 In the **Clip Art** task pane, click the **Results should be arrow**. Be sure the **Illustrations** check box is selected, and then click as necessary to clear the *Photographs*, *Videos*, and *Audio* check boxes. Click the **Results should be** arrow again to collapse the list. Be sure the **Include Office.com content** check box is selected.

4 In the **Clip Art** task pane, click the **Go** button. Locate the image of the three white arrows in a blue circle. Click on the image to insert it, and then compare your screen with Figure 3.26.

Recall that when you insert a graphic, it is inserted as an inline object; that is, it is treated as a character in a line of text. Here, the inserted clip art becomes the first character in the nameplate.

Figure 3.26

Clip Art task pane

Search term

Selected image

Image inserted in document

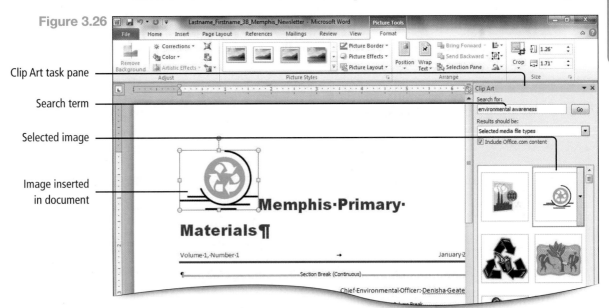

5 **Close** ☒ the **Clip Art** task pane. With the image still selected, on the **Format tab**, in the **Size group**, click in the **Shape Height** box, type **1** and then press Enter. In the **Arrange group**, click the **Wrap Text** button, and then click **Square**.

6 Point to the image to display the 🔀 pointer, and then drag the image to the right so that the bottom edge aligns slightly above *January 2016*, and the right side aligns with the right margin. Recall that you can press the arrow keys as necessary to move the image in small, precise increments.

7 Compare your screen with Figure 3.27, and then **Save** 🖫 the document.

Figure 3.27

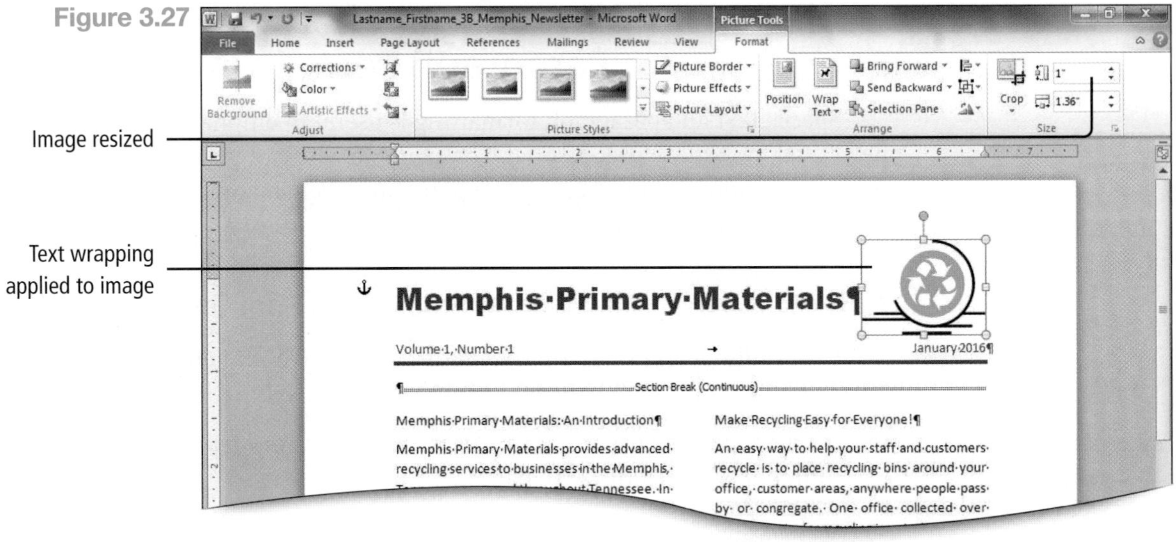

Image resized

Text wrapping applied to image

Activity 3.12 | Inserting a Screenshot

A *screenshot* is an image of an active window on your computer that you can paste into a document. Screenshots are especially useful when you want to insert an image of a Web site into a document you are creating in Word. You can insert a screenshot of any open window on your computer.

1 In the second column, click to position the insertion point at the beginning of the paragraph that begins *You can make*. Open your Internet browser, and then in the address bar type **www.epa.gov/osw/conserve/rrr** and press Enter. Maximize ⬚ the browser window, if necessary.

2 From the taskbar, redisplay your **3B_Memphis_Newletter** document.

3 On the **Insert tab**, in the **Illustrations group**, click the **Screenshot** button.

All of your open windows display in the Available Windows gallery and are available to paste into the document.

4 In the **Screenshot** gallery, click the browser window that contains the EPA site to insert the screenshot at the insertion point, and notice that the image resizes to fit between the column margins. Compare your screen with Figure 3.28. **Save** ⬚ the document.

Figure 3.28

Screenshot inserted in document

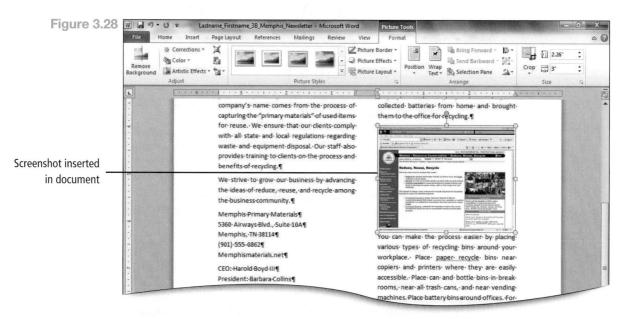

Objective 5 | Use Special Character and Paragraph Formatting

Special text and paragraph formatting is useful to emphasize text, and it makes your newsletter look more professional. For example, you can place a border around one or more paragraphs or add shading to a paragraph. When adding shading, use light colors; dark shading can make the text difficult to read.

Activity 3.13 | Applying the Small Caps Font Effect

For headlines and titles, *small caps* is an attractive font effect. The effect changes lowercase letters to uppercase letters, but with the height of lowercase letters.

1 At the top of the first column, select the paragraph *Memphis Primary Materials: An Introduction* including the paragraph mark.

2 Right-click the selected text, and then from the shortcut menu, click **Font**. In the **Font** dialog box, click the **Font color arrow**, and then under **Theme Colors**, in the fifth column, click the last color—**Blue, Accent 1, Darker 50%**.

3 Under **Font style**, click **Bold**. Under **Size**, click **18**. Under **Effects**, select the **Small caps** check box. Compare your screen with Figure 3.29.

> The Font dialog box provides more options than are available on the Ribbon and enables you to make several changes at the same time. In the Preview box, the text displays with the selected formatting options applied.

Figure 3.29

Small caps effect selected

Selected text

Preview of changes to text

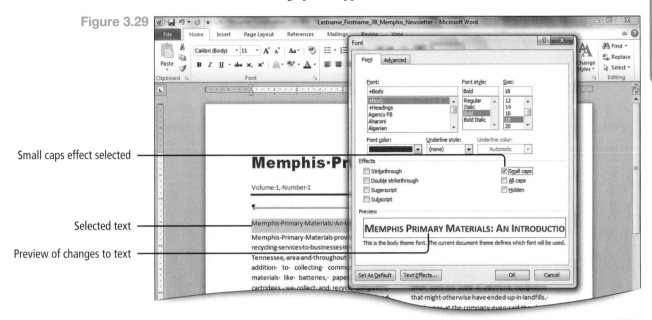

4 Click **OK**. Right-click the selected text, and then on the Mini toolbar, click **Center** ☰.

5 With the text still selected, right-click, and then on the Mini toolbar, click the **Format Painter** button ✍. Then, with the ✍I pointer, at the top of the second column, select the paragraph *Make Recycling Easy for Everyone!* to apply the same formats. Notice that the column title wraps placing a single word on the second line.

6 Position the insertion point to the right of the word *Recycling*, and then press Del to remove the space. Hold down Shift and then press Enter.

> Holding down Shift while pressing Enter inserts a ***manual line break***, which moves the text to the right of the insertion point to a new line while keeping the text in the same paragraph. A ***line break indicator***, in the shape of a bent arrow, indicates that a manual line break was inserted.

7 Compare your screen with Figure 3.30, and then **Save** 🖫 the document.

Figure 3.30

Manual line break inserted

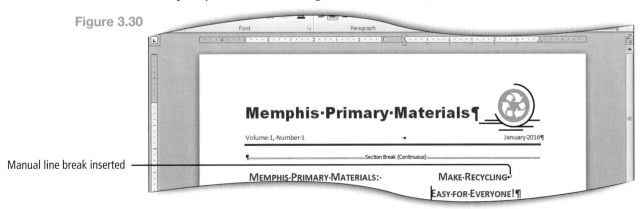

Activity 3.14 | Adding a Border and Shading to a Paragraph

Paragraph borders provide strong visual cues to the reader. Paragraph shading can be used with or without borders. When used with a border, light shading can be very effective in drawing the reader's eye to the text.

1 In the first column, in the paragraph that begins *We strive to grow*, click to position the insertion point at the end of the paragraph, and then press [Enter] one time.

2 At the bottom of the column, select the nine lines of company information, beginning with *Memphis Primary Materials* and ending with the paragraph that begins *Chief Environmental*. On the Mini toolbar, apply **Bold** [B] and **Center** [≣].

3 With the text still selected, on the **Home tab**, in the **Paragraph group**, click the **Borders button arrow** [⊞ ▾], and then click **Borders and Shading**.

4 In the **Borders and Shading** dialog box, be sure the **Borders tab** is selected. Under **Setting**, click **Shadow**. If necessary, click the **Color arrow**, and then in the fifth column, click the last color—**Blue, Accent 1, Darker 50%**. Click the **Width arrow**, and then click **3 pt**. Compare your screen with Figure 3.31.

In the lower right portion of the Borders and Shading dialog box, the *Apply to* box displays *Paragraph*. The *Apply to* box directs where the border will be applied—in this instance, the border will be applied only to the selected paragraphs.

Figure 3.31

Preview of paragraph border

Shadow border selected

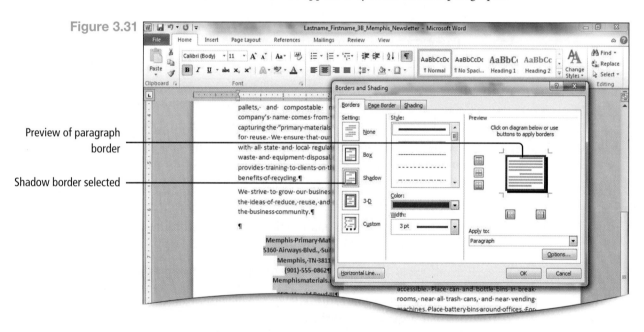

Note | Adding Simple Borders to Text

You can add simple borders from the Borders button gallery, located in the Paragraph group. This button offers less control over the border appearance, however, because the line thickness and color applied will match whatever was last used on this computer. The Borders and Shading dialog box enables you to make your own custom selections.

---

5 At the top of the **Borders and Shading** dialog box, click the **Shading tab**.

6 Click the **Fill arrow**, and then in the fifth column, click the second color—**Blue, Accent 1, Lighter 80%**. Notice that the shading change is reflected in the Preview area on the right side of the dialog box.

7   At the bottom of the **Borders and Shading** dialog box, click **OK**. Click anywhere in the document to deselect the text, and then compare your screen with Figure 3.32.

Figure 3.32

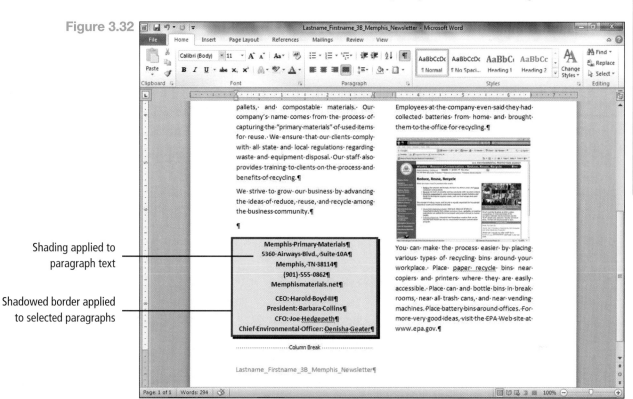

Shading applied to paragraph text

Shadowed border applied to selected paragraphs

8   From **Backstage** view, display the **Document Panel**.

9   In the **Author** box, delete any text and then type your firstname and lastname. In the **Subject** box, type your course name and section number, and in the **Keywords** box, type **newsletter, January Close** ☒ the **Document Panel**.

10 Press ⌷Ctrl⌷ + ⌷F2⌷ to view the **Print Preview**. **Close** the preview, make any necessary corrections, and then click **Save** 🔲. **Exit** Word; hold this file until you complete this Project.

Objective 6 | Create Mailing Labels Using Mail Merge

Word's *mail merge* feature joins a *main document* and a *data source* to create customized letters or labels. The main document contains the text or formatting that remains constant. For labels, the main document contains the formatting for a specific label size. The data source contains information including the names and addresses of the individuals for whom the labels are being created. Names and addresses in a data source might come from a Word table, an Excel spreadsheet, or an Access database.

The easiest way to perform a mail merge is to use the Mail Merge Wizard, which asks you questions and, based on your answers, walks you step by step through the mail merge process.

Activity 3.15 | Opening the Mail Merge Wizard Template

In this activity, you will open the data source for the mail merge, which is a Word table containing names and addresses.

1 **Start** Word and display a new blank document. Display formatting marks and rulers. **Save** the document in your **Word Chapter 3** folder as **Lastname_Firstname_3B_Mailing_Labels**

2 With your new document open on the screen, **Open** the file **w03B_Addresses**. **Save** the address file in your **Word Chapter 3** folder as **Lastname_Firstname_3B_Addresses** and then add the file name to the footer.

This document contains a table of addresses. The first row contains the column names. The remaining rows contain the names and addresses.

3 Click to position the insertion point in the last cell in the table, and then press Tab to create a new row. Enter the following information, and then compare your table with Figure 3.33:

First Name	**John**
Last Name	**Wisniewski**
Address 1	**1226 Snow Road**
Address 2	**#234**
City	**Lakeland**
State	**TN**
ZIP Code	**38002**

Figure 3.33

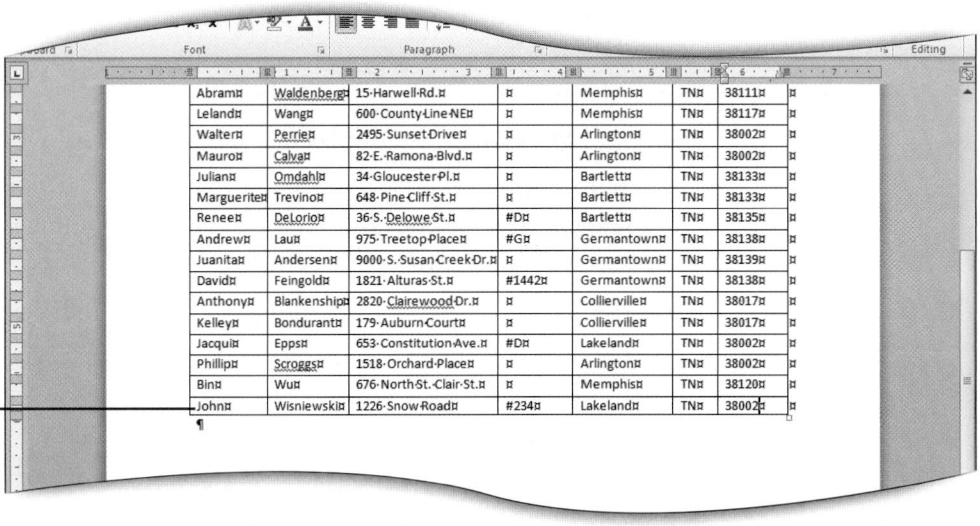

Abram	Waldenberg	15 Harwell Rd.		Memphis	TN	38111
Leland	Wang	600 County Line NE		Memphis	TN	38117
Walter	Perrie	2495 Sunset Drive		Arlington	TN	38002
Mauro	Calva	82 E. Ramona Blvd.		Arlington	TN	38002
Julian	Omdahl	34 Gloucester Pl.		Bartlett	TN	38133
Marguerite	Trevino	648 Pine Cliff St.		Bartlett	TN	38133
Renee	DeLorio	36 S. Delowe St.	#D	Bartlett	TN	38135
Andrew	Lau	975 Treetop Place	#G	Germantown	TN	38138
Juanita	Andersen	9000 S. Susan Creek Dr.		Germantown	TN	38139
David	Feingold	1821 Alturas St.	#1442	Germantown	TN	38138
Anthony	Blankenship	2820 Clairewood Dr.		Collierville	TN	38017
Kelley	Bondurant	179 Auburn Court		Collierville	TN	38017
Jacqui	Epps	653 Constitution Ave.	#D	Lakeland	TN	38002
Phillip	Scroggs	1518 Orchard Place		Arlington	TN	38002
Bin	Wu	676 North St. Clair St.		Memphis	TN	38120
John	Wisniewski	1226 Snow Road	#234	Lakeland	TN	38002

Font
Paragraph
Editing
New record added to address list

4 **Save**, and then **Close** the table of addresses. Be sure your blank **Lastname_Firstname_3B_Mailing_Labels** document displays.

5 Click the **Mailings tab**. In the **Start Mail Merge group**, click the **Start Mail Merge** button, and then click **Step by Step Mail Merge Wizard** to display the **Mail Merge** task pane.

6 Under **Select document type**, click the **Labels** option button. At the bottom of the task pane, click **Next: Starting document** to display Step 2 of 6 of the Mail Merge Wizard.

7 Under **Select starting document**, be sure **Change document layout** is selected, and then under **Change document layout**, click **Label options**.

8 In the **Label Options** dialog box, under **Printer information**, click the **Tray arrow**, and then click **Default tray (Automatically Select)**—the exact wording may vary depending on your printer, but select the *Default* or *Automatic* option—to print the labels on regular paper rather than manually inserting labels in the printer.

9 Under **Label information**, click the **Label vendors arrow**, and then click **Avery US Letter**. Under **Product number**, scroll about halfway down the list, and then click **5160 Easy Peel Address Labels**. Compare your screen with Figure 3.34.

> The Avery 5160 address label is a commonly used label. The precut sheets contain three columns of 10 labels each—for a total of 30 labels per sheet.

Figure 3.34

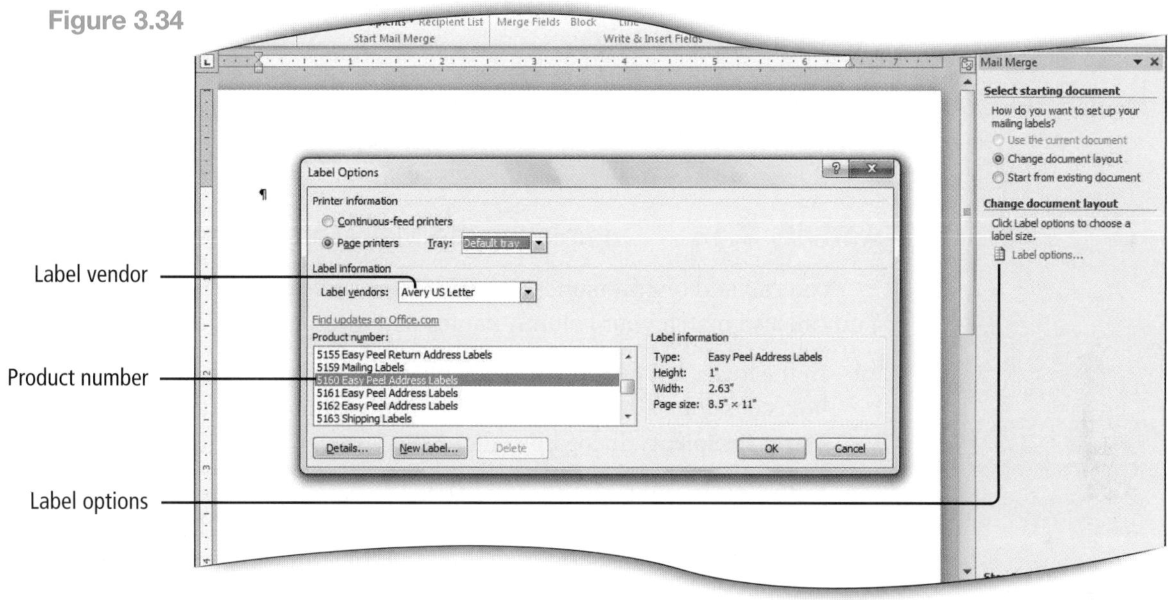

Label vendor

Product number

Label options

10 At the bottom of the **Label Options** dialog box, click **OK**. If a message box displays, click OK to set up the labels. At the bottom of the task pane, click **Next: Select recipients**.

> The label page is set up with three columns and ten rows. The label borders may or may not display on your screen, depending on your settings. Here in Step 3 of the Mail Merge Wizard, you must identify the recipients—the data source. For your recipient data source, you can choose to use an existing list—for example, a list of names and addresses that you have in an Access database, an Excel worksheet, a Word table, or your Outlook contacts list. If you do not have an existing data source, you can type a new list at this point in the wizard.

11 If gridlines do not display, click the **Layout tab**. In the **Table group**, click the **View Gridlines** button, and then notice that each label is outlined with a dashed line. If you cannot see the right and left edges of the page, in the status bar, click the **Zoom Out** button as necessary to see the right and left edges of the label sheet on your screen.

12 Under **Select recipients**, be sure the **Use an existing list** option button is selected. Under **Use an existing list**, click **Browse**.

13 Navigate to your **Word Chapter 3** folder, select your **Lastname_Firstname_3B_ Addresses** file, and then click **Open** to display the **Mail Merge Recipients** dialog box.

> In the Mail Merge Recipients dialog box, the column headings are formed from the text in the first row of your Word table of addresses. Each row of information that contains data for one person is referred to as a *record*. The column headings—for example, *Last_Name* and *First_Name*—are referred to as **fields**. An underscore replaces the spaces between words in the field name headings.

14 Compare your screen with Figure 3.35.

Figure 3.35

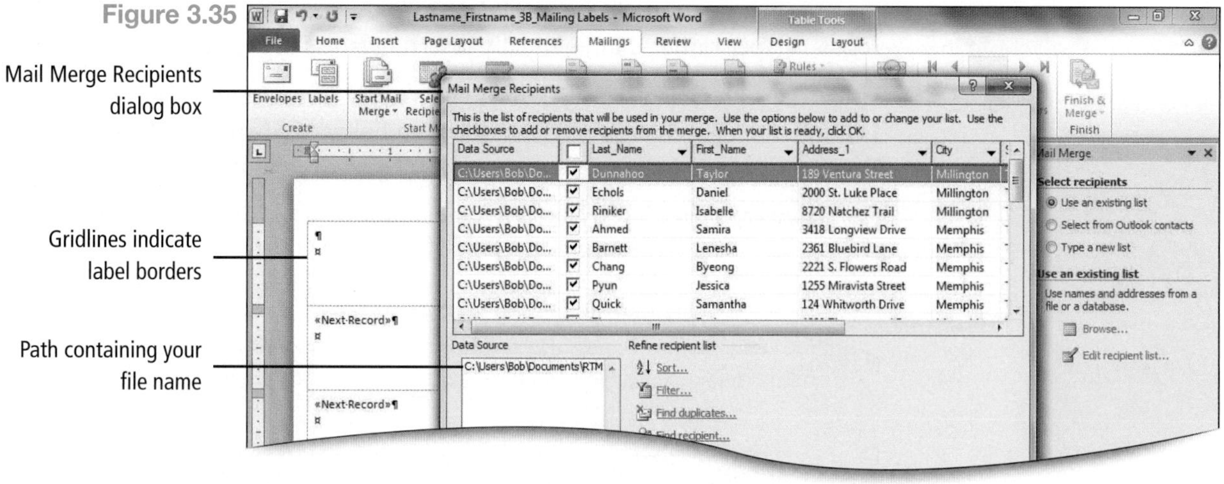

Mail Merge Recipients dialog box

Gridlines indicate label borders

Path containing your file name

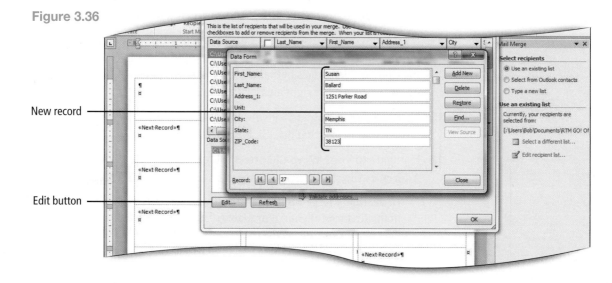

Activity 3.16 | Completing the Mail Merge Wizard

You can add or edit names and addresses while completing the Mail Merge Wizard. You can also match your column names with preset names used in Mail Merge.

1 In the lower left portion of the **Mail Merge Recipients** dialog box, in the **Data Source** box, click the path that contains your file name. Then, at the bottom of the **Mail Merge Recipients** dialog box, click **Edit**.

2 In the upper right corner of the **Data Form** dialog box, click **Add New**. In the blank record, type the following, pressing Tab to move from field to field, and then compare your **Data Form** dialog box with Figure 3.36.

First_Name	**Susan**
Last_Name	**Ballard**
Address_1	**1251 Parker Road**
Unit:	
City	**Memphis**
State	**TN**
ZIP_Code	**38123**

Figure 3.36

New record

Edit button

3 In the lower right corner of the **Data Form** dialog box, click **Close**. Scroll to the end of the recipient list to confirm that the record for *Susan Ballard* that you just added is in the list. At the bottom of the **Mail Merge Recipients** dialog box, click **OK**.

4 At the bottom of the **Mail Merge** task pane, click **Next: Arrange your labels**.

5 Under **Arrange your labels**, click **Address block**. In the **Insert Address Block** dialog box, under **Specify address elements**, examine the various formats for names. If necessary, under *Insert recipient's name in this format*, select the *Joshua Randall Jr.* format. Compare your dialog box with Figure 3.37.

Figure 3.37

Format selected

Preview of address block

Match Fields button

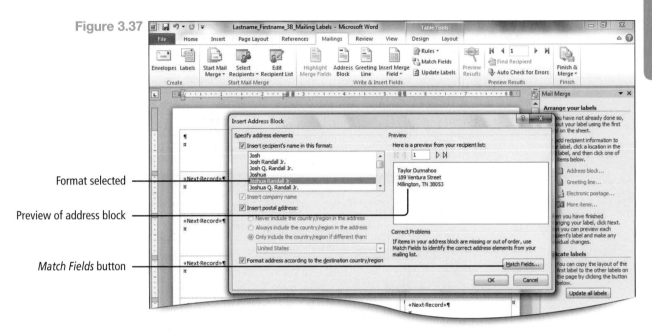

6 In the lower right corner of the **Insert Address Block** dialog box, click **Match Fields**.

If your field names are descriptive, the Mail Merge program will identify them correctly, as is the case with most of the information in the *Required for Address Block* section. However, the Address 2 field is unmatched—in the source file, this column is named *Unit*.

7 Scroll down and examine the dialog box, and then compare your screen with Figure 3.38.

Figure 3.38

Address 2 unmatched

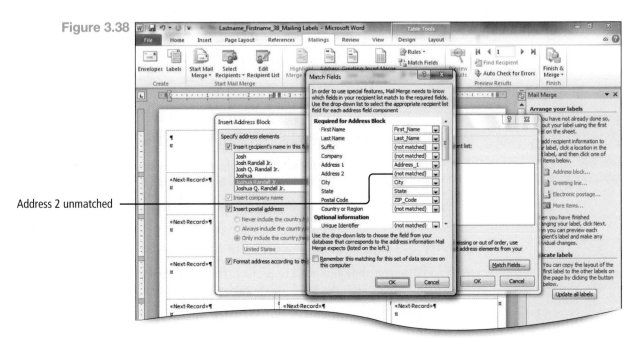

8 Click the **Address 2 arrow**, and then from the list of available fields, click **Unit** to match the Mail Merge field with the field in your data source.

9 At the bottom of the **Match Fields** dialog box, click **OK**. At the bottom of the **Insert Address Block** dialog box, click **OK**.

> Word inserts the Address block in the first label space surrounded by double angle brackets. The *AddressBlock* field name displays, which represents the address block you saw in the Preview area of the Insert Address Block dialog box.

10 In the task pane, under **Replicate labels**, click **Update all labels** to insert an address block in each label space for each subsequent record.

11 At the bottom of the task pane, click **Next: Preview your labels**. Notice that for addresses with four lines, the last line of the address is cut off.

12 Press Ctrl + A to select all of the label text, click the **Page Layout tab**, and then in the **Paragraph group**, click in the **Spacing Before** box. Type **3** and press Enter.

13 Click in any label to deselect, and notice that 4-line addresses are no longer cut off. Compare your screen with Figure 3.39.

Figure 3.39

Preview of mailing labels

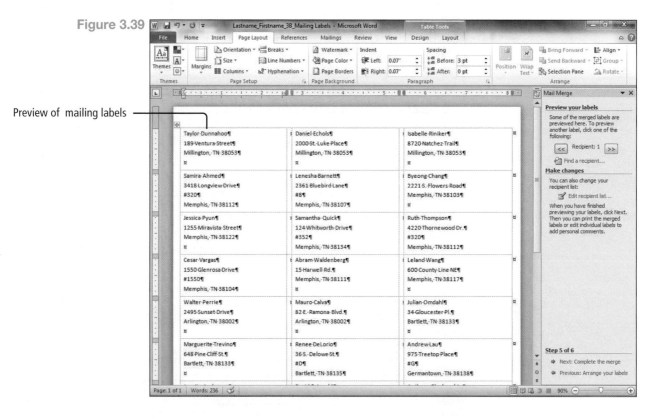

14 At the bottom of the task pane, click **Next: Complete the merge**.

> Step 6 of the Mail Merge task pane displays. At this point you can print or edit your labels, although this is done more easily in the document window.

15 **Save** your labels, and then **Close** the **Mail Merge** task pane.

Activity 3.17 │ Previewing and Printing the Mail Merge Document

If you discover that you need to make further changes to your labels, you can still make them even though the Mail Merge task pane is closed.

1 Add the file name to the footer, close the footer area, and then move to the top of Page 2. Click anywhere in the empty table row, click the **Layout tab**, in the **Rows & Columns group**, click the **Delete** button, and then click **Delete Rows**.

> Adding footer text to a label sheet replaces the last row of labels on a page with the footer text, and moves the last row of labels to the top of the next page. In this instance, a blank second page is created, which you can delete by deleting the blank row.

2 Press Ctrl + F2 to display the **Print Preview**. Notice that the labels do not display in alphabetical order.

3 Click the **Mailings tab**, and then in the **Start Mail Merge group**, click the **Edit Recipient List** button to display the list of names and addresses.

4 In the **Mail Merge Recipients** dialog box, click the **Last_Name** field heading, and notice that the names are sorted alphabetically by the recipient's last name.

> Mailing labels are often sorted by either last name or by ZIP Code.

5 Click the **Last_Name** field heading again, and notice that the last names are sorted in descending order. Click the **Last_Name** field one more time to return to ascending order, and then click **OK**. Press Ctrl + Home, and then compare your screen with Figure 3.40.

Figure 3.40

Labels in alphabetical order

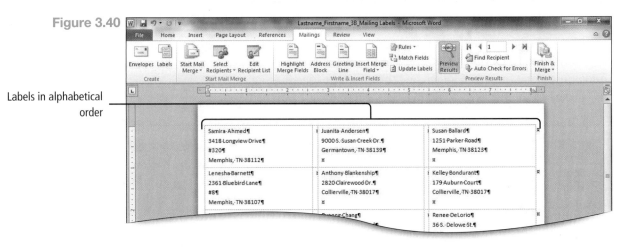

6 From **Backstage** view, display the **Document Panel**. In the **Author** box, delete any text and then type your firstname and lastname. In the **Subject** box, type your course name and section number, and in the **Keywords** box type **newsletter mailing labels** **Close** ☒ the **Document Panel**.

7 Click **Save** 🖫. Display **Backstage** view, and then click the **Print tab**. Examine the **Print Preview** on the right side of the window.

8 As directed by your instructor, print or submit electronically.

> If you print, the labels will print on whatever paper is in the printer; unless you have preformatted labels available, the labels will print on a sheet of paper. Printing the labels on plain paper enables you to proofread the labels before you print them on more expensive label sheets.

9 **Close** the document, click **Yes** to save the data source, and then if necessary, click **Save** to save the labels.

10 In addition to your labels and address document, print or submit your **3B_Memphis_ Newsletter** document as directed. **Exit** Word.

 You have completed Project 3B ————————————————

GO! Beyond Office

Objective | Create a Document Using the Word Web App

Office Web Apps are available either in Windows Live by signing in with your personal Windows Live ID or on a SharePoint site for individuals in organizations that have installed and configured Office Web Apps on a SharePoint site. You do not need to have Office 2010 installed on your computer to use Office Web Apps.

Personal use of Office Web Apps is free, and requires only a Windows Live ID and a computer with an Internet connection and supported browser software. *Business use of Office Web Apps* requires a SharePoint site with appropriate software and a SharePoint user ID provided by the organization.

> **Alert! | Working with Web-Based Applications and Services**
>
> Computer programs and services on the Web receive continuous updates and improvements. Thus, the steps to complete this Web-based Activity may differ from the ones shown. You can often look at the screens and the information presented to determine how to complete the Activity.

Activity | Creating a Document Using the Word Web App

In this activity, you will create a document using the Word Web App, open the document in Microsoft Word, insert text from a modified version of the student file you used in Project 3B, and then edit the document in the Word Web App. You will save the document on your SkyDrive.

1 Open your browser, go to **live.com** and then sign in with your Windows Live ID. At the top of the window, click **SkyDrive**. Click your **GO! Beyond Office-Word** folder to make it the active folder, and then near the top of the window, to the right of **Create**, click the **Word icon**.

2 In the **Name** box, with *Document1* highlighted, using your own name type **Lastname_Firstname_3B_Newsletter** and then at the end of the **Name** box, notice that your document will be created in the *.docx* file format. Click **Save**.

Because Office Web Apps use the standard file formats of the desktop version of Office 2010, you will have *high-fidelity viewing* of documents. Documents created in the desktop version of Office 2010 and opened in the corresponding Office Web App, will retain images, footnotes, table borders, text effects, and so on.

3 With the insertion point blinking, type **Madison Primary Materials** and then press Enter. Type **Volume 1, Number 1**

4 Select the first line of text. On the **Home tab**, in the **Font group**, click the **Font Size button arrow**, and then click **24**. Click the **Bold** button B . In the **Paragraph group**, click the **Center** button ≡ .

5 Select the second line of text. In the **Font group**, click the **Font Size button arrow,** and then click **14**. In the **Paragraph group**, click the **Center** button ≡ . Position the insertion point at the end of the paragraph and then press Enter two times. **Save** 💾 your document.

6 On the **File tab**, click **Open in Word**. When the **Open Document** dialog box displays, click **OK**. Click the name of your **3B_Newsletter** document to open it again, and then, if necessary, at the top of the window, click Open in Word. If necessary, click OK, and then sign in again if asked to do so.

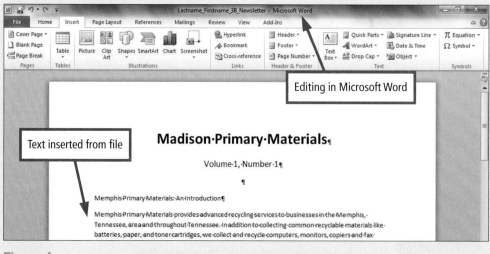

Figure A

7 Position the insertion point in the blank paragraph at the bottom of the document. On the **Insert tab**, in the **Text group**, click the **Object button arrow**, and then click **Text from File**. Locate and **Insert** the **w03B_Newsletter** student file. Delete the blank paragraph at the bottom of the document. Move to the top of the document, and then compare your screen with Figure A.

8 Select all of the text you just inserted. In the **Page Layout group**, on the **Page Setup tab**, click the **Columns** button, and then click **Two**. With the text still selected, on the **Home tab**, in the **Paragraph group**, click the **Justify** button ▤.

9 In the second column, position the insertion point in the blank paragraph. On the **Insert tab**, in the **Illustrations group**, click the **Picture** button. Locate the file **w03B_Picture**, and then click **Insert**.

10 From the **File tab**, **Exit** Word, saving your changes when prompted. In your browser, in your SkyDrive, click your **3B_Newsletter** to open it, and then at the top of the window, click **Edit in Browser**.

11 Near the top of the document, locate and select the short paragraph *Memphis Primary Materials: An Introduction*. In the **Font group**, click the **Bold** button ⓑ. In the **Paragraph group**, click the **Center** button ▤. Near the bottom of the document, select the paragraph *Make Recycling Easy for Everyone!* and apply **Bold** and **Center**.

12 On the **View tab**, click the **Reading View** button. **Save** your changes when prompted. Compare your screen with Figure B.

13 Display the **Start** menu 🟢, and then click **All Programs**. On the list of programs, click the **Accessories** folder, and then click **Snipping Tool**. In the **Snipping Tool** dialog box, click the **New arrow**. On the displayed list, click **Full-screen Snip**.

14 On the **Snipping Tool** markup window toolbar, click the **Save Snip** button 🖫. In the **Save As** dialog box, navigate to your USB drive and open your **Word Chapter 3** folder. Be sure the **Save as type** box displays **JPEG file**. In the **File name** box, type **Lastname_Firstname_3B_Newsletter_Snip** and then click **Save**. Close all open windows, and then submit the file as directed.

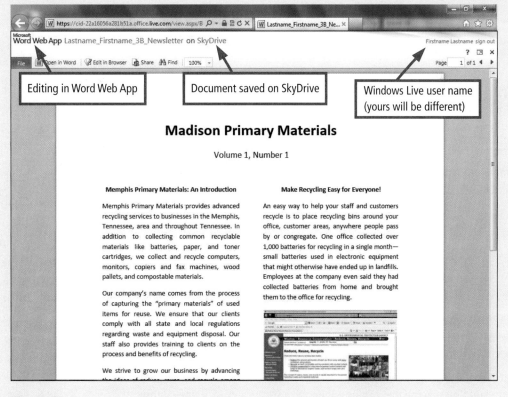

Figure B

Content-Based Assessments

Summary

In this chapter, you created a research paper using the MLA style. You added a header, footnotes, citations, and a bibliography, and changed the footnote style. You created a newsletter that used multiple columns. You added a column break, a page break, and a manual line break. You added special font effects, and added a border and shading to a paragraph. Finally, you used the Mail Merge Wizard to create a set of mailing labels for the newsletter.

Key Terms

Matching

Match each term in the second column with its correct definition in the first column by writing the letter of the term on the blank line in front of the correct definition.

_____ 1. A manual that contains standards for the design and writing of documents.

_____ 2. One of two commonly used style guides for formatting research papers.

_____ 3. An image of an active window on your computer that you can paste into a document.

_____ 4. In a research paper, information that expands on the topic, but that does not fit well in the document text.

_____ 5. In a research paper, a note placed at the bottom of the page.

_____ 6. In a research paper, a note placed at the end of a document or chapter.

_____ 7. A list of cited works in a report or research paper, also referred to as *Works Cited*, *Sources*, or *References*, depending upon the report style.

_____ 8. In the MLA style, a list of cited works placed at the end of a research paper or report.

_____ 9. A group of formatting commands, such as font, font size, font color, paragraph alignment, and line spacing that can be applied to a paragraph with one command.

_____ 10. A note, inserted into the text of a research paper that refers the reader to a source in the bibliography.

_____ 11. In the MLA style, a citation that refers to items on the *Works Cited* page, and which is placed in parentheses; the citation includes the last name of the author or authors, and the page number in the referenced source.

A American Psychological Association (APA)

B Bibliography

C Citation

D Endnote

E Footnote

F Hanging indent

G Manual column break

H Manual page break

I Note

J Page break indicator

K Parenthetical reference

L Screenshot

M Style

N Style guide

O Works Cited

Content-Based Assessments

_____ 12. The action of forcing a page to end and placing subsequent text at the top of the next page.

_____ 13. A dotted line with the text *Page Break* that indicates where a manual page break was inserted.

_____ 14. An indent style in which the first line of a paragraph extends to the left of the remaining lines, and that is commonly used for bibliographic entries.

_____ 15. An artificial end to a column to balance columns or to provide space for the insertion of other objects.

Multiple Choice

Circle the correct answer.

1. Column text that is aligned to both the left and right margins is referred to as:
   A. centered   B. justified   C. indented

2. The banner on the front page of a newsletter that identifies the publication is the:
   A. heading   B. nameplate   C. title

3. A portion of a document that can be formatted differently from the rest of the document is a:
   A. tabbed list   B. paragraph   C. section

4. A font effect, commonly used in titles, that changes lowercase text into uppercase letters using a reduced font size is:
   A. Small Caps   B. Level 2 Head   C. Bevel

5. To end a line before the normal end of the line, without creating a new paragraph, hold down the [Shift] key while pressing the:
   A. [Enter] key   B. [Ctrl] key   C. [Alt] key

6. The nonprinting symbol that displays where a manual line break is inserted is the:
   A. short arrow   B. bent arrow   C. anchor

7. In mail merge, the document that contains the text or formatting that remains constant is the:
   A. data source   B. mailing list   C. main document

8. In mail merge, the list of variable information, such as names and addresses, that is merged with a main document to create customized form letters or labels is the:
   A. data source   B. mailing list   C. main document

9. In mail merge, a row of information that contains data for one person is a:
   A. record   B. field   C. label

10. To perform a mail merge using Word's step-by-step guided process, use the:
    A. Mail Merge Template   B. Mail Merge Management Source   C. Mail Merge Wizard

NOTES

Creating a Worksheet and Charting Data

OUTCOMES

At the end of this chapter you will be able to:

OBJECTIVES

Mastering these objectives will enable you to:

PROJECT 1A
Create a sales report with an embedded column chart and sparklines.

PROJECT 1B
Calculate the value of an inventory.

rangizzz/Shutterstock

In This Chapter

In this chapter, you will use Microsoft Excel 2010 to create and analyze data organized into columns and rows. After entering data in a worksheet, you can perform calculations, analyze the data to make logical decisions, and create charts.

In this chapter, you will create and modify Excel workbooks. You will practice the basics of worksheet design, create a footer, enter and edit data in a worksheet, chart data, and then save, preview, and print workbooks. You will also construct formulas for mathematical operations.

The projects in this chapter relate to **Texas Spectrum Wireless**, which provides accessories and software for all major brands of cell phones, smartphones, PDAs, MP3 players, and portable computers. The company sells thousands of unique products in their retail stores, which are located throughout Texas and the southern United States. They also sell thousands of items each year through their Web site, and offer free shipping and returns to their customers. The company takes pride in offering unique categories of accessories such as waterproof and ruggedized gear.

Project 1A Sales Report with Embedded Column Chart and Sparklines

myitlab
Project 1A Training

In Activities 1.01 through 1.16, you will create an Excel worksheet for Roslyn Thomas, the President of Texas Spectrum Wireless. The worksheet displays the first quarter sales of wireless accessories for the current year, and includes a chart to visually represent the data. Your completed worksheet will look similar to Figure 1.1.

Project Files

For Project 1A, you will need the following file:

New blank Excel workbook

You will save your workbook as:

Lastname_Firstname_1A_Quarterly_Sales

Project Results

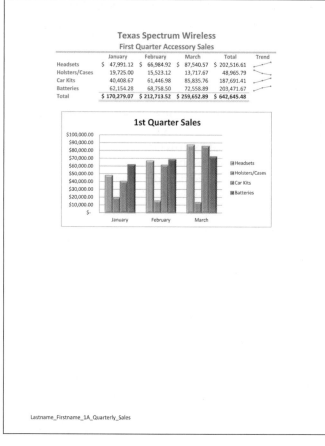

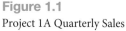

Figure 1.1
Project 1A Quarterly Sales

Objective 1 | Create, Save, and Navigate an Excel Workbook

On startup, Excel displays a new blank *workbook*—the Excel document that stores your data—which contains one or more pages called a *worksheet*. A worksheet—or *spreadsheet*—is stored in a workbook, and is formatted as a pattern of uniformly spaced horizontal rows and vertical columns. The intersection of a column and a row forms a box referred to as a *cell*.

Activity 1.01 | Starting Excel and Naming and Saving a Workbook

1 **Start** Excel. In the lower right corner of the window, if necessary, click the Normal button ▦, and then to the right, locate the zoom—magnification—level.

> Your zoom level should be 100%, although some figures in this textbook may be shown at a higher zoom level.

Another Way

Use the keyboard shortcut F12 to display the Save As dialog box.

2 In the upper left corner of your screen, click the **File tab** to display **Backstage** view, click **Save As**, and then in the **Save As** dialog box, navigate to the location where you will store your workbooks for this chapter.

3 In your storage location, create a new folder named **Excel Chapter 1** Open the new folder to display its folder window, and then in the **File name** box, notice that *Book1* displays as the default file name.

4 In the **File name** box, click *Book1* to select it, and then using your own name, type **Lastname_Firstname_1A_Quarterly_Sales** being sure to include the underscore (Shift + -) instead of spaces between words. Compare your screen with Figure 1.2.

Figure 1.2

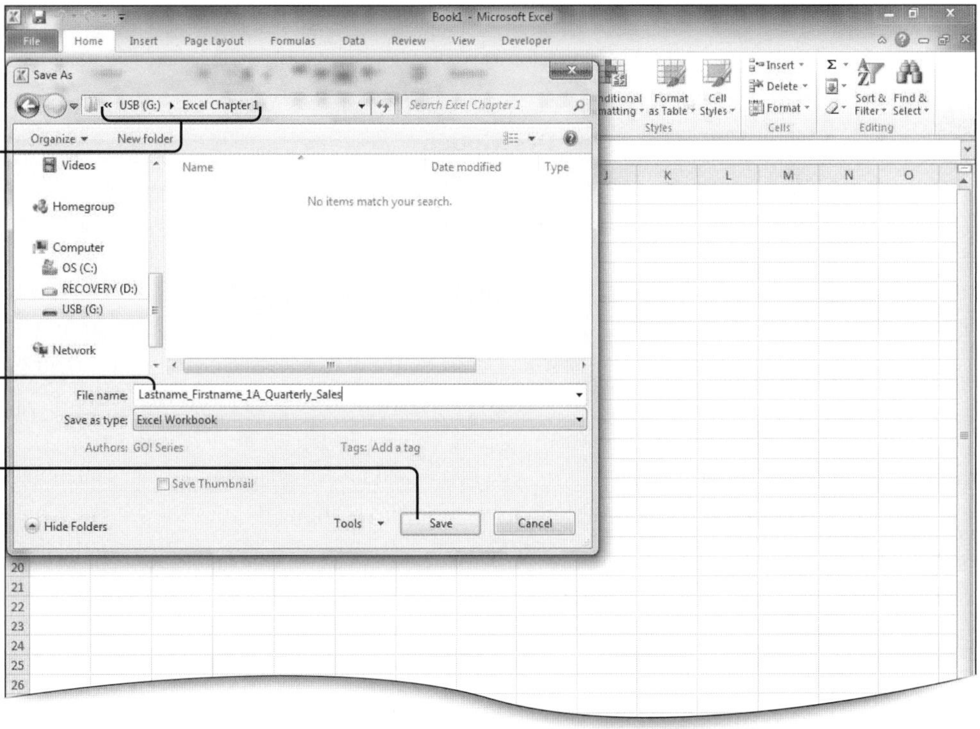

Path to your new *Excel Chapter 1* folder in address bar (yours may vary)

File name with your name and underscores between words

Save button

5 Click **Save**. Compare your screen with Figure 1.3, and then take a moment to study the Excel window parts in the table in Figure 1.4.

Figure 1.3

Workbook-level buttons
Name Box
Formula Bar
Worksheet grid area
Vertical window split box
Expand horizontal scroll bar button
Status bar
Sheet tabs and Insert Worksheet button
Sheet tab scrolling buttons

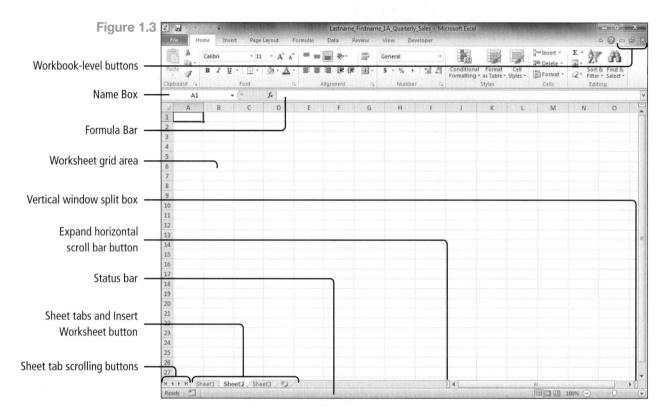

Parts of the Excel Window

Screen Part	Description
Expand horizontal scroll bar button	Increases the width of the horizontal scroll bar.
Formula Bar	Displays the value or formula contained in the active cell; also permits entry or editing.
Sheet tabs and Insert Worksheet button	Identify the worksheets in a workbook and inserts an additional worksheet.
Name Box	Displays the name of the selected cell, table, chart, or object.
Sheet tab scrolling buttons	Display sheet tabs that are not in view when there are numerous sheet tabs.
Status bar	Displays the current cell mode, page number, worksheet information, view and zoom buttons, and for numerical data, common calculations such as Sum and Average.
Vertical window split box	Splits the worksheet into two vertical views of the same worksheet.
Workbook-level buttons	Minimize, close, or restore the previous size of the displayed workbook.
Worksheet grid area	Displays the columns and rows that intersect to form the worksheet's cells.

Figure 1.4

Activity 1.02 | Navigating a Worksheet and a Workbook

1 Take a moment to study Figure 1.5 and the table in Figure 1.6 to become familiar with the Excel workbook window.

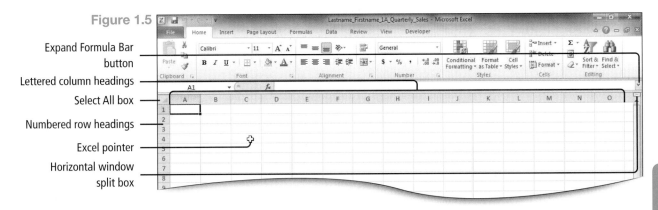

Figure 1.5

Expand Formula Bar button
Lettered column headings
Select All box
Numbered row headings
Excel pointer
Horizontal window split box

Excel Workbook Window Elements

Workbook Window Element	Description
Excel pointer	Displays the pointer in Excel.
Expand Formula Bar button	Increases the height of the Formula Bar to display lengthy cell content.
Horizontal window split box	Splits the worksheet into two horizontal views of the same worksheet.
Lettered column headings	Indicate the column letter.
Numbered row headings	Indicate the row number.
Select All box	Selects all the cells in a worksheet.

Figure 1.6

2 In the lower right corner of the screen, in the horizontal scroll bar, click the **right scroll arrow** one time to shift **column A** out of view.

> A *column* is a vertical group of cells in a worksheet. Beginning with the first letter of the alphabet, *A*, a unique letter identifies each column—this is called the *column heading*. Clicking one of the horizontal scroll bar arrows shifts the window either left or right one column at a time.

3 Point to the **right scroll arrow**, and then hold down the left mouse button until the columns begin to scroll rapidly to the right; release the mouse button when you begin to see pairs of letters as the column headings.

4 Slowly drag the horizontal scroll box to the left, and notice that just above the scroll box, ScreenTips with the column letters display as you drag. Drag the horizontal scroll box left or right—or click the left or right scroll arrow—as necessary to position **column Z** near the center of your screen.

> Column headings after column Z use two letters starting with AA, AB, and so on through ZZ. After that, columns begin with three letters beginning with AAA. This pattern provides 16,384 columns. The last column is XFD.

5 In the lower left portion of your screen, click the **Sheet2 tab**.

> The second worksheet displays and is the active sheet. Column A displays at the left.

6 In the vertical scroll bar, click the **down scroll arrow** one time to move **Row 1** out of view.

A *row* is a horizontal group of cells. Beginning with number 1, a unique number identifies each row—this is the *row heading*, located at the left side of the worksheet. A single worksheet has 1,048,576 rows.

7 In the lower left corner, click the **Sheet1 tab**.

The first worksheet in the workbook becomes the active worksheet. By default, new workbooks contain three worksheets. When you save a workbook, the worksheets are contained within it and do not have separate file names.

8 Use the skills you just practiced to scroll horizontally to display **column A**, and if necessary, **row 1**.

Objective 2 | Enter Data in a Worksheet

Cell content, which is anything you type in a cell, can be one of two things: either a *constant value*—referred to simply as a *value*—or a *formula*. A formula is an equation that performs mathematical calculations on values in your worksheet. The most commonly used values are *text values* and *number values*, but a value can also include a date or a time of day.

Activity 1.03 | Entering Text and Using AutoComplete

A text value, also referred to as a *label*, usually provides information about number values in other worksheet cells. For example, a title such as First Quarter Accessory Sales gives the reader an indication that the data in the worksheet relates to information about sales of accessories during the three-month period January through March.

1 Click the **Sheet1 tab** to make it the active sheet. Point to and then click the cell at the intersection of **column A** and **row 1** to make it the *active cell*—the cell is outlined in black and ready to accept data.

The intersecting column letter and row number form the *cell reference*—also called the *cell address*. When a cell is active, its column letter and row number are highlighted. The cell reference of the selected cell, *A1*, displays in the Name Box.

2 With cell **A1** as the active cell, type the worksheet title **Texas Spectrum Wireless** and then press Enter. Compare your screen with Figure 1.7.

Text or numbers in a cell are referred to as *data*. You must confirm the data you type in a cell by pressing Enter or by some other keyboard movement, such as pressing Tab or an arrow key. Pressing Enter moves the selection to the cell below.

Figure 1.7

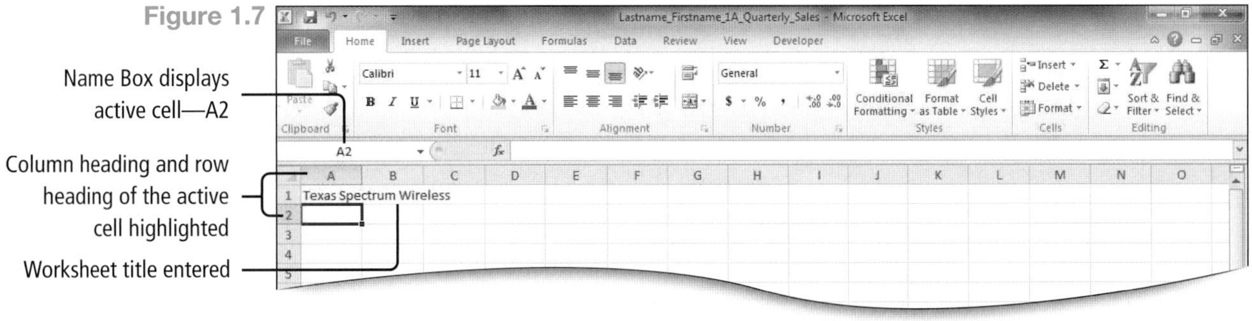

Name Box displays
active cell—A2

Column heading and row
heading of the active
cell highlighted

Worksheet title entered

3 In cell **A1**, notice that the text does not fit; the text spills over and displays in cells **B1** and **C1** to the right.

> If text is too long for a cell and cells to the right are empty, the text will display. If the cells to the right contain other data, only the text that will fit in the cell displays.

4 In cell **A2**, type the worksheet subtitle **First Quarter Accessory Sales** and then press [Enter]. Compare your screen with Figure 1.8.

Figure 1.8

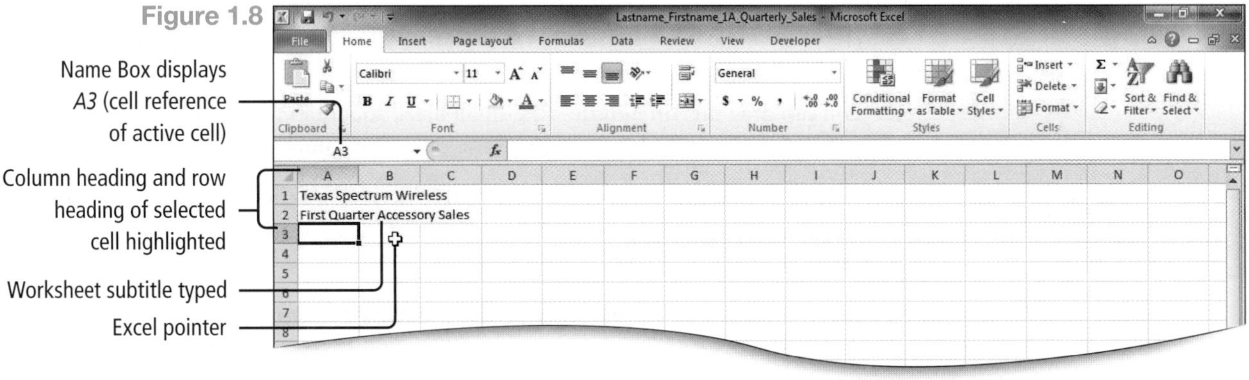

Name Box displays
A3 (cell reference
of active cell)

Column heading and row
heading of selected
cell highlighted

Worksheet subtitle typed

Excel pointer

5 Press [Enter] again to make cell **A4** the active cell. In cell **A4**, type **Headsets** which will form the first row title, and then press [Enter].

> The text characters that you typed align at the left edge of the cell—referred to as *left alignment*—and cell A5 becomes the active cell. Left alignment is the default for text values.

6 In cell **A5**, type **H** and notice the text from the previous cell displays.

> If the first characters you type in a cell match an existing entry in the column, Excel fills in the remaining characters for you. This feature, called *AutoComplete*, assists only with alphabetic values.

7 Continue typing the remainder of the row title **olsters/Cases** and press [Enter].

> The AutoComplete suggestion is removed when the entry you are typing differs from the previous value.

Another Way

Use the keyboard shortcut [Ctrl] + [S] to Save changes to your workbook.

8 In cell **A6**, type **Car Kits** and press [Enter]. In cell **A7**, type **Batteries** and press [Enter]. In cell **A8**, type **Total** and press [Enter]. On the Quick Access Toolbar, click **Save** 🖫.

Activity 1.04 | Using Auto Fill and Keyboard Shortcuts

1 Click cell **B3**. Type **J** and notice that when you begin to type in a cell, on the **Formula Bar**, the **Cancel** and **Enter** buttons become active, as shown in Figure 1.9.

Figure 1.9

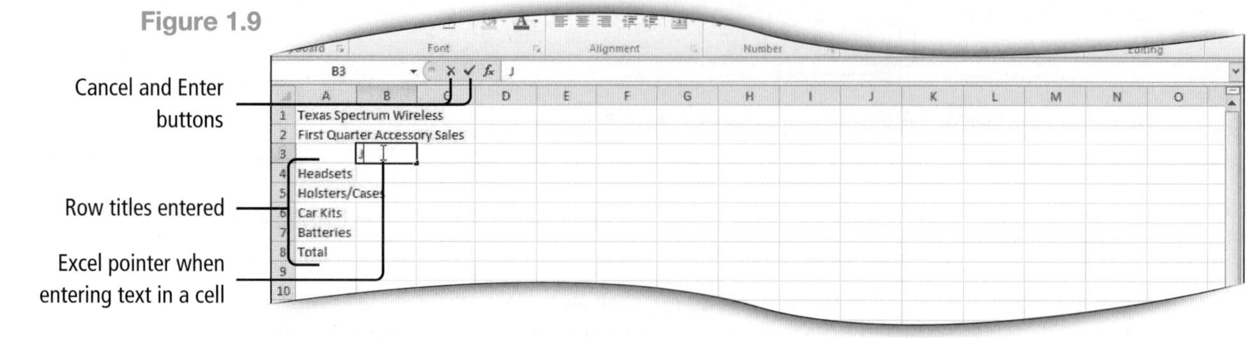

Cancel and Enter buttons

Row titles entered

Excel pointer when entering text in a cell

2 Continue to type **anuary** On the **Formula Bar**, notice that values you type in a cell also display there. Then, on the **Formula Bar**, click the **Enter** button ✓ to confirm the entry and keep cell **B3** active.

3 With cell **B3** active, locate the small black square in the lower right corner of the selected cell.

> You can drag this *fill handle*—the small black square in the lower right corner of a selected cell—to adjacent cells to fill the cells with values based on the first cell.

4 Point to the **fill handle** until the ⊞ pointer displays, hold down the left mouse button, drag to the right to cell **D3**, and as you drag, notice the ScreenTips *February* and *March*. Release the mouse button.

5 Under the text that you just filled, click the **Auto Fill Options** button ⊞▾ that displays, and then compare your screen with Figure 1.10.

> *Auto Fill* generates and extends a *series* of values into adjacent cells based on the value of other cells. A series is a group of things that come one after another in succession; for example, *January, February, March*.
>
> The Auto Fill Options button displays options to fill the data; options vary depending on the content and program from which you are filling, and the format of the data you are filling.
>
> *Fill Series* is selected, indicating the action that was taken. Because the options are related to the current task, the button is referred to as being *context sensitive*.

Figure 1.10

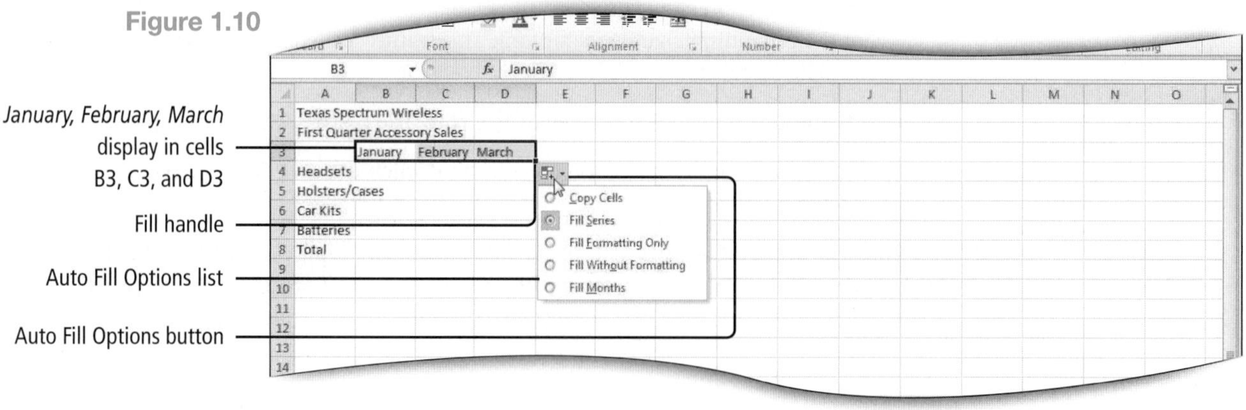

January, February, March display in cells B3, C3, and D3

Fill handle

Auto Fill Options list

Auto Fill Options button

6 Click in any cell to cancel the display of the Auto Fill Options list.

> The list no longer displays; the button will display until you perform some other screen action.

7　Press `Ctrl` + `Home`, which is the keyboard shortcut to make cell **A1** active.

8　On the Quick Access Toolbar, click **Save** 🖫 to save the changes you have made to your workbook, and then take a moment to study the table in Figure 1.11 to become familiar with additional keyboard shortcuts with which you can navigate the Excel worksheet.

Keyboard Shortcuts to Navigate the Excel Window

To Move the Location of the Active Cell:	Press:
Up, down, right, or left one cell	`↑`, `↓`, `→`, `←`
Down one cell	`Enter`
Up one cell	`Shift` + `Enter`
Up one full screen	`PageUp`
Down one full screen	`PageDown`
To column A of the current row	`Home`
To the last cell in the last column of the active area (the rectangle formed by all the rows and columns in a worksheet that contain entries)	`Ctrl` + `End`
To cell A1	`Ctrl` + `Home`
Right one cell	`Tab`
Left one cell	`Shift` + `Tab`

Figure 1.11

Activity 1.05 │ Aligning Text and Adjusting the Size of Columns

1　In the **column heading area**, point to the vertical line between **column A** and **column B** to display the ⊞ pointer, press and hold down the left mouse button, and then compare your screen with Figure 1.12.

A ScreenTip displays information about the width of the column. The default width of a column is 64 *pixels*. A pixel, short for *picture element*, is a point of light measured in dots per square inch. Sixty-four pixels equal 8.43 characters, which is the average number of digits that will fit in a cell using the default font. The default font in Excel is Calibri and the default font size is 11.

Figure 1.12

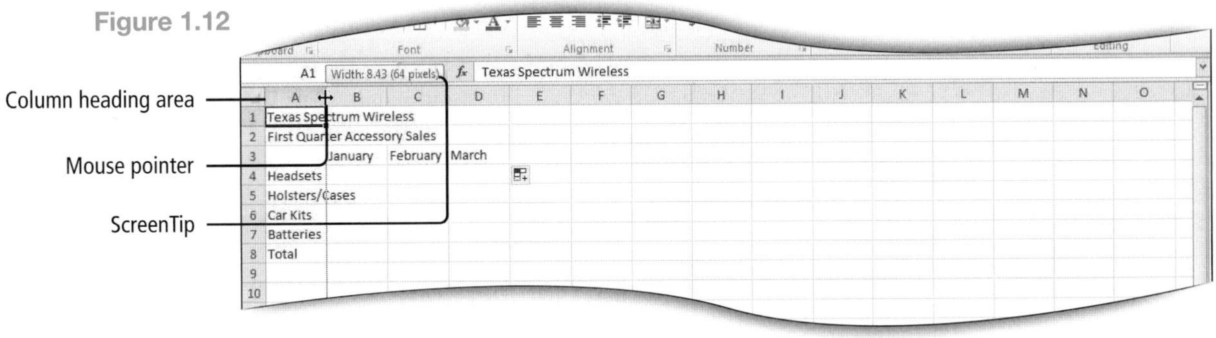

Column heading area

Mouse pointer

ScreenTip

2 Drag to the right, and when the number of pixels indicated in the ScreenTip reaches **100 pixels**, release the mouse button. If you are not satisfied with your result, click Undo ⤾ on the Quick Access Toolbar and begin again.

> This width accommodates the longest row title in cells A4 through A8—*Holsters/Cases*. The worksheet title and subtitle in cells A1 and A2 span more than one column and still do not fit in column A.

3 Point to cell **B3** and then drag across to select cells **B3**, **C3**, and **D3**. Compare your screen with Figure 1.13; if you are not satisfied with your result, click anywhere and begin again.

> The three cells, B3 through D3, are selected and form a ***range***—two or more cells on a worksheet that are adjacent (next to each other) or nonadjacent (not next to each other). This range of cells is referred to as *B3:D3*. When you see a colon (:) between two cell references, the range includes all the cells between the two cell references.

> A range of cells that is selected in this manner is indicated by a dark border, and Excel treats the range as a single unit so you can make the same changes to more than one cell at a time. The selected cells in the range are highlighted except for the first cell in the range, which displays in the Name Box.

Figure 1.13

First cell in selected range—B3—displays in Name Box

Column A widened to 100 pixels

Range B3:D3 selected

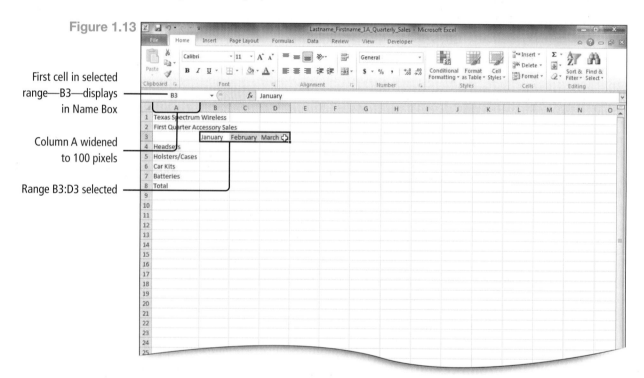

4 With the range **B3:D3** selected, point anywhere over the selected range, right-click, and then on the Mini toolbar, click the **Center** button ▤. On the Quick Access Toolbar, click **Save** 💾.

> The column titles *January, February, March* align in the center of each cell.

Activity 1.06 | Entering Numbers

To type number values, use either the number keys across the top of your keyboard or the numeric keypad if you have one—laptop computers may not have a numeric keypad.

1 Under *January*, click cell **B4**, type **47991.12** and then on the **Formula Bar**, click the **Enter** button ☑ to maintain cell **B4** as the active cell. Compare your screen with Figure 1.14.

By default, *number* values align at the right edge of the cell. The default **number format**—a specific way in which Excel displays numbers—is the **general format**. In the default general format, whatever you type in the cell will display, with the exception of trailing zeros to the right of a decimal point. For example, in the number 237.50 the *0* following the *5* is a trailing zero.

Data that displays in a cell is the **displayed value**. Data that displays in the Formula Bar is the **underlying value**. The number of digits or characters that display in a cell—the displayed value—depends on the width of the column. Calculations on numbers will always be based on the underlying value, not the displayed value.

Figure 1.14

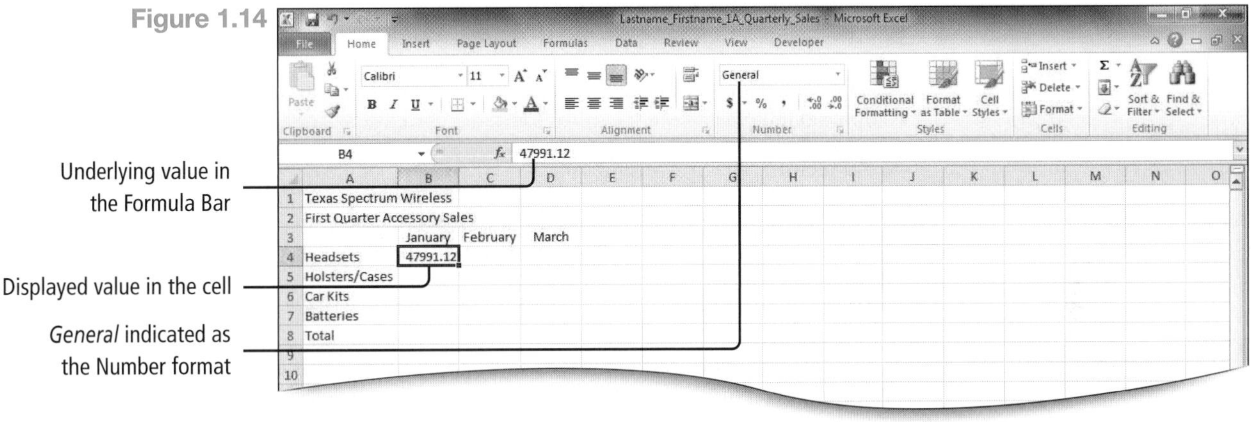

Underlying value in the Formula Bar

Displayed value in the cell

General indicated as the Number format

2 Press Tab to make cell **C4** active. Then, enter the remaining sales numbers as shown by using the following technique: Press Tab to confirm your entry and move across the row, and then press Enter at the end of a row to move to the next row.

	January	February	March
Headsets	47991.12	66984.92	87540.57
Holsters/Cases	19725	15523.12	13717.67
Car Kits	40408.67	61446.98	85835.76
Batteries	62154.28	68758.50	72558.89

3 Compare the numbers you entered with Figure 1.15 and then **Save** 🖫 your workbook.

In the default general format, trailing zeros to the right of a decimal point will not display. For example, when you type *68758.50*, the cell displays 68758.5 instead.

Figure 1.15

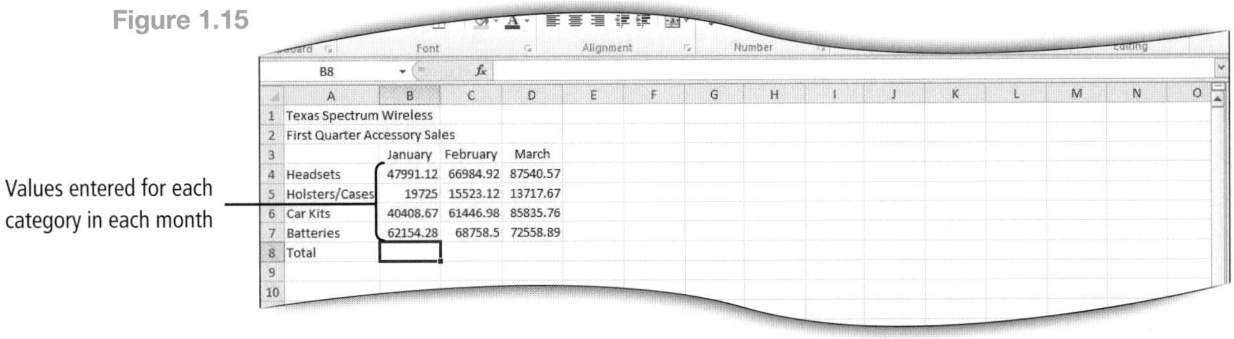

Values entered for each category in each month

Objective 3 | Construct and Copy Formulas and Use the SUM Function

A cell contains either a constant value (text or numbers) or a formula. A formula is an equation that performs mathematical calculations on values in other cells, and then places the result in the cell containing the formula. You can create formulas or use a *function*—a prewritten formula that looks at one or more values, performs an operation, and then returns a value.

Activity 1.07 | Constructing a Formula and Using the SUM Function

In this activity, you will practice three different ways to sum a group of numbers in Excel.

1 Click cell **B8** to make it the active cell and type **=**

The equal sign (=) displays in the cell with the insertion point blinking, ready to accept more data.

All formulas begin with the = sign, which signals Excel to begin a calculation. The Formula Bar displays the = sign, and the Formula Bar Cancel and Enter buttons display.

2 At the insertion point, type **b4** and then compare your screen with Figure 1.16.

A list of Excel functions that begin with the letter *B* may briefly display—as you progress in your study of Excel, you will use functions of this type. A blue border with small corner boxes surrounds cell B4, which indicates that the cell is part of an active formula. The color used in the box matches the color of the cell reference in the formula.

Figure 1.16

Cell B4 outlined in blue to show it is part of an active formula

Cell B8 displays the beginning of the formula, with *b4* in blue to match outlined cell

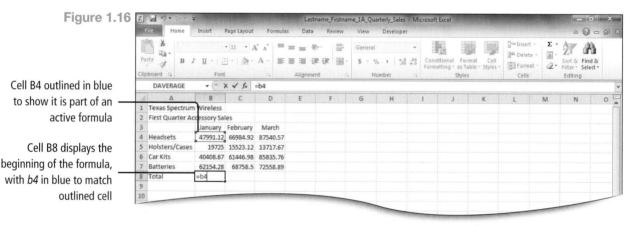

3 At the insertion point, type **+** and then type **b5**

A border of another color surrounds cell B5, and the color matches the color of the cell reference in the active formula. When typing cell references, it is not necessary to use uppercase letters.

4 At the insertion point, type **+b6+b7** and then press [Enter].

The result of the formula calculation—*170279.1*—displays in the cell. Recall that in the default General format, trailing zeros do not display.

5 Click cell **B8** again, look at the **Formula Bar**, and then compare your screen with Figure 1.17.

> The formula adds the values in cells B4 through B7, and the result displays in cell B8. In this manner, you can construct a formula by typing. Although cell B8 displays the *result* of the formula, the formula itself displays in the Formula Bar. This is referred to as the **underlying formula**.
>
> Always view the Formula Bar to be sure of the exact content of a cell—*a displayed number may actually be a formula*.

Figure 1.17

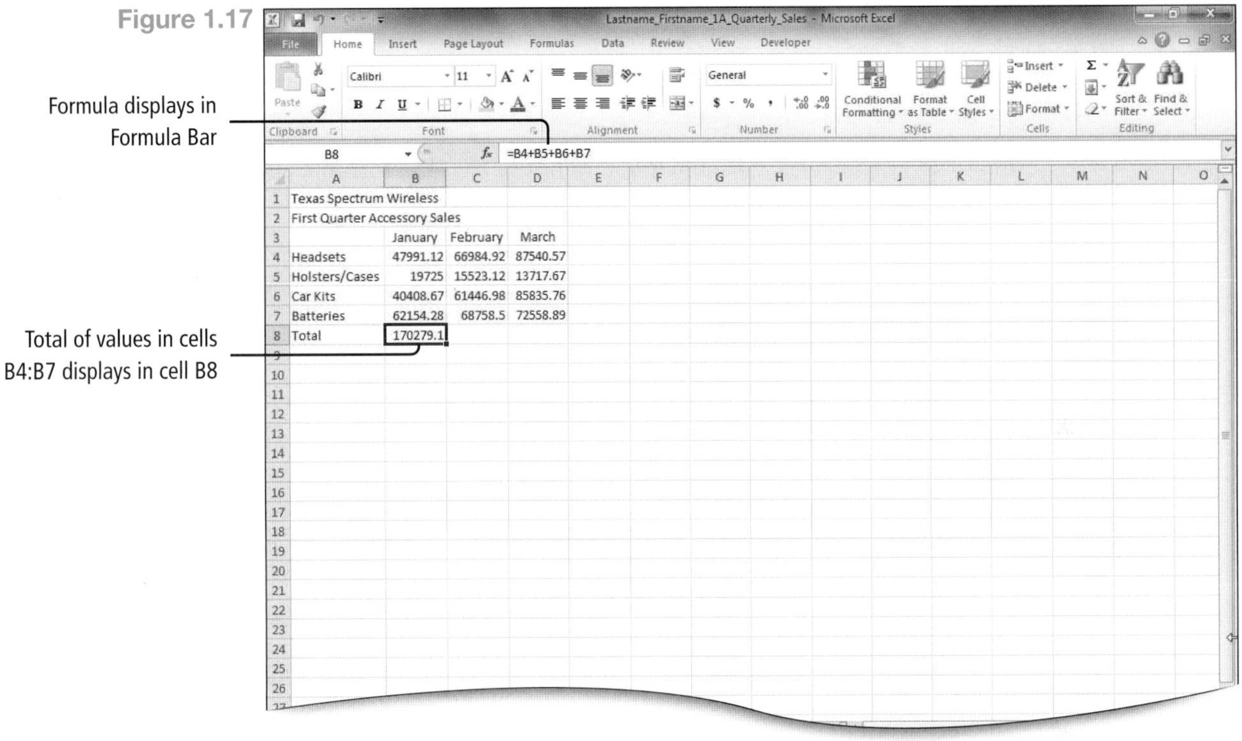

Formula displays in
Formula Bar

Total of values in cells
B4:B7 displays in cell B8

	A	B	C	D
1	Texas Spectrum Wireless			
2	First Quarter Accessory Sales			
3		January	February	March
4	Headsets	47991.12	66984.92	87540.57
5	Holsters/Cases	19725	15523.12	13717.67
6	Car Kits	40408.67	61446.98	85835.76
7	Batteries	62154.28	68758.5	72558.89
8	Total	170279.1		

B8 =B4+B5+B6+B7

6 Click cell **C8** and type **=** to signal the beginning of a formula. Then, point to cell **C4** and click one time.

> The reference to the cell C4 is added to the active formula. A moving border surrounds the referenced cell, and the border color and the color of the cell reference in the formula are color coded to match.

7 At the insertion point, type **+** and then click cell **C5**. Repeat this process to complete the formula to add cells **C4** through **C7**, and then press [Enter].

> The result of the formula calculation—*212713.5*—displays in the cell. This method of constructing a formula is the **point and click method**.

Another Way

Use the keyboard shortcut [Alt] + [=]; or, on the Formulas tab, in the Function Library group, click the AutoSum button.

8 Click cell **D8**. On the **Home tab**, in the **Editing group**, click the **Sum** button Σ, and then compare your screen with Figure 1.18.

> **SUM** is an Excel function—a prewritten formula. A moving border surrounds the range D4:D7 and *=SUM(D4:D7)* displays in cell D8.
>
> The = sign signals the beginning of a formula, *SUM* indicates the type of calculation that will take place (addition), and *(D4:D7)* indicates the range of cells on which the sum calculation will be performed. A ScreenTip provides additional information about the action.

Figure 1.18

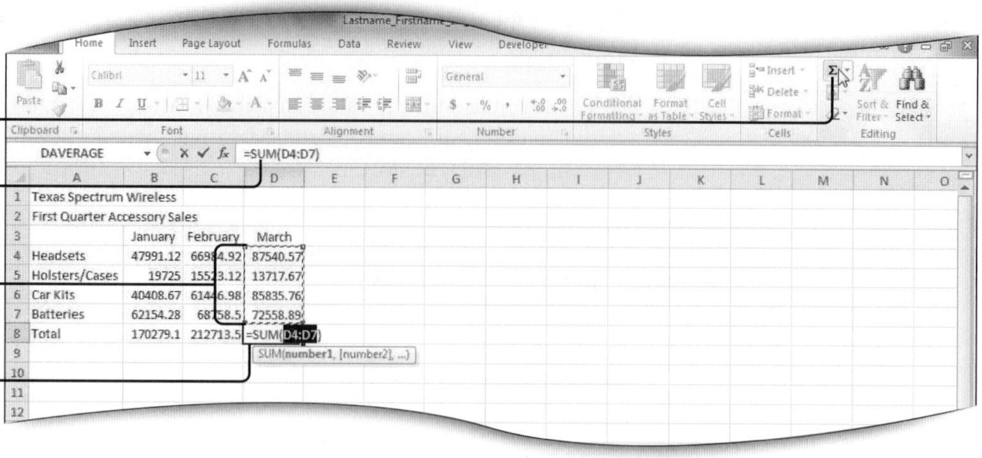

Sum button —

Formula displays in Formula Bar —

Proposed range to sum surrounded by moving border

SUM function formula and range to sum display in cell

9   Look at the **Formula Bar**, and notice that the formula also displays there. Then, look again at the cells surrounded by the moving border.

> When you activate the *Sum function*, Excel first looks *above* the active cell for a range of cells to sum. If no range is above the active cell, Excel will look to the *left* for a range of cells to sum. If the proposed range is not what you want to calculate, you can select a different group of cells.

10 Press Enter to construct a formula by using the prewritten SUM function.

> Your total is *259652.9*. Because the Sum function is frequently used, it has its own button in the Editing group on the Home tab of the Ribbon. A larger version of the button also displays on the Formulas tab in the Function Library group. This button is also referred to as *AutoSum*.

11 Notice that the totals in the range **B8:D8** display only *one* decimal place. Click **Save** 🖫.

> Number values that are too long to fit in the cell do *not* spill over into the unoccupied cell to the right in the same manner as text values. Rather, Excel rounds the number to fit the space.

> *Rounding* is a procedure that determines which digit at the right of the number will be the last digit displayed and then increases it by one if the next digit to its right is 5, 6, 7, 8, or 9.

Activity 1.08 │ Copying a Formula by Using the Fill Handle

You have practiced three ways to create a formula—by typing, by using the point-and-click technique, and by using a Function button from the Ribbon. You can also copy formulas. When you copy a formula from one cell to another, Excel adjusts the cell references to fit the new location of the formula.

1   Click cell **E3**, type **Total** and then press Enter.

> The text in cell E3 is centered because the centered format continues from the adjacent cell.

2   With cell **E4** as the active cell, hold down Alt, and then press =. Compare your screen with Figure 1.19.

> Alt + = is the keyboard shortcut for the Sum function. Recall that Excel first looks above the selected cell for a proposed range of cells to sum, and if no data is detected, Excel looks to the left and proposes a range of cells to sum.

Figure 1.19

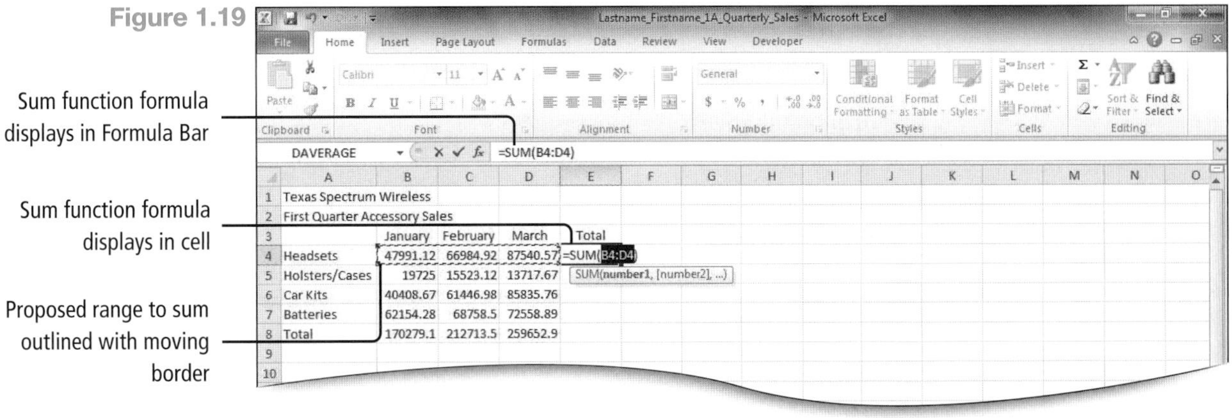

Sum function formula displays in Formula Bar

Sum function formula displays in cell

Proposed range to sum outlined with moving border

3 On the **Formula Bar**, click the **Enter** button ☑ to display the result and keep cell **E4** active.

> The total dollar amount of *Headsets* sold in the quarter is *202516.6*. In cells E5:E8, you can see that you need a formula similar to the one in E4, but formulas that refer to the cells in row 5, row 6, and so on.

4 With cell **E4** active, point to the fill handle in the lower right corner of the cell until the ⊞ pointer displays. Then, drag down through cell **E8**; if you are not satisfied with your result, on the Quick Access Toolbar, click Undo ↺ and begin again. Compare your screen with Figure 1.20.

Figure 1.20

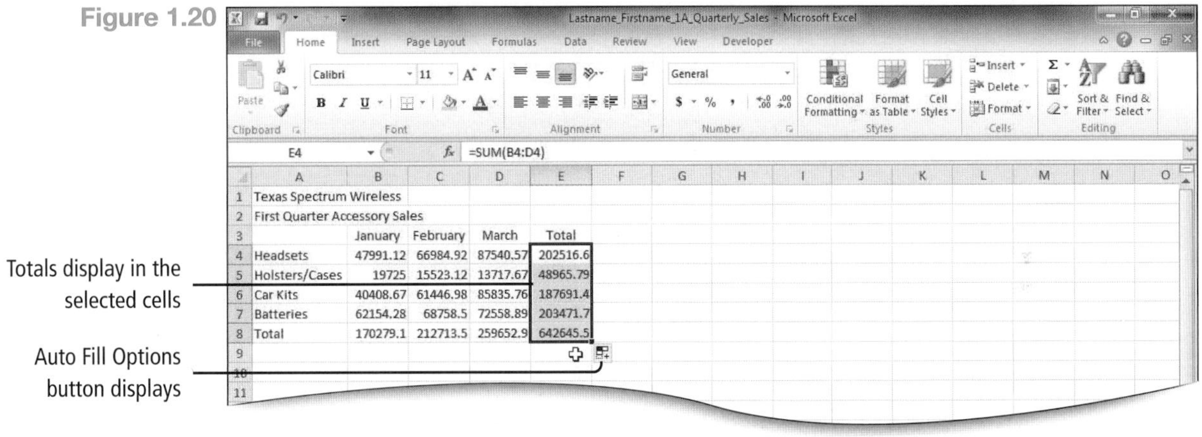

Totals display in the selected cells

Auto Fill Options button displays

5 Click cell **E5**, look at the **Formula Bar**, and notice the formula *=SUM(B5:D5)*. Click cell **E6**, look at the **Formula Bar**, and then notice the formula *=SUM(B6:D6)*.

> In each row, Excel copied the formula but adjusted the cell references *relative to* the row number. This is called a *relative cell reference*—a cell reference based on the relative position of the cell that contains the formula and the cells referred to.

> The calculation is the same, but it is performed on the cells in that particular row. Use this method to insert numerous formulas into spreadsheets quickly.

6 Click cell **F3,** type **Trend** and then press Enter. **Save** 🖫 your workbook.

Objective 4 | Format Cells with Merge & Center and Cell Styles

Format—change the appearance of—cells to make your worksheet attractive and easy to read.

Activity 1.09 | Using Merge & Center and Applying Cell Styles

Another Way

Select the range, right-click over the selection, and then on the Mini toolbar, click the Merge & Center button.

1 Select the range **A1:F1**, and then in the **Alignment group**, click the **Merge & Center** button. Then, select the range **A2:F2** and click the **Merge & Center** button.

The *Merge & Center* command joins selected cells into one larger cell and centers the contents in the new cell; individual cells in the range B1:F1 and B2:F2 can no longer be selected—they are merged into cell A1 and A2 respectively.

2 Click cell **A1**. In the **Styles group**, click the **Cell Styles** button, and then compare your screen with Figure 1.21.

A *cell style* is a defined set of formatting characteristics, such as font, font size, font color, cell borders, and cell shading.

Figure 1.21

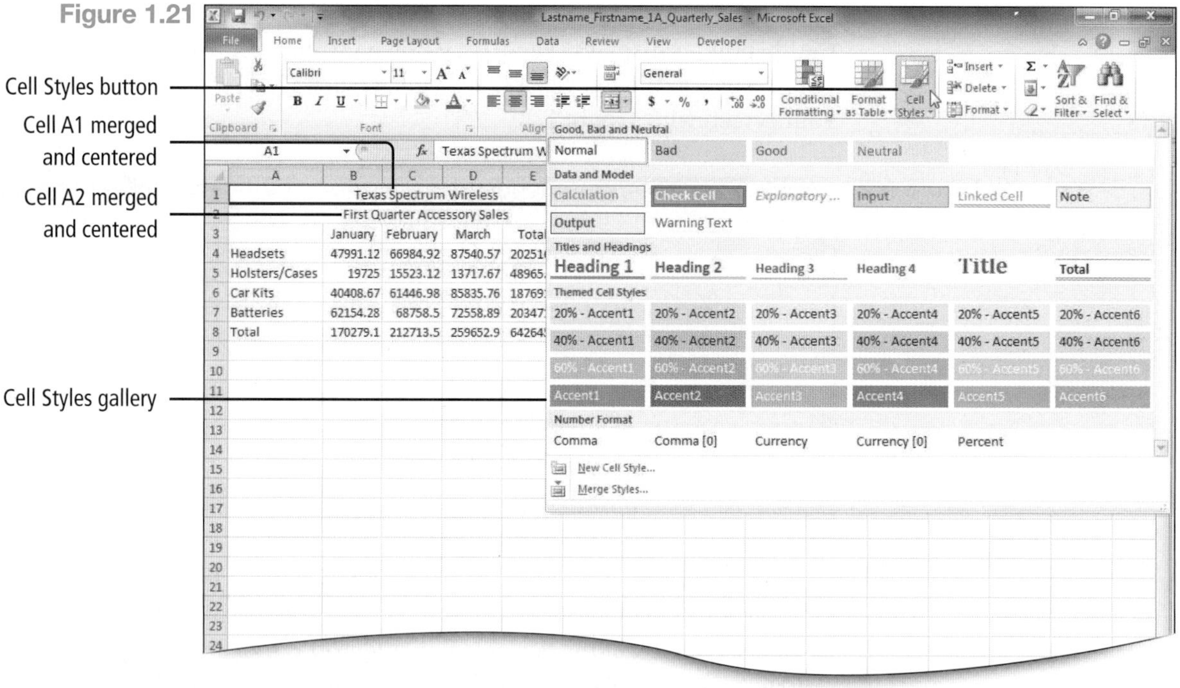

Cell Styles button

Cell A1 merged and centered

Cell A2 merged and centered

Cell Styles gallery

3 In the displayed gallery, under **Titles and Headings**, click **Title** and notice that the row height adjusts to accommodate this larger font size.

4 Click cell **A2**, display the **Cell Styles** gallery, and then under **Titles and Headings**, click **Heading 1**.

Use cell styles to maintain a consistent look in a worksheet and across worksheets in a workbook.

5 Select the range **B3:F3**, hold down Ctrl, and then select the range **A4:A8** to select the column titles and the row titles.

Use this technique to select two or more ranges that are nonadjacent—not next to each other.

6 Display the **Cell Styles** gallery, click **Heading 4** to apply this cell style to the column titles and row titles, and then **Save** 🔲 your workbook.

Another Way

In the Name Box type b4:e4,b8:e8 and then press Enter.

Activity 1.10 | Formatting Financial Numbers

1 Select the range **B4:E4**, hold down Ctrl, and then select the range **B8:E8**.

This range is referred to as *b4:e4,b8:e8* with a comma separating the references to the two nonadjacent ranges.

Another Way

Display the Cell Styles gallery, and under Number Format, click Currency.

2 On the **Home tab**, in the **Number group**, click the **Accounting Number Format** button $\boxed{\$\ \cdot}$. Compare your screen with Figure 1.22.

The *Accounting Number Format* applies a thousand comma separator where appropriate, inserts a fixed U.S. dollar sign aligned at the left edge of the cell, applies two decimal places, and leaves a small amount of space at the right edge of the cell to accommodate a parenthesis when negative numbers are present. Excel widens the columns to accommodate the formatted numbers.

Figure 1.22

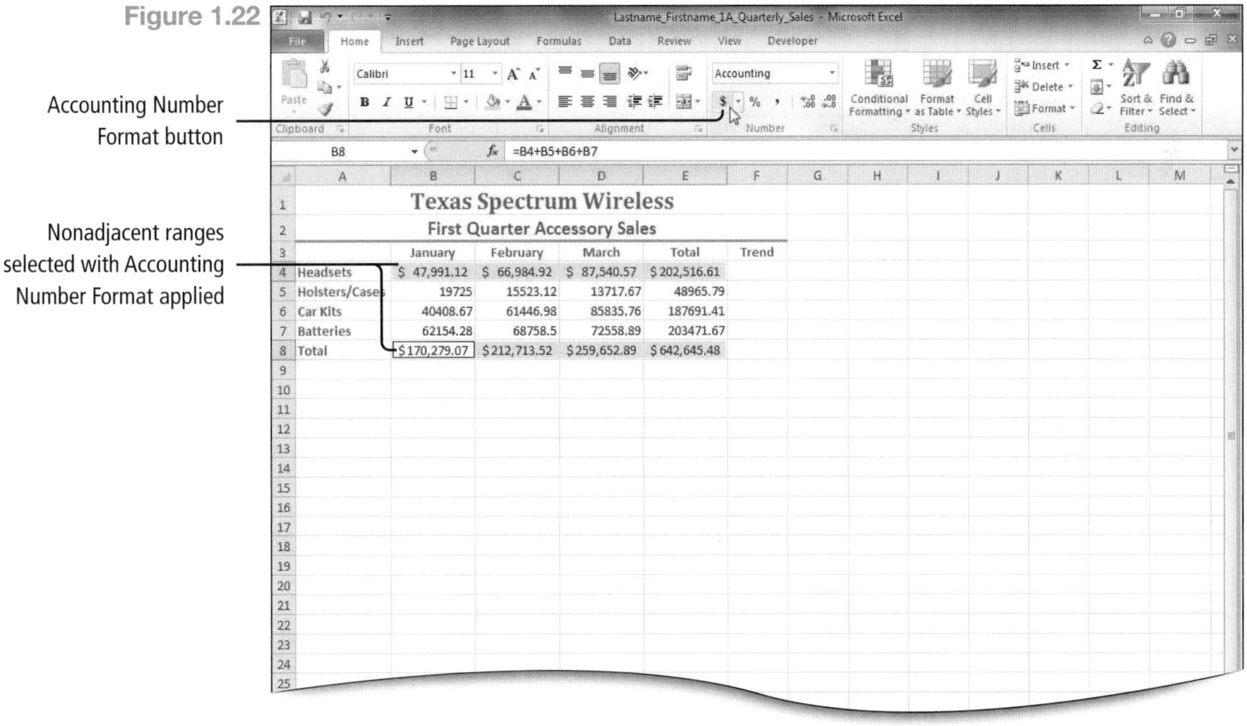

Accounting Number Format button

Nonadjacent ranges selected with Accounting Number Format applied

3 Select the range **B5:E7**, and then in the **Number group**, click the **Comma Style** button $\boxed{\,\cdot\,}$.

The *Comma Style* inserts thousand comma separators where appropriate and applies two decimal places. Comma Style also leaves space at the right to accommodate a parenthesis when negative numbers are present.

When preparing worksheets with financial information, the first row of dollar amounts and the total row of dollar amounts are formatted in the Accounting Number Format; that is, with thousand comma separators, dollar signs, two decimal places, and space at the right to accommodate a parenthesis for negative numbers, if any. Rows that are *not* the first row or the total row should be formatted with the Comma Style.

4 Select the range **B8:E8**. From the **Styles group**, display the **Cell Styles** gallery, and then under **Titles and Headings**, click **Total**. Click any blank cell to cancel the selection, and then compare your screen with Figure 1.23.

> This is a common way to apply borders to financial information. The single border indicates that calculations were performed on the numbers above, and the double border indicates that the information is complete. Sometimes financial documents do not display values with cents; rather, the values are rounded up. You can do this by selecting the cells, and then clicking the Decrease Decimal button two times.

Figure 1.23

Comma style applied to range B5:E7

Total format applied to total row

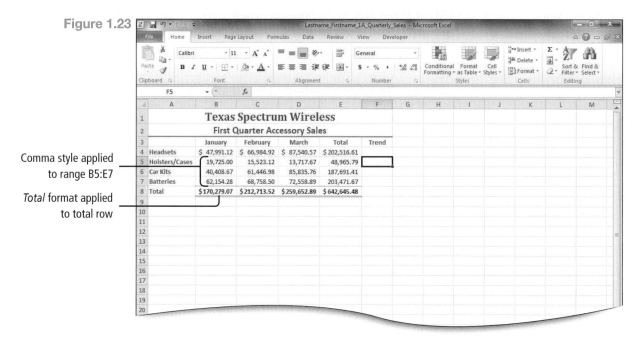

5 Click the **Page Layout tab**, and then in the **Themes group**, click **Themes**. Click the **Composite** theme, and notice that the cell styles change to match the new theme. Click **Save** ⊟.

> Recall that a theme is a predefined set of colors, fonts, lines, and fill effects that look good together.

Objective 5 | Chart Data to Create a Column Chart and Insert Sparklines

A ***chart*** is a graphic representation of data in a worksheet. Data presented as a chart is easier to understand than a table of numbers. ***Sparklines*** are tiny charts embedded in a cell and give a visual trend summary alongside your data. A sparkline makes a pattern more obvious to the eye.

Activity 1.11 | Charting Data in a Column Chart

In this activity, you will create a ***column chart*** showing the monthly sales of accessories by category during the first quarter. A column chart is useful for illustrating comparisons among related numbers. The chart will enable the company president, Rosalyn Thomas, to see a pattern of overall monthly sales.

1 Select the range **A3:D7**. Click the **Insert tab**, and then in the **Charts group**, click **Column** to display a gallery of Column chart types.

> When charting data, typically you should *not* include totals—include only the data you want to compare. By using different ***chart types***, you can display data in a way that is meaningful to the reader—common examples are column charts, pie charts, and line charts.

2 On the gallery of column chart types, under **2-D Column**, point to the first chart to display the ScreenTip *Clustered Column*, and then click to select it. Compare your screen with Figure 1.24.

> A column chart displays in the worksheet, and the charted data is bordered by colored lines. Because the chart object is selected—surrounded by a border and displaying sizing handles—contextual tools named *Chart Tools* display and add contextual tabs next to the standard tabs on the Ribbon.

Figure 1.24

Chart Tools display three additional tabs—*Design, Layout, Format*

Border and sizing handles indicate chart is selected

Charted data range bordered by colored lines (green = legend, blue = columns, purple = category labels)

Clustered column chart displays in worksheet

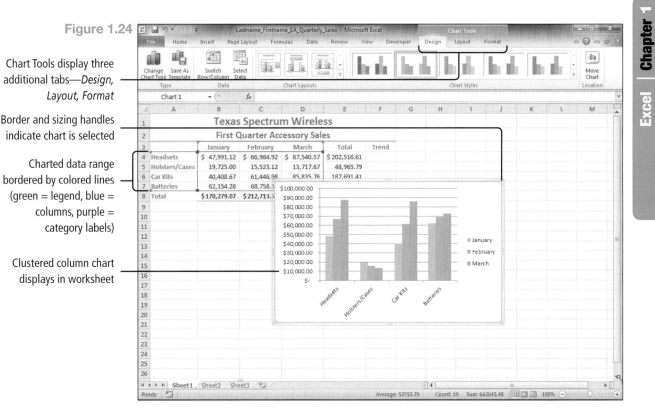

3 Point to the top border of the chart to display the pointer, and then drag the upper left corner of the chart just inside the upper left corner of cell **A10**, approximately as shown in Figure 1.25.

> Based on the data you selected in your worksheet, Excel constructs a column chart and adds ***category labels***—the labels that display along the bottom of the chart to identify the category of data. This area is referred to as the ***category axis*** or the ***x-axis***. Excel uses the row titles as the category names.

> On the left, Excel includes a numerical scale on which the charted data is based; this is the ***value axis*** or the ***y-axis***. On the right, a ***legend***, which identifies the patterns or colors that are assigned to the categories in the chart, displays.

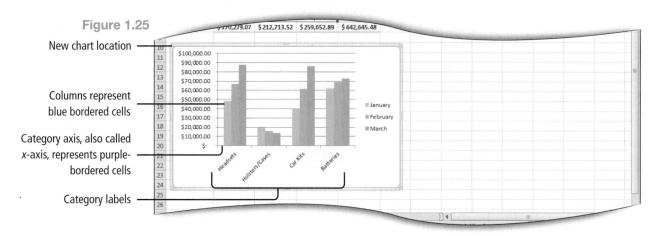

Figure 1.25

New chart location

Columns represent blue bordered cells

Category axis, also called x-axis, represents purple-bordered cells

Category labels

4 On the Ribbon, locate the contextual tabs under **Chart Tools—Design**, **Layout**, and **Format**.

> When a chart is selected, Chart Tools become available and three tabs provide commands for working with the chart.

5 Locate the group of cells bordered in blue.

> Each of the twelve cells bordered in blue is referred to as a ***data point***—a value that originates in a worksheet cell. Each data point is represented in the chart by a ***data marker***—a column, bar, area, dot, pie slice, or other symbol in a chart that represents a single data point.

> Related data points form a ***data series***; for example, there is a data series for *January*, for *February*, and for *March*. Each data series has a unique color or pattern represented in the chart legend.

6 On the **Design tab** of the Ribbon, in the **Data group**, click the **Switch Row/Column** button, and then compare your chart with Figure 1.26.

> In this manner, you can easily change the categories of data from the row titles, which is the default, to the column titles. Whether you use row or column titles as your category names depends on how you want to view your charted data. Here, the president wants to see monthly sales and the breakdown of product categories within each month.

Figure 1.26

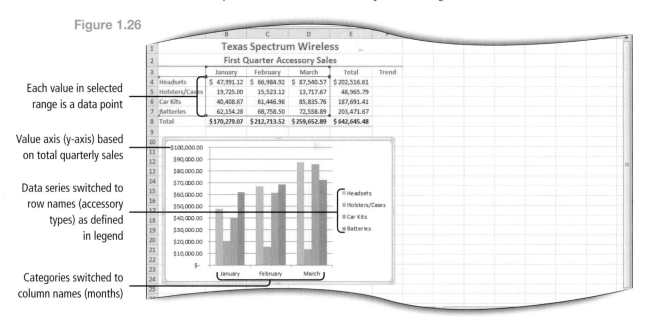

Each value in selected range is a data point

Value axis (y-axis) based on total quarterly sales

Data series switched to row names (accessory types) as defined in legend

Categories switched to column names (months)

7 On the **Design tab**, in the **Chart Layouts group**, locate and click the **More** button ⊡. Compare your screen with Figure 1.27.

In the *Chart Layouts gallery*, you can select a predesigned *chart layout*—a combination of chart elements, which can include a title, legend, labels for the columns, and the table of charted cells.

Figure 1.27

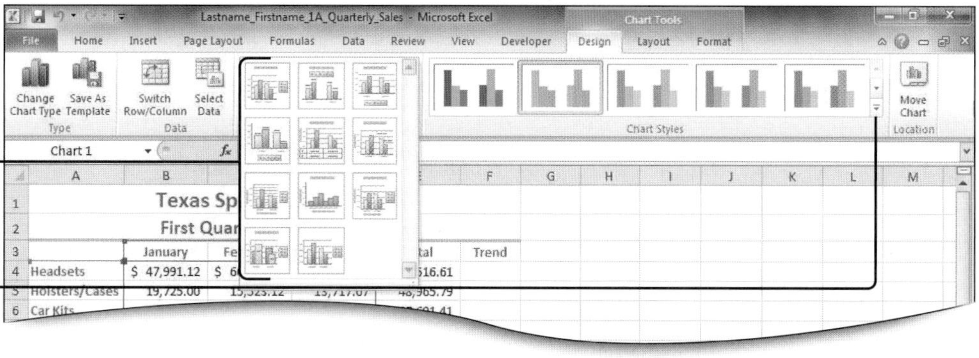

Chart Layouts gallery

More buttons in Chart Styles group

8 Click several different layouts to see the effect on your chart, and then using the ScreenTips as your guide, locate and click **Layout 1**.

9 In the chart, click anywhere in the text *Chart Title* to select the title box, watch the **Formula Bar** as you type **1st Quarter Sales** and then press Enter to display the new chart title.

10 Click in a white area just slightly *inside* the chart border to deselect the chart title. On the **Design tab**, in the **Chart Styles group**, click the **More** button ⊡. Compare your screen with Figure 1.28.

The *Chart Styles gallery* displays an array of pre-defined *chart styles*—the overall visual look of the chart in terms of its colors, backgrounds, and graphic effects such as flat or beveled columns.

Figure 1.28

Chart Styles gallery

Title added to chart ——————— 1st Quarter Sales

11 Using the ScreenTips as your guide, locate and click **Style 26**.

This style uses a white background, formats the columns with theme colors, and applies a beveled effect. With this clear visual representation of the data, the president can see the sales of all product categories in each month, and can see that the sale of headsets and car kits has risen quite markedly during the quarter.

Excel | Chapter 1

12 Click any cell to deselect the chart, and notice that the *Chart Tools* no longer display in the Ribbon. Click **Save** 🔲 , and then compare your screen with Figure 1.29.

> Contextual tabs display when an object is selected, and then are removed from view when the object is deselected.

Figure 1.29

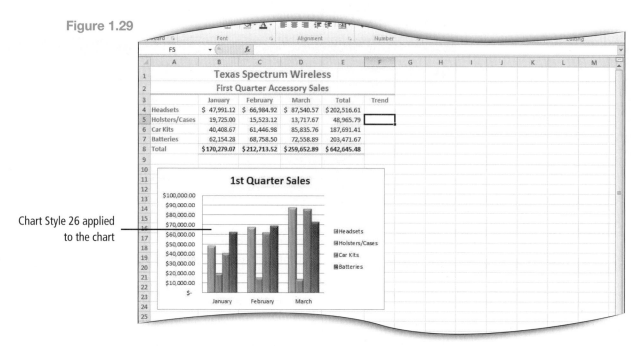

Chart Style 26 applied to the chart

Activity 1.12 | Creating and Formatting Sparklines

By creating sparklines, you provide a context for your numbers. Your readers will be able to see the relationship between a sparkline and its underlying data quickly.

> **Another Way**
>
> In the worksheet, select the range F4:F7 to insert it into the Location Range box.

1 Select the range **B4:D7**. Click the **Insert tab**, and then in the **Sparklines group**, click **Line**. In the displayed **Create Sparklines** dialog box, notice that the selected range *B4:D7* displays.

2 With the insertion point blinking in the **Location Range** box, type **f4:f7** Compare your screen with Figure 1.30.

Figure 1.30

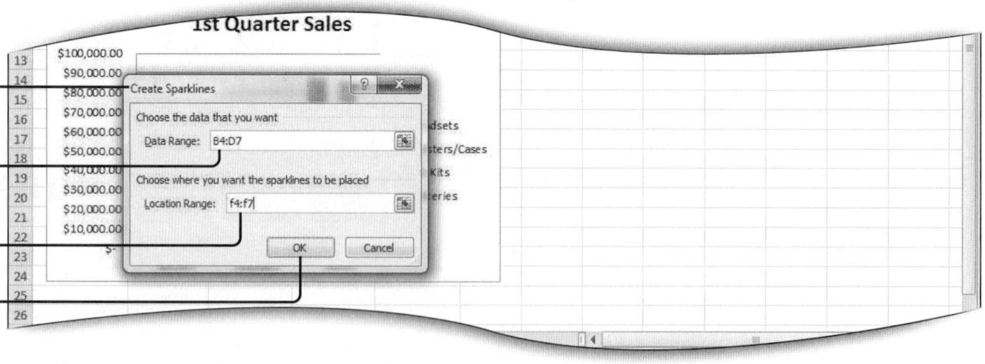

Create Sparklines dialog box

Data Range indicates your selected data

Location Range typed

OK button

3 Click **OK** to insert the trend lines in the range F4:F7, and then on the **Design tab**, in the **Show group**, click the **Markers** check box to select it.

> Alongside each row of data, the sparkline provides a quick visual trend summary for sales of each accessory item over the three-month period. For example, you can see instantly that of the four items, only Holsters/Cases had declining sales for the period.

4 In the **Style group**, click the **More** button ⊡. In the second row, click the fourth style—**Sparkline Style Accent 4, Darker 25%**. Click cell **A1** to deselect the range. Click **Save** 🖫. Compare your screen with Figure 1.31.

Use markers, colors, and styles in this manner to further enhance your sparklines.

Figure 1.31

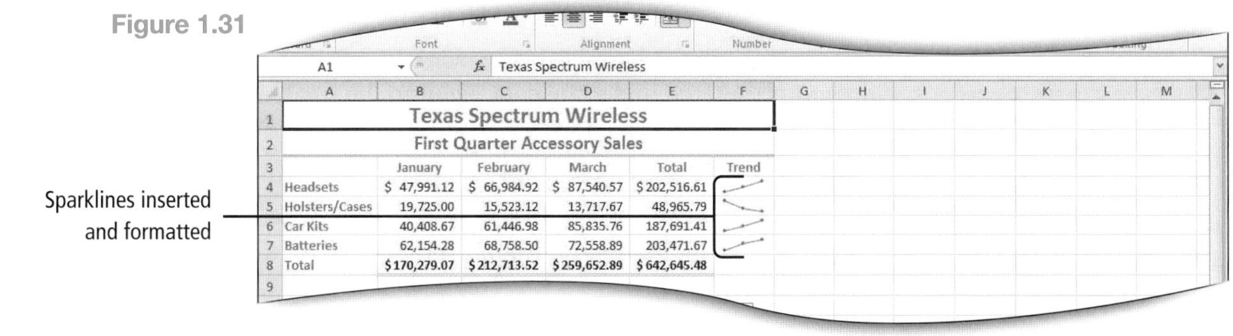

Sparklines inserted and formatted

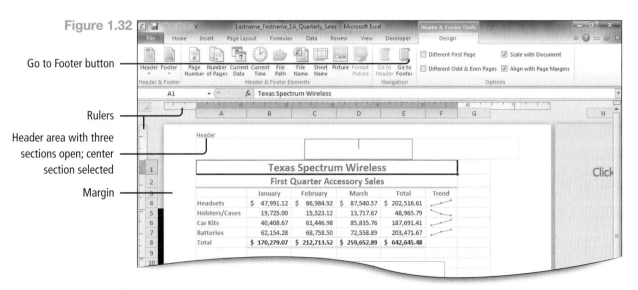

Objective 6 | Print, Display Formulas, and Close Excel

Use *Page Layout view* and the commands on the Page Layout tab to prepare for printing.

Activity 1.13 | Changing Views, Creating a Footer, and Using Print Preview

For each Excel project in this textbook, you will create a footer containing your name and the project name.

1 Be sure the chart is *not* selected. Click the **Insert tab**, and then in the **Text group**, click the **Header & Footer** button to switch to Page Layout view and open the **Header area**. Compare your screen with Figure 1.32.

In Page Layout view, you can see the edges of the paper of multiple pages, the margins, and the rulers. You can also insert a header or footer by typing in the areas indicated and use the Header & Footer Tools.

Figure 1.32

Go to Footer button

Rulers

Header area with three sections open; center section selected

Margin

2 On the **Design tab**, in the **Navigation group**, click **Go to Footer** to open the **Footer area**, and then click just above the word *Footer* to place the insertion point in the **left section** of the **Footer area**.

3 In the **Header & Footer Elements group**, click the **File Name** button to add the name of your file to the footer—&*[File]* displays in the left section of the **Footer area**. Then, click in a cell just above the footer to exit the **Footer area** and view your file name.

4 Scroll up to see your chart, click a corner of the chart to select it, and then see if the chart is centered under the data. *Point* to the small dots on the right edge of the chart; compare your screen with Figure 1.33.

Figure 1.33

Horizontal resize pointer

Border indicates chart is selected

5 Drag the pointer to the right so that the right border of the chart is just inside the right border of **column F**. Be sure the left and right borders of the chart are just slightly **inside** the left border of **column A** and the right border of **column F**—adjust as necessary.

6 Click any cell to deselect the chart. Click the **Page Layout tab**, in the **Page Setup group**, click the **Margins** button, and then at the bottom of the **Margins** gallery, click **Custom Margins**. In the **Page Setup** dialog box, under **Center on page**, select the **Horizontally** check box.

This action will center the data and chart horizontally on the page, as shown in the Preview area.

7 In the lower right corner of the **Page Setup** dialog box, click **OK**. In the upper left corner of your screen, click the **File tab** to display **Backstage** view. On the **Info tab**, on the right under the screen thumbnail, click **Properties**, and then click **Show Document Panel**.

8 In the **Author** box, replace the existing text with your firstname and lastname. In the **Subject** box, type your course name and section number. In the **Keywords** box type **accessory sales** and then **Close** ☒ the **Document Information Panel**.

Another Way
Press Ctrl + F2 to view the Print Preview.

9 **Click the File tab** to redisplay **Backstage** view, and then on the left, click the **Print tab** to view the Print commands and the **Print Preview**. Compare your screen with Figure 1.34.

Figure 1.34

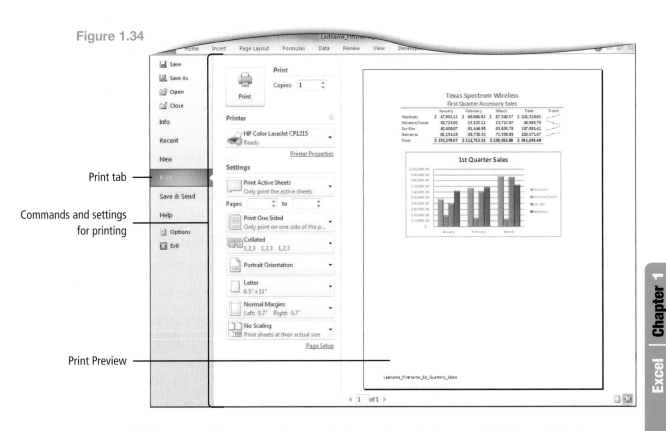

Print tab

Commands and settings for printing

Print Preview

10 Note any adjustments that need to be made, and then on the Ribbon, click the **Home tab** to close Backstage view and return to the worksheet. In the lower right corner of your screen, click the **Normal** button 🔲 to return to the Normal view, and then press [Ctrl] + [Home] to return to cell **A1**.

> The *Normal view* maximizes the number of cells visible on your screen and keeps the column letters and row numbers closer. The vertical dotted line between columns indicates that as currently arranged, only the columns to the left of the dotted line will print on the first page. The exact position of the vertical line may depend on your default printer setting.

11 Make any necessary adjustments, and then **Save** 🔲 your workbook.

Activity 1.14 | Deleting Unused Sheets in a Workbook

A new Excel workbook contains three blank worksheets. It is not necessary to delete unused sheets, but doing so saves storage space and removes any doubt that additional information is in the workbook.

1 At the bottom of your worksheet, click the **Sheet2 tab** to display the second worksheet in the workbook and make it active.

Another Way

On the Home tab, in the Cells group, click the Delete button arrow, and then click Delete Sheet.

2 Hold down [Ctrl], and then click the **Sheet3 tab**. Release [Ctrl], and then with both sheets selected (the tab background is white), point to either of the selected sheet tabs, right-click, and then on the shortcut menu, click **Delete**.

> Excel deletes the two unused sheets from your workbook. If you attempt to delete a worksheet with data, Excel will display a warning and permit you to cancel the deletion. *Sheet tabs* are labels along the lower border of the Excel window that identify each worksheet.

Activity 1.15 | Printing a Worksheet

1 Click **Save** 🖫.

2 Display **Backstage** view and on the left click the Print tab. Under **Print**, be sure **Copies** indicates *1*. Under **Settings**, verify that *Print Active Sheets* displays. Compare your screen with Figure 1.35.

Figure 1.35

Copies indicates *1*

Print Active Sheets

Print Preview

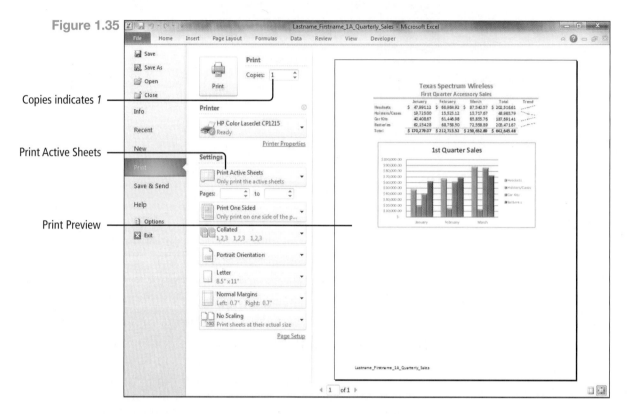

3 To print on paper, be sure that a printer is available to your system, and then in the **Print group**, click the **Print** button. To create an electronic printout, on the Backstage tabs, click the **Save & Send tab**, under **File Types** click **Create PDF/XPS Document**, and then on the right, click **Create PDF/XPS**. In the **Publish as PDF or XPS** dialog box, navigate to your storage location, and then click the **Publish** button to create the PDF file. Close the Adobe window.

Activity 1.16 | Displaying, Printing, and Hiding Formulas

When you type a formula in a cell, the cell displays the *results* of the formula calculation. Recall that this value is called the displayed value. You can view and print the underlying formulas in the cells. When you do so, a formula often takes more horizontal space to display than the result of the calculation.

1 If necessary, redisplay your worksheet. Because you will make some temporary changes to your workbook, on the Quick Access Toolbar, click **Save** 🖫 to be sure your work is saved up to this point.

> **Another Way**
>
> Hold down Ctrl, and then press ` (usually located below Esc).

2 On the **Formulas tab**, in the **Formula Auditing group**, click the **Show Formulas** button. Then, in the **column heading area**, point to the **column A** heading to display the ↓ pointer, hold down the left mouse button, and then drag to the right to select columns **A:F**. Compare your screen with Figure 1.36.

Figure 1.36

Dotted line shows page break

Underlying formulas displayed

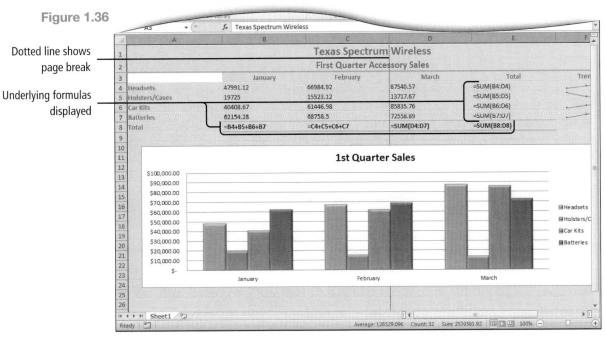

Note | Turning the Display of Formulas On and Off

The Show Formulas button is a toggle button. Clicking it once turns the display of formulas on—the button will glow orange. Clicking the button again turns the display of formulas off.

3 Point to the column heading boundary between any two of the selected columns to display the ⊞ pointer, and then double-click to AutoFit the selected columns.

> *AutoFit* adjusts the width of a column to fit the cell content of the *widest* cell in the column.

Another Way

In the Scale to Fit group, click the Dialog Box Launcher button to display the Page tab of the Page Setup dialog box. Then, under Scaling, click the Fit to option button.

4 On the **Page Layout tab**, in the **Page Setup group**, click **Orientation**, and then click **Landscape**. In the **Scale to Fit** group, click the **Width arrow**, and then click **1 page** to scale the data to fit onto one page.

> *Scaling* shrinks the width (or height) of the printed worksheet to fit a maximum number of pages, and is convenient for printing formulas. Although it is not always the case, formulas frequently take up more space than the actual data.

Another Way

In the Page Setup group, click the Dialog Box Launcher button to display the Page tab of the Page Setup dialog box. Then, under Orientation, click the Landscape option button.

5 In the **Page Setup group**, click the **Dialog Box Launcher** button ⬚. In the **Page Setup** dialog box, click the **Margins tab**, and then under **Center on page**, if necessary, click to select the **Horizontally** check box.

6 Click **OK** to close the dialog box. Check to be sure your chart is centered below the data and the left and right edges are slightly inside column A and column F—drag a chart edge and then deselect the chart if necessary. Display the **Print Preview**, and then submit your worksheet with formulas displayed, either printed or electronically, as directed by your instructor.

7 Click the **File tab** to display **Backstage** view, click **Close**, and when prompted, click **Don't Save** so that you do *not* save the changes you made—displaying formulas, changing column widths and orientation, and scaling—to print your formulas.

8 In the upper right corner of your screen, click the **Close** button ⬚ to exit Excel.

End **You have completed Project 1A**

GO! Beyond Office

Objective | Upload an Excel Worksheet to SkyDrive and Edit a Worksheet Using the Excel Web App

Recall that Windows Live SkyDrive is a free file storage and file sharing service provided by Windows Live—a collection of programs and services for individuals that work together and includes Hotmail e-mail, Live Messenger instant messaging, applications such as Photo Gallery and Movie Maker, the Office Web Apps, and mobile phone applications. The Excel Web App enables you to work with worksheets directly on the Web site where the worksheet is stored.

> **Alert! | Working with Web-Based Applications and Services**
>
> Computer programs and services on the Web receive continuous updates and improvements. Thus, the steps to complete this Web-based Activity may differ from the ones shown. You can often look at the screens and the information presented to determine how to complete the Activity.

Activity | Uploading an Excel Worksheet to Your SkyDrive and Editing a Worksheet Using the Excel Web App

In this activity, you will upload a worksheet to your SkyDrive, and then you will edit the worksheet using the Excel Web App.

1 Launch your Web browser, navigate to **www.live.com**, and then sign in to your Windows Live account. If you do not have a Windows Live account, refer to GO! Beyond Word Project 1A to create the account.

2 At the top of the screen, click **SkyDrive**, and then to the right of *Create*, click the **Create folder** button. In the **Name** box, type **GO! Beyond Office-Excel** and then click **Next**.

3 On the **Add documents to GO! Beyond Office - Excel** screen, click the text *select documents from your computer*. Navigate to your **Excel Chapter 1** folder, and then click your **Lastname_Firstname_1A_Quarterly_Sales** file. In the lower right corner of the dialog box, click **Open**.

4 When the upload is complete, in the lower left corner, click **Continue** to return to your **GO! Beyond Office-Excel** folder.

Your Lastname_Firstname_1A_Quarterly_Sales file displays in the folder.

5 Click your **Lastname_Firstname_1A_Quarterly_Sales** file one time to open the Excel file in your browser window. Above the worksheet, click **Edit in Browser**, and then compare your screen with Figure A.

The worksheet displays in the Excel Web App, which includes Home, Insert, and View tabs with several groups. In the Excel Web App, you can edit and format cells; insert charts, tables, cells, columns, and rows; and you can modify and insert formulas.

Figure A

GO! Beyond Office

6 Click cell **B6**, type **50100.89** and then press Enter. Notice that the chart is updated.

7 In cell **C4**, type **72984.92** and then press Enter. In cell **D7**, type **81622.34** and then press Enter.

As each new value is entered, the chart and the worksheet totals update. You can share this worksheet with others who do not have the Microsoft Office Excel 2010 program so that they can view and edit the worksheet.

8 Click the edge of the chart to select it. On the **Design tab**, in the **Labels group**, click the **Chart Title** button, and then click **Edit Chart Title**. In the **Title text** box, click after the *r* in the word *Quarter*. Press Spacebar, and then type **Accessory** Click **OK** to change the chart title. Compare your screen with Figure B.

9 Display the **Start** menu 🌐, and then click **All Programs**. On the list of programs, click the **Accessories folder**, and then click **Snipping Tool**. In the **Snipping Tool** dialog box, click the **New arrow**. On the displayed list, click **Full-screen Snip**, and then click the **Save Snip** button 💾. In the **Save As** dialog box, navigate to your **Excel Chapter 1** folder, be sure the **Save as type** box displays **JPEG file**, and then in the **File name** box, type **Lastname_Firstname_1A_Web_Snip** Click **Save**. **Close** ❎ the **Snipping Tool** window, sign out of your Windows Live account, close all open windows, and then submit your snip file as directed.

In the Excel Web App, it is not necessary to save your file because changes are saved automatically.

Figure B

Project 1B Inventory Valuation

myitlab
Project 1B Training

Project Activities

In Activities 1.17 through 1.24, you will create a workbook for Josette Lovrick, Operations Manager, which calculates the retail value of an inventory of car convenience products. Your completed worksheet will look similar to Figure 1.37.

Project Files

For Project 1B, you will need the following file:

New blank Excel workbook

You will save your workbook as:

Lastname_Firstname_1B_Car_Products

Project Results

Texas Spectrum Wireless

Car Products Inventory Valuation

As of December 31

	Warehouse Location	Quantity In Stock	Retail Price	Total Retail Value	Percent of Total Retail Value
Antenna Signal Booster	Dallas	1,126	$ 19.99	$ 22,508.74	8.27%
Car Power Port Adapter	Dallas	3,546	19.49	69,111.54	25.39%
Repeater Antenna	Houston	1,035	39.99	41,389.65	15.21%
SIM Card Reader and Writer	Houston	2,875	16.90	48,587.50	17.85%
Sticky Dash Pad	Houston	3,254	11.99	39,015.46	14.33%
Window Mount GPS Holder	Dallas	2,458	20.99	51,593.42	18.95%
Total Retail Value for All Products				$ 272,206.31	

Lastname_Firstname_1B_Car_Products

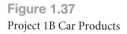

Figure 1.37
Project 1B Car Products

Objective 7 | Check Spelling in a Worksheet

In Excel, the spelling checker performs similarly to the other Microsoft Office programs.

Activity 1.17 | Checking Spelling in a Worksheet

1 **Start** Excel and display a new blank workbook. In cell **A1**, type **Texas Spectrum Wireless** and press [Enter]. In cell **A2**, type **Car Products Inventory** and press [Enter].

2 On the Ribbon, click the **File tab** to display **Backstage** view, click **Save As**, and then in the **Save As** dialog box, navigate to your **Excel Chapter 1** folder. As the **File name**, type **Lastname_Firstname_1B_Car_Products** and then click **Save**.

3 Press [Tab] to move to cell **B3**, type **Quantity** and press [Tab]. In cell **C3**, type **Average Cost** and press [Tab]. In cell **D3**, type **Retail Price** and press [Tab].

4 Click cell **C3**, and then look at the **Formula Bar**. Notice that in the cell, the displayed value is cut off; however, in the **Formula Bar**, the entire text value—the underlying value—displays. Compare your screen with Figure 1.38.

> Text that is too long to fit in a cell spills over to cells on the right only if they are empty. If the cell to the right contains data, the text in the cell to the left is truncated. The entire value continues to exist, but is not completely visible.

Figure 1.38

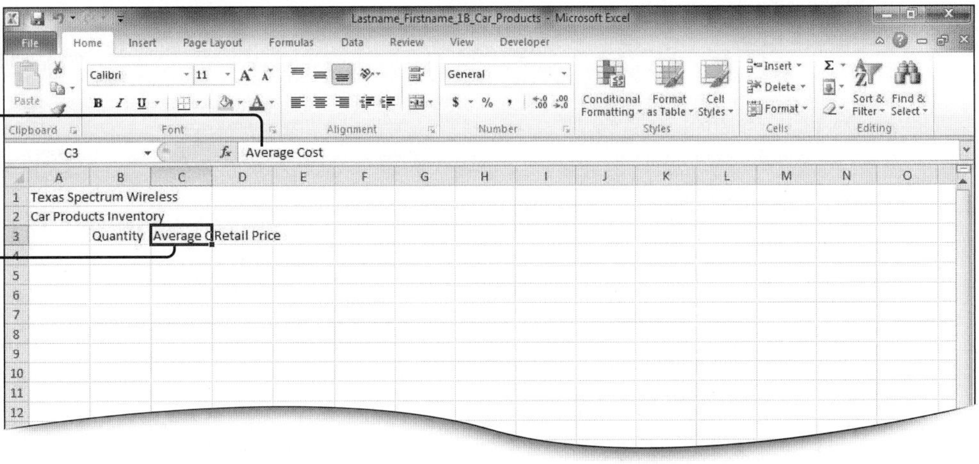

Entire contents of C3 display in Formula Bar

Cell C3 active, text cut off

5 Click cell **E3**, type **Total Retail Value** and press [Tab]. In cell **F3**, type **Percent of Total Retail Value** and press [Enter].

6 Click cell **A4**. *Without* correcting the spelling error, type **Antena Signal Booster** Press [Enter]. In the range **A5:A10**, type the remaining row titles shown below. Then compare your screen with Figure 1.39.

> **Car Power Port Adapter**
>
> **Repeater Antenna**
>
> **SIM Card Reader and Writer**
>
> **Sticky Dash Pad**
>
> **Window Mount GPS Holder**
>
> **Total Retail Value for All Products**

Figure 1.39

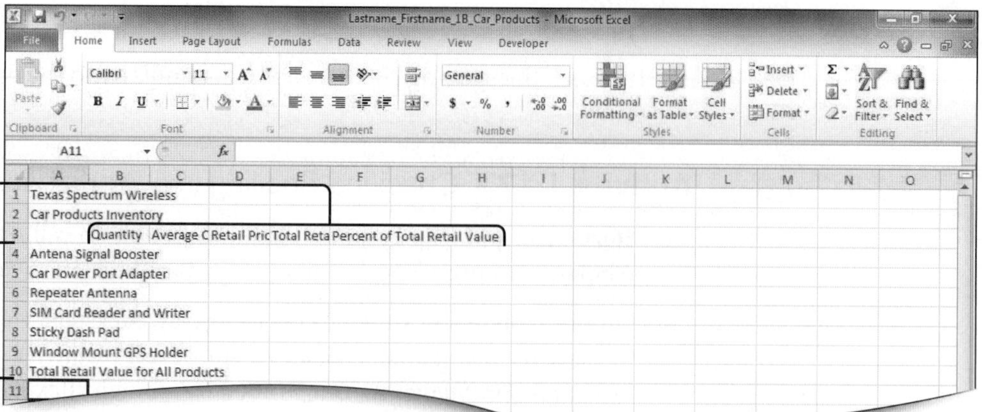

Column titles

Row titles

7 In the **column heading area**, point to the right boundary of **column A** to display the ⊞ pointer, and then drag to the right to widen **column A** to 215 pixels.

8 Select the range **A1:F1**, **Merge & Center** 🔳 the text, and then from the **Cell Styles** gallery, apply the **Title** style.

9 Select the range **A2:F2**, **Merge & Center** 🔳 the text, and then from the **Cell Styles** gallery, apply the **Heading 1** style. Press Ctrl + Home to move to the top of your worksheet.

> **Another Way**
>
> Press F7, which is the keyboard shortcut for the Spelling command.

10 With cell **A1** as the active cell, click the **Review tab**, and then in the **Proofing group**, click the **Spelling** button. Compare your screen with Figure 1.40.

Figure 1.40

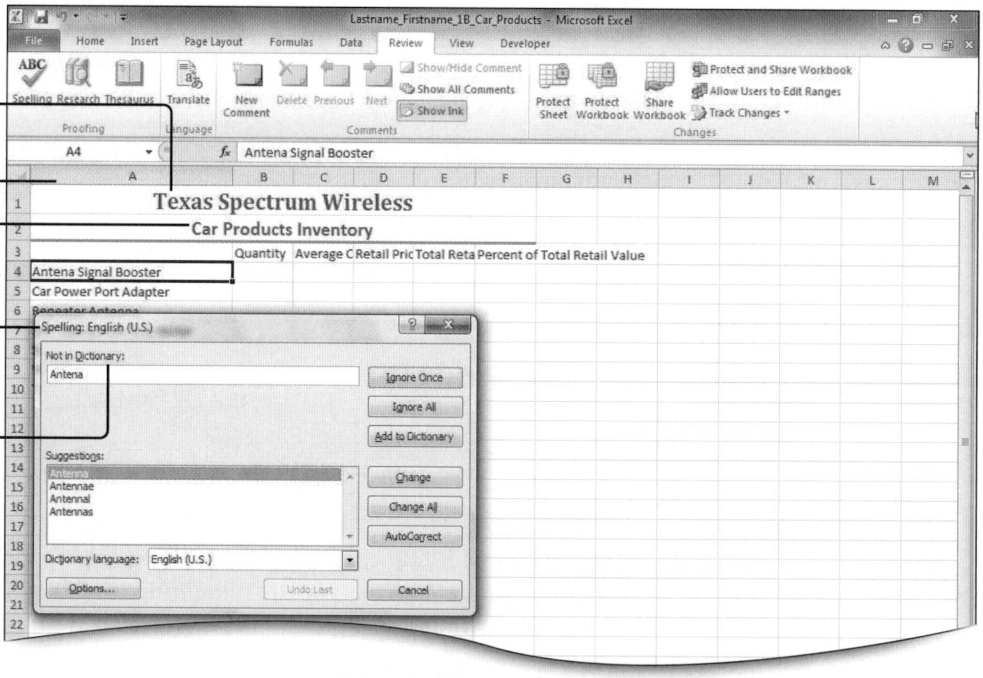

Worksheet title formatted with Title style

Column A widened to 215 pixels

Worksheet subtitle formatted with Heading 1 style

Spelling dialog box

Word indicated as *Not in Dictionary*

> **Alert! | Does a Message Display Asking if You Want to Continue Checking at the Beginning of the Sheet?**
>
> If a message displays asking if you want to continue checking at the beginning of the sheet, click Yes. The Spelling command begins its checking process with the currently selected cell and moves to the right and down. Thus, if your active cell was a cell after A4, this message may display.

11 In the **Spelling** dialog box, under **Not in Dictionary**, notice the word *Antena*.

The spelling tool does not have this word in its dictionary. Under *Suggestions*, Excel provides a list of suggested spellings.

12 Under **Suggestions**, click **Antenna**, and then click the **Change** button.

Antena, a typing error, is changed to *Antenna*. A message box displays *The spelling check is complete for the entire sheet*—unless you have additional unrecognized words. Because the spelling check begins its checking process starting with the currently selected cell, it is good practice to return to cell A1 before starting the Spelling command.

13 Correct any other errors you may have made. When the message displays, *The spelling check is complete for the entire sheet*, click **OK**. Save 🔲 your workbook.

Objective 8 | Enter Data by Range

You can enter data by first selecting a range of cells. This is a time-saving technique, especially if you use the numeric keypad to enter the numbers.

Activity 1.18 | Entering Data by Range

1 Select the range **B4:D9**, type **1126** and then press `Enter`.

The value displays in cell B4, and cell B5 becomes the active cell.

2 With cell **B5** active in the range, and pressing `Enter` after each entry, type the following, and then compare your screen with Figure 1.41:

> 4226
> 1035
> 2875
> 3254
> 2458

After you enter the last value and press `Enter`, the active cell moves to the top of the next column within the selected range. Although it is not required to enter data in this manner, you can see that selecting the range before you enter data saves time because it confines the movement of the active cell to the selected range.

Figure 1.41

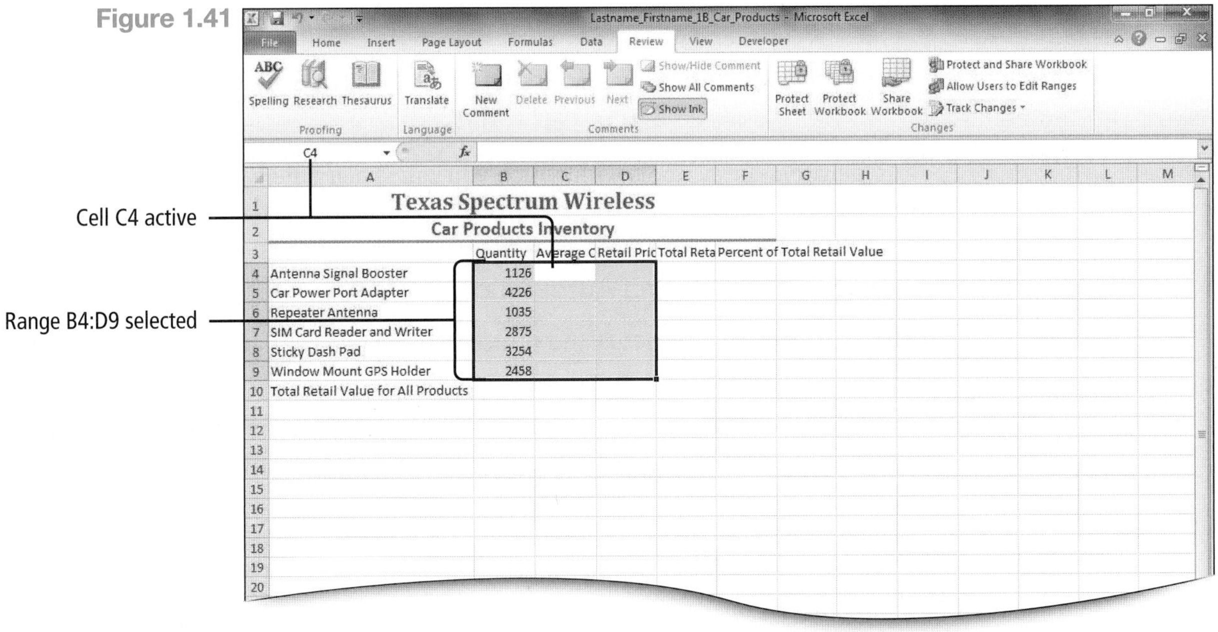

Cell C4 active

Range B4:D9 selected

3 With the selected range still active, from the following table, beginning in cell **C4** and pressing Enter after each entry, enter the data for the **Average Cost** column and then the **Retail Price** column. If you prefer, deselect the range to enter the values—typing in a selected range is optional.

Average Cost	Retail Price
9.75	19.99
9.25	19.49
16.90	39.99
9.55	16.90
4.20	12.99
10.45	20.99

Recall that the default number format for cells is the *General* number format, in which numbers display exactly as you type them and trailing zeros do not display, even if you type them.

4 Click any blank cell, and then compare your screen with Figure 1.42. Correct any errors you may have made while entering data, and then click **Save** 💾.

Figure 1.42

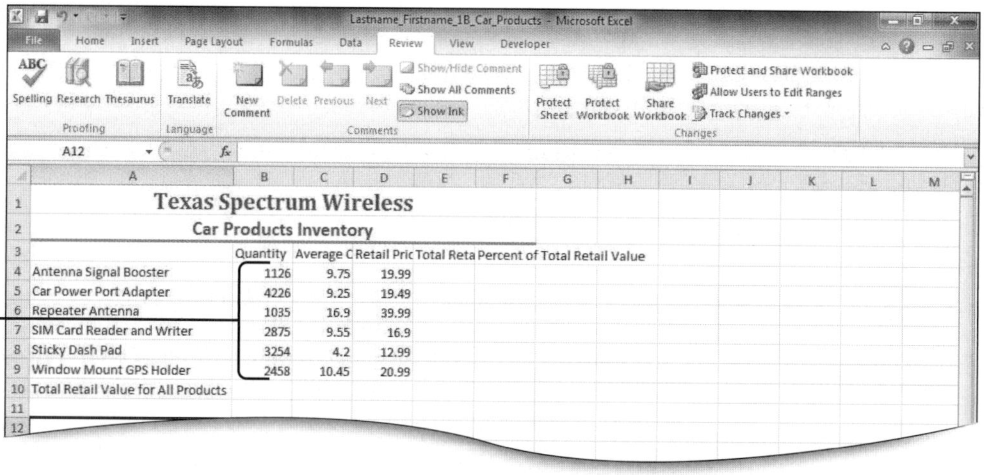

Data entered

Objective 9 | Construct Formulas for Mathematical Operations

Operators are symbols with which you can specify the type of calculation you want to perform in a formula.

Activity 1.19 | Using Arithmetic Operators

1 Click cell **E4**, type **=b4*d4** and notice that the two cells are outlined as part of an active formula. Then press Enter.

The *Total Retail Value* of all *Antenna Signal Booster* items in inventory—*22508.74*—equals the *Quantity* (1,126) times the *Retail Price* (selling price) of 19.99. In Excel, the asterisk (*) indicates multiplication.

2 Take a moment to study the symbols you will use to perform basic mathematical operations in Excel, as shown in the table in Figure 1.43, which are referred to as *arithmetic operators*.

Symbols Used in Excel for Arithmetic Operators	
Operator Symbol	**Operation**
+	Addition
-	Subtraction (also negation)
*	Multiplication
/	Division
%	Percent
^	Exponentiation

Figure 1.43

3 Click cell **E4**.

> You can see that in cells E5:E9, you need a formula similar to the one in E4, but one that refers to the cells in row 5, row 6, and so forth. Recall that you can copy formulas and the cell references will change *relative to* the row number.

4 With cell **E4** selected, position your pointer over the fill handle in the lower right corner of the cell until the + pointer displays. Then, drag down through cell **E9** to copy the formula.

Another Way

Select the range, display the Cell Styles gallery, and then under Number Format, click Comma [0].

5 Select the range **B4:B9**, and then on the **Home tab**, in the **Number group**, click the **Comma Style** button ⟨,⟩. Then, in the **Number group**, click the **Decrease Decimal** button ⟨.00→.0⟩ two times to remove the decimal places from these values.

> Comma Style formats a number with two decimal places; because these are whole numbers referring to quantities, no decimal places are necessary.

6 Select the range **E4:E9**, and then at the bottom of your screen, in the status bar, notice the displayed values for **Average**, **Count**, and **Sum**—*48118.91833*, *6* and *288713.51*.

> When you select numerical data, three calculations display in the status bar by default—Average, Count, and Sum. Here, Excel indicates that if you averaged the selected values, the result would be *48118.91833*, there are 6 cells in the selection that contain values, and that if you added the values the result would be 288713.51.

7 Click cell **E10**, in the **Editing group**, click the **Sum** button ⟨Σ⟩, notice that Excel selects a range to sum, and then press Enter to display the total *288713.5*.

8 Select the range **C5:E9** and apply the **Comma Style** ⟨,⟩; notice that Excel widens **column E**.

9 Select the range **C4:E4**, hold down Ctrl, and then click cell **E10**. Release Ctrl and then apply the **Accounting Number Format** ⟨$ ▾⟩. Notice that Excel widens the columns as necessary.

10 Click cell **E10**, and then from the **Cell Styles** gallery, apply the **Total** style. Click any blank cell, and then compare your screen with Figure 1.44.

Figure 1.44

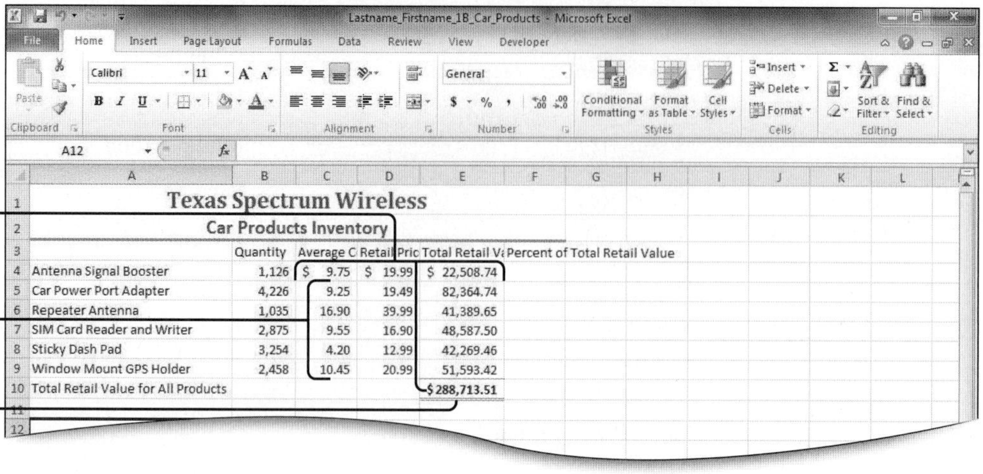

Accounting Number Format applied to C4:E4, E10

Comma Style applied to C5:E9

Total style applied to E10

11 Save 💾 your workbook.

More Knowledge | Multiple Status Bar Calculations

You can display a total of six calculations on the status bar. To add additional calculations—Minimum, Maximum, and Numerical Count (the number of selected cells that contain a number value)—right-click on the status bar, and then click the additional calculations that you want to display.

Activity 1.20 | Copying Formulas Containing Absolute Cell References

In a formula, a relative cell reference refers to a cell by its position *in relation to* the cell that contains the formula. An ***absolute cell reference***, on the other hand, refers to a cell by its *fixed* position in the worksheet, for example, the total in cell E10.

A relative cell reference automatically adjusts when a formula is copied. In some calculations, you do *not* want the cell reference to adjust; rather, you want the cell reference to remain the same when the formula is copied.

1 Click cell **F4**, type **=** and then click cell **E4**. Type **/** and then click cell **E10**.

The formula *=E4/E10* indicates that the value in cell E4 will be *divided* by the value in cell E10. Why? Because Ms. Lovrick wants to know the percentage by which each product's Total Retail Value makes up the Total Retail Value for All Products.

Arithmetically, the percentage is computed by dividing the *Total Retail Value* for each product by the *Total Retail Value for All Products*. The result will be a percentage expressed as a decimal.

2 Press [Enter]. Click cell **F4** and notice that the formula displays in the **Formula Bar**. Then, point to cell **F4** and double-click.

The formula, with the two referenced cells displayed in color and bordered with the same color, displays in the cell. This feature, called the ***range finder***, is useful for verifying formulas because it visually indicates which workbook cells are included in a formula calculation.

3 Press [Enter] to redisplay the result of the calculation in the cell, and notice that approximately 8% of the total retail value of the inventory is made up of Antenna Signal Boosters.

4 Click cell **F4** again, and then drag the fill handle down through cell **F9**. Compare your screen with Figure 1.45.

> Each cell displays an error message—*#DIV/0!* and a green triangle in the upper left corner of each cell indicates that Excel detects an error.

> Like a grammar checker, Excel uses rules to check for formula errors and flags errors in this manner. Additionally, the Auto Fill Options button displays, from which you can select formatting options for the copied cells.

Figure 1.45

Auto Fill Options button

Cells F5:F9 display error message and green triangles

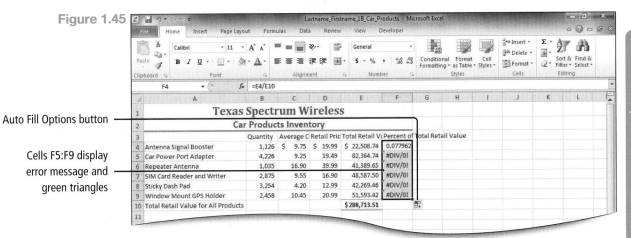

5 Click cell **F5**, and to the left of the cell, point to the **Error Checking** button ⬦ to display its ScreenTip—*The formula or function used is dividing by zero or empty cells.*

> In this manner, Excel suggests the cause of an error.

6 Look at the **Formula Bar** and examine the formula.

> The formula is *=E5/E11*. The cell reference to *E5* is correct, but the cell reference following the division operator (/) is *E11*, and E11 is an *empty* cell.

7 Click cell **F6**, point to the **Error Checking** button ⬦, and in the **Formula Bar** examine the formula.

> Because the cell references are relative, Excel builds the formulas by increasing the row number for each equation. But in this calculation, the divisor must always be the value in cell E10—the *Total Retail Value for All Products*.

8 Point to cell **F4**, and then double-click to place the insertion point within the cell.

Another Way
Edit the formula so that it indicates *=E4/$E$10*

9 Within the cell, use the arrow keys as necessary to position the insertion point to the left of *E10*, and then press [F4]. Compare your screen with Figure 1.46.

> Dollar signs ($) display, which changes the reference to cell E10 to an absolute cell reference. The use of the dollar sign to denote an absolute reference is not related in any way to whether or not the values you are working with are currency values. It is simply the symbol that Excel uses to denote an absolute cell reference.

Figure 1.46

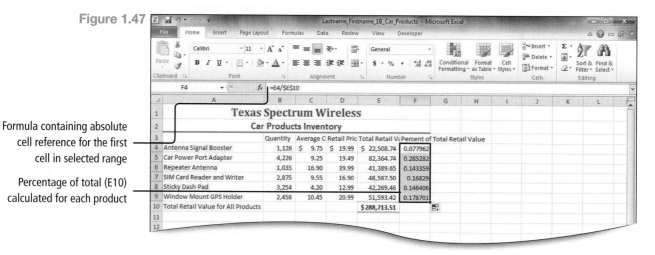

Edited formula with dollar
signs denoting an absolute
cell reference

10 On the **Formula Bar**, click the **Enter** button ✔ so that **F4** remains the active cell. Then, drag the fill handle to copy the new formula down through cell **F9**. Compare your screen with Figure 1.47.

Figure 1.47

Formula containing absolute
cell reference for the first
cell in selected range

Percentage of total (E10)
calculated for each product

11 Click cell **F5**, examine the formula in the **Formula Bar**, and then examine the formulas for cells **F6**, **F7**, **F8**, and **F9**.

For each formula, the cell reference for the *Total Retail Value* of each product changed relative to its row; however, the value used as the divisor—*Total Retail Value for All Products* in cell F10—remained absolute. Thus, using either relative or absolute cell references, it is easy to duplicate formulas without typing them.

12 Save 🖫 your workbook.

More Knowledge | Calculate a Percentage if You Know the Total and the Amount

Using the equation *amount/total = percentage*, you can calculate the percentage by which a part makes up a total—with the percentage formatted as a decimal. For example, if on a test you score 42 points correctly out of 50, your percentage of correct answers is 42/50 = 0.84 or 84%.

Objective 10 | Edit Values in a Worksheet

Excel performs calculations on numbers; that is why you use Excel. If you make changes to the numbers, Excel automatically *re*-calculates. This is one of the most powerful and valuable features of Excel.

Activity 1.21 | Editing Values in a Worksheet

You can edit text and number values directly within a cell or on the Formula Bar.

1 In cell **E10**, notice the column total *$288,713.51*. Then, click cell **B5**, and to change its value type **3546** Watch cell **E5** and press `Enter`.

> Excel formulas *re-calculate* if you change the value in a cell that is referenced in a formula. It is not necessary to delete the old value in a cell; selecting the cell and typing a new value replaces the old value with your new typing.

> The *Total Retail Value* of all *Car Power Port Adapters* items recalculates to *69,111.54* and the total in cell E10 recalculates to *$275,460.31*. Additionally, all of the percentages in column F recalculate.

2 Point to cell **D8**, and then double-click to place the insertion point within the cell. Use the arrow keys to move the insertion point to left or right of *2*, and use either `Del` or `Backspace` to delete *2* and then type **1** so that the new Retail Price is *11.99*.

3 Watch cell **E8** and **E10** as you press `Enter`, and then notice the recalculation of the formulas in those two cells.

> Excel recalculates the value in cell E8 to *39,015.46* and the value in cell E10 to *$272,206.31*. Additionally, all of the percentages in column F recalculate because the *Total Retail Value for All Products* recalculated.

4 Point to cell **A2** so that the ⊕ pointer is positioned slightly to the right of the word *Inventory*, and then double-click to place the insertion point in the cell. Edit the text to add the word **Valuation** pressing `Spacebar` as necessary, and then press `Enter`.

5 Click cell **B3**, and then in the **Formula Bar**, click to place the insertion point after the letter *y*. Press `Spacebar` one time, type **In Stock** and then on the **Formula Bar**, click the **Enter** button ✓. Click **Save** 🖫, and then compare your screen with Figure 1.48.

> Recall that if text is too long to fit in the cell and the cell to the right contains data, the text is truncated—cut off—but the entire value still exists as the underlying value.

Figure 1.48

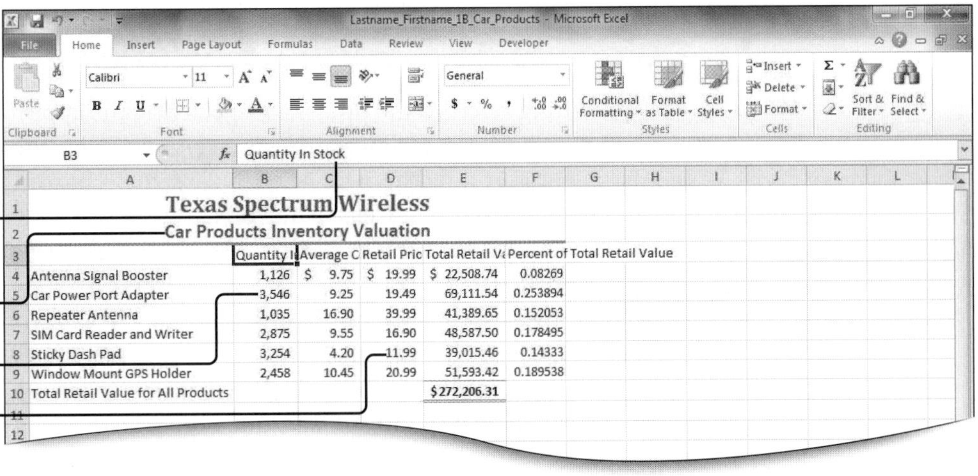

In Stock added to column title

Valuation added to subtitle

New value in cell B5

New value in cell D8

Excel | Chapter 1

Activity 1.22 | Formatting Cells with the Percent Style

A percentage is part of a whole expressed in hundredths. For example, 75 cents is the same as 75 percent of one dollar. The Percent Style button formats the selected cell as a percentage rounded to the nearest hundredth.

1 Click cell **F4**, and then in the **Number group**, click the **Percent Style** button %.

Your result is 8%, which is *0.08269* rounded to the nearest hundredth and expressed as a percentage. Percent Style displays the value of a cell as a percentage.

2 Select the range **F4:F9**, right-click over the selection, and then on the Mini toolbar, click the **Percent Style** button %, click the **Increase Decimal** button two times, and then click the **Center** button.

Percent Style may not offer a percentage precise enough to analyze important financial information—adding additional decimal places to a percentage makes data more precise.

3 Click any cell to cancel the selection, **Save** your workbook, and then compare your screen with Figure 1.49.

Figure 1.49

F4:F9 formatted with Percent Style and two decimal places

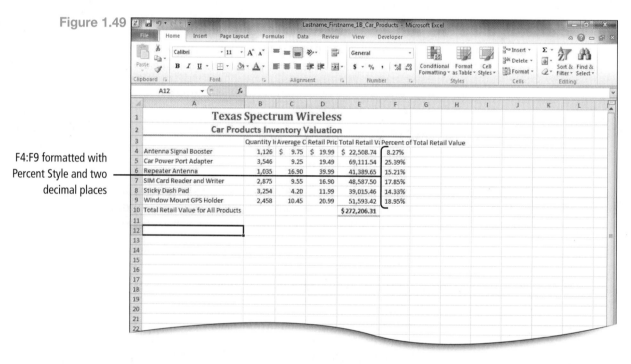

Objective 11 | Format a Worksheet

Formatting refers to the process of specifying the appearance of cells and the overall layout of your worksheet. Formatting is accomplished through various commands on the Ribbon, for example, applying Cell Styles, and also from shortcut menus, keyboard shortcuts, and the Format Cells dialog box.

Activity 1.23 | Inserting and Deleting Rows and Columns

1 In the **row heading area** on the left side of your screen, point to the row heading for **row 3** to display the ➡ pointer, and then right-click to simultaneously select the row and display a shortcut menu.

Another Way

Select the row, on the Home tab, in the Cells group, click the Insert button arrow, and then click Insert Sheet Rows. Or, select the row and click the Insert button—the default setting of the button inserts a new sheet row above the selected row.

2 On the displayed shortcut menu, click **Insert** to insert a new **row 3**.

The rows below the new row 3 move down one row, and the Insert Options button displays. By default, the new row uses the formatting of the row *above*.

3 Click cell **E11**. On the **Formula Bar**, notice that the range changed to sum the new range **E5:E10**. Compare your screen with Figure 1.50.

If you move formulas by inserting additional rows or columns in your worksheet, Excel automatically adjusts the formulas. Excel adjusted all of the formulas in the worksheet that were affected by inserting this new row.

Figure 1.50

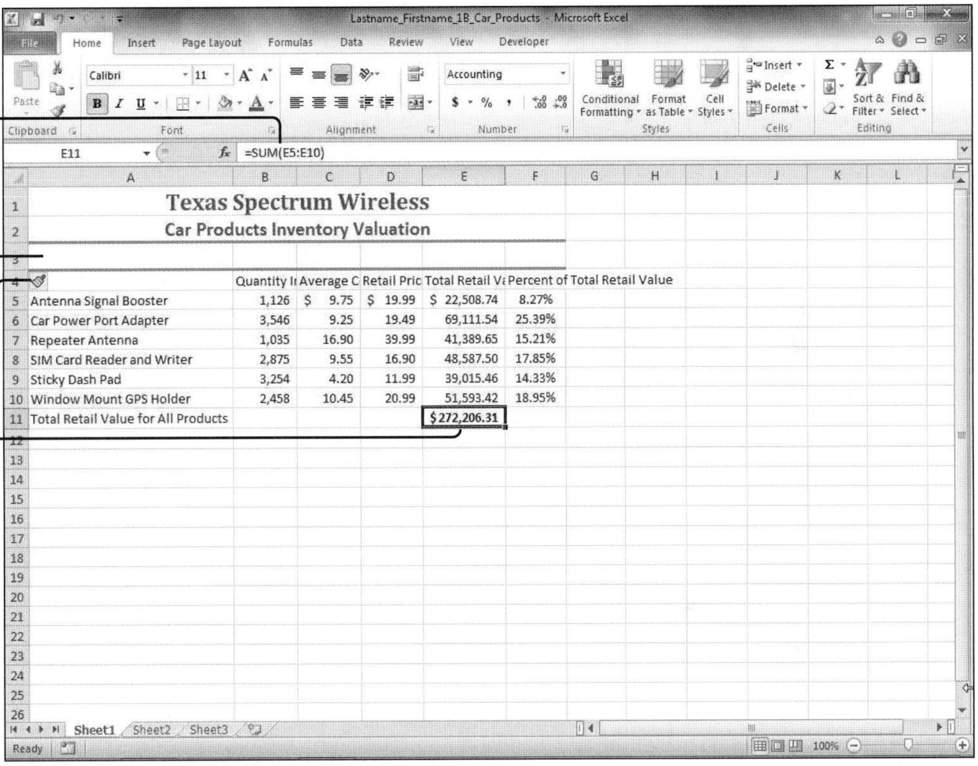

Formula Bar displays the formula in E11

New row 3 inserted

Insert Options button

Cell E11 selected

4 Click cell **A3**, type **As of December 31** and then on the **Formula Bar**, click the **Enter** button ✓ to maintain **A3** as the active cell. **Merge & Center** 🔲 the text across the range **A3:F3**, and then apply the **Heading 2** cell style.

5 In the **column heading area**, point to **column B** to display the ⬇ pointer, right-click, and then click **Insert**.

By default, the new column uses the formatting of the column to the *left*.

6 Click cell **B4**, type **Warehouse Location** and then press Enter.

7 In cell **B5**, type **Dallas** and then type **Dallas** again in cells **B6** and **B10**. Use AutoComplete to speed your typing by pressing Enter as soon as the AutoComplete suggestion displays. In cells **B7**, **B8**, and **B9**, type **Houston**

Another Way

Select the column, on the Home tab, in the Cells group, click the Insert button arrow, and then click Insert Sheet Columns. Or, select the column and click the Insert button—the default setting of the button inserts a new sheet column to the right of the selected column.

8 In the **column heading area**, point to **column D**, right-click, and then click **Delete**.

The remaining columns shift to the left, and Excel adjusts all the formulas in the worksheet accordingly. You can use a similar technique to delete a row in a worksheet.

9 Compare your screen with Figure 1.51, and then **Save** 💾 your workbook.

Figure 1.51

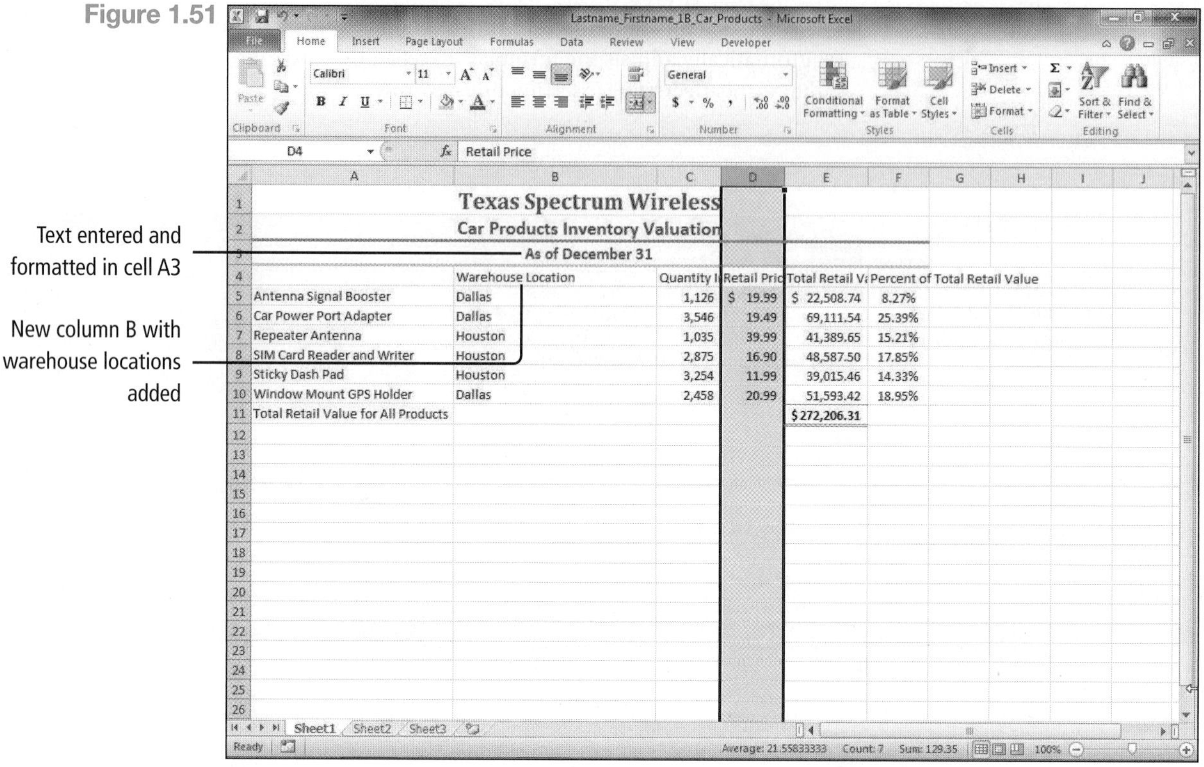

Text entered and formatted in cell A3

New column B with warehouse locations added

Activity 1.24 | Adjusting Column Widths and Wrapping Text

Use the Wrap Text command to display the contents of a cell on multiple lines.

1 In the **column heading area**, point to the **column B** heading to display the ↓ pointer, and then drag to the right to select **columns B:F**.

2 With the columns selected, in the **column heading area**, point to the right boundary of any of the selected columns to display the ↔ pointer, and then drag to set the width to **90 pixels**.

Use this technique to format multiple columns or rows simultaneously.

3 Select the range **B4:F4** that comprises the column headings, and then on the **Home tab**, in the **Alignment group**, click the **Wrap Text** button 📋. Notice that the row height adjusts.

4 With the range **B4:F4** still selected, in the **Alignment group**, click the **Center** button ≡ and the **Middle Align** button ≡. With the range **B4:F4** still selected, apply the **Heading 4** cell style.

The Middle Align command aligns text so that it is centered between the top and bottom of the cell.

5 Select the range **B5:B10**, right-click, and then on the shortcut menu, click the **Center** button ▤. Click cell **A11**, and then from the **Cell Styles** gallery, under **Themed Cell Styles**, click **40% - Accent1**. Click any blank cell, and then compare your screen with Figure 1.52.

Figure 1.52

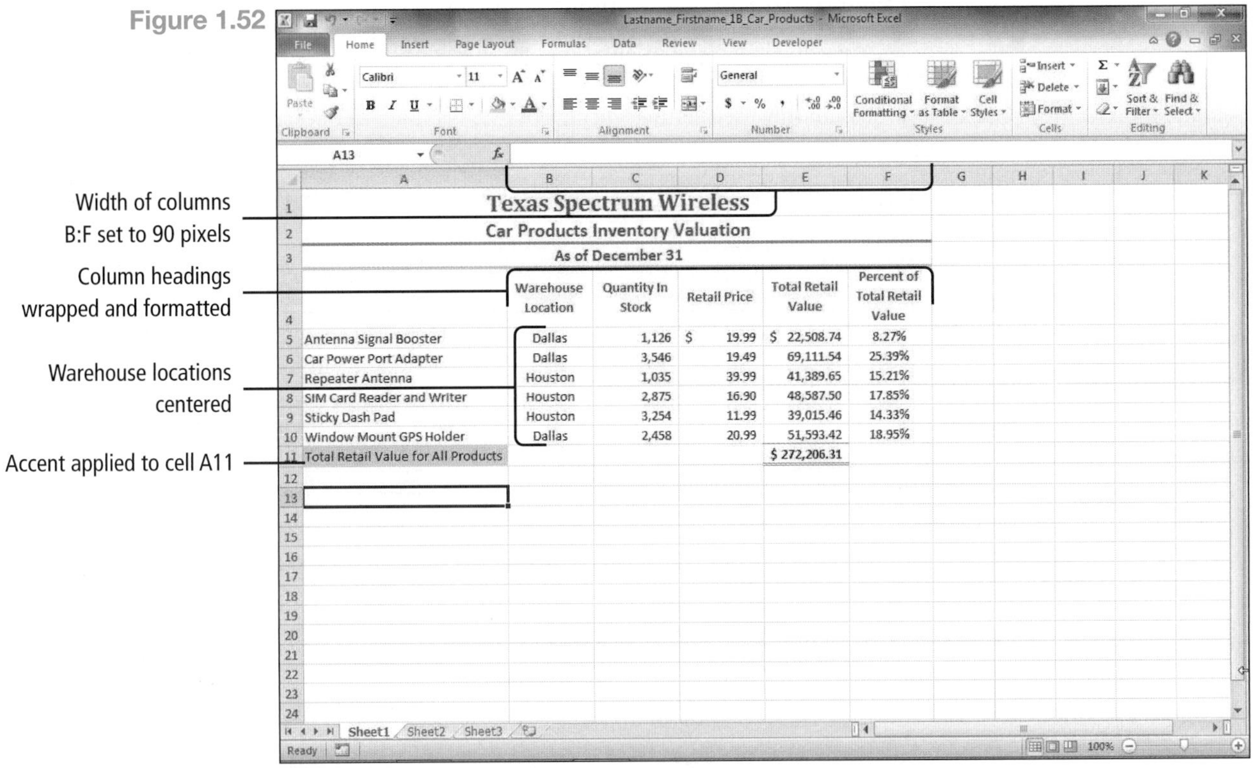

Width of columns B:F set to 90 pixels

Column headings wrapped and formatted

Warehouse locations centered

Accent applied to cell A11

6 Click the **Insert tab**, and then in the **Text group**, click **Header & Footer** to switch to Page Layout view and open the **Header area**.

7 In the **Navigation group**, click the **Go to Footer** button to move to the bottom of the page and open the **Footer area**, and then click just above the word *Footer* to place the insertion point in the **left section** of the **Footer area**.

8 In the **Header & Footer Elements group**, click the **File Name** button to add the name of your file to the footer—&*[File]* displays in the left section of the **Footer area**. Then, click in a cell above the footer to exit the **Footer area** and view your file name.

9 Click the **Page Layout tab**, in the **Page Setup group**, click the **Margins** button, and then at the bottom of the **Margins gallery**, click **Custom Margins**. In the **Page Setup** dialog box, under **Center on page**, select the **Horizontally** check box; click **OK**.

10 In the upper left corner of your screen, click **File** to display **Backstage** view. On the **Info tab**, on the right under the screen thumbnail, click **Properties**, and then click **Show Document Panel**.

11 In the **Author** box, replace the existing text with your firstname and lastname. In the **Subject** box, type your course name and section number. In the **Keywords** box, type **car products, inventory** and then **Close** ☒ the **Document Information Panel**.

12 Press [Ctrl] + [F2] to view the **Print Preview**. At the bottom of the **Print Preview**, click the **Next Page** button [▶], and notice that as currently formatted, the worksheet occupies two pages.

13 In the center panel, under **Settings**, click **Portrait Orientation**, and then click **Landscape Orientation**. Compare your screen with Figure 1.53.

> You can change the orientation on the Page Layout tab, or here, in the Print Preview. Because it is in the Print Preview that you will often see adjustments that need to be made, commonly used settings display on the Print tab in Backstage view.

Figure 1.53

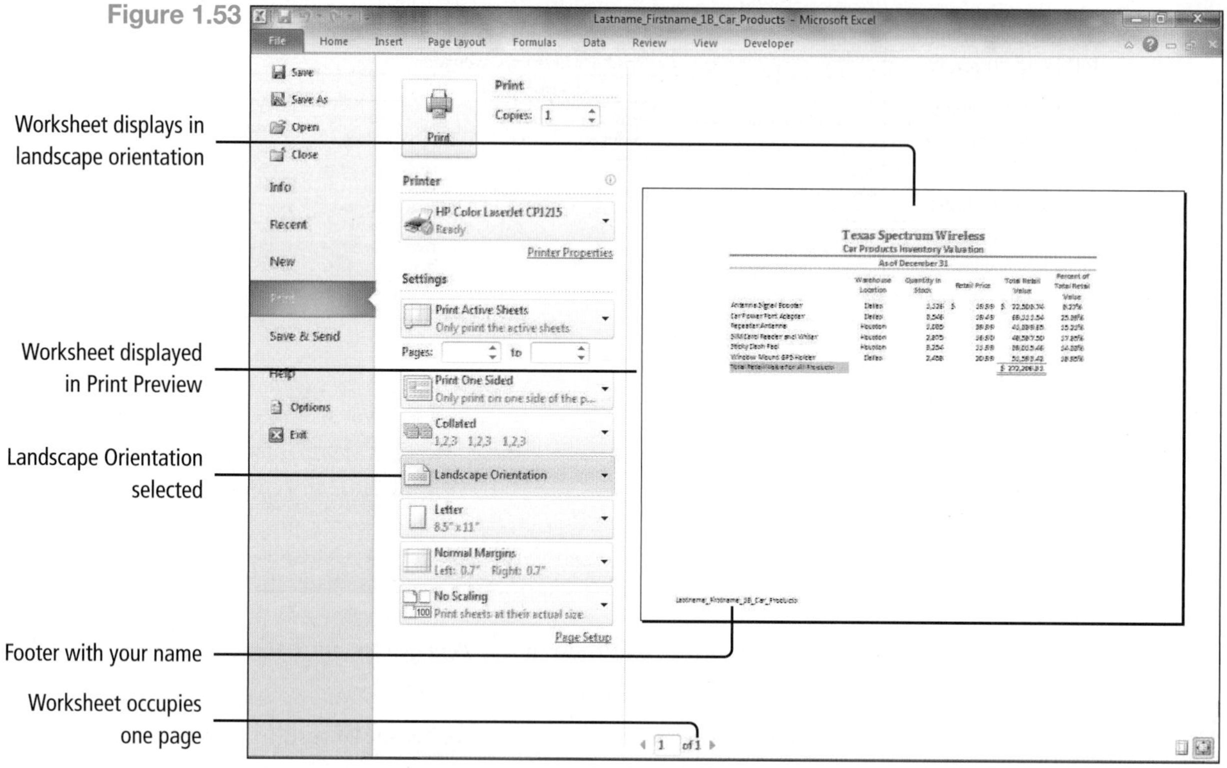

Worksheet displays in landscape orientation

Worksheet displayed in Print Preview

Landscape Orientation selected

Footer with your name

Worksheet occupies one page

14 Note any additional adjustments or corrections that need to be made, and then on the Ribbon, click **Home** to redisplay your worksheet. In the lower right corner of your screen, on the right side of the status bar, click the **Normal** button [▦] to return to the Normal view, and then press [Ctrl] + [Home] to return to cell **A1**.

15 Make any necessary corrections. Then, at the bottom of your worksheet, click the **Sheet2 tab** to make it the active worksheet. Hold down [Ctrl], and then click the **Sheet3 tab**. Release [Ctrl], and then with both sheets selected (tab background is white), point to either of the selected sheet tabs, right-click, and click **Delete** to delete the unused sheets in the workbook.

16 Save your workbook.

17 Print or submit your worksheet electronically as directed by your instructor. If required by your instructor, print or create an electronic version of your worksheet with formulas displayed using the instructions in Activity 1.16 in Project 1A.

18 Close your workbook and close Excel.

End **You have completed Project 1B** ——————————————

GO! Beyond Office

Objective | Create a Link in the OneNote Web App to an Excel Workbook Stored on SkyDrive

OneNote is a Microsoft application with which you can create a digital notebook that gives you a single location where you can gather and organize information in the form of notes. The OneNote Web App enables you to share your OneNote notebooks on the Web.

Alert! | **Working with Web-Based Applications and Services**

Computer programs and services on the Web receive continuous updates and improvements. Thus, the steps to complete this Web-based Activity may differ from the ones shown. You can often look at the screens and the information presented to determine how to complete the Activity.

Activity | Creating a Link in the OneNote Web App to an Excel Workbook Stored on a SkyDrive

In this activity, you will upload a workbook to your SkyDrive, and then create a link to it in a OneNote Web App notebook. Then you will add notes regarding the workbook to your notebook.

1 **Start** Excel, and then open your **Lastname_Firstname_1B_Car_Products** workbook.

2 On the **File tab**, click **Save & Send**, and then click **Save to Web**. On the right, click the **Sign In** button, and then sign in to your Windows Live account. If you do not have a Windows Live account, refer to GO! Beyond Word Project 1A to create the account, and create a folder in that account named GO! Beyond Office-Excel.

3 Under **Windows Live SkyDrive**, click your **GO! Beyond Office-Excel** folder, click the **Save As** button, and then wait a moment for the **Save As** dialog box to display. Click **Save**.

In the Excel status bar, a progress bar and message indicate that the file is being uploaded to the server.

4 When the file upload is complete, **Close** Excel.

5 Launch your Web browser, navigate to **www.live.com**, and then log in to your **Windows Live account**.

6 At the top of the screen, click **SkyDrive**, and then click your **GO! Beyond Office-Excel** folder. Compare your screen with Figure A.

In the folder, your Lastname_Firstname_1B_Car_Products file displays along with any other files you have uploaded to this location.

7 Near the top of the window, to the right of *Create*, click the **OneNote notebook** icon. In the **Name** box, with the text *Notebook1* selected, using your own name

Figure A

type **Lastname_Firstname_1B_Notebook** and then click **Save**.

The OneNote Web App displays a new notebook stored on the SkyDrive. A *notebook* is a collection of files organized by major divisions called *sections*. Each section contains pages where notes are inserted. On the left, the navigation pane indicates that this notebook has one Untitled Section and Page.

8 In the **Navigation pane**, point to the text *Untitled Section*, and then right-click. On the shortcut menu, click **Rename**. In the **Enter a section name** box, type **Excel** and then click **OK** to rename the section.

9 With the insertion point blinking in the blank **Untitled Page** box, type **Car Products Information for Sales Managers** to rename the Untitled Page.

Below the page title, the date and time display to keep track of when you create the notes.

10 Click approximately one inch below the time that displays on your page, and then type **This report will inform sales managers about some of the latest products in this line.** Press Enter.

11 At the top of the **OneNote Web App** window, following your notebook name, click the text *SkyDrive*, which is an active link, and notice that your OneNote notebook and your Excel workbook display in your **GO! Beyond Office-Excel** folder.

12 Point to the file name of your **Lastname_Firstname_1B_Car_Products** workbook to display the 👆 pointer, and then click to display the worksheet in your browser window.

13 In your Web browser address bar, click one time to select the Web address of your worksheet.

On your keyboard, press Ctrl + C to copy the address.

14 At the top of the Excel Web App window, click the text *SkyDrive*, and then click your **Lastname_Firstname_1B_Notebook** to open your OneNote notebook. Notice that the text you typed and the formatting you applied display, even though you did not save the notebook.

OneNote saves your work as it is entered. You do not need to save your work.

15 Click below the sentence that you typed on the page. On the **Insert tab**, in the **Links group**, click **Link**. In the displayed **Link** dialog box, with the insertion point blinking in the **Address** box, press Ctrl + V to paste the link to your presentation in the **Address** box.

16 Click in the **Display text** box, type **Car Products Information Report** and then click the **Insert** button.

The text you typed displays in blue, underlined text, indicating that the text is a link.

17 Start the **Snipping Tool**, and then create a **Full-screen Snip**. On the **Snipping Tool markup window toolbar**, click the **Save Snip** button 🖫. In the **Save As** dialog box, navigate to your **Excel Chapter 1** folder. Be sure the **Save as type** box displays **JPEG file**. In the **File name** box, type **Lastname_Firstname_1B_OneNote_Snip** and then click **Save**. **Close** the **Snipping Tool** window.

18 Point to the link that you inserted, hold down Ctrl, and then click to open the Excel workbook in the Excel Web App. Then close the window, sign out of your Windows Live account, and close all windows. Submit your snip file as directed.

Content-Based Assessments

Summary

In this chapter, you used Microsoft Excel 2010 to create and analyze data organized into columns and rows and to chart and perform calculations on the data. By organizing your data with Excel, you will be able to make calculations and create visual representations of your data in the form of charts.

Key Terms

Matching

Match each term in the second column with its correct definition in the first column by writing the letter of the term on the blank line in front of the correct definition.

_____ 1. An Excel file that contains one or more worksheets.

_____ 2. Another name for a worksheet.

_____ 3. The intersection of a column and a row.

A Cell

B Cell address

C Cell content

D Chart

E Column

Content-Based Assessments

_____	4.	The labels along the lower border of the Excel window that identify each worksheet.	**F** Constant value
_____	5.	A vertical group of cells in a worksheet.	**G** Data
_____	6.	A horizontal group of cells in a worksheet.	**H** Fill handle
_____	7.	Anything typed into a cell.	**I** Formula
_____	8.	Information such as numbers, text, dates, or times of day that you type into a cell.	**J** Number value
_____	9.	Text or numbers in a cell that are not a formula.	**K** Row
_____	10.	An equation that performs mathematical calculations on values in a worksheet.	**L** Sheet tabs
_____	11.	A constant value consisting of only numbers.	**M** Spreadsheet
_____	12.	Another name for a cell reference.	**N** Value
_____	13.	Another name for a constant value.	**O** Workbook
_____	14.	The small black square in the lower right corner of a selected cell.	
_____	15.	The graphic representation of data in a worksheet.	

Multiple Choice

Circle the correct answer.

1. On startup, Excel displays a new blank:
   A. document **B.** workbook **C.** grid

2. An Excel window element that displays the value or formula contained in the active cell is the:
   A. name box **B.** status bar **C.** formula bar

3. An Excel window element that displays the name of the selected cell, table, chart, or object is the:
   A. name box **B.** status bar **C.** formula bar

4. A box in the upper left corner of the worksheet grid that selects all the cells in a worksheet is the:
   A. name box **B.** select all box **C.** split box

5. A cell surrounded by a black border and ready to receive data is the:
   A. active cell **B.** address cell **C.** reference cell

6. The feature that generates and extends values into adjacent cells based on the values of selected cells is:
   A. AutoComplete **B.** Auto Fill **C.** fill handle

7. The default format that Excel applies to numbers is the:
   A. comma format **B.** accounting format **C.** general format

8. The data that displays in the Formula Bar is referred to as the:
   A. constant value **B.** formula **C.** underlying value

9. The type of cell reference that refers to cells by their fixed position in a worksheet is:
   A. absolute **B.** relative **C.** exponentiation

10. Tiny charts embedded in a cell that give a visual trend summary alongside your data are:
    A. embedded charts **B.** sparklines **C.** chart styles

Content-Based Assessments

Apply **1A** skills from these Objectives:

1 Create, Save, and Navigate an Excel Workbook
2 Enter Data in a Worksheet
3 Construct and Copy Formulas and Use the SUM Function
4 Format Cells with Merge & Center and Cell Styles
5 Chart Data to Create a Column Chart and Insert Sparklines
6 Print, Display Formulas, and Close Excel

Skills Review | Project **1C** Laptop Sales

In the following Skills Review, you will create a new Excel worksheet with a chart that summarizes the third quarter sales of laptop computers. Your completed worksheet will look similar to Figure 1.54.

Project Files

For Project 1C, you will need the following file:

New blank Excel workbook

You will save your workbook as:

Lastname_Firstname_1C_Laptop_Sales

Project Results

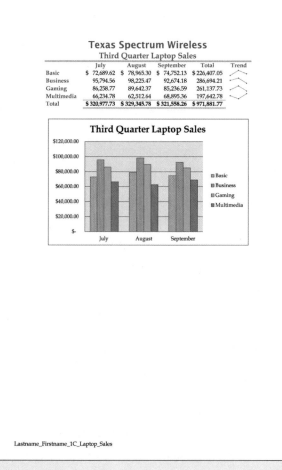

Figure 1.54

(Project 1C Laptop Sales continues on the next page)

Content-Based Assessments

1 **Start** Excel. Click the **File tab** to display **Backstage** view, click **Save As**, and then in the **Save As** dialog box, navigate to your **Excel Chapter 1** folder. In the **File name** box, using your own name, type **Lastname_Firstname_1C_Laptop_Sales** and then press Enter.

a. With cell **A1** as the active cell, type the worksheet title **Texas Spectrum Wireless** and then press Enter. In cell **A2**, type the worksheet subtitle **Third Quarter Laptop Sales** and then press Enter.

b. Click in cell **A4**, type **Basic** and then press Enter. In cell **A5**, type **Business** and then press Enter. In cell **A6**, type **Gaming** and then press Enter. In cell **A7**, type **Multimedia** and then press Enter. In cell **A8**, type **Total** and then press Enter.

c. Click cell **B3**. Type **July** and then in the **Formula Bar**, click the **Enter** button to keep cell **B3** the active cell. With **B3** as the active cell, point to the fill handle in the lower right corner of the selected cell, drag to the right to cell **D3**, and then release the mouse button to enter the text *August* and *September*.

d. Press Ctrl + Home, to make cell **A1** the active cell. In the **column heading area**, point to the vertical line between **column A** and **column B** to display the ✛ pointer, hold down the left mouse button, and drag to the right to increase the column width to **120 pixels**.

e. Point to cell **B3**, and then drag across to select cells **B3** and **C3** and **D3**. With the range **B3:D3** selected, point anywhere over the selected range, right-click, and then on the Mini toolbar, click the **Center** button.

f. Click cell **B4**, type **72689.62** and press Tab to make cell **C4** active. Enter the remaining values, as shown below in **Table 1**, pressing Tab to move across the rows and Enter to move down the columns.

2 Click cell **B8** to make it the active cell and type **=**

a. At the insertion point, type **b4** and then type **+** Type **b5** and then type **+b6+b7** Press Enter. Your result is *320977.7*.

b. Click in cell **C8**. Type **=** and then click cell **C4**. Type **+** and then click cell **C5**. Repeat this process to complete the formula to add cells **C4** through **C7**, and then press Enter. Your result is *329345.8*.

c. Click cell **D8**. On the **Home tab**, in the **Editing group**, click the **Sum** button, and then press Enter to construct a formula by using the SUM function. Your result is *321558.3*. You can use any of these methods to add values; the Sum button is the most efficient.

d. In cell **E3** type **Total** and press Enter. With cell **E4** as the active cell, hold down Alt, and then press =. On the **Formula Bar**, click the **Enter** button to display the result and keep cell **E4** active.

e. With cell **E4** active, point to the fill handle in the lower right corner of the cell. Drag down through cell **E8**, and then release the mouse button to copy the formula with relative cell references down to sum each row.

3 Click cell **F3**. Type **Trend** and then press Enter.

a. Select the range **A1:F1**, and then on the **Home tab**, in the **Alignment group**, click the **Merge & Center** button. Select the range **A2:F2**, and then click the **Merge & Center** button.

b. Click cell **A1**. In the **Styles group**, click the **Cell Styles** button. Under **Titles and Headings**, click **Title**. Click cell **A2**, display the **Cell Styles** gallery, and then click **Heading 1**.

c. Select the range **B3:F3**, hold down Ctrl, and then select the range **A4:A8**. From the **Cell Styles** gallery, click **Heading 4** to apply this cell style to the column and row titles.

d. Select the range **B4:E4**, hold down Ctrl, and then select the range **B8:E8**. On the **Home tab**, in the **Number group**, click the **Accounting Number Format** button. Select the range **B5:E7**, and then in the **Number group**, click the **Comma Style** button. Select the range **B8:E8**. From the **Styles group**,

Table 1

	July	August	September
Basic	72689.62	**78965.30**	**74752.13**
Business	**95794.56**	**98225.47**	**92674.18**
Gaming	**86258.77**	**89642.37**	**85236.59**
Multimedia	**66234.78**	**62512.64**	**68895.36**

--→ (Return to Step 2)

(Project 1C Laptop Sales continues on the next page)

display the **Cell Styles** gallery, and then under **Titles and Headings**, click **Total**.

e. On the Ribbon, click the **Page Layout tab**, and then from the **Themes group**, click the **Themes** button to display the **Themes** gallery. Click the **Apex** theme.

4 Select the range **A3:D7**. Click the **Insert tab**, and then in the **Charts group**, click **Column**. From the gallery of column chart types, under **2-D Column**, click the first chart—**Clustered Column**.

a. On the Quick Access Toolbar, click the **Save** button to be sure that you have saved your work up to this point. Point to the top border of the chart to display the 🔳 pointer, and then drag to position the chart inside the upper left corner of cell **A10**.

b. On the **Design tab**, in the **Data group**, click the **Switch Row/Column** button so that the months display on the Horizontal (Category) axis and the types of laptops display in the legend.

c. On the **Design tab**, in the **Chart Layouts group**, click the first layout—**Layout 1**.

d. In the chart, click anywhere in the text *Chart Title* to select the text box. Type **Third Quarter Laptop Sales** and then press Enter.

e. Click anywhere in the chart so that the chart title text box is not selected. On the **Design tab**, in the **Chart Styles group**, click the **More** button. Using the ScreenTips as your guide, locate and click **Style 34**.

f. Point to the lower right corner of the chart to display the 🔳 pointer, and then drag down and to the right so that the lower right border of the chart is positioned just inside the lower right corner of cell **F26**.

5 Select the range **B4:D7**. Click the **Insert tab**, and then in the **Sparklines group**, click **Line**. In the **Create Sparklines** dialog box, in the **Location Range** box, type **f4:f7** and then click **OK** to insert the sparklines.

a. On the **Design tab**, in the **Show group**, select the **Markers** check box to display markers in the sparklines.

b. On the **Design tab**, in the **Style group**, click the **More** button, and then in the second row, click the fourth style—**Sparkline Style Accent 4, Darker 25%**.

6 On the **Insert tab**, in the **Text group**, click **Header & Footer** to switch to **Page Layout** view and open the **Header** area.

a. In the **Navigation group**, click the **Go to Footer** button to open the Footer area. Click just above the word *Footer* to place the insertion point in the **left section** of the Footer.

b. In the **Header & Footer Elements group**, click the **File Name** button, and then click in a cell just above the footer to exit the Footer area.

7 On the right side of the status bar, click the **Normal** button to return to Normal view, and then press Ctrl + Home to make cell **A1** active.

a. Click the **File tab**, and then on the right, click **Properties**. Click **Show Document Panel**, and then in the **Author** box, delete any text and type your firstname and lastname. In the **Subject** box, type your course name and section number, and in the **Keywords** box, type **laptop sales Close** the Document Information Panel.

b. At the bottom of your worksheet, click the **Sheet2** tab. Hold down Ctrl, and then click the **Sheet3** tab. With both sheets selected, point to either of the selected sheet tabs, right-click, and then click **Delete** to delete the unused sheets.

c. Click the **Page Layout tab**. In the **Page Setup group**, click the **Margins** button, and then at the bottom of the **Margins** gallery, click **Custom Margins**. In the **Page Setup** dialog box, under **Center on page**, select the **Horizontally** check box.

d. In the lower right corner of the **Page Setup** dialog box, click **OK**. On the **File tab**, click **Print** to view the **Print Preview**. Click the **Home tab** to return to Normal view and if necessary, make any corrections and resize and move your chart so that it is centered under the worksheet.

e. On the Quick Access Toolbar, click the **Save** button to be sure that you have saved your work up to this point.

f. Print or submit your workbook electronically as directed by your instructor. If required by your instructor, print or create an electronic version of your worksheets with formulas displayed by using the instructions in Activity 1.16. **Exit** Excel without saving so that you do not save the changes you made to print formulas.

End You have completed Project **1C**

Apply 1B skills from these Objectives:

- **7** Check Spelling in a Worksheet
- **8** Enter Data by Range
- **9** Construct Formulas for Mathematical Operations
- **10** Edit Values in a Worksheet
- **11** Format a Worksheet

Skills Review | Project 1D Laptop Bags

In the following Skills Review, you will create a worksheet that summarizes the inventory of laptop messenger-style bags. Your completed worksheet will look similar to Figure 1.55.

Project Files

For Project 1D, you will need the following file:

New blank Excel workbook

You will save your workbook as:

Lastname_Firstname_1D_Laptop_Bags

Project Results

Texas Spectrum Wireless

Laptop Messenger-Style Bag Inventory

As of June 30

	Material	Quantity in Stock	Retail Price	Total Retail Value	Percent of Total Retail Value
Notebook Bag	Fabric	56	$ 39.99	$ 2,239.44	4.30%
Biker Messenger Bag	Leather	120	84.99	10,198.80	19.60%
Reaction Bag	Fabric	115	42.95	4,939.25	9.49%
Divider Bag	Fabric	245	88.95	21,792.75	41.89%
Women's Tote	Leather	75	76.95	5,771.25	11.09%
Pinstripe Messenger	Fabric	187	37.89	7,085.43	13.62%
Total Retail Value for All Products				$ 52,026.92	

Lastname_Firstname_1D_Laptop_Bags

Figure 1.55

(Project 1D Laptop Bags continues on the next page)

NOTES

Using Functions, Creating Tables, and Managing Large Workbooks

OUTCOMES

At the end of this chapter you will be able to:

OBJECTIVES

Mastering these objectives will enable you to:

PROJECT 2A

Analyze inventory by applying statistical and logical calculations to data and by sorting and filtering data.

1. Use the SUM, AVERAGE, MEDIAN, MIN, and MAX Functions (p. 367)
2. Move Data, Resolve Error Messages, and Rotate Text (p. 371)
3. Use COUNTIF and IF Functions and Apply Conditional Formatting (p. 373)
4. Use Date & Time Functions and Freeze Panes (p. 378)
5. Create, Sort, and Filter an Excel Table (p. 380)
6. Format and Print a Large Worksheet (p. 383)

Ronald Sumners/Shutterstock

In This Chapter

In this chapter, you will use the Statistical functions to calculate the average of a group of numbers, and use other Logical and Date & Time functions. You will use the counting functions and apply conditional formatting to make data easy to visualize. In this chapter, you will also create a table and analyze the table's data by sorting and filtering the data. You will summarize a workbook that contains multiple worksheets.

The projects in this chapter relate to **Laurales Herbs and Spices**. After ten years as an Executive Chef, Laura Morales started her own business, which offers quality products for cooking, eating, and entertaining in retail stores and online. In addition to herbs and spices, there is a wide variety of condiments, confections, jams, sauces, oils, and vinegars. Later this year, Laura will add a line of tools, cookbooks, and gift baskets. The company name is a combination of Laura's first and last names, and also the name of an order of plants related to cinnamon.

Project 2A Inventory Status Report

Project Activities

In Activities 2.01 through 2.15, you will edit a worksheet for Laura Morales, President, detailing the current inventory of flavor products at the Oakland production facility. Your completed worksheet will look similar to Figure 2.1.

Project Files

For Project 2A, you will need the following file:

e02A_Flavor_Inventory

You will save your workbook as:

Lastname_Firstname_2A_Flavor_Inventory

Project Results

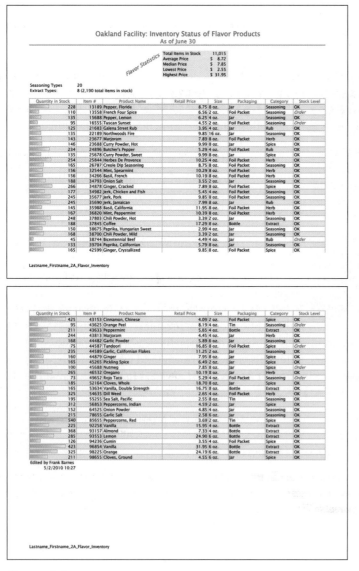

Figure 2.1

Project 2A Flavor Inventory

Objective 1 | Use the SUM, AVERAGE, MEDIAN, MIN, and MAX Functions

A *function* is a predefined formula—a formula that Excel has already built for you—that performs calculations by using specific values in a particular order or structure. *Statistical functions*, which include the AVERAGE, MEDIAN, MIN, and MAX functions, are useful to analyze a group of measurements.

Activity 2.01 | Using the SUM and AVERAGE Functions

Laura has a worksheet with information about the inventory of flavor product types currently in stock at the Oakland facility. In this activity, you will use the SUM and AVERAGE functions to gather information about the product inventory.

1. **Start** Excel. From **Backstage** view, display the **Open** dialog box, and then from the student files that accompany this textbook, locate and open **e02A_Flavor_Inventory**. Click the **File tab** to redisplay **Backstage** view, and then click **Save As**. In the **Save As** dialog box, navigate to the location where you are storing your projects for this chapter.

2. Create a new folder named **Excel Chapter 2** open the new folder, and then in the **File name** box, type **Lastname_Firstname_2A_Flavor_Inventory** Click **Save** or press Enter.

3. Scroll down. Notice that the worksheet contains data related to types of flavor products in inventory, including information about the *Quantity in Stock, Item #, Product Name, Retail Price, Size, Packaging,* and *Category*.

4. Leave row 3 blank, and then in cell **A4**, type **Total Items in Stock** In cell **A5**, type **Average Price** In cell **A6**, type **Median Price**

5. Click cell **B4**. Click the **Formulas tab**, and then in the **Function Library group**, click the **AutoSum** button. Compare your screen with Figure 2.2.

   The *SUM function* that you have used is a predefined formula that adds all the numbers in a selected range of cells. Because it is frequently used, there are several ways to insert the function.

   For example, you can insert the function from the Home tab's Editing group, by using the keyboard shortcut Alt + =, from the Function Library group on the Formulas tab, and also from the Math & Trig button in that group.

Figure 2.2

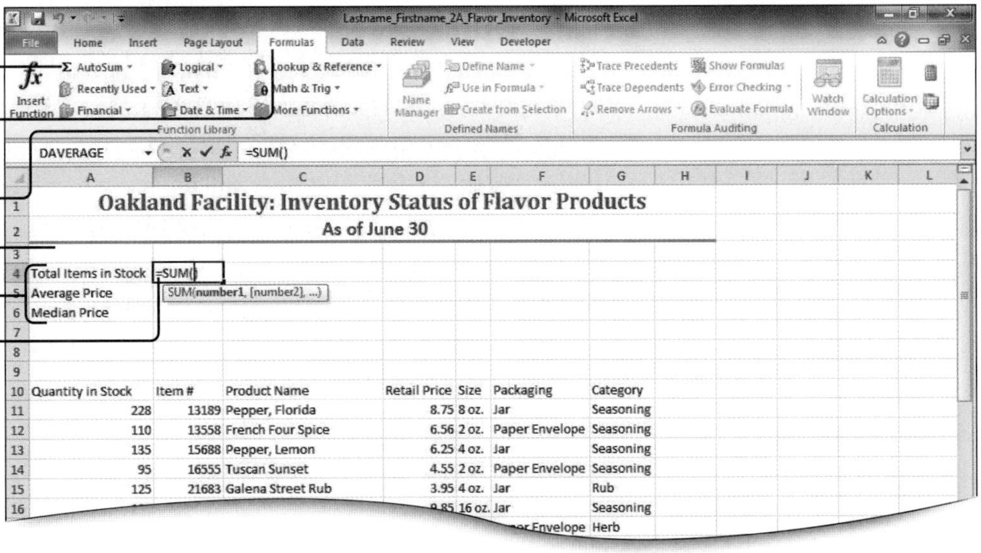

AutoSum button
Formulas tab
Function Library group
Row 3 blank
Row titles entered
SUM function in cell B4

6 With the insertion point blinking in the function, select the range **A11:A65**, dragging down as necessary, and then press [Enter]. Scroll up to view the top of your worksheet, and notice your result in cell **B4**, *11015*.

7 Click cell **B4** and look at the **Formula Bar**: Compare your screen with Figure 2.3.

> *SUM* is the name of the function. The values in parentheses are the **arguments**—the values that an Excel function uses to perform calculations or operations. In this instance, the argument consists of the values in the range A11:A65.

Figure 2.3

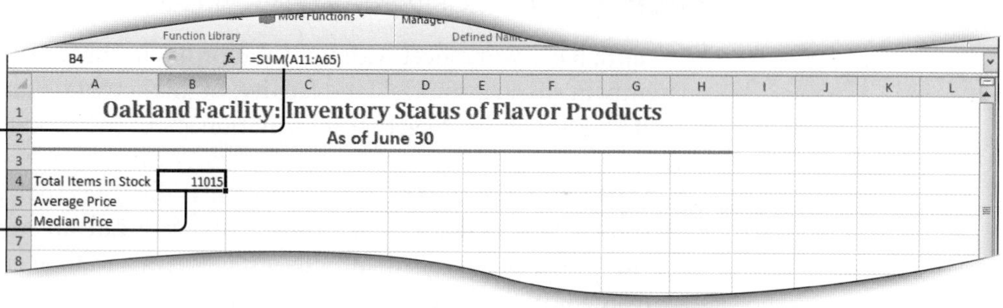

Function and arguments display in Formula Bar

Result of SUM function displays in B4

8 Click cell **B5**. In the **Function Library group**, click the **More Functions** button, point to **Statistical**, point to **AVERAGE**, and notice the ScreenTip. Compare your screen with Figure 2.4.

> The ScreenTip describes how the AVERAGE function will compute the calculation.

Figure 2.4

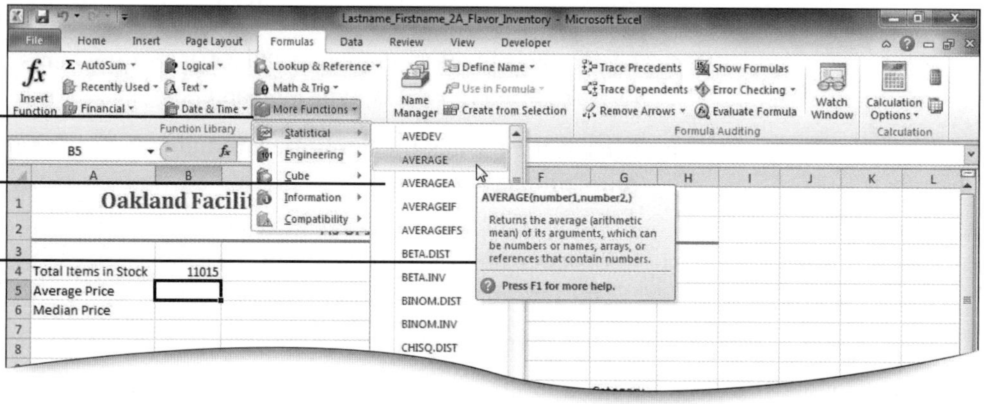

More Functions button

Statistical functions

ScreenTip describes function

9 Click **AVERAGE**, and then if necessary, drag the title bar of the **Function Arguments** dialog box down and to the right so you can view the **Formula Bar** and cell **B5**.

> The *AVERAGE function* adds a group of values, and then divides the result by the number of values in the group.

> In the cell, the Formula Bar, and the dialog box, Excel proposes to average the value in cell B4. Recall that Excel functions will propose a range if data is above or to the left of a selected cell.

Another Way

Alternatively, with the existing text selected, select the range D11:D65 and press [Enter].

10 In the **Function Arguments** dialog box, notice that *B4* is highlighted. Press [Del] to delete the existing text, type **d11:d65** and then compare your screen with Figure 2.5.

> Because you want to average the values in the range D11:D65—and not cell B4—you must edit the proposed range in this manner.

Figure 2.5

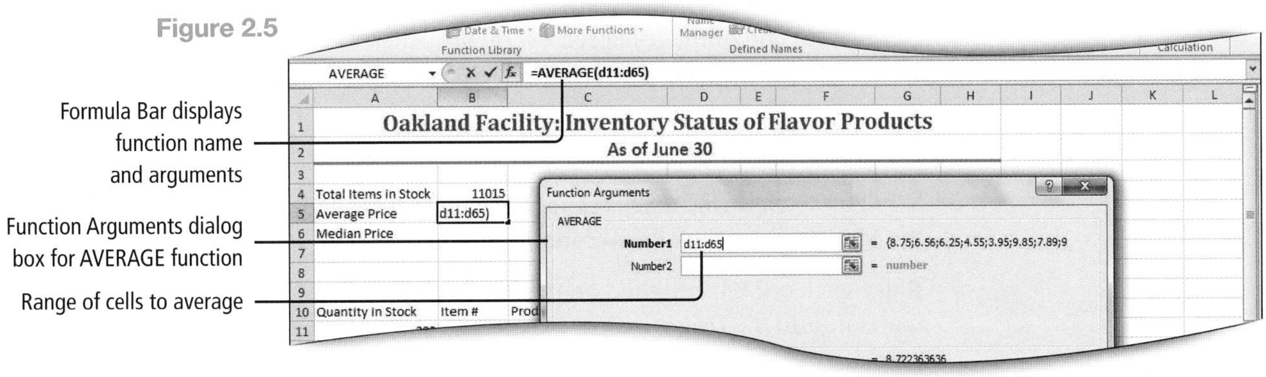

Formula Bar displays function name and arguments

Function Arguments dialog box for AVERAGE function

Range of cells to average

11 In the **Function Arguments** dialog box, click **OK**, and then **Save** 💾.

The result indicates that the average Retail Price of all products is *8.72*.

Activity 2.02 | Using the MEDIAN Function

The *MEDIAN function* is a statistical function that describes a group of data—you may have seen it used to describe the price of houses in a particular geographical area. The MEDIAN function finds the middle value that has as many values above it in the group as are below it. It differs from AVERAGE in that the result is not affected as much by a single value that is greatly different from the others.

1 Click cell **B6**. In the **Function Library group**, click the **More Functions** button, display the list of **Statistical** functions, scroll down as necessary, and then click **MEDIAN**.

2 In the **Function Arguments** dialog box, to the right of the **Number 1** box, click the **Collapse Dialog** button 📷.

The dialog box collapses to a small size with space only for the first argument so you can see more of your data.

3 Select the range **D11:D65**, and then compare your screen with Figure 2.6.

When indicating which cells you want to use in the function's calculation—known as *defining the arguments*—you can either select the values with your mouse or type the range of values, whichever you prefer.

Figure 2.6

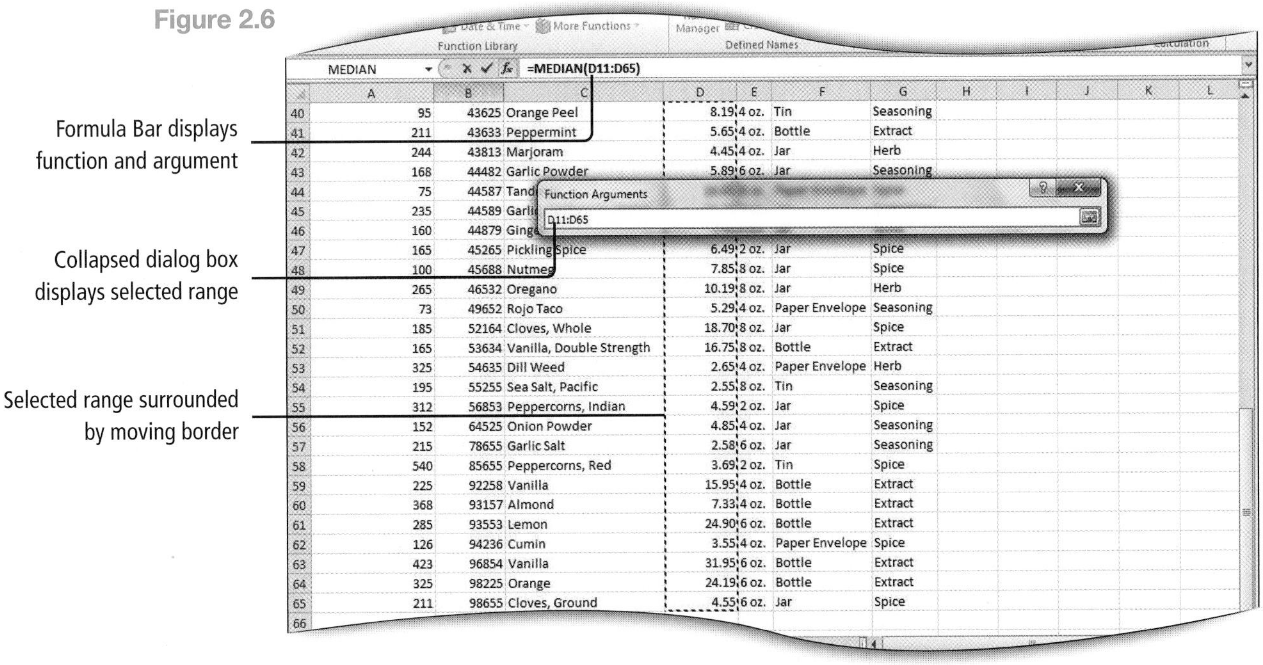

Formula Bar displays function and argument

Collapsed dialog box displays selected range

Selected range surrounded by moving border

Excel | Chapter 2

Another Way

Press Enter to expand the dialog box.

4 At the right end of the collapsed dialog box, click the **Expand Dialog** button 🔲 to expand the dialog box to its original size, and then click **OK** to display *7.85*.

> In the range of prices, 7.85 is the middle value. Half of all flavor products are priced *above* 7.85 and half are priced *below* 7.85.

5 Scroll up to view **row 1**. Select the range **B5:B6** and right-click over the selection. On the Mini toolbar, click the **Accounting Number Format** button $ ▾ .

6 Right-click cell **B4**, and then on the Mini toolbar, click the **Comma Style** button ▾ one time and the **Decrease Decimal** button ▾ two times. Click **Save** 🔲 and compare your screen with Figure 2.7.

Figure 2.7

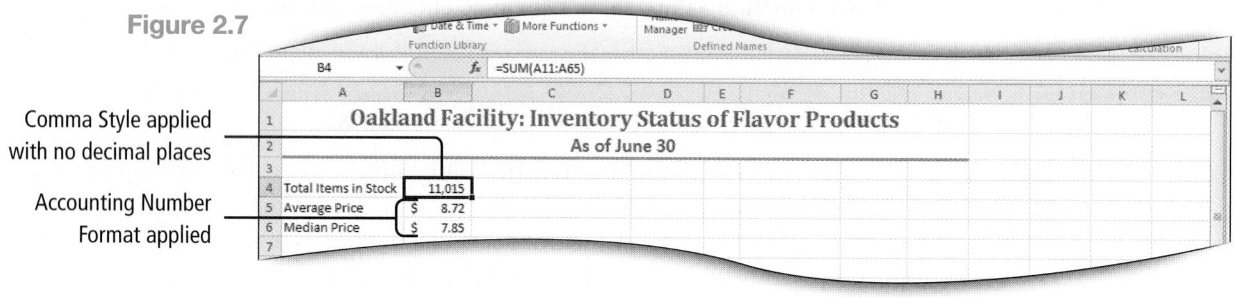

Comma Style applied
with no decimal places

Accounting Number
Format applied

Activity 2.03 | Using the MIN and MAX Functions

The statistical *MIN function* determines the smallest value in a selected range of values. The statistical *MAX function* determines the largest value in a selected range of values.

1 In cell **A7**, type **Lowest Price** and then in cell **A8**, type **Highest Price**

2 Click cell **B7**. On the **Formulas tab**, in the **Function Library group**, click the **More Functions** button, display the list of **Statistical** functions, scroll as necessary, and then click **MIN**.

3 At the right end of the **Number1** box, click the **Collapse Dialog** button 🔲, select the range **D11:D65**, and then click the **Expand Dialog** button 🔲. Click **OK**.

> The lowest Retail Price is *2.55*.

4 Click cell **B8**, and then by using a similar technique, insert the **MAX** function to determine the highest **Retail Price**—*31.95*.

5 Select the range **B7:B8** and apply the **Accounting Number Format** $ ▾ , click **Save** 🔲, and then compare your screen with Figure 2.8.

Figure 2.8

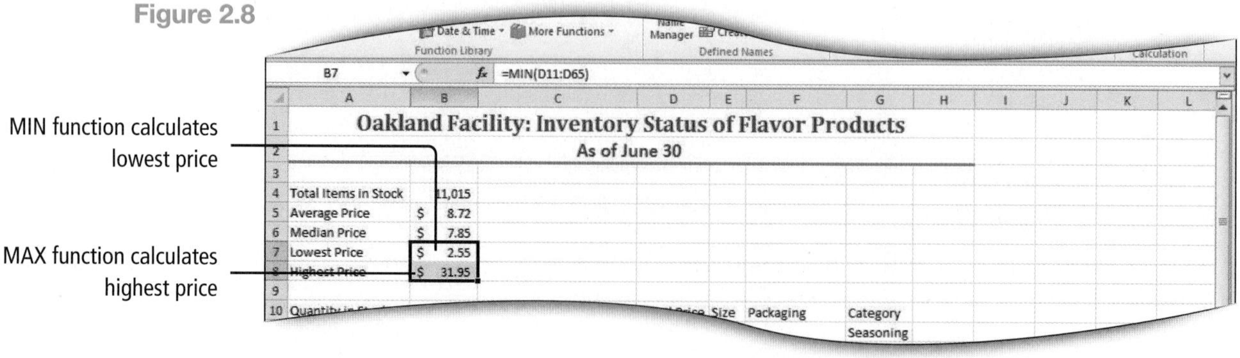

MIN function calculates
lowest price

MAX function calculates
highest price

Objective 2 | Move Data, Resolve Error Messages, and Rotate Text

When you move a formula, the cell references within the formula do not change, no matter what type of cell reference you use.

If you move cells into a column that is not wide enough to display number values, Excel will display a message so that you can adjust as necessary.

You can reposition data within a cell at an angle by rotating the text.

Activity 2.04 | Moving Data and Resolving a # # # # # Error Message

1 Select the range **A4:B8**. Point to the right edge of the selected range to display the 🔧 pointer, and then compare your screen with Figure 2.9.

Figure 2.9

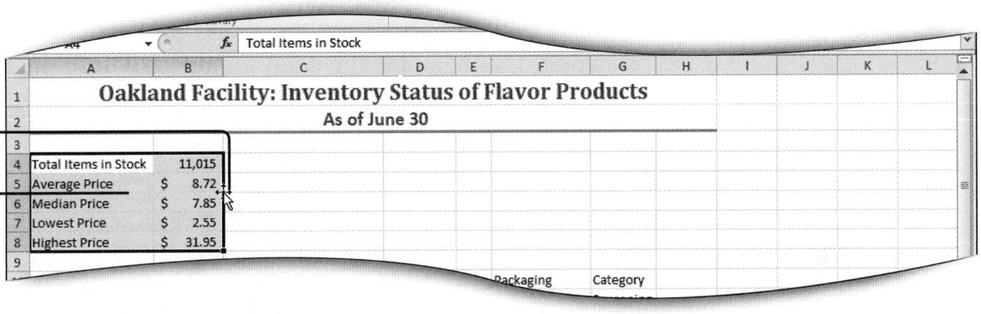

Move pointer

Selected range

2 Drag the selected range to the right until the ScreenTip displays *D4:E8*, release the mouse button, and then notice that a series of # symbols displays in **column E**. Point to any of the cells that display # symbols, and then compare your screen with Figure 2.10.

Using this technique, cell contents can be moved from one location to another; this is referred to as *drag and drop*.

If a cell width is too narrow to display the entire number, Excel displays the ##### error, because displaying only a portion of a number would be misleading. The underlying values remain unchanged and are displayed in the Formula Bar for the selected cell. An underlying value also displays in the ScreenTip if you point to a cell containing # symbols.

Figure 2.10

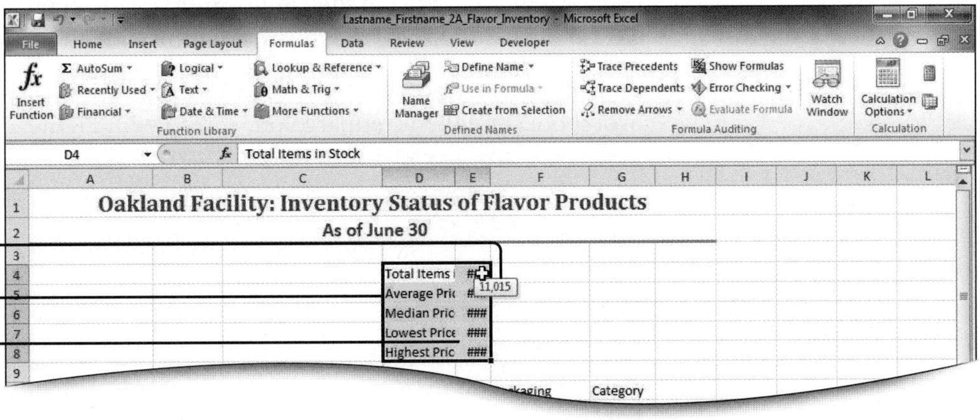

ScreenTip indicates underlying value

Range moved to D4:E8

symbols display

3 Select **column E** and widen it to **50** pixels, and notice that two cells are still not wide enough to display the cell contents.

4 In the **column heading area**, point to the right boundary of **column E** to display the ⊞ pointer. Double-click to AutoFit the column to accommodate the widest entry.

5 Using the same technique, AutoFit **column D** to accommodate the widest text entry.

6 Select the range **D4:E8**. On the **Home tab**, in the **Styles group**, display the **Cell Styles** gallery. Under **Themed Cell Styles**, click **20%-Accent1**. Click **Save** 🖫.

Activity 2.05 | Rotating Text

Rotated text is useful to draw attention to data on your worksheet.

Another Way

Type the number of degrees directly into the Degrees box or use the spin box arrows to set the number.

1 In cell **C6**, type **Flavor Statistics** Select the range **C4:C8**, right-click over the selection, and then on the shortcut menu, click **Format Cells**. In the **Format Cells** dialog box, click the **Alignment tab**. Under **Text control**, select the **Merge cells** check box.

2 In the upper right portion of the dialog box, under **Orientation**, point to the **red diamond**, and then drag the diamond upward until the **Degrees** box indicates **30**. Compare your screen with Figure 2.11.

Figure 2.11

Range of cells moved and formatted

Format Cells dialog box

Orientation set to 30 degrees

Merge cells selected

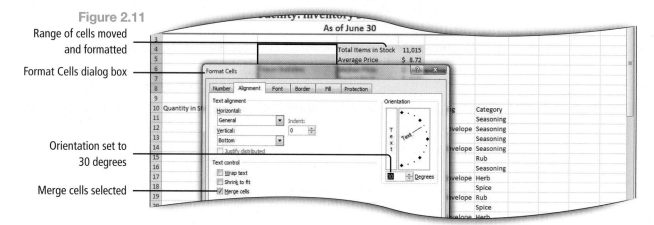

3 In the lower right corner of the **Format Cells** dialog box, click **OK**.

4 With the merged cell still selected, on the **Home tab**, in the **Font group**, change the **Font Size** 11 ▾ to **14**, and then apply **Bold** **B** and **Italic** *I*. Click the **Font Color arrow** **A** ▾, and then in the fourth column, click the first color—**Dark Blue, Text 2**.

5 In the **Alignment group**, apply **Align Text Right** ▤. Click cell **A1**, **Save** 🖫 your workbook, and then compare your screen with Figure 2.12.

Figure 2.12

Text rotated and formatted

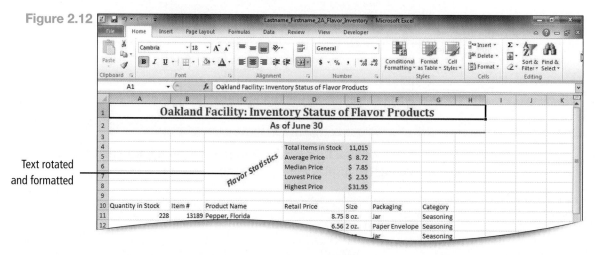

Objective 3 | Use COUNTIF and IF Functions and Apply Conditional Formatting

Recall that statistical functions analyze a group of measurements. Another group of Excel functions, referred to as *logical functions*, test for specific conditions. Logical functions typically use conditional tests to determine whether specified conditions—called *criteria*—are true or false.

Activity 2.06 | Using the COUNTIF Function

The *COUNTIF function* is a statistical function that counts the number of cells within a range that meet the given condition—the criteria that you provide. The COUNTIF function has two arguments—the range of cells to check and the criteria.

The seasonings of Laurales Herbs and Spices will be featured on an upcoming segment of a TV shopping channel. In this activity, you will use the COUNTIF function to determine the number of *seasoning* products currently available in inventory.

1   In the **row heading area**, point to **row 9** and right-click to select the row and display the shortcut menu. Click **Insert**, and then press F4 two times to repeat the last action and thus insert three blank rows.

> F4 is useful to repeat commands in Microsoft Office programs. Most commands can be repeated in this manner.

2   From the **row heading area**, select **rows 9:11**. On the **Home tab**, in the **Editing group**, click the **Clear** button ⬜, and then click **Clear Formats** to remove the blue accent color in columns D and E from the new rows.

> When you insert rows or columns, formatting from adjacent rows or columns repeats in the new cells.

3   Click cell **E4**, look at the **Formula Bar**, and then notice that the arguments of the **SUM** function adjusted and refer to the appropriate cells in rows 14:68.

> The referenced range updates to *A14:A68* after you insert the three new rows. In this manner, Excel adjusts the cell references in a formula relative to their new locations.

4   In cell **A10**, type **Seasoning Types:** and then press Tab.

5   With cell **B10** as the active cell, on the **Formulas tab**, in the **Function Library group**, click the **More Functions** button, and then display the list of **Statistical** functions. Click **COUNTIF**.

> Recall that the COUNTIF function counts the number of cells within a range that meet the given condition.

6 In the **Range** box, click the **Collapse Dialog** button ▣, select the range **G14:G68**, and then at the right end of the collapsed dialog box, click the **Expand Dialog** button ▣. Click in the **Criteria** box, type **Seasoning** and then compare your screen with Figure 2.13.

Figure 2.13

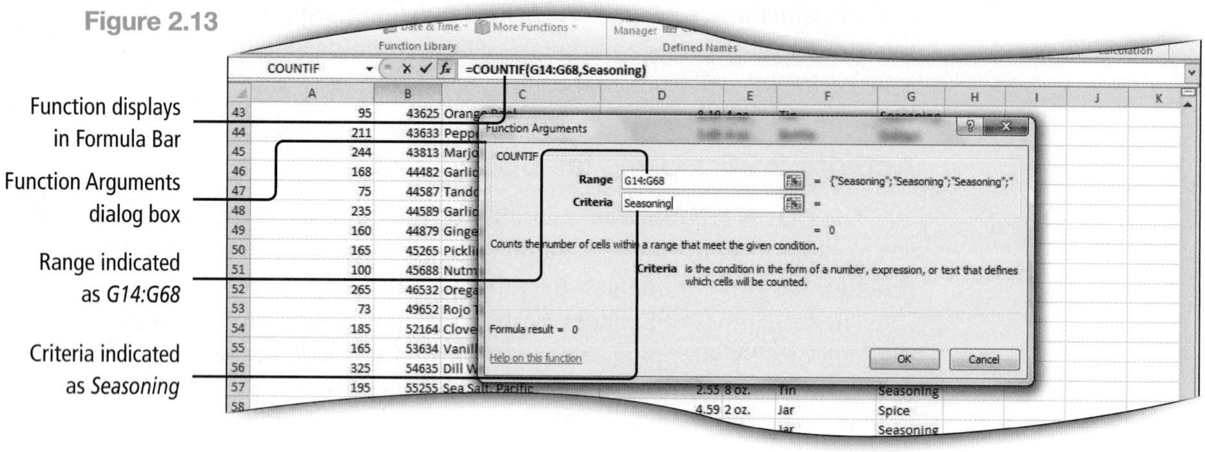

Function displays in Formula Bar

Function Arguments dialog box

Range indicated as *G14:G68*

Criteria indicated as *Seasoning*

7 In the lower right corner of the **Function Arguments** dialog box, click **OK**.

There are *20* different *Seasoning* products available to feature on the TV show.

8 On the **Home tab**, in the **Alignment group**, click **Align Text Left** ▤ to place the result closer to the row title. **Save** ▣ your workbook.

Activity 2.07 | Using the IF Function

A ***logical test*** is any value or expression that you can evaluate as being true or false. The ***IF function*** uses a logical test to check whether a condition is met, and then returns one value if true, and another value if false.

For example, *C14=228* is an expression that can be evaluated as true or false. If the value in cell C14 is equal to 228, the expression is true. If the value in cell C14 is not 228, the expression is false.

In this activity, you will use the IF function to determine the inventory levels and determine if more products should be ordered.

1 Click cell **H13**, type **Stock Level** and then press Enter.

2 In cell **H14**, on the **Formulas tab**, in the **Function Library group**, click the **Logical** button, and then in the list, click **IF**. Drag the title bar of the **Function Arguments** dialog box up or down to view **row 14** on your screen.

3 With the insertion point in the **Logical_test** box, click cell **A14**, and then type **<125**

This logical test will look at the value in cell A14, which is *228*, and then determine if the number is less than 125. The expression *<125* includes the < ***comparison operator***, which means *less than*. Comparison operators compare values.

4 Examine the table in Figure 2.14 for a list of comparison operator symbols and their definitions.

Comparison Operators

Comparison Operator	Symbol Definition
=	Equal to
>	Greater than
<	Less than
>=	Greater than or equal to
<=	Less than or equal to
<>	Not equal to

Figure 2.14

5 Press Tab to move the insertion point to the **Value_if_true** box, and then type **Order**

> If the result of the logical test is true—the Quantity in Stock is less than 125—cell H14 will display the text *Order* indicating that additional product must be ordered.

6 Click in the **Value_if_false** box, type **OK** and then compare your dialog box with Figure 2.15.

> If the result of the logical test is false—the Quantity in Stock is *not* less than 125—then Excel will display *OK* in the cell.

Figure 2.15

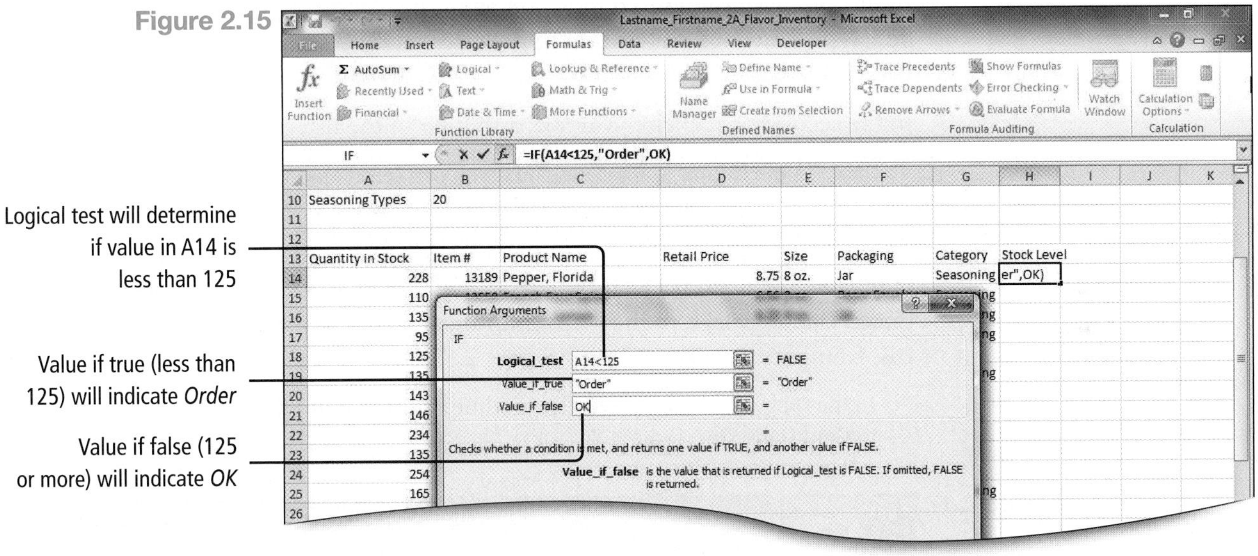

Logical test will determine if value in A14 is less than 125

Value if true (less than 125) will indicate *Order*

Value if false (125 or more) will indicate *OK*

7 Click **OK** to display the result *OK* in cell **H14**.

8 Using the fill handle, copy the function in cell **H14** down through cell **H68**. Then scroll as necessary to view cell **A18**, which indicates *125*. Look at cell **H18** and notice that the **Stock Level** is indicated as *OK*. **Save** your workbook. Compare your screen with Figure 2.16.

> The comparison operator indicated <125 (less than 125) and thus a value of *exactly* 125 is indicated as OK.

Figure 2.16

Function copied in column H

Cell H18 indicates *OK*

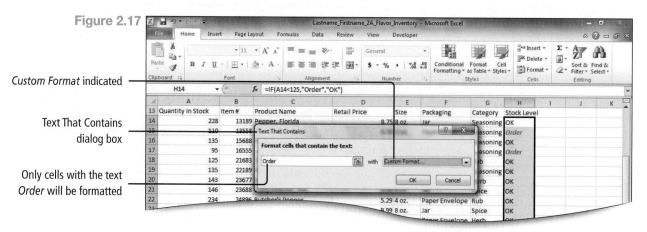

Activity 2.08 | Applying Conditional Formatting by Using Highlight Cells Rules and Data Bars

A ***conditional format*** changes the appearance of a cell based on a condition—a criteria. If the condition is true, the cell is formatted based on that condition; if the condition is false, the cell is *not* formatted. In this activity, you will use conditional formatting as another way to draw attention to the Stock Level of products.

1 Be sure the range **H14:H68** is selected. On the **Home tab**, in the **Styles group**, click the **Conditional Formatting** button. In the list, point to **Highlight Cells Rules**, and then click **Text that Contains**.

2 In the **Text That Contains** dialog box, with the insertion point blinking in the first box, type **Order** and notice that in the selected range, the text *Order* displays with the default format—Light Red Fill with Dark Red Text.

3 In the second box, click the **arrow**, and then in the list, click **Custom Format**.

Here, in the Format Cells dialog box, you can select any combination of formats to apply to the cell if the condition is true. The custom format you specify will be applied to any cell in the selected range if it contains the text *Order*.

4 On the **Font tab**, under **Font style**, click **Bold Italic**. Click the **Color arrow**, and then under **Theme Colors**, in the sixth column, click the first color—**Red, Accent 2**. Click **OK**. Compare your screen with Figure 2.17.

In the range, if the cell meets the condition of containing *Order*, the font color will change to Bold Italic, Red, Accent 2.

Figure 2.17

Custom Format indicated

Text That Contains dialog box

Only cells with the text *Order* will be formatted

5 In the **Text That Contains** dialog box, click **OK**.

6 Select the range **A14:A68**. In the **Styles group**, click the **Conditional Formatting** button. Point to **Data Bars**, and then under **Gradient Fill**, click **Orange Data Bar**. Click anywhere to cancel the selection; click 🖫. Compare your screen with Figure 2.18.

A ***data bar*** provides a visual cue to the reader about the value of a cell relative to other cells. The length of the data bar represents the value in the cell. A longer bar represents a higher value and a shorter bar represents a lower value. Data bars are useful for identifying higher and lower numbers quickly within a large group of data, such as very high or very low levels of inventory.

Figure 2.18

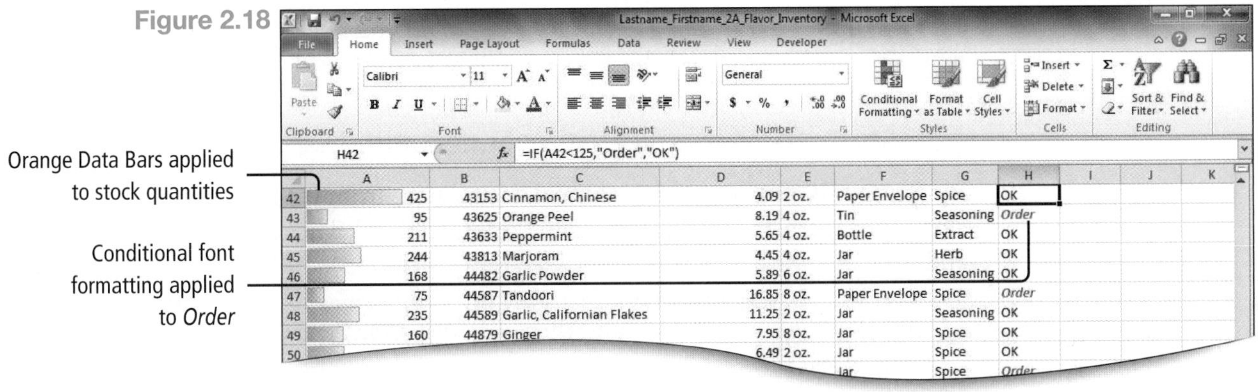

Orange Data Bars applied to stock quantities

Conditional font formatting applied to *Order*

Activity 2.09 | Using Find and Replace

The ***Find and Replace*** feature searches the cells in a worksheet—or in a selected range—for matches, and then replaces each match with a replacement value of your choice.

Comments from customers on the company's blog indicate that, for dried herbs and seasonings, customers prefer a sealable foil packet rather than a paper envelope. Thus, all products of this type have been repackaged. In this activity, you will replace all occurrences of *Paper Envelope* with *Foil Packet*.

1 Select the range **F14:F68**.

Restrict the find and replace operation to a specific range in this manner, especially if there is a possibility that the name occurs elsewhere.

2 On the **Home tab**, in the **Editing group**, click the **Find & Select** button, and then click **Replace**.

3 Type **Paper Envelope** to fill in the **Find what** box. In the **Replace with** box, type **Foil Packet** and then compare your screen with Figure 2.19.

Figure 2.19

Find & Select button in Editing group

Find *Paper Envelope*

Replace with *Foil Packet*

Replace All button

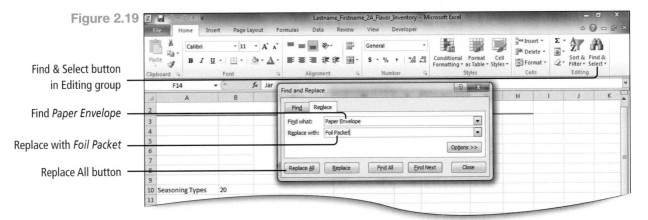

4 Click the **Replace All** button. In the message box, notice that 19 replacements were made, and then click **OK**. In the lower right corner of the **Find and Replace** dialog box, click the **Close** button. Click **Save** 🖫.

Objective 4 | Use Date & Time Functions and Freeze Panes

Excel can obtain the date and time from your computer's calendar and clock and display this information on your worksheet.

By freezing or splitting panes, you can view two areas of a worksheet and lock rows and columns in one area. When you freeze panes, you select the specific rows or columns that you want to remain visible when scrolling in your worksheet.

Activity 2.10 | Using the NOW Function to Display a System Date

The *NOW function* retrieves the date and time from your computer's calendar and clock and inserts the information into the selected cell. The result is formatted as a date and time.

1 Scroll down as necessary, and then click cell **A70**. Type **Edited by Frank Barnes** and then press Enter.

2 With cell **A71** as the active cell, on the **Formulas tab**, in the **Function Library group**, click the **Date & Time** button. In the list of functions, click **NOW**. Compare your screen with Figure 2.20.

Figure 2.20

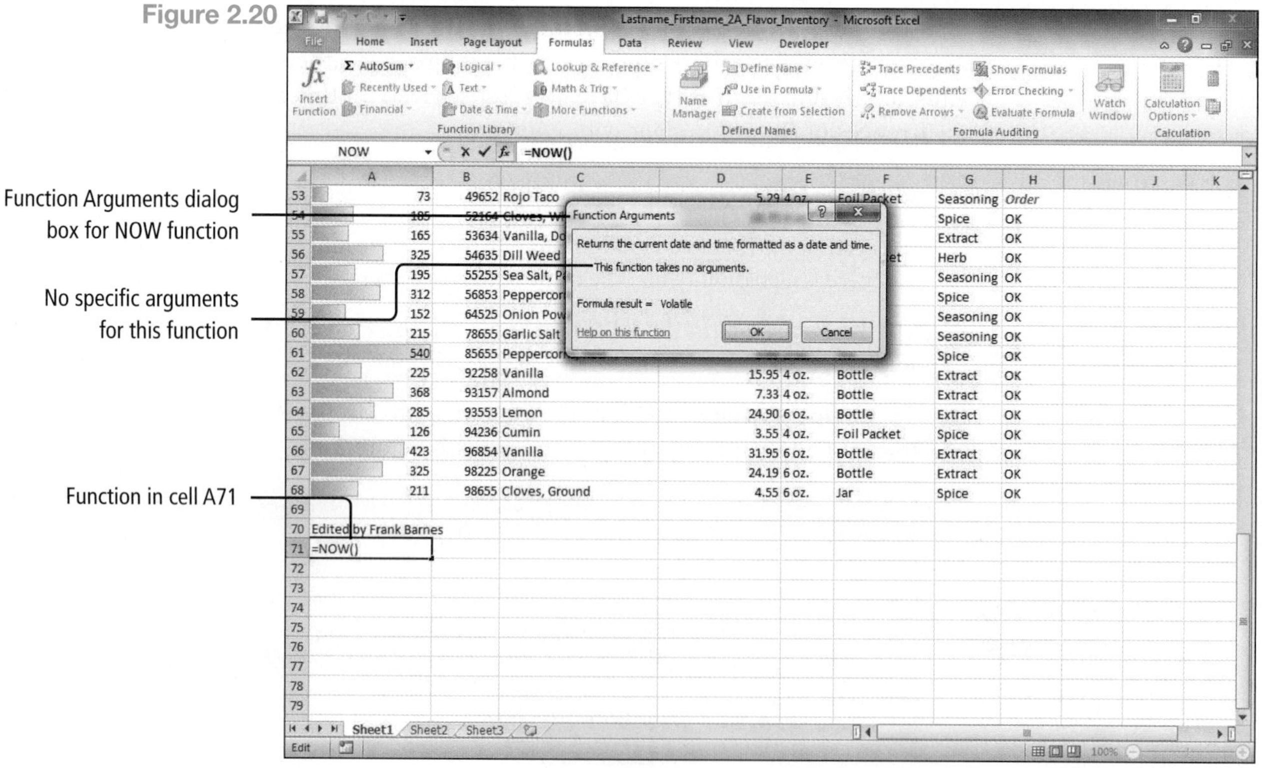

Function Arguments dialog box for NOW function

No specific arguments for this function

Function in cell A71

3 Read the description in the **Function Arguments** dialog box, and notice that this result is *Volatile*.

> The Function Arguments dialog box displays a message indicating that this function does not require an argument. It also states that this function is **volatile**, meaning the date and time will not remain as entered, but rather the date and time will automatically update each time you open this workbook.

4 In the **Function Arguments** dialog box, click **OK** to close the dialog box to display the current date and time in cell **A71**. **Save** 🖫 your workbook.

More Knowledge | **NOW Function Recalculates Each Time a Workbook Opens**

The NOW function updates each time the workbook is opened. With the workbook open, you can force the NOW function to update by pressing F9 , for example, to update the time.

Activity 2.11 | Freezing and Unfreezing Panes

In a large worksheet, if you scroll down more than 25 rows or scroll beyond column O (the exact row number and column letter varies, depending on your screen resolution), you will no longer see the top rows or first column of your worksheet where identifying information about the data is usually placed. You will find it easier to work with your data if you can always view the identifying row or column titles.

The **Freeze Panes** command enables you to select one or more rows or columns and then freeze (lock) them into place. The locked rows and columns become separate panes. A **pane** is a portion of a worksheet window bounded by and separated from other portions by vertical or horizontal bars.

1 Press Ctrl + Home to make cell **A1** the active cell. Scroll down until **row 40** displays at the top of your Excel window, and notice that all of the identifying information in the column titles is out of view.

2 Press Ctrl + Home again, and then from the **row heading area**, select **row 14**. Click the **View tab**, and then in the **Window group**, click the **Freeze Panes** button. In the list, click **Freeze Panes**. Click any cell to deselect the row, and then notice that a line displays along the upper border of **row 14**.

> By selecting row 14, the rows above—rows 1–13—are frozen in place and will not move as you scroll down.

3 Watch the row numbers below **row 13**, and then begin to scroll down to bring **row 40** into view again. Notice that rows 1:13 are frozen in place. Compare your screen with Figure 2.21.

> The remaining rows of data continue to scroll. Use this feature when you have long or wide worksheets.

Figure 2.21

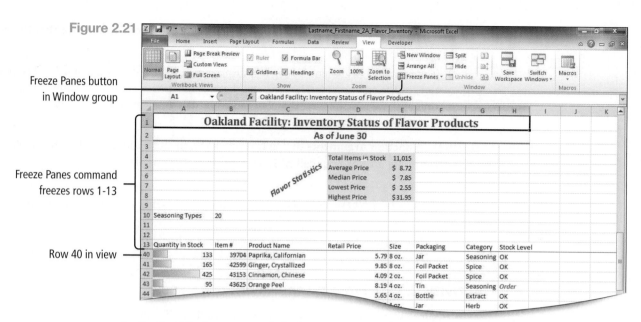

Freeze Panes button in Window group

Freeze Panes command freezes rows 1-13

Row 40 in view

4 In the **Window group**, click the **Freeze Panes** button, and then click **Unfreeze Panes** to unlock all rows and columns. **Save** 🖫 your workbook.

More Knowledge | Freeze Columns or Freeze Both Rows and Columns

You can freeze columns that you want to remain in view on the left. Select the column to the right of the column(s) that you want to remain in view while scrolling to the right, and then click the Freeze Panes command. You can also use the command to freeze both rows and columns; click a *cell* to freeze the rows *above* the cell and the columns to the *left* of the cell.

Objective 5 | Create, Sort, and Filter an Excel Table

To analyze a group of related data, you can convert a range of cells to an *Excel table*. An Excel table is a series of rows and columns that contains related data that is managed independently from the data in other rows and columns in the worksheet.

Activity 2.12 | Creating an Excel Table

1 Be sure that you have applied the Unfreeze Panes command—no rows on your worksheet are locked. Then, click any cell in the data below row 13.

> **Another Way**
> Select the range of cells that make up the table, including the header row, and then click the Table button.

2 Click the **Insert tab**. In the **Tables group**, click the **Table** button. In the **Create Table** dialog box, if necessary, click to select the **My table has headers** check box, and then compare your screen with Figure 2.22.

The column titles in row 13 will form the table headers. By clicking in a range of contiguous data, Excel will suggest the range as the data for the table. You can adjust the range if necessary.

Figure 2.22

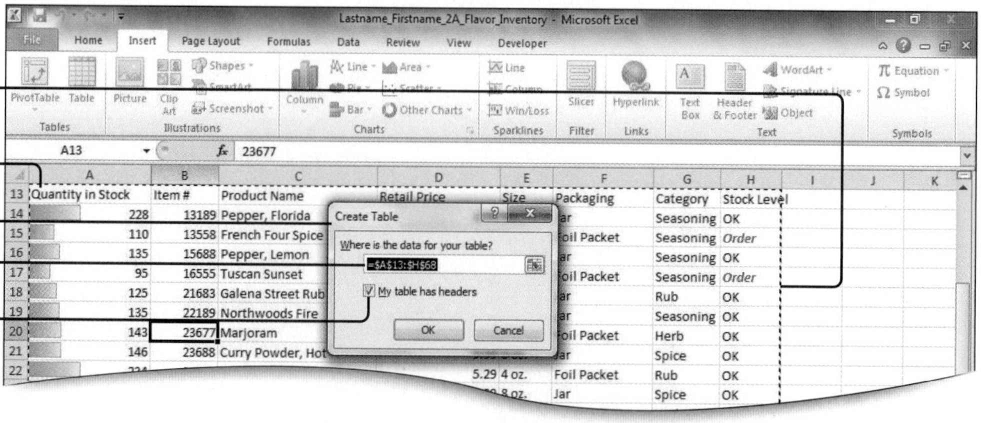

Moving border surrounds range

Column titles will form table headers

Create Table dialog box

Range of data selected

Check box selected

3 Click **OK**. With the range still selected, on the Ribbon notice that the **Table Tools** are active.

4 On the **Design tab**, in the **Table Styles group**, click the **More** button ⬇, and then under **Light**, locate and click **Table Style Light 16**.

5 Press Ctrl + Home. Click **Save** 🖫, and then compare your screen with Figure 2.23.

> Sorting and filtering arrows display in the table's header row.

Figure 2.23

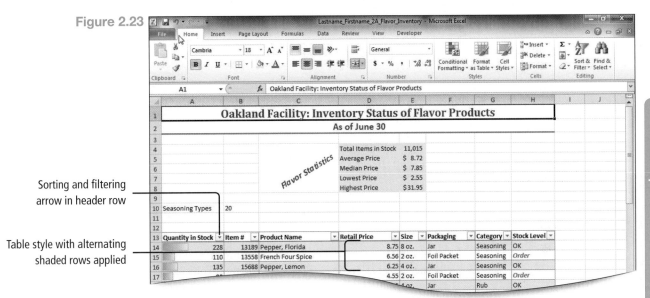

Sorting and filtering arrow in header row

Table style with alternating shaded rows applied

Activity 2.13 | Sorting and Filtering an Excel Table

You can *sort* tables—arrange all the data in a specific order—in ascending or descending order. You can *filter* tables—display only a portion of the data based on matching a specific value—to show only the data that meets the criteria that you specify.

1 In the header row of the table, click the **Retail Price arrow**, and then on the menu, click **Sort Smallest to Largest**. Next to the arrow, notice the small **up arrow** indicating an ascending (smallest to largest) sort.

> The rows in the table are sorted from the lowest retail price to highest retail price.

2 In the table's header row, click the **Category arrow**. On the menu, click **Sort A to Z**. Next to the arrow, notice the small **up arrow** indicating an ascending (A to Z) sort.

> The rows in the table are sorted alphabetically by Category.

3 Click the **Category arrow** again, and then sort from **Z to A**.

> The rows in the table are sorted in reverse alphabetic order by Category name, and the small arrow points downward, indicating a descending (Z to A) sort.

4 Click the **Category arrow** again. On the menu, click the **(Select All)** check box to clear all the check boxes. Click to select only the **Extract** check box, and then click **OK**. Compare your screen with Figure 2.24.

> Only the rows containing *Extract* in the Category column display—the remaining rows are hidden from view. A small funnel—the filter icon—indicates that a filter is applied to the data in the table. Additionally, the row numbers display in blue to indicate that some rows are hidden from view. A filter hides entire rows in the worksheet.

Figure 2.24

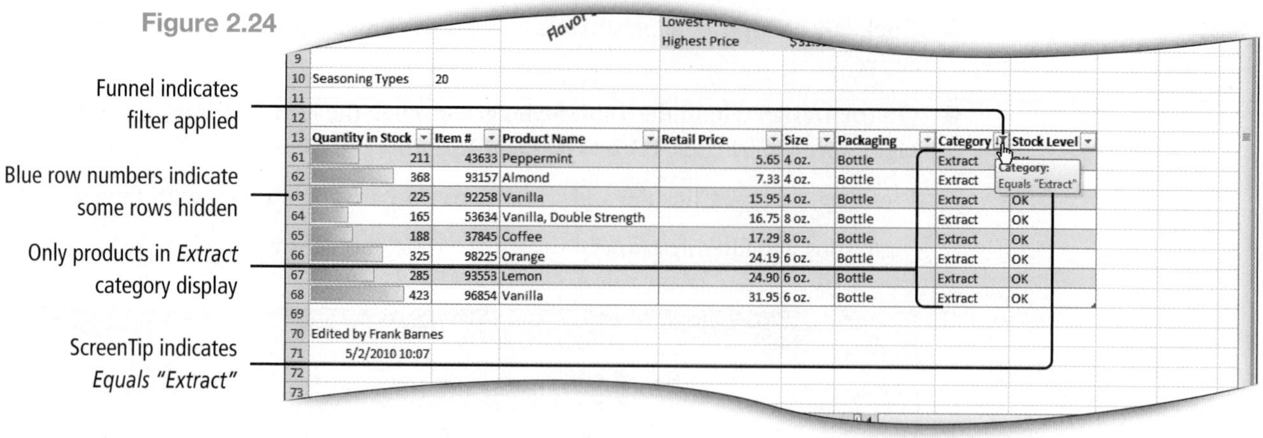

Funnel indicates filter applied

Blue row numbers indicate some rows hidden

Only products in *Extract* category display

ScreenTip indicates *Equals "Extract"*

5 Point to the **Category arrow**, and notice that *Equals "Extract"* displays to indicate the filter criteria.

6 Click any cell in the table so that the table is selected. On the Ribbon, click the **Design tab**, and then in the **Table Style Options group**, select the **Total Row** check box.

> *Total* displays in cell A69. In cell H69, the number 8 indicates that eight rows currently display.

7 Click cell **A69**, click the **arrow** that displays to the right of cell **A69**, and then in the list, click **Sum**.

> Excel sums only the visible rows in Column A, and indicates that 2190 products in the Extract category are in stock. In this manner, you can use an Excel table to quickly find information about a group of data.

8 Click cell **A11**, type **Extract Types:** and press Tab. In cell **B11**, type **8 (2,190 total items in stock)** and then press Enter.

9 In the table header row, click the **Category arrow**, and then on the menu, click **Clear Filter From "Category"**.

> All the rows in the table redisplay. The Z to A sort on Category remains in effect.

10 Click the **Packaging arrow**, click the **(Select All)** check box to clear all the check boxes, and then click to select the **Foil Packet** check box. Click **OK**.

11 Click the **Category arrow**, click the **(Select All)** check box to clear all the check boxes, and then click the **Herb** check box. Click **OK**, and then compare your screen with Figure 2.25.

> By applying multiple filters, Laura can quickly determine that seven items in the Herb category are packaged in foil packets with a total of 1,346 such items in stock.

Figure 2.25

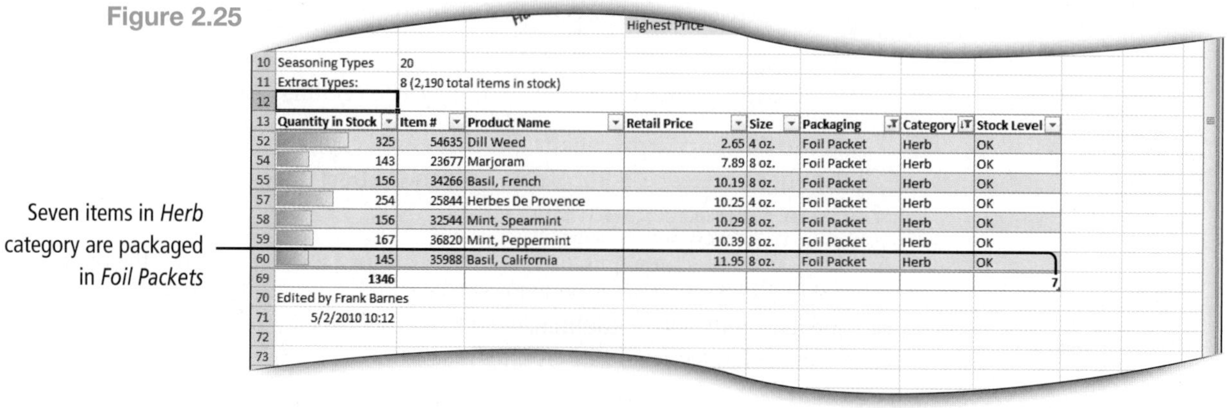

Seven items in *Herb* category are packaged in *Foil Packets*

12 Click the **Category arrow**, and then click **Clear Filter From "Category"**. Use the same technique to remove the filter from the **Packaging** column.

13 In the table header row, click the **Item# arrow**, and then click **Sort Smallest to Largest**, which will apply an ascending sort to the data using the *Item#* column. **Save** 💾 your workbook.

Activity 2.14 | Converting a Table to a Range of Data

When you are finished answering questions about the data in a table by sorting, filtering, and totaling, you can convert the table into a normal range. Doing so is useful if you want to use the feature only to apply an attractive Table Style to a range of cells. For example, you can insert a table, apply a Table Style, and then convert the table to a normal range of data but keep the formatting.

> **Another Way**
>
> With any table cell selected, right-click, point to Table, and then click Convert to Range.

1 Click anywhere in the table to activate the table and display the **Table Tools** on the Ribbon. On the **Design tab**, in the **Table Style Options group**, click the **Total Row** check box to clear the check mark and remove the Total row from the table.

2 On the **Design tab**, in the **Tools group**, click the **Convert to Range** button. In the message box, click **Yes**. Click **Save** 💾, and then compare your screen with Figure 2.26.

Figure 2.26

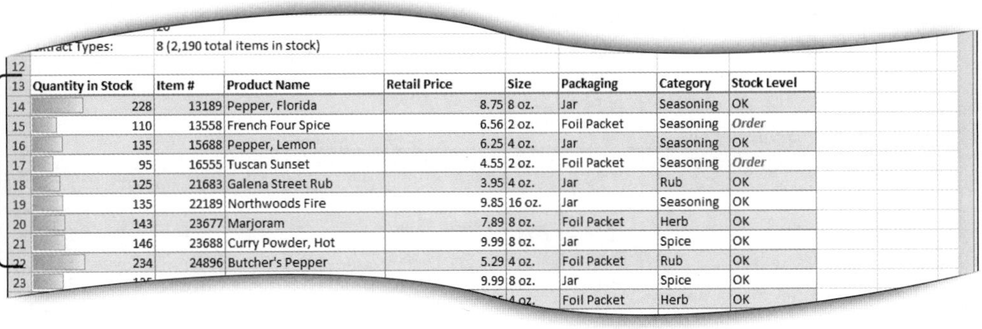

Table converted to a normal range, color and shading formats remain

	Quantity in Stock	Item #	Product Name	Retail Price	Size	Packaging	Category	Stock Level
	Contract Types:		8 (2,190 total items in stock)					
13	Quantity in Stock	Item #	Product Name	Retail Price	Size	Packaging	Category	Stock Level
14	228	13189	Pepper, Florida	8.75	8 oz.	Jar	Seasoning	OK
15	110	13558	French Four Spice	6.56	2 oz.	Foil Packet	Seasoning	Order
16	135	15688	Pepper, Lemon	6.25	4 oz.	Jar	Seasoning	OK
17	95	16555	Tuscan Sunset	4.55	2 oz.	Foil Packet	Seasoning	Order
18	125	21683	Galena Street Rub	3.95	4 oz.	Jar	Rub	OK
19	135	22189	Northwoods Fire	9.85	16 oz.	Jar	Seasoning	OK
20	143	23677	Marjoram	7.89	8 oz.	Foil Packet	Herb	OK
21	146	23688	Curry Powder, Hot	9.99	8 oz.	Jar	Spice	OK
22	234	24896	Butcher's Pepper	5.29	4 oz.	Foil Packet	Rub	OK
23				9.99	8 oz.	Jar	Spice	OK
					4 oz.	Foil Packet	Herb	OK

Objective 6 | Format and Print a Large Worksheet

A worksheet might be too wide, too long—or both—to print on a single page. Use Excel's *Print Titles* and *Scale to Fit* commands to create pages that are attractive and easy to read.

The Print Titles command enables you to specify rows and columns to repeat on each printed page. Scale to Fit commands enable you to stretch or shrink the width, height, or both, of printed output to fit a maximum number of pages.

Activity 2.15 | Printing Titles and Scaling to Fit

1 Press Ctrl + Home to display the top of your worksheet. Select the range **A13:H13**. On the **Home tab**, from the **Styles group**, apply the **Heading 4** cell style, and then apply **Center** ≡.

2 On the **Insert tab**, in the **Text group**, click **Header & Footer**. In the **Navigation group**, click the **Go to Footer** button, and then click just above the word *Footer*.

3 In the **Header & Footer Elements group**, click the **File Name** button to add the name of your file to the footer—& *[File]* displays. Then, click in a cell just above the footer to exit the Footer and view your file name.

4 Delete the unused sheets **Sheet2** and **Sheet3**. On the right edge of the status bar, click the **Normal** button 🔳, and then press ⌃Ctrl + ⌂Home to display the top of your worksheet.

> Dotted lines indicate where the pages would break if printed as currently formatted; these dotted lines display when you switch from Page Layout view to Normal view.

5 On the **Page Layout tab**, in the **Themes group**, click the **Themes** button, and then click **Concourse**.

6 In the **Page Setup group**, click **Margins**, and then at the bottom, click **Custom Margins**. In the **Page Setup** dialog box, under **Center on page**, select the **Horizontally** check box, and then click **OK**.

7 In the **Page Setup group**, click **Orientation**, and then click **Landscape**. Press ⌃Ctrl + F2 to display the **Print Preview**. At the bottom of the **Print Preview**, click the **Next Page** button ▶. Compare your screen with Figure 2.27.

> As currently formatted, the worksheet will print on five pages, and the columns will span multiple pages. Additionally, after Page 1, no column titles are visible to identify the data in the columns.

Figure 2.27

No identifying column titles at top of page

Additional columns not visible on this page

Page 2 indicated

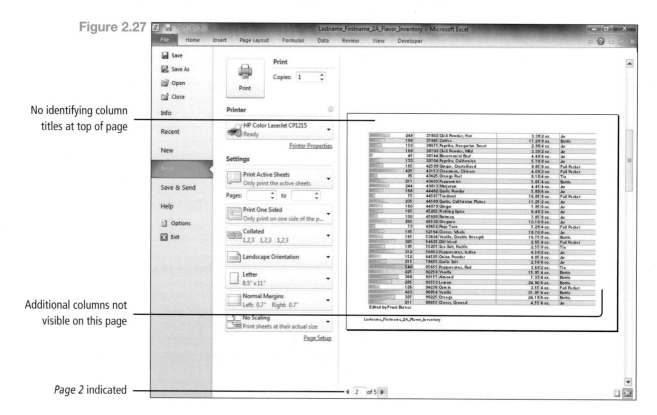

8 Click **Next Page** ▶ two times to display **Page 4**, and notice that two columns move to an additional page.

9 On the Ribbon, click **Page Layout** to redisplay the worksheet. In the **Page Setup group**, click the **Print Titles** button. Under **Print titles**, click in the **Rows to repeat at top** box, and then at the right, click the **Collapse Dialog** button 🔲.

10 From the **row heading area**, select **row 13**, and then click the **Expand Dialog** button 🔲. Click **OK** to print the column titles in row 13 at the top of every page.

Adding the titles on each page increases the number of pages to 6.

Another Way

With the worksheet displayed, on the Page Layout tab, in the Scale to Fit group, click the Width button arrow, and then click 1 page.

---▸ **11** Press Ctrl + F2 to display the **Print Preview**. In the center panel, at the bottom of the **Settings group**, click the **Scaling** button, and then on the displayed list, point to **Fit All Columns on One Page**. Compare your screen with Figure 2.28.

This action will shrink the width of the printed output to fit all the columns on one page. You can make adjustments like this on the Page Layout tab, or here, in the Print Preview.

Figure 2.28

Settings group

Fit All Columns on One Page command

Scaling button

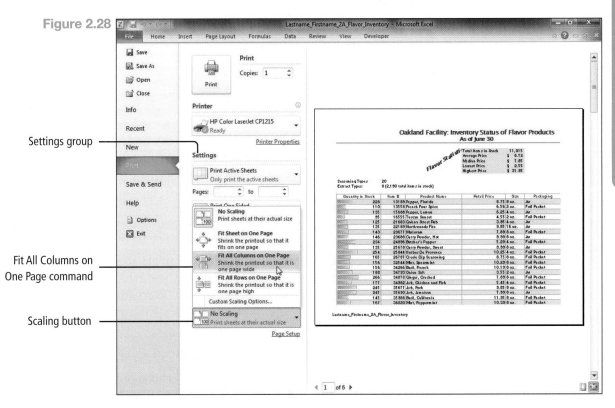

12 Click **Fit All Columns on One Page**. Notice in the **Print Preview** that all the columns display on one page.

13 At the bottom of the **Print Preview**, click the **Next Page** button ▶ one time. Notice that the output will now print on two pages and that the column titles display at the top of **Page 2**. Compare your screen with Figure 2.29.

Figure 2.29

Column titles display on Page 2

Page 2 of 2 indicated

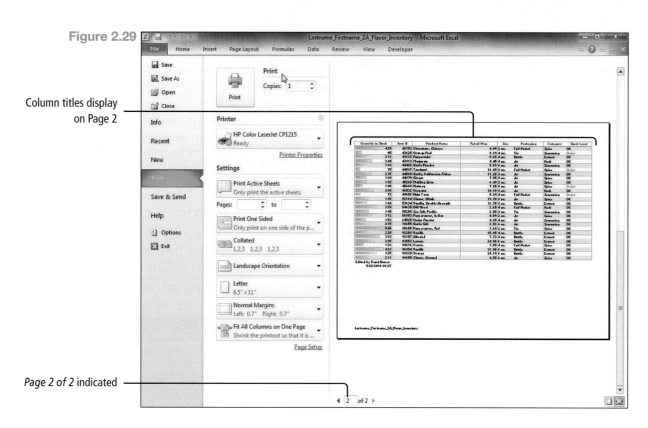

14 In **Backstage** view, click the **Info tab**. On the right, under the document thumbnail, click **Properties**, and then click **Show Document Panel**. In the **Author** box, replace the existing text with your firstname and lastname. In the **Subject** box, type your course name and section number. In the **Keywords** box, type **inventory, Oakland** and then **Close** ⊠ the **Document Information Panel**.

15 **Save** your workbook, and then print or submit electronically as directed.

16 If required by your instructor, print or create an electronic version of your worksheets with formulas displayed by using the instructions in Activity 1.16, and then **Close** ⊠ Excel without saving so that you do not save the changes you made to print formulas.

More Knowledge | Scaling for Data That Is Slightly Larger Than the Printed Page

If your data is just a little too large to fit on a printed page, you can scale the worksheet to make it fit. Scaling reduces both the width and height of the printed data to a percentage of its original size or by the number of pages that you specify. To adjust the printed output to a percentage of its actual size, for example to 80%, on the Page Layout tab, in the Scale to Fit group, click the Scale arrows to select a percentage.

End **You have completed Project 2A**

NOTES

GO! Beyond Office

Objective | Use SDExplorer to Copy a File to SkyDrive

SDExplorer is a free extension for Windows Explorer that enables you to perform everyday operations with your files on your Microsoft Live SkyDrive as if they were on your own computer. You need not install any additional programs or ActiveX components to use SDExplorer.

SDExplorer will make working with SkyDrive easier and more efficient. It keeps your SkyDrive account readily available. The Base edition is free; for information about the paid edition, go to **www.cloudstorageexplorer.com**.

> **Alert! | Working with Web-Based Applications and Services**
>
> Computer programs and services on the Web receive continuous updates and improvements. Thus, the steps to complete this Web-based Activity may differ from the ones shown. You can often look at the screens and the information presented to determine how to complete the Activity.

Activity | Using SDExplorer to Perform Common Operations with Your Documents Stored on SkyDrive

In this activity, you will install and use SDExplorer. If you are unable to install new software on the computer at which you are working, you can study the steps and try the project on another computer on which you have permission to install new software.

1 Launch your browser and go to **www.cloudstorageexplorer.com** Near the top of the screen, click **FREE DOWNLOAD** and then scroll down slightly and click the **Free download** button. In the **File Download** dialog box, click **Run**. If necessary, click Run and if a User Account Control message displays, click Yes.

Various technical experts have verified the safety of this product for your computer.

2 In the **Setup** window, click **Next**, click the **I accept the agreement** option button and click **Next**. Click **Next**

again, and then click **Install**. Click **Next** to check for updates, and then click **Finish**. If you want to do so, print the Notepad file that displays, which includes some tips for using SDExplorer. **Close** ⬛ Notepad.

3 **Close** ⬛ your browser window. On the taskbar, click the **Windows Explorer** icon 🗔, and then on the left, in the **navigation pane**, click **Computer**. Compare your screen with Figure A.

In your Computer window, the SDExplorer System Folder displays under Other.

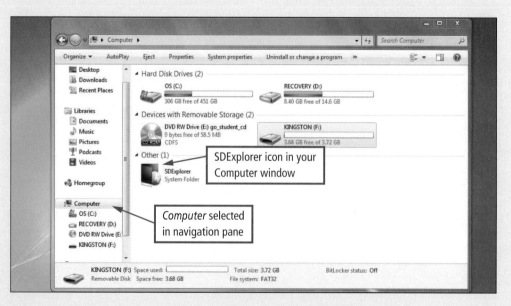

Figure A

4 Double-click the **SDExplorer** icon, and then in the displayed window, sign in to your Windows Live account. Notice that your SkyDrive folders display in a manner similar to Windows Explorer.

5 Point to the title bar of the **SDExplorer** window to display the ⬚ pointer. Drag to the right until your mouse pointer is positioned at the right edge of your screen so that the window snaps into place and fills half of the screen vertically.

6 On the taskbar, point to the **Windows Explorer** icon ⬚, right-click, and then click **Windows Explorer** to open a *second* window. Point to the Windows Explorer title bar to display the ⬚ pointer, and then drag the window to the *left* edge of your screen until it snaps into place and fills half the screen vertically.

7 In the left window, in the **navigation pane**, double-click to open the location of your **Excel Chapter 2** folder, and then open the folder.

8 *Point* to your **Lastname_Firstname_2A_Flavor_Inventory** file, drag it to the right and into the right window until your pointer is on top of your **GO! Beyond Office-Excel** folder as shown in Figure B, and then release the mouse button.

This action places a copy of the file from your Excel Chapter 2 folder to your SkyDrive folder.

9 In the window on the right, on the toolbar, click **Sign out** to sign out of your Windows Live account,

and then click **Yes**. **Close** ⬚ the remaining Windows Explorer window.

10 Launch your browser, go to **www.live.com** and then sign in to your account. At the top of the screen, click **SkyDrive**. Click your **GO! Beyond Office-Excel** folder to confirm that your **Lastname_Firstname_2A_Flavor_Inventory** file was copied there.

If you are comfortable using SDExplorer, which is not a Microsoft product but is known to be secure, leave SDExplorer installed on your computer and use it when it is convenient to do so. If you prefer to uninstall this software, do so from the Control Panel as described in Step 13.

11 Start the **Snipping Tool**, and then create a **Full-screen Snip**. On the **Snipping Tool** markup window toolbar, click the **Save Snip** button ⬚. In the **Save As** dialog box, navigate to your **Excel Chapter 2** folder. Be sure the **Save as type** box displays **JPEG file**. In the **File name** box, type **Lastname_Firstname_2A_SDExplorer_Snip** and then click **Save**. **Close** the **Snipping Tool** window.

12 Sign out of your Windows Live account, and then close all windows. Submit your snip file as directed.

13 If you want to uninstall SDExplorer from your computer, click Start, click Control Panel, under Programs, click Uninstall a program, on the displayed list click SDExplorer, and then at the top of the window, click Uninstall.

Figure B

Left window displays your Excel Chapter 2 folder

File being copied to your SkyDrive folder using SDExplorer

NOTES

Analyzing Data with Pie Charts, Line Charts, and What-If Analysis Tools

OUTCOMES

At the end of this chapter you will be able to:

OBJECTIVES

Mastering these objectives will enable you to:

PROJECT 3A

Present budget data in a pie chart.

1. Chart Data with a Pie Chart (p. 393)
2. Format a Pie Chart (p. 396)
3. Edit a Workbook and Update a Chart (p. 402)
4. Use Goal Seek to Perform What-If Analysis (p. 403)

PROJECT 3B

Make projections using what-if analysis and present projections in a line chart.

5. Design a Worksheet for What-If Analysis (p. 411)
6. Answer What-If Questions by Changing Values in a Worksheet (p. 418)
7. Chart Data with a Line Chart (p. 421)

osmera.com/Shutterstock

In This Chapter

In this chapter, you will work with two different types of commonly used charts that make it easy to visualize data. You will create a pie chart in a separate chart sheet to show how the parts of a budget contribute to a total budget. You will also practice using parentheses in a formula, calculate the percentage rate of an increase, answer what-if questions, and then chart data in a line chart to show the flow of data over time. In this chapter you will also practice formatting the axes in a line chart.

The projects in this chapter relate to **The City of Orange Blossom Beach**, a coastal city located between Fort Lauderdale and Miami. The city's access to major transportation provides both residents and businesses an opportunity to compete in the global marketplace. Each year the city welcomes a large number of tourists who enjoy the warm climate and beautiful beaches, and who embark on cruises from this major cruise port. The city encourages best environmental practices and partners with cities in other countries to promote sound government at the local level.

Project 3A Budget Pie Chart

Project Activities

In Activities 3.01 through 3.11, you will edit a worksheet for Lila Darius, City Manager, that projects expenses from the city's general fund for the next fiscal year, and then present the data in a pie chart. Your completed worksheet will look similar to Figure 3.1.

Project Files

For Project 3A, you will need the following file:

e03A_Fund_Expenses

You will save your workbook as:

Lastname_Firstname_3A_Fund_Expenses

Project Results

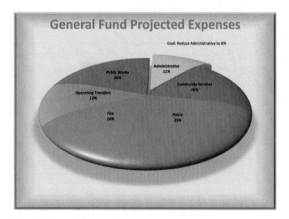

Lastname_Firstname_3A_Fund_Expenses

Figure 3.1
Project 3A Fund Expenses

Objective 1 | Chart Data with a Pie Chart

A *pie chart* shows the relationship of each part to a whole. The size of each pie slice is equal to its value compared to the total value of all the slices. The pie chart style charts data that is arranged in a single column or single row, and shows the size of items in a single data series proportional to the sum of the items. Whereas a column or bar chart can have two or more data series in the chart, a pie chart can have only one data series.

Consider using a pie chart when you have only one data series to plot, you do not have more than seven categories, and the categories represent parts of a total value.

Activity 3.01 | Creating a Pie Chart and a Chart Sheet

A *fund* is a sum of money set aside for a specific purpose. In a municipal government like the City of Orange Blossom Beach, the *general fund* is money set aside for the normal operating activities of the city, such as police, fire, and administering the everyday functions of the city.

1 **Start** Excel. From the student files that accompany this textbook, open **e03A_Fund_Expenses**. From **Backstage view**, display the **Save As** dialog box. Navigate to the location where you are storing projects for this chapter.

2 Create a new folder named **Excel Chapter 3** and open the new folder. In the **File name** box, type **Lastname_Firstname_3A_Fund_Expenses** Click **Save** or press Enter.

> The worksheet indicates the expenses for the current year and the projected expenses for the next fiscal year.

3 Click cell **D5**, and then type **=** to begin a formula.

4 Click cell **C5**, which is the first value that is part of the total Projected Expenses, to insert it into the formula. Type **/** to indicate division, and then click cell **C11**, which is the total Projected Expenses.

> Recall that to determine the percentage by which a value makes up a total, you must divide the value by the total. The result will be a percentage expressed as a decimal.

5 Press F4 to make the reference to the value in cell **C11** absolute, which will enable you to copy the formula. Compare your screen with Figure 3.2.

> Recall that an *absolute cell reference* refers to a cell by its fixed position in the worksheet. The reference to cell C5 is a *relative cell reference*, because when you copy the formula, you want the reference to change *relative* to its row.
>
> Recall also that dollar signs display to indicate that a cell reference is absolute.

Figure 3.2

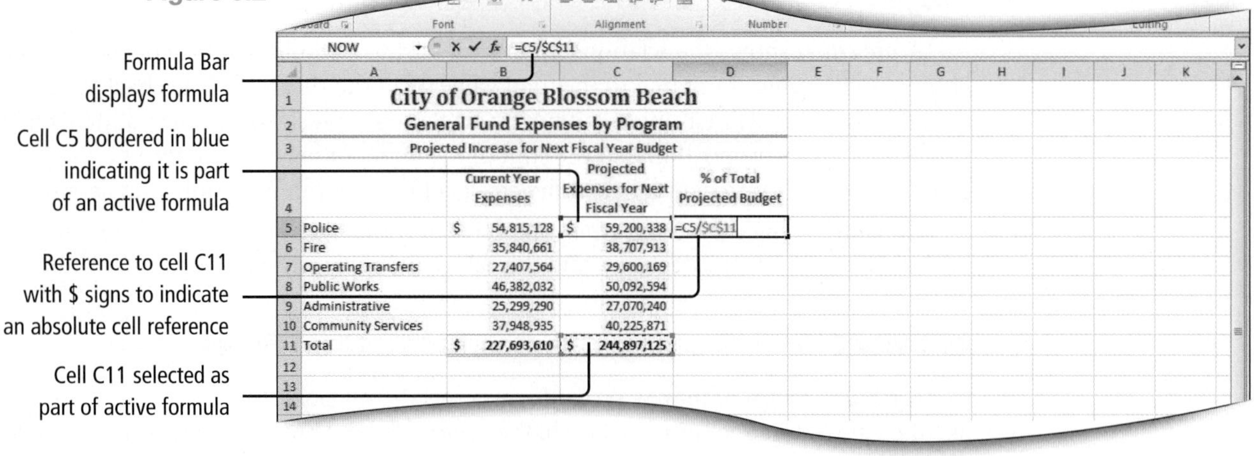

Formula Bar displays formula

Cell C5 bordered in blue indicating it is part of an active formula

Reference to cell C11 with $ signs to indicate an absolute cell reference

Cell C11 selected as part of active formula

Figure 3.2

6 On the **Formula Bar**, click the **Enter** button ✓ to confirm the entry and to keep cell **D5** the active cell. Copy the formula down through cell **D10**, and then compare your screen with Figure 3.3.

Figure 3.3

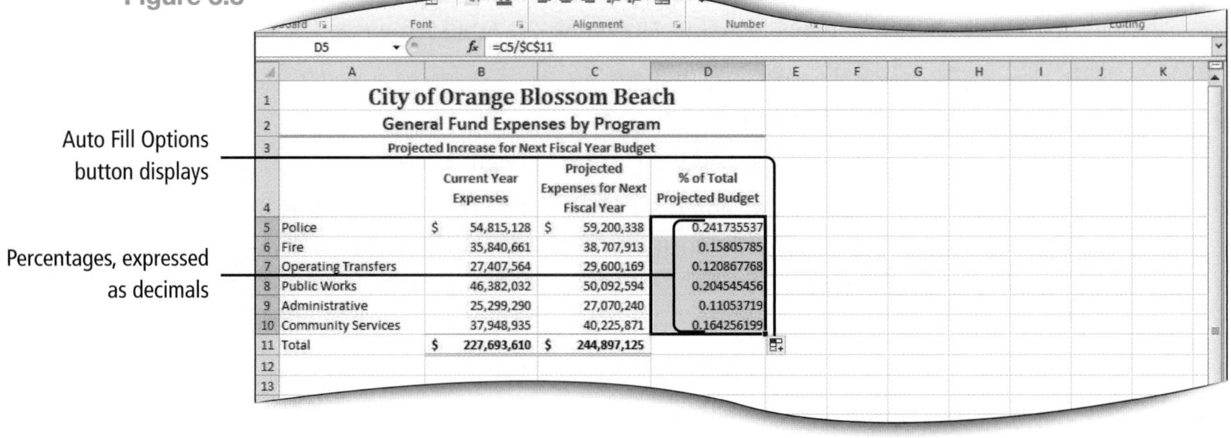

Auto Fill Options button displays

Percentages, expressed as decimals

Figure 3.3

7 With the range **D5:D10** still selected, right-click over the selection, and then on the Mini toolbar, click the **Percent Style** button % and the **Center** ☰ button. Click cell **A1** to cancel the selection, and then **Save** 🖫 your workbook. Compare your screen with Figure 3.4.

Figure 3.4

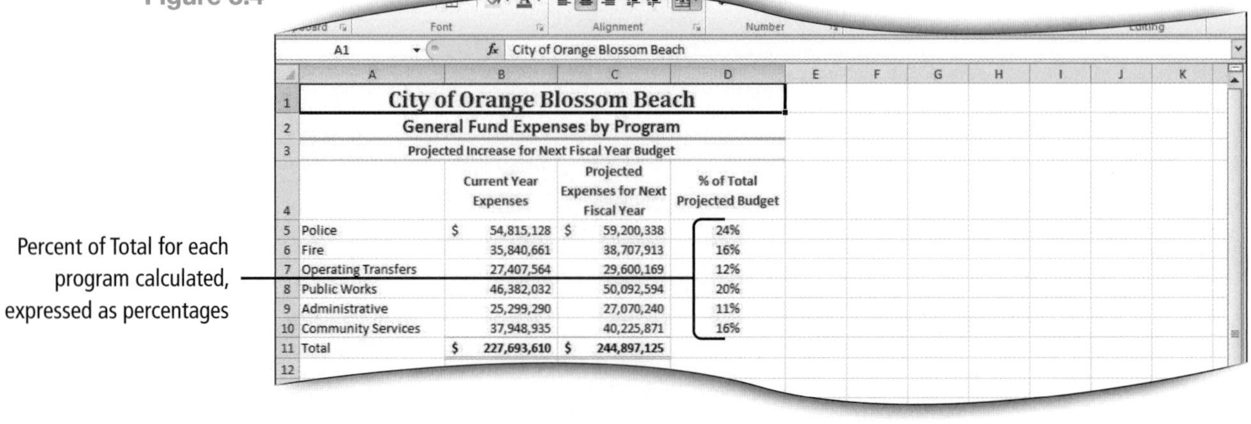

Percent of Total for each program calculated, expressed as percentages

Figure 3.4

8 Select the range **A5:A10**, hold down Ctrl, and then select the range **C5:C10** to select the nonadjacent ranges with the program names and the projected expense for each program.

> To create a pie chart, you must select two ranges. One range contains the labels for each slice of the pie chart, and the other range contains the values that add up to a total. The two ranges must have the same number of cells and the range with the values should *not* include the cell with the total.

> The program names (Police, Fire, and so on) are the category names and will identify the slices of the pie chart. Each projected expense is a *data point*—a value that originates in a worksheet cell and that is represented in a chart by a *data marker*. In a pie chart, each pie slice is a data marker. Together, the data points form the *data series*—related data points represented by data markers—and determine the size of each pie slice.

9 With the nonadjacent ranges selected, click the **Insert tab**, and then in the **Charts group**, click **Pie**. Under **3-D Pie**, click the first chart—**Pie in 3-D**—to create the chart on your worksheet.

10 On the **Design tab**, at the right end of the Ribbon in the **Location group**, click the **Move Chart** button. In the **Move Chart** dialog box, click the **New sheet** option button.

11 In the **New sheet** box, replace the highlighted text *Chart1* by typing **Projected Expenses Chart** and then click **OK** to display the chart on a separate worksheet in your workbook. Compare your screen with Figure 3.5.

> The pie chart displays on a separate new sheet in your workbook, and a *legend* identifies the pie slices. Recall that a legend is a chart element that identifies the patterns or colors assigned to the categories in the chart.

> A *chart sheet* is a workbook sheet that contains only a chart; it is useful when you want to view a chart separately from the worksheet data. The sheet tab indicates *Projected Expenses Chart*.

Figure 3.5

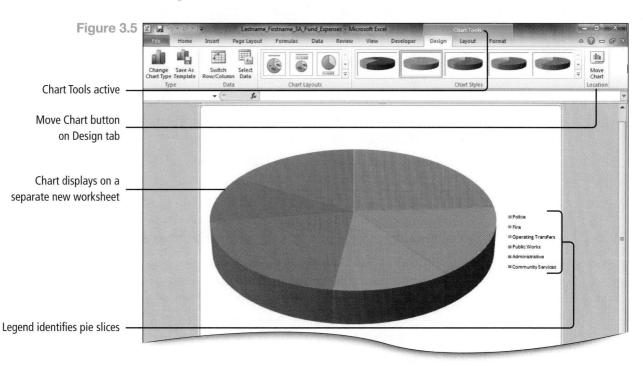

Chart Tools active

Move Chart button on Design tab

Chart displays on a separate new worksheet

Legend identifies pie slices

Objective 2 | Format a Pie Chart

Activity 3.02 | Applying Percentages to Labels in a Pie Chart

In your worksheet, for each expense, you calculated the percent of the total in column D. These percentages can also be calculated by the Chart feature and added to the pie slices as labels.

1 On the Ribbon under **Chart Tools**, click the **Layout tab**, and then in the **Labels group**, click the **Chart Title** button. On the displayed list, click **Above Chart**.

2 With the **Chart Title** box selected, watch the **Formula Bar** as you type **General Fund Projected Expenses** and then press Enter to create the new chart title in the box.

3 Point to the chart title text, right-click to display the Mini toolbar, and then change the **Font Size** to **36** and change the **Font Color** ▲▼ to **Olive Green, Accent 1, Darker 25%**—in the fifth column, the fifth color. Compare your screen with Figure 3.6.

Figure 3.6

Text displays in Formula Bar as you type

New chart title text entered and formatted

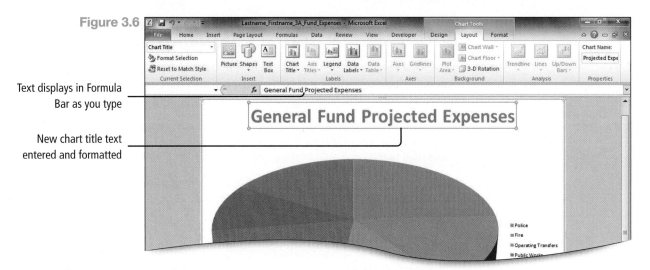

4 In the **Labels group**, click the **Legend** button, and then click **None**.

> The chart expands to fill the new space. In a pie chart, it is usually more effective to place the labels within, or close to, each pie slice. Because you will place the program names (the categories) on the pie slices, a legend is unnecessary.

5 In the **Labels group**, click the **Data Labels** button, and then at the bottom, click **More Data Label Options**.

6 In the **Format Data Labels** dialog box, on the left, be sure **Label Options** is selected. On the right, under **Label Contains**, click as necessary to select the **Category Name** and **Percentage** check boxes. *Clear* any other check boxes in this group. Under **Label Position**, click the **Center** option button.

> In the worksheet, you calculated the percent of the total in column D. Here, the percentage will be calculated by the Chart feature and added to the chart as a label.

7 In the lower right corner of the **Format Data Labels** dialog box, click **Close**, and notice that all of the data labels are selected and display both the category name and the percentage.

8 Point to any of the selected labels, right-click to display the Mini toolbar, and then change the **Font Size** to **11**, apply **Bold** B , and apply **Italic** I .

9 **Save** 🖫 your workbook. Press Esc to deselect the labels, and then compare your screen with Figure 3.7.

Figure 3.7

Data labels on pie slices replace legend; labels include category name and percentage; data labels centered in slice, 11 pt font, bold and italic

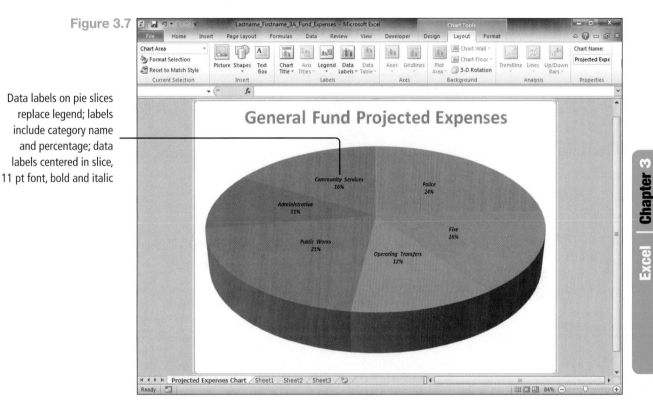

Activity 3.03 | Formatting a Pie Chart with 3-D

3-D, which is short for *three-dimensional*, refers to an image that appears to have all three spatial dimensions—length, width, and depth.

1 Click in any pie slice outside of the label to select the entire pie; notice that selection handles display on the outside corners of each slice.

2 Click the **Format tab**. In the **Shape Styles group**, click the **Shape Effects** button, point to **Bevel**, and then at the bottom of the gallery, click **3-D Options**.

3 In the **Format Data Series** dialog box, on the right, under **Bevel**, click the **Top** button. In the displayed gallery, under **Bevel**, point to the first button to display the ScreenTip *Circle*. Click the **Circle** button. Then click the **Bottom** button, and apply the **Circle** bevel.

> *Bevel* is a shape effect that uses shading and shadows to make the edges of a shape appear to be curved or angled.

4 In the four **Width** and **Height** spin boxes, type **512 pt** and then compare your screen with Figure 3.8.

Figure 3.8

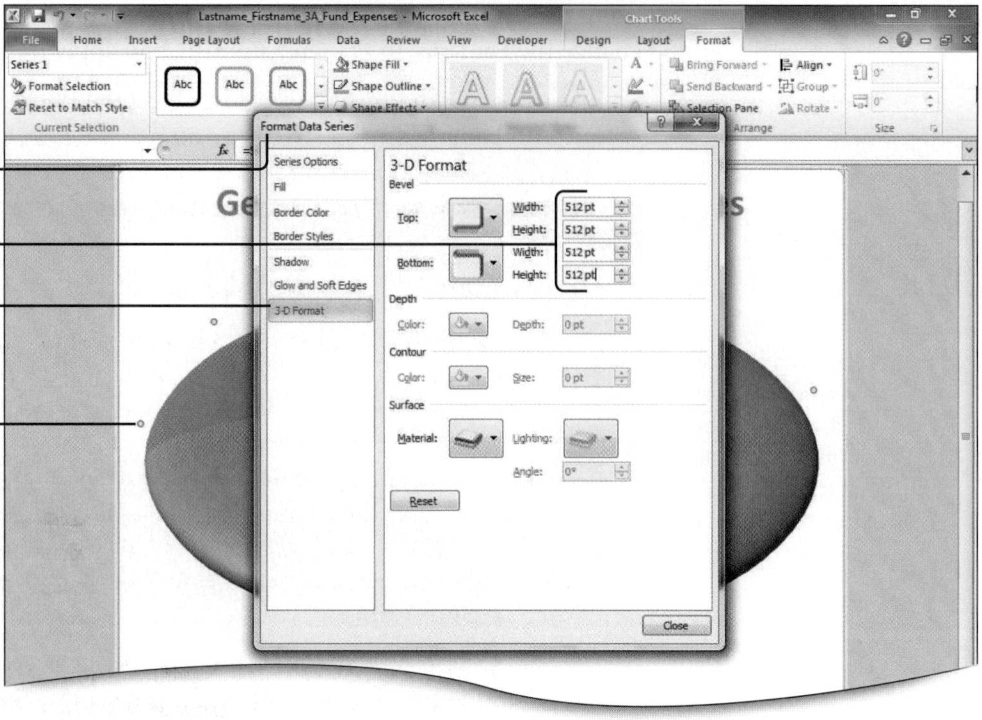

Format Data Series dialog box

Spin box Widths and Heights set to *512 pt*

3-D Format selected

Selection handles surround pie

5 In the lower portion of the dialog box, under **Surface**, click the **Material** button. Under **Standard**, click the third button—**Plastic**. In the lower right corner, click **Close**.

6 With the pie still selected, on the **Format tab**, in the **Shape Styles group**, click **Shape Effects**, and then point to **Shadow**. At the bottom of the displayed gallery, scroll if necessary, and then under **Perspective**, click the third button, which displays the ScreenTip *Below* to display a shadow below the pie chart. Click **Save** 🔲.

Activity 3.04 | Rotating a Pie Chart

The order in which the data series in pie charts are plotted in Excel is determined by the order of the data on the worksheet. To gain a different view of the chart, you can rotate the chart within the 360 degrees of the circle of the pie shape to present a different visual perspective of the chart.

1 Notice the position of the **Fire** and **Police** slices in the chart. Then, with the pie chart still selected—sizing handles surround the pie—point anywhere in the pie and right-click. On the displayed shortcut menu, click **Format Data Series**.

Another Way

Drag the slider to 100.

2 In the **Format Data Series** dialog box, on the left, be sure **Series Options** is selected. On the right, under **Angle of first slice**, click in the box and type **100** to rotate the chart 100 degrees to the right.

3 Close the **Format Data Series** dialog box. Click **Save** 🔲, and then compare your screen with Figure 3.9.

Rotating the chart can provide a better perspective to the chart. Here, rotating the chart in this manner emphasizes that the Fire and Police programs represent a significant portion of the total expenses.

Figure 3.9

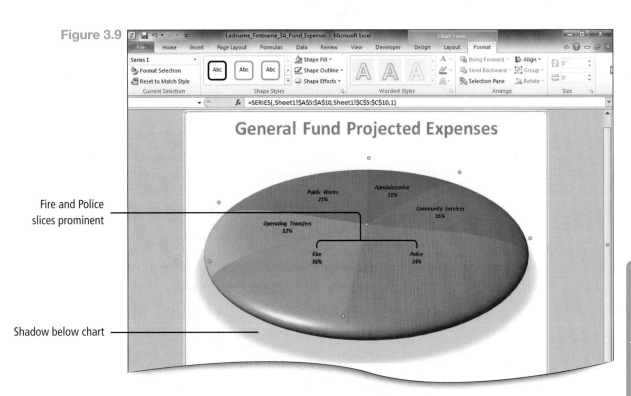

Fire and Police slices prominent

Shadow below chart

Activity 3.05 | Exploding and Coloring a Pie Slice

You can pull out—*explode*—one or more slices of a pie chart to emphasize a specific slice or slices. Additionally, there is a different chart type you can select if you want *all* the slices to explode and emphasize all the individual slices of a pie chart—the exploded pie or exploded pie in 3-D chart type. The exploded pie chart type displays the contribution of *each* value to the total, while at the same time emphasizing individual values.

1 Press Esc to deselect all chart elements. Click any slice to select the entire pie, and then click the **Administrative** slice to select only that slice. Compare your screen with Figure 3.10.

Figure 3.10

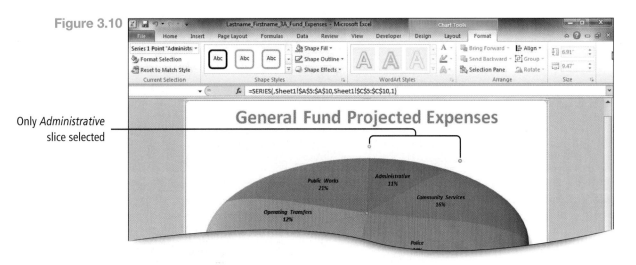

Only *Administrative* slice selected

2 Point to the **Administrative** slice to display the ⬚ pointer, and then drag the slice slightly upward and away from the center of the pie, as shown in Figure 3.11, and then release the mouse button.

Figure 3.11

Move pointer

Dotted lines indicate
position of slice as
you move it

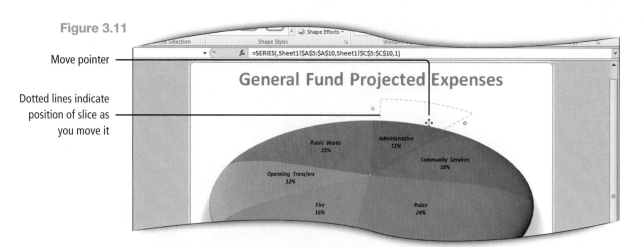

3   With the **Administrative** slice still selected, point to the slice and right-click, and then on the shortcut menu, click **Format Data Point**.

4   In the **Format Data Point** dialog box, on the left, click **Fill**. On the right, under **Fill**, click the **Solid fill** option button.

5   Click the **Color arrow**, and then under **Theme Colors**, in the seventh column, click the fourth color—**Gold, Accent 3, Lighter 40%**.

6   In the lower right corner of the **Format Data Point** dialog box, click the **Close** button.

Activity 3.06 | Formatting the Chart Area

The entire chart and all of its elements comprise the ***chart area***.

1   Point to the white area just inside the border of the chart to display the ScreenTip *Chart Area*. Click one time.

2   On the **Format tab**, in the **Shape Styles group**, click the **Shape Effects** button, point to **Bevel**, and then under **Bevel**, in the second row, click the third bevel—**Convex**.

3   Press Esc to deselect the chart element and view this effect—a convex beveled frame around your entire chart—and then compare your screen with Figure 3.12.

Figure 3.12

Convex beveled frame
surrounds chart sheet

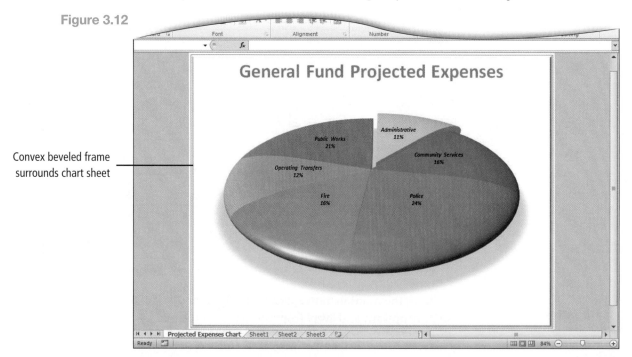

4   Point slightly inside the border of the chart to display the ScreenTip *Chart Area*, right-click, and then on the shortcut menu, click **Format Chart Area**.

5   In the **Format Chart Area** dialog box, on the left, be sure that **Fill** is selected. On the right, under **Fill**, click the **Gradient fill** option button.

6   Click the **Preset colors** arrow, and then in the second row, click the last preset, **Fog**. Click the **Type arrow**, and then click **Path**. Click the **Close** button.

7   Compare your screen with Figure 3.13, and then **Save** 💾 your workbook.

Figure 3.13

Chart area formatted with *Fog* gradient

Bevel effect added to chart area

Border indicates that the chart is selected

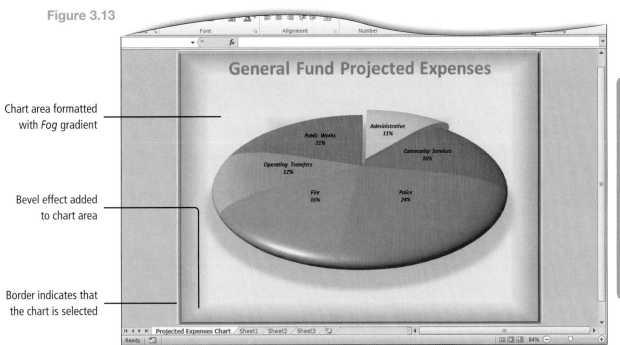

Activity 3.07 | Inserting a Text Box in a Chart

A **text box** is a movable, resizable container for text or graphics.

1   With the Chart Area still selected, click the **Layout tab**, and then in the **Insert group**, click the **Text Box** button, and then move the pointer into the chart area.

2   Position the displayed 🔽 pointer under the *c* in *Projected* and about midway between the title and the pie—above the *Administrative* slice. Hold down the left mouse button, and then drag down and to the right approximately as shown in Figure 3.14; your text box need not be precise.

Figure 3.14

Text Box button

Text box drawn

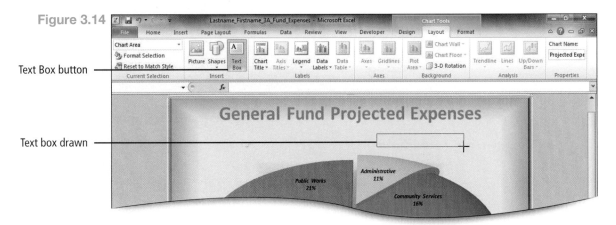

3 With the insertion point blinking inside the text box, type **Goal: Reduce Administrative to 8%** Press (Esc) or click outside the chart area to deselect the chart element, and then compare your screen with Figure 3.15.

Figure 3.15

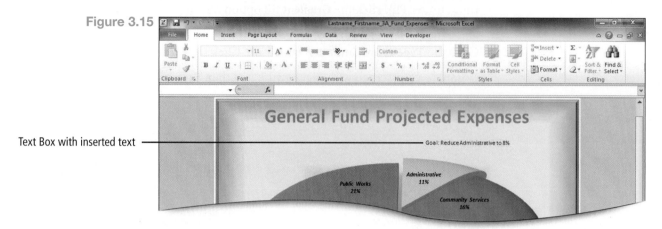

Text Box with inserted text ——————————————————————— General Fund Projected Expenses

4 If necessary, select and then adjust or move your text box. **Save** 💾 your workbook.

Objective 3 | Edit a Workbook and Update a Chart

Activity 3.08 | Editing a Workbook and Updating a Chart

If you edit the data in your worksheet, the chart data markers—in this instance the pie slices—will adjust automatically to accurately represent the new values.

1 On the pie chart, notice that *Police* represents 24% of the total projected expenses.

2 In the sheet tab area at the bottom of the workbook, click the **Sheet1 tab** to redisplay the worksheet.

> **Another Way**
>
> Double-click the cell to position the insertion point in the cell and edit.

3 Click cell **C5**, and then in **Formula Bar**, change *59,200,338* to **62,200,388**

4 Press (Enter), and notice that the total in cell **C11** recalculates to *$247,897,175* and the percentages in **column D** also recalculate.

5 Display the **Projected Expenses Chart** sheet. Notice that the pie slices adjust to show the recalculation—*Police* is now *25%* of the projected expenses. Click **Save** 💾, and then compare your screen with Figure 3.16.

Figure 3.16

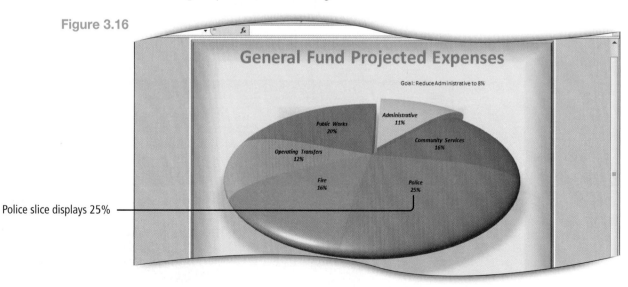

Police slice displays 25% ——————————————

Activity 3.09 | Inserting WordArt in a Worksheet

WordArt is a gallery of text styles with which you can create decorative effects, such as shadowed or mirrored text. In an Excel worksheet, WordArt can be effective if you plan to display your worksheet in a PowerPoint presentation, or if readers will be viewing the worksheet data online.

1 In the sheet tab area at the bottom of the workbook, click the **Sheet1 tab** to redisplay the worksheet. Click the **Insert tab**, and then in the **Text group**, click the **WordArt** button.

2 In the WordArt gallery, in the last row, click the last style—**Fill – Olive Green, Accent 1, Metal Bevel, Reflection**.

The WordArt indicating *YOUR TEXT HERE* displays in the worksheet.

3 With the WordArt selected, type **general fund expenses** and then point anywhere on the dashed border surrounding the WordArt object. Click the dashed border one time to change it to a solid border, indicating that all of the text is selected.

4 On the **Home tab**, in the **Font group**, change the **Font Size** to **28**.

5 Point to the WordArt border to display the [pointer], and then drag to position the upper left corner of the WordArt approximately as shown in Figure 3.17. If necessary, hold down Ctrl and press any of the arrow keys on your keyboard to move the WordArt object into position in small increments. Click any cell to deselect the WordArt, and then click **Save** [icon].

Figure 3.17

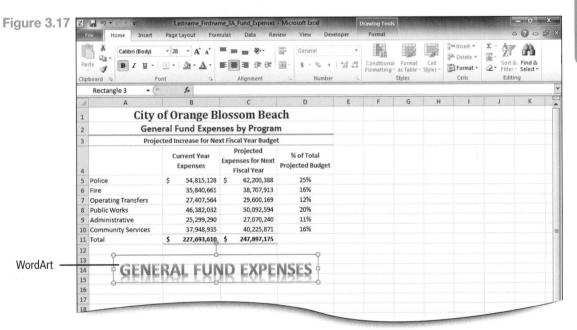

Objective 4 | Use Goal Seek to Perform What-If Analysis

Activity 3.10 | Using Goal Seek to Perform What-If Analysis

The process of changing the values in cells to see how those changes affect the outcome of formulas in your worksheet is referred to as *what-if analysis*. A what-if analysis tool that is included with Excel is *Goal Seek*, which finds the input needed in one cell to arrive at the desired result in another cell.

1 In cell **A17**, type **Goal: To Reduce Administrative Expenses from 11% to 8% of Total Expenses** Merge and center the text across the range **A17:D17**, and then apply the **Heading 3** Cell Style.

2 In cell **A18**, type **Goal Amount:** and press Enter.

3 Select the range **C9:D9**, right-click over the selection, and then click **Copy**. Point to cell **B18**, right-click, and then under **Paste Options**, click the **Paste** button 📋.

4 Press Esc to cancel the moving border, click cell **C18**, and then compare your screen with Figure 3.18.

Figure 3.18

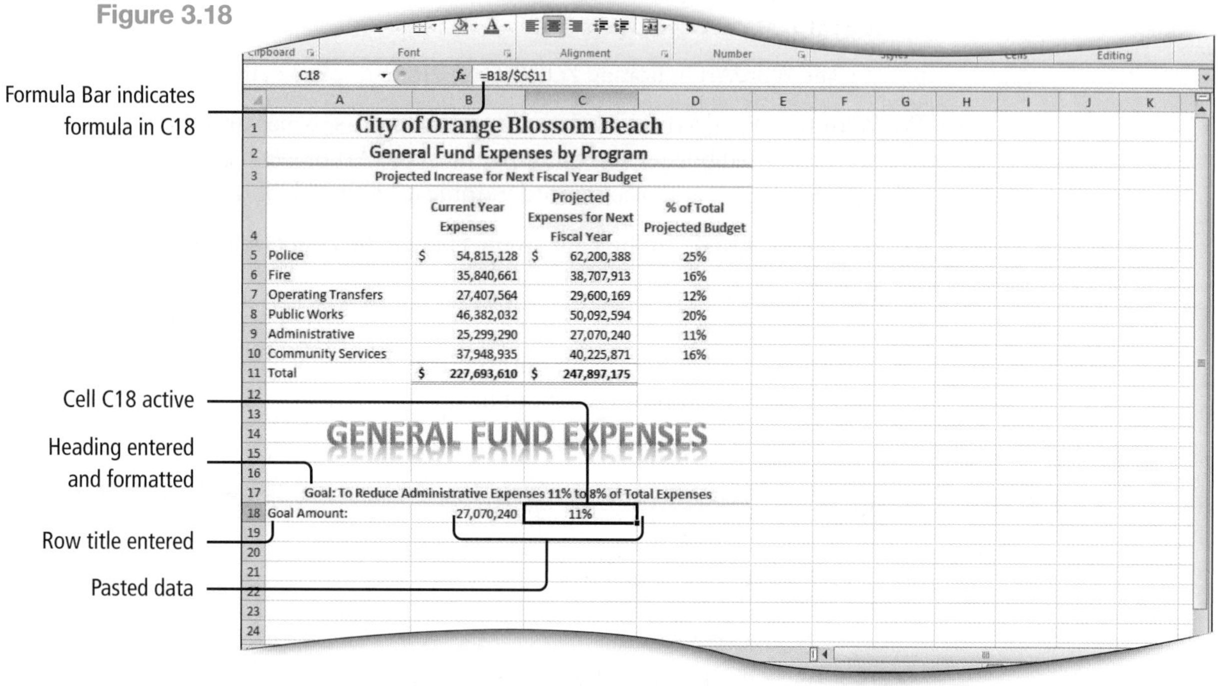

Formula Bar indicates formula in C18

Cell C18 active

Heading entered and formatted

Row title entered

Pasted data

	A	B	C	D	E
C18			fx =B18/$C$11		
1	**City of Orange Blossom Beach**				
2	**General Fund Expenses by Program**				
3	Projected Increase for Next Fiscal Year Budget				
4		Current Year Expenses	Projected Expenses for Next Fiscal Year	% of Total Projected Budget	
5	Police	$ 54,815,128	$ 62,200,388	25%	
6	Fire	35,840,661	38,707,913	16%	
7	Operating Transfers	27,407,564	29,600,169	12%	
8	Public Works	46,382,032	50,092,594	20%	
9	Administrative	25,299,290	27,070,240	11%	
10	Community Services	37,948,935	40,225,871	16%	
11	Total	$ 227,693,610	$ 247,897,175		
17	Goal: To Reduce Administrative Expenses 11% to 8% of Total Expenses				
18	Goal Amount:	27,070,240	11%		

GENERAL FUND EXPENSES

5 Be sure cell **C18** is the active cell. On the **Data tab**, in the **Data Tools group**, click the **What-If Analysis** button, and then click **Goal Seek**.

6 In the **Goal Seek** dialog box, notice that the active cell, **C18**, is indicated in the **Set cell** box. Press Tab to move to the **To value** box, and then type **8%**

C18 is the cell in which you want to set a specific value; 8% is the percentage of the total expenses that you want to budget for Administrative expenses. The Set cell box contains the formula that calculates the information you seek.

7 Press Tab to move the insertion point to the **By changing cell** box, and then click cell **B18**. Compare your screen with Figure 3.19.

Cell B18 contains the value that Excel changes to reach the goal. Excel formats this cell as an absolute cell reference.

Figure 3.19

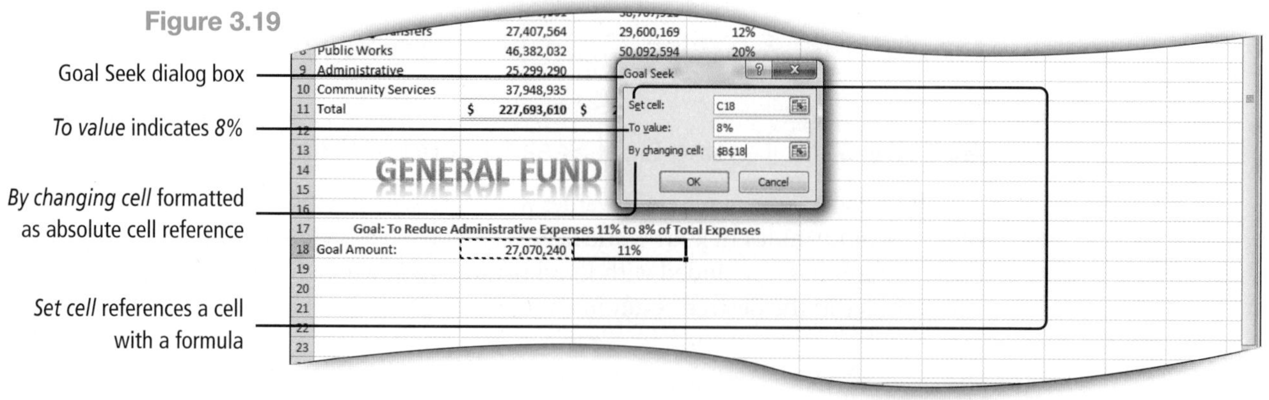

Goal Seek dialog box

To value indicates 8%

By changing cell formatted as absolute cell reference

Set cell references a cell with a formula

	A	B	C	D
	Transfers	27,407,564	29,600,169	12%
8	Public Works	46,382,032	50,092,594	20%
9	Administrative	25,299,290		
10	Community Services	37,948,935		
11	Total	$ 227,693,610	$	
17	Goal: To Reduce Administrative Expenses 11% to 8% of Total Expenses			
18	Goal Amount:	27,070,240	11%	

GENERAL FUND

Goal Seek
Set cell: C18
To value: 8%
By changing cell: $B$18
OK   Cancel

8. Click **OK**. In the displayed **Goal Seek Status** dialog box, click **OK**.

9. Select the range **A18:C18**. From the **Home tab**, display the **Cell Styles** gallery. Under **Themed Cell Styles**, apply **20% - Accent3**. Click cell **B18**, and then from the **Cell Styles** gallery, at the bottom of the gallery under **Number Format**, apply the **Currency [0]** cell style.

10. Press [Ctrl] + [Home], click **Save** 💾, and then compare your screen with Figure 3.20.

> Excel calculates that the City must budget for *$19,831,774* in Administrative expenses in order for this item to become 8% of the total projected budget.

Figure 3.20

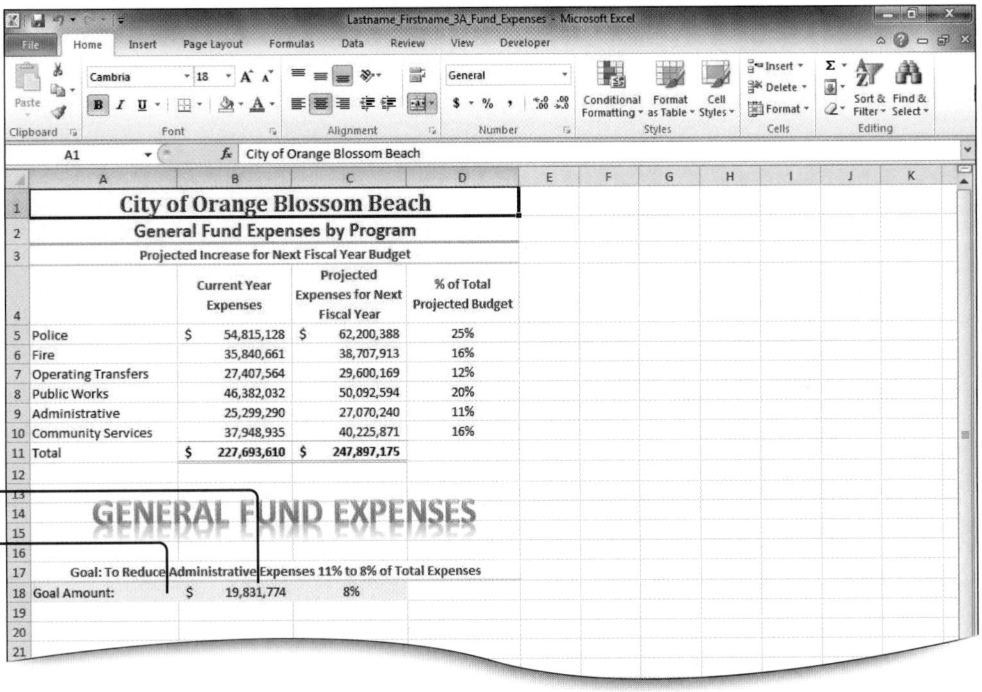

Goal of *$19,831,774*

Accent shading applied

Activity 3.11 | Preparing and Printing a Workbook with a Chart Sheet

Another Way
Right-click the sheet tab, click Rename, type, and press [Enter].

1. With your worksheet displayed, in the sheet tab area, double-click *Sheet1* to select the text, and then type **Projected Expenses Data** and press [Enter].

2. Select **Sheet2** and **Sheet3**, right-click over the selected tabs, and then click **Delete** to delete the unused sheets.

3. On the **Insert tab**, click **Header & Footer**. In the **Navigation group**, click the **Go to Footer** button, click in the **left section** above the word *Footer*, and then in the **Header & Footer Elements group**, click the **File Name** button.

4. Click in a cell above the footer to deselect the **Footer area** and view your file name. On the **Page Layout tab**, in the **Page Setup group**, click the **Margins** button, and then at the bottom click **Custom Margins**.

5. In the displayed **Page Setup** dialog box, under **Center on page**, select the **Horizontally** check box. Click **OK**, and then on the status bar, click the **Normal** button 🔲 to return to Normal view.

> Recall that after displaying worksheets in Page Layout View, dotted lines display to indicate the page breaks when you return to Normal view.

6. Press [Ctrl] + [Home] to move to the top of the worksheet.

7 Click the **Projected Expenses Chart** sheet tab to display the chart sheet. On the **Insert tab**, in the **Text group**, click **Header & Footer** to display the **Header/Footer tab** of the **Page Setup** dialog box.

8 In the center of the **Page Setup** dialog box, click **Custom Footer**. With the insertion point blinking in the **Left section**, in the row of buttons in the middle of the dialog box, locate and click the **Insert File Name** button. Compare your screen with Figure 3.21.

> Use the Page Setup dialog box in this manner to insert a footer on a chart sheet, which has no Page Layout view in which you can see the Header and Footer areas.

Figure 3.21

Page Setup dialog box ⎯

Footer dialog box ⎯

Insert File Name button ⎯

Left section displays *&[File]* ⎯

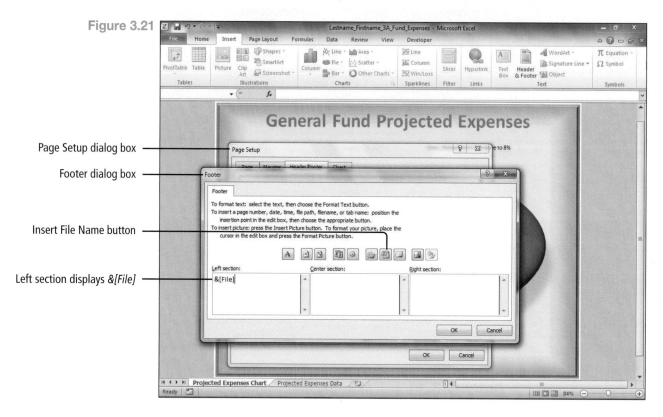

9 Click **OK** two times. Display **Backstage** view, on the right under the thumbnail, click **Properties**, and then click **Show Document Panel**. In the **Author** box, replace the existing text with your firstname and lastname. In the **Subject** box, type your course name and section number. In the **Keywords** box type **general fund, expenses, pie chart** and then **Close** × the **Document Information Panel**.

10 Right-click either of the sheet tabs, and then click **Select All Sheets**. Verify that *[Group]* displays in the title bar.

> Recall that by selecting all sheets, you can view all of the workbook pages in Print Preview.

11 Press Ctrl + F2 to display the **Print Preview**. Examine the first page, and then at the bottom of the **Print Preview**, click the **Next Page** ▶ button to view the second page of your workbook.

Note | Printing a Chart Sheet Uses More Toner

Printing a chart that displays on a chart sheet will use more toner or ink than a small chart that is part of a worksheet. If you are printing your work, check with your instructor to verify whether or not you should print the chart sheet.

12 Click **Save** to redisplay the workbook. Print or submit electronically as directed by your instructor.

13 If you are directed to submit printed formulas, refer to Activity 1.16 in Project 1A to do so.

14 If you printed your formulas, be sure to redisplay the worksheet by clicking the Show Formulas button to turn it off. **Close** the workbook. If you are prompted to save changes, click **No** so that you do not save the changes to the worksheet that you used for printing formulas. **Close** Excel.

More Knowledge | Setting the Default Number of Sheets in a New Workbook

By default, the number of new worksheets in a new workbook is three, but you can change this default number. From Backstage view, display the Excel Options dialog box, click the General tab, and then under When creating new workbooks, change the number in the Include this many sheets box.

End **You have completed Project 3A**

GO! Beyond Office

Objective | Create a JPEG Photo of a Chart and Upload to a
OneNote Web App Notebook

Recall that *OneNote* is a Microsoft application with which you can create a digital notebook that gives you a single location where you can gather and organize information in the form of notes. The OneNote Web App enables you to share your OneNote notebooks on the Web.

> **Alert!** | **Working with Web-Based Applications and Services**
>
> Computer programs and services on the Web receive continuous updates and improvements. Thus, the steps to complete this Web-based Activity may differ from the ones shown. You can often look at the screens and the information presented to determine how to complete the Activity.

Activity | Creating a JPEG Photo of a Chart and Uploading It to a OneNote Web App
Notebook

In this activity, you will create a JPEG image of a chart, and then upload the image to a OneNote Web App notebook.

1 From your **Excel Chapter 3** folder, open your file **Lastname_Firstname_3A_Fund_Expenses** and display the **Projected Expenses Chart** worksheet.

2 Start the **Snipping Tool**, click the **New arrow**, and then click **Rectangular Snip**. With the ⊞ pointer, point to the upper left corner of the chart, hold down the left mouse button, and then drag down to the lower right corner of the chart to create a red rectangle around the chart as shown in Figure A.

3 On the **Snipping Tool** markup window toolbar, click the **Save Snip** button 🖫. In the **Save As** dialog box, navigate to your **Excel Chapter 3** folder. Be sure the **Save as type** box displays **JPEG file**. In the **File name** box, type **Lastname_ Firstname_3A_Expenses_Chart** and then click **Save**. **Close** ✖ the **Snipping Tool** window and **Close** ✖ Excel.

4 Launch your browser, navigate to **www.live.com** and then sign in to your **Windows Live** account. At the top of the screen, click **SkyDrive**. Click your **GO! Beyond**

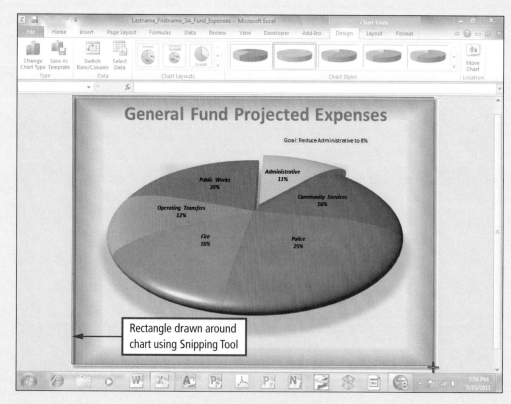

Figure A

Office-Excel folder to open it; if necessary, create this folder.

5 In the upper portion of the screen, to the right of **Create**, click the **OneNote notebook** button to create a new notebook. In the **Name** box, using your own name, type **Lastname_Firstname_3A_Notebook** and then click the **Save** button.

6 Point to the text *Untitled Section*, right-click, click **Rename**, and then in the **Enter a section name** box, type **Fund Management** Click **OK**.

7 With the insertion point blinking at the top of the notebook page, type **Chart of Expenses** and press Enter. With the insertion point in the blank page, on the Ribbon, click the **Insert tab**, and then in the **Pictures group**, click **Picture**.

8 In the **Choose File to Upload** dialog box, navigate to your **Excel Chapter 3** folder, and then click the **3A_Expenses_Chart** JPEG file that you created with the Snipping Tool. Click **Open**.

Use this technique to insert a picture to store in a OneNote notebook.

9 If the picture is selected, click below to position the insertion point under the chart picture. Click the **Home tab**, and then in the **Tags group**, click the **Tag** button to display a list of tags. Click **Important**. With the insertion

point blinking to the right of the tag—a gold star—type **Attention Council Members: The expenses from the General Fund will be discussed at the August City Council meeting.** Compare your screen with Figure B.

Note tags can help you locate specific information quickly. A note tag is both a descriptive term representing a category, such as *Important* or *To Do*, and a related icon that can be associated with a specific note. When this notebook on the SkyDrive is shared with all of the City Council members, each will be able to view the chart and see that it is important.

10 Start the **Snipping Tool**, and then create a **Full-screen Snip**. On the **Snipping Tool** markup window toolbar, click the **Save Snip** button. In the **Save As** dialog box, navigate to your **Excel Chapter 3** folder. Be sure the **Save as type** box displays **JPEG file**. In the **File name** box, type **Lastname_Firstname_3A_Chart_Snip** and then click **Save**. **Close** the **Snipping Tool** window.

11 On the Ribbon, click the **File tab**, and then click **Close**.

Recall that OneNote saves your work automatically and continuously while you take notes, when you switch to another page or section, or when you close a section or a notebook. You need not save notes manually.

12 Sign out of your Windows Live account, and then close all windows. Submit your snip file as directed.

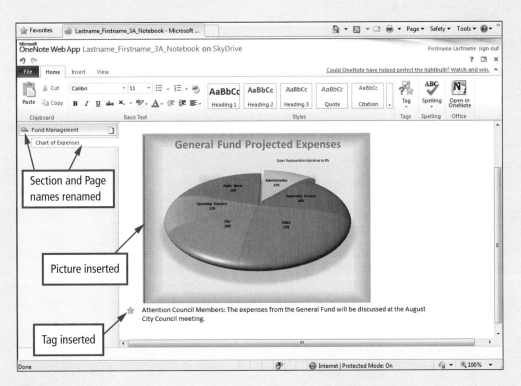

Figure B

Project 3B Growth Projection with Line Chart

myitlab
Project 3B Training

Project Activities

In Activities 3.12 through 3.19, you will assist Lila Darius, City Manager, in creating a worksheet to estimate future population growth based on three possible growth rates. You will also create a line chart to display past population growth. Your resulting worksheet and chart will look similar to Figure 3.22.

Project Files

For Project 3B, you will need the following files:

e03B_Population_Growth
e03B_Beach

You will save your workbook as:

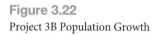

Lastname_Firstname_3B_Population_Growth

Project Results

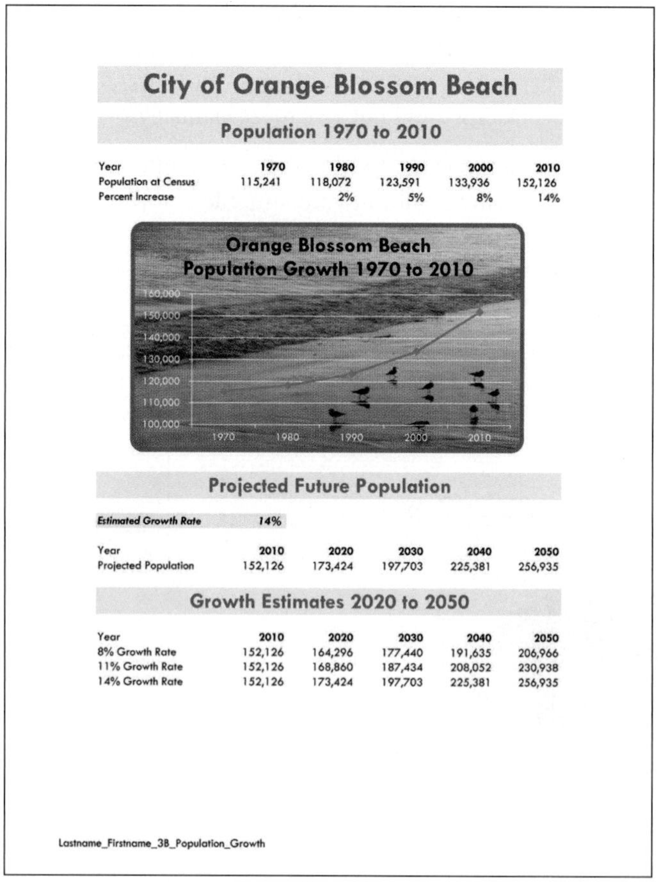
City of Orange Blossom Beach
Population 1970 to 2010
Year 1970 1980 1990 2000 2010
Population at Census 115,241 118,072 123,591 133,936 152,126
Percent Increase 2% 5% 8% 14%
Orange Blossom Beach
Population Growth 1970 to 2010
160,000
150,000
140,000
130,000
120,000
110,000
100,000
1970 1980 1990 2000 2010
Projected Future Population
Estimated Growth Rate 14%
Year 2010 2020 2030 2040 2050
Projected Population 152,126 173,424 197,703 225,381 256,935
Growth Estimates 2020 to 2050
Year 2010 2020 2030 2040 2050
8% Growth Rate 152,126 164,296 177,440 191,635 206,966
11% Growth Rate 152,126 168,860 187,434 208,052 230,938
14% Growth Rate 152,126 173,424 197,703 225,381 256,935
Lastname_Firstname_3B_Population_Growth

Figure 3.22
Project 3B Population Growth

Objective 5 | Design a Worksheet for What-If Analysis

Excel recalculates; if you change the value in a cell referenced in a formula, Excel automatically recalculates the result of the formula. Thus, you can change cell values to see *what* would happen *if* you tried different values. Recall that this process of changing the values in cells to see how those changes affect the outcome of formulas in your worksheet is referred to as what-if analysis.

Activity 3.12 | Using Parentheses in a Formula to Calculate a Percentage Rate of Increase

Ms. Darius has the city's population figures for the past five 10-year census periods. In each 10-year census period, the population has increased. In this activity, you will construct a formula to calculate the *percentage rate of increase*—the percent by which one number increases over another number—for each 10-year census period since 1970. From this information, future population growth can be estimated.

1   **Start** Excel. From your student files, open the file **e03B_Population_Growth**. From **Backstage** view, display the **Save As** dialog box. Navigate to your **Excel Chapter 3** folder, in the **File name** box, name the file **Lastname_Firstname_3B_Population_ Growth** and then click **Save** or press Enter.

2   Leave **row 4** blank, and then click cell **A5**. Type **Year** and then press Tab. In cell **B5**, type **1970** and then press Tab.

3   In cell **C5**, type **1980** and then press Tab. Select the range **B5:C5**, and then drag the fill handle to the right through cell **F5** to extend the series to 2010.

> By establishing a pattern of 10-year intervals with the first two cells, you can use the fill handle to continue the series. The AutoFill feature will do this for any pattern that you establish with two or more cells.

4   With the range **B5:F5** still selected, right-click over the selection, and then on the Mini toolbar, click **Bold** B. Compare your screen with Figure 3.23.

Figure 3.23

AutoFill used to fill 10-year periods to create column titles

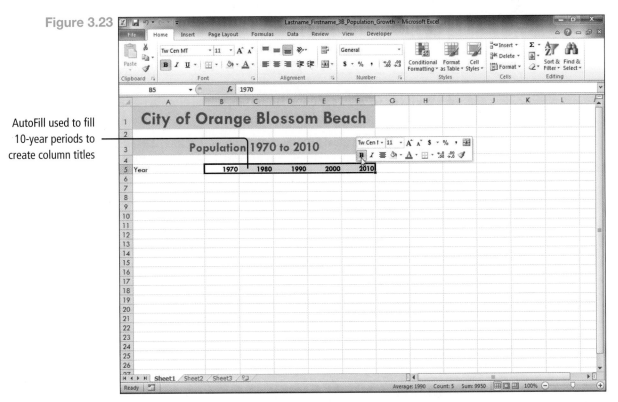

5 In cell **A6**, type **Population at Census** and press Enter. In cell **A7**, type **Percent Increase** and press Enter.

6 Click cell **B6**, and then beginning in cell **B6**, and pressing Tab to move across the row, enter the following values for the population in the years listed:

1970	1980	1990	2000	2010
115241	118072	123591	133936	152126

7 Select the range **B6:F6**, right-click, on the Mini toolbar, click **Comma Style** , and then click **Decrease Decimal** two times.

8 Click cell **C7**. Being sure to include the parentheses, type **=(c6-b6)/b6** and then on the **Formula Bar**, click the **Enter** button ✓ to keep cell **C7** active; your result is *0.02456591* (or *0.02*). Compare your screen with Figure 3.24.

> Recall that as you type, a list of Excel functions that begin with the letter *C* and *B* may briefly display. This is *Formula AutoComplete*, an Excel feature which, after typing an = (equal sign) and the beginning letter or letters of a function name, displays a list of function names that match the typed letter(s). In this instance, the letters represent cell references, *not* the beginning of a function name.

Figure 3.24

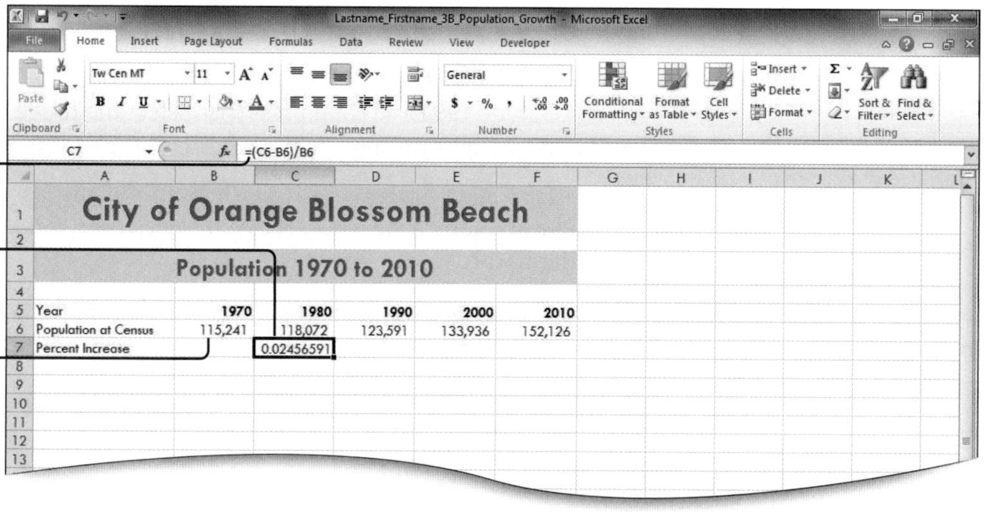

Formula Bar displays formula

Formula result in cell C7 (yours may display *0.02*)

Values entered for population, Comma Style with no decimals applied

9 With cell **C7** active, on the **Home tab**, in the **Number group**, click the **Percent Style** button %, and then examine the formula in the **Formula Bar**.

> The mathematical formula *rate = amount of increase/base* is used to calculated the percentage rate of population increase from 1970 to 1980. The formula is applied as follows:

> First, determine the *amount of increase* by subtracting the *base*—the starting point represented by the 1970 population—from the 1980 population. Thus, the *amount of increase* = 118,072 – 115,241 or 2,831. Between 1970 and 1980, the population increased by 2,831 people. In the formula, this calculation is represented by *C6-B6*.

> Second, calculate the *rate*—what the amount of increase (2,831) represents as a percentage of the base (1970's population of 115,241). Determine this by dividing the amount of increase (2,831) by the base (115,241). Thus, 2,831 divided by 115,241 is equal to 0.02456591 or, when formatted as a percent, 2%.

10 In the **Formula Bar**, locate the parentheses enclosing *C6-B6*.

> Excel follows a set of mathematical rules called the *order of operations*, which has four basic parts:
>
> - Expressions within parentheses are processed first.
> - Exponentiation, if present, is performed before multiplication and division.
> - Multiplication and division are performed before addition and subtraction.
> - Consecutive operators with the same level of precedence are calculated from left to right.

11 Click cell **D7**, type **=** and then by typing, or using a combination of typing and clicking cells to reference them, construct a formula similar to the one in cell **C7** to calculate the rate of increase in population from 1980 to 1990. Compare your screen with Figure 3.25.

> Recall that the first step is to determine the *amount of increase*—1990 population minus 1980 population—and then to write the calculation so that Excel performs this operation first; that is, place it in parentheses.
>
> The second step is to divide the result of the calculation in parentheses by the *base*—the population for 1980.

Figure 3.25

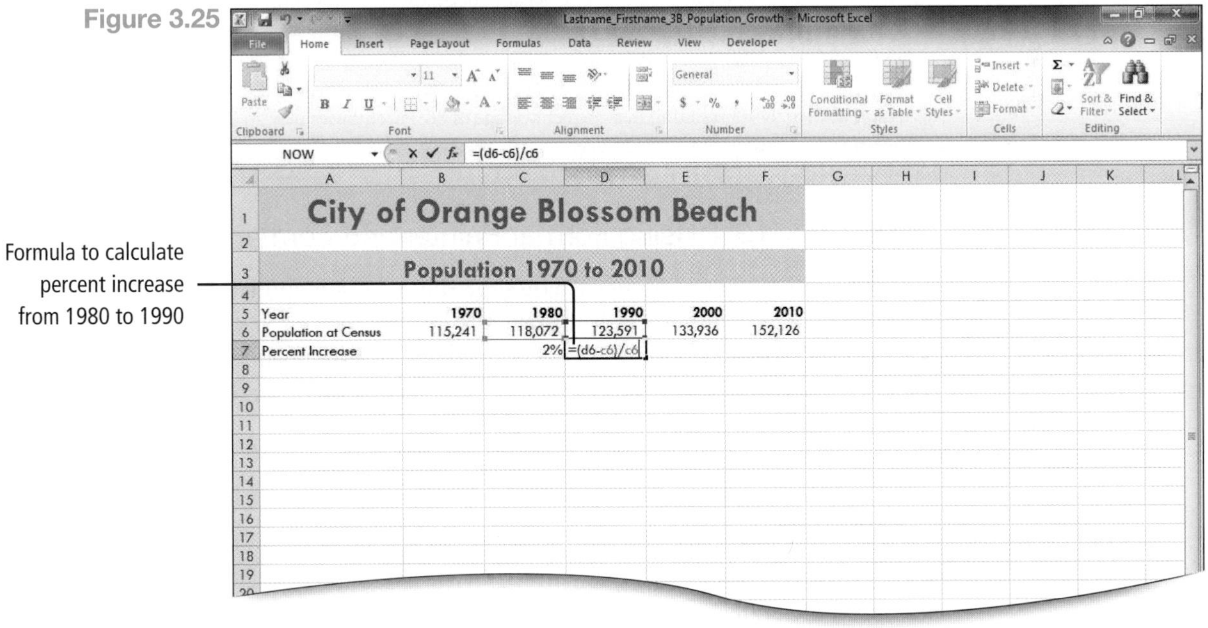

Formula to calculate percent increase from 1980 to 1990

12 Press Enter; your result is *0.04674267* (or *0.05*). Format cell **D7** with the **Percent Style** %.

> Your result is *5%*; Excel rounds up or down to format percentages.

13 With cell **D7** selected, drag the fill handle to the right through cell **F7**. Click any empty cell to cancel the selection, **Save** your workbook, and then compare your screen with Figure 3.26.

> Because this formula uses relative cell references—that is, for each year, the formula is the same but the values used are relative to the formula's location—you can copy the formula in this manner. For example, the result for 1990 uses the 1980 population as the base, the result for 2000 uses the 1990 population as the base, and the result for 2010 uses the 2000 population as the base.
>
> The formula results show the percent of increase for each 10-year period between 1970 and 2010. You can see that in each 10-year period, the population has grown as much as 14%—from 2000 to 2010—and as little as 2%—from 1970 to 1980.

Figure 3.26

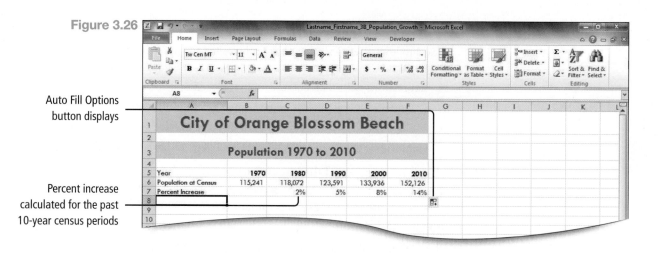

Auto Fill Options button displays

Percent increase calculated for the past 10-year census periods

---

More Knowledge | Use of Parentheses in a Formula

When writing a formula in Excel, use parentheses to communicate the order in which the operations should occur. For example, to average three test scores of 100, 50, and 90 that you scored on three different tests, you would add the test scores and then divide by the number of test scores in the list. If you write this formula as =100+50+90/3, the result would be 180, because Excel would first divide 90 by 3 and then add 100+50+30. Excel would do so because the order of operations states that multiplication and division are calculated *before* addition and subtraction.

The correct way to write this formula is =(100+50+90)/3. Excel will add the three values, and then divide the result by 3, or 240/3 resulting in a correct average of 80. Parentheses play an important role in ensuring that you get the correct result in your formulas.

Activity 3.13 | Using Format Painter and Formatting as You Type

You can format numbers as you type them. When you type numbers in a format that Excel recognizes, Excel automatically applies that format to the cell. Recall that once applied, cell formats remain with the cell, even if the cell contents are deleted. In this activity, you will format cells by typing the numbers with percent signs and use Format Painter to copy text (non-numeric) formats.

1 Leave **row 8** blank, and then click cell **A9**. Type **Projected Future Population** and then press Enter.

> **Another Way**
>
> On the Home tab, in the Clipboard group, click the Format Painter button.

2 Point to cell **A3**, right-click, on the Mini toolbar, click the **Format Painter** button, and then click cell **A9**.

> The format of cell A3 is *painted*—applied to—cell A9, including the merging and centering of the text across the range A9:F9.

3 Leave **row 10** blank, and then click cell **A11**, type **Estimated Growth Rate** and then press Enter.

4 Leave **row 12** blank, and then click cell **A13**. Type **Year** and then in cell **A14**, type **Projected Population**

5 In cell **B13**, type **2010** and then press Tab. In cell **C13**, type **2020** and then press Tab.

6 Select the range **B13:C13**, and then drag the fill handle through cell **F13** to extend the pattern of years to *2050*. Apply **Bold** to the selected range. Compare your screen with Figure 3.27.

Figure 3.27

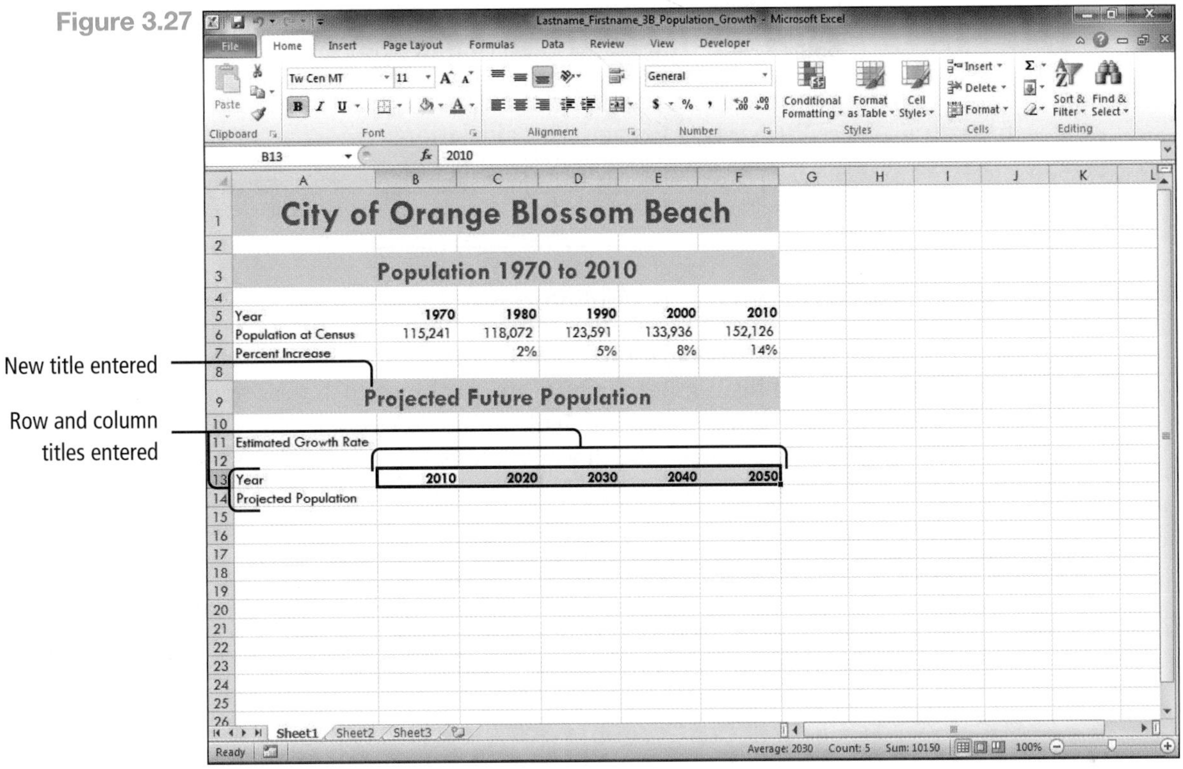

New title entered

Row and column
titles entered

7 Click cell **B14**, and then on the **Home tab**, in the **Number group**, notice that the **Number Format** box indicates *General*. Then, being sure to type the comma, type **152,126**

8 On the **Formula Bar**, click the **Enter** button ✓ to keep the cell active, and then in the **Number group**, notice that the format changed to *Number*.

9 Press Del, and then in the **Number group**, notice that the *Number* format is still indicated.

> Recall that deleting the contents of a cell does not delete the cell's formatting.

10 *Without* typing a comma, in cell **B14**, type **152126** and then press Enter.

> The comma displays even though you did not type it. When you type a number and include a formatting symbol such as a comma or dollar sign, Excel applies the format to the cell. Thus, if you delete the contents of the cell and type in the cell again, the format you established remains applied to the cell. This is referred to as *format as you type*.

11 Examine the format of the value in cell **B14**, and then compare it to the format in cell **B6** where you used the **Comma Style** button to format the cell. Notice that the number in cell **B14** is flush with the right edge of the cell, but the number in cell **B6** leaves a small amount of space on the right edge.

> When you type commas as you enter numbers, Excel applies the *Number* format, which does *not* leave a space at the right of the number for a closing parenthesis in the event of a negative number. This is different from the format that is applied when you use the *Comma Style* button on the Ribbon or Mini toolbar, as you did for the numbers entered in row 6. Recall that the Comma Style format applied from either the Ribbon or the Mini toolbar leaves space on the right for a closing parenthesis in the event of a negative number.

12 In cell **B11**, type **8%** Select the range **A11:B11**, and then from the Mini toolbar, apply **Bold** [B] and **Italic** [I]. **Save** [💾] your workbook.

More Knowledge | Percentage Calculations

When you type a percentage into a cell—for example *8%*—the percentage format, without decimal points, displays in both the cell and the Formula Bar. Excel will, however, use the decimal value of *0.08* for actual calculations.

Activity 3.14 | Calculating a Value After an Increase

A growing population results in increased use of city services. Thus, city planners in Orange Blossom Beach must estimate how much the population will increase in the future. The calculations you made in the previous activity show that the population has increased at varying rates during each 10-year period from 1970 to 2010, ranging from a low of 2% to a high of 14% per 10-year census period.

Population data from the state and surrounding areas suggests that future growth will trend close to that of the recent past. To plan for the future, Ms. Darius wants to prepare three forecasts of the city's population based on the percentage increases in 2000, in 2010, and for a percentage increase halfway between the two; that is, for 8%, 11%, and 14%. In this activity, you will calculate the population that would result from an 8% increase.

1 Click cell **C14**. Type **=b14*(100%+b11)** and then on the **Formula Bar**, click the **Enter** [✓] button to display a result of *164296.08*. Compare your screen with Figure 3.28.

This formula calculates what the population will be in the year 2020 assuming an increase of 8% over 2010's population. Use the mathematical formula *value after increase = base ×* *percent for new value* to calculate a value after an increase as follows:

First, establish the *percent for new value*. The **percent for new value = base percent +** **percent of increase**. The *base percent* of 100% represents the base population and the *percent of increase* in this instance is 8%. Thus, the population will equal 100% of the base year plus 8% of the base year. This can be expressed as 108% or 1.08. In this formula, you will use 100% + the rate in cell B11, which is 8%, to equal 108%.

Second, enter a reference to the cell that contains the *base*—the population in 2010. The base value resides in cell B14—*152,126*.

Third, calculate the *value after increase*. Because in each future 10-year period the increase will be based on 8%—an absolute value located in cell B11—this cell reference can be formatted as absolute by typing dollar signs.

Figure 3.28

Formula includes absolute reference to cell B11

Formula result

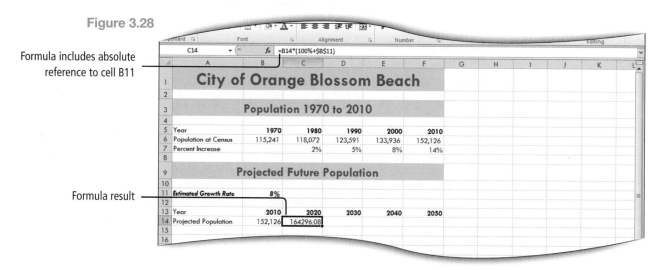

416 **Excel** | Chapter 3: Analyzing Data with Pie Charts, Line Charts, and What-If Analysis Tools

2 With cell **C14** as the active cell, drag the fill handle to copy the formula to the range **D14:F14**.

3 Point to cell **B14**, right-click, click the **Format Painter** 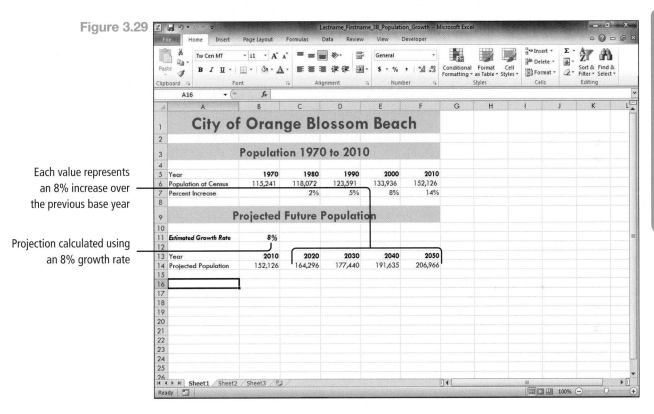 button, and then select the range **C14:F14**. Click an empty cell to cancel the selection, click **Save** and then compare your screen with Figure 3.29.

> This formula uses a relative cell address—B14—for the *base*; the population in the previous 10-year period is used in each of the formulas in cells D14:F14 as the *base* value. Because the reference to the *percent of increase* in cell B11 is an absolute reference, each *value after increase* is calculated with the value from cell B11.

> The population projected for 2020—*164,296*—is an increase of 8% over the population in 2010. The projected population in 2030—*177,440*—is an increase of 8% over the population in 2020 and so on.

Figure 3.29

Each value represents an 8% increase over the previous base year

Projection calculated using an 8% growth rate

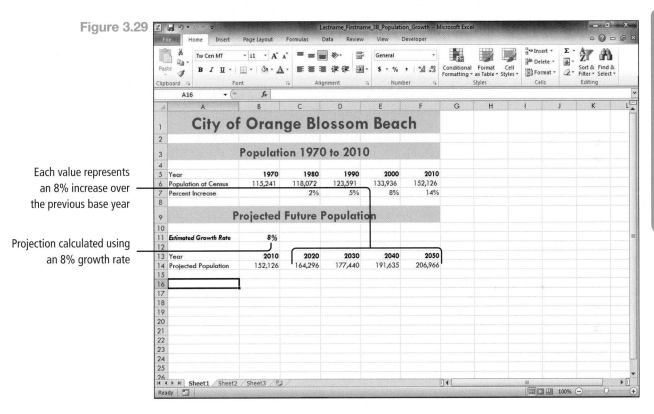

More Knowledge | Percent Increase or Decrease

The basic formula for calculating an increase or decrease can be done in two parts. First determine the percent by which the base value will be increased or decreased, and then add or subtract the results to the base. The formula can be simplified by using (1+amount of increase) or (1–amount of decrease), where 1, rather than 100%, represents the whole. Thus, the formula used in Step 1 of Activity 3.14 could also be written =b14*(1+b11), or =(b14*b11)+b14.

Objective 6 | Answer What-If Questions by Changing Values in a Worksheet

If a formula depends on the value in a cell, you can see what effect it will have if you change the value in that cell. Then, you can copy the value computed by the formula and paste it into another part of the worksheet where you can compare it to other values.

Activity 3.15 | Answering What-If Questions and Using Paste Special

A growth rate of 8% in each 10-year period will result in a population of almost 207,000 people by 2050. The city planners will likely ask: *What if* the population grows at the highest rate (14%)? *What if* the population grows at a rate that is halfway between the 2000 and 2010 rates (11%)?

Because the formulas are constructed to use the growth rate displayed in cell B11, Ms. Darius can answer these questions quickly by entering different percentages into that cell. To keep the results of each set of calculations so they can be compared, you will paste the results of each what-if question into another area of the worksheet.

1 Leave **row 15** blank, and then click cell **A16**. Type **Growth Estimates 2020 to 2050** and then press Enter. Use **Format Painter** ☑ to copy the format from cell **A9** to cell **A16**.

2 Select the range **A11:B11**, right-click to display the Mini toolbar, click the **Fill Color button arrow** ◇ ▾, and then under **Theme Colors**, in the first column, click the third color—**White, Background 1, Darker 15%**.

3 Leave **row 17** blank, and then in the range **A18:A21**, type the following row titles:

Year

8% Growth Rate

11% Growth Rate

14% Growth Rate

> **Another Way**
>
> Press Ctrl + C; or, on the Home tab, in the Clipboard group, click the Copy button.

4 Select the range **B13:F13**, right-click over the selection, and then on the shortcut menu, click **Copy**.

5 Point to cell **B18**, right-click, and then on the shortcut menu, under **Paste Options**, click the **Paste** button 📋.

Recall that when pasting a group of copied cells to a target range, you need only point to or select the first cell of the range.

6 Select and **Copy** the range **B14:F14**, and then **Paste** it beginning in cell **B19**.

7 Click cell **C19**. On the **Formula Bar**, notice that the *formula* was pasted into the cell, as shown in Figure 3.30.

> This is *not* the desired result. The actual *calculated values*—not the formulas—are needed in the range.

Figure 3.30

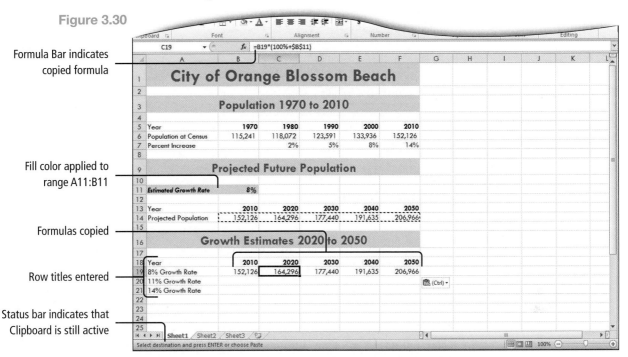

Formula Bar indicates copied formula

Fill color applied to range A11:B11

Formulas copied

Row titles entered

Status bar indicates that Clipboard is still active

8 On the Quick Access Toolbar, click the **Undo** button. With the range **B14:F14** still copied to the Clipboard—as indicated by the message in the status bar and the moving border—point to cell **B19**, and then right-click to display the shortcut menu.

9 Under **Paste Options**, point to **Paste Special** to display another gallery, and then under **Paste Values**, point to the **Values & Number Formatting** button to display the ScreenTip as shown in Figure 3.31.

> The ScreenTip *Values & Number Formatting (A)* indicates that you can paste the *calculated values* that result from the calculation of formulas along with the formatting applied to the copied cells. *(A)* is the keyboard shortcut for this command.

Figure 3.31

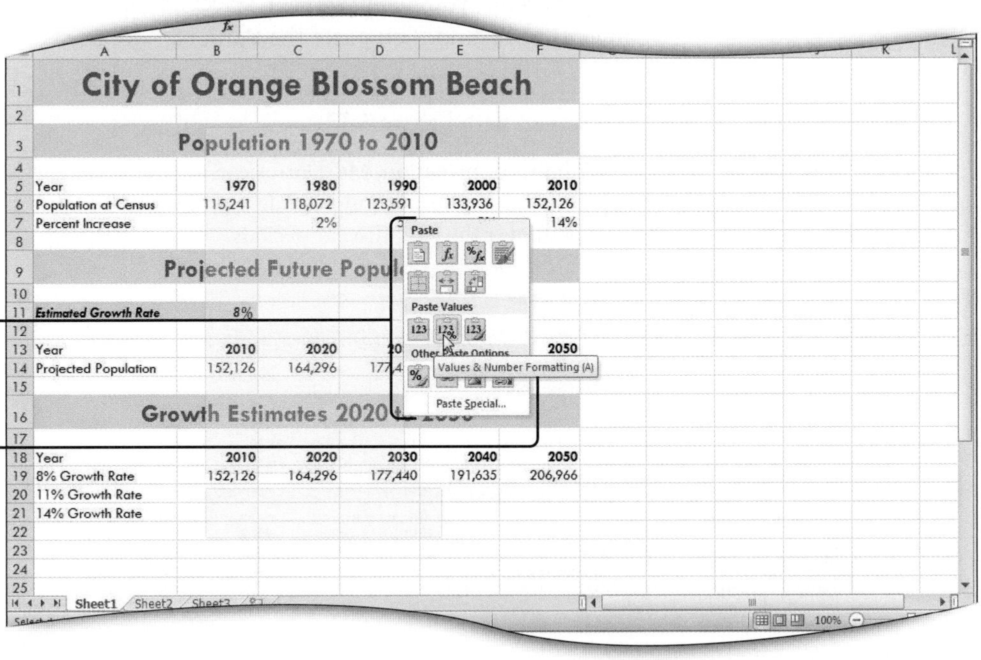

Gallery of Paste Special buttons

Values & Number Formatting ScreenTip

10 Click the **Values & Number Formatting** button 🔢, click cell **C19** and notice on the **Formula Bar** that the cell contains a *value*, not a formula. Press [Esc] to cancel the moving border. Compare your screen with Figure 3.32.

> The calculated estimates based on an 8% growth rate are pasted along with their formatting.

Figure 3.32

Formula Bar indicates the value

	A	B	C	D	E	F	G	H	I	J	K
	C19		164296.08								
1	**City of Orange Blossom Beach**										
2											
3		**Population 1970 to 2010**									
4											
5	Year	1970	1980	1990	2000	2010					
6	Population at Census	115,241	118,072	123,591	133,936	152,126					
7	Percent Increase		2%	5%	8%	14%					
8											
9		**Projected Future Population**									
10											
11	*Estimated Growth Rate*	8%									
12											
13	Year	2010	2020	2030	2040	2050					
14	Projected Population	152,126	164,296	177,440	191,635	206,966					
15											
16		**Growth Estimates 2020 to 2050**									
17											
18	Year	2010	2020	2030	2040	2050					
19	8% Growth Rate	152,126	164,296	177,440	191,635	206,966					
20	11% Growth Rate										
21	14% Growth Rate										
22											

11 Click cell **B11**. Type **11** and then watch the values in **C14:F14** *recalculate* as, on the **Formula Bar**, you click the **Enter** button ✓.

> The value *11%* is halfway between 8% and 14%—the growth rates from the two most recent 10-year periods.

12 Select and **Copy** the new values in the range **B14:F14**. Point to cell **B20**, right-click, and then on the shortcut menu, point to **Paste Special**. Under **Paste Values**, click the **Values & Number Formatting** button 🔢.

13 In cell **B11**, change the percentage by typing **14** and then press [Enter]. Notice that the projected values in **C14:F14** recalculate.

14 Using the skills you just practiced, select and copy the recalculated values in the range **B14:F14**, and then paste the **Values & Number Formatting** to the range **B21:F21**.

15 Press [Esc] to cancel the moving border, click cell **A1**, click **Save** 💾, and then compare your screen with Figure 3.33.

> With this information, Ms. Darius can answer several what-if questions about the future population of the city and provide a range of population estimates based on the rates of growth over the past 10-year periods.

Figure 3.33

			2%	5%			
9		**Projected Future Population**					
10							
11	*Estimated Growth Rate*	*14%*					
12							
13	Year	2010	2020	2030	2040	2050	
14	Projected Population	152,126	173,424	197,703	225,381	256,935	
15							
16		**Growth Estimates 2020 to 2050**					
17							
18	Year	2010	2020	2030	2040	2050	
19	8% Growth Rate	152,126	164,296	177,440	191,635	206,966	
20	11% Growth Rate	152,126	168,860	187,434	208,052	230,938	
21	14% Growth Rate	152,126	173,424	197,703	225,381	256,935	
22							

Values copied for each what-if question

Objective 7 | Chart Data with a Line Chart

A *line chart* displays trends over time. Time is displayed along the bottom axis and the data point values connect with a line. The curve and direction of the line make trends obvious to the reader.

Whereas the columns in a column chart and the pie slices in a pie chart emphasize the distinct values of each data point, the line in a line chart emphasizes the flow from one data point value to the next.

Activity 3.16 | Inserting Multiple Rows and Creating a Line Chart

So that city council members can see how the population has increased over the past five census periods, in this activity, you will chart the actual population figures from 1970 to 2010 in a line chart.

1 In the **row header area**, point to **row 8** to display the ➡ pointer, and then drag down to select **rows 8:24**. Right-click over the selection, and then click **Insert** to insert the same number of blank rows as you selected. Compare your screen with Figure 3.34.

Use this technique to insert multiple rows quickly.

Figure 3.34

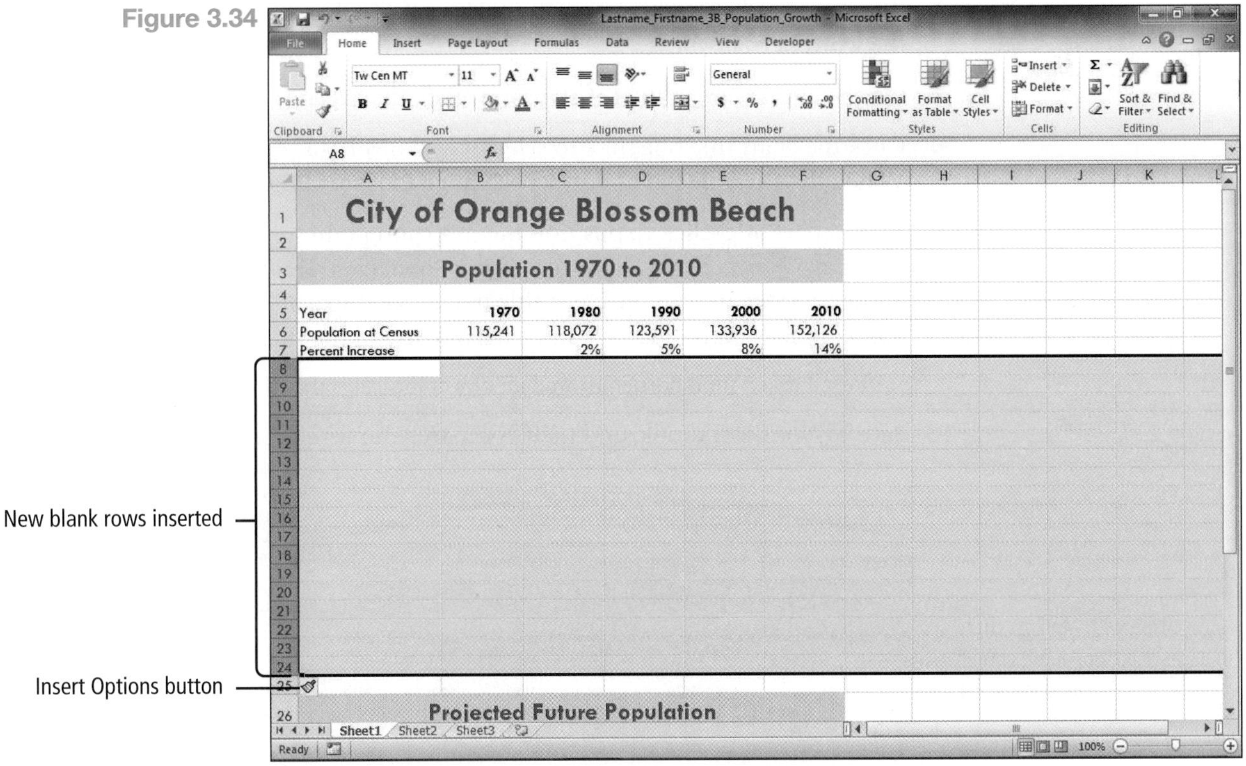

New blank rows inserted

Insert Options button

2 Near **row 25**, click the **Insert Options** button ⬧, and then click the **Clear Formatting** option button to clear any formatting from these rows.

You will use this blank area in which to position your line chart.

3 Select the range **A6:F6**. On the **Insert tab**, in the **Charts group**, click the **Line** button.

4 In the displayed gallery of line charts, in the second row, point to the first chart type to display the ScreenTip *Line with Markers*. Compare your screen with Figure 3.35.

Figure 3.35

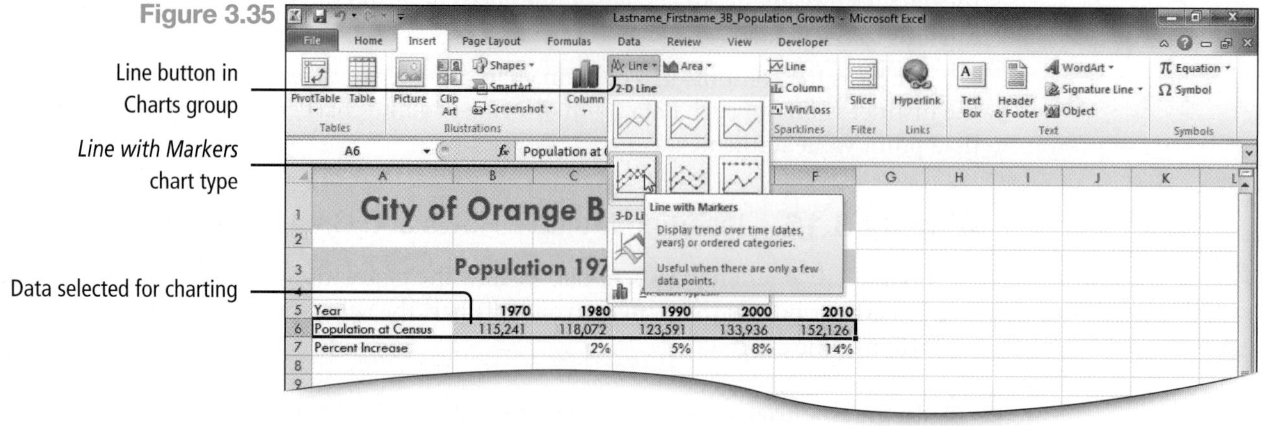

Line button in Charts group

Line with Markers chart type

Data selected for charting

5 Click the **Line with Markers** chart type to create the chart as an embedded chart in the worksheet.

6 Point to the border of the chart to display the ⬚ pointer, and then drag the chart so that its upper left corner is positioned in cell **A9**, aligned approximately under the *t* in the word *Percent* above.

7 On the **Layout tab**, in the **Labels group**, click the **Legend** button, and then click **None**.

8 Click the chart title one time to select it and display a solid border around the title. Watch the **Formula Bar** as you type **Orange Blossom Beach** and then press Enter.

9 In the chart title, click to position the insertion point following the *h* in *Beach*, and then press Enter to begin a new line. Type **Population Growth 1970 to 2010** Click the dashed border around the chart title to change it to a solid border, right-click, and then on the Mini toolbar, change the **Font Size** of the title to **20**.

Recall that a solid border around an object indicates that the entire object is selected.

10 **Save** 🖫 your workbook, and then compare your screen with Figure 3.36.

Figure 3.36

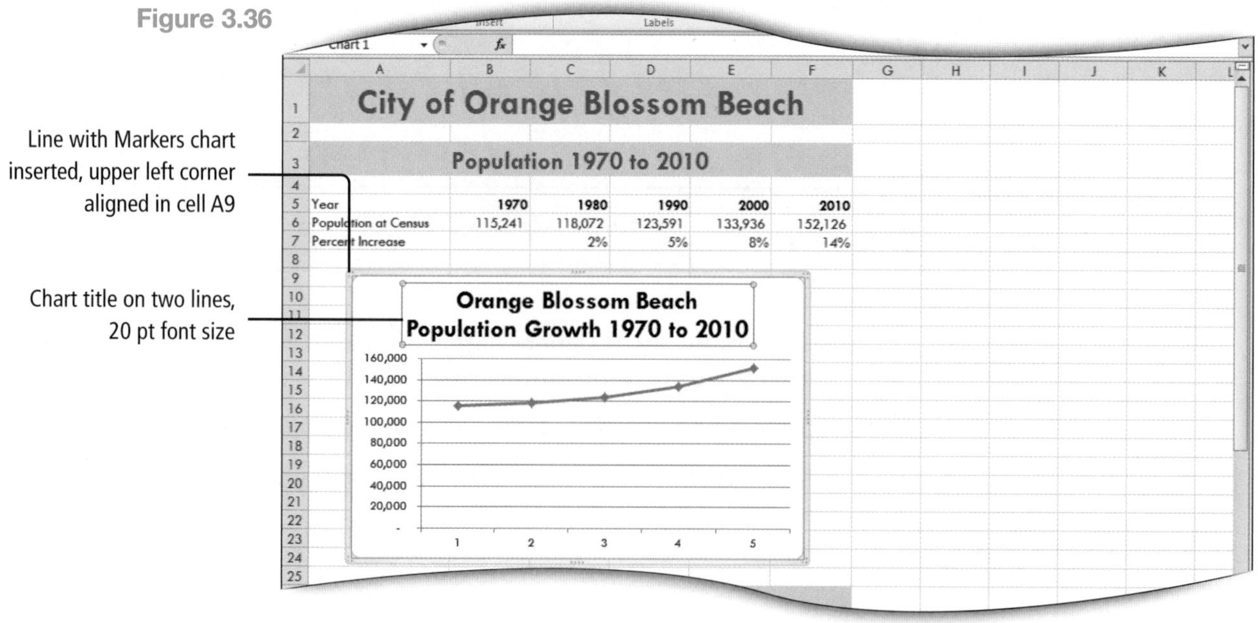

Line with Markers chart inserted, upper left corner aligned in cell A9

Chart title on two lines, 20 pt font size

Activity 3.17 | Formatting Axes in a Line Chart

An *axis* is a line that serves as a frame of reference for measurement; it borders the chart *plot area*. The plot area is the area bounded by the axes, including all the data series. Recall that the area along the bottom of a chart that identifies the categories of data is referred to as the *category axis* or the *x-axis*. Recall also that the area along the left side of a chart that shows the range of numbers for the data points is referred to as the *value axis* or the *y-axis*.

In this activity, you will change the category axis to include the names of the 10-year census periods and adjust the numeric scale of the value axis.

Another Way

At the bottom of the chart, point to any of the numbers 1 through 5 to display the ScreenTip *Horizontal (Category) Axis*. Right-click, and then from the shortcut menu, click Select Data.

1 Be sure the chart is still selected—a pale frame surrounds the chart area. Click the **Design tab**, and then in the **Data group**, click the **Select Data** button.

2 On the right side of the displayed **Select Data Source** dialog box, under **Horizontal (Category) Axis Labels**, locate the **Edit** button, as shown in Figure 3.37.

Figure 3.37

Select Data Source dialog box

Edit button to edit labels on the category axis

Category axis requires labels to identify each 10-year period

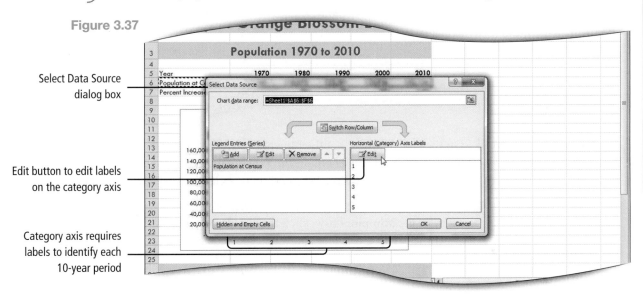

3 In the right column, click the **Edit** button. If necessary, drag the title bar of the **Axis Labels** dialog box to the right of the chart so that it is not blocking your view of the data, and then select the years in the range **B5:F5**. Compare your screen with Figure 3.38.

Figure 3.38

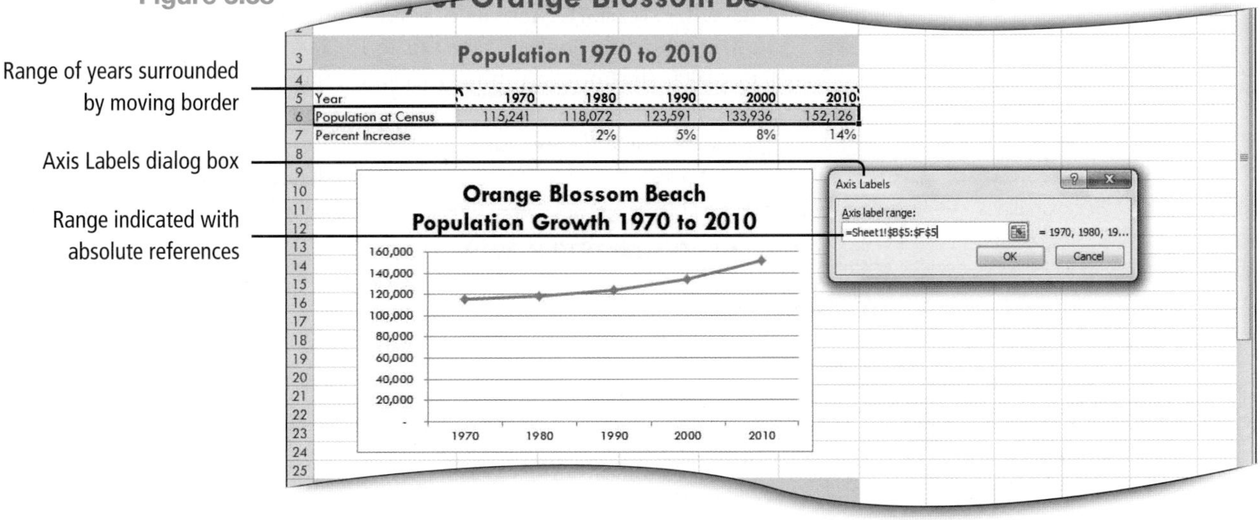

Range of years surrounded by moving border

Axis Labels dialog box

Range indicated with absolute references

Project 3B: Growth Projection with Line Chart | **Excel** 423

4 In the **Axis Labels** dialog box, click **OK**, and notice that in the right column of the **Select Data Source** dialog box, the years display as the category labels. Click **OK** to close the **Select Data Source** dialog box. Compare your screen with Figure 3.39.

Figure 3.39

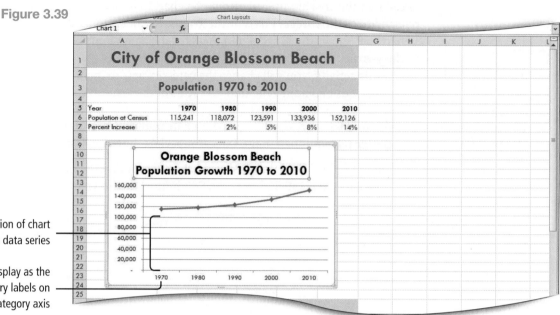

Lower portion of chart unused by the data series

Years display as the category labels on the category axis

Another Way

On the left side of the chart, point to any of the numbers to display the ScreenTip *Vertical (Value) Axis*, and then right-click. From the shortcut menu, click Format Axis.

5 On the chart, notice that the blue line—the data series—does not display in the lower portion of the chart. Then, on the **Layout tab**, in the **Axes group**, click the **Axes** button. Point to **Primary Vertical Axis**, and then click **More Primary Vertical Axis Options**.

6 In the **Format Axis** dialog box, on the left, be sure **Axis Options** is selected. On the right, in the **Minimum** row, click the **Fixed** option button. In the box to the right, select the existing text *0.0*, and then type **100000**

Because none of the population figures are under 100,000, changing the Minimum number to 100,000 will enable the data series to occupy more of the plot area.

7 In the **Major unit** row, click the **Fixed** option button, select the text in the box to the right *20000.0*, and then type **10000** In the lower right corner, click **Close**. **Save** your workbook, and then compare your screen with Figure 3.40.

The *Major unit* value determines the spacing between *tick marks* and thus between the gridlines in the plot area. Tick marks are the short lines that display on an axis at regular intervals. By default, Excel started the values at zero and increased in increments of 20,000. By setting the Minimum value on the value axis to 100,000 and changing the Major unit from 20,000 to 10,000, the line chart shows a clearer trend in the population growth.

Figure 3.40

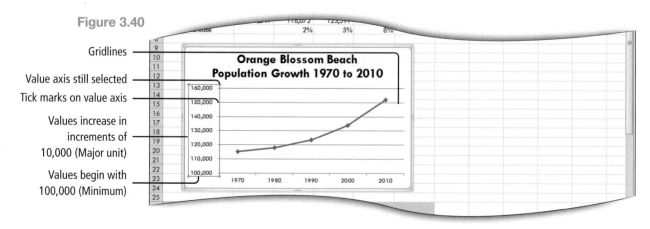

Gridlines

Value axis still selected

Tick marks on value axis

Values increase in increments of 10,000 (Major unit)

Values begin with 100,000 (Minimum)

Activity 3.18 | Formatting the Chart and Plot Areas

An Excel chart has two background elements—the plot area and the chart area—which, by default display a single fill color. To add visual appeal to a chart, you can insert a graphic image as the background.

When formatting chart elements, there are several ways to display the dialog boxes that you need. You can right-click the area you want to format and choose a command on the shortcut menu. In this activity, you will use the Chart Elements box in the Current Selection group on the Format tab of the Ribbon, which is convenient if you are changing the format of a variety of chart elements.

1 Click the **Format tab**, and then in the **Current Selection group**, point to the small arrow to the right of the first item in the group to display the ScreenTip *Chart Elements*. Compare your screen with Figure 3.41.

From the ***Chart Elements box***, you can select a chart element so that you can format it.

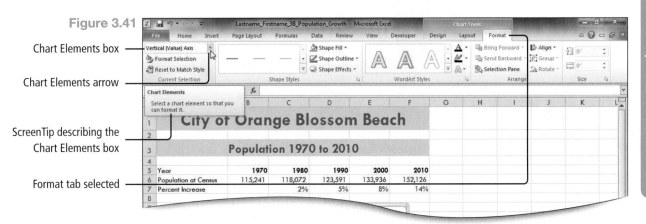

Figure 3.41

Chart Elements box

Chart Elements arrow

ScreenTip describing the Chart Elements box

Format tab selected

2 Click the **Chart Elements arrow**, and then from the displayed list, click **Chart Area**. Directly below the **Chart Elements** box, click the **Format Selection** button.

The Format Chart Area dialog box displays. Use this technique to select the chart element that you want to format, and then click the Format Selection button to display the appropriate dialog box.

3 In the **Format Chart Area** dialog box, on the left, be sure that **Fill** is selected.

4 On the right, under **Fill**, click the **Picture or texture fill** option button, and then under **Insert from**, click the **File** button. In the **Insert Picture** dialog box, navigate to your student files, and then insert the picture **e03B_Beach**. Leave the dialog box open, and then compare your screen with Figure 3.42.

Figure 3.42

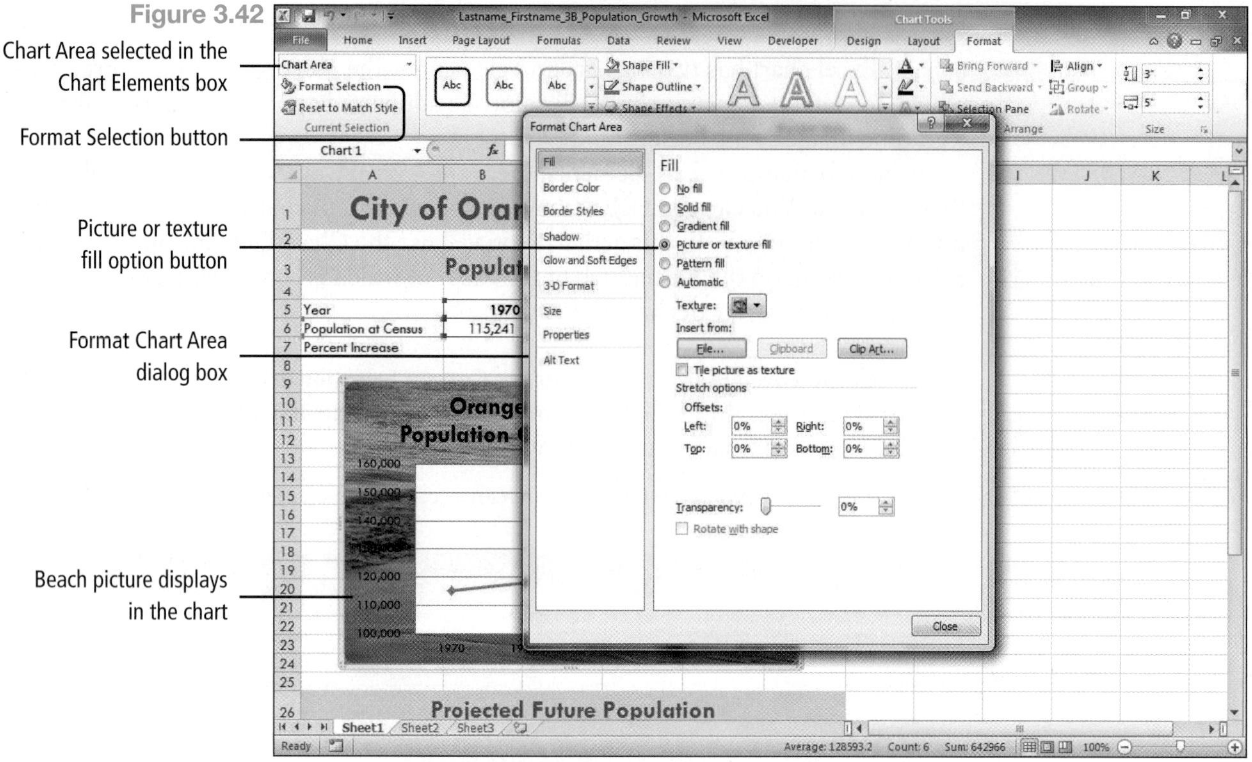

Chart Area selected in the
Chart Elements box

Format Selection button

Picture or texture
fill option button

Format Chart Area
dialog box

Beach picture displays
in the chart

5 In the **Format Chart Area** dialog box, on the left, click **Border Color**, on the right click the **Solid line** option button, click the **Color arrow**, and then under **Theme Colors**, in the fourth column, click the first color—**Dark Teal, Text 2**.

6 On the left, click **Border Styles**. On the right, select the text in the **Width** box and type **4 pt** At the bottom select the **Rounded corners** check box, and then **Close** the dialog box.

> A 4 pt teal border with rounded corners frames the chart.

7 In the **Current Selection group**, click the **Chart Elements arrow**, on the list click **Plot Area**, and then click the **Format Selection** button.

8 In the **Format Plot Area** dialog box, on the left, be sure that **Fill** is selected, and then on the right, click the **No fill** option button. **Close** the dialog box.

> The fill is removed from the plot area so that the picture is visible as the background.

9 Click the **Chart Elements arrow**, on the list click **Vertical (Value) Axis**, and then click the **Format Selection** button.

10 In the **Format Axis** dialog box, on the left click **Line Color**, on the right click the **Solid line** option button, click the **Color arrow**, and then click the first color—**White, Background 1**. Compare your screen with Figure 3.43.

> The vertical line with tick marks displays in white.

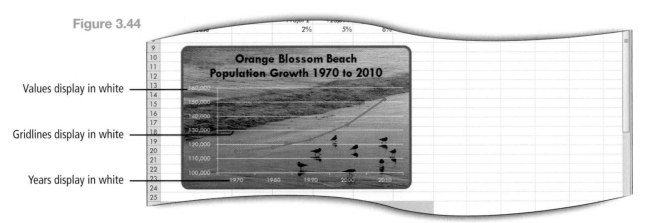

Figure 3.43

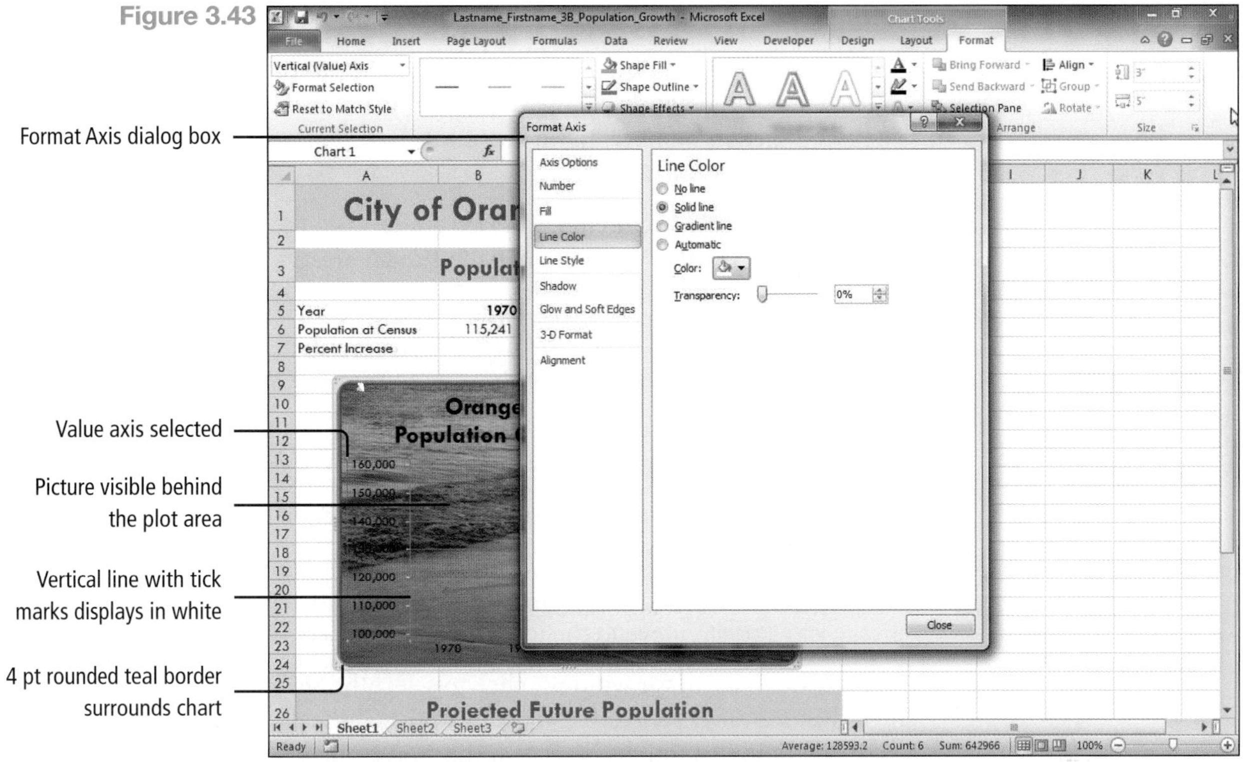

Format Axis dialog box

Value axis selected

Picture visible behind the plot area

Vertical line with tick marks displays in white

4 pt rounded teal border surrounds chart

11 **Close** the dialog box. From the **Chart Elements** box, select the **Vertical (Value) Axis Major Gridlines**, and then click **Format Selection**. Change the **Line Color** to a **Solid line**, and then apply the **White, Background 1** color. **Close** the dialog box.

12 From the **Chart Elements** list, select the **Horizontal (Category) Axis**, and then click **Format Selection**. In the **Format Axis** dialog box, change the **Line Color** to a **Solid line**, and then apply the **White, Background 1** color. **Close** the dialog box.

13 Point to any of the numbers on the vertical value axis, right-click, and then on the Mini toolbar, change the **Font Color** [A ▾] to **White, Background 1**. Point to any of the years on the horizontal category axis, right-click, and then change the **Font Color** [A ▾] to **White, Background 1**.

> For basic text-formatting changes—for example changing the size, font, style, or font color—you must leave the Chart Tools on the Ribbon and use commands from the Home tab or the Mini toolbar.

14 Click any cell to deselect the chart, press [Ctrl] + [Home] to move to the top of your worksheet, click **Save** [🖫], and then compare your screen with Figure 3.44.

Figure 3.44

Values display in white

Gridlines display in white

Years display in white

Activity 3.19 | Preparing and Printing Your Worksheet

1 From **Backstage** view, display the **Document Panel**. In the **Author** box, replace the existing text with your firstname and lastname. In the **Subject** box, type your course name and section number. In the **Keywords** box, type **population** and then **Close** [×] the **Document Information Panel**.

2 Click the **Insert tab**, and then in the **Text group**, click the **Header & Footer** button to switch to **Page Layout View** and open the **Header area**.

3 In the **Navigation group**, click the **Go to Footer** button, click just above the word *Footer*, and then in the **Header & Footer Elements group**, click the **File Name** button. Click in a cell just above the footer to exit the **Footer area** and view your file name.

4 Click the **Page Layout tab**. In the **Page Setup group**, click the **Margins** button, and then at the bottom of the **Margins** gallery, click **Custom Margins**.

5 In the displayed **Page Setup** dialog box, under **Center on page**, select the **Horizontally** check box. Click **OK** to close the dialog box.

6 On the status bar, click the **Normal** button ⊞ to return to Normal view, and then press Ctrl + Home to move to the top of your worksheet.

7 At the lower edge of the window, click to select the **Sheet2 tab**, hold down Ctrl, and then click the **Sheet3 tab** to select the two unused sheets. Right-click over the selected sheet tabs, and then on the displayed shortcut menu, click **Delete**.

8 **Save** 🖫 your workbook before printing or submitting. Press Ctrl + F2 to display the **Print Preview** to check your worksheet. Compare your screen with Figure 3.45.

Figure 3.45

Completed worksheet in Print Preview

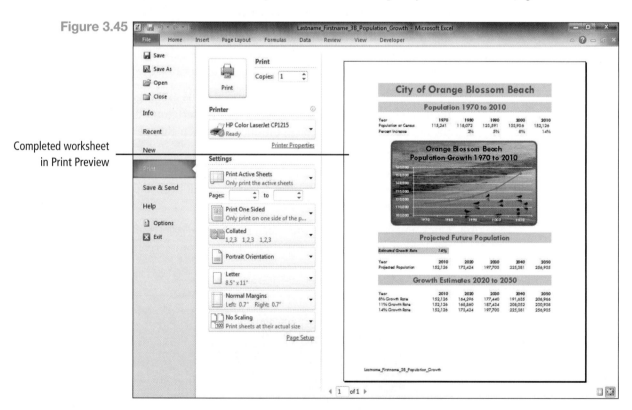

9 If necessary, return to the worksheet to make any necessary adjustments or corrections, and then **Save**.

10 Print or submit electronically as directed. If you are directed to submit printed formulas, refer to Activity 1.16 to do so.

11 If you printed your formulas, be sure to redisplay the worksheet by clicking the Show Formulas button to turn it off. From **Backstage** view, click **Close**. If the dialog box displays asking if you want to save changes, click **No** so that you do *not* save the changes you made for printing formulas. **Close** Excel.

End You have completed Project 3B ————————————————

GO! Beyond Office

Objective | Convert an Excel Worksheet to a Google Docs Spreadsheet

Google Docs is Google's free, Web-based word processor, spreadsheet, slide show, form, and data storage service. You can convert an Excel worksheet to a Google Docs spreadsheet.

> **Alert! | Working with Web-Based Applications and Services**
>
> Computer programs and services on the Web receive continuous updates and improvements. Thus, the steps to complete this Web-based Activity may differ from the ones shown. You can often look at the screens and the information presented to determine how to complete the Activity.

Activity | Converting an Excel Worksheet to a Google Docs Spreadsheet

In this activity, you will convert an Excel worksheet to a Google Docs spreadsheet.

1 If you do *not* have a Google account, skip to Step 2. Otherwise, start your Web browser. In the address bar, type **http://docs.google.com** and then press [Enter]. On the right side of the window, sign into your Google account and display the Google docs page. Now skip to Step 3.

2 Start your Web browser. In the address bar, type **http://docs.google.com** and then press [Enter]. On the right side of the window, click **Sign up for a new Google Account**. On the **Google accounts Sign up** page, under **Use your email provider** you already have, click **Windows Live Hotmail**. On the **Windows Live** page, sign in to your account. In the **Allow Access** page, click **Yes**. Under **Email**

address, click the **Save and continue** button to create the account and display the Google docs page.

3 Compare your screen with Figure A.

On the left side of the Google docs page are folders where you can organize your Google docs files and buttons that display options for creating new files and uploading files from your computer. In the center of the page, files that are stored in the selected folder display. Your screen may display files that you have created in Google docs. On the right, when a file is selected, a preview and other document information will display.

Figure A

4 On the left side of your screen, click the **Upload** button 📤, and then click **Files**. Navigate to your **Excel Chapter 3** folder, and then select **Lastname_Firstname_3B_Population_Growth**. Click **Open**. If the Upload settings message box displays, if necessary select the first check box, and then click **Start Upload** to display a message box that indicates the upload progress of your file.

5 When the title bar of the message box indicates *Upload complete*, **Close** ⊠ the message box.

At the top of the window, a yellow bar indicates that the upload is complete and in the center of your screen, your file name displays.

6 Click your **Lastname_Firstname_3B_Population Growth** file to open the file in Google docs.

The worksheet displays column letters and row numbers, data, and a chart. If necessary, maximize your window.

7 Click the edge of the chart to select it, and notice that in its upper left corner, *Chart 1* displays. Click **Chart 1** to display a menu, and then click **Delete chart**.

8 Select the range **A9:A25**. Click the **Edit menu**, and then click **Delete rows 9 - 25**.

The selected rows are deleted so that the *Projected Future Population* data displays below the *Population 1970 to 2010* data. The *Estimated Growth Rate* text in cell A11 does not display fully because column A is not wide enough to accommodate the text.

9 Point to the column divider between **columns A** and **B** to display the ⟷ pointer. Drag to the right about

one-quarter of an inch and then release the mouse button to widen the column. If the entire *Estimated Growth Rate* text does not fully display, widen the column again until it does.

10 Scroll down to view the lower portion of the spreadsheet. Below the spreadsheet, in the **Add** box, type **30** and then click **Add** to add 30 additional rows to the spreadsheet.

11 Select the range **A18:F21**. Click the **Insert menu**, and then click **Chart**. Under **Recommended charts**, click **column chart**, and then under **Data**, select the **Use row 18 as headers** check box so that the years display in the legend. Click the **Customize tab**, and then in the **Chart title** box, type **Growth Estimates 2010 to 2050**

12 In the lower left corner of the **Chart Editor**, click the **Insert** button to insert the chart. Select the chart, and then point to the upper chart area so that a small hand pointer displays. Drag down to position the chart in **row 23**. Compare your screen with Figure B.

13 With the entire chart displayed in the spreadsheet, display the **Start** menu 🏁, and then click **All Programs**. On the list of programs, click the **Accessories folder**, and then click **Snipping Tool**. In the **Snipping Tool** dialog box, click the **New arrow**. On the displayed list, click **Full-screen Snip**, and then click the **Save Snip** button 💾. In the **Save As** dialog box, navigate to your **Excel Chapter 3** folder, be sure the **Save as type** box displays **JPEG file**, and then in the **File name** box, type **Lastname_Firstname_3B_Google_Docs_Snip** Click **Save**. Sign out of your Google account. **Close** all open windows, and then submit your snip file as directed.

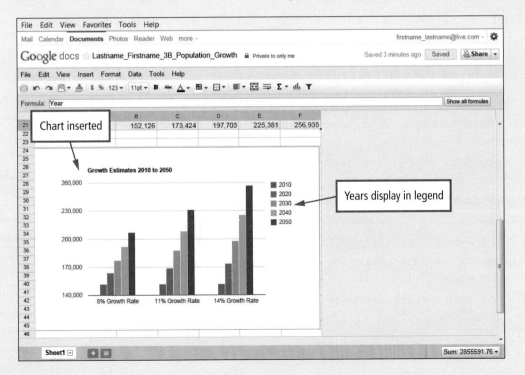

Figure B

Content-Based Assessments

Summary

In this chapter, you created a pie chart to show how the parts of a budget contribute to a total budget. Then you formatted the pie chart attractively and used Goal Seek. You also practiced using parentheses in a formula, calculating the percentage rate of an increase, answering what-if questions, and charting data in a line chart to show the flow of data over time.

Key Terms

Matching

Match each term in the second column with its correct definition in the first column by writing the letter of the term on the blank line in front of the correct definition.

_____ 1. A chart that shows the relationship of each part to a whole.

_____ 2. The term used to describe money set aside for the normal operating activities of a government entity such as a city.

_____ 3. In a formula, the address of a cell based on the relative position of the cell that contains the formula and the cell referred to.

_____ 4. A column, bar, area, dot, pie slice, or other symbol in a chart that represents a single data point.

_____ 5. A workbook sheet that contains only a chart.

_____ 6. A shape effect that uses shading and shadows to make the edges of a shape appear to be curved or angled.

_____ 7. The entire chart and all of its elements.

_____ 8. The process of changing the values in cells to see how those changes affect the outcome of formulas in a worksheet.

_____ 9. The mathematical formula to calculate a rate of increase.

A Axis

B Bevel

C Category axis

D Chart area

E Chart sheet

F Data marker

G Format as you type

H General Fund

I Order of operations

J Pie chart

K Rate = amount of increase/base

L Relative cell reference

M Tick marks

N Value axis

O What-if analysis

_____ 10. The mathematical rules for performing multiple calculations within a formula.

_____ 11. The Excel feature by which a cell takes on the formatting of the number typed into the cell.

_____ 12. A line that serves as a frame of reference for measurement and that borders the chart plot area.

_____ 13. The area along the bottom of a chart that identifies the categories of data; also referred to as the x-axis.

_____ 14. A numerical scale on the left side of a chart that shows the range of numbers for the data points; also referred to as the y-axis.

_____ 15. The short lines that display on an axis at regular intervals.

Multiple Choice

Circle the correct answer.

1. A sum of money set aside for a specific purpose is a:
   A. value axis   B. fund   C. rate

2. A cell reference that refers to a cell by its fixed position in a worksheet is referred to as being:
   A. absolute   B. relative   C. mixed

3. A value that originates in a worksheet cell and that is represented in a chart by a data marker is a data:
   A. point   B. cell   C. axis

4. Related data points represented by data markers are referred to as the data:
   A. slices   B. set   C. series

5. The action of pulling out a pie slice from a pie chart is called:
   A. extract   B. explode   C. plot

6. A gallery of text styles with which you can create decorative effects, such as shadowed or mirrored text is:
   A. WordArt   B. shape effects   C. text fill

7. The percent by which one number increases over another number is the percentage rate of:
   A. decrease   B. change   C. increase

8. A chart type that displays trends over time is a:
   A. pie chart   B. line chart   C. column chart

9. The area bounded by the axes of a chart, including all the data series, is the:
   A. chart area   B. plot area   C. axis area

10. The x-axis is also known as the:
    A. category axis   B. value axis   C. data axis

Excel | Chapter 3

Content-Based Assessments

Apply **3A** skills from these Objectives:

1 Chart Data with a Pie Chart
2 Format a Pie Chart
3 Edit a Workbook and Update a Chart
4 Use Goal Seek to Perform What-If Analysis

Skills Review | Project **3C** Improvement Expenditures

In the following Skills Review, you will edit a worksheet for Jennifer Carson, City Finance Manager, which details the city general fund facilities improvement expenditures. Your completed worksheets will look similar to Figure 3.46.

Project Files

For Project 3C, you will need the following file:

e03C_Improvement_Expenditures

You will save your workbook as:

Lastname_Firstname_3C_Improvement_Expenditures

Project Results

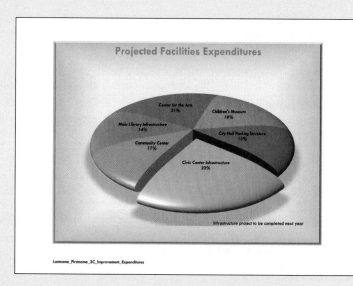

City of Orange Blossom Beach
General Fund Facilities Improvement Expenditures

	Projection for Next Fiscal Year Budget		
	Current Year Expenses	Projected Expenses for Next Fiscal Year	% of Total Projected Expenses
Center for the Arts	$ 752,600	$ 925,000	21%
Children's Museum	938,450	768,420	18%
City Hall Parking Structure	320,740	568,750	13%
Civic Center Infrastructure	897,500	974,650	23%
Community Center	355,250	476,850	11%
Main Library Infrastructure	378,750	597,560	14%
Total	$ 3,643,290	$ 4,311,230	

FACILITIES IMPROVEMENT EXPENDITURES

Projection: Main Library Infrastructure to Decrease from 14% to 12%

| Projected Amount: | $ 517,348 | 12% |

Lastname_Firstname_3C_Improvement_Expenditures

Figure 3.46

(Project 3C Improvement Expenditures continues on the next page)

Content-Based Assessments

1 **Start** Excel. From your student files, open the file **e03C_Improvement_Expenditures**. Save the file in your **Excel Chapter 3** folder as **Lastname_Firstname_3C_Improvement_Expenditures**

a. Click cell **D5**, and then type = to begin a formula. Click cell **C5**, type / and then click cell **C11**. Press F4 to make the reference to the value in cell **C11** absolute. On the **formula bar**, click the **Enter** button, and then fill the formula down through cell **D10**.

b. With the range **D5:D10** selected, right-click over the selection, and then on Mini toolbar, click the **Percent Style** button and the **Center** button.

2 Select the nonadjacent ranges **A5:A10** and **C5:C10** to select the expense names and the projected expenses. Click the **Insert tab**, and then in the **Charts group**, click **Pie**. Under **3-D Pie**, click the first chart—**Pie in 3-D**.

a. On the **Design tab**, in the **Location group**, click the **Move Chart** button. In the **Move Chart** dialog box, click the **New sheet** option button. In the **New sheet** box, replace the highlighted text *Chart1* by typing **Projected Expenditures Chart** and then click **OK**.

b. On the **Layout tab**, in the **Labels group**, click the **Chart Title** button, and then click **Above Chart**. With the **Chart Title** box selected, type **Projected Facilities Expenditures** and then press Enter to create the new chart title.

c. Point to the chart title text, and then right-click to display the Mini toolbar. Change the **Font Size** to **28** and change the **Font Color** to **Blue-Gray, Accent 1**—in the fifth column, the first color.

d. Click in a white area of the chart to deselect the chart title. On the **Layout tab**, in the **Labels group**, click the **Legend** button, and then click **None**.

e. In the **Labels group**, click the **Data Labels** button, and then click **More Data Label Options**. In the **Format Data Labels** dialog box, on the left, be sure **Label Options** is selected. On the right, under **Label Contains**, click as necessary to select the **Category Name** and **Percentage** check boxes. *Clear* any other check boxes in this group. Under **Label Position**, click the **Center** option button. Click **Close**.

f. Point to any of the selected labels, right-click to display the Mini toolbar, and then change the **Font Size** to **12**. Apply **Bold** and **Italic**.

3 Click in any pie slice outside of the label to select the entire pie. Click the **Format tab**, and then in the **Shape Styles group**, click the **Shape Effects** button. Point to **Bevel**, and then at the bottom of the gallery, click **3-D Options**.

a. In the **Format Data Series** dialog box, on the right, under **Bevel**, click the **Top** button. In the gallery, under **Bevel**, in the first row, click the first button—**Circle**. Then click the **Bottom** button, and apply the **Circle** bevel. In the four **Width** and **Height** spin boxes, type **512**

b. In the lower portion of the dialog box, under **Surface**, click the **Material** button. Under **Standard**, click the third button—**Plastic**. In the lower right corner, click the **Close** button.

c. On the **Format tab**, in the **Shape Styles group**, click **Shape Effects**, and then point to **Shadow**. Under **Perspective**, click the third button—**Below**.

d. With the pie chart still selected, point anywhere in the pie and right-click. On the displayed shortcut menu, click **Format Data Series**. In the **Format Data Series** dialog box, on the left, be sure **Series Options** is selected. On the right, click in the box under **Angle of first slice**, change *0* to **300** to move the largest slice—*Civic Center Infrastructure*—to the front of the pie. Click **Close**.

e. Click in the area outside of the chart sheet to deselect all chart elements. Then, on the pie chart, click the outer edge of the **Civic Center Infrastructure** slice one time to select the pie chart, and then click the **Civic Center Infrastructure** slice again to select only that slice.

f. Point to the **Civic Center Infrastructure** slice, and then explode the slice by dragging it slightly away from the center of the pie.

g. With the **Civic Center Infrastructure** slice still selected, point to the slice and right-click. On the shortcut menu, click **Format Data Point**. In the displayed **Format Data Point** dialog box, on the left, click **Fill**. On the right, under **Fill**, click the **Solid fill** option button. Click the **Color arrow**, and then under **Theme Colors**, in the fifth column, click the fourth color—**Blue-Gray, Accent 1, Lighter 40%**. Click **Close**.

(Project 3C Improvement Expenditures continues on the next page)

Excel | Chapter 3

4 Point to the white area just inside the border of the chart to display the ScreenTip **Chart Area**, and then click one time.

a. On the **Format tab**, in the **Shape Styles** group, click the **Shape Effects** button, point to **Bevel**, and then under **Bevel**, in the second row, click the third bevel—**Convex**.

b. With the chart area still selected, right-click in a white area at the outer edge of the chart, and then on the shortcut menu, click **Format Chart Area**. In the **Format Chart Area** dialog box, on the left, be sure that **Fill** is selected. On the right, under **Fill**, click the **Gradient fill** option button. Click the **Preset colors** arrow, and then in the third row, click the fourth preset, **Parchment**. Click the **Type arrow**, and then click **Path**. Click the **Close** button.

c. Click the **Layout tab**, and then in the **Insert group**, click the **Text Box** button. Position the pointer near the lower center of the **Civic Center Infrastructure** slice. Hold down the left mouse button, and then drag down and to the right so that the text box is approximately one-half inch high and its right edge aligns with the right edge of the *Civic Center Infrastructure* slice. With the insertion point blinking inside the text box, type **Infrastructure project to be completed next year** Select the text and then on the Mini toolbar, change the **Font Size** to **12**. If necessary, use the sizing handles to widen the text box so that the text displays on one line.

5 In the sheet tab area at the bottom of the workbook, click the **Sheet1 tab** to redisplay the worksheet.

a. Click the **Insert tab**, and then in the **Text group**, click the **WordArt** button.

b. In the **WordArt** gallery, in the last row, click the last style—**Fill – Blue-Gray, Accent 1, Metal Bevel, Reflection**. Type **facilities improvement expenditures** and then point anywhere on the dashed border surrounding the WordArt object. Click the dashed border one time to change it to a solid border, indicating that all of the text is selected. Right-click the border to display the Mini toolbar, and then change the **Font Size** to **24**.

c. Drag to position the upper left corner of the WordArt in cell **A13**, centered below the worksheet.

6 In cell **A17**, type **Projection: Main Library Infrastructure to Decrease from 14% to 12%** and then **Merge & Center** the text across the range **A17:D17**. Apply the **Heading 3** cell style.

a. In cell **A18**, type **Projected Amount:** and press Enter. Select the range **C10:D10**, right-click over the selection, and then click **Copy**. Point to cell **B18**, right-click, and then under **Paste Options**, click the **Paste** button. Press Esc to cancel the moving border.

b. Click cell **C18**. On the **Data tab**, in the **Data Tools group**, click the **What-If Analysis** button, and then click **Goal Seek**. In the **Goal Seek** dialog box, press Tab to move to the **To value** box, and then type **12%**

c. Press Tab to move the insertion point to the **By changing cell** box, and then click cell **B18**. Click **OK**. In the displayed **Goal Seek Status** dialog box, click **OK**.

d. Select the range **A18:C18**. From the **Home tab**, display the **Cell Styles** gallery. Under **Themed Cell Styles**, apply **40% - Accent3**. Click cell **B18**, and then from the **Cell Styles** gallery, apply the **Currency [0]** cell style.

7 With your worksheet displayed, in the sheet tab area, double-click *Sheet1* to select the text, and then type **Projected Expenditure Data** and press Enter.

a. On the **Insert tab**, in the **Text group**, click **Header & Footer**. In the **Navigation group**, click the **Go to Footer** button, click in the **left section** above the word *Footer*, and then in the **Header & Footer Elements group**, click the **File Name** button. Click in a cell above the footer to deselect the **Footer area** and view your file name.

b. On the **Page Layout tab**, in the **Page Setup group**, click the **Margins** button, and then at the bottom of the **Margins gallery**, click **Custom Margins**. In the **Page Setup** dialog box, under **Center on page**, select the **Horizontally** check box. Click **OK**, and then on the status bar, click the **Normal** button. Press Ctrl + Home to move to the top of your worksheet.

c. Click the **Projected Expenditures Chart** sheet tab to display the chart sheet. On the **Insert tab**, click **Header & Footer**. In the center of the **Page Setup** dialog box, click **Custom Footer**. With the insertion point blinking in the **Left section**, in the row of buttons

(Project 3C Improvement Expenditures continues on the next page)

Content-Based Assessments

in the middle of the dialog box, locate and click the **Insert File Name** button. Click **OK** two times.

d. Right-click either of the sheet tabs, and then click **Select All Sheets**. From **Backstage** view, show the **Document Information Panel**. In the **Author** box, replace the existing text with your firstname and lastname. In the **Subject** box, type your course name and section number. In the **Keywords** box type **facilities expenditures Close** the **Document Information Panel**.

e. With the two sheets still grouped, press Ctrl + F2 to display the **Print Preview**, and then view the two pages of your workbook.

f. **Save** your workbook. Print or submit electronically as directed by your instructor. If required by your instructor, print or create an electronic version of your worksheets with formulas displayed by using the instructions in Activity 1.16, and then **Close** Excel without saving so that you do not save the changes you made to print formulas.

End **You have completed Project 3C** ————————————

NOTES

Getting Started with Access Databases

OUTCOMES
At the end of this chapter you will be able to:

OBJECTIVES
Mastering these objectives will enable you to:

PROJECT 1A
Create a new database.

1. Identify Good Database Design (p. 441)
2. Create a Table and Define Fields in a New Database (p. 442)
3. Change the Structure of Tables and Add a Second Table (p. 454)
4. Create and Use a Query, Form, and Report (p. 464)
5. Save and Close a Database (p. 470)

PROJECT 1B
Create a database from a template.

6. Create a Database Using a Template (p. 475)
7. Organize Objects in the Navigation Pane (p. 479)
8. Create a New Table in a Database Created with a Template (p. 481)
9. Print a Report and a Table in a Database Created with a Template (p. 483)

Jaimie Duplass/Shutterstock

In This Chapter

In this chapter, you will use Microsoft Access 2010 to organize a collection of related information. Access is a powerful program that enables you to organize, search, sort, retrieve, and present information in a professional-looking manner. You will create new databases, enter data into Access tables, and create a query, form, and report—all of which are Access objects that make a database useful. In this chapter, you will also create a database from a template provided with the Access program. The template creates a complete database that you can use as provided, or you can modify it to suit your needs. Additional templates are available from the Microsoft Online Web site. For your first attempt at a database, consider using a template.

The projects in this chapter relate to **Capital Cities Community College**, which is located in the Washington D. C. metropolitan area. The college provides high-quality education and professional training to residents in the cities surrounding the nation's capital. Its four campuses serve over 50,000 students and offer more than 140 certificate programs and degrees at the associate's level. CapCCC has a highly acclaimed Distance Education program and an extensive Workforce Development program. The college makes positive contributions to the community through cultural and athletic programs and partnerships with businesses and non-profit organizations.

Project 1A Contact Information Database with Two Tables

myitlab
Project 1A Training

Project Activities

In Activities 1.01 through 1.17, you will assist Dr. Justin Mitrani, Vice President of Instruction at Capital Cities Community College, in creating a new database for tracking the contact information for students and faculty members. Your completed database objects will look similar to Figure 1.1.

Project Files

For Project 1A, you will need the following files:

> New blank Access database
> a01A_Students (Excel workbook)
> a01A_Faculty (Excel workbook)

You will save your database as:

> Lastname_Firstname_1A_Contacts

Project Results

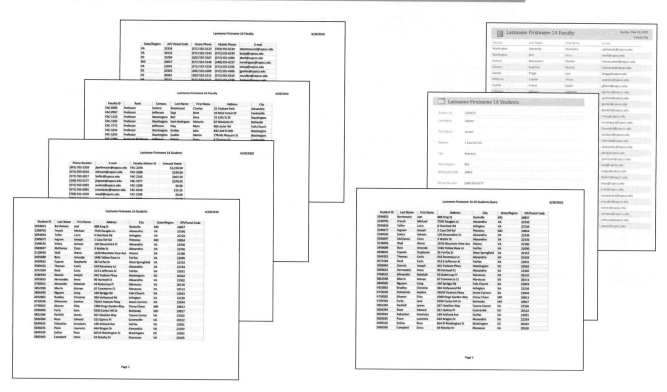

Figure 1.1
Project 1A Contacts

Objective 1 | Identify Good Database Design

A *database* is an organized collection of *data*—facts about people, events, things, or ideas—related to a specific topic or purpose. *Information* is data that is organized in a useful manner. Your personal address book is a type of database, because it is a collection of data about one topic—the people with whom you communicate. A simple database of this type is called a *flat database* because it is not related or linked to any other collection of data. Another example of a simple database is a list of movie DVDs. You do not keep information about your DVDs in your address book because the data is not related to your addresses.

A more sophisticated type of database is a *relational database*, because multiple collections of data in the database are related to one another; for example, data about the students, the courses, and the faculty members at a college. Microsoft Access 2010 is a relational *database management system*—also referred to as a *DBMS*—which is software that controls how related collections of data are stored, organized, retrieved, and secured.

Activity 1.01 | Using Good Design Techniques to Plan a Database

The first step in creating a new database is to determine the information you want to keep track of, and then ask yourself, *What questions should this database be able to answer for me?* The purpose of a database is to store the data in a manner that makes it easy for you to get the information you need by asking questions. For example, in the Contacts database for Capital Cities Community College, the questions to be answered might include:

How many students are enrolled at Capital Cities Community College?

How many faculty members teach in the Accounting Department?

Which and how many students live in Arlington, Virginia?

Which and how many students have a balance owed?

Which and how many students are majoring in Information Systems Technology?

Tables are the foundation of an Access database because all of the data is stored in one or more tables. A table is similar in structure to an Excel worksheet; that is, data is organized into rows and columns. Each table row is a *record*—all of the categories of data pertaining to one person, place, thing, event, or idea. Each table column is a *field*—a single piece of information for every record. For example, in a table storing student contact information, each row forms a record for only one student. Each column forms a field for a single piece of information for every record; for example, the student ID number for all students.

When organizing the fields of information in your database, break each piece of information into its smallest useful part. For example, create three fields for the name of a student—one field for the last name, one field for the first name, and one field for the middle name or initial.

The *first principle of good database design* is to organize data in the tables so that *redundant*—duplicate—data does not occur. For example, record the contact information for students in only *one* table, because if the address for a student changes, the change can be made in just one place. This conserves space, reduces the likelihood of errors when recording the new data, and does not require remembering all of the different places where the address is stored.

The *second principle of good database design* is to use techniques that ensure the accuracy of data when it is entered into the table. Typically, many different people enter data into a database—think of all the people who enter data at your college. When entering a state in a contacts database, one person might enter the state as *Virginia* and another might enter the state as *VA*. Use design techniques to help those who enter data into a database do so in a consistent and accurate manner.

Normalization is the process of applying design rules and principles to ensure that your database performs as expected. Taking the time to plan and create a database that is well designed will ensure that you can retrieve meaningful information from the database.

The tables of information in a relational database are linked or joined to one another by a *common field*—a field in one or more tables that stores the same data. For example, the Student Contacts table includes the Student ID, name, and address of every student. The Student Activities table includes the name of each club, and the Student ID—but not the name or address—of each student in each club. Because the two tables share a common field—Student ID—you can create a list of names and addresses of all the students in the Photography Club. The names and addresses are stored in the Student Contacts table, and the Student IDs of the Photography Club members are stored in the Student Activities table.

Objective 2 | Create a Table and Define Fields in a New Database

There are two methods to create a new Access database: create a new database using a *database template*—a preformatted database designed for a specific purpose—or create a new database from a *blank database*. A blank database has no data and has no database tools; you create the data and the tools as you need them.

Regardless of the method you use, you must name and save the database before you can create any *objects* in it. Objects are the basic parts of a database; you create objects to store your data and to work with your data. The most common database objects are tables, forms, and reports. Think of an Access database as a container for the objects that you will create.

Activity 1.02 | Starting with a New Database

1 **Start** Access. Take a moment to compare your screen with Figure 1.2 and study the parts of the Microsoft Access window described in the table in Figure 1.3.

From this Access starting point in Backstage view, you can open an existing database, create a new blank database, or create a new database from a template.

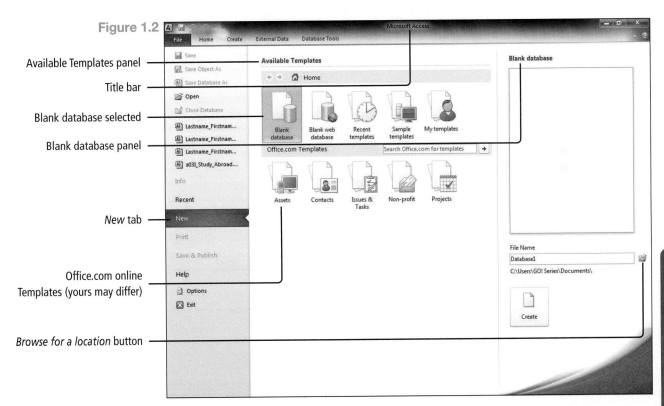

Figure 1.2

- Available Templates panel
- Title bar
- Blank database selected
- Blank database panel
- *New* tab
- Office.com online Templates (yours may differ)
- *Browse for a location* button

Microsoft Access Opening Window

Window Part	Description
Available Templates panel	Displays alternative methods of creating a database.
Blank database	Starts a new blank database.
Blank database panel	Displays when *Blank database* button is selected under Available Templates.
Browse for location button	Enables you to select a storage location for the database.
New tab	Displays, when active in Backstage view, the various methods by which you can create a new database.
Office.com Templates	Displays template categories available from the Office.com Web site.
Title bar	Displays the Quick Access Toolbar, program name, and program-level buttons.

Figure 1.3

2 On the right, under **Blank database**, to the right of the **File Name** box, click the **Browse** button 📷. In the **File New Database** dialog box, navigate to the location where you are saving your databases for this chapter, create a new folder named **Access Chapter 1** and then notice that *Database1* displays as the default file name—the number at the end of your file name might differ if you have saved a database previously with the default name. In the **File New Database** dialog box, click **Open**.

3 In the **File name** box, replace the existing text with **Lastname_Firstname_1A_Contacts** Press Enter, and then compare your screen with Figure 1.4.

On the right, the name of your database displays in the File Name box, and the drive and folder where the database is stored displays under the File Name box. An Access database has the file extension *.accdb*.

Figure 1.4

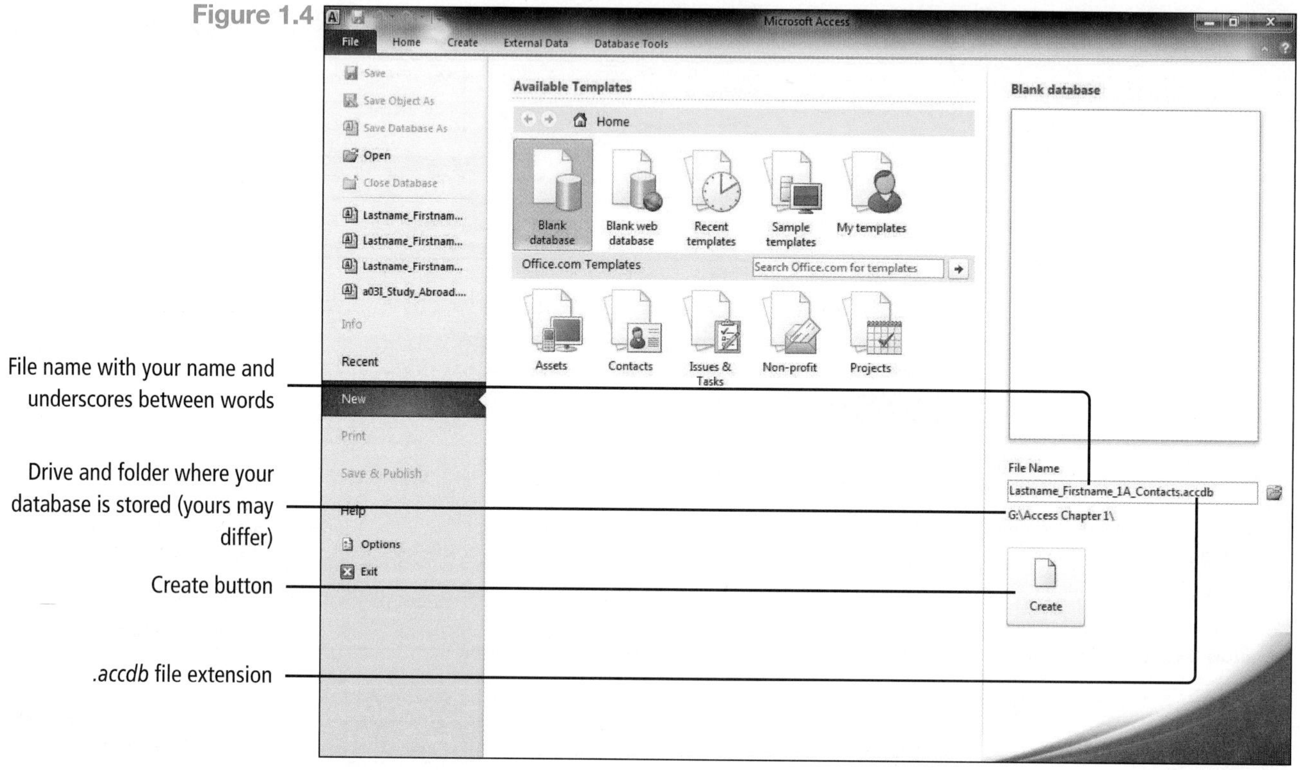

File name with your name and underscores between words

Drive and folder where your database is stored (yours may differ)

Create button

.accdb file extension

4 Under the **File Name** box, click the **Create** button, compare your screen with Figure 1.5, and then take a moment to study the screen elements described in the table in Figure 1.6.

Access creates the new database and opens *Table1*. Recall that a table is an Access object that stores your data in columns and rows, similar to the format of an Excel worksheet. Table objects are the foundation of a database because tables store the actual data.

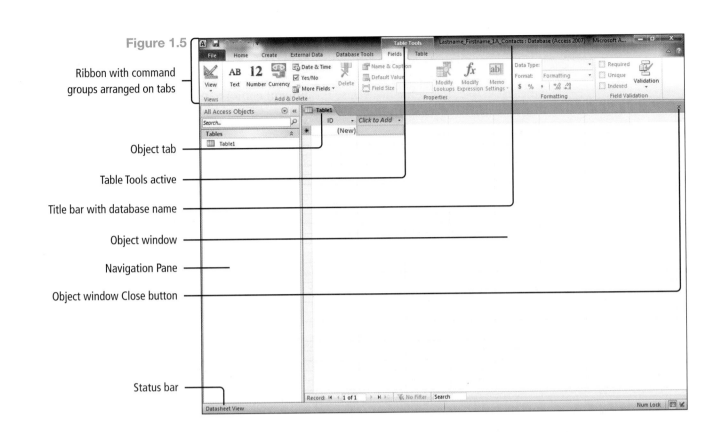

Figure 1.5

Ribbon with command groups arranged on tabs

Object tab

Table Tools active

Title bar with database name

Object window

Navigation Pane

Object window Close button

Status bar

Parts of the Access Database Window

Window Part	Description
Navigation Pane	Displays the database objects; from here you open the database objects to display in the object window at the right.
Object tab	Identifies and enables you to select the open object.
Object window	Displays the active or open object (table, query, or other object).
Object window Close button	Closes the active object (table, query, or other object).
Ribbon with command groups arranged on tabs	Groups the commands for performing related database tasks on tabs.
Status bar	Indicates the active view and the status of actions occurring within the database on the left; provides buttons to switch between Datasheet view and Design view on the right.
Table Tools	Provides tools for working with a table object; Table Tools are available only when a table is displayed.
Title bar	Displays the name of your database.

Figure 1.6

Activity 1.03 | Assigning the Data Type and Name to Fields

After you have saved and named your database, the next step is to consult your database plan, and then create the tables in which to enter your data. Limit the data in each table to *one* subject. For example, in this project, your database will have two tables—one for student contact information and one for faculty contact information.

Recall that each column in a table is a field and that field names display at the top of each column of the table. Recall also that each row in a table is a record—all of the data pertaining to one person, place, thing, event, or idea. Each record is broken up into its smallest usable parts—the fields. Use meaningful names to name fields; for example, *Last Name*.

1 Notice the new blank table that displays in Datasheet view, and then take a moment to study the elements of the table's object window. Compare your screen with Figure 1.7.

The table displays in **Datasheet view**, which displays the data as columns and rows similar to the format of an Excel worksheet. Another way to view a table is in **Design view**, which displays the underlying design—the **structure**—of the table's fields. The **object window** displays the open object—in this instance, the table object.

In a new blank database, there is only one object—a new blank table. Because you have not yet named this table, the object tab displays a default name of *Table1*. Access creates the first field and names it *ID*. In the ID field, Access assigns a unique sequential number—each number incremented by one—to each record as it is entered into the table.

Figure 1.7

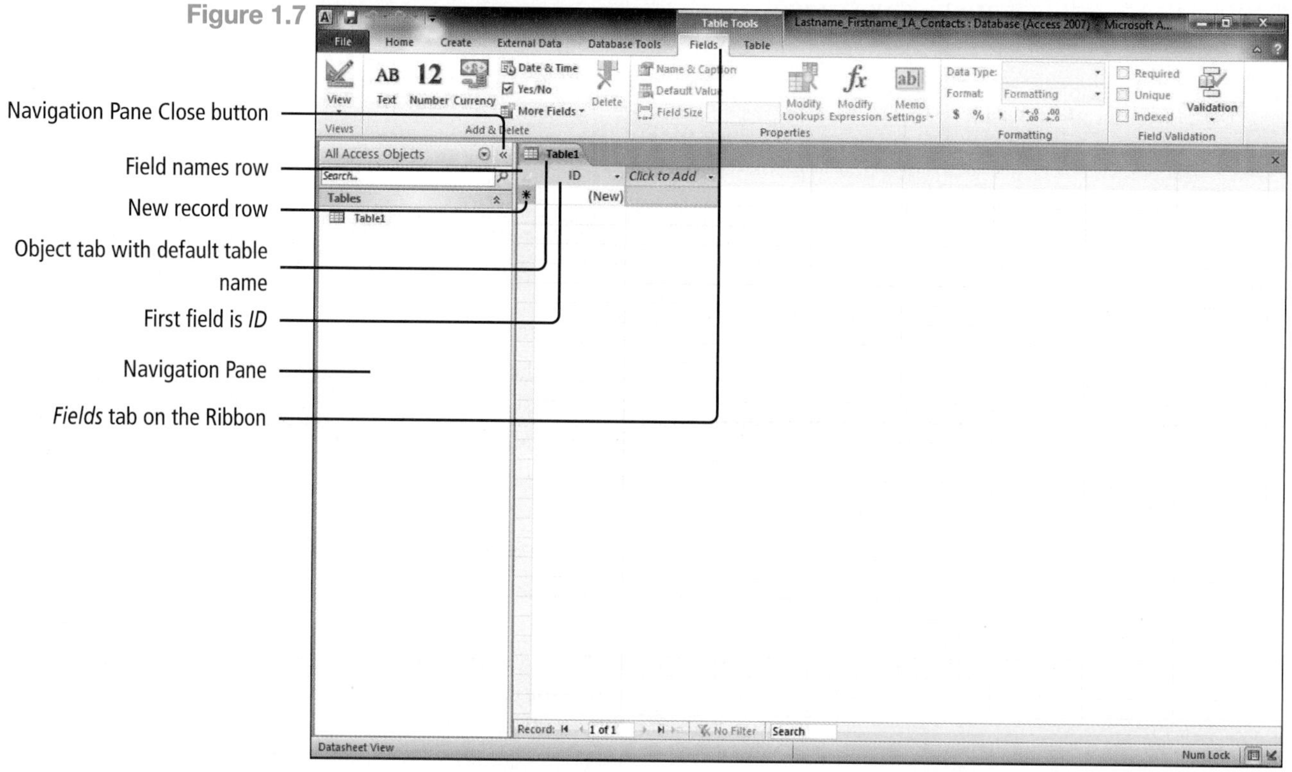

Navigation Pane Close button

Field names row

New record row

Object tab with default table name

First field is *ID*

Navigation Pane

Fields tab on the Ribbon

2 In the **Navigation Pane**, click the **Open/Close** button ⟪ to collapse the **Navigation Pane** to a narrow bar on the left and to display more of the table.

The **Navigation Pane** is an area of the Access window that displays and organizes the names of the objects in a database. From the Navigation Pane, you can open objects for use.

Another Way
To the right of *Click to Add*, click the arrow.

3 In the field names row, click anywhere in the text *Click to Add* to display a list of data types. Compare your screen with Figure 1.8.

Data type is the characteristic that defines the kind of data that you can type in a field, such as numbers, text, or dates. A field in a table can have only one data type. Part of your database design should include deciding on the data type of each field. After you have selected the data type, you can name the field.

Figure 1.8

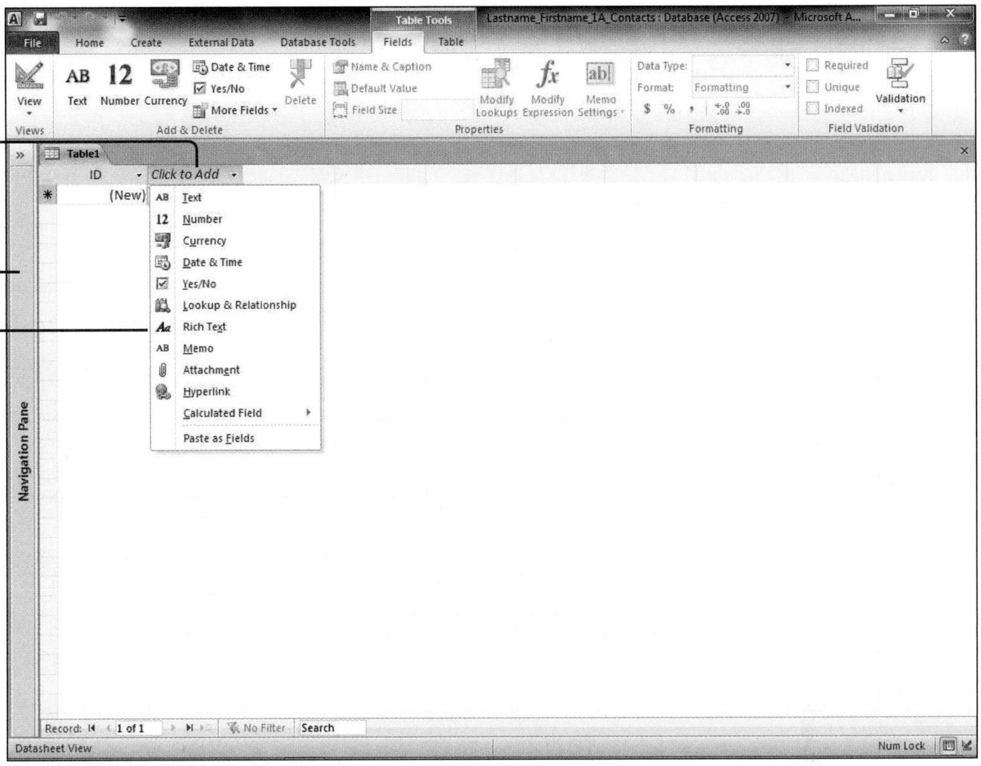

Click to display data types

Navigation Pane closed

List of data types

4 In the list of data types, click **Text**, and notice that in the second column, *Click to Add* changes to *Field1*, which is selected. Type **Last Name** and then press [Enter].

> The second column displays *Last Name* as the field name, and the data type list displays in the third column. The **Text data type** describes text, a combination of text and numbers, or numbers that are not used in calculations, such as a ZIP code.

Another Way

With the list of data types displayed, type *T* to select Text.

---

5 In the third field name box, click **Text**, type **First Name** and then press [Enter]. In the fourth field name box, click **Text**, type **Middle Initial** and then press [Enter].

6 Using the technique you just practiced, create the remaining fields as follows by first selecting the data type, then typing the field name, and then pressing [Enter]. The field names in the table will display on one line.

> The ZIP/Postal Code field is assigned a data type of Text because the number is never used in a calculation. The Amount Owed field is assigned a data type of Currency; the **Currency data type** describes monetary values and numeric data used in mathematical calculations involving data with one to four decimal places. Access automatically adds a U.S. dollar sign ($) and two decimal places to all of the numbers in the fields with a data type of *Currency*.

Data Type		Text	Text	Text	**Text**	Text	Text	Text	Text	Text	Text	Currency
Field Name	ID	Last Name	First Name	Middle Initial	**Address**	City	State/ Region	ZIP/Postal Code	Phone Number	E-mail	Faculty Advisor ID	Amount Owed

7 If necessary, by using the horizontal scroll bar at the bottom of the screen, scroll to the left to bring the first column into view. Compare your screen with Figure 1.9.

> Access automatically created the ID field, and you created 11 additional fields in the table. The horizontal scroll bar indicates that there are additional fields that are not displayed on the screen—your screen width may vary.

Access | Chapter 1

Figure 1.9

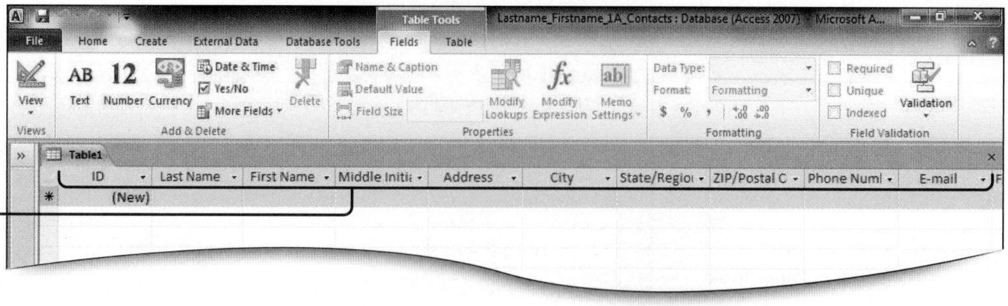

Twelve fields created—scroll
to the left to display *ID* and
Last Name fields

Activity 1.04 | Renaming Fields and Changing Data Types in a Table

Another Way

Right-click the field
name, and then on the
shortcut menu, click
Rename Field.

1 Click anywhere in the text *ID*. In the **Properties group**, click the **Name & Caption** button. In the **Enter Field Properties** dialog box, in the **Name** box, change *ID* to **Student ID** and then click **OK**.

The field name *Student ID* is a better description of the data in this field. In the Enter Field Properties dialog box, the ***Caption*** property is used to display a name for a field other than that listed as the field name. Many database designers do not use spaces in field names; instead, they might name a field LastName—with no spaces—and then create a caption for that field so it displays with spaces in tables, forms, and reports. In the Enter Field Properties dialog box, you can also provide a description for the field if you want to do so.

2 In the **Formatting group**, notice that the **Data Type** for the **Student ID** field is *AutoNumber*. Click the **Data Type arrow**, click **Text**, and then compare your screen with Figure 1.10.

In the new record row, the Student ID field is selected. By default, Access creates an ID field for all new tables and sets the data type for the field to AutoNumber. The ***AutoNumber data type*** describes a unique sequential or random number assigned by Access as each record is entered. By changing the data type of this field from *AutoNumber* to *Text,* you can enter a custom student ID number.

When records in a database have *no* unique value, for example the names in your address book, the AutoNumber data type is a useful way to automatically create a unique number so that you have a way to ensure that every record is different from the others.

Figure 1.10

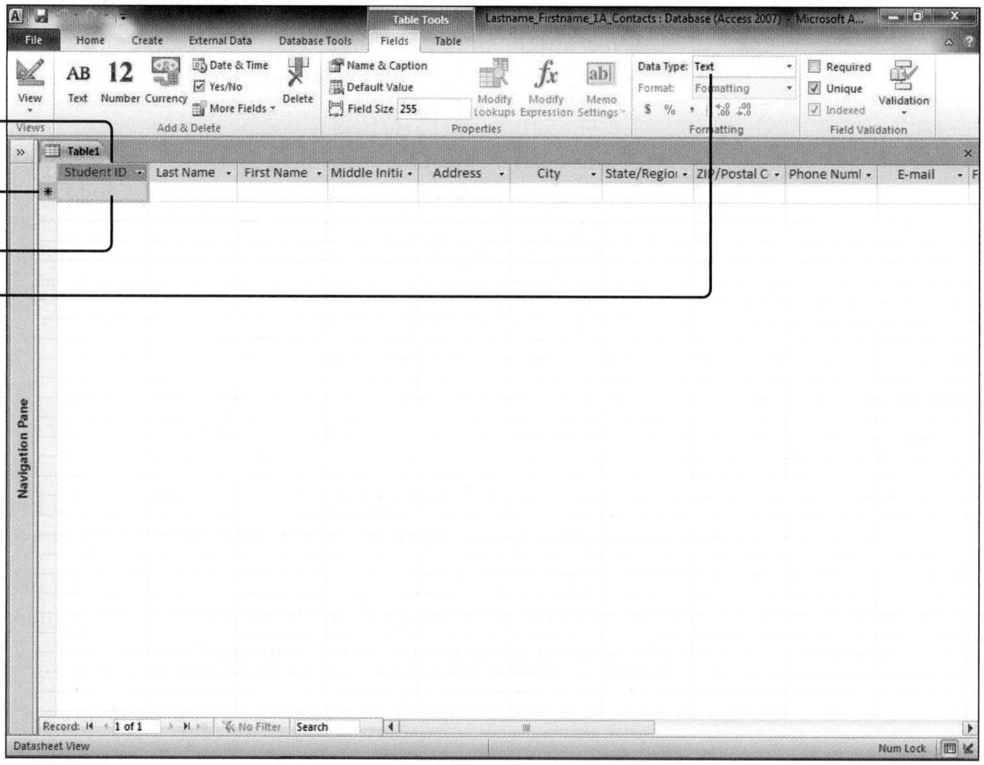

Field renamed

New record row—indicated
by asterisk

Selected field

Data type indicates *Text*

Activity 1.05 | Adding a Record to a Table

A new address book is not useful until you fill it with names, addresses, and phone numbers. Likewise, a new database is not useful until you **populate** it—fill one or more tables with data. You can populate a table with records by typing data directly into the table.

> **Another Way**
>
> Press Tab to move to the next field.

1 In the new record row, click in the **Student ID** field to display the insertion point, type **1238765** and then press Enter. Compare your screen with Figure 1.11.

The pencil icon 🖉 in the **record selector box**—the small box at the left of a record in Datasheet view that, when clicked, selects the entire record—indicates that a record is being entered or edited.

Figure 1.11

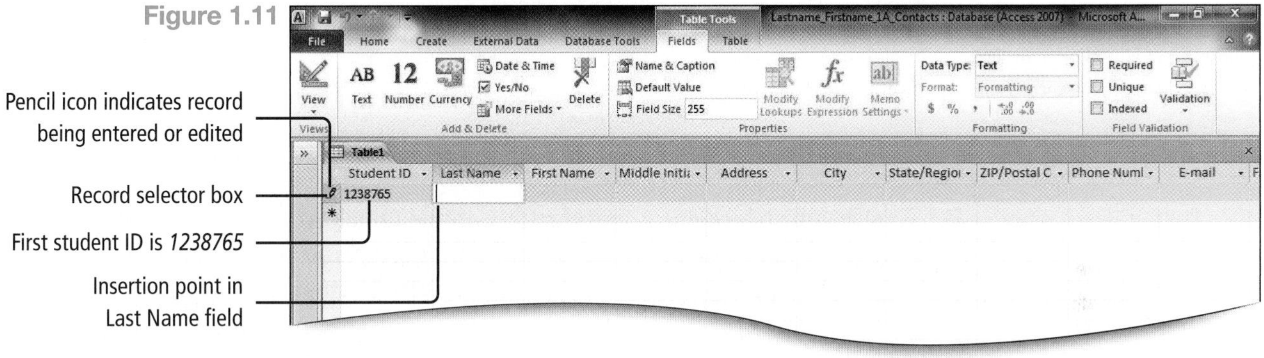

Pencil icon indicates record being entered or edited

Record selector box

First student ID is *1238765*

Insertion point in Last Name field

2 With the insertion point positioned in the **Last Nam**e field, type **Fresch** and then press Enter.

> **Note | Correct Typing Errors**
>
> Correct typing errors by using the techniques you have practiced in other Office applications. For example, use Backspace to remove characters to the left, Del to remove characters to the right, or select the text you want to replace and type the correct information. Press Esc to exit out of a record that has not been completely entered.

3 In the **First Name** field, type **Michael** and then press Enter.

4 In the **Middle Initial** field, type **B** and then press Enter.

5 In the **Address** field, type **7550 Douglas Ln** and then press Enter.

Do not be concerned if the data does not completely display in the column. As you progress in your study of Access, you will adjust the column widths so that you can view all of the data.

6 Continue entering data in the fields as indicated below, pressing Enter to move to the next field.

City	State/Region	ZIP/Postal Code	Phone Number	E-mail	Faculty Advisor ID
Alexandria	**VA**	**22336**	**(571) 555-0234**	**mfresch@capccc.edu**	**FAC-2289**

> **Note | Format for Typing Telephone Numbers in Access**
>
> Access does not require any specific format for typing telephone numbers in a database. The examples in this project use the format of Microsoft Outlook. Using such a format facilitates easy transfer of Outlook information to and from Access.

7 In the **Amount Owed** field, type **150** and then press [Enter]. Compare your screen with Figure 1.12.

> Pressing [Enter] or [Tab] in the last field moves the insertion point to the next row to begin a new record. As soon as you move to the next row, Access saves the record—you do not have to take any specific action to save a record.

Figure 1.12

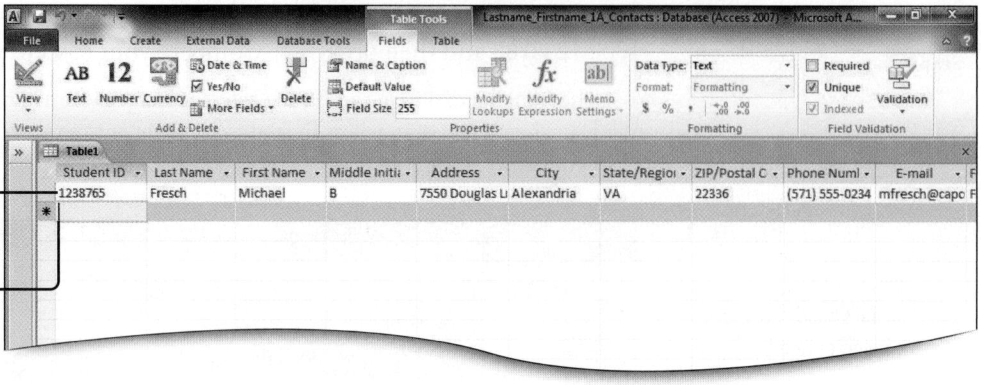

First record entered and saved

Insertion point blinking in first field of new record row

8 To give your table a meaningful name, on the Quick Access Toolbar, click the **Save** button. In the **Save As** dialog box, in the **Table Name** box, using your own name, replace the highlighted text by typing **Lastname Firstname 1A Students**

> Save each database object with a name that identifies the data that it contains. When you save objects within a database, it is not necessary to use underscores. Your name is included as part of the object name so that you and your instructor can identify your printouts or electronic files.

9 In the **Save As** dialog box, click **OK**, and then notice that the object tab displays the new table name you just typed.

> **More Knowledge | Renaming a Table**
>
> To change the name of a table, close the table, display the Navigation Pane, right-click the table name, and then on the shortcut menu, click Rename. Type the new name or edit as you would any selected text.

Activity 1.06 | Adding Additional Records to a Table

1 In the new record row, click in the **Student ID** field, and then enter the contact information for the following two additional students, pressing [Enter] or [Tab] to move from field to field. The data in each field will display on one line in the table.

Student ID	Last Name	First Name	Middle Initial	Address	City	State/ Region	ZIP/ Postal Code	Phone Number	E-mail	Faculty Advisor ID	Amount Owed
2345677	Ingram	Joseph	S	1 Casa Del Sol	Potomac	MD	20854	(240) 555-0177	jingram@ capccc.edu	FAC-2377	378.5
3456689	Bass	Amanda	J	1446 Yellow Rose Ln	Fairfax	VA	22030	(703) 555-0192	abass@ capccc.edu	FAC-9005	0

2 Compare your screen with Figure 1.13.

Figure 1.13

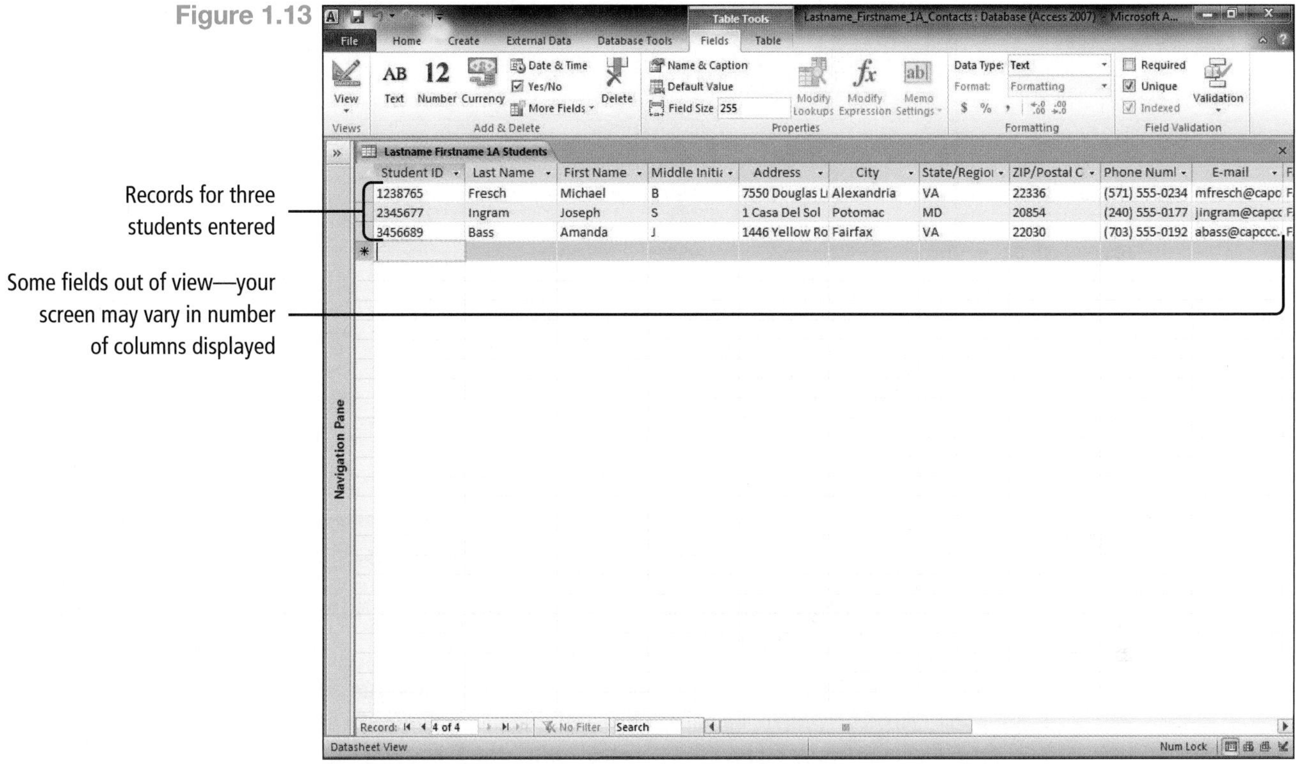

Records for three students entered

Some fields out of view—your screen may vary in number of columns displayed

Activity 1.07 | Importing Data from an Excel Workbook into an Existing Access Table

When you create a database table, you can type the records directly into a table. You can also *import* data from a variety of sources. Importing is the process of copying data from one source or application to another application. For example, you can import data from a Word table or an Excel worksheet into an Access database because the data is arranged in columns and rows, similar to a table in Datasheet view.

In this activity, you will *append*—add on—data from an Excel spreadsheet to your *1A Students* table. To append data, the table must already be created, and it must be closed.

1 In the upper right corner of the table, below the Ribbon, click the **Object Close** ☒ button to close your **1A Students** table. Notice that no objects are open.

2 On the Ribbon, click the **External Data tab.** In the **Import & Link group**, click the **Excel** button. In the **Get External Data - Excel Spreadsheet** dialog box, click the **Browse** button.

3 In the **File Open** dialog box, navigate to your student files, locate and double-click the Excel file **a01A_Students**, and then compare your screen with Figure 1.14.

> **Another Way**
>
> Select the file name, and in the lower right area of the dialog box, click Open.

The path to the *source file*—the file being imported—displays in the File name box. There are three options for importing data from an Excel workbook—import the data into a *new* table in the current database, append a copy of the records to an existing table, or link the data from Excel to a linked table. A *link* is a connection to data in another file. When linking, Access creates a table that maintains a link to the source data.

Access | Chapter 1

Figure 1.14

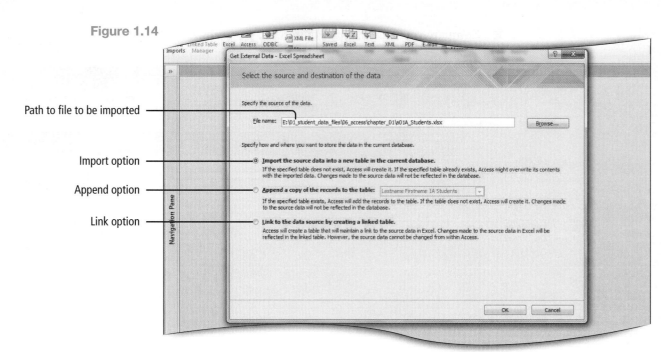

Path to file to be imported

Import option

Append option

Link option

4 Click the **Append a copy of the records to the table** option button, and then in the box to its right, click the **arrow**.

Currently your database has only one table, so no other tables display on the list. However, when a database has multiple tables, here you can select the table to which you want to append records. The table into which you import or append data is referred to as the *destination table*.

5 Press Esc to cancel the list, and then in the lower right corner of the dialog box, click **OK.** Compare your screen with Figure 1.15.

The first screen of the Import Spreadsheet Wizard displays, and the presence of scroll bars indicates that records and fields are out of view in this window. To append records from an Excel worksheet to an existing database table, the field names in the Excel worksheet must be identical to the field names in the table, and that is true in this table.

Figure 1.15

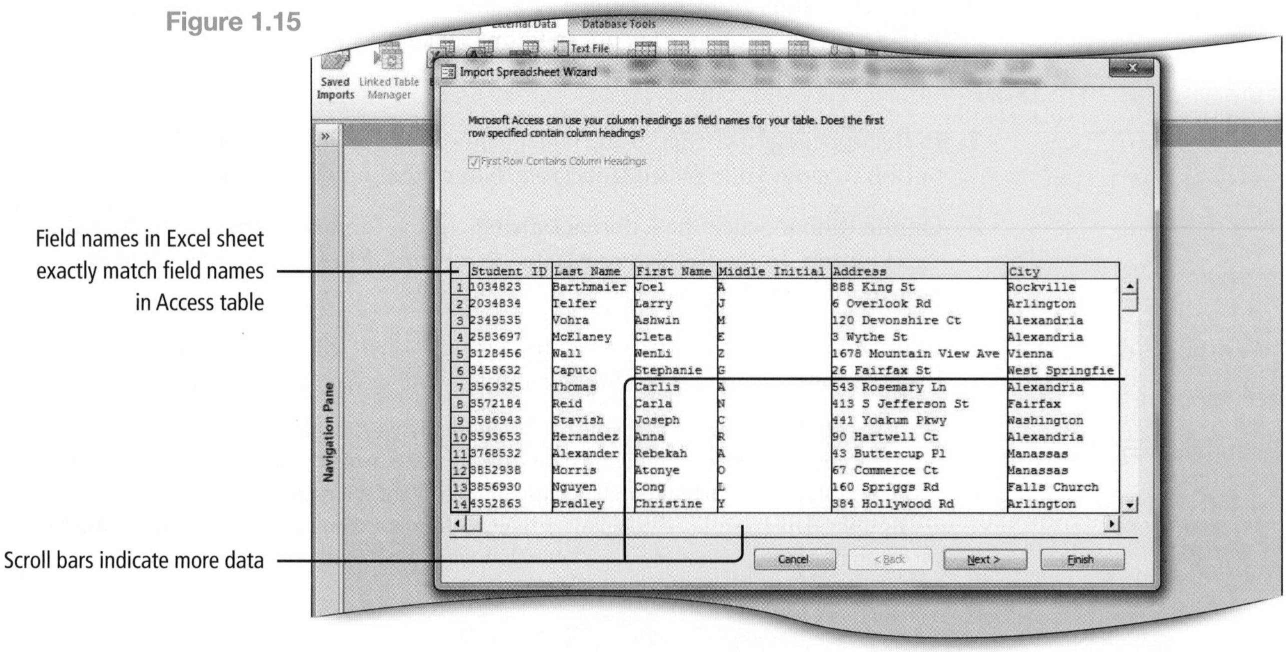

Field names in Excel sheet
exactly match field names
in Access table

Scroll bars indicate more data

6 In the lower right corner, click **Next.** Notice that the name of your table displays under **Import to Table.** In the lower right corner, click **Finish.**

7 In the **Get External Data - Excel Spreadsheet** dialog box, click **Close**, and then **Open** [»] the **Navigation Pane**.

8 Point to the right edge of the **Navigation Pane** to display the [↔] pointer. Drag to the right to widen the pane to display the entire table name, and then compare your screen with Figure 1.16.

Figure 1.16

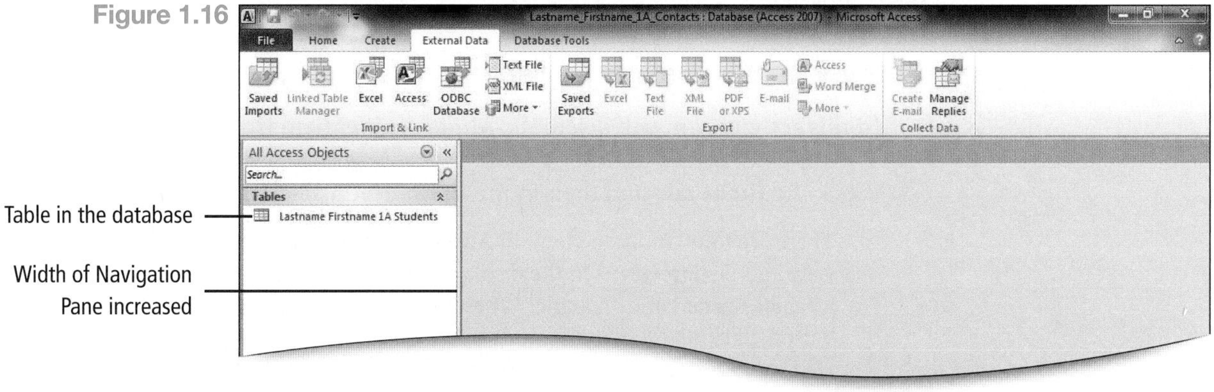

Table in the database

Width of Navigation Pane increased

Another Way

To open an object from the Navigation Pane, right-click the object name, and then on the shortcut menu, click Open.

9 In the **Navigation Pane**, double-click your **1A Students** table to open the table in Datasheet view, and then **Close** [«] the **Navigation Pane**.

10 At the bottom left corner of your screen, locate the navigation area, and notice that there are a total of **26** records in the table—you created three records and imported 23 additional records. Compare your screen with Figure 1.17.

The records from the Excel worksheet display in your table, and the first record is selected. The *navigation area* indicates the number of records in the table and contains controls (arrows) with which you can navigate among the records.

Figure 1.17

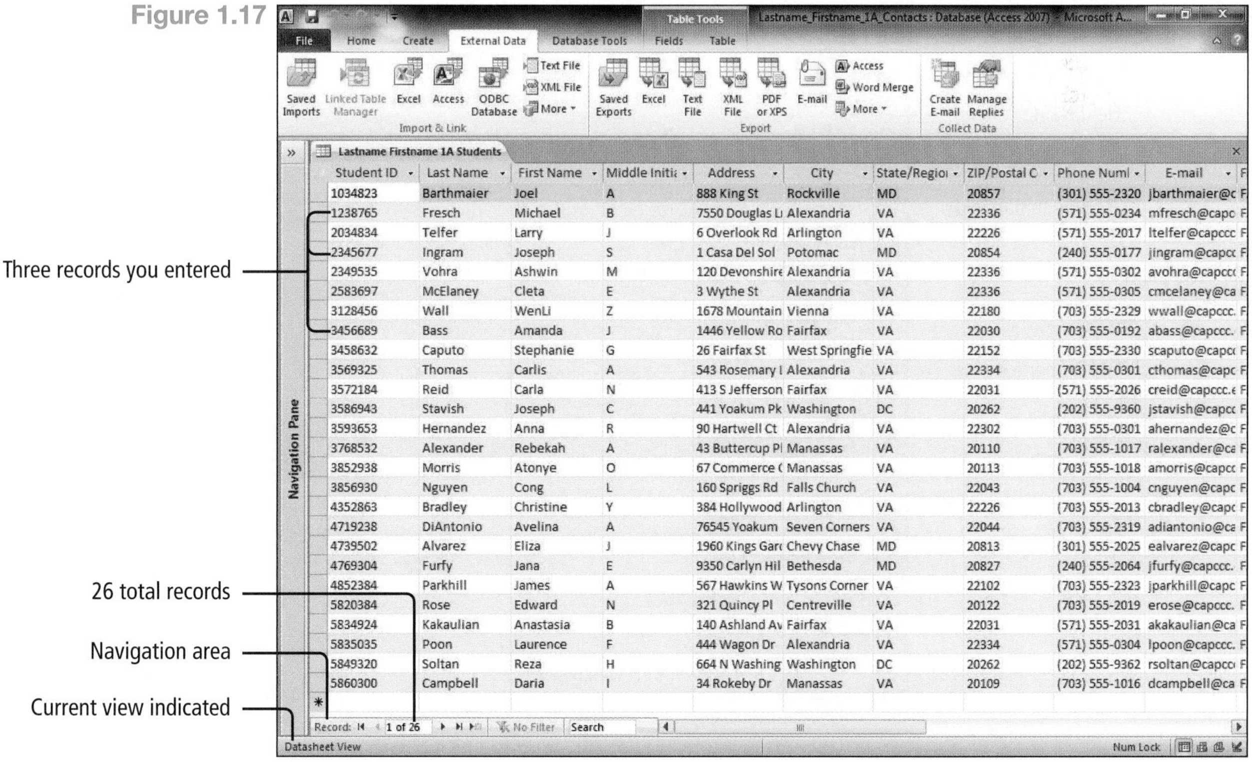

Three records you entered

26 total records

Navigation area

Current view indicated

Access | Chapter 1

Objective 3 | Change the Structure of Tables and Add a Second Table

Recall that the structure of a table is the underlying design, including field names and data types. You can create a table or modify a table in Datasheet view. To define and modify fields, many database experts prefer to work in Design view, where you have many additional options for defining the fields in a table.

Activity 1.08 | Deleting a Table Field in Design View

In this activity, you will delete the *Middle Initial* field from the table.

1 Click the **Home tab**, and then in the **Views group**, click the **View button arrow**.

There are four common views in Access, but two that you will use often are Datasheet view and Design view. On the displayed list, Design view is represented by a picture of a pencil, a ruler, and an angle. When one of these four icons is displayed on the View button, clicking the View button will display the table in the view represented by the icon. Datasheet view displays the table data in rows and columns.

2 On the list, click **Design View**, and then compare your screen with Figure 1.18.

Design view displays the underlying design—the structure—of the table and its fields. In Design view, you cannot view the data; you can view only the information about each field's characteristics. Each field name is listed, along with its data type. A column to add a Description—information about the data in the field—is provided.

In the Field Properties area, you can make additional decisions about how each individual field looks and behaves. For example, you can set a specific field size.

Figure 1.18

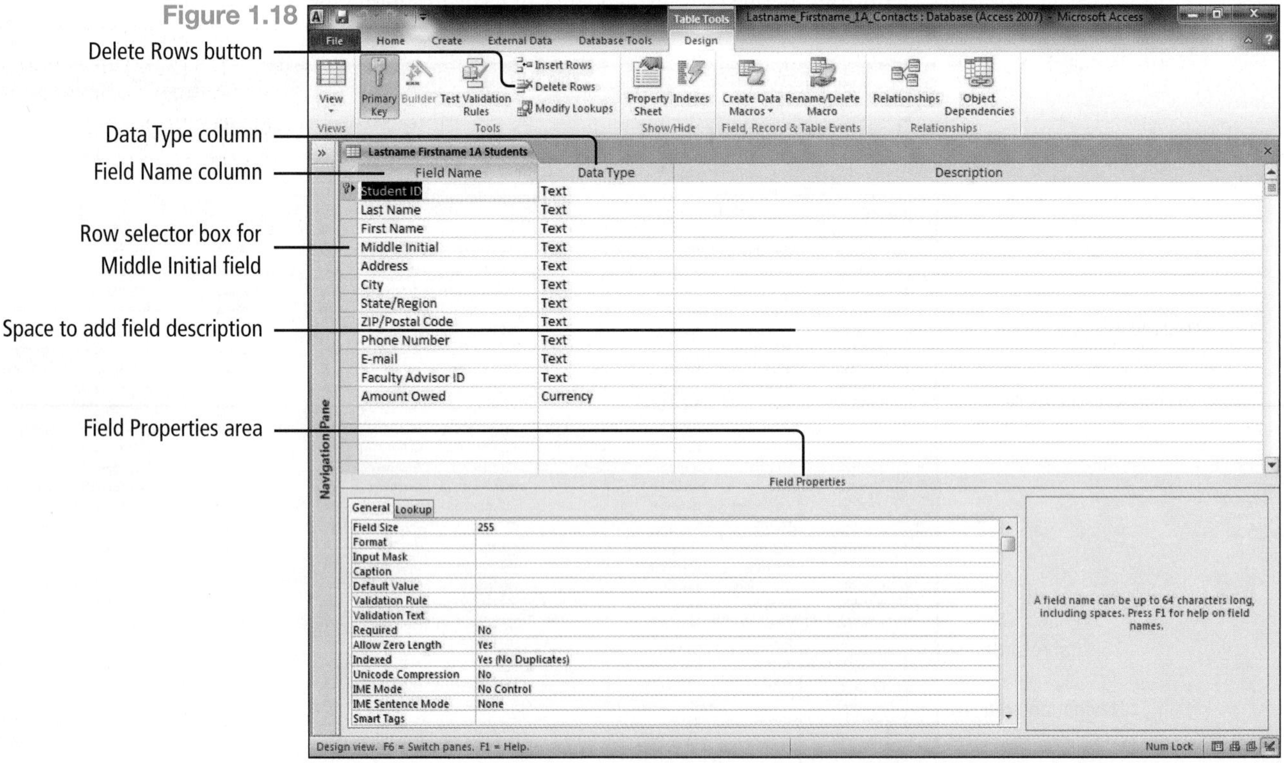

3 In the **Field Name** column, to the left of **Middle Initial**, point to the row selector box to display the **→** pointer, and then click one time to select the entire row.

Another Way

Right-click the selected row and click Delete Rows.

4 On the **Design tab**, in the **Tools group**, click the **Delete Rows** button, read the message in the message box, and then click **Yes**.

Deleting a field deletes both the field and its data; you cannot undo this action. Thus, Access prompts you to be sure you want to proceed. If you change your mind after deleting a field, you must add the field back into the table and then reenter the data in that field for every record.

Activity 1.09 | Modifying a Field Size and Adding a Description

Typically, many individuals enter data into a table. For example, at your college many Registration Assistants enter and modify student and course information daily. Two ways to help reduce errors are to restrict what can be typed in a field and to add descriptive information.

1 With your table still displayed in **Design** view, in the **Field Name** column, click anywhere in the **State/Region** field name.

2 In the lower portion of the screen, under **Field Properties**, click **Field Size** to select the text *255*, type **2** and then compare your screen with Figure 1.19.

This action limits the size of the State/Region field to no more than two characters—the size of the two-letter state abbreviations provided by the United States Postal Service. *Field properties* control how the field displays and how data can be entered in the field. You can define properties for every field in the Field Properties area.

The default field size for a text field is 255. Limiting the field size property to 2 ensures that only two characters can be entered for each state. However, this does not prevent someone from entering two characters that are incorrect. Setting the proper data type for the field and limiting the field size are two ways to *help* to reduce errors.

Figure 1.19

State/Region field selected

Field Size indicates *2*

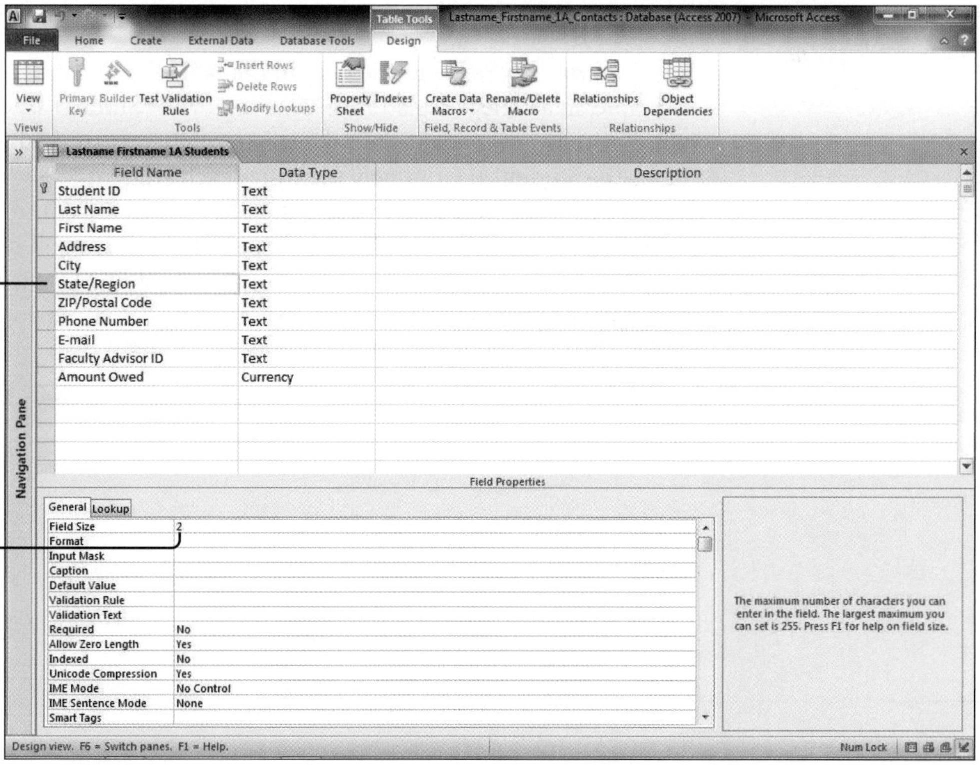

3 In the **State/Region** row, click in the **Description** box, type **Two-character state abbreviation** and then press (Enter).

> Descriptions for fields in a table are optional. Include a description if the field name does not provide an obvious explanation of the field. Information typed in the description area displays on the left side of the status bar in Datasheet view when the field is active, providing additional information to individuals who are entering data.
>
> When you enter a description for a field, a Property Update Options button displays below the text you typed, which enables you to copy the description for the field to all other database objects that use this table as an underlying source.

4 Click in the **Student ID** field name box. Using the technique you practiced, in the **Field Properties** area, change the **Field Size** to **7**

> By limiting the field size to seven characters, which is the maximum number of characters in a Student ID, you help to ensure the accuracy of the data.

5 In the **Student ID** row, click in the **Description** box, and then type **Seven-digit Student ID number**

6 Click in the **Faculty Advisor ID** field name box. In the **Field Properties** area, change the **Field Size** to **8** In the **Description** box for this field, type **Eight-character ID of faculty member assigned as advisor** and then press (Enter).

7 On the Quick Access Toolbar, click the **Save** button 🖫 to save the design changes to your table, and then notice the message.

> The message indicates that the field size property of one or more fields has changed to a shorter size. If more characters are currently present in the Student ID, State/Region, or Faculty Advisor ID than you have allowed, the data could be *truncated*—cut off or shortened—because the fields were not previously restricted to a specific number of characters.

8 In the message box, click **Yes**.

Activity 1.10 | Viewing a Primary Key in Design View

Primary key refers to the field in the table that uniquely identifies a record. For example, in a college registration database, your Student ID number uniquely identifies you—no other student at the college has your exact student number. In the 1A Students table, the Student ID uniquely identifies each student.

When you create a table using the Blank database command, by default Access designates the first field as the primary key field. It is good database design practice to establish a primary key for every table, because doing so ensures that you do not enter the same record more than once. You can imagine the confusion if another student at your college had the same Student ID number as you do.

1 With your table still displayed in Design view, in the **Field Name** column, click in the **Student ID** box. To the left of the box, notice the small icon of a key, as shown in Figure 1.20.

> Access automatically designates the first field as the primary key field, but you can set any field as the primary key by clicking in the box to the left of the field name, and then clicking the Primary Key button.

Figure 1.20

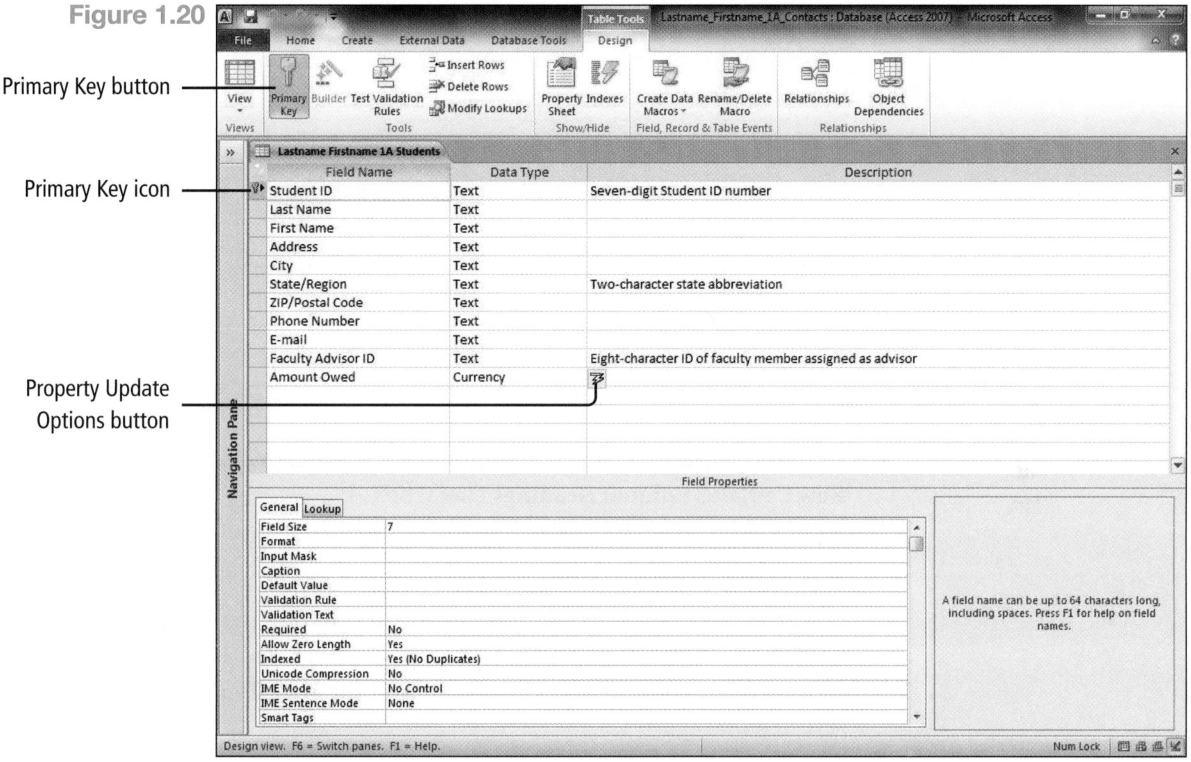

Primary Key button

Primary Key icon

Property Update Options button

2 On the **Design tab**, in the **Views group**, notice that the **View** button contains a picture of a Datasheet, indicating that clicking the button will return you to Datasheet view. Click the **View** button.

Activity 1.11 | Adding a Second Table to a Database by Importing an Excel Spreadsheet

Many Microsoft Office users track data in an Excel spreadsheet. The sorting and filtering capabilities of Excel are useful for a simple database where all the information resides in one large Excel spreadsheet. However, Excel is limited as a database management tool because it cannot *relate* the information in multiple spreadsheets in a way in which you could ask a question and get a meaningful result. Data in an Excel spreadsheet can easily become an Access table by importing the spreadsheet, because Excel's format of columns and rows is similar to that of an Access table.

1 On the Ribbon, click the **External Data tab**, and then in the **Import & Link group**, click the **Excel** button. In the **Get External Data – Excel Spreadsheet** dialog box, to the right of the **File name** box, click **Browse**.

2 In the **File Open** dialog box, navigate to your student files, and then double-click **a01A_Faculty.** Compare your screen with Figure 1.21.

Figure 1.21

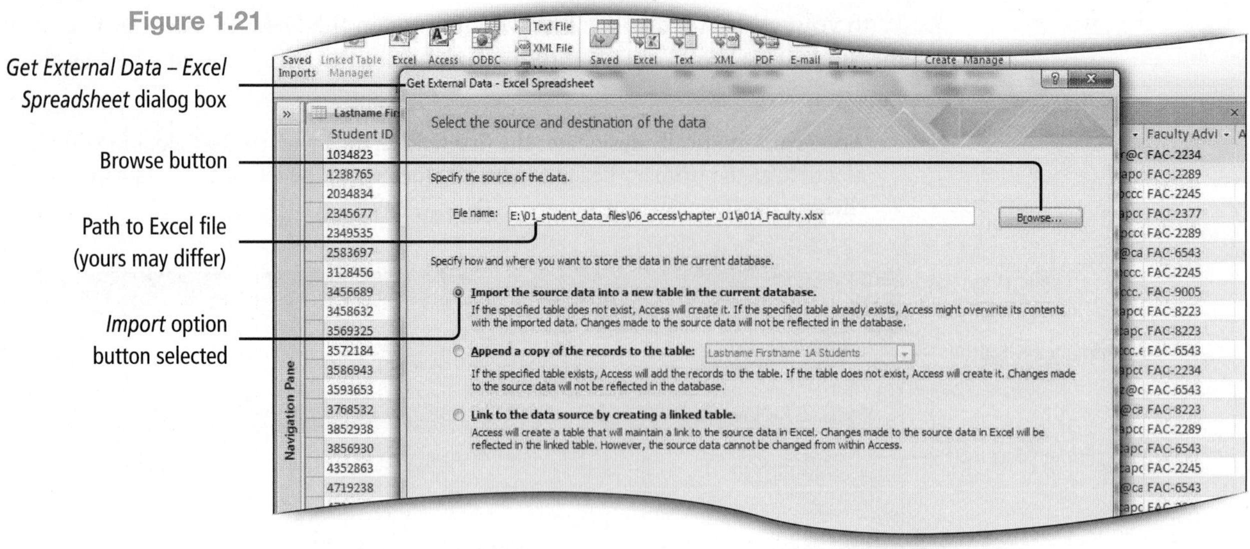

Get External Data – Excel Spreadsheet dialog box

Browse button

Path to Excel file (yours may differ)

Import option button selected

3 Be sure that the **Import the source data into a new table in the current database** option button is selected, and then click **OK**.

The Import Spreadsheet Wizard opens and displays the spreadsheet data.

4 In the upper left portion of the **Import Spreadsheet Wizard** dialog box, select the **First Row Contains Column Headings** check box.

The Excel data is framed, indicating that the first row of Excel column titles will become the Access table field names, and the remaining rows will become the individual records in the new Access table.

5 Click **Next.** Notice that the first column—*Faculty ID*—is selected, and in the upper portion of the Wizard, the **Field Name** and the **Data Type** display. Compare your screen with Figure 1.22.

Here you can review and change the field properties for each field (column). You can also identify fields in the spreadsheet that you do not want to import into the Access table by selecting the Do not import field (Skip) check box.

Figure 1.22

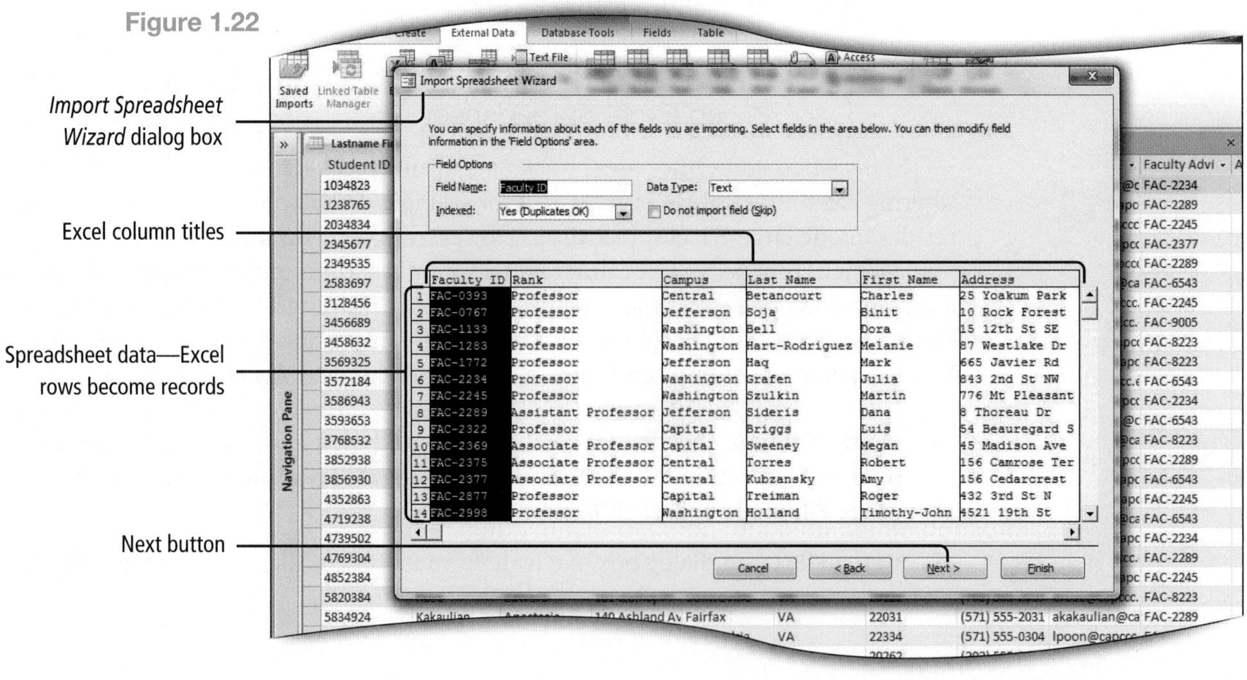

Import Spreadsheet Wizard dialog box

Excel column titles

Spreadsheet data—Excel rows become records

Next button

6   Click **Next.** In the upper portion of the Wizard, click the **Choose my own primary key** option button, and then be sure that **Faculty ID** displays.

> In the new table, Faculty ID will be the primary key. No two faculty members have the same Faculty ID. By default, Access selects the first field as the primary key, but you can click the arrow to select a different field.

7   Click **Next.** In the **Import to Table** box, type **Lastname Firstname 1A Faculty** and then click **Finish**.

8   In the **Get External Data – Excel Spreadsheet** dialog box, click **Close**, and then **Open** [»] the **Navigation Pane**.

9   In the **Navigation Pane**, double-click your **1A Faculty** table to open it in Datasheet view, and then **Close** [«] the **Navigation Pane**.

10 Click in the **ZIP/Postal Code** field, and then on the Ribbon, click the **Fields tab.** In the **Formatting group**, change the **Data Type** to **Text.** Compare your screen with Figure 1.23.

> The data from the *a01A_Faculty* worksheet displays in your *1A Faculty* table in the database. The navigation area indicates that there are 30 records in the table. Recall that if a field contains numbers that are not used in calculations, the data type should be set to Text. When you import data from an Excel spreadsheet, check the data types of all fields to ensure they are correct.

Figure 1.23

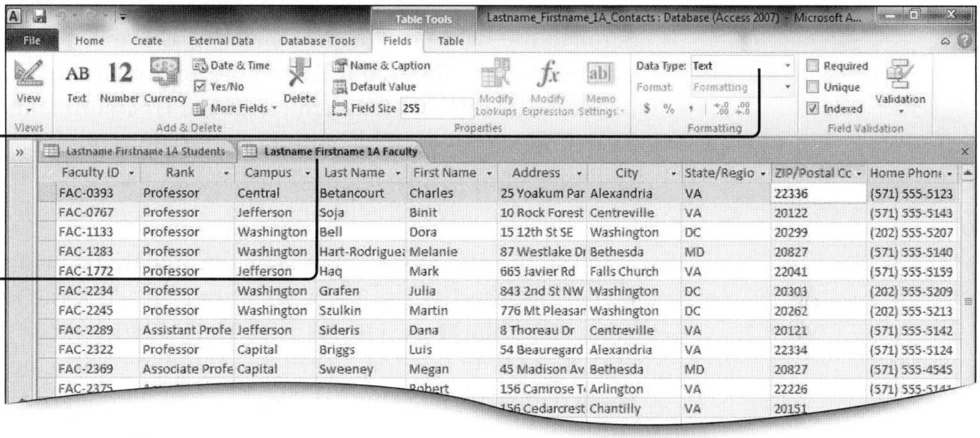

ZIP/Postal Code data type changed to Text

Table created by importing Excel spreadsheet

Activity 1.12 | Adjusting Column Widths

By using techniques similar to those you use for Excel worksheets, you can adjust the widths of Access fields that display in Datasheet view.

1   In the object window, click the **object tab** for your **1A Students** table.

> Clicking the object tabs along the top of the object window enables you to display open objects to work with them. All of the columns are the same width regardless of the amount of data in the field, the field size that was set, or the length of the field name. If you print the table as currently displayed, some of the data or field names will not fully print until you adjust the column widths.

2 In the field names row, point to the right edge of the **Address** field to display the ⬌ pointer, and then compare your screen with Figure 1.24.

Figure 1.24

Pointer positioned on right edge of Address field

3 With your ⬌ pointer positioned as shown in Figure 1.24, double-click the right edge of the **Address** field.

> The column width of the Address field widens to fully display the longest entry in the field. In this manner, the width of a column can be increased or decreased to fit its contents in the same manner as a column in an Excel worksheet. In Access this is referred to as *Best Fit*.

4 Point to the **Phone Number** field name to display the ⬇ pointer, right-click to select the entire column and display a shortcut menu, and then click **Field Width.** In the **Column Width** dialog box, click **Best Fit**.

5 Scroll to the right until the last three fields display. Point to the **E-mail** field name to display the ⬇ pointer, hold down the left mouse button, and then drag to the right to select this column, the **Faculty Advisor ID** column, and the **Amount Owed** column. By double-clicking the ⬌ pointer on the right boundary of any of the selected columns, or by displaying the Field Width dialog box from the shortcut menu, apply **Best Fit** to the selected columns.

6 Scroll all the way to the left to view the **Student ID** field. To the left of the *Student ID* field name, click the **Select All** button ▫. Click the **Home tab**, and in the **Records group**, click the **More** button. Click **Field Width**, and in the **Column Width** dialog box, click **Best Fit**. In the first record, scroll to the right as necessary, click in the **Amount Owed** field, and then compare your screen with Figure 1.25.

> In this manner, you can adjust all of the column widths at one time. After applying Best Fit, be sure to click in any field to remove the selection from all of the records; otherwise, the layout changes will not be saved with the table. Adjusting the width of columns does not change the data in the table's records; it changes only the *display* of the data.

Figure 1.25

Select All button

More button

City	State/Region	ZIP/Postal Code	Phone Number	E-mail	Faculty Advisor ID	Amount Owed	Click to Add
Rockville	MD	20857	(301) 555-2320	jbarthmaier@capccc.edu	FAC-2234	$3,210.00	
Alexandria	VA	22336	(571) 555-0234	mfresch@capccc.edu	FAC-2289	$150.00	
Arlington	VA	22226	(571) 555-2017	ltelfer@capccc.edu	FAC-2245	$402.50	
Potomac	MD	20854	(240) 555-0177	jingram@capccc.edu	FAC-2377	$378.50	
Alexandria	VA	22336	(571) 555-0302	avohra@capccc.edu	FAC-2289	$0.00	
Alexandria	VA	22336	(571) 555-0305	cmcelaney@capccc.edu	FAC-6543	$15.15	
Vienna	VA	22180	(703) 555-2329	wwall@capccc.edu	FAC-2245	$0.00	
Fairfax	VA	22030	(703) 555-0192	abass@capccc.edu	FAC-9005	$0.00	
West Springfield	VA	22152	(703) 555-2330	scaputo@capccc.edu	FAC-8223	$0.00	
Alexandria	VA	22334	(703) 555-0301	cthomas@capccc.edu	FAC-8223	$0.00	
Fairfax	VA	22031	(571) 555-2026	creid@capccc.edu	FAC-6543	$1,232.00	
Washington	DC	20262	(202) 555-9360	jstavish@capccc.edu	FAC-2234	$26.25	
Alexandria	VA	22302	(703) 555-0301	ahernandez@capccc.edu	FAC-6543	$896.25	
Manassas			(703) 555-1017	ralexander@capccc.edu	FAC-8223	$0.00	
				amorris@capccc.edu	FAC-2289		

7   On the Quick Access Toolbar, click the **Save** button 🖫 to save the table design changes—changing the column widths.

> If you do not save the table after making design changes, Access will prompt you to save when you close the table.

Activity 1.13 | Printing a Table

Although a printed table does not look as professional as a printed report, there are times when you will want to print a table. For example, you may need a quick reference or want to proofread the data that has been entered.

1   On the Ribbon, click the **File tab** to display **Backstage** view, click the **Print** tab, click **Print Preview**, and then compare your screen with Figure 1.26.

Figure 1.26

Print Preview window

Next Page button

Page 1 displays

Navigation area—used to move from page to page

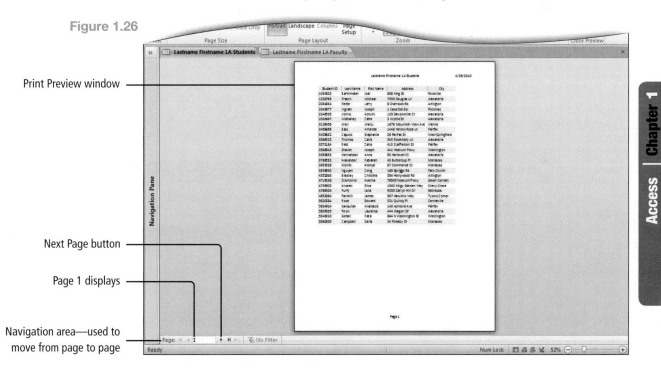

2   In the lower left corner, click the **Next Page** button ▶ two times. Point to the top of the page to display the 🔍 pointer, click one time to zoom in, and then compare your screen with Figure 1.27.

> The display enlarges, and the Zoom Out pointer displays. The third page of the table displays the last two field columns. The Next Page button is dimmed, indicating there are no more pages. The Previous Page button is darker, indicating that pages exist before this page.

Figure 1.27

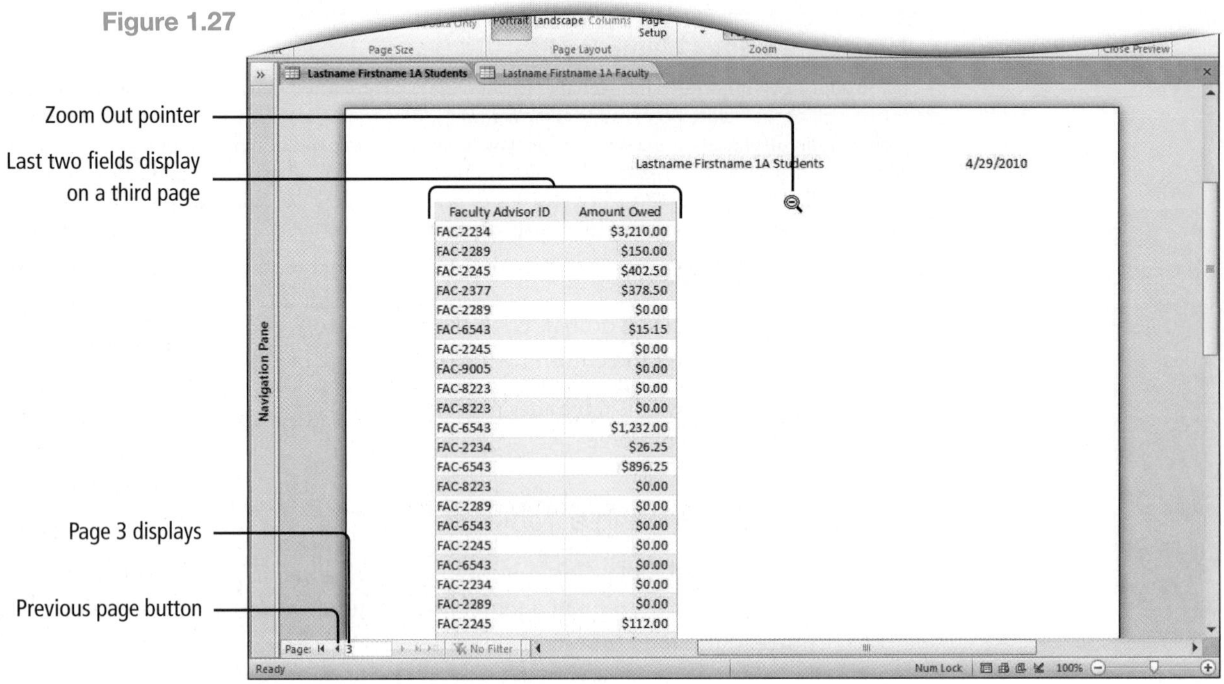

Zoom Out pointer

Last two fields display
on a third page

Page 3 displays

Previous page button

Another Way

Click the 🔍 pointer
to zoom back to Fit to
Window view.

3 On the Ribbon, in the **Zoom group**, click the **Zoom** button to zoom back to Fit to
Window view.

4 In the **Page Layout group**, click the **Landscape** button. In the navigation area, click
the **Previous Page** button ◀ to display **Page 1**, and then compare your screen with
Figure 1.28.

> The orientation of the printout changes, the table name and current date display at the
> top of the page, and the page number displays at the bottom. The change in orientation
> from portrait to landscape is not saved with the table. Each time you print, you must
> check the margins, page orientation, and other print parameters to print as you intend.

Figure 1.28

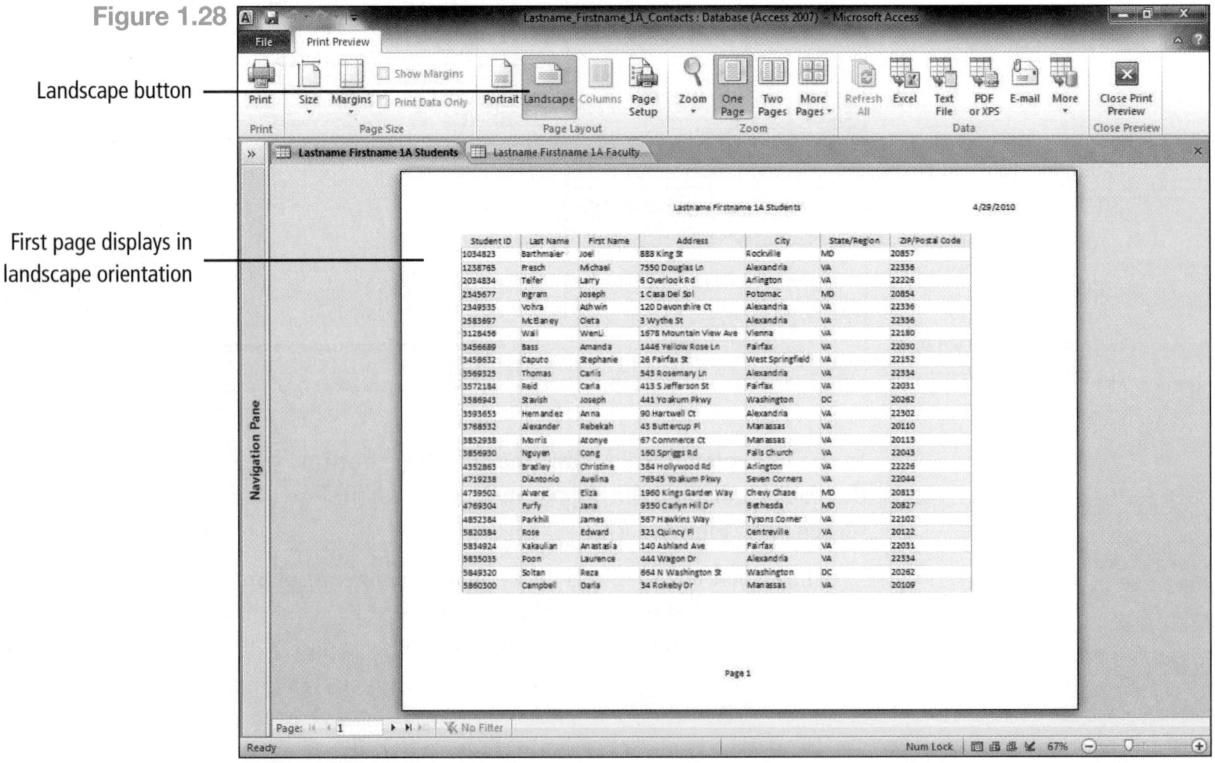

Landscape button

First page displays in
landscape orientation

5 On the **Print Preview tab**, in the **Print group**, click the **Print** button. In the **Print** dialog box, under **Print Range**, verify that the **All** option button is selected. Under **Copies**, verify that the **Number of Copies** is **1.** Compare your screen with Figure 1.29.

Figure 1.29

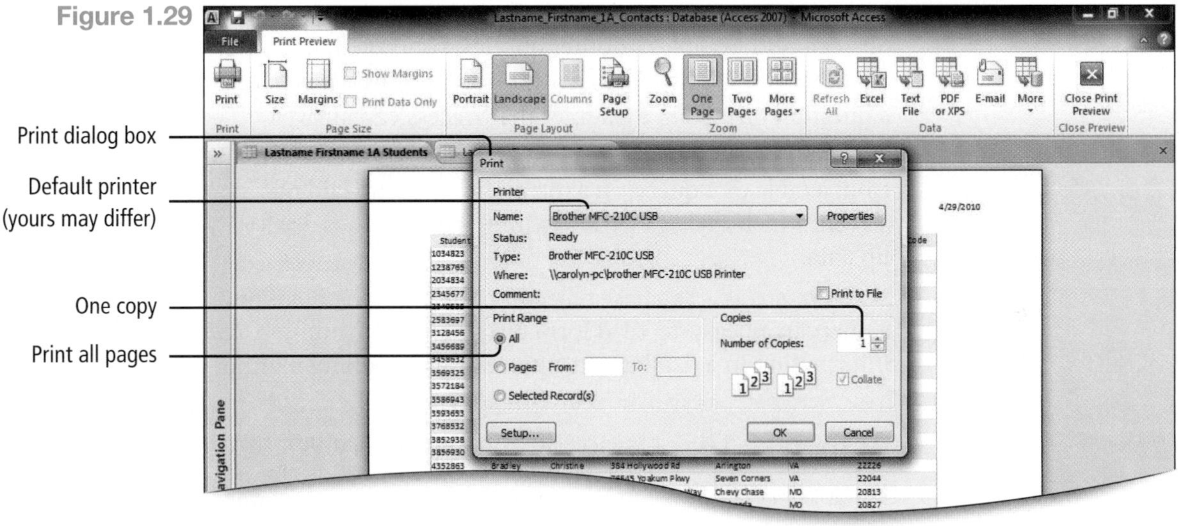

Print dialog box

Default printer
(yours may differ)

One copy

Print all pages

6 Determine how your instructor wants you to submit your work for this project—on paper or electronically. If submitting electronically, determine if, in addition to submitting your Access database, you are to create and submit electronic printouts of individual database objects.

7 To print on paper, in the **Print** dialog box, click **OK**, and then in the **Close Preview group**, click the **Close Print Preview** button. This printout will have two pages. To create an electronic PDF printout of this table object, in the Print dialog box, click Cancel, and then follow the steps in the following Note—or follow the specific directions provided by your instructor.

8 At the far right edge of the object window, click the **Close Object** button ☒ to close the **1A Students** table.

9 With your **1A Faculty** table displayed, to the left of the **Faculty ID** field name, click the **Select All** button ☐ to select all of the columns. On the **Home tab**, in the **Records group**, click the **More** button. Click **Field Width**, and in the **Column Width** dialog box, click **Best Fit**. Click in any field in the table to remove the selection, and then **Save** 🖫 the table.

10 Display the table in **Print Preview.** Change the **Orientation** to **Landscape.** If directed to do so by your instructor, create a paper or electronic printout, and then **Close Print Preview**—two pages result.

11 Click the **Close Object** button ⊠.

> All of your database objects—the *1A Students* table and the *1A Faculty* table—are closed; the object window is empty.

Objective 4 | Create and Use a Query, Form, and Report

A *query* is a database object that retrieves specific data from one or more database objects—either tables or other queries—and then, in a single datasheet, displays only the data that you specify. Because the word *query* means *to ask a question*, think of a query as a question formed in a manner that Access can answer.

A *form* is an Access object with which you can enter data, edit data, or display data from a table or a query. In a form, the fields are laid out in an attractive format on the screen, which makes working with the database easier for those who must enter and look up data.

A *report* is a database object that displays the fields and records from a table or a query in an easy-to-read format suitable for printing. Create reports to *summarize* information in a database in a professional-looking manner.

Activity 1.14 | Using the Simple Query Wizard to Create a Query

A *select query* is one type of Access query. A select query, also called a *simple select query*, retrieves (selects) data from one or more tables or queries and then displays the selected data in a datasheet. A select query creates subsets of data to answer specific questions; for example, *Which students live in Arlington, VA?*

The objects from which a query selects its data are referred to as the query's *data source*. In this activity, you will create a simple select query using a *wizard*. A wizard is a feature in Microsoft Office programs that walks you step by step through a process. The process involves choosing the data source, and then indicating the fields you want to include in the query result. The query—the question that you want to ask—is *What is the name, complete mailing address, and Student ID of every student?*

1 Click the **Create tab**, and then in the **Queries group**, click the **Query Wizard** button. In the **New Query** dialog box, click **Simple Query Wizard**, and then click **OK.** Compare your screen with Figure 1.30.

Figure 1.30

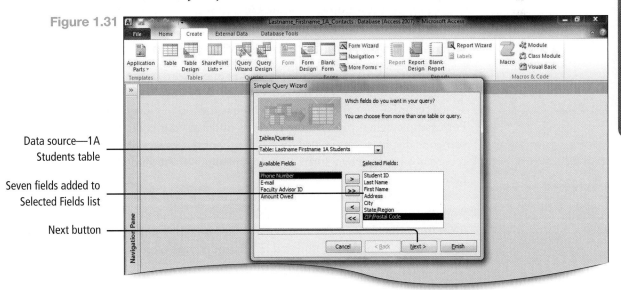

Simple Query Wizard dialog box

Tables/Queries arrow

Add Field button

No database objects display in object window—all are closed

2 Click the **Tables/Queries arrow**, and then click your **Table: 1A Students**.

To create a query, first choose the data source—the object from which to select data. The name and complete mailing address of every student is stored in the 1A Students table, so this table will be your data source.

3 Under **Available Fields**, click **Student ID**, and then click the **Add Field** button ![>] to move the field to the **Selected Fields** list on the right. Point to the **Last Name** field, and then double-click to add the field to the **Selected Fields** list.

Use either method to add fields to the Selected Fields list. Fields can be added in any order.

4 By using the **Add Field** button ![>] or by double-clicking the field name, add the following fields to the **Selected Fields** list: **First Name**, **Address**, **City**, **State/Region**, and **ZIP/Postal Code.** Compare your screen with Figure 1.31.

Choosing these seven fields will answer the question, *What is the Student ID, name, and address of every student?*

Figure 1.31

Data source—1A Students table

Seven fields added to Selected Fields list

Next button

5 Click **Next.** In the **Simple Query Wizard** dialog box, click in the **What title do you want for your query?** box. Edit as necessary so that the query name, using your own last and first name, is **Lastname Firstname 1A All Students Query** and then compare your screen with Figure 1.32.

Access | Chapter 1

Figure 1.32

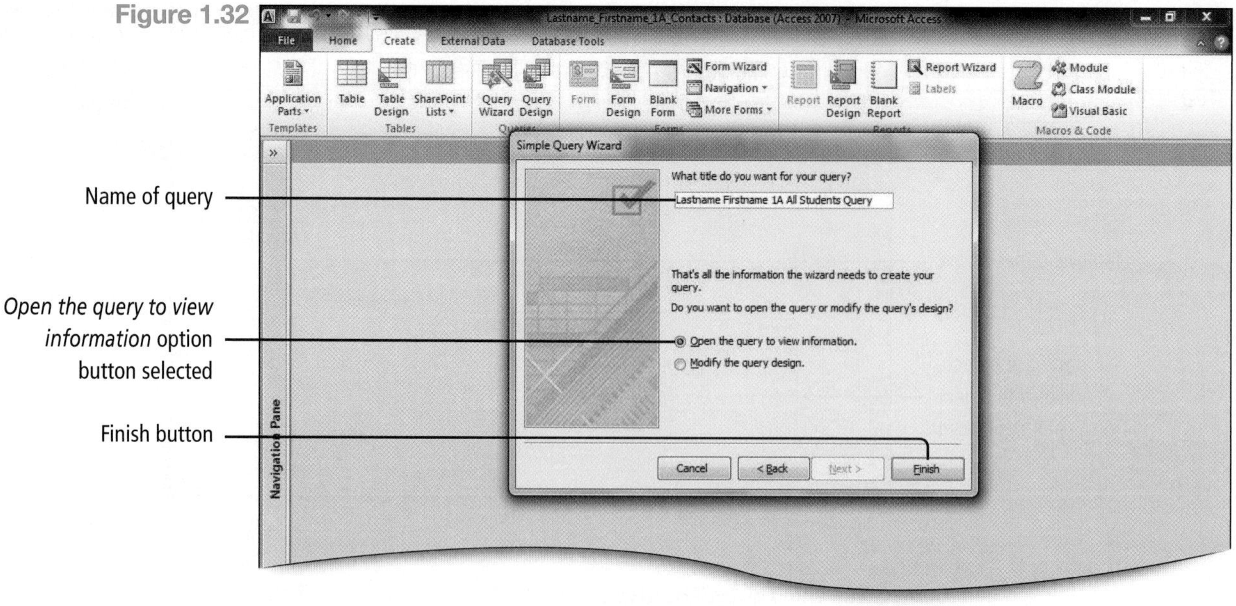

Name of query —

Open the query to view
information option
button selected

Finish button —

6 Click **Finish.**

> Access *runs* the query—performs the actions indicated in your query design by searching the records in the data source you selected, and then finding the records that match specified criteria. The records that match the criteria display in a datasheet. A select query *selects*—pulls out and displays—*only* the information from the data source that you requested, including the specified fields.

> In the object window, Access displays every student record in Datasheet view, but displays *only* the seven fields that you moved to the Selected Fields list in the Simple Query Wizard dialog box.

7 If necessary, apply Best Fit to the columns and then Save the query. Display the query in **Print Preview.** Change the **Orientation** to **Landscape**, and then create a paper or electronic printout as instructed. **Close** the **Print Preview.**

8 In the object window, click the **Close Object** button ☒ to close the query.

Activity 1.15 │ Creating and Printing a Form

One type of Access form displays only one record in the database at a time. Such a form is useful not only to the individual who performs the data entry—typing in the actual records—but also to anyone who has the job of viewing information in a database. For example, when you visit the Records office at your college to obtain a transcript, someone displays your record on a screen. For the viewer, it is much easier to look at one record at a time, using a form, than to look at all of the student records in the database table.

The Form command on the Ribbon creates a form that displays all of the *fields* from the underlying data source (table)—one record at a time. You can use this new form immediately, or you can modify it. Records that you create or edit in a form are automatically added to or updated in the underlying table or tables.

1 **Open** ▸▸ the **Navigation Pane.** Increase the width of the **Navigation Pane** so that all object names display fully. Notice that a table displays a datasheet icon, and a query displays an icon of two overlapping datasheets. Right-click your **1A Students** table to display a menu as shown in Figure 1.33.

Figure 1.33

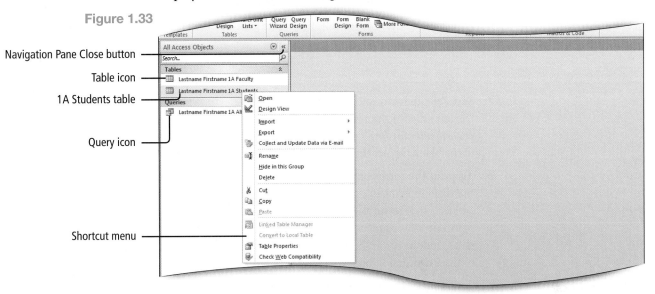

Navigation Pane Close button

Table icon

1A Students table

Query icon

Shortcut menu

2 On the shortcut menu, click **Open** to display the table in the object window, and then **Close** ◂◂ the **Navigation Pane** to maximize your object space.

3 Scroll to the right, and notice that there are 11 fields in the table. On the **Create tab**, in the **Forms group**, click the **Form** button. Compare your screen with Figure 1.34.

Access creates a form based on the currently selected object—the 1A Students table. Access creates the form in a simple top-to-bottom format, with all 11 fields in the record lined up in a single column.

The form displays in *Layout view*—the Access view in which you can make changes to a form or to a report while the object is open. Each field displays the data for the first student record in the table—*Joel Barthmaier*.

Figure 1.34

Form object icon

First record, for *Joel Barthmaier*, displays

Layout View button active

Next record button

Total number of records is 26

Navigation buttons to move among records

Lastname Firstname 1A Students

Student ID	1034823
Last Name	Barthmaier
First Name	Joel
Address	888 King St
City	Rockville
State/Region	MD
ZIP/Postal Code	20857
Phone Number	(301) 555-2320
E-mail	jbarthmaier@capccc.edu
Faculty Advisor ID	FAC-2234
Amount Owed	$3,210.00

Record: ◂ 1 of 26 ▸ ▸▸ ◦ No Filter Search

Layout View

Num Lock

4 At the right edge of the status bar, notice that the **Layout View** button ⊞ is active, indicating that the form is displayed in Layout view.

Another Way

On the Home tab, in the Views group, click the View button, which displays an icon of a form.

5 At the right edge of the status bar, click the **Form View** button ▦.

In *Form view*, you can view the records, but you cannot change the layout or design of the form.

6 In the navigation area, click the **Next record** button ▸ three times. The fourth record—for *Joseph Ingram*—displays.

You can use the navigation buttons to scroll among the records to display any single record.

7 **Save** 🖫 the form with the default name—*Lastname Firstname 1A Students*. Along the left edge of the record, under ▸, click anywhere in the narrow gray bar—the *record selector bar*—to select only the record for *Joseph Ingram*. Notice that the bar turns black, indicating that the record is selected.

8 To print the form for *Joseph Ingram* only, click the **File tab**, and then click **Print**—do *not* display Print Preview. Instead, click **Print**. In the **Print** dialog box, in the lower left corner, click **Setup**. Click the **Columns tab**, change the **Width** to **7.5** so that the form prints on one page, and then click **OK**. The maximum column width that you can enter is dependent upon the printer that is installed on your system. In the lower left corner of the **Print** dialog box, click the **Selected Record(s)** option button, and then click **OK**.

Note | To Print a Single Form in PDF

To create a PDF electronic printout of a single record in a form, change the column width to 7.5 as described in step 8 above, and then in the Print dialog box, click Cancel. On the left edge of the form, click the Record Selector bar so that it is black—selected. On the Ribbon click the External Data tab. In the Export group, click the PDF or XPS button. Navigate to your chapter folder, and then in the lower left corner of the dialog box, if necessary, select the Open file after publishing check box. In the lower right corner of the dialog box, click the Options button. In the Options dialog box, under Range, click the Selected records option button, click OK, and then click Publish. Close the Adobe Reader or Acrobat window.

---

9 **Close** ✕ the form. Notice that your **1A Students** table remains open.

Activity 1.16 | Creating, Modifying, and Printing a Report

1 **Open** ⟩⟩ the **Navigation Pane**, and then open your **1A Faculty** table by double-clicking the table name or by right-clicking and clicking Open from the shortcut menu. **Close** ⟨⟨ the **Navigation Pane**.

2 Click the **Create tab**, and then in the **Reports group**, click the **Report** button.

When you click the Report button, Access generates the report in Layout view and includes all of the fields and all of the records in the table, and does so in a format suitable for printing. Dotted lines indicate how the report would break across pages if you print it. In Layout view, you can make quick changes to the report layout.

Another Way

Right-click the field. From the shortcut menu, click Select Entire Column, and then press Del.

3 Click the **Faculty ID** field name, and then on the Ribbon, click the **Arrange tab.** In the **Rows & Columns group**, click the **Select Column** button, and then press Del. Using the same technique, delete the **Rank** field.

The Faculty ID and Rank fields and data are deleted, and the report readjusts the fields.

4 Click the **Address** field name, and then use the scroll bar at the bottom of the screen to scroll to the right to display the **Mobile Phone** field; be careful not to click in the report. Hold down Shift and then click the **Mobile Phone** field name to select all of the fields from *Address* through *Mobile Phone*. With all the field names selected—surrounded by a colored border—in the **Row & Columns group**, click the **Select Column** button, and then press Del.

Use this technique to select and delete multiple columns in Layout view.

5 Scroll to the left, and notice that you can see all of the remaining fields. In any record, click in the **E-mail** field. Point to the right edge of the field box to display the ↔ pointer. Drag to the right slightly to increase the width of the field so that all E-mail addresses display on one line.

6 Click the **Last Name** field name. On the Ribbon, click the **Home tab.** In the **Sort & Filter group**, click the **Ascending** button. Compare your screen with Figure 1.35.

By default, tables are sorted in ascending order by the primary key field, which is the Faculty ID field. You can change the default and sort any field in either ascending order or descending order. The sort order does not change in the underlying table, only in the report.

Figure 1.35

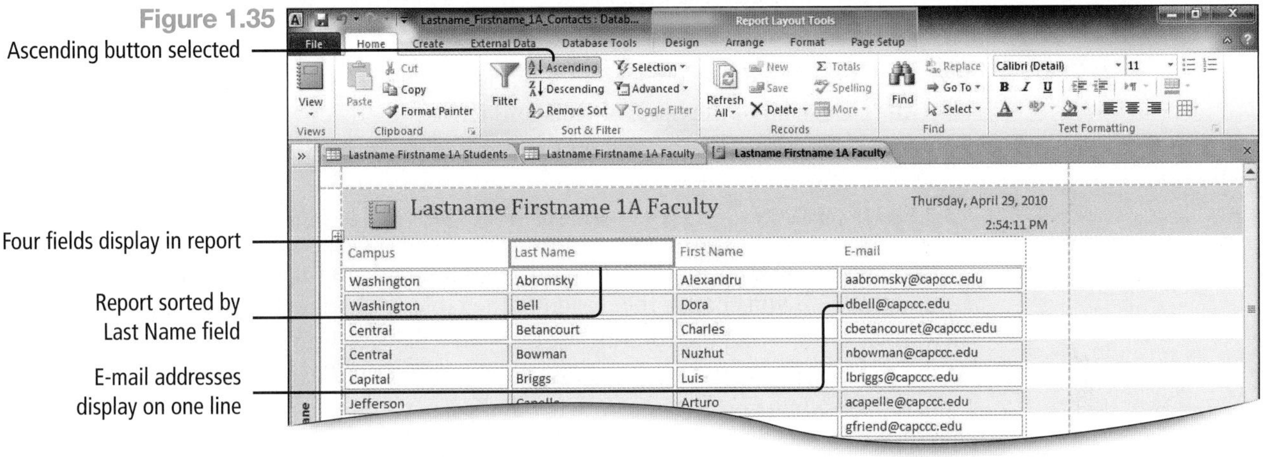

Ascending button selected

Four fields display in report

Report sorted by Last Name field

E-mail addresses display on one line

7 Click the **Save** button 🖫. In the **Report Name** box, add **Report** to the end of the suggested name, and then click **OK**.

8 Display the report in **Print Preview.** In the **Zoom group**, click the **Two Pages** button, and then compare your screen with Figure 1.36.

The report will print on two pages because the page number at the bottom of the report is located beyond the right margin of the report.

Figure 1.36

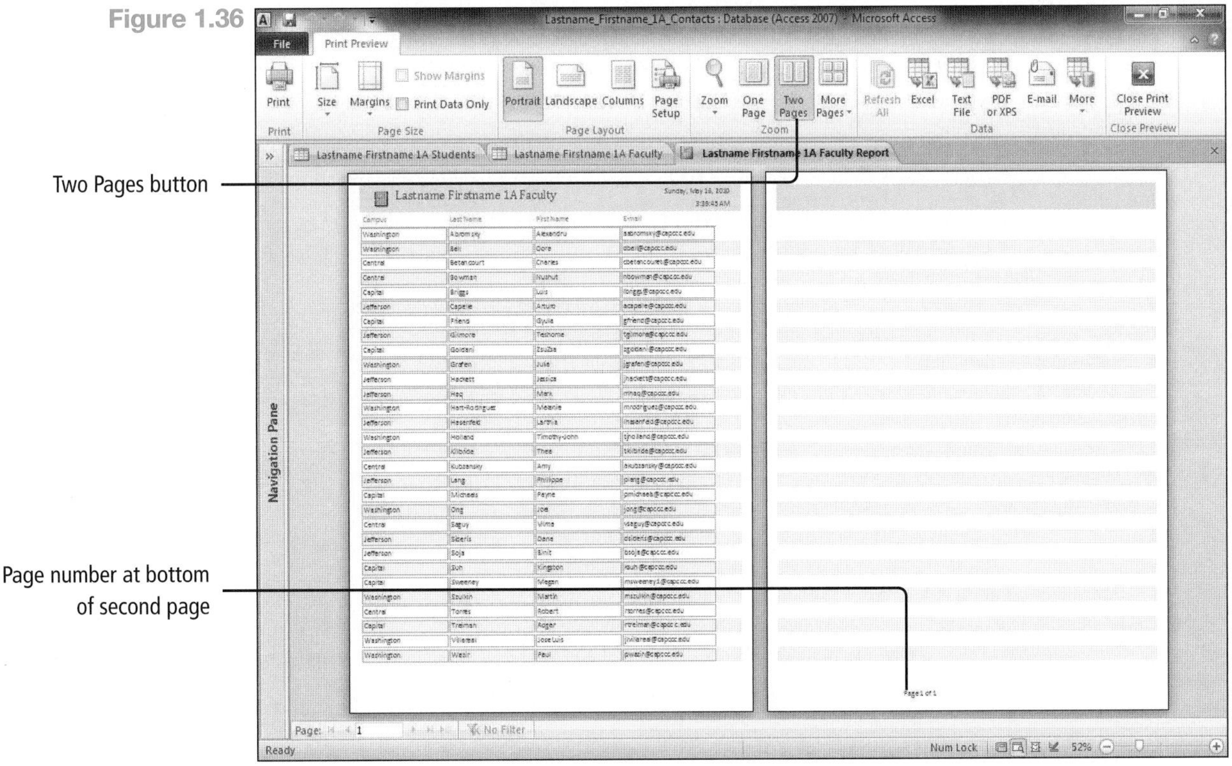

Two Pages button

Page number at bottom of second page

9 In the **Close Preview group**, click the **Close Print Preview button**. Scroll down to the bottom of the report, and then scroll to the right to display the page number. Click the page number—**Page 1 of 1**—and then press Del.

10 Display the report in **Print Preview** and notice that the report will print on one page. In the **Zoom group**, click the **One Page** button. **Save** 🖫 the changes to the design of the report, and then create a paper or electronic printout as instructed. At the right end of the Ribbon, click the **Close Print Preview** button.

> The default margins of a report created with the Report tool are 0.25 inch. Some printers require a greater margin so your printed report may result in two pages—you will learn to adjust this later. Also, if a printer is not installed on your system, the report may print on two pages.

11 Along the top of the object window, right-click any object tab, and then click **Close All** to close all of the open objects and leave the object window empty.

Objective 5 | Save and Close a Database

When you close an Access table, any changes made to the records are saved automatically. If you change the design of the table or change the layout of the Datasheet view, such as adjusting the column widths, you will be prompted to save the design changes. At the end of your Access session, close your database and exit Access. If the Navigation Pane is open when you close Access, it will display when you reopen the database.

Activity 1.17 | Closing and Saving a Database

1 **Open** ⏵ the **Navigation Pane.** Notice that your report object displays with a green report icon. Compare your screen with Figure 1.37.

Figure 1.37

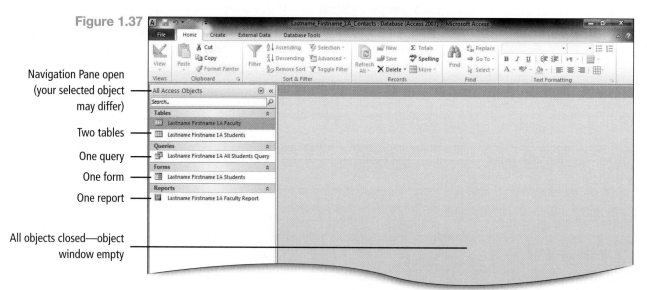

Navigation Pane open (your selected object may differ)

Two tables

One query

One form

One report

All objects closed—object window empty

Another Way

In the upper right corner of the window, click the Close button.

2 Display **Backstage** view, click **Close Database**, and then click **Exit**. As directed by your instructor, submit your database and the five paper or electronic printouts—two tables, one query, one form, and one report—that are the results of this project.

End **You have completed Project 1A** ————————————

GO! Beyond Office

Objective | Export an Access Table to an Excel File, Save to Your SkyDrive, and Share the File

Recall that Windows Live SkyDrive is a free file storage and file sharing service provided by Windows Live—a collection of programs and services for individuals and that work together. You can save a database to SkyDrive—so long as the database is no larger than 50 MB—and then share the database. This enables others to download the database to their computers. You can export a database object to an Excel worksheet, a PDF file, or a text file, and then save the file to SkyDrive.

> **Alert! | Working with Web-Based Applications and Services**
>
> Computer programs and services on the Web receive continuous updates and improvements. Thus, the steps to complete this Web-based Activity may differ from the ones shown. You can often look at the screens and the information presented to determine how to complete the Activity.

Activity | Exporting an Access Table to an Excel File, Saving the File to Your SkyDrive, and Sharing the File

In this activity, you will *export*—copy data from one file into another file—your 1A Students table to an Excel file, create a folder on your Windows Live SkyDrive, upload your 1A_Students_xcel file to the folder, and then share the Excel file.

1 If you have a yahoo.com e-mail account, or if you created one in GO! Beyond PowerPoint 1B, skip to Step 2. Otherwise, start your Web browser. In the address bar, type **www.yahoo.com** and then on the left side of the Yahoo! window, click **Mail**. At the bottom of the **Sign in to Yahoo** box, click **Create New Account**, and then follow the steps to create a Yahoo! ID. Close your Web browser.

2 **Start** Access. In **Backstage** view, click **Open**. Navigate to your **Access Chapter 1** folder, and then open your **1A_Contacts** database. If necessary, on the Message Bar, click Enable Content. In the **Navigation Pane**, click your **1A Students** table.

3 On the Ribbon, click the **External Data tab**, and then in the **Export group**, click the **Excel** button. In the **Export - Excel Spreadsheet** dialog box, click the **Browse** button, and then navigate to your **Access Chapter 1** folder.

In the **File name** box, select the text, type **Lastname_Firstname_1A_Students_Excel** and then click **Save**.

4 In the **Export – Excel Spreadsheet** dialog box, under **Specify export options**, select the first two check boxes—**Export data with formatting and layout** and **Open the destination file after the export operation is complete**—and then click **OK**. Compare your screen to Figure A, notice that the table displays in an Excel spreadsheet, and then **Close** Excel.

5 In the **Export – Excel Spreadsheet** dialog box, click **Close**—you need not save the export steps. Click the **File tab** to display **Backstage** view, click **Close Database**, and then click **Exit** to close the Access program.

6 Launch your Web browser, go to **www.live.com**, and then sign in to your Windows Live account. If you do not have a Windows Live account, refer to GO! Beyond

Figure A

GO! Beyond Office

Word 1A to create the account. After you have signed in to your account, at the top of the screen, click **SkyDrive**.

Your SkyDrive opens and may display several folders depending on what you may have previously uploaded to SkyDrive.

7 Near the top of the screen, to the right of **Create**, click the **Create folder** button. In the **Name** box, select the existing text, type **GO! Beyond Office-Access** and then click **Next**.

The newly created folder opens, and you can either drag documents to the folder or select documents from your computer to add to the folder.

8 Click the text **select documents from your computer**. In the **Open** dialog box, navigate to your **Access Chapter 1** folder, and then double-click your **1A_Students_Excel** file to upload it to your SkyDrive folder.

9 In the lower left corner of the screen, click **Continue** to display the contents of your GO! Beyond Office-Access folder.

By default, folders that you create are shared with only you unless you change the sharing arrangement. One purpose for uploading documents to SkyDrive is to share documents with others for collaboration, for comment, for editing, or for downloading. *Permissions* grant access to the files within your folder to others. In SkyDrive, permissions are set at the *folder* level.

10 On the right side of the screen, under **Sharing**, click **Edit permissions**.

11 Under **Add additional people**, with the insertion point blinking in the **Enter a name or an email address** box, type your complete **Yahoo! e-mail address**; for example, Firstname_Lastname@yahoo.com and then press Enter.

The Yahoo! e-mail address displays below the *Enter a name or an email address* box. An X displays to its left,

which you can click if you choose to delete permission for the person whose e-mail address you entered. To the right of the e-mail address, you can display a list of Permission levels.

12 To the right of your Yahoo! e-mail address, click the **arrow**, and if necessary, select **Can add, edit details, and delete files**.

This permission level enables the person with this e-mail address to make changes to the folder. If you set the *Can view files permission level*, the person with whom the folder is shared is restricted to viewing only—he or she cannot make any changes in the folder.

13 In the lower left corner, click **Save**. In the **Send a notification for GO! Beyond Office-Access** page, click the **Send** button to notify this individual that you have shared this folder with him or her.

14 Display the **Start** menu 🪟, and then click **All Programs**. On the list of programs, click the **Accessories** folder, and then click **Snipping Tool**. In the **Snipping Tool** dialog box, click the **New arrow**. On the list, click **Full-screen Snip**.

15 On the **Snipping Tool** markup window toolbar, click the **Save Snip** button 💾. In the **Save As** dialog box, navigate to your **Access Chapter 1** folder. Be sure the **Save as type** box displays **JPEG file**. In the **File name** box, type **Lastname_Firstname_1A_Access_Snip** and then click **Save**. **Close** ❎ the **Snipping Tool** window.

16 Sign out of your Windows Live account. Open your Yahoo! account, and notice that you have an e-mail message indicating that the folder was shared with you. If you do not see the e-mail message, look in your Yahoo! Spam folder. Compare your screen with Figure B, log out of your Yahoo! account, and then close all windows. Submit your snip file as directed by your instructor.

E-mail message indicating that a folder was shared

Figure B

Project 1B Student Workshops Database

myitlab
Project 1B Training

Project Activities

In Activities 1.18 through 1.23, you will assist Dr. Kirsten McCarty, Vice President of Student Services, by creating a database to store information about student workshops presented by Capital Cities Community College. You will use a database template that tracks event information, add workshop information to the database, and then print the results. Your completed report and table will look similar to Figure 1.38.

Project Files

For Project 1B, you will need the following files:

> New Access database using the Events template
> a01B_Workshops (Excel workbook)

You will save your database as:

> Lastname_Firstname_1B_Student_Workshops

Project Results

Lastname Firstname 1B Workshop Locations   4/29/2010

Room ID	Campus/Location	Room	Seats	Room Arrangement	Equipment
CAP-01	Capital Campus	C202	50	Lecture/Classroom	Smart Board
CEN-01	Central Campus	H248	20	U-shaped	White Board
JEFF-01	Jefferson Campus	J123	150	Theater	Computer Projector, Surround Sound, & Microphones
JEFF-02	Jefferson Campus	A15	25	U-shaped	25 Computers, Projector
WASH-01	Washington Campus	A15	35	Lecture/Classroom	Computer Projector

Lastname Firstname All Events

Thursday, April 29, 2010   4:33:47 PM

Title	Start Time	End Time	Location	
Your Cyber Reputation	3/9/2016 7:00:00 PM	3/9/2016 9:00:00 PM	Jefferson Campus	
Internet Safety				
Writing a Research Paper	3/10/2016 4:00:00 PM	3/10/2016 6:00:00 PM	Washington Campu	
Computer Skills				
Resume Writing	3/18/2016 2:00:00 PM	3/18/2016 4:00:00 PM	Capital Campus	
Job Skills				
Careers in the Legal Profession	3/19/2016 2:00:00 PM	3/19/2016 4:00:00 PM	Central Campus	
Careers				
Transferring to a 4-Year University	4/8/2016 11:00:00 AM	4/8/2016 12:30:00 PM	Jefferson Campus	
Transfer				
Financial Aid	4/14/2016 7:00:00 PM	4/14/2016 8:30:00 PM	Central Campus	
CC Info				
Sensitivity Training	4/15/2016 8:00:00 AM	4/15/2016 9:00:00 AM	Capital Campus	
Human Behavior				
Preparing for the Job Interview	4/15/2016 12:30:00 PM	4/15/2016 2:00:00 PM	Capital Campus	
Job Skills				
Class Note Taking	4/18/2016 12:30:00 PM	4/18/2016 1:30:00 PM	Central Campus	
Study Skills				
Managing Time and Stress	4/18/2016 6:00:00 PM	4/18/2016 7:30:00 PM	Washington Campu	
Study Skills				
Work Smart at Your Computer	4/20/2016 10:00:00 AM	4/20/2016 11:00:00 AM	Jefferson Campus	
Computer Skills				
Preparing for Tests	4/20/2016 4:00:00 PM	4/20/2016 5:00:00 PM	Central Campus	
Study Skills				

Page 1 of 1

Figure 1.38
Project 1B Student Workshops

Objective 6 | Create a Database Using a Template

A database template contains pre-built tables, queries, forms, and reports to perform a specific task, such as tracking a large number of events. For example, your college may hold events such as athletic contests, plays, lectures, concerts, and club meetings. Using a predefined template, your college Activities Director can quickly create a database to manage these events. The advantage of using a template to start a new database is that you do not have to create the objects—all you need to do is enter your data and modify the pre-built objects to suit your needs.

The purpose of the database in this project is to track the student workshops offered by Capital Cities Community College. The questions to be answered might include:

What workshops will be offered and when will they be offered?

In what rooms and campus locations will the workshops be held?

Which workshop locations have a computer projector for PowerPoint presentations?

Activity 1.18 | Creating a New Database Using a Template

1 **Start** Access. Under **Available Templates**, click **Sample templates.** If necessary, scroll down to locate and then click **Events.** Compare your screen with Figure 1.39.

Sample templates are stored on your computer; they are included with the Access program.

Figure 1.39

2 On the right side of the screen, to the right of the **File Name** box, click the **Browse** button, and then navigate to your **Access Chapter 1** folder.

3 At the bottom of the **File New Database** dialog box, select the text in the **File name** box. Using your own name, type **Lastname_Firstname_1B_Student_Workshops** and then press (Enter).

4 In the lower right corner of your screen, click the **Create** button.

Access creates the *1B Student Workshops* database, and the database name displays in the title bar. A predesigned *form*—Event List—displays in the object window. Although you can enter events for any date, when you open the database in the future, the Event List will display only those events for the current date and future dates.

5 Under the Ribbon, on the **Message Bar**, a Security Warning displays. On the **Message Bar**, click the **Enable Content** button.

Databases provided by Microsoft are safe to use on your computer.

Activity 1.19 │ Building a Table by Entering Records in a Multiple Items Form

The purpose of a form is to simplify the entry of data into a table—either for you or for others who enter data. In Project 1A, you created a simple form that enabled you to display or enter records in a table one record at a time. The Events template creates a *Multiple Items form*, a form that enables you to display or enter *multiple* records in a table, but still with an easier and simplified layout than typing directly into the table itself.

1 Click in the first empty **Title** field. Type **Your Cyber Reputation** and then press (Tab). In the **Start Time** field, type **3/9/16 7p** and then press (Tab).

Access formats the date and time. As you enter dates and times, a small calendar displays to the right of the field, which you can click to select a date instead of typing.

2 In the **End Time** field, type **3/9/16 9p** and then press (Tab). In the **Description** field, type **Internet Safety** and then press (Tab). In the **Location** field, type **Jefferson Campus** and then press (Tab) three times to move to the **Title** field in the new record row. Compare your screen with Figure 1.40.

Because the workshops have no unique value, Access uses the AutoNumber data type of the ID field to assign a unique, sequential number to each record. In the navigation area, each record is identified as a task, rather than a record or page.

Figure 1.40

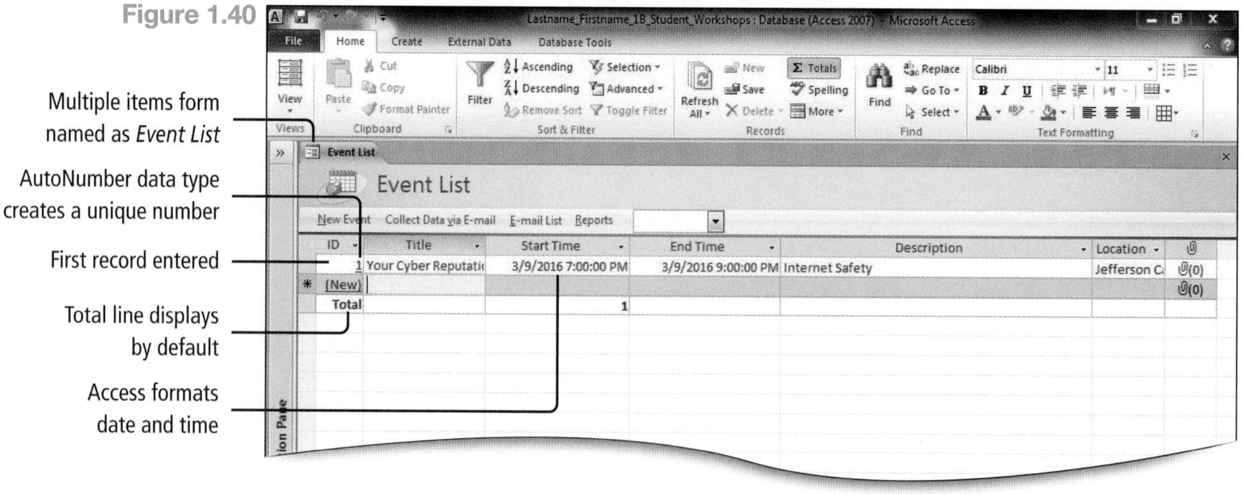

Multiple items form named as *Event List*

AutoNumber data type creates a unique number

First record entered

Total line displays by default

Access formats date and time

3 Directly above the field names row, click **New Event**.

A *single-record form* displays, similar to the simple form you created in Project 1A. A single-record form enables you to display or enter one record at a time into a table.

4 Using Tab to move from field to field, enter the following record—press Tab three times to move from the **End Time** field to the **Description** field. Compare your screen with Figure 1.41.

Title	Location	Start Time	End Time	Description
Writing a Research Paper	**Washington Campus**	**3/10/16 4p**	**3/10/16 6p**	**Computer Skills**

Figure 1.41

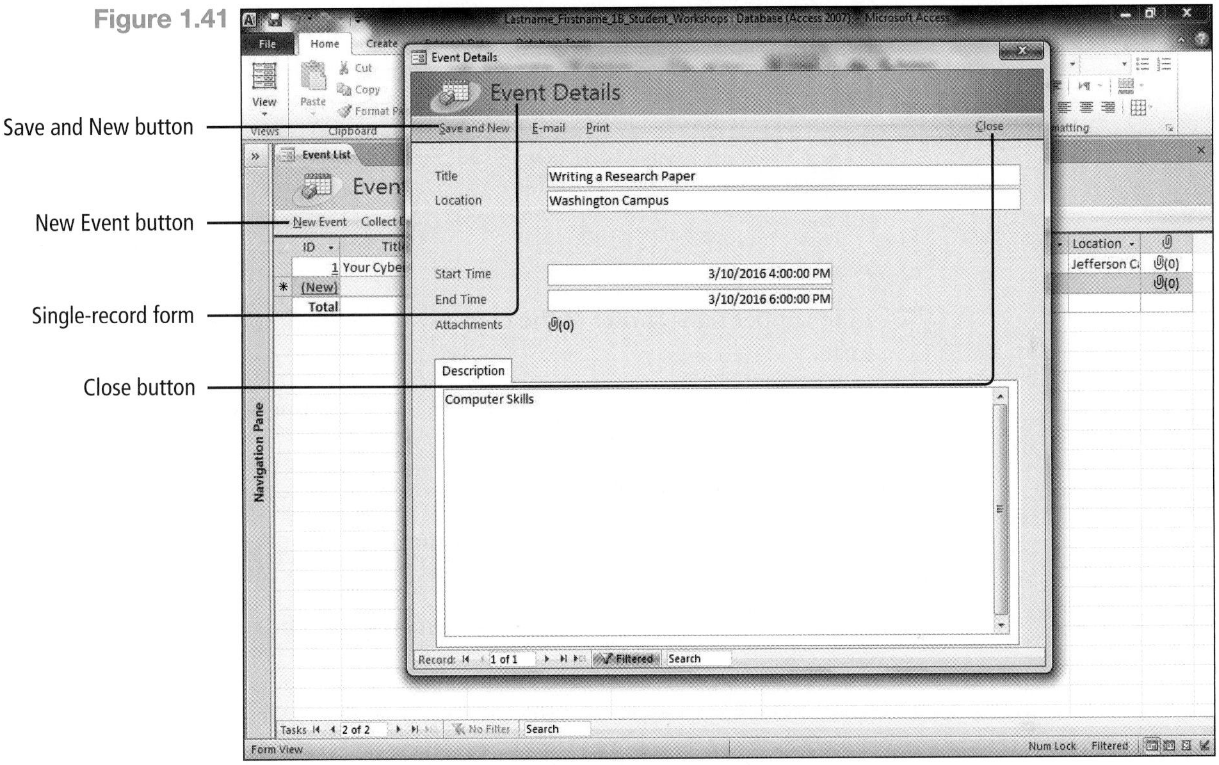

Save and New button
New Event button
Single-record form
Close button

5 In the upper right corner of the single-record form, click **Close**, and notice that the new record displays in the Multiple Items form.

6 Using either the rows on the Multiple Items form or the New Event single-record form, enter the following records, and then compare your screen with Figure 1.42.

ID	Title	Start Time	End Time	Description	Location
3	**Resume Writing**	**3/18/16 2p**	**3/18/16 4p**	**Job Skills**	**Capital Campus**
4	**Careers in the Legal Profession**	**3/19/16 2p**	**3/19/16 4p**	**Careers**	**Central Campus**

> **Alert! | Does a Single Record Form Open?**
>
> In the Multiple Items form, pressing Enter three times at the end of a row to begin a new record may display the single-record New Event form. If you prefer to use the Multiple Items form, close the single-record form and continue entering records, using the Tab key to move from field to field.

Figure 1.42

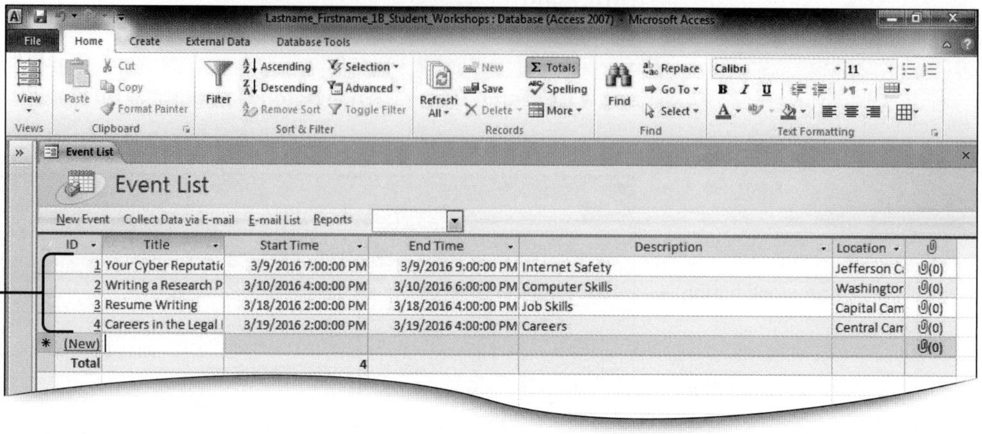

Four records entered in form

7. In the upper right corner of the object window, click **Close** to close the **Event List** form.

8. On the Ribbon, click the **External Data tab.** In the **Import & Link group**, click the **Excel** button.

   Recall that you can populate a table by importing data from an Excel workbook.

9. In the **Get External Data – Excel Spreadsheet** dialog box, click the **Browse** button. Navigate to your student files, and then double-click **a01B_Workshops**.

10. Click the second option button—**Append a copy of the records to the table**—and then click **OK**.

11. Click **Next**, click **Finish**, and then **Close** the dialog box.

12. **Open** » the **Navigation Pane.** Double-click **Event List** to open the form that displays data stored in the Events table, and then **Close** « the **Navigation Pane**.

13. To the left of the **ID** field name, click the **Select All** button to select all of the columns.

> **Another Way**
>
> With the columns selected, in the field heading row, point to the right edge of any of the selected columns, and then double-click to apply Best Fit to all of the selected columns.

14. In the field names row, point to any of the selected field names, right-click, and then click **Field Width.** In the **Column Width** dialog box, click **Best Fit.** Notice that the widths of all of the columns are adjusted to accommodate the longest entry in the column. If you scroll to the right and some of the column widths did not adjust, select those columns and then follow the directions given in the Another Way box. Access applies Best Fit to the columns that are displayed in the window or for the width of the computer screen.

15. In the first record, click in the **Title** field to deselect the columns. **Save** the form, and then compare your screen with Figure 1.43.

    Eight additional records display—those imported from the a01B_Workshops Excel workbook.

Figure 1.43

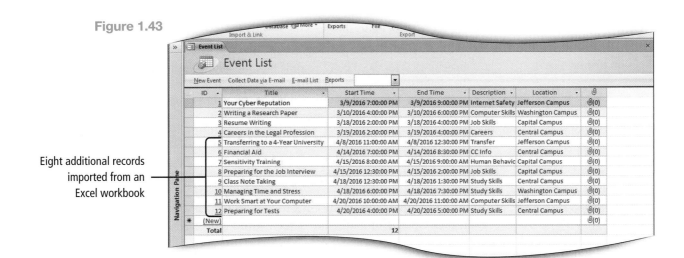

Eight additional records imported from an Excel workbook

Objective 7 | Organize Objects in the Navigation Pane

Use the Navigation Pane to organize database objects, to open them, and to perform common tasks like renaming an object.

Activity 1.20 | Organizing Database Objects in the Navigation Pane

The Navigation Pane groups and displays your database objects and can do so in predefined arrangements. In this activity, you will group your database objects using the *Tables and Related Views* category, which groups objects by the table to which they are related. This grouping is useful because you can easily determine the data source table of queries, forms, and reports.

1 **Open** ⟫ the **Navigation Pane.** At the top of the **Navigation Pane**, click the **Navigation arrow** ⊙. In the list, under **Navigate To Category**, click **Tables and Related Views**.

2 Confirm that *Events* displays in the bar under the Search box at the top of the **Navigation Pane.** Compare your screen with Figure 1.44.

The icons to the left of the objects listed in the Navigation Pane indicate that the Events template created a number of objects for you—among them, one table titled *Events*, one query, two forms, and five reports. The Event List Multiple Items form, which is currently displayed in the object window, is included in the Navigation Pane. All of the objects were created using the underlying data source, which is the Events table.

Figure 1.44

One table
One query
Two forms
Five reports

Another Way
Double-click the table name to open it in the object window.

3 In the **Navigation Pane**, point to the **Events** *table*, right-click, and then click **Open**.

The Events table is the active object in the object window. Use the Navigation Pane to open objects for use. The 12 records that you entered using the Multiple Items *form* and by importing from an Excel workbook display in the *table*. Tables are the foundation of your database because your data must be stored in a table. You can enter records directly into a table or you can use a form to enter records.

4 In the object window, click the **Event List tab** to bring the form into view and make it the active object.

Recall that a form presents a more user-friendly screen for entering records into a table.

Another Way
Double-click the report name to open it.

5 In the **Navigation Pane**, right-click the *report* (green icon) named **Current Events**, and then click **Open.** Compare your screen with Figure 1.45.

An advantage of using a template to begin a database is that many objects, such as attractively formatted reports, are already designed for you.

Figure 1.45

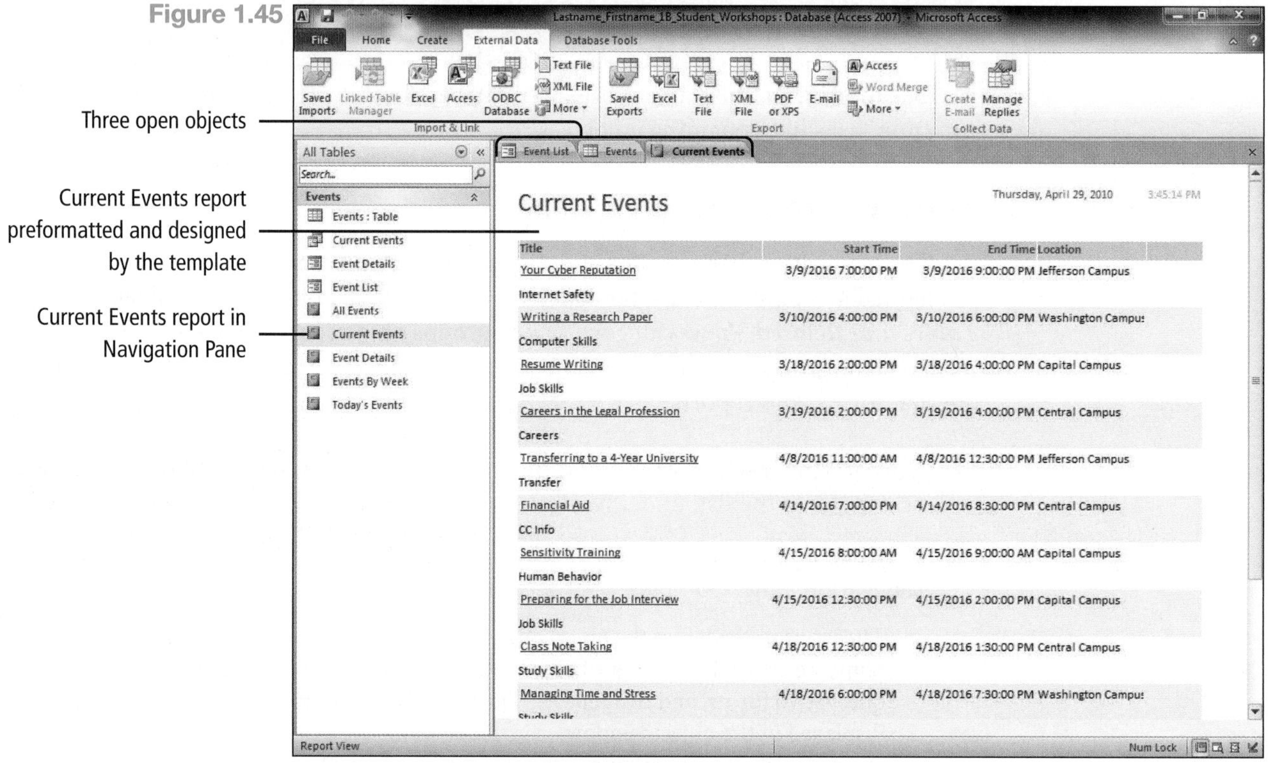

Three open objects

Current Events report preformatted and designed by the template

Current Events report in Navigation Pane

6 In the object window, **Close** ⊠ the **Current Events** report.

7 From the **Navigation Pane**, open the **Events By Week** report.

In this predesigned report, the events are displayed by week. After entering records in the form or table, the preformatted reports are updated with the records from the table.

8 **Close** ⊠ the **Events By Week** report, and then **Close** ⊠ the remaining two open objects. **Close** « the **Navigation Pane**.

Objective 8 | Create a New Table in a Database Created with a Template

The Events database template created only one table—the *Events* table. Although the database was started from a template and contains other objects, you can add additional objects as needed.

Activity 1.21 | Creating a New Table and Changing Its Design

Dr. McCarty has information about the various locations where workshops are held. For example, for the Jefferson campus, she has information about the room, seating arrangements, number of seats, and audio-visual equipment. In the Events table, workshops are scheduled in rooms at each of the four campuses. It would not make sense to store information about the campus rooms multiple times in the same table. It is *not* considered good database design to have duplicate information in a table.

When data in a table becomes redundant, it is usually an indication that you need a new table to contain the information about the topic. In this activity, you will create a table to track the workshop locations and the equipment and seating arrangements in each location.

1 On the Ribbon, click the **Create tab.** In the **Tables group**, click the **Table** button.

2 Click the **Click to Add arrow**, click **Text**, type **Campus/Location** and then press Enter.

3 In the third column, click **Text**, type **Room** and then press Enter. In the fourth column, click **Text**, type **Seats** and then press Enter. In the fifth column, click **Text**, type **Room Arrangement** and then press Enter. In the sixth column, click **Text**, type **Equipment** and then press ↓.

> The table has six fields. Access creates the first field in the table—the ID field—to ensure that every record has a unique value.

4 Right-click the **ID** field name, and then click **Rename Field.** Type **Room ID** and then press Enter. On the **Fields tab**, in the **Formatting group**, click the **Data Type arrow**, and then click **Text.** In the **Field Validation group**, notice that **Unique** is selected.

> Recall that, by default, Access creates the ID field with the AutoNumber data type so that the field can be used as the primary key. Here, this field will store a unique room ID that is a combination of letters, symbols, and numbers, so it is appropriate to change the data type to Text. In Datasheet view, the primary key field is identified by the selection of the Unique check box.

5 In the new record row, click in the **Room ID** field, type **JEFF-01** and then press Tab. In the **Campus/Location** field, type **Jefferson Campus** and then press Tab. In the **Room** field, type **J123** and then press Tab. In the **Seats** field, type **150** and then press Tab. In the **Room Arrangement** field, type **Theater** and then press Tab. In the **Equipment** field, type **Computer Projector, Surround Sound, & Microphones** and then press Tab to move to the new record row. Compare your screen with Figure 1.46.

Recall that Access saves the record when you move to another row within the table. You can press either Tab or Enter to move to another field in a table.

Figure 1.46

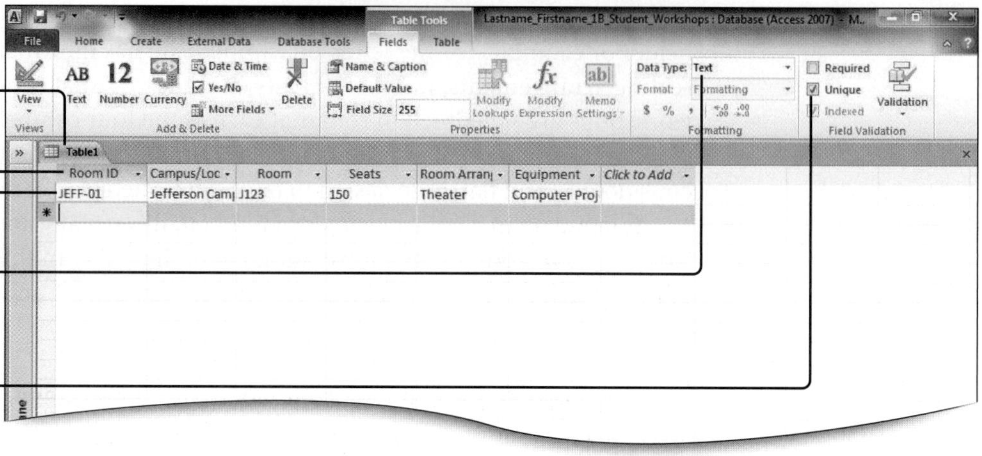

New table
Renamed field
First record entered
Room ID field assigned data type of *Text*
Selected field—Room ID—indicated as primary key field

6 In the **Views group**, click the **View** button to switch to **Design** view. In the **Save As** dialog box, save the table as **Lastname Firstname 1B Workshop Locations** and then click **OK**.

7 In the **Field Name** column, to the left of the **Room ID** box, notice the key icon.

In Design view, the key icon indicates the field—Room ID—that is identified as the primary key.

8 In the **Views group**, click the **View** button to switch to **Datasheet** view.

9 Enter the following records in the table:

Room ID	Campus/Location	Room	Seats	Room Arrangement	Equipment
WASH-01	Washington Campus	A15	35	Lecture/Classroom	Computer Projector
CAP-01	Capital Campus	C202	50	Lecture/Classroom	Smart Board
CEN-01	Central Campus	H248	20	U-shaped	White Board
JEFF-02	Jefferson Campus	A15	25	U-shaped	25 Computers, Projector

10 To the left of the **Room ID** field name, click the **Select All** button ☐ to select all of the columns. On the **Home tab**, in the **Records group**, click the **More** button. Click **Field Width**, and in the **Column Width** dialog box, click **Best Fit**. Click in any field to remove the selection, and then **Save** 💾 the changes to the table. In the object window, **Close** ☒ the **1B Workshop Locations** table.

11 **Open** ⟫ the **Navigation Pane**, and then locate the name of your new table. Point to the right edge of the **Navigation Pane** to display the ⟷ pointer. Drag to the right to display the entire table name, and then compare your screen with Figure 1.47.

Recall that as currently arranged, the Navigation Pane organizes the objects by Tables and Related Views. In Figure 1.47, the Events table is listed first, followed by its related objects, and then the Workshop Locations table is listed. In its current view, the tables are sorted in ascending order by name; therefore, your table may be listed before the Events table depending on your last name.

Figure 1.47

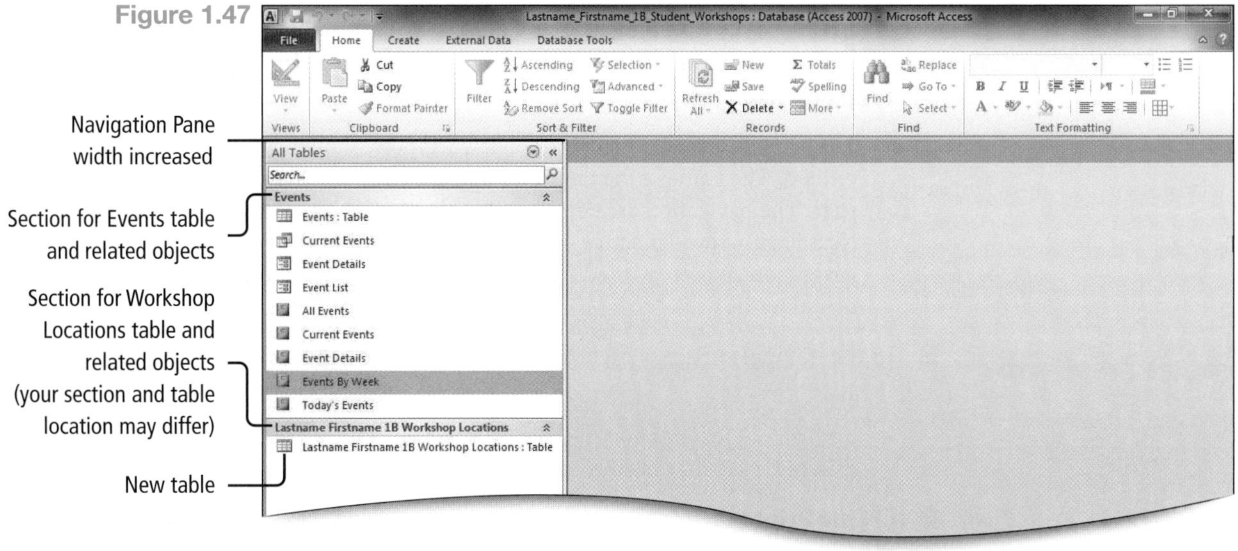

Navigation Pane
width increased

Section for Events table
and related objects

Section for Workshop
Locations table and
related objects
(your section and table
location may differ)

New table

Objective 9 | Print a Report and a Table in a Database Created with a Template

Recall that an advantage to starting a new database with a template, instead of from a blank database, is that many report objects are already created for you.

Activity 1.22 | Viewing and Printing a Report

1 From the **Navigation Pane**, open the **Event Details** *report* (not the form).

The pre-built Event Details report displays in an attractively arranged format.

2 **Close** the **Event Details** report. Open the **All Events** report. In the lower right corner of the status bar, click the **Layout View** button. At the top of the report, click on the text *All Events* to display a colored border, and then click to the left of the letter *A* to place the insertion point there. Using your own name, type **Lastname Firstname** and then press Spacebar. Press Enter, and then **Save** the report.

Each report displays the records in the table in different useful formats.

> **Another Way**
>
> Right-click the object tab, and then click Print Preview.

3 Display **Backstage** view, click **Print**, and then click **Print Preview.** In the navigation area, notice that the navigation arrows are dimmed, which indicates that this report will print on one page.

4 Create a paper or electronic printout as instructed, **Close Print Preview**, and then **Close** the report.

Activity 1.23 | Printing a Table

When printing a table, use the Print Preview command to determine if the table will print on one page or if you need to adjust column widths, margins, or the orientation. Recall that there will be occasions when you want to print a table for a quick reference or for proofreading. For a more professional-looking format, and for more options to format the output, create and print a report.

Access | Chapter 1

1 From the **Navigation Pane**, open your **1B Workshop Locations** table. **Close** ⟪
the **Navigation Pane.** Display **Backstage** view, click **Print**, and then click
Print Preview.

> The table displays in the Print Preview window, showing how it will look when it is
> printed. The name of the table and the date the table is printed display at the top of the
> page. The navigation area displays *1* in the Pages box, and the right-pointing arrow—the
> Next Page arrow—is active. Recall that when a table is in the Print Preview window, the
> navigation arrows are used to navigate from one page to the next, rather than from one
> record to the next.

2 In the navigation area, click the **Next Page** button ▶.

> The second page of the table displays the last field column. Whenever possible, try to
> print all of the fields horizontally on one page. Of course, if there are many records, more
> than one page may be needed to print all of the records.

3 On the **Print Preview tab**, in the **Page Layout group**, click the **Landscape** button, and
then compare your screen with Figure 1.48. Notice that the entire table will print on
one page.

Figure 1.48

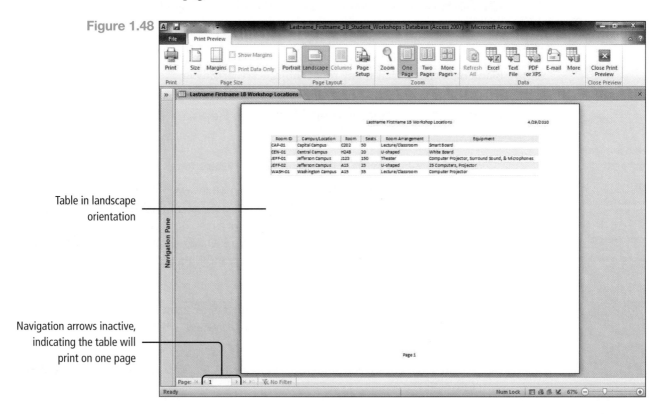

Table in landscape
orientation

Navigation arrows inactive,
indicating the table will
print on one page

4 Create a paper or electronic printout if instructed to do so, and then **Close Print Preview**.

5 **Close** ⊠ the **1B Workshop Locations** table. For the convenience of the next person opening the database, **Open** ⏵⏵ the **Navigation Pane.** In **Backstage** view, click **Close Database**, and then click **Exit** to close the Access program. As directed by your instructor, submit your database and the two paper or electronic printouts—one report and one table—that are the results of this project.

End **You have completed Project 1B** ————————————————————

GO! Beyond Office

Objective | Export an Access Table to Excel, Save to Google Docs, and Share the Spreadsheet

Recall that Google Docs is Google's free, Web-based word processor, spreadsheet, slide show, form, and data storage service. You can export Access database objects to Excel, upload the Excel file to Google Docs, and then edit and share the file in Google Docs. You can also import the file back into an Access database file.

> **Alert!** | **Working with Web-Based Applications and Services**
>
> Computer programs and services on the Web receive continuous updates and improvements. Thus, the steps to complete this Web-based Activity may differ from the ones shown. You can often look at the screens and the information presented to determine how to complete the Activity.

Activity | Exporting an Access Table to an Excel Spreadsheet, Saving to Google Docs, Adding a Record, and Sharing the Spreadsheet

In this activity, you will export your 1B Workshop Locations table to an Excel spreadsheet, and then upload the exported spreadsheet to Google Docs. You will enter a new record in the spreadsheet, format the spreadsheet, and then share the spreadsheet.

1 **Start** Access. In **Backstage** view, click **Open**, navigate to your **Access Chapter 1** folder, and then open your **1B_Student_Workshops** database. If necessary, on the Message Bar, click Enable Content. In the **Navigation Pane**, click your **1B Workshop Locations** table.

2 On the Ribbon, click the **External Data tab**, and then in the **Export group**, click the **Excel** button. In the **Export - Excel Spreadsheet** dialog box, click the **Browse** button, and then navigate to your **Access Chapter 1** folder. In the **File name** box, select the text, type **Lastname_Firstname_1B_Workshop_Locations** and then click **Save**.

3 In the **Export – Excel Spreadsheet** dialog box, under **Specify export options**, select the first two check boxes— **Export data with formatting and layout** and **Open the destination file after the export operation is complete**— and then click **OK**. Notice that Excel opens and the exported spreadsheet displays six fields and five records.

4 **Close** [x] your **1B_Workshop_Locations** Excel file. **Close** the **Export - Excel Spreadsheet** dialog box, click the **File tab**, click **Close Database**, and then click **Exit** to close the Access program.

5 Launch your Web browser, and then navigate to **http://docs.google.com** If you do not have a Google Docs account, follow the steps in the Excel 3B GO! Beyond Office project. On the **Google Docs** page, in the **Email** box, type your e-mail address that you use for Google Docs. In the **Password** box, type your password, and then click **Sign in**.

Your Google Docs Home page displays and may display several files depending on what have previously uploaded to Google Docs.

6 In the upper left portion of your screen, click the **Upload** button, and then click **Files**. In the **Select file(s) to upload by docs.google.com** dialog box, navigate to your **Access Chapter 1** folder, and then double-click your **1B_Workshop_Locations** Excel file. In the **Upload settings** dialog box, click **Start upload** to accept the default settings. In the lower right corner, the status of the upload displays until the entire file is uploaded. In the **Upload complete** message box, click the **Close** button [x], and notice that your **1B_Workshop_Locations** workbook is listed in Google Docs.

7 Click your **1B_Workshop_Locations** document to open it in Google Docs in a format similar to Excel. If necessary, maximize the window. Click in **Cell A7**, type **CAP-02** and then press [Tab]. In **Cell B7**, type **Capital Campus** and then press [Tab]. In **Cell C7,** type **B101** and then press [Tab]. In **Cell D7**, type **25** and then press [↓] to move to the next record. Compare your screen with Figure A.

The new record displays in a slightly smaller font size than the other records, and in Cell D7, *25* is aligned at the right side of the cell because Google Docs has formatted it as a number rather than text. On Row 7, there is no border surrounding the cells.

8 Above **Row 1**, and to the left of **Column A**, click in the small box bordered in blue on two sides, which functions as the **Select All** button, and notice that the entire spreadsheet is selected.

9 On the Google Docs menu bar, click **Format**, and then click **Clear formatting**, to change the font size of all cells to 10 pt, to remove the cell borders, and to remove the formatting of the field names.

10 Click in the column heading for **Column D** to select the column. On the Google Docs menu bar, click **Format**, point to **Number**, and then at the bottom of the displayed menu, click **Plain text** to format every number in this field as text.

Recall that in Access, numbers that are not used in calculations should be formatted as Text. Clearing the formatting enables new records to be entered into the spreadsheet in the same format as the existing records.

11 At the top of the page, in the black command bar, click **Documents** to return to your Home page. Point to your **1B_Workshop_Locations** spreadsheet, and then on the right side, click **Actions**. In the list, click **Share**, and then in the submenu, click **Share**.

12 In the **Sharing settings** dialog box, click in the **Add people** box, and then type the address of your Windows Live e-mail account. Click the **Can edit** arrow and notice the two permission levels you can assign—*Can edit* and *Can view*. Be sure that **Can edit** is selected, and then click in the **Optional: include a personal message** box. Type

This document is shared with you. and be sure that the **Send email notifications (recommended)** check box is selected. Click the **Share & Save** button. In the **Sharing settings** dialog box, click **Close**.

You can change the permission level in the Sharing settings dialog box so that only the owner of the file— you—can change sharing permissions. Only the owner can delete files from Google Docs.

13 Display the **Start** menu 🌐, and then click **All Programs**. On the list of programs, click the **Accessories** folder, and then click **Snipping Tool**. In the **Snipping Tool** dialog box, click the **New arrow**. On the displayed list, click **Full-screen Snip**.

14 On the **Snipping Tool** markup window toolbar, click the **Save Snip** button 💾. In the **Save As** dialog box, navigate to your **Access Chapter 1** folder, and open that folder. Be sure the **Save as type** box displays **JPEG file**. In the **File name** box, type **Lastname_Firstname_1B_ Access_Google_Docs_Snip** and then click **Save**. **Close** ❎ the **Snipping Tool** window.

15 In the upper right corner of your Google Docs page, to the right of your e-mail name, click the **arrow**, and then click **Sign out**. If there is no arrow, first click your user name. **Close** your Web browser, and then submit your snip file as directed.

Figure A

Content-Based Assessments

Summary

Microsoft Access 2010 is a database management system that uses various objects—tables, forms, queries, reports—to organize information. Data is stored in tables in which you establish fields, set the data type and field size, and create a primary key. Data from a database can be reported and printed.

Key Terms

Matching

Match each term in the second column with its correct definition in the first column by writing the letter of the term on the blank line in front of the correct definition.

_____ 1. An organized collection of facts about people, events, things, or ideas related to a specific topic.

_____ 2. Facts about people, events, things, or ideas.

_____ 3. Data that is organized in a useful manner.

_____ 4. A simple database file that is not related or linked to any other collection of data.

_____ 5. The database object that stores the data, and which is the foundation of an Access database.

_____ 6. A table row that contains all of the categories of data pertaining to one person, place, thing, event, or idea.

_____ 7. A single piece of information that is stored in every record and represented by a column in a table.

_____ 8. A principle stating that data is organized in tables so that there is no redundant data.

A Common field

B Data

C Database

D Field

E First principle of good database design

F Flat database

G Information

H Navigation Pane

I Normalization

J Object window

K Objects

L Populate

Content-Based Assessments

_____ 9. A principle stating that techniques are used to ensure the accuracy of data entered into a table.

_____ 10. The process of applying design rules and principles to ensure that a database performs as expected.

_____ 11. A field in one or more tables that stores the same data.

_____ 12. The basic parts of a database; for example tables, forms, queries, and reports.

_____ 13. The window area that organizes the database objects and from which you open objects.

_____ 14. The window area that displays each open object on its own tab.

_____ 15. The action of filling a database with records.

M Record

N Second principle of good database design

O Table

Multiple Choice

Circle the correct answer.

1. The Access view that displays data in columns and rows like an Excel worksheet is:
   - **A.** Datasheet view
   - **B.** Design view
   - **C.** Layout view

2. The characteristic that defines the kind of data you can enter into a field is the:
   - **A.** data source
   - **B.** data type
   - **C.** field property

3. The box at the left of a record in Datasheet view that you click to select an entire record is the:
   - **A.** link
   - **B.** navigation area
   - **C.** record selector box

4. To add on to the end of an object, such as to add records to the end of an existing table, is to:
   - **A.** append
   - **B.** import
   - **C.** run

5. Characteristics of a field that control how the field displays and how data is entered are:
   - **A.** data sources
   - **B.** data types
   - **C.** field properties

6. The field that uniquely identifies a record in a table is known as the:
   - **A.** attachments field
   - **B.** common field
   - **C.** primary key

7. The underlying design of a table is referred to as the:
   - **A.** caption
   - **B.** source file
   - **C.** structure

8. The object that retrieves specific data and then displays only the data that you specify is a:
   - **A.** form
   - **B.** query
   - **C.** report

9. The object that displays fields and records from a table or query in a printable format is a:
   - **A.** form
   - **B.** query
   - **C.** report

10. Information repeated in a database in a manner that indicates poor design is said to be:
    - **A.** relational
    - **B.** redundant
    - **C.** truncated

Apply **1A** skills from these Objectives:

1 Identify Good Database Design

2 Create a Table and Define Fields in a New Database

3 Change the Structure of Tables and Add a Second Table

4 Create and Use a Query, Form, and Report

5 Save and Close a Database

Skills Review | Project **1C** College Administrators

In the following Skills Review, you will create a database to store information about the administrators of Capital Cities Community College and their departments. Your completed database objects will look similar to Figure 1.49.

Project Files

For Project 1C, you will need the following files:

New blank Access database
a01C_Administrators (Excel workbook)
a01C_Departments (Excel workbook)

You will save your database as:

Lastname_Firstname_1C_College_Administrators

Project Results

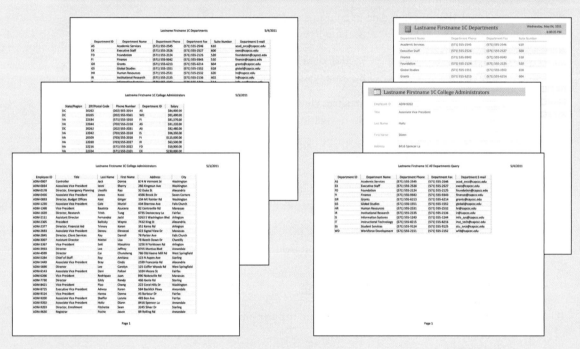

Figure 1.49

(Project 1C College Administrators continues on the next page)

Content-Based Assessments

1 **Start** Access. Click **Blank database**, and then in the lower right corner, click the **Browse** button. In the **File New Database** dialog box, navigate to your **Access Chapter 1** folder, and then in the **File name** box, replace the existing text with **Lastname_Firstname_1C_College_Administrators** Press [Enter], and then in the lower right corner, click **Create**.

a. **Close** the **Navigation Pane**. Click in the text *Click to Add*. Click **Text**, type **Title** and then press [Enter].

b. In the third field name box, click **Text**, type **Last Name** and then press [Enter]. In the fourth field name box, click **Text**, type **First Name** and then press [Enter]. In the fifth field name box, click **Text**, type **Middle Initial** and then press [Enter]. Create the remaining fields as shown in **Table 1**, pressing [Enter] after the last field name.

c. Scroll as necessary to view the first field. Click the **ID** field name. In the **Properties group**, click the **Name & Caption** button. In the **Enter Field Properties** dialog box, in the **Name** box, change *ID* to **Employee**

ID and then click **OK**. In the **Formatting group**, click the **Data Type arrow**, and then click **Text**.

d. In the first record row, click in the **Employee ID** field, type **ADM-9200** and press [Enter]. In the **Title** field, type **Associate Vice President** and press [Enter]. In the **Last Nam**e field, type **Shaffer** In the **First Name** field, type **Lonnie** In the **Middle Initial** field, type **J** In the **Address** field, type **489 Ben Ave**

e. Continue entering data in the fields as shown in **Table 2**, pressing [Enter] to move to the next field and to the next row.

f. Click **Save**, and then in the **Table Name** box, using your own name, replace the selected text by typing **Lastname Firstname 1C College Administrators** and then click **OK**.

2 Scroll, if necessary, to view the first field. In the new record row, click in the **Employee ID** field, and then enter the information for two additional college administrators as shown in **Table 3**, pressing [Enter] to move from field to field.

Table 1

Data Type						Text	Text	Text	Text	Text	Text	Currency
Field Name	ID	Title	Last Name	First Name	Middle Initial	Address	City	State/Region	ZIP/Postal Code	Phone Number	Department ID	Salary

(Return to Step 1-c)

Table 2

City	State/Region	ZIP/Postal Code	Phone Number	Department ID	Salary
Fairfax	VA	22038	(571) 555-6185	AS	98602

(Return to Step 1-f)

Table 3

Employee ID	Title	Last Name	First Name	Middle Initial	Address	City	State/Region	ZIP/Postal Code	Phone Number	Department ID	Salary
ADM-9201	Associate Vice President	Holtz	Diann	S	8416 Spencer La	Annandale	VA	22003	(571) 555-1077	AS	101524
ADM-9202	Director, Enrollment	Fitchette	Sean	H	3245 Silver Dr	Sterling	VA	20152	(703) 555-9012	SS	45070

(Return to Step 2-a)

(Project 1C College Administrators continues on the next page)

Access | Chapter 1

a. **Close** your **1C College Administrators** table. On the **External Data tab**, in the **Import & Link group**, click the **Excel** button. In the **Get External Data - Excel Spreadsheet** dialog box, click the **Browse** button. In the **File Open** dialog box, navigate to your student data files, and then double-click the **a01C_Administrators** Excel file.

b. Click **Append a copy of the records to the table**, and then click **OK**. Click **Next**, click **Finish**, and then click **Close**. **Open** the **Navigation Pane**, and then widen it so that you can view the entire table name. In the **Navigation Pane**, double-click your **1C College Administrators** table to open it, and then **Close** the **Navigation Pane**—30 total records display.

3 Click the **Home tab**, and then in the **Views group**, click the **View** button to switch to **Design** view.

a. To the left of **Middle Initial**, point to the row selector box, and then click to select the entire row. On the **Design tab**, in the **Tools group**, click the **Delete Rows** button, and then click **Yes**.

b. Click anywhere in the **State/Region** field name, and then under **Field Properties**, set the **Field Size** to **2** In the **State/Region** row, click in the **Description** box, and then type **Two-character state abbreviation**

c. Click in the **Employee ID** field name box, set the **Field Size** to **8** and in the **Description** box, type **Eight-character Employee ID** Then **Save** the design of your table; click **Yes**. On the **Design tab**, in the **Views group**, click the **View** button to switch to **Datasheet** view.

4 On the Ribbon, click the **External Data tab**, and then in the **Import & Link group**, click the **Excel** button. In the **Get External Data – Excel Spreadsheet** dialog box, click the **Browse** button. Navigate to your student data files, and then double-click **a01C_Departments**. Be sure that the **Import the source data into a new table in the current database** option button is selected, and then click **OK**.

a. In the **Import Spreadsheet Wizard** dialog box, click to select the **First Row Contains Column Headings** check box, and then click **Next**.

b. Click **Next** again. Click the **Choose my own primary key** option button, and to the right, be sure that *Department ID* displays. Click **Next**. In the **Import to Table** box, type **Lastname Firstname**

1C Departments and then click **Finish**. Click **Close**, **Open** the **Navigation Pane**, and then open your **1C Departments** table—12 records display. **Close** the **Navigation Pane**.

c. At the top of the object window, click the **1C College Administrators tab**. To the left of the **Employee ID** field name, click the **Select All** button. Click the **Home tab**, and in the **Records group**, click the **More** button. Click **Field Width**, and in the **Column Width** dialog box, click **Best Fit**. Click in any field, and then **Save** the table.

d. Display **Backstage** view, click **Print**, and then click **Print Preview**. In the **Page Layout group**, click the **Landscape** button. Create a paper or electronic printout as directed by your instructor; two pages result. Click **Close Print Preview**, and then **Close** your **1C College Administrators** table.

e. With your **1C Departments** table displayed, to the left of the **Department ID** field name, click the **Select All** button, and then apply **Best Fit** to all of the columns. Click in any field, **Save** the table, and then display the table in **Print Preview**. Change the **Orientation** to **Landscape**. Create a paper or electronic printout as directed—one page results. **Close Print Preview**, and then **Close** your **1C Departments** table.

5 On the **Create tab**, in the **Queries group**, click the **Query Wizard** button. In the **New Query** dialog box, click **Simple Query Wizard**, and then click **OK**. Click the **Tables/Queries arrow**, and then be sure your **Table: 1C Departments** is selected.

a. Under **Available Fields**, click **Department ID**, and then click the **Add Field** button to move the field to the **Selected Fields** list on the right. Using either the **Add Field** button or by double-clicking, add the following fields to the **Selected Fields** list: **Department Name**, **Department Phone**, **Department Fax**, and **Department E-mail**. The query will answer the question, *What is the Department ID, Department Name, Department Phone number, Department Fax number, and Department E-mail address of every department?*

(Project 1C College Administrators continues on the next page)

Content-Based Assessments

b. Click **Next**. In the **Simple Query Wizard** dialog box, change the query title to **Lastname Firstname 1C All Departments Query** and then click **Finish** to run the query.

c. Display the query in **Print Preview**. Change the **Orientation** to **Landscape**. Create a paper or electronic printout as directed—one page results. **Close Print Preview**, and then **Close** the query.

d. **Open** the **Navigation Pane**, open your **1C College Administrators** table, and then **Close** the **Navigation Pane**. The table contains 11 fields. On the **Create tab**, in the **Forms group**, click the **Form** button. Click **Save**, and then in the **Save As** dialog box, accept the default name for the form—*Lastname Firstname 1C College Administrators*—by clicking **OK**. In the navigation area, click the **Last Record** button, and then click the **Previous Record** button two times to display the record for *Diann Holtz*. At the left edge of the form, click the gray **record selector bar** to select only this record. By using the instructions in Activity 1.15, print or create an electronic printout of this record as directed. **Close** the form object. Your **1C College Administrators** table object remains open.

6 **Open** the **Navigation Pane**, open your **1C Departments** table, and then **Close** the **Navigation Pane**. On the **Create tab**, in the **Reports group**, click the **Report** button.

a. In the field names row at the top of the report, click the **Department ID** field name. Hold down Ctrl, and then click the **Department E-Mail** field name. On the **Arrange tab**, in the **Rows & Columns group**, click the **Select Column** button, and then press Del.

b. If necessary, scroll to the left, and then click in the **Department Phone** field name. By using the ↔

pointer, decrease the width of the field until there is about **0.25 inch** of space between the **Department Phone** field and the **Department Fax** field. Decrease the widths of the **Department Fax** and **Suite Number** fields in a similar manner. Be sure that the width of the report is within the dotted boundaries.

c. Click the **Department Name** field name. On the Ribbon, click the **Home tab**. In the **Sort & Filter group**, click the **Ascending** button to sort the report in alphabetic order by Department Name.

d. **Save** the report as **Lastname Firstname 1C Departments Report** and then click **OK**. Display the report in **Print Preview**. In the **Zoom group**, click the **Two Pages** button, and notice that the report will print on two pages because the page number is beyond the right margin of the report. **Close Print Preview**. With the report displayed in **Layout** view, if necessary, scroll down and to the right to display the page number—**Page 1 of 1**. Click the page number, press Del, and then **Save** the changes to the report.

e. Display the report in **Print Preview**, and notice that the report will print on one page. In the **Zoom group**, click the **One Page** button. Create a paper or electronic printout of the report as directed. Click **Close Print Preview**. Along the top of the object window, right click any **object tab**, and then click **Close All** to close all of the open objects, leaving the object window empty.

f. **Open** the **Navigation Pane**. If necessary, increase the width of the **Navigation Pane** so that all object names display fully. Display **Backstage** view, click **Close Database**, and then click **Exit**. As directed by your instructor, submit your database and the five paper or electronic printouts—two tables, one query, one form, and one report—that are the results of this project.

End **You have completed Project 1C**

Access | Chapter 1

NOTES

Sort and Query a Database

OUTCOMES

At the end of this chapter you will be able to:

PROJECT 2A

Sort and query a database.

OBJECTIVES

Mastering these objectives will enable you to:

1. Open an Existing Database (p. 497)
2. Create Table Relationships (p. 498)
3. Sort Records in a Table (p. 503)
4. Create a Query in Design View (p. 506)
5. Create a New Query from an Existing Query (p. 509)
6. Sort Query Results (p. 510)
7. Specify Criteria in a Query (p. 512)

In This Chapter

lightpoet/Shutterstock

In this chapter, you will sort Access database tables and create and modify queries. To convert data into meaningful information, you must manipulate your data in a way that you can answer questions. One question might be: *Which students have a grade point average of 3.0 or higher?* With such information, you could send information about scholarships or internships to selected students.

Questions can be answered by sorting the data in a table or by creating a query. Queries enable you to isolate specific data in database tables by limiting the fields that display and by setting conditions that limit the records to those that match specified conditions. You can also use a query to create a new field that is calculated by using one or more existing fields.

The projects in this chapter relate to **Capital Cities Community College**, which is located in the Washington D. C. metropolitan area. The college provides high-quality education and professional training to residents in the cities surrounding the nation's capital. Its four campuses serve over 50,000 students and offer more than 140 certificate programs and degrees at the associate's level. CapCCC has a highly acclaimed Distance Education program and an extensive Workforce Development program. The college makes positive contributions to the community through cultural and athletic programs and partnerships with businesses and non-profit organizations.

Project 2A Instructors and Courses Database

Project 1A Training

Project Activities

In Activities 2.01 through 2.13, you will assist Carolyn Judkins, the Dean of the Business and Information Technology Division at the Jefferson Campus, in locating information about instructors and courses in the Division. Your results will look similar to Figure 2.1.

Project Files

For Project 2A, you will need the following file:

a02A_Instructors_Courses

You will save your database as:

Lastname_Firstname_2A_Instructors_Courses

Project Results

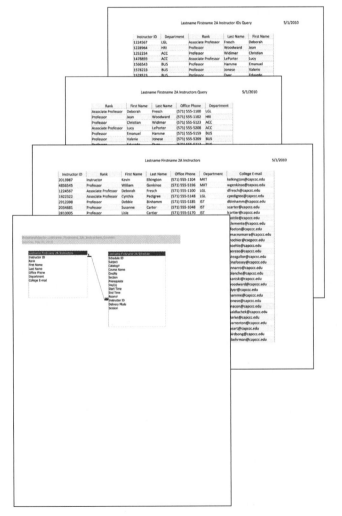

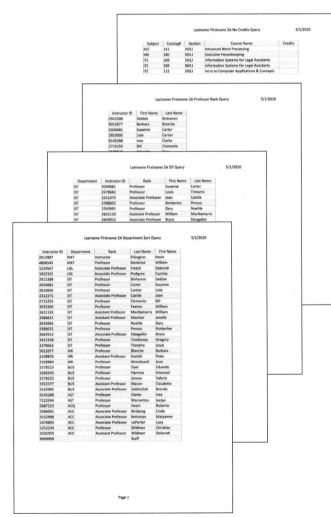

Figure 2.1
Project 2A Instructors and Courses

Objective 1 | Open an Existing Database

There will be instances in which you may want to work with a database and still keep the *original* version of the database. Like the other Microsoft Office 2010 applications, you can open a database file and save it with a new name.

Activity 2.01 | Opening and Renaming an Existing Database

1 **Start** Access. In **Backstage** view, click **Open**. Navigate to the student data files for this textbook, and then open the **a02A_Instructors_Courses** Access database.

2 Click the **File tab** to return to **Backstage** view, and then click **Save Database As.** In the **Save As** dialog box, navigate to the location where you are saving your databases for this chapter. Create a new folder named **Access Chapter 2** and then click **Open**.

3 In the **File name** box, select the file name, to which *1* has been added at the end. Edit as necessary to name the database **Lastname_Firstname_2A_Instructors_Courses** and then press [Enter].

Use this technique when you want to keep a copy of the original database file.

4 On the **Message Bar**, notice the **Security Warning**. In the **Navigation Pane**, notice that this database contains two table objects. Compare your screen with Figure 2.2.

Figure 2.2

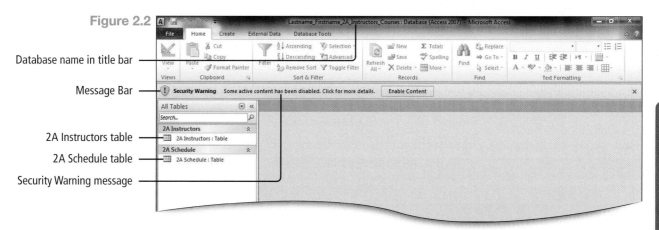

Database name in title bar
Message Bar
2A Instructors table
2A Schedule table
Security Warning message

Activity 2.02 | Resolving Security Alerts and Renaming Tables

The *Message Bar* is the area below the Ribbon that displays information such as security alerts when there is potentially unsafe, active content in an Office document that you open. Settings that determine the alerts that display on your Message Bar are set in the Access *Trust Center*, which is an area of Access where you can view the security and privacy settings for your Access installation.

You may or may not be able to change the settings in the Trust Center, depending upon decisions made within your organization's computing environment. You can display the Trust Center from Options, which is available in Backstage view.

1 On the **Message Bar**, click the **Enable Content** button.

When working with the student files that accompany this textbook, repeat these actions each time you see this security warning. Databases for this textbook are safe to use on your computer.

2 In the **Navigation Pane**, right-click the **2A Instructors** table, and then click **Rename**. With the table name selected and using your own name, type **Lastname Firstname 2A Instructors** and then press [Enter] to rename the table. Using the same technique, **Rename** the **2A Schedule** table to **Lastname Firstname 2A Schedule**

> Including your name in the table enables you and your instructor to easily identify your work, because Access includes the table name in the header of printed and PDF pages.

3 Point to the right edge of the **Navigation Pane** to display the ⟷ pointer. Drag to the right to widen the pane until both table names display fully.

Objective 2 | Create Table Relationships

Access databases are relational databases because the tables in the database can relate—actually connect—to other tables through common fields. Recall that common fields are fields that contain the same data in more than one table.

After you have a table for each subject in your database, you must provide a way to connect the data in the tables when you need meaningful information. To do this, create common fields in related tables, and then define table relationships. A *relationship* is an association that you establish between two tables based on common fields. After the relationship is established, you can create a query, a form, or a report that displays information from more than one table.

Activity 2.03 | Creating Table Relationships and Enforcing Referential Integrity

In this activity, you will create a relationship between two tables in the database.

1 Double-click your **2A Instructors** table to open it in the object window and examine its contents. Then open your **2A Schedule** table and examine its contents.

> In the 2A Instructors table, *Instructor ID* is the primary key field, which ensures that each instructor will appear in the table only one time. No two instructors have the same Instructor ID.

> In the 2A Schedule table, *Schedule ID* is the primary key field. Every scheduled course section during an academic term has a unique Schedule ID. The 2A Schedule table includes the *Instructor ID* field, which is the common field between the 2A Schedule table and the 2A Instructors table.

2 In the **2A Schedule** table, scroll to the right to display the Instructor ID field, and then compare your screen with Figure 2.3.

> Because *one* instructor can teach *many* different courses, *one* Instructor ID number can be present *many* times in the 2A Schedule table. This relationship between each instructor and the courses is known as a *one-to-many relationship*. This is the most common type of relationship in Access.

Figure 2.3

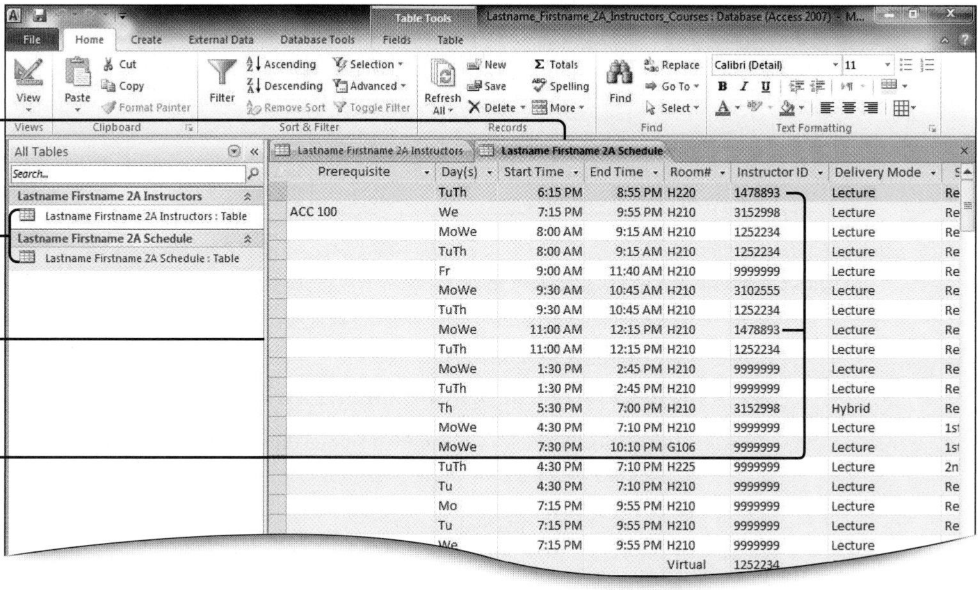

Two table objects open
in the object window;
2A Schedule table active

Tables renamed

Navigation Pane width
increased so that both
table names are visible

Instructor teaches
more than one course

3   In the upper right corner of the object window, click **Close** [×] two times to close
    each table. Click the **Database Tools tab**, and then in the **Relationships group**, click the
    Relationships button. Compare your screen with Figure 2.4.

    The Show Table dialog box displays in the Relationships window. In the Show Table dialog
    box, the Tables tab displays all of the table objects in the database. Your two tables are listed.

Figure 2.4

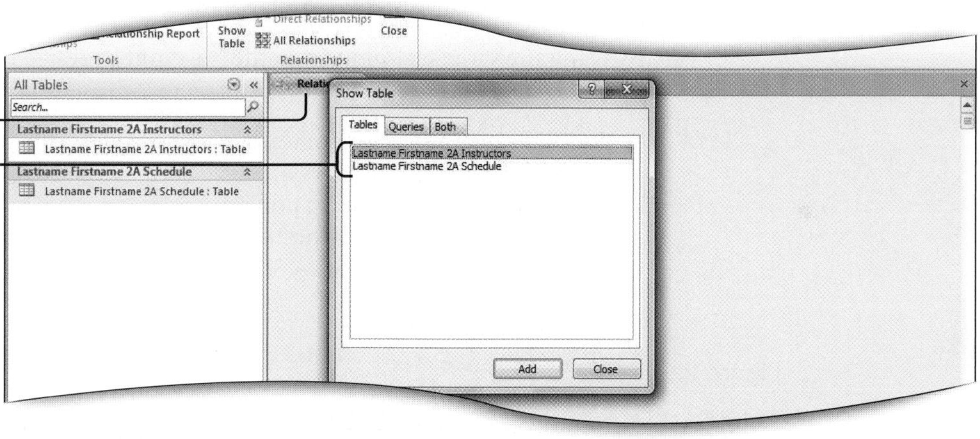

Relationships window

Two tables in database

4   Point to the title bar of the **Show Table** dialog box, and then drag down and to
    the right slightly to move the **Show Table** dialog box away from the top of the
    Relationships window.

    Moving the Show Table dialog box enables you to see the tables as they are added to the
    Relationships window.

5   In the **Show Table** dialog box, click your **2A Instructors** table, and then at the bottom
    of the dialog box, click **Add**. In the **Show Table** dialog box, double-click your **2A
    Schedule** table to add the table to the **Relationships** window. In the **Show Table** dialog
    box, click **Close**, and then compare your screen with Figure 2.5.

    You can use either technique to add a table to the Relationships window. A *field list*—a
    list of the field names in a table—for each of the two table objects displays, and each
    table's primary key is identified. Although this database currently has only two tables,
    larger databases can have many tables. Scroll bars in a field list indicate that there are
    fields that are not currently in view.

Access | Chapter 2

Figure 2.5

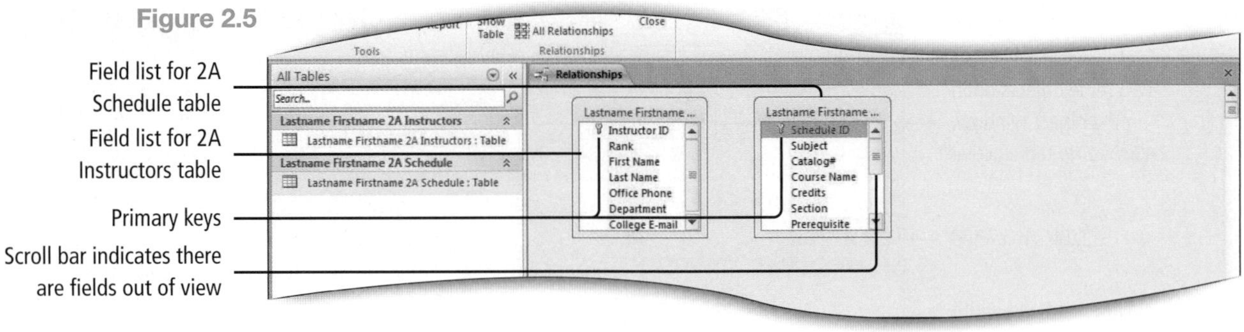

Field list for 2A Schedule table

Field list for 2A Instructors table

Primary keys

Scroll bar indicates there are fields out of view

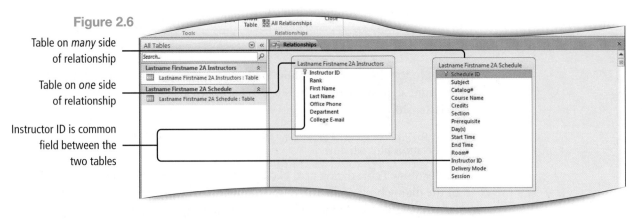

Alert! | Are There More Than Two Field Lists in the Relationships Window?

If you double-click a table more than one time, a duplicate field list displays in the Relationships window. To remove a field list from the Relationships window, right-click the title bar of the field list, and then click Hide Table. Alternatively, click anywhere in the field list, and then on the Design tab, in the Relationships group, click the Hide Table button.

---

6   In the **2A Schedule** field list—the field list on the right—point to the title bar to display the pointer. Drag the field list to the right until there are about 2 inches between the field lists.

7   In the **2A Instructors** field list—the field list on the left—point to the lower right corner of the field list to display the pointer, and then drag down and to the right to increase the height and width of the field list until the entire name of the table in the title bar displays and all of the field names display.

> This action enables you to see all of the available fields and removes the vertical scroll bar.

8   By using the same technique and the pointer, resize the **2A Schedule** field list so that all of the field names and the table name display as shown in Figure 2.6.

> Recall that *one* instructor can teach *many* scheduled courses. This arrangement of the tables on your screen displays the *one table* on the left side and the *many table* on the right side. Recall also that the primary key in each table is the field that uniquely identifies the record in each table. In the 2A Instructors table, each instructor is uniquely identified by the Instructor ID. In the 2A Schedule table, each scheduled course section is uniquely identified by the Schedule ID.

Figure 2.6

Table on *many* side of relationship

Table on *one* side of relationship

Instructor ID is common field between the two tables

Note | The Field That Is Highlighted Does Not Matter

After you rearrange the two field lists in the Relationships window, the highlighted field indicates the active field list, which is the list you moved last. This is of no consequence for completing the activity.

Another Way

On the Design tab, in the Tools group, click the Edit Relationships button. In the Edit Relationships dialog box, click Create New, and then in the Create New dialog box, designate the tables and fields that will create the relationship.

9 In the **2A Instructors** field list, point to **Instructor ID**, hold down the left mouse button, and then drag down and to the right into the **2A Schedule** field list until the pointer's arrow is on top of **Instructor ID**. Then release the mouse button to display the **Edit Relationships** dialog box.

As you drag, a small graphic displays to indicate that you are dragging a field from one field list to another. A table relationship works by matching data in two fields—the common field. In these two tables, the common field has the same name—*Instructor ID*. Common fields are not required to have the same names; however, they must have the same data type and field size.

10 Point to the title bar of the **Edit Relationships** dialog box, and then drag the dialog box below the two field lists as shown in Figure 2.7.

Both tables include the Instructor ID field—the common field between the two tables. By dragging, you create the *one-to-many* relationship. In the 2A Instructors table, Instructor ID is the primary key. In the 2A Schedule table, Instructor ID is referred to as the **foreign key** field. The foreign key is the field in the related table used to connect to the primary key in another table. The field on the *one* side of the relationship is typically the primary key.

Figure 2.7

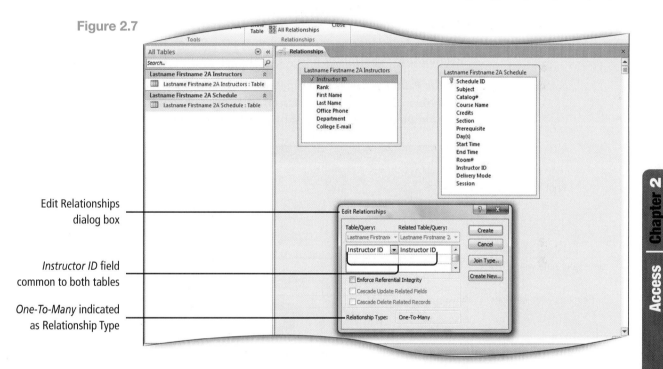

Edit Relationships dialog box

Instructor ID field common to both tables

One-To-Many indicated as Relationship Type

11 In the **Edit Relationships** dialog box, click to select the **Enforce Referential Integrity** check box.

Referential integrity is a set of rules that Access uses to ensure that the data between related tables is valid. Enforcing referential integrity ensures that an instructor cannot be added to the 2A Schedules table if the Instructor ID is *not* included in the 2A Instructors table. Similarly, enforcing referential integrity ensures that you cannot delete an instructor from the 2A Instructors table if there is a course listed in the 2A Schedule table for that instructor.

12 In the **Edit Relationships** dialog box, click the **Create** button, and then compare your screen with Figure 2.8.

A **join line**—the line joining two tables—displays between the two tables. On the join line, *1* indicates the *one* side of the relationship, and the infinity symbol (∞) indicates the *many* side of the relationship. These symbols display when referential integrity is enforced.

Access | Chapter 2

Figure 2.8

1 indicates one side of the relationship

Join line connects the two common fields, creating the relationship

∞ indicates many side of the relationship

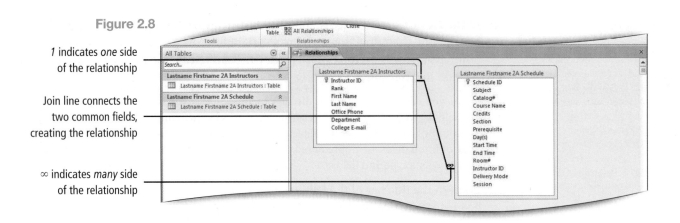

Activity 2.04 | Printing a Relationship Report and Displaying Subdatasheet Records

The Relationships window provides a map of how your database tables are related, and you can print this information as a report.

1 With the **Relationships** window open, on the **Design tab**, in the **Tools group**, click the **Relationship Report** button to create the report and display it in Print Preview.

2 On the **Print Preview tab**, in the **Page Size group**, click the **Margins** button, and then click **Normal**. Compare your screen with Figure 2.9. If instructed to do so, create a paper or electronic printout of this relationship report.

Figure 2.9

Print Preview tab
Margins button

Database name and date (your date will differ)

Field lists with join lines

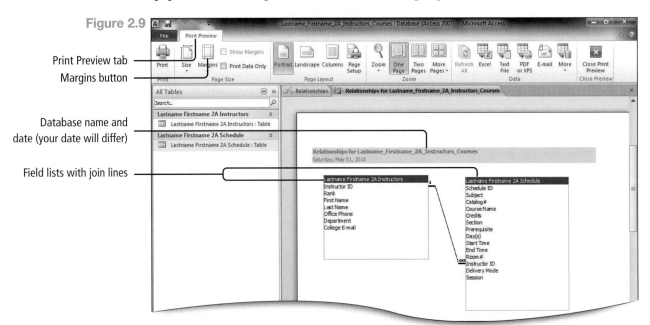

3 On the **Quick Access Toolbar**, click the **Save** button 🔲 to save the report. In the **Save As** dialog box, click **OK** to accept the default name.

The report name displays in the Navigation Pane under *Unrelated Objects*. Because the report is just a map of the relationships, and not a report containing actual records, it is not associated with any of the tables.

4 In the object window, **Close** ✕ the report, and then **Close** ✕ the **Relationships** window.

5 From the **Navigation Pane**, open your **2A Instructors** table, and then **Close** [«] the **Navigation Pane**. For the first record—*Instructor ID 1224567*—on the left side of the record, click the **plus sign** (+), and then compare your screen with Figure 2.10.

Plus signs to the left of a record in a table indicate that *related* records exist in another table. Clicking the plus sign displays the related records in a **subdatasheet**. In the first record, for *Deborah Fresch*, you can see that related records exist in the 2A Schedule table—she is teaching five LGL courses that are listed in the schedule. The plus sign displays because you created a relationship between the two tables using the Instructor ID field—the common field.

Figure 2.10

Course sections from the 2A Schedule table for *Associate Professor Deborah Fresch*

Plus sign indicates that related records may exist in another table

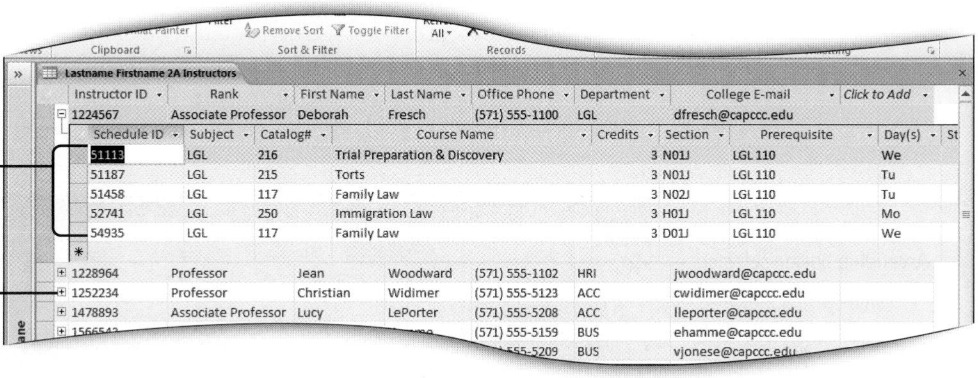

6 For the first record, click the **minus sign** (−) to collapse the subdatasheet.

> **More Knowledge | Other Types of Relationships: One-to-One and Many-to-Many**
>
> There are other relationships you can create using the same process in the Relationships window. The type of relationship is determined by the placement of the primary key field. A one-to-one relationship exists between two tables when a record in one table is related to a single record in a second table. In this case, both tables use the same field as the primary key. This is most often used when data is placed in a separate table because access to the information is restricted.
>
> You can also create a many-to-many relationship between tables, where many records in one table can be related to many records in another table. For example, many students can enroll in many courses. To create a many-to-many relationship, you must create a third table that contains the primary key fields from both tables. These primary key fields are then joined to their related fields in the other tables. In effect, you create multiple one-to-one relationships.

Objective 3 | Sort Records in a Table

Sorting is the process of arranging data in a specific order based on the value in a field. For example, you can sort the names in your address book alphabetically by each person's last name, or you can sort your DVD collection by the date of purchase. Initially, records in an Access table display in the order they are entered into the table. When a primary key is established, the records display in order based on the primary key field.

Activity 2.05 | Sorting Records in a Table in Ascending or Descending Order

In the following activity, you will determine the departments of the faculty in the Business and Information Technology Division by sorting the data. You can sort data in either *ascending order* or *descending order*. Ascending order sorts text alphabetically (A to Z) and sorts numbers from the lowest number to the highest number. Descending order sorts text in reverse alphabetical order (Z to A) and sorts numbers from the highest number to the lowest number.

1 Notice that the records in the **2A Instructors** table are sorted in ascending order by **Instructor ID**, which is the primary key field.

Another Way

On the Home tab, in the Sort & Filter group, click the Ascending button.

2 In the field names row, click the **Department arrow**, click **Sort A to Z**, and then compare your screen with Figure 2.11.

To sort records in a table, click the arrow to the right of the field name in the column on which you want to sort, and then choose the sort order. After a field is sorted, a small arrow in the field name box indicates its sort order. The small arrow in the field name points up, indicating an ascending sort; and in the Ribbon, the Ascending button is selected.

The records display in alphabetical order by Department. Because the department names are now grouped together, you can quickly scroll the length of the table to see the instructors in each department. The first record in the table has no data in the Department field because the Instructor ID number 9999999 is reserved for Staff, a designation that is used until a scheduled course has been assigned to a specific instructor.

Figure 2.11

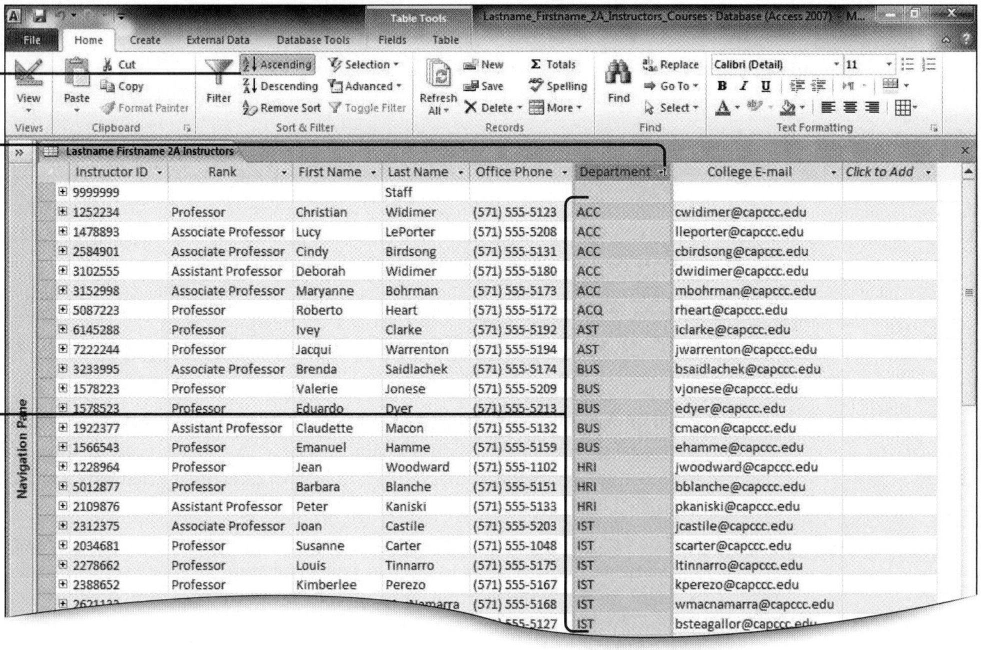

Ascending button selected

Small arrow indicates order by which the field is sorted

Records sorted alphabetically by Department

3 On the **Home tab**, in the **Sort & Filter group**, click the **Remove Sort** button to clear the sort and return the records to the default sort order, which is by the primary key field—*Instructor ID.*

4 Click the **Last Name arrow**, and then click **Sort Z to A.**

The records in the table are sorted by last name in reverse alphabetical order. The small arrow in the Field name box points down, indicating a descending sort. On the Ribbon, the Descending button is selected.

5 In the **Sort & Filter group**, click the **Remove Sort** button.

Activity 2.06 | Sorting Records in a Table on Multiple Fields

To sort a table on two or more fields, first identify the fields that will act as the *outermost sort field* and the *innermost sort field*. The outermost sort field is the first level of sorting, and the innermost sort field is the second level of sorting. For example, you might want to sort first by the Last Name field, which would be the outermost sort field, and then by the First Name field, which would be the innermost sort field. After you identify your outermost and innermost sort fields, sort the innermost field first, and then sort the outermost field.

In this activity, you will sort the records in descending order by the department name. Within each department name, you will sort the records in ascending order by last name.

1 In the **Last Name** field, click any record. In the **Sort & Filter group**, click the **Ascending** button.

The records are sorted in ascending alphabetical order by Last Name—the innermost sort field.

2 Point anywhere in the **Department** field, and then right-click. From the shortcut menu, click **Sort Z to A**. Compare your screen with Figure 2.12.

The records are sorted in descending alphabetical order first by Department—the *outermost* sort field—and then within a specific Department grouping, the sort continues in ascending alphabetical order by Last Name—the *innermost* sort field. The records are sorted on multiple fields using both ascending and descending order.

Figure 2.12

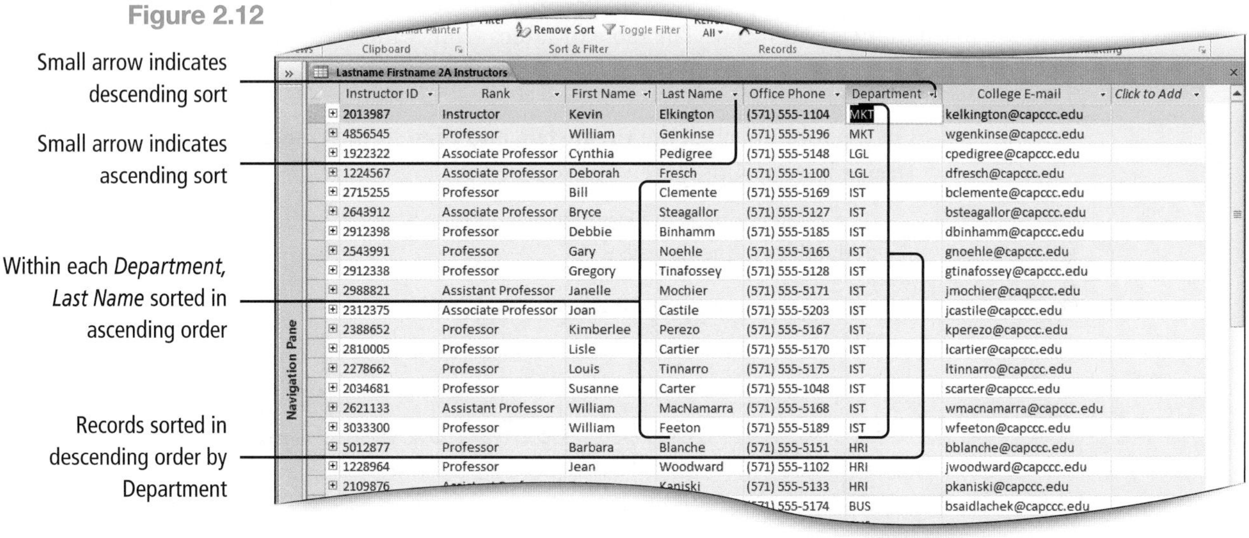

Small arrow indicates descending sort

Small arrow indicates ascending sort

Within each *Department*, *Last Name* sorted in ascending order

Records sorted in descending order by Department

3 Display **Backstage** view, click **Print**, and then click **Print Preview**. In the **Page Layout** group, click the **Landscape** button. In the **Zoom group**, click the **Two Pages** button, and notice that the table will print on two pages.

4 On the **Print Preview tab**, in the **Print group**, click the **Print** button. Under **Print Range**, click the **Pages** option button. In the **From** box, type **1** and then in the **To** box, type **1** to print only the first page. If directed to submit a paper copy, click OK or create an electronic copy as instructed. To create a PDF of only the first page, in the Data group, click PDF or XPS, click the Options button, and then indicate *Page 1 to 1*. In the **Close Preview group**, click the **Close Print Preview** button.

5 In the object window, **Close** ☒ the table. In the message box, click **Yes** to save the changes to the sort order.

6 **Open** ➤ the **Navigation Pane**, and then open the **2A Instructors** table. Notice the table was saved with the sort order you specified.

7 In the **Sort & Filter group**, click the **Remove Sort** button. **Close** ☒ the table, and in the message box, click **Yes** to save the table with the sort removed. **Close** ➤ the **Navigation Pane**.

> Generally, tables are not stored with the data sorted. Instead, queries are created that sort the data; and then reports are created to display the sorted data.

Objective 4 | Create a Query in Design View

Recall that a ***select query*** is a database object that retrieves (selects) specific data from one or more tables and then displays the specified data in Datasheet view. A query answers a question such as *Which instructors teach courses in the IST department?* Unless a query has already been set up to ask this question, you must create a new query.

Database users rarely need to see all of the records in all of the tables. That is why a query is so useful; it creates a ***subset*** of records—a portion of the total records—according to your specifications and then displays only those records.

Activity 2.07 | Creating a New Select Query in Design View

Previously, you created a query using the Query Wizard. To create complex queries, use Query Design view. The table or tables from which a query selects its data is referred to as the ***data source***.

1 On the Ribbon, click the **Create tab**, and then in the **Queries group**, click the **Query Design** button. Compare your screen with Figure 2.13.

> A new query opens in Design view and the Show Table dialog box displays, which lists both tables in the database.

Figure 2.13

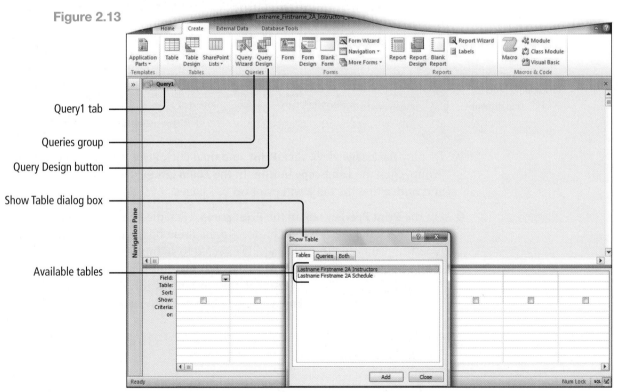

Query1 tab

Queries group

Query Design button

Show Table dialog box

Available tables

2 In the **Show Table** dialog box, double-click **2A Instructors**, and then **Close** the **Show Table** dialog box.

> A field list for the 2A Instructors table displays in the upper area of the Query window. The Instructor ID field is the primary key field in this table. The Query window has two parts: the *table area* (upper area), which displays the field lists for tables that are used in the query, and the *design grid* (lower area), which displays the design of the query.

> **Alert!** | **Is There More Than One Field List in the Query Window?**
>
> If you double-click a table more than one time, a duplicate field list displays in the Query window. To remove a field list from the Query window, right-click the title bar of the field list, and then click Remove Table.

3 Point to the lower right corner of the field list to display the ⬔ pointer, and then drag down and to the right to expand the field list, displaying all of the field names and the table name. In the **2A Instructors** field list, double-click **Rank**, and then look at the design grid.

> The Rank field name displays in the design grid in the Field row. You limit the fields that display when the query is run by placing only the desired field names in the design grid.

4 In the **2A Instructors** field list, point to **First Name**, hold down the left mouse button, and then drag down into the design grid until the ⬔ pointer displays in the **Field** row in the second column. Release the mouse button, and then compare your screen with Figure 2.14.

> This is a second way to add field names to the design grid. As you drag the field, a small rectangular shape attaches to the mouse pointer. When you release the mouse button, the field name displays in the Field row.

Figure 2.14

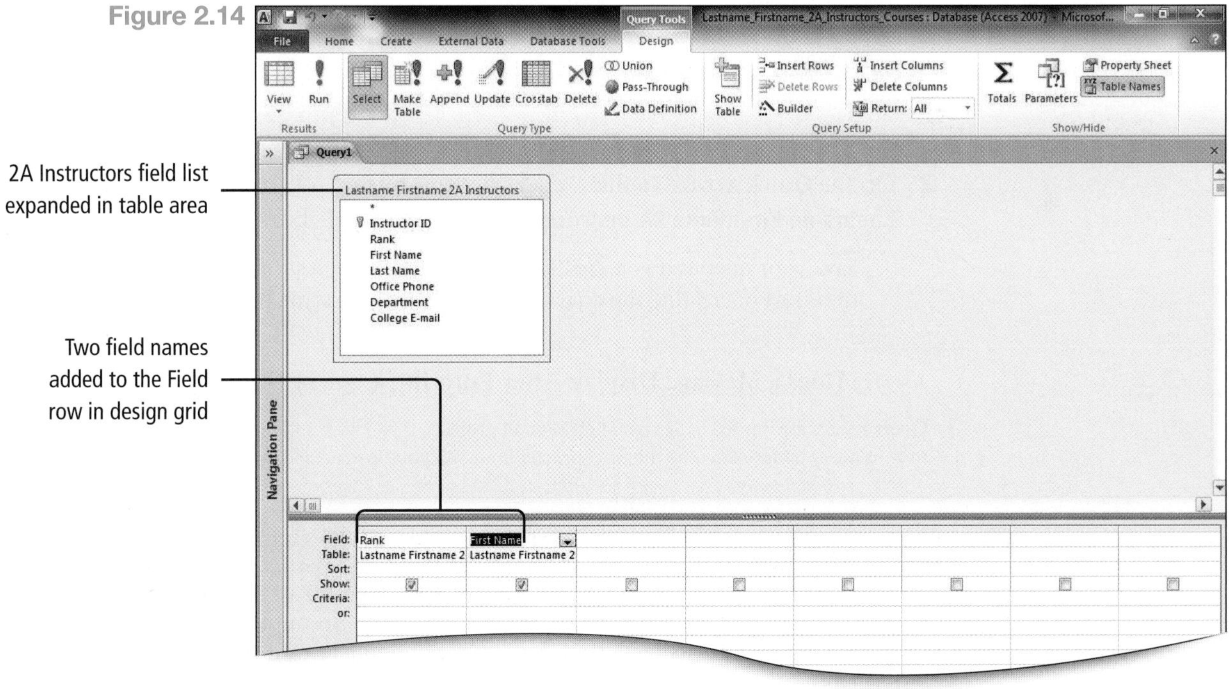

2A Instructors field list expanded in table area

Two field names added to the Field row in design grid

5 In design grid, in the **Field** row, click in the third column, and then click the **arrow** that displays. From the list, click **Last Name** to add the field to the design grid, which is a third way to add a field to the design grid.

6 Using one of the techniques you just practiced, add the **Office Phone** field to the fourth column and the **Department** field to the fifth column in the design grid.

Activity 2.08 | Running, Saving, Printing, and Closing a Query

After you create a query, you *run* it to display the results. When you run a query, Access looks at the records in the table (or tables) you have included in the query, finds the records that match the specified conditions (if any), and displays only those records in a datasheet. Only the fields that you have added to the design grid display in the query results. The query always runs using the current table or tables, presenting the most up-to-date information.

> **Another Way**
>
> On the Design tab, in the Results group, click the View button to automatically start the Run command.

1 On the **Design tab**, in the **Results group**, click the **Run** button, and then compare your screen with Figure 2.15.

This query answers the question, *What is the Rank, First Name, Last Name, Office Phone number, and Department of all of the instructors in the 2A Instructors table?* A query is a subset of the records in one or more tables, arranged in Datasheet view, using the fields and conditions that you specify. The five fields that you specified in the design grid display in columns, and the records from the 2A Instructors table display in rows.

Figure 2.15

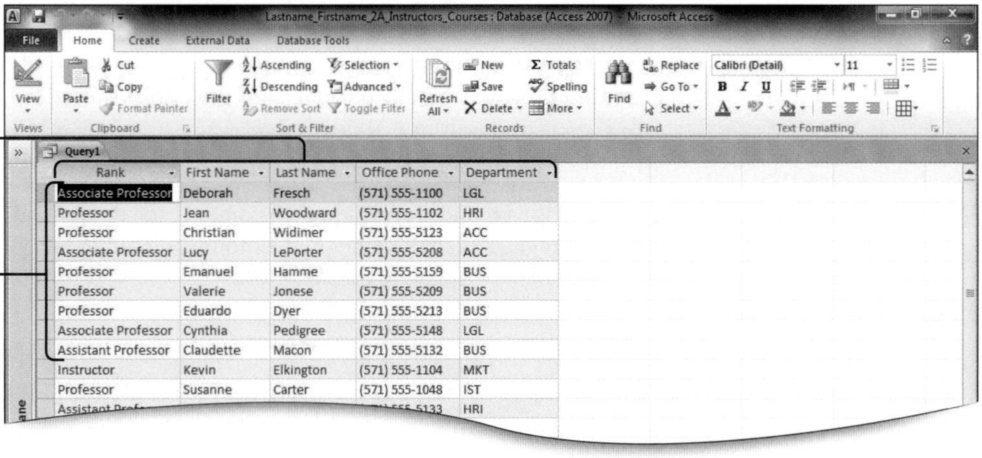

Five fields specified in design grid

Records displayed in rows

2 On the **Quick Access Toolbar**, click the **Save** button. In the **Save As** dialog box, type **Lastname Firstname 2A Instructors Query** and then click **OK**.

Save your queries if you are likely to ask the same question again; doing so will save you the effort of creating the query again to answer the same question.

Alert! | Does a Message Display After Entering a Query Name?

Query names are limited to 64 characters. For all projects, if you have a long last name or first name that results in your query name exceeding the 64-character limit, ask your instructor how you should abbreviate your name.

---

3 Display **Backstage** view, click **Print**, and then click **Print Preview**. Create a paper or electronic printout if instructed to do so, and then **Close Print Preview**.

Queries answer questions and gather information from the data in the tables. Queries are typically created as a basis for a report, but query results can be printed like any other table of data.

4 **Close** ⊠ the query. **Open** » the **Navigation Pane**, and then notice that the **2A Instructors Query** object displays under the **2A Instructors** table object.

> The new query name displays in the Navigation Pane under the table with which it is related—the 2A Instructors table. Only the design of the query is saved. The records still reside in the table object. Each time you open the query, Access runs it again and displays the results based on the data stored in the related table(s). Thus, the results of a query always reflect the latest information in the related table(s).

Objective 5 | Create a New Query from an Existing Query

You can create a new query from scratch or you can open an existing query, save it with new name, and modify the design to suit your needs. Using an existing query saves you time if your new query uses all or some of the same fields and conditions in an existing query.

Activity 2.09 | Creating a New Query from an Existing Query

1 From the **Navigation Pane**, open your **2A Instructors Query** by either double-clicking the name or by right-clicking and clicking Open.

> The query runs, opens in Datasheet view, and displays the records from the 2A Instructors table as specified in the query design grid.

2 Display **Backstage** view, and then click **Save Object As**. In the **Save As** dialog box, type **Lastname Firstname 2A Instructor IDs Query** and then click **OK**. Click the **Home tab**, and then in the **Views group**, click the **View** button to switch to **Design** view.

> A new query, based on a copy of the 2A Instructors Query, is created and displays in the object window and in the Navigation Pane under its data source—the 2A Instructors table.

3 **Close** « the **Navigation Pane**. In the design grid, point to the thin gray selection bar above the **Office Phone** field name until the ↓ pointer displays. Click to select the **Office Phone** column, and then press Del.

> This action deletes the field from the query design only—it has no effect on the field in the underlying 2A Instructors table. The Department field moves to the left. Similarly, you can select multiple fields and delete them at one time.

4 From the gray selection bar, select the **First Name** column. In the selected column, point to the selection bar to display the ▯ pointer, and then drag to the right until a dark vertical line displays on the right side of the **Last Name** column. Release the mouse button to position the **First Name** field in the third column.

> To rearrange fields in the query design, select the field to move, and then drag it to a new position in the design grid.

5 Using the technique you just practiced, move the **Department** field to the left of the **Rank** field.

6 From the field list, drag the **Instructor ID** field down to the first column in the design grid until the ▯ pointer displays, and then release the mouse button. Compare your screen with Figure 2.16.

> The Instructor ID field displays in the first column, and the remaining four fields move to the right. Use this method to insert a field to the left of a field already displayed in the design grid.

Figure 2.16

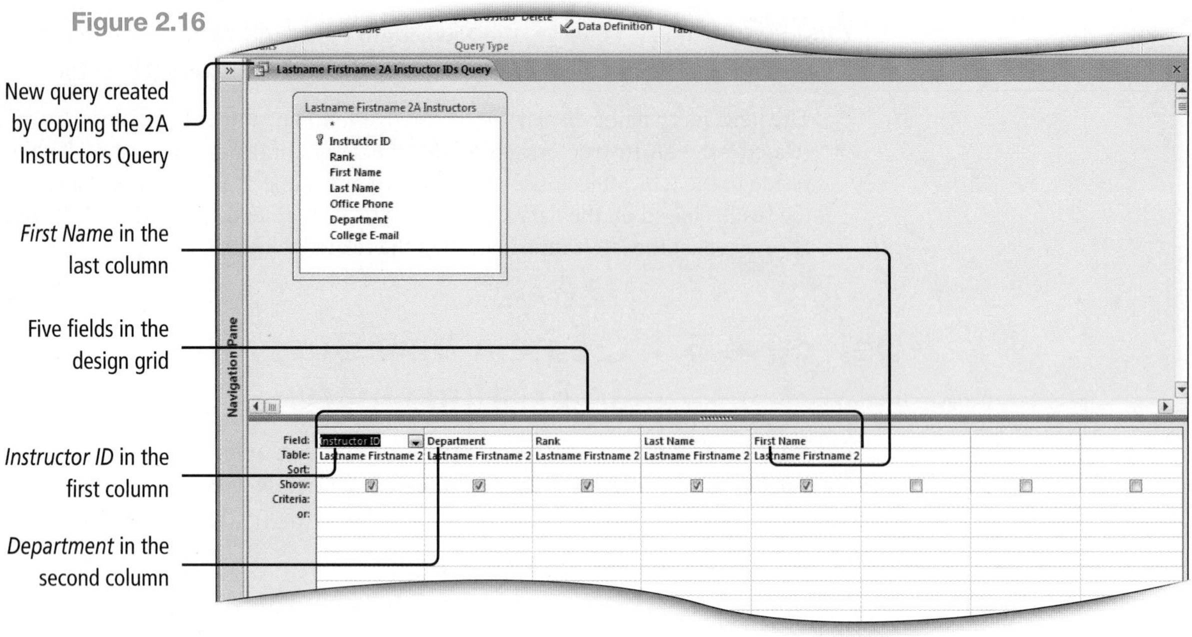

New query created by copying the 2A Instructors Query

First Name in the last column

Five fields in the design grid

Instructor ID in the first column

Department in the second column

7 On the **Design tab**, in the **Results group**, click the **Run** button.

This query answers the question, *What is the Instructor ID, Department, Rank, Last Name, and First Name for every instructor in the 2A Instructors table?* The results of the query are a subset of the records contained in the 2A Instructors table. The records are sorted by the primary key field—Instructor ID.

8 From **Backstage** view, display the query in **Print Preview**. Create a paper or electronic printout if instructed to do so, and then **Close Print Preview**.

9 **Close** ☒ the query, and in the message box, click **Yes** to save the changes to the design—deleting a field, moving two fields, and adding a field. **Open** ☒ the **Navigation Pane**.

The query is saved and closed. The new query name displays in the Navigation Pane under the related table. Recall that when you save a query, only the *design* of the query is saved; the records reside in the related table object or objects.

Objective 6 | Sort Query Results

You can sort the results of a query in ascending or descending order in either Datasheet view or Design view. Use Design view if your query results should display in a specified sort order, or if you intend to use the sorted results in a report.

Activity 2.10 | Sorting Query Results

In this activity, you will save an existing query with a new name, and then sort the query results by using the Sort row in Design view.

1 On the **Navigation Pane**, click your **2A Instructor IDs Query**. Display **Backstage** view, and then click **Save Object As**. In the **Save As** dialog box, type **Lastname Firstname 2A Department Sort Query** and then click **OK**. Click the **Home tab**, and then drag the right edge of the **Navigation Pane** to the right to increase its width so that the names of the new query and the relationship report display fully.

Access creates a new query, based on a copy of your 2A Instructors ID Query; that is, the new query includes the same fields in the same order as the query on which it is based.

2 In the **Navigation Pane**, right-click your **2A Department Sort Query**, and then click **Design View**. **Close** ⊠ the **Navigation Pane**.

3 In the design grid, in the **Sort** row, click in the **Last Name** field to display the insertion point and an arrow. Click the **Sort arrow**, and then in the list, click **Ascending**. Compare your screen with Figure 2.17.

Figure 2.17

Sort row in design grid ——

Ascending sort added to Last Name field ——

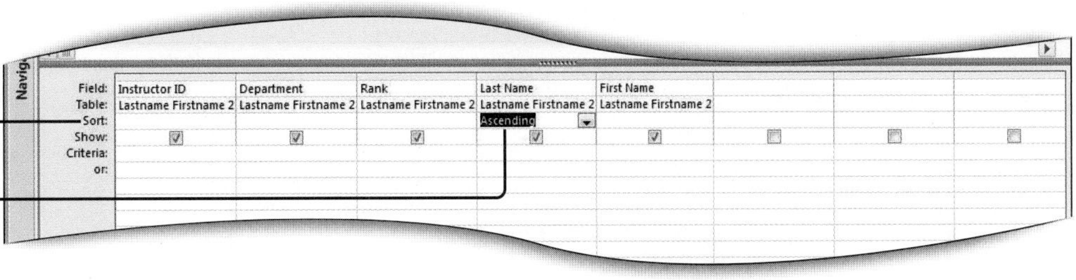

4 On the **Design tab** in the **Results group**, click the **Run** button.

In the query result, the records are sorted in ascending alphabetical order by the Last Name field, and two instructors have the same last name of *Widimer*.

5 On the **Home tab** in the **Views group**, click the **View** button to switch to **Design** view.

6 In the **Sort** row, click in the **First Name** field, click the **Sort arrow**, and then click **Ascending**. **Run** the query.

In the query result, the records are sorted first by the Last Name field. If instructors have the same last name, then Access sorts those records by the First Name field. The two instructors with the last name of *Widimer* are sorted by their first names.

7 Switch to **Design** view. In the **Sort** row, click in the **Department** field, click the **Sort arrow**, and then click **Descending**. **Run** the query; if necessary, scroll down to display the last records, and then compare your screen with Figure 2.18.

In Design view, fields with a Sort designation are sorted from left to right. That is, the sorted field on the left becomes the outermost sort field, and the sorted field on the right becomes the innermost sort field.

Thus, the records are sorted first in descending alphabetical order by the Department field—the leftmost sort field. Then, within each same department name field, the Last Names are sorted in ascending alphabetical order. And, finally, within each same last name field, the First Names are sorted in ascending alphabetical order.

If you run a query and the sorted results are not what you intended, be sure that the fields are displayed from left to right according to the groupings that you desire.

Figure 2.18

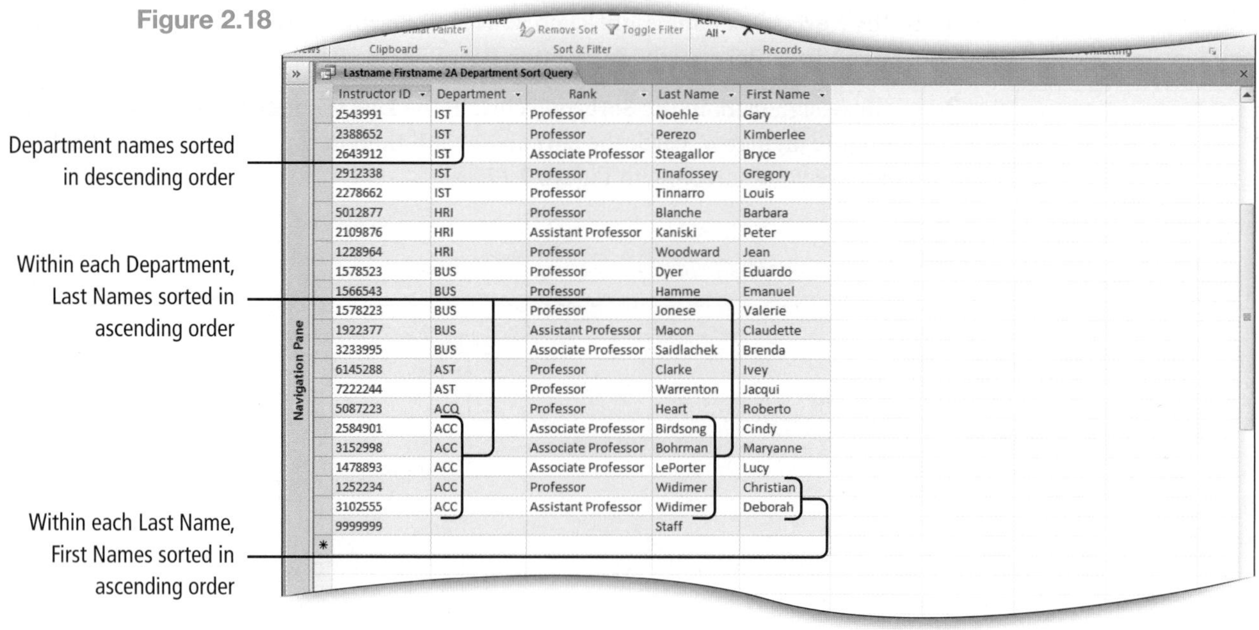

Department names sorted
in descending order

Within each Department,
Last Names sorted in
ascending order

Within each Last Name,
First Names sorted in
ascending order

8 Display the query in **Print Preview**. Create a paper or electronic printout if instructed to do so, and then **Close Print Preview**. **Close** [X] the query. In the message box, click **Yes** to save the changes to the query design.

More Knowledge | **Sorting**

If you add a sort order to the *design* of a query, it remains as a permanent part of the query design. If you use the sort buttons in the Datasheet view, they will override the sort order of the query design, and can be saved as part of the query. A sort order designated in Datasheet view does not display in the Sort row of the query design grid.

Objective 7 | Specify Criteria in a Query

Queries locate information in a database based on *criteria* that you specify as part of the query. Criteria are conditions that identify the specific records for which you are looking.

Criteria enable you to ask a more specific question; therefore, you will get a more specific result. For example, if you want to find out how many instructors are in the IST department, limit the results to that specific department, and then only the records that match the specified department will display.

Activity 2.11 | Specifying Text Criteria in a Query

In this activity, you will assist Dean Judkins by creating a query to answer the question *How many instructors are in the IST Department?*

1 Be sure that all objects are closed and that the **Navigation Pane** is closed. Click the **Create tab**, and then in the **Queries group**, click the **Query Design** button.

2 In the **Show Table** dialog box, **Add** the **2A Instructors** table to the table area, and then **Close** the **Show Table** dialog box.

3 Expand the field list to display all of the fields and the table name. Add the following fields to the design grid in the order given: **Department**, **Instructor ID**, **Rank**, **First Name**, and **Last Name**.

4 In the **Criteria** row of the design grid, click in the **Department** field, type **IST** and then press Enter. Compare your screen with Figure 2.19.

Access places quotation marks around the criteria to indicate that this is a **_text string_**—a sequence of characters. Use the Criteria row to specify the criteria that will limit the results of the query to your exact specifications. The criteria is not case sensitive; so you can type *ist* instead of IST.

Figure 2.19

Five fields added to the design grid

Criteria row in design grid

Criteria under Department—Access adds quotation marks

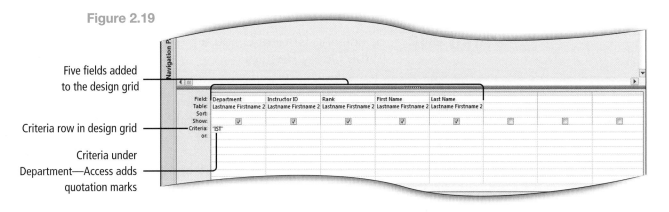

Note | Pressing Enter After Adding Criteria

If you press Enter or click in another column or row in the query design grid after you have added your criteria, you can see how Access alters the criteria so it can interpret what you have typed. Sometimes, there is no change, such as when you add criteria to a number or currency field. Other times, Access may capitalize a letter or add quotation marks or other symbols to clarify the criteria. Whether or not you press Enter after adding criteria has no effect on the query results. It is used here to help you see how the program behaves.

---

5 **Run** the query, and then compare your screen with Figure 2.20.

Thirteen records display that meet the specified criteria—records that have *IST* in the Department field.

Figure 2.20

Thirteen records match Department *IST* criteria

Department	Instructor ID	Rank	First Name	Last Name
IST	2034681	Professor	Susanne	Carter
IST	2278662	Professor	Louis	Tinnarro
IST	2312375	Associate Professor	Joan	Castile
IST	2388652	Professor	Kimberlee	Perezo
IST	2543991	Professor	Gary	Noehle
IST	2621133	Assistant Professor	William	MacNamarra
IST	2643912	Associate Professor	Bryce	Steagallor
IST	2715255	Professor	Bill	Clemente
IST	2810005	Professor	Lisle	Cartier
IST	2912338	Professor	Gregory	Tinafossey
IST	2912398	Professor	Debbie	Binhamm
IST	2988821	Assistant Professor	Janelle	Mochier
IST	3033300	Professor	William	Feeton

Alert! | Do Your Query Results Differ?

If you mistype the criteria, or enter it under the wrong field, or make some other error, the result will display no records. This indicates that there are no records in the table that match the criteria as you entered it. If this occurs, return to Design view and re-examine the query design. Verify that the criteria is typed in the Criteria row, under the correct field, and without typing errors. Then run the query again.

Access | Chapter 2

6 Save 🖫 the query as **Lastname Firstname 2A IST Query** and then display the query in **Print Preview**. Create a paper or electronic printout if instructed to do so, and then **Close Print Preview**.

7 Close ☒ the query, **Open** ⧉ the **Navigation Pane**, and then notice that the **2A IST Query** object displays under the **2A Instructors** table—its data source.

> Recall that queries in the Navigation Pane display an icon of two overlapping tables.

Activity 2.12 | Specifying Criteria Using a Field Not Displayed in the Query Results

So far, all of the fields that you included in the query design have also been included in the query results. It is not required to have every field in the query display in the results. In this activity, you will create a query to answer the question, *Which instructors have a rank of Professor?*

1 Close ⧉ the **Navigation Pane**. Click the **Create tab**, and then in the **Queries group**, click the **Query Design** button.

2 From the **Show Table** dialog box, **Add** the **2A Instructors** table to the table area, and then **Close** the dialog box. Expand the field list.

3 Add the following fields, in the order given, to the design grid: **Instructor ID**, **First Name**, **Last Name**, and **Rank**.

4 In the **Sort** row, in the **Last Name** field, click the **Sort arrow**; click **Ascending**.

5 In the **Criteria** row, click in the **Rank** field, type **professor** and then press Enter. Compare your screen with Figure 2.21.

> Recall that criteria is not case sensitive. As you start typing *professor*, a list of functions display, from which you can select if including a function in your criteria. When you press Enter, the insertion point moves to the next criteria box and quotation marks are added around the text string that you entered.

Figure 2.21

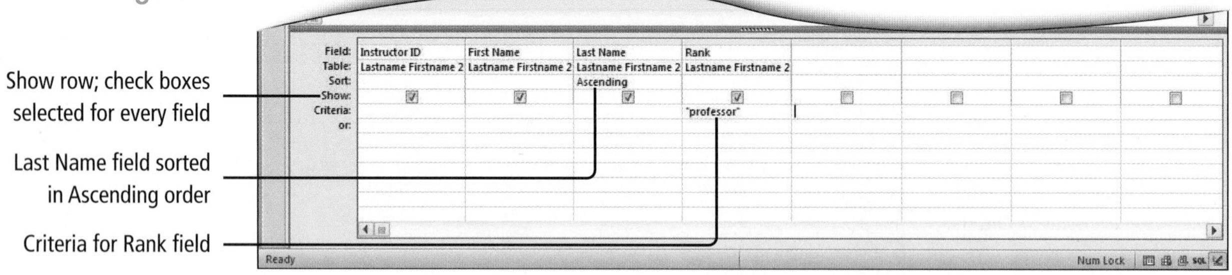

Show row; check boxes selected for every field

Last Name field sorted in Ascending order

Criteria for Rank field

6 In the design grid, in the **Show** row, notice that the check box is selected for every field. **Run** the query to view the query results.

> Nineteen records meet the criteria. In the Rank column each record displays *Professor*, and the records are sorted in ascending alphabetical order by the Last Name field.

7 Switch to **Design** view. In the design grid, under **Rank**, in the **Show** row, click to clear the check box.

> Because it is repetitive and not particularly useful to have *Professor* display for each record in the query results, clear this check box so that the field does not display. However, you should run the query before clearing the Show check box to be sure that the correct records display.

8 **Run** the query, and then notice that the *Rank* field does not display.

> The query results display the same 19 records, but the *Rank* field does not display. Although the Rank field is still included in the query criteria for the purpose of identifying specific records, it is not necessary to display the field in the results. When appropriate, clear the Show check box to avoid cluttering the query results with data that is not useful.

9 **Save** 🖫 the query as **Lastname Firstname 2A Professor Rank Query** and then display the query in **Print Preview**. Create a paper or electronic printout if instructed to do so, and then **Close Print Preview**. **Close** ☒ the query.

Activity 2.13 | Using *Is Null* Criteria to Find Empty Fields

Sometimes you must locate records where data is *missing*. You can locate such records by using *Is Null*—empty—as the criteria in a field. Additionally, you can display only the records where a value *has* been entered in a field by using *Is Not Null* as the criteria, which will exclude records where the specified field is empty. In this activity, you will design a query to find out *Which scheduled courses have no credits listed?*

1 Click the **Create tab**. In the **Queries group**, click the **Query Design** button. Add the **2A Schedule** table to the table area, **Close** the **Show Table** dialog box, and then expand the field list.

2 Add the following fields to the design grid in the order given: **Subject**, **Catalog#**, **Section**, **Course Name**, and **Credits**.

3 In the **Criteria** row, click in the **Credits** field, type **is null** and then press [Enter].

> Access capitalizes *is null*. The criteria *Is Null* examines the field and looks for records that do *not* have any values entered in the Credits field.

4 In the **Sort** row, click in the **Subject** field, click the **Sort arrow**, and then click **Ascending**. **Sort** the **Catalog#** field in **Ascending** order, and then **Sort** the **Section** field in **Ascending** order. Compare your screen with Figure 2.22.

Figure 2.22

Three fields sorted in ascending alphabetical order

Is Null criteria in Credits field

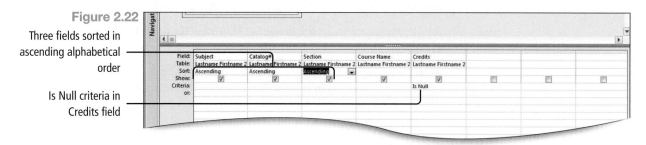

5 **Run** the query, and then compare your screen with Figure 2.23.

Five scheduled courses do not have credits listed—the Credits field is empty. The records are sorted in ascending order first by the Subject field, then by the Catalog # field, and then by the Section. Using the information displayed in the query results, a course scheduler can more easily locate the records in the table to enter the credits.

Figure 2.23

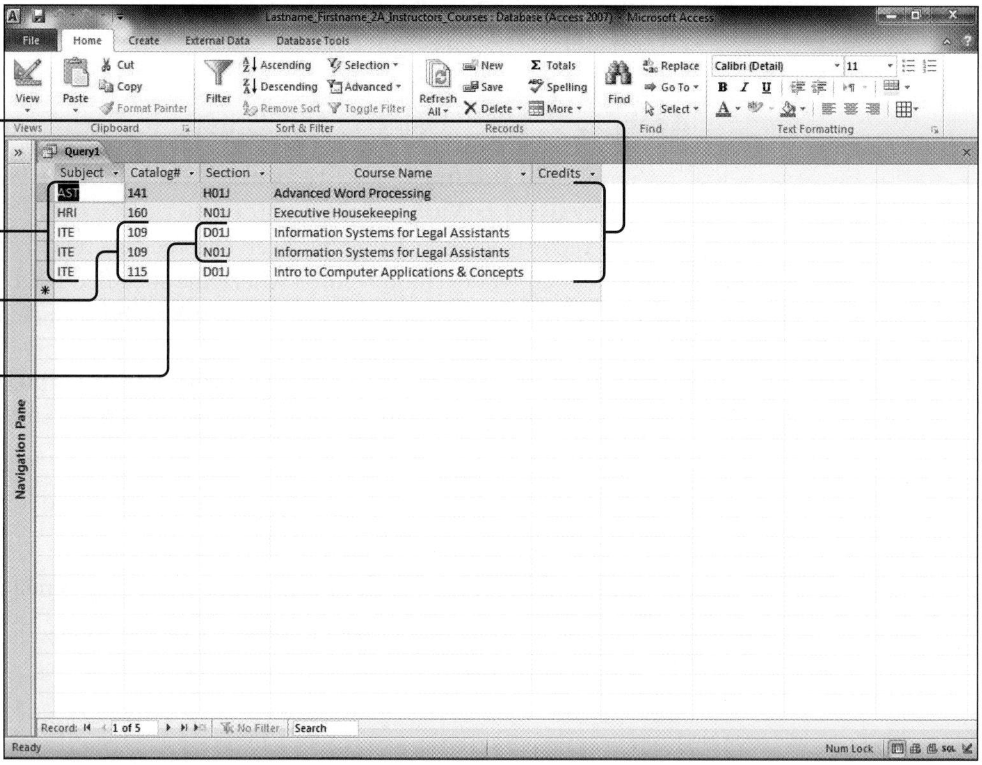

Credits field empty (null) for five courses

Sorted first by Subject

Within Subject, sorted by Catalog#

Within Catalog#, sorted by Section

6 **Save** 🖫 the query as **Lastname Firstname 2A No Credits Query** and then display the query in **Print Preview**. Create a paper or electronic printout if instructed to do so, and then **Close Print Preview**.

7 **Close** ☒ the query. **Open** �» the **Navigation Pane**, and then notice that the **2A No Credits Query** object displays under the **2A Schedule** table object, which is the query's data source.

8 From **Backstage** view, click **Close Database**, and then click **Exit** to close the Access program. As directed by your instructor, submit your database and the eight paper or electronic printouts—relationship report, sorted table, and six queries—that are the results of this project.

End **You have completed Project 2A** ———————————————————

Access | Chapter 2

GO! Beyond Office

Objective | Export an Access Query to a PDF File and Save to Your SkyDrive

When you have information that you want to share with others, you can upload files to your Windows Live SkyDrive. Some files can be opened in SkyDrive; some can only be downloaded. Because database files are typically large files, and storage space is limited on SkyDrive, you can export database objects and then upload those files to SkyDrive.

> **Alert!** | **Working with Web-Based Applications and Services**
>
> Computer programs and services on the Web receive continuous updates and improvements. Thus, the steps to complete this Web-based Activity may differ from the ones shown. You can often look at the screens and the information presented to determine how to complete the Activity.

Activity | Exporting an Access Table to a PDF File, Saving the File to Your SkyDrive, and Adding Comments

In this activity, you will export your 2A No Credits Query object to a PDF file, and then upload your 2A_No_Credits_Query pdf file to your GO! Beyond Office-Access folder on your SkyDrive. Recall that PDF stands for Portable Document Format—a file format that creates an image that preserves the look of your file, but that cannot be easily changed. The results of the query will be available for individuals with whom you have shared the folder that stores the file.

1 **Start** Access. In **Backstage** view, click **Open**. Navigate to your **Access Chapter 2** folder, and then open your **2A_Instructors_Courses** database. If necessary, on the Message Bar, click Enable Content. In the **Navigation Pane**, click your **2A No Credits Query** object.

2 On the Ribbon, click the **External Data tab**, and then in the **Export group**, click the **PDF or XPS** button. In the **Publish as PDF or XPS** dialog box, navigate to your **Access Chapter 2** folder. In the **File name** box, select the text, type **Lastname_Firstname_2A_No_Credits_Query** and then be sure that the **Open file after publishing** check box is selected and the **Minimum size (publishing online)** option button is selected. Click **Publish**.

3 Compare your screen with Figure A, and notice that the document opens in either Adobe Acrobat or Adobe Reader. Notice the displayed records, and then **Close**

your **2A_No_Credits_Query.pdf** file. In the **Export - PDF** dialog box, click **Close**. From **Backstage** view, click **Close Database**, and then click **Exit** to close the Access program.

4 Launch your Web browser, navigate to **www.live.com**, sign in to your Windows Live account, and then at the top of the screen, click **SkyDrive**. If you do not have a Windows Live ID, follow the steps in the GO! Beyond Office project at the end of Word Project 1A to create your account.

Your SkyDrive opens and may display several folders depending on what you have previously uploaded to SkyDrive.

5 Click your **GO! Beyond Office-Access** folder to open it. If necessary, create the folder.

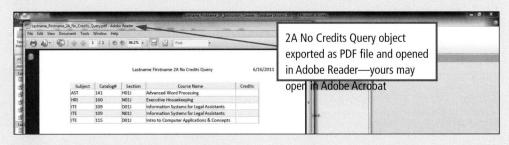

2A No Credits Query object exported as PDF file and opened in Adobe Reader—yours may open in Adobe Acrobat

Figure A

6 With the folder open, at the top of the screen click **Add files**. In the **Add documents to GO! Beyond Office-Access** window, click the text *select documents from your computer*. In the **Open** dialog box, navigate to your **Access Chapter 2** folder, and then click **Open**. Double-click your **2A_No_Credits_Query** PDF file to upload the file to your SkyDrive folder.

7 In the lower left corner, click **Continue**. With the list of files in the folder displayed, on the right, under **Comments**, click in the **Add a comment** box. Type **This query displays courses in the schedule that do not have credits assigned to them.** and then click **Add**.

Individuals who have been granted permissions to the folder can add comments to documents. You might ask for suggestions and receive comments from those with whom you have shared the file.

8 Click the document name, and then in the **File Download** dialog box, click **Open** to display the query as a PDF file. **Close** your **2A_No_Credits_Query.pdf** file.

9 Display the **Start** menu, and then click **All Programs**. On the list of programs, click the **Accessories** folder, and then click **Snipping Tool**. In the **Snipping Tool** dialog box, click the **New arrow**. On the displayed list, click **Full-screen Snip**.

10 On the **Snipping Tool** markup window toolbar, click the **Save Snip** button. In the **Save As** dialog box, navigate to your **Access Chapter 2**, be sure the **Save as type** box displays **JPEG file**, and then in the **File name** box, type **Lastname_Firstname_2A_Access_SkyDrive_Snip** Click **Save**, and then **Close** the **Snipping Tool** window.

11 Sign out of your Windows Live account. **Close** your Web browser, and then submit your snip file as directed.

NOTES

Getting Started with Microsoft Office PowerPoint

OUTCOMES

At the end of this chapter you will be able to:

PROJECT 1A
Create a new PowerPoint presentation.

PROJECT 1B
Edit and format a PowerPoint presentation.

OBJECTIVES

Mastering these objectives will enable you to:

1. Create a New Presentation (p. 523)
2. Edit a Presentation in Normal View (p. 527)
3. Add Pictures to a Presentation (p. 534)
4. Print and View a Presentation (p. 537)

5. Edit an Existing Presentation (p. 545)
6. Format a Presentation (p. 549)
7. Use Slide Sorter View (p. 552)
8. Apply Slide Transitions (p. 555)

Hawaiian Waterfall/Shutterstock

In This Chapter

In this chapter you will study presentation skills, which are among the most important skills you will learn. Good presentation skills enhance your communications—written, electronic, and interpersonal. In this technology-enhanced world, communicating ideas clearly and concisely is a critical personal skill. Microsoft PowerPoint 2010 is presentation software with which you create electronic slide presentations. Use PowerPoint to present information to your audience effectively. You can start with a new, blank presentation and add content, pictures, and themes, or you can collaborate with colleagues by inserting slides that have been saved in other presentations.

The projects in this chapter relate to **Lehua Hawaiian Adventures**. Named for the small, crescent-shaped island that is noted for its snorkeling and scuba diving, Lehua Hawaiian Adventures offers exciting but affordable adventure tours. Hiking tours go off the beaten path to amazing remote places on the islands. If you prefer to ride into the heart of Hawaii, try the cycling tours. Lehua Hawaiian Adventures also offers Jeep tours. Whatever you prefer—mountain, sea, volcano—our tour guides are experts in the history, geography, culture, and flora and fauna of Hawaii.

Project 1A Company Overview

Project Activities

In Activities 1.01 through 1.13, you will create the first four slides of a new presentation that Lehua Hawaiian Adventures tour manager Carl Kawaoka is developing to introduce the tour services that the company offers. Your completed presentation will look similar to Figure 1.1.

Project Files

For Project 1A, you will need the following files:

> New blank PowerPoint presentation
> p01A_Helicopter
> p01A_Beach

You will save your presentation as:

> Lastname_Firstname_1A_LHA_Overview

Project Results

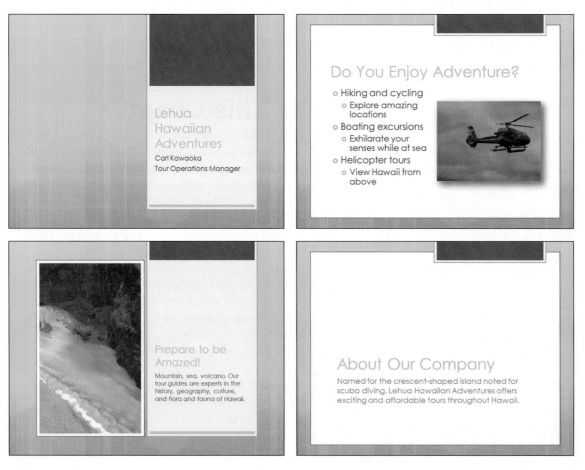

Figure 1.1
Project 1A LHA Overview

Objective 1 | Create a New Presentation

Microsoft PowerPoint 2010 is software with which you can present information to your audience effectively. You can edit and format a blank presentation by adding text, a presentation theme, and pictures.

Activity 1.01 | Identifying Parts of the PowerPoint Window

In this activity, you will start PowerPoint and identify the parts of the PowerPoint window.

1 **Start** ⊕ PowerPoint to display a new blank presentation in Normal view, and then compare your screen with Figure 1.2.

Normal view is the primary editing view in PowerPoint where you write and design your presentations. Normal view includes the Notes pane, the Slide pane, and the Slides/Outline pane.

Figure 1.2

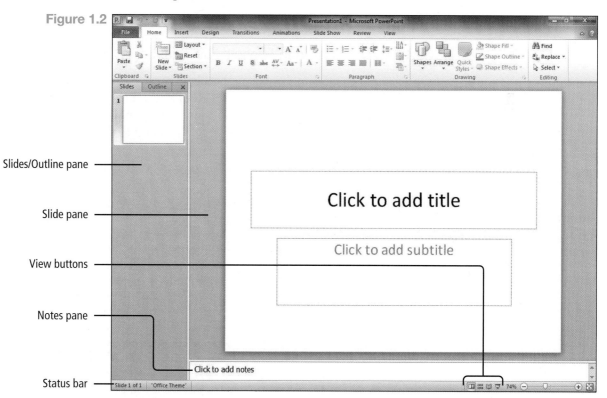

Slides/Outline pane

Slide pane

View buttons

Notes pane

Status bar

2 Take a moment to study the parts of the PowerPoint window described in the table in Figure 1.3.

PowerPoint | Chapter 1

Microsoft PowerPoint Screen Elements	
Screen Element	**Description**
Notes pane	Displays below the Slide pane and provides space for you to type notes regarding the active slide.
Slide pane	Displays a large image of the active slide.
Slides/Outline pane	Displays either the presentation in the form of miniature images called *thumbnails* (Slides tab) or the presentation outline (Outline tab).
Status bar	Displays, in a horizontal bar at the bottom of the presentation window, the current slide number, number of slides in a presentation, theme, View buttons, Zoom slider, and Fit slide to current window button; you can customize this area to include additional helpful information.
View buttons	Control the look of the presentation window with a set of commands.

Figure 1.3

Activity 1.02 | Entering Presentation Text and Saving a Presentation

On startup, PowerPoint displays a new blank presentation with a single *slide*—a *title slide* in Normal view. A presentation slide—similar to a page in a document—can contain text, pictures, tables, charts, and other multimedia or graphic objects. The title slide is the first slide in a presentation and provides an introduction to the presentation topic.

1 In the *Slide pane*, click in the text *Click to add title*, which is the title *placeholder*.

A placeholder is a box on a slide with dotted or dashed borders that holds title and body text or other content such as charts, tables, and pictures. This slide contains two placeholders, one for the title and one for the subtitle.

2 Type **Lehua Hawaiian Adventures** point to *Lehua*, and then right-click. On the shortcut menu, click **Ignore All** so *Lehua* is not flagged as a spelling error in this presentation. Compare your screen with Figure 1.4.

Recall that a red wavy underline indicates that the underlined word is not in the Microsoft Office dictionary.

Figure 1.4

Red wavy underline no longer displays

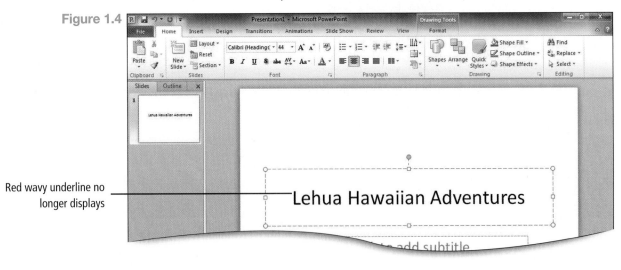

3 Click in the subtitle placeholder, and then type **Carl Kawaoka**

4 Press Enter to create a new line in the subtitle placeholder. Type **Tour Manager**

5 Right-click **Kawaoka**, and then on the shortcut menu, click **Ignore All**. Compare your screen with Figure 1.5.

Figure 1.5

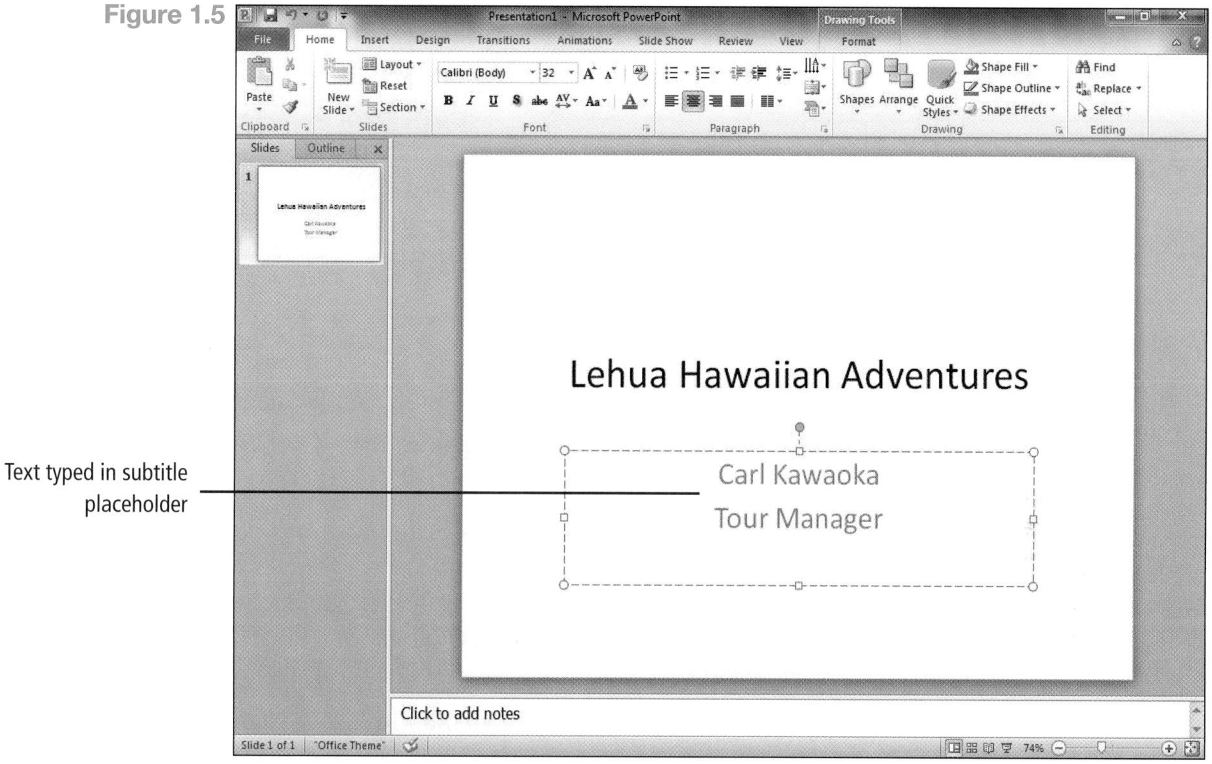

Text typed in subtitle placeholder

6 In the upper left corner of your screen, click the **File tab** to display **Backstage** view, click **Save As**, and then in the **Save As** dialog box, navigate to the location where you will store your files for this chapter. Create a new folder named **PowerPoint Chapter 1** In the **File name** box, replace the existing text with **Lastname_Firstname_1A_LHA_ Overview** and then click **Save**.

Activity 1.03 | Applying a Presentation Theme

A *theme* is a set of unified design elements that provides a look for your presentation by applying colors, fonts, and effects.

1 On the Ribbon, click the **Design tab**. In the **Themes group**, click the **More** button to display the **Themes** gallery. Compare your screen with Figure 1.6.

Figure 1.6

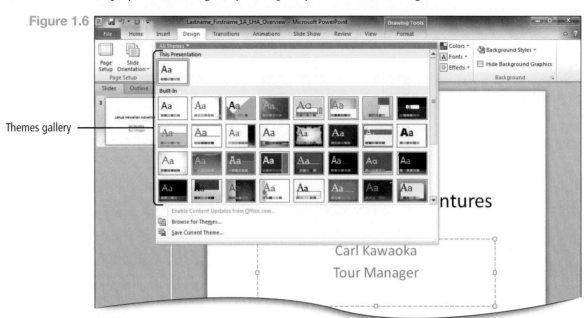

Themes gallery

2 Under **Built-In,** point to several of the themes and notice that a ScreenTip displays the name of each theme and the Live Preview feature displays how each theme would look if applied to your presentation.

> The first theme that displays is the Office theme. Subsequent themes are arranged alphabetically.

3 Use the ScreenTips to locate the theme with the green background—**Austin**—as shown in Figure 1.7.

Figure 1.7

Austin theme

ScreenTip displayed

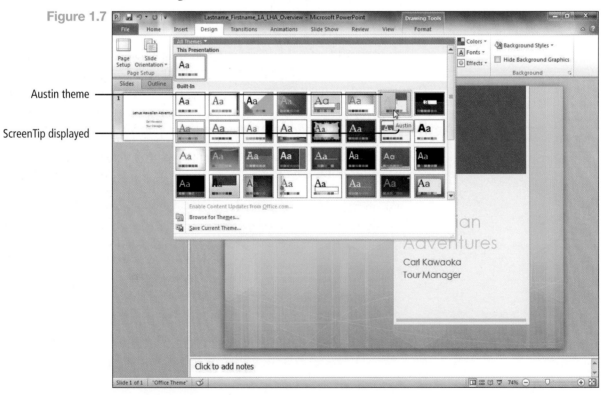

4 Click the **Austin** theme to change the presentation theme and then **Save** your presentation.

Objective 2 | Edit a Presentation in Normal View

Editing is the process of modifying a presentation by adding and deleting slides or by changing the contents of individual slides.

Activity 1.04 | Inserting a New Slide

To insert a new slide in a presentation, display the slide that will precede the slide that you want to insert.

1 On the **Home tab**, in the **Slides group**, point to the **New Slide** button. Compare your screen with Figure 1.8.

The New Slide button is a split button. Recall that clicking the main part of a split button performs a command and clicking the arrow opens a menu, list, or gallery. The upper, main part of the New Slide button, when clicked, inserts a slide without displaying any options. The lower part—the New Slide button arrow—when clicked, displays a gallery of slide *layouts*. A layout is the arrangement of elements, such as title and subtitle text, lists, pictures, tables, charts, shapes, and movies, on a slide.

Figure 1.8

New Slide button

New Slide button arrow

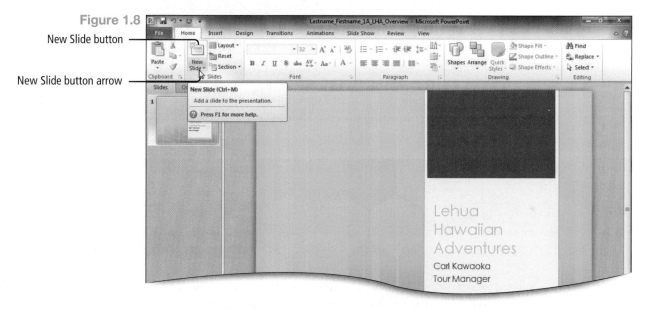

2 In the **Slides group**, click the lower portion of the New Slide button—the **New Slide button arrow**—to display the gallery, and then compare your screen with Figure 1.9.

Figure 1.9

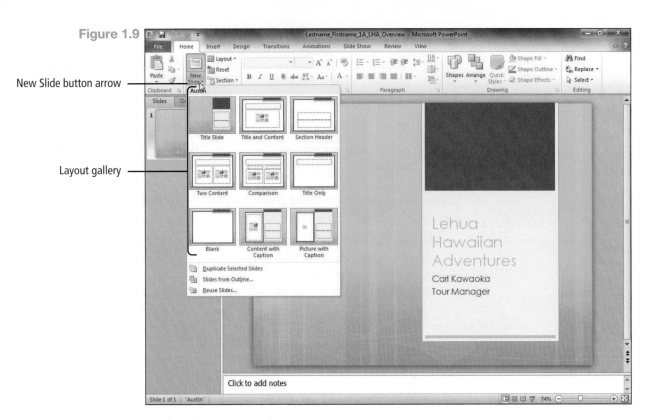

New Slide button arrow

Layout gallery

3 In the gallery, click the **Two Content** layout to insert a new slide. Notice that the new blank slide displays in the **Slide pane** and in the *Slides/Outline pane*. Compare your screen with Figure 1.10.

Figure 1.10

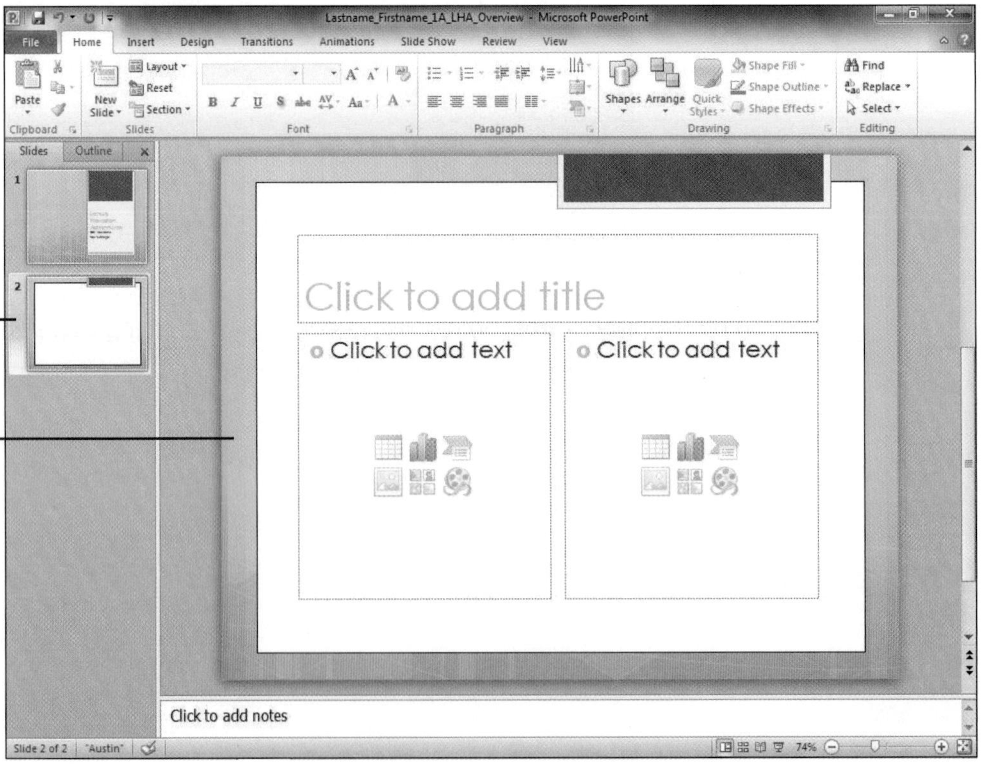

Slide 2 thumbnail

New slide with Two Content layout

4 In the **Slide pane**, click the text *Click to add title*, and then type **Do You Enjoy Adventure?**

5 On the left side of the slide, click anywhere in the content placeholder. Type **Hiking and cycling** and then press [Enter].

6 Type **Explore locations** and then compare your screen with Figure 1.11.

Figure 1.11

Slide title

Text typed in content placeholder

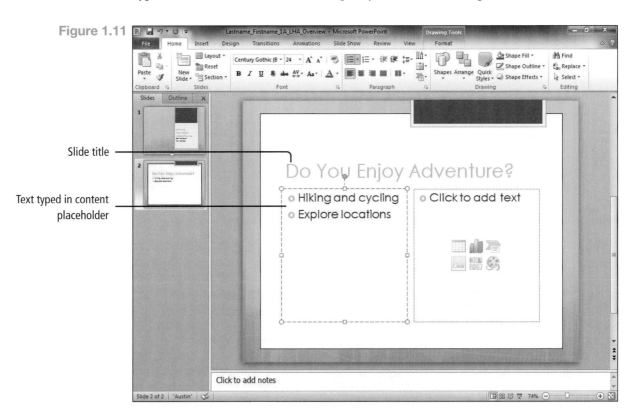

7 Save 💾 your presentation.

Activity 1.05 | Increasing and Decreasing List Levels

Text in a PowerPoint presentation is organized according to *list levels*. List levels, each represented by a bullet symbol, are similar to outline levels. On a slide, list levels are identified by the bullet style, indentation, and the size of the text.

The first level on an individual slide is the title. Increasing the list level of a bullet point increases its indent and results in a smaller text size. Decreasing the list level of a bullet point decreases its indent and results in a larger text size.

1 On **Slide 2**, if necessary, click at the end of the last bullet point after the word *locations*, and then press Enter to insert a new bullet point.

2 Type **Boating excursions** and then press Enter.

3 Press Tab, and then notice that the green bullet is indented. Type **Exhilarate your senses while at sea**

By pressing Tab at the beginning of a bullet point, you can increase the list level and indent the bullet point.

4   Press Enter. Notice that a new bullet point displays at the same level as the previous bullet point. Then, on the **Home tab**, in the **Paragraph group**, click the **Decrease List Level** button. Type **Helicopter tours** and then compare your screen with Figure 1.12.

The Decrease List Level button promotes the bullet point. The text size increases and the text is no longer indented.

Figure 1.12

Decrease List Level button

List level of bullet point increased

List level of bullet point decreased

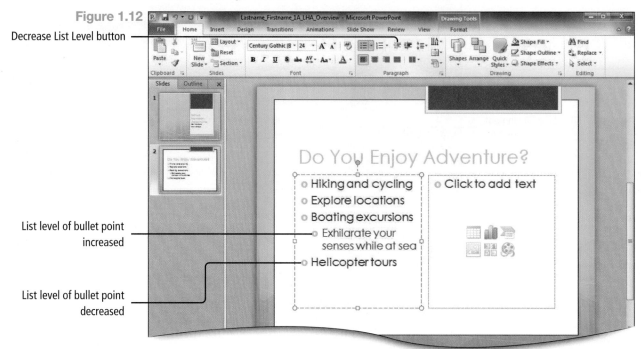

5   Press Enter, and then press Tab to increase the list level. Type **View Hawaii from above**

6   Click anywhere in the second bullet point—*Explore locations*. On the **Home tab**, in the **Paragraph group**, click the **Increase List Level** button. Compare your screen with Figure 1.13.

The bullet point is indented and the size of the text decreases.

Figure 1.13

Increase List Level button

List level of two bullet points increased

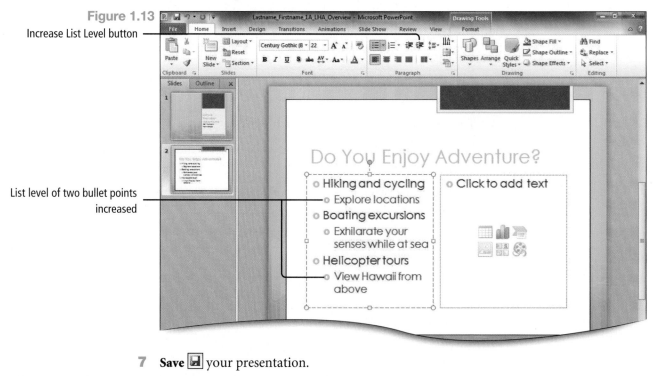

7   **Save** your presentation.

Activity 1.06 | Adding Speaker's Notes to a Presentation

Recall that when a presentation is displayed in Normal view, the Notes pane displays below the Slide pane. Use the Notes pane to type speaker's notes that you can print below a picture of each slide. Then, while making your presentation, you can refer to these printouts while making a presentation, thus reminding you of the important points that you want to discuss during the presentation.

1 With **Slide 2** displayed, on the **Home tab**, in the **Slides group**, click the **New Slide button arrow** to display the **Slide Layout** gallery, and then click **Section Header**.

> The section header layout changes the look and flow of a presentation by providing text placeholders that do not contain bullet points.

2 Click in the title placeholder, and then type **About Our Company**

3 Click in the content placeholder below the title, and then type **Named for the crescent-shaped island noted for scuba diving, Lehua Hawaiian Adventures offers exciting and affordable tours throughout Hawaii.** Compare your screen with Figure 1.14.

Figure 1.14

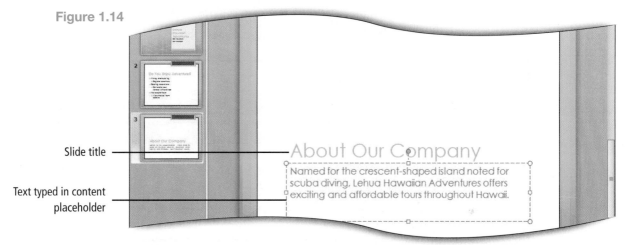

Slide title

Text typed in content placeholder

4 Below the slide, click in the **Notes pane**. Type **Lehua Hawaiian Adventures is based in Honolulu but has offices on each of the main Hawaiian islands.** Compare your screen with Figure 1.15, and then **Save** your presentation.

Figure 1.15

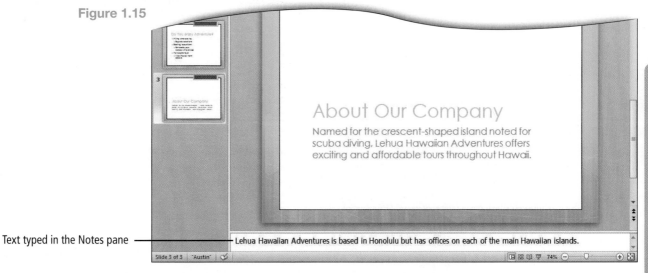

Text typed in the Notes pane

Activity 1.07 | Displaying and Editing Slides in the Slide Pane

To edit a presentation slide, display the slide in the Slide pane.

1 Look at the **Slides/Outline pane**, and then notice that the presentation contains three slides. At the right side of the PowerPoint window, in the vertical scroll bar, point to the scroll box, and then hold down the left mouse button to display a ScreenTip indicating the slide number and title.

2 Drag the scroll box up until the ScreenTip displays *Slide: 2 of 3 Do You Enjoy Adventure?* Compare your slide with Figure 1.16, and then release the mouse button to display **Slide 2**.

Figure 1.16

3 In the second bullet point, click at the end of the word *Explore*. Press Spacebar, and then type **amazing** Compare your screen with Figure 1.17.

The placeholder text is resized to fit within the placeholder. The AutoFit Options button displays.

Figure 1.17

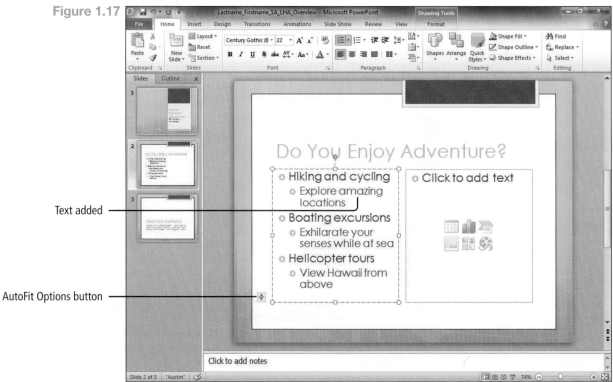

4 Click the **AutoFit Options** button, and then click **AutoFit Text to Placeholder**.

The *AutoFit Text to Placeholder* option keeps the text contained within the placeholder by reducing the size of the text. The *Stop Fitting Text to This Placeholder* option turns off the AutoFit option so that the text can flow beyond the placeholder border; the text size remains unchanged.

5 Below the vertical scroll bar, locate the **Previous Slide** ⬆ and **Next Slide** ⬇ buttons as shown in Figure 1.18.

Figure 1.18

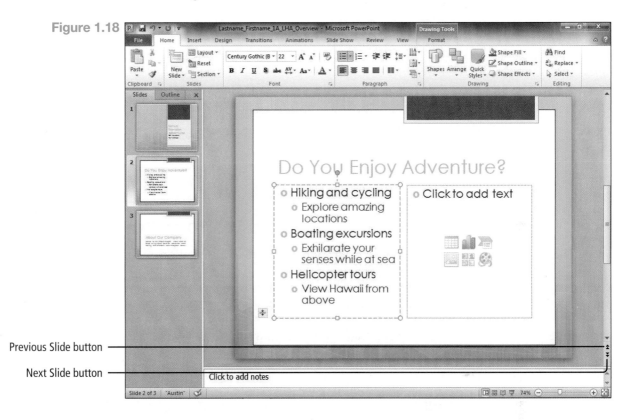

Previous Slide button

Next Slide button

6 In the vertical scroll bar, click the **Previous Slide** button ⬆ so that **Slide 1** displays. Then click the **Next Slide** button ⬇ two times until **Slide 3** displays.

By clicking the Next Slide or the Previous Slide buttons, you can scroll through your presentation one slide at a time.

7 On the left side of the PowerPoint window, in the **Slides/Outline pane**, point to **Slide 1**, and then notice that a ScreenTip displays the slide title. Compare your screen with Figure 1.19.

In the Slides/Outline pane, the slide numbers display to the left of the slide thumbnails.

Figure 1.19

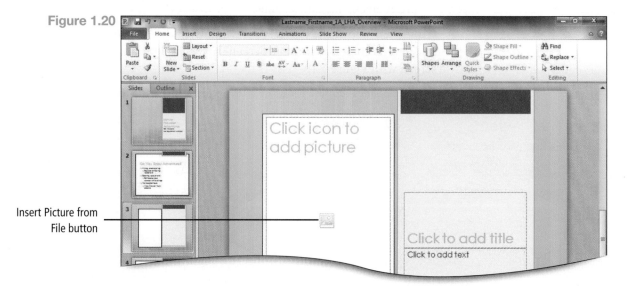

ScreenTip displays slide title

8 Click **Slide 1** to display it in the **Slide pane**, and then in the slide subtitle, click at the end of the word *Tour*. Press Spacebar, and then type **Operations**

Clicking a slide thumbnail is the most common method used to display a slide in the Slide pane.

9 **Save** 🖬 your presentation.

Objective 3 | Add Pictures to a Presentation

Photographic images add impact to a presentation and help the audience visualize the message you are trying to convey.

Activity 1.08 | Inserting a Picture from a File

Many slide layouts in PowerPoint accommodate digital picture files so that you can easily add pictures you have stored on your system or on a portable storage device.

1 In the **Slides/Outline pane**, click **Slide 2** to display it in the **Slide pane**. On the **Home tab**, in the **Slides group**, click the **New Slide button arrow** to display the **Slide Layout** gallery. Click **Picture with Caption** to insert a new **Slide 3**. Compare your screen with Figure 1.20.

In the center of the large picture placeholder, the *Insert Picture from File* button displays.

Figure 1.20

Insert Picture from File button

2 In the picture placeholder, click the **Insert Picture from File** button ![icon] to open the **Insert Picture** dialog box. Navigate to the location in which your student files are stored, click **p01A_Beach**, then click **Insert** to insert the picture in the placeholder.

3 To the right of the picture, click in the title placeholder. Type **Prepare to be Amazed!**

4 Below the title, click in the caption placeholder, and then type **Mountain, sea, volcano. Our tour guides are experts in the history, geography, culture, and flora and fauna of Hawaii.** Compare your screen with Figure 1.21.

Figure 1.21

Inserted picture

Title

Caption

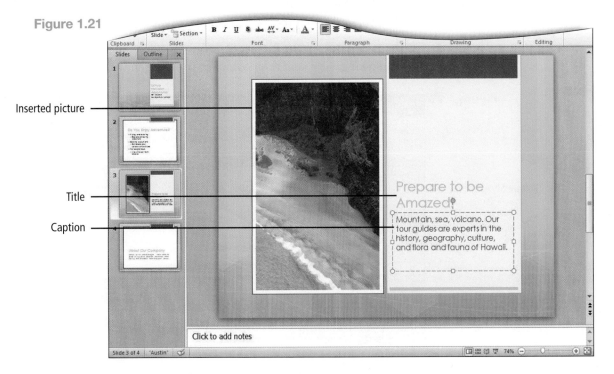

5 Display **Slide 2**. In the placeholder on the right side of the slide, click the **Insert Picture from File** button ![icon]. Navigate to your student files, and then click **p01A_ Helicopter**. Click **Insert**, and then compare your screen with Figure 1.22.

Small circles and squares—*sizing handles*—surround the inserted picture and indicate that the picture is selected and can be modified or formatted. The *rotation handle*—a green circle above the picture—provides a way to rotate a selected image.

Figure 1.22

Rotation handle

Sizing handles

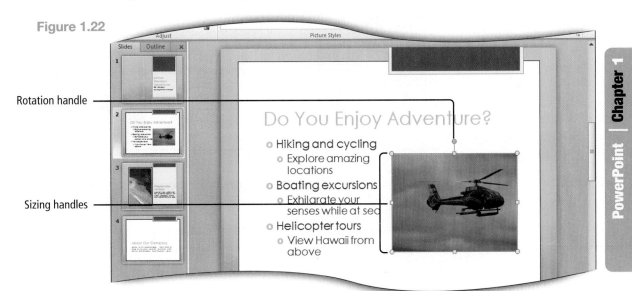

6 Save 🖫 the presentation.

Activity 1.09 | Applying a Style to a Picture

The Picture Tools add the Format tab to the Ribbon, which provides numerous *styles* that you can apply to your pictures. A style is a collection of formatting options that you can apply to a picture, text, or an object.

1 With **Slide 2** displayed, if necessary, click the picture of the helicopter to select it. On the Ribbon, notice that the Picture Tools are active and the Format tab displays.

2 On the **Format tab**, in the **Picture Styles group**, click the **More** button 🔽 to display the **Picture Styles** gallery, and then compare your screen with Figure 1.23.

Figure 1.23

Picture Styles gallery

3 In the gallery, point to several of the picture styles to display the ScreenTips and to view the effect on your picture. In the first row, click **Drop Shadow Rectangle**.

4 Click in a blank area of the slide, and then compare your screen with Figure 1.24.

Figure 1.24

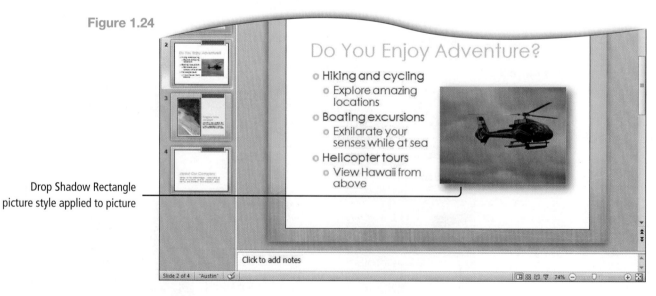

Drop Shadow Rectangle picture style applied to picture

5 **Save** 🖫 the presentation.

Activity 1.10 | Applying and Removing Picture Artistic Effects

Artistic effects are formats applied to images that make pictures resemble sketches or paintings.

1 With **Slide 2** displayed, select the picture of the helicopter.

2 Click the **Format tab**, and then in the **Adjust group**, click the **Artistic Effects** button to display the **Artistic Effects** gallery. Compare your screen with Figure 1.25.

Figure 1.25

Artistic Effects button

Artistic Effects gallery

3 In the gallery, point to several of the artistic effects to display the ScreenTips and to have Live Preview display the effect on your picture. Then, in the second row, click the **Paint Strokes** effect.

4 With the picture still selected, on the **Format tab**, in the **Adjust group**, click the **Artistic Effects** button to display the gallery. In the first row, click the first effect— **None**—to remove the effect from the picture and restore the previous formatting.

5 **Save** 🖫 the presentation.

Objective 4 | Print and View a Presentation

Activity 1.11 | Viewing a Slide Show

When you view a presentation as an electronic slide show, the entire slide fills the computer screen, and an audience can view your presentation if your computer is connected to a projection system.

1 On the Ribbon, click the **Slide Show tab**. In the **Start Slide Show group**, click the **From Beginning** button.

> The first slide fills the screen, displaying the presentation as the audience would see it if your computer was connected to a projection system.

Another Way

Press F5 to start the slide show from the beginning. Or, display the first slide you want to show and click the Slide Show button on the lower right side of the status bar; or press Shift + F5.

PowerPoint | Chapter 1

2 Click the left mouse button or press Spacebar to advance to the second slide.

3 Continue to click or press Spacebar until the last slide displays, and then click or press Spacebar one more time to display a black slide.

> After the last slide in a presentation, a *black slide* displays, indicating that the presentation is over.

4 With the black slide displayed, click the left mouse button or press Spacebar to exit the slide show and return to the presentation.

Activity 1.12 | Inserting Headers and Footers

A *header* is text that prints at the top of each sheet of *slide handouts* or *notes pages*. Slide handouts are printed images of slides on a sheet of paper. Notes pages are printouts that contain the slide image on the top half of the page and notes that you have created on the Notes pane in the lower half of the page.

In addition to headers, you can insert *footers*—text that displays at the bottom of every slide or that prints at the bottom of a sheet of slide handouts or notes pages.

1 Click the **Insert tab**, and then in the **Text group**, click the **Header & Footer** button to display the **Header and Footer** dialog box.

2 In the **Header and Footer** dialog box, click the **Notes and Handouts tab**. Under **Include on page**, select the **Date and time** check box, and as you do so, watch the Preview box in the lower right corner of the Header and Footer dialog box.

> The Preview box indicates the placeholders on the printed Notes and Handouts pages. The two narrow rectangular boxes at the top of the Preview box indicate placeholders for the header text and date. When you select the Date and time check box, the placeholder in the upper right corner is outlined, indicating the location in which the date will display.

3 If necessary, click the Update automatically option button so that the current date prints on the notes and handouts each time the presentation is printed.

4 If necessary, *clear* the Header check box to omit this element. Notice that in the **Preview** box, the corresponding placeholder is not selected.

5 Select the **Page number** and **Footer** check boxes, and then notice that the insertion point displays in the **Footer** box. Using your own name, type **Lastname_Firstname_1A_LHA_Overview** so that the file name displays as a footer, and then compare your dialog box with Figure 1.26.

Figure 1.26

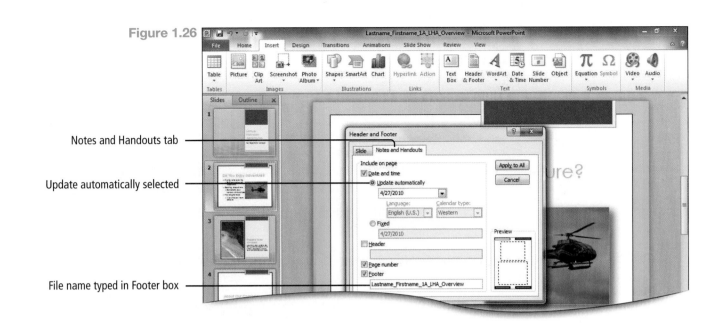

Notes and Handouts tab

Update automatically selected

File name typed in Footer box

6　In the upper right corner of the dialog box, click **Apply to All**. **Save** 🖫 your presentation.

> **More Knowledge | Adding Footers to Slides**
>
> You can also add footers to the actual slides, which will display during your presentation, by using the Slide tab in the Header and Footer dialog box. Headers cannot be added to individual slides.

Activity 1.13 | Printing a Presentation

Use Backstage view to preview the arrangement of slides on the handouts and notes pages.

1　Display **Slide 1**. Click the **File tab** to display **Backstage** view, and then click the **Print tab**.

The Print tab in Backstage view displays the tools you need to select your settings and also to view a preview of your presentation. On the right, Print Preview displays your presentation exactly as it will print.

2　In the **Settings group**, click **Full Page Slides**, and then compare your screen with Figure 1.27.

The gallery displays either the default print setting—Full Page Slides—or the most recently selected print setting. Thus, on your system, this button might indicate the presentation Notes Pages, Outline, or one of several arrangements of slide handouts—depending on the most recently used setting.

Figure 1.27

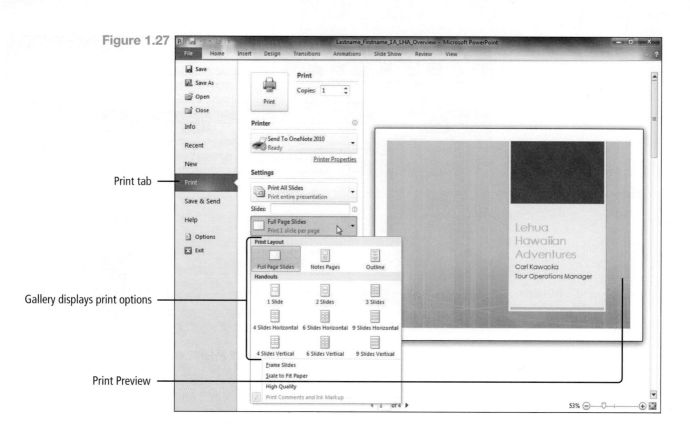

Print tab

Gallery displays print options

Print Preview

3 In the gallery, under **Handouts**, click **4 Slides Horizontal**. Notice that the **Print Preview** on the right displays the slide handout, and that the current date, file name, and page number display in the header and footer.

In the Settings group, the Portrait Orientation option displays so that you can change the print orientation from Portrait to Landscape. The Portrait Orientation option does not display when Full Page Slides is chosen.

4 To print your handout, be sure your system is connected to a printer, and then in the **Print group**, click the **Print** button.

The handout will print on your default printer—on a black and white printer, the colors will print in shades of gray. Backstage view closes and your file redisplays in the PowerPoint window.

5 Click the **File tab** to display **Backstage** view, and then click the **Print tab**. In the **Settings group**, click **4 Slides Horizontal**, and then under **Print Layout**, click **Notes Pages** to view the presentation notes for **Slide 1**; recall that you created notes for **Slide 4**.

Indicated below the Notes page are the current slide number and the number of pages that will print when Notes page is selected. You can use the Next Page and Previous Page arrows to display each Notes page in the presentation.

6 At the bottom of the **Print Preview**, click the **Next Page** button ▶ three times so that **Page 4** displays. Compare your screen with Figure 1.28.

The notes that you created for Slide 4 display below the image of the slide.

Figure 1.28

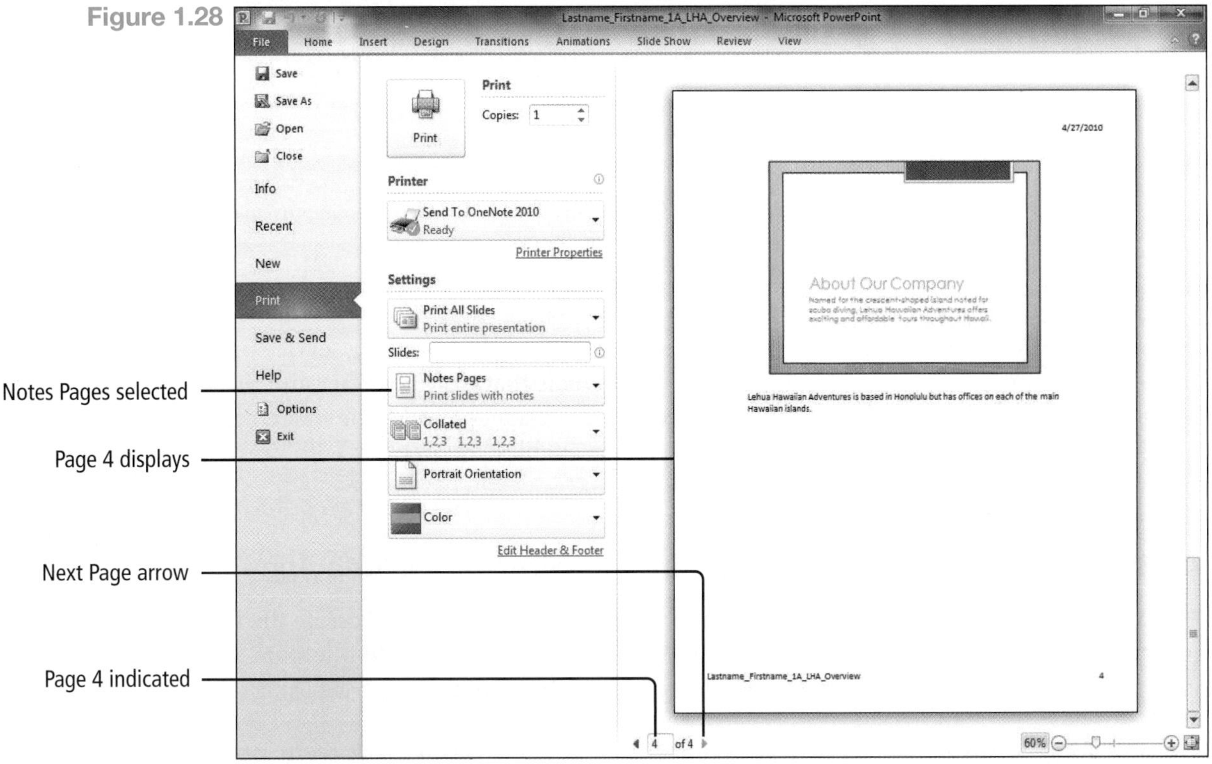

Notes Pages selected

Page 4 displays

Next Page arrow

Page 4 indicated

7 In the **Settings group**, click in the **Slides** box, and then type **4** so that only the Notes pages for **Slide 4** will print. In the **Settings group**, click **Notes Pages**, and then below the gallery, select **Frame Slides**. In the **Print group**, click the **Print** button to print the Notes page.

8 Click the **File tab** to redisplay **Backstage** view, be sure the **Info tab** is active, and then in the third panel, click **Properties**. Click **Show Document Panel**, and then in the **Author** box, delete any text and type your firstname and lastname.

9 In the **Subject** box, type your course name and section number. In the **Keywords** box, type **company overview** and then **Close** ☒ the Document Information Panel.

10 **Save** 🖫 your presentation. On the right end of the title bar, click the **Close** button ☒ to close the presentation and close PowerPoint.

End You have completed Project 1A ————————————

GO! Beyond Office

> **Alert!** | **Working with Web-Based Applications and Services**
>
> Computer programs and services on the Web receive continuous updates and improvements. Thus, the steps to complete this Web-based Activity may differ from the ones shown. You can often look at the screens and the information presented to determine how to complete the Activity.

Recall that Windows Live SkyDrive is a free file storage and file sharing service provided by Windows Live—a collection of programs and services for individuals that work together and includes Hotmail e-mail, Live Messenger instant messaging, applications such as Photo Gallery and Movie Maker, the Office Web Apps, and mobile phone applications. The PowerPoint Web App enables you to work with presentations directly on the Web site where the presentation is stored.

Activity | Creating a New Presentation in the PowerPoint Web App

In this activity, you will navigate to your Windows Live SkyDrive and create the first two slides of a presentation using the PowerPoint Web App. You will apply a theme, add one slide, and insert a picture from your student data files. You will save the file in your SkyDrive folder and create snips of the slides that you create.

1 Launch your Web browser, navigate to **www.live.com** and then log in to your Windows Live account. If you do not have a Windows Live account, refer to Go! Beyond Word Project 1A to create the account.

2 At the top of the window, click **SkyDrive**. To the right of **Create**, click the **Create folder** button. In the **Name** box, type **GO! Beyond Office-PowerPoint** and then click **Next**.

Recall that you can share files on your SkyDrive with others. You will save your PowerPoint file for this activity in this folder. In the displayed window, you can add documents to your SkyDrive so that you can store them or share them with others.

3 In the lower portion of the screen, click **Continue**.

4 At the top of the window, to the right of **Create**, click the **PowerPoint** icon to display the **New Microsoft PowerPoint presentation** window.

To create a presentation using the PowerPoint Web App, you must first name the new presentation.

5 In the **Name** box, type **Lastname_Firstname_1A_ Lehua_Web** and then click **Save**.

A new presentation displays in the PowerPoint Web App and the Select Theme gallery opens. The themes available

in the PowerPoint Web App are the same as the themes in PowerPoint 2010.

6 In the **Select Theme** gallery, scroll as necessary to locate, and then click **Austin**. Click **Apply** to change the presentation theme.

7 Click in the title placeholder—scroll bars may display around the placeholder.

In the PowerPoint Web App, content placeholders do not expand to accommodate text while you are typing. To view text that you have typed that does not display, use the scroll bars.

8 Type **Lehua Hawaiian Adventures** and then click in a blank area of the slide to cancel the selection and notice that the scroll bars no longer display.

9 Click in the subtitle placeholder. Type **Carl Kawaoka** and then press Enter. Type **Tour Operations Director** and then click in a blank area of the slide.

In the PowerPoint Web App, the window displays similar to the PowerPoint 2010 window. On the left, a Navigation pane displays, enabling you to click on a slide to display it in the Slide pane. Below the Slide pane, a Notes pane displays.

10 On the **Home tab**, in the **Slides group**, click the **New Slide** button, and then click **Two Content**. Click **Add Slide** to insert a slide with the Two Content layout.

11 Click in the title placeholder, and then type **Do You Enjoy Adventure?** Click in the content placeholder on the left side of the slide to enter the title text, and then if necessary, click in the left side content placeholder again to activate the placeholder. Type **Helicopter tours** and then press Enter. On the **Home tab**, in the **Paragraph group**, click the **Increase List Level** button. Type **View Hawaii from above** and then press Enter.

12 On the **Home tab**, in the **Paragraph group**, click the **Decrease List Level** button. Type **Boating tours** and then press Enter. On the **Home tab**, in the **Paragraph group**, click the **Increase List Level** button. Type **Explore the coast in a rigid hull inflatable raft**

13 Click in the placeholder on the right side of the slide. In the placeholder, click the **Insert Picture from File** button. Navigate to your student data files, and then insert **p01A_Helicopter**.

The picture is inserted and is selected, as indicated by the border surrounding the image. A picture inserted in the PowerPoint Web App cannot be moved or sized.

14 With the picture selected, on the **Format tab**, click the **Picture Styles** scroll bar to display the gallery. Notice that the picture styles that display are the same picture styles that display in PowerPoint 2010.

15 In the third row, click the first style—**Rotated, White**.

16 Click in the title placeholder, and then select the title text—*Do You Enjoy Adventure?* On the **Home tab**, in the **Font group**, click the **Font arrow**, and then click **Corbel**. With the title still selected, on the **Home tab**, in the **Font group**, click the **Bold** button B and the **Italic** button I. Click the **Font Size button arrow**, and then click **54**.

Click anywhere in a blank area of the slide to cancel the selection and view your changes.

17 Display the **Start** menu, and then click **All Programs**. On the list of programs, click the **Accessories folder**, and then click **Snipping Tool**. In the **Snipping Tool** dialog box, click the **New arrow**. On the displayed list, click **Full-screen Snip**.

18 On the **Snipping Tool** markup window toolbar, click the **Save Snip** button. In the **Save As** dialog box, navigate to your **PowerPoint Chapter 1** folder. Be sure the **Save as type** box displays **JPEG file**. In the **File name** box, type **Lastname_Firstname_1A_Slide2_Snip** and then click **Save. Close** the **Snipping Tool** window.

19 In the **Navigation pane**, click **Slide 1** to display it in the Slide pane. Below the slide, click the text *Click to add notes*.

The Notes pane expands so that you have space to type notes for the slide.

20 Type **Lehua Hawaiian Adventures has offices on each of the major islands in Hawaii.**

21 Display the **Start** menu, and then click **All Programs**. On the list of programs, click the **Accessories folder**, and then click **Snipping Tool**. In the **Snipping Tool** dialog box, click the **New arrow**. On the displayed list, click **Full-screen Snip**.

22 On the **Snipping Tool** markup window toolbar, click the **Save Snip** button. In the **Save As** dialog box, navigate to your **PowerPoint Chapter 1** folder. Be sure the **Save as type** box displays **JPEG file**. In the **File name** box, type **Lastname_Firstname_1A_Slide1_Snip** and then click **Save. Close** the **Snipping Tool** window and the PowerPoint Web App, and then submit the snip files as directed.

You do not need to save your presentation; all changes will be saved when the Web App is closed.

Project 1B New Product Announcement

myitlab
Project 1B Training

Project Activities

In Activities 1.14 through 1.23, you will combine two presentations that the marketing team at Lehua Adventure Travels developed describing their new Ecotours. You will combine the presentations by inserting slides from one presentation into another, and then you will rearrange and delete slides. You will also apply font formatting and slide transitions to the presentation. Your completed presentation will look similar to Figure 1.29.

Project Files

For Project 1B, you will need the following files:

> p01B_Ecotours
> p01B_Slides

You will save your presentation as:

> Lastname_Firstname_1B_Ecotours

Project Results

Figure 1.29
Project 1B—Ecotours

Objective 5 | Edit an Existing Presentation

Recall that editing refers to the process of adding, deleting, and modifying presentation content. You can edit presentation content in either the Slide pane or the Slides/Outline pane.

Activity 1.14 | Displaying and Editing the Presentation Outline

You can display the presentation outline in the Slides/Outline pane and edit the presentation text. Changes that you make in the outline are immediately displayed in the Slide pane.

1 **Start** PowerPoint. From your student files, open **p01B_Ecotours**. On the **File tab**, click **Save As**, navigate to your **PowerPoint Chapter 1** folder, and then using your own name, save the file as **Lastname_Firstname_1B_Ecotours**

2 In the **Slides/Outline pane**, click the **Outline tab** to display the presentation outline. If necessary, below the Slides/Outline pane, drag the scroll box all the way to the left so that the slide numbers display. Compare your screen with Figure 1.30.

The outline tab is wider than the Slides tab so that you have additional space to type your text. Each slide in the outline displays the slide number, slide icon, and the slide title in bold.

Figure 1.30

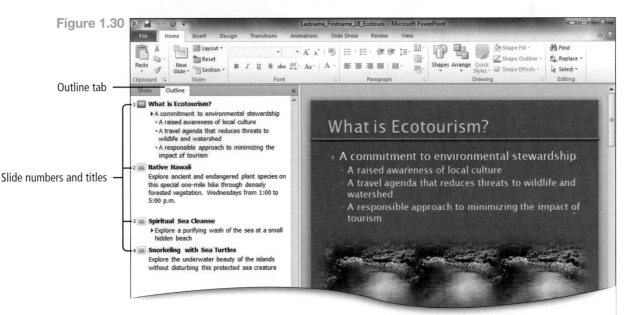

Outline tab

Slide numbers and titles

3 In the **Outline tab**, in **Slide 1**, select the last three bullet points, and then compare your screen with Figure 1.31.

Figure 1.31

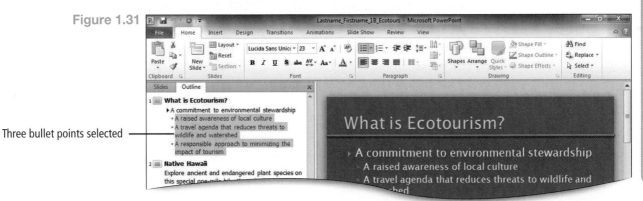

Three bullet points selected

PowerPoint | Chapter 1

4 On the **Home tab**, in the **Paragraph group**, click the **Decrease List Level** button ![decrease list level icon] one time to decrease the list level of the selected bullet points.

When you type in the outline or change the list level, the changes also display in the Slide pane.

5 In the **Outline tab**, click anywhere in **Slide 3**, and then click at the end of the last bullet point after the word *beach*. Press Enter to create a new bullet point at the same list level as the previous bullet point. Type **Offered Tuesdays and Thursdays one hour before sunset, weather permitting**

6 Press Enter to create a new bullet point. Type **Fee: $30** and then compare your screen with Figure 1.32.

Figure 1.32

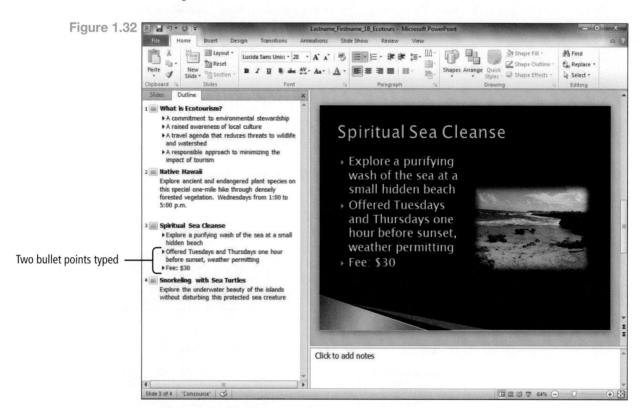

Two bullet points typed

7 In the **Slides/Outline pane**, click the **Slides tab** to display the slide thumbnails, and then **Save** ![save icon] the presentation.

You can type text in the Slide tab or in the Outline tab. Displaying the Outline tab enables you to view the entire flow of the presentation.

Activity 1.15 | Inserting Slides from an Existing Presentation

Presentation content is commonly shared among group members in an organization. Rather than re-creating slides, you can insert slides from an existing presentation into the current presentation. In this activity, you will insert slides from an existing presentation into your 1B_Ecotours presentation.

1 Display **Slide 1**. On the **Home tab**, in the **Slides group**, click the **New Slide button arrow** to display the **Slide Layout** gallery and additional commands for inserting slides. Compare your screen with Figure 1.33.

Figure 1.33

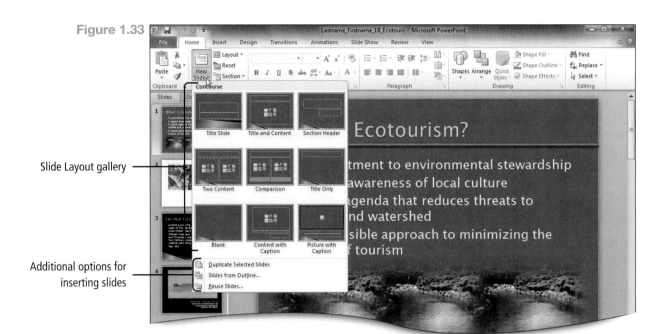

Slide Layout gallery

Additional options for inserting slides

2 Below the gallery, click **Reuse Slides** to open the Reuse Slides pane on the right side of the PowerPoint window.

3 In the **Reuse Slides** pane, click the **Browse** button, and then click **Browse File**. In the **Browse** dialog box, navigate to the location where your student files are stored, and then double-click **p01B_Slides** to display the slides in the Reuse Slides pane.

4 At the bottom of the **Reuse Slides** pane, select the **Keep source formatting** check box, and then compare your screen with Figure 1.34.

By selecting the *Keep source formatting* check box, you retain the formatting applied to the slides when inserted into the existing presentation. When the *Keep source formatting* check box is cleared, the theme formatting of the presentation in which the slides are inserted is applied.

Figure 1.34

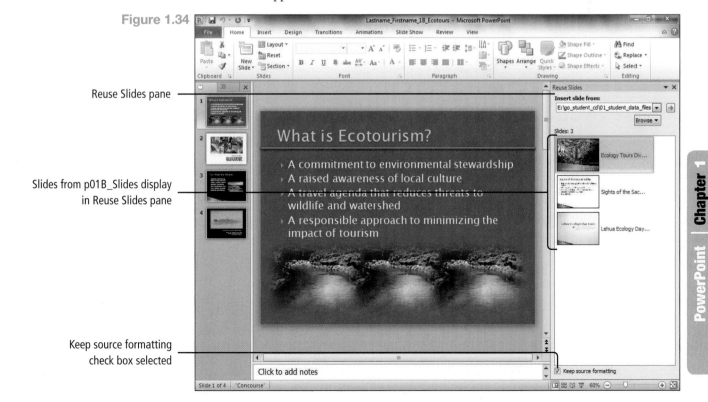

Reuse Slides pane

Slides from p01B_Slides display in Reuse Slides pane

Keep source formatting check box selected

PowerPoint | Chapter 1

5 In the **Reuse Slides** pane, point to each slide to view a zoomed image of the slide and a ScreenTip displaying the file name and the slide title.

6 In the **Reuse Slides** pane, click the first slide—**Ecology Tours Division**—to insert the slide into the current presentation after Slide 1, and then notice that the original slide background formatting is retained.

> **Note** | Inserting Slides
>
> You can insert slides into your presentation in any order; remember to display the slide that will precede the slide that you want to insert.

7 In your **1B_Ecotours** presentation, in the **Slides/Outline pane**, click **Slide 5** to display it in the **Slide pane**.

8 In the **Reuse Slides** pane, click the second slide and then click the third slide to insert both slides after **Slide 5**.

Your presentation contains seven slides.

9 On **Slide 7**, point to *Lehua*, and then right-click to display the shortcut menu. Click **Ignore all**. Use the same technique to ignore the spelling of the word *Ecotour*. Compare your screen with Figure 1.35.

Figure 1.35

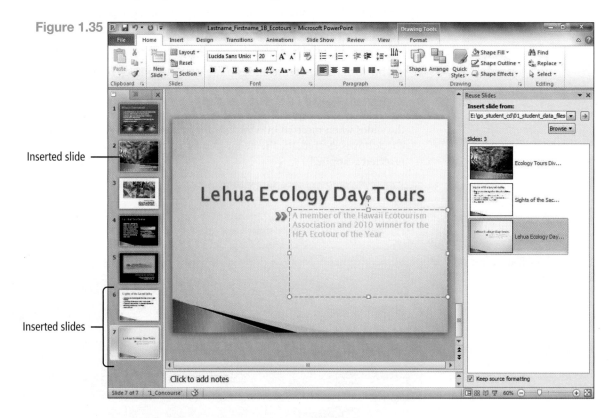

10 **Close** ⊠ the **Reuse Slides** pane; click **Save** 🖫.

> **More Knowledge** | Inserting All Slides
>
> You can insert all of the slides from an existing presentation into the current presentation at one time. In the Reuse Slides pane, right-click one of the slides that you want to insert, and then click Insert All Slides.

Activity 1.16 | Finding and Replacing Text

The Replace command enables you to locate all occurrences of specified text and replace it with alternative text.

1 Display **Slide 1**. On the **Home tab**, in the **Editing group**, click the **Replace** button. In the **Replace** dialog box, in the **Find what** box, type **Ecology** and then in the **Replace with** box, type **Eco** Compare your screen with Figure 1.36.

Figure 1.36

Replace button

Find what box

Replace with box

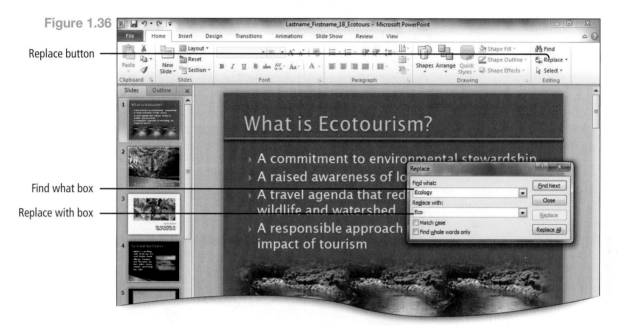

2 In the **Replace** dialog box, click the **Replace All** button.

A message box displays indicating the number of replacements that were made.

3 In the message box, click **OK**, **Close** ⊠ the **Replace** dialog box, and then click **Save** 🖫.

Objective 6 | Format a Presentation

Formatting refers to changing the appearance of the text, layout, and design of a slide. You will find it easiest to do most of your formatting changes in PowerPoint in the Slide pane.

Activity 1.17 | Changing Fonts, Font Sizes, Font Styles, and Font Colors

Recall that a font is a set of characters with the same design and shape and that fonts are measured in points. Font styles include bold, italic, and underline, and you can apply any combination of these styles to presentation text. Font styles and font color are useful to provide emphasis and are a visual cue to draw the reader's eye to important text.

1. On the right side of the **Slides/Outline pane**, drag the scroll box down until **Slide 7** displays, and then click **Slide 7** to display it in the **Slides** pane.

   When a presentation contains a large number of slides, a scroll box displays to the right of the slide thumbnails so that you can scroll and then select the thumbnails.

2. Select the title text—*Lehua Eco Day Tours*. Point to the Mini toolbar, and then click the **Font button arrow** to display the available fonts. Click **Arial Black**.

3. Select the light green text in the placeholder below the title, and then on the Mini toolbar, change the **Font** to **Arial Black** and the **Font Size** to **28**. Then, click the **Font Color button arrow** , and compare your screen with Figure 1.37.

   The colors in the top row of the color gallery are the colors associated with the presentation theme—*Concourse*. The colors in the rows below the first row are light and dark variations of the theme colors.

Figure 1.37

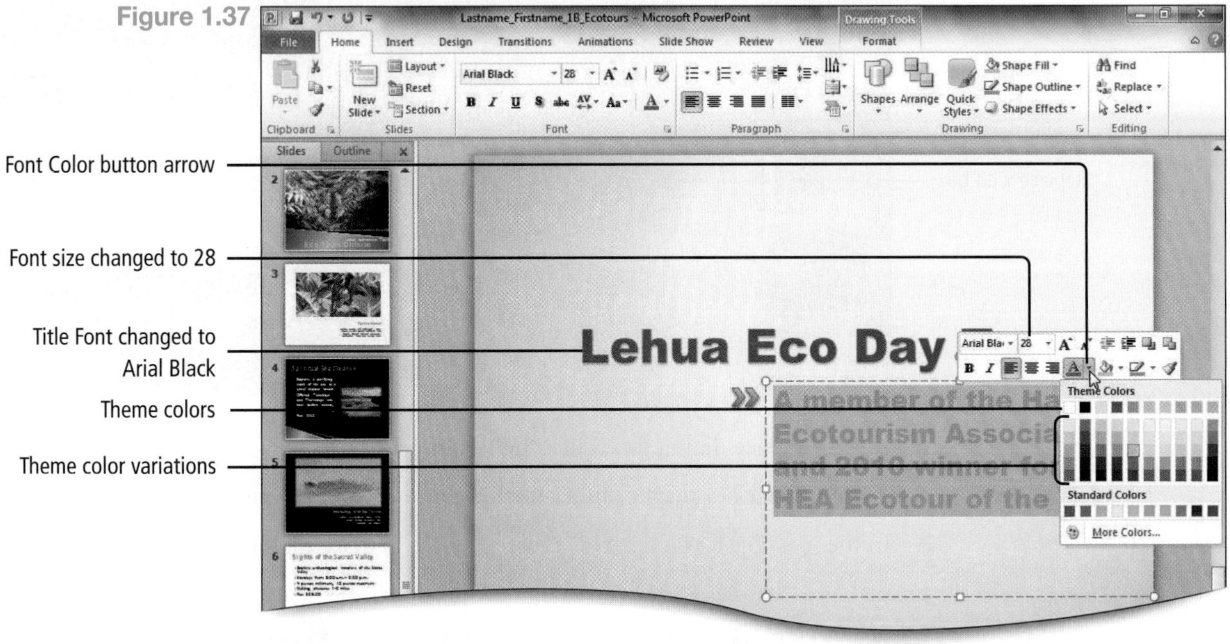

Labels: Font Color button arrow; Font size changed to 28; Title Font changed to Arial Black; Theme colors; Theme color variations

4. Point to several of the colors and notice that a ScreenTip displays the color name and Live Preview displays the selected text in the color to which you are pointing.

5. In the second column of colors, click the first color—**Black, Text 1**—to change the font color. Notice that on the Home tab and Mini toolbar, the lower part of the Font Color button displays the most recently applied font color—Black.

   When you click the Font Color button instead of the Font Color button arrow, the color displayed in the lower part of the Font Color button is applied to selected text without displaying the color gallery.

6. Display **Slide 2**, and then select the title *Eco Tours Division*. On the Mini toolbar, click the **Font Color button** to apply the font color **Black, Text 1** to the selection. Select the subtitle—*Lehua Adventure Tours*—and then change the **Font Color** to **Black, Text 1**. Compare your screen with Figure 1.38.

Figure 1.38

Font color changed
to black

7 Display **Slide 3**, and then select the title—*Native Hawaii*. From the Mini toolbar, apply **Bold** B and **Italic** I , and then **Save** your presentation.

Activity 1.18 | Aligning Text and Changing Line Spacing

In PowerPoint, ***text alignment*** refers to the horizontal placement of text within a placeholder. You can align left, centered, right, or justified.

1 Display **Slide 2**. Click anywhere in the title—*Eco Tours Division*.

2 On the **Home tab**, in the **Paragraph group**, click the **Align Text Right** button to right align the text within the placeholder.

3 Display **Slide 7**. Click anywhere in the text below the title. In the **Paragraph group**, click the **Line Spacing** button . In the list, click **1.5** to change from single-spacing between lines to one-and-a-half spacing between lines. **Save** your presentation, and then compare your screen with Figure 1.39.

Figure 1.39

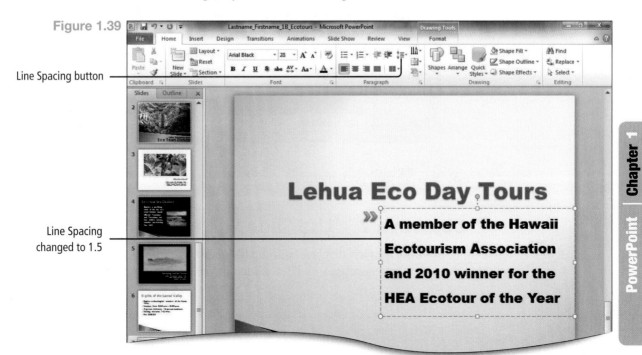

Line Spacing button

Line Spacing
changed to 1.5

PowerPoint | Chapter 1

Activity 1.19 | Modifying Slide Layout

Recall that the slide layout defines the placement of the content placeholders on a slide. PowerPoint includes predefined layouts that you can apply to your slide for the purpose of arranging slide elements.

For example, a Title Slide contains two placeholder elements—the title and the subtitle. When you design your slides, consider the content that you want to include, and then choose a layout with the elements that will display the message you want to convey in the best way.

1 Display **Slide 3**. On the **Home tab**, in the **Slides group**, click the **Layout** button to display the **Slide Layout** gallery. Notice that *Content with Caption* is selected.

> The selection indicates the layout of the current slide.

2 Click **Picture with Caption** to change the slide layout, and then compare your screen with Figure 1.40.

> The Picture with Caption layout emphasizes the picture more effectively than the Content with Caption layout.

Figure 1.40

3 Save 🖫 your presentation.

Objective 7 | Use Slide Sorter View

Slide Sorter view displays thumbnails of all of the slides in a presentation. Use Slide Sorter view to rearrange and delete slides and to apply formatting to multiple slides.

Activity 1.20 | Deleting Slides in Slide Sorter View

Another Way

On the Ribbon, click the View tab, and then in the Presentation Views group, click Slide Sorter.

1 In the lower right corner of the PowerPoint window, click the **Slide Sorter** button 🔳 to display all of the slide thumbnails.

2 Compare your screen with Figure 1.41.

Your slides may display larger or smaller than those shown in Figure 1.41.

Figure 1.41

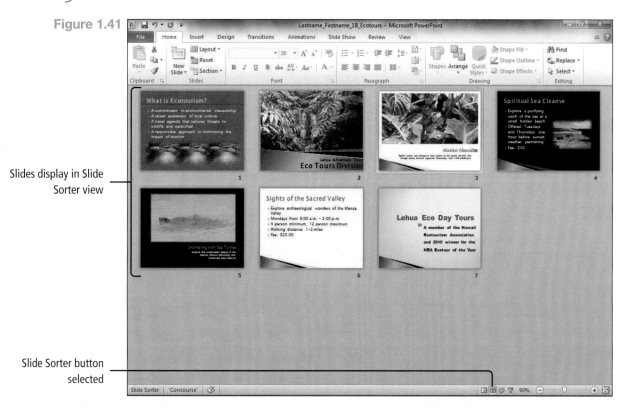

Slides display in Slide Sorter view

Slide Sorter button selected

3 Click **Slide 6**, and notice that a thick outline surrounds the slide, indicating that it is selected. On your keyboard, press ⌨Del to delete the slide. Click **Save** 🔳.

Activity 1.21 | Moving Slides in Slide Sorter View

1 With the presentation displayed in Slide Sorter view, point to **Slide 2**. Hold down the left mouse button, and then drag the slide to the left until the vertical move bar and pointer indicating the position to which the slide will be moved is positioned to the left of **Slide 1**, as shown in Figure 1.42.

Figure 1.42

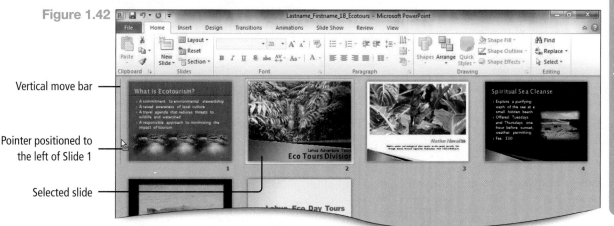

Vertical move bar

Pointer positioned to the left of Slide 1

Selected slide

2 Release the mouse button to move the slide to the Slide 1 position in the presentation.

3 Click **Slide 4**, hold down Ctrl, and then click **Slide 5**. Compare your screen with Figure 1.43.

Both slides are outlined, indicating that both are selected. By holding down Ctrl, you can create a group of selected slides.

Figure 1.43

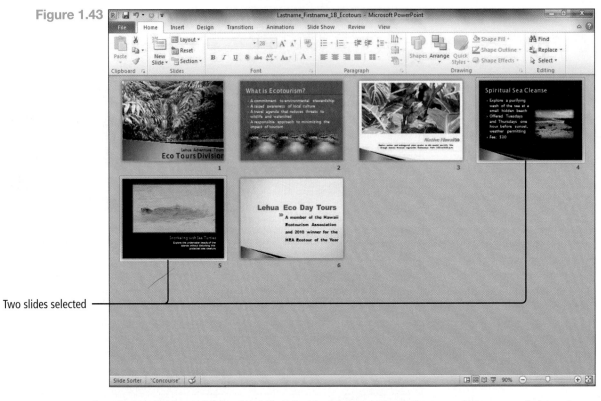

Two slides selected

4 Point to either of the selected slides, hold down the left mouse button, and then drag to position the vertical move bar to the left of **Slide 3**. Release the mouse button to move the two slides, and then compare your screen with Figure 1.44.

Figure 1.44

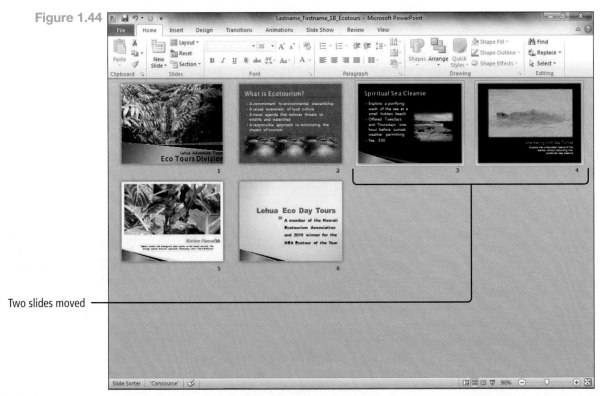

Two slides moved

5 In the status bar, click the **Normal** button ⬛ to return to Normal view. **Save** 💾 your presentation.

Objective 8 | Apply Slide Transitions

Slide transitions are the motion effects that occur in Slide Show view when you move from one slide to the next during a presentation. You can choose from a variety of transitions, and you can control the speed and method with which the slides advance.

Activity 1.22 | Applying Slide Transitions to a Presentation

1 Display **Slide 1**. On the **Transitions tab**, in the **Transition to This Slide group**, click the **More** button ⬛ to display the **Transitions** gallery. Compare your screen with Figure 1.45.

Figure 1.45

Transitions gallery ⎯⎯⎯

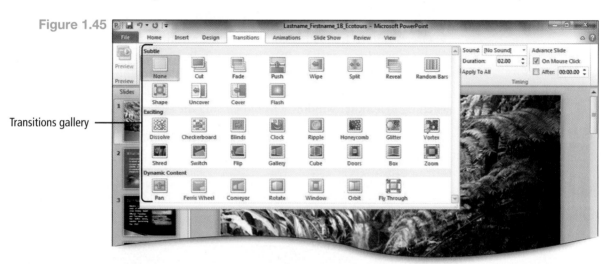

2 Under **Exciting**, click **Doors** to apply and view the transition. In the **Transition to This Slide group**, click the **Effect Options** button to display the directions from which the slide enters the screen. Click **Horizontal**.

The Effect Options vary depending upon the selected transition and include the direction from which the slide enters the screen or the shape in which the slide displays during the transition.

3 In the **Timing group**, notice that the **Duration** box displays *01.40*, indicating that the transition lasts 1.40 seconds. Click the **Duration** box **up spin arrow** two times so that *01.75* displays. Under **Advance Slide**, verify that the **On Mouse Click** check box is selected; select it if necessary. Compare your screen with Figure 1.46.

When the On Mouse Click option is selected, the presenter controls when the current slide advances to the next slide by clicking the mouse button or by pressing (Spacebar).

Figure 1.46

On Mouse Click check box selected ⎯⎯⎯

Doors transition selected ⎯⎯⎯

Duration changed to *01.75* ⎯⎯⎯

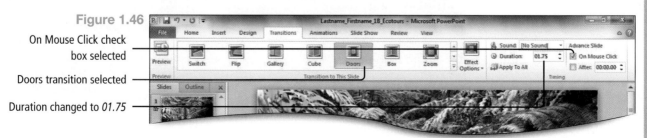

4 In the **Timing group**, click the **Apply To All** button so that the Doors, Horizontal with a Duration of 1.75 seconds transition is applied to all of the slides in the presentation. Notice that in the Slides/Outline pane, a star displays below the slide number providing a visual cue that a transition has been applied to the slide.

5 Click the **Slide Show tab**. In the **Start Slide Show group**, click the **From Beginning** button, and then view your presentation, clicking the mouse button to advance through the slides. When the black slide displays, click the mouse button one more time to display the presentation in Normal view. **Save** your presentation ▣.

More Knowledge | Applying Multiple Slide Transitions

You can apply more than one type of transition in your presentation by displaying the slides one at a time, and then clicking the transition that you want to apply instead of clicking the Apply To All button.

Activity 1.23 | Displaying a Presentation in Reading View

Organizations frequently conduct online meetings when participants are unable to meet in one location. The *Reading view* in PowerPoint displays a presentation in a manner similar to a slide show but the taskbar, title bar, and status bar remain available in the presentation window. Thus, a presenter can easily facilitate an online conference by switching to another window without closing the slide show.

> **Another Way**
>
> On the View tab, in the Presentation Views group, click Reading View.

1 In the lower right corner of the PowerPoint window, click the **Reading View** button ▣. Compare your screen with Figure 1.47.

In Reading View, the status bar contains the Next and Previous buttons, which are used to navigate in the presentation, and the Menu button which is used to print, copy, and edit slides.

Figure 1.47

Slide displays in Reading View

Reading View button

Next button

Menu button

Previous button

Lehua Adventure Tours
Eco Tours Division

2 In the status bar, click the **Next** button to display **Slide 2**. Press [Spacebar] to display **Slide 3**. Click the left mouse button to display **Slide 4**. In the status bar, click the **Previous** button to display **Slide 3**.

Another Way

Press [Esc] to exit Reading view and return to Normal view.

3 In the status bar, click the **Menu** button to display the Reading view menu, and then click **End Show** to return to Normal view.

4 On the **Insert tab**, in the **Text group**, click the **Header & Footer** button, and then click the **Notes and Handouts tab**. Under **Include on page**, select the **Date and time** check box, and if necessary, select **Update automatically**. Clear the **Header** check box, and then select the **Page number** and **Footer** check boxes. In the **Footer** box, using your own name, type **Lastname_Firstname_1B_Ecotours** and then click **Apply to All**.

5 Display **Backstage** view, and then on the right, click **Properties**. Click **Show Document Panel**, and then in the **Author** box, delete any text and type your firstname and lastname. In the **Subject** box, type your course name and section number, and in the **Keywords** box, type **ecotours, ecotourism Close** the Document Information Panel.

6 **Save** your presentation ![save icon]. Submit your presentation electronically or print **Handouts, 6 Slides Horizontal**, as directed by your instructor.

7 **Close** the presentation and **Exit** PowerPoint.

More Knowledge | Broadcasting a Slide Show

You can broadcast a slide show to remote viewers by using the PowerPoint Broadcast Service or another broadcast service. To broadcast a slide show, on the Slide Show tab, in the Start Slide Show group, click Broadcast Slide Show, and then follow the instructions in the Broadcast Slide Show dialog box to start the broadcast.

End You have completed Project 1B ——————————————————

GO! Beyond Office

Objective | Save Presentation Slides as Pictures, Import Pictures to Windows Live Photo Gallery, and Upload Pictures to Flickr

Recall that Windows Live Essentials is a set of free programs available on the Microsoft Web site. **Windows Live Photo Gallery** is a Windows Live Essentials photo organizing tool to view, manage, share, and edit digital photos and videos. You can save PowerPoint presentation slides as pictures and then share the pictures using the Windows Live Photo Gallery.

> **Alert!** | Working with Web-Based Applications and Services
>
> Computer programs and services on the Web receive continuous updates and improvements. Thus, the steps to complete this Web-based Activity may differ from the ones shown. You can often look at the screens and the information presented to determine how to complete the Activity.

Activity | Saving Presentation Slides as Pictures and Importing Pictures to Windows Live Photo Gallery

In this activity, you will create a Yahoo! and Flickr account. Then, you will save the first slide of a PowerPoint presentation as a picture in the JPEG file format and upload the picture to Windows Live Photo Gallery.

1 If you have a Yahoo! e-mail address, skip to Step 2. Otherwise, start your Web browser. In the address bar, type **www.yahoo.com** and then on the left, click **Mail**. Click **Create New Account** and then follow the steps to create an account.

2 If you have a Flickr account, skip to Step 3. Otherwise, in your browser address bar, type **www.flickr.com** and then click **Sign Up**. Enter your **Yahoo! ID** and **password** and then follow the steps to create a Flickr account. **Close** your browser window.

3 **Start** PowerPoint. On the **File tab**, click **Open**, and then navigate to your **PowerPoint Chapter 1** folder. **Open** your PowerPoint Chapter 1 folder, and then open your **Lastname_Firstname_1B_Ecotours** file.

4 With **Slide 1** displayed, click the **File tab**, and then click **Save As**. If you are saving your work to a USB flash drive, be sure that the flash drive and your **PowerPoint Chapter 1** folder display in the **Save As** dialog box address bar. If you are saving your work to your hard drive, navigate to the Pictures folder.

5 Click the **Save as type arrow** to display a list of file formats to save your presentation.

6 Click **JPEG File Interchange Format**, and then click **Save**.

7 In the displayed message box, click the **Current Slide Only** button to save the current slide—Slide 1—as a picture with the .jpg extension. **Exit** PowerPoint.

8 From the **Start** menu, click **All Programs**, and then click **Windows Live Photo Gallery**.

On the left side of the window is a Navigation pane in which you can choose the location from which to view your pictures and videos. To the right of the Navigation pane, pictures in your Pictures and Videos folders display and are grouped according to when they were last modified.

9 If you saved your picture to the Pictures folder, skip to Step 11. If you saved your picture to your USB flash drive, continue with Step 10.

10 At the left of the Windows Live Photo Gallery window, in the **Navigation bar**, under **Devices**, click your **USB flash drive**. In the **Import Photos and Videos** dialog box, click **Review, organize, and group items to import**, and then click **Next**. In the **Import Photos and Videos** dialog box, *clear* the **Select all** check box, and then select the check box to the left of the image of **Slide 1**. Click **Import**. If a message displays, **Close** the message.

11 If necessary, on the left click My Pictures, and then click the picture of slide 1 so that it is selected as indicated by the blue rounded rectangle surrounding the image.

You can organize your photos using flags, captions, ratings, and tags. *Tags* are descriptive words that make photos and videos easier to organize and find.

12 Verify that the picture of slide 1 is selected. On the **Home tab**, in the **Organize group**, click the **Descriptive tag** button. On the right side of the window, under **Descriptive tags**, type **eco tours**

13 Under **Geotag**, click **Add geotag**. Type **Hawaii** and then notice that below the word *Hawaii*, the text *HI, United States* displays. Click **HI, United States** to enter the geotag.

Use *geotags* to identify places where photos were taken.

14 Under **Caption**, click **Add caption**. Type **Eco Tours Division Slide 1** and then press Enter.

15 On the **Home tab**, in the **Organize group**, click the **Flag** button. Click the **Rate** button, and then click **5 stars**.

The tags, caption, rating, and flag display in the pane at the right side of the Windows Live Photo Gallery window.

16 On the **Home tab**, in the **Quick find group**, click the **Flagged** button.

Pictures that are flagged, including your slide 1 picture, display. Above the flagged images, a Search by box indicates the folder in which the search was performed and the Flagged criteria.

17 In the **Search by** box, click the **Cancel search** button ☒ to redisplay all the pictures.

18 If necessary, select your slide 1 picture. On the **Edit tab**, click the **View file** button to display a zoomed view of your picture. On the **Edit tab**, in the **Adjustments group**, click the **Color button arrow**, and then under **Choose color adjustment**, in the third row, click the last color adjustment—**High temperature, low tint**.

19 Display the **Start** menu ⊕, and then click **All Programs**. On the list of programs, click the **Accessories folder**, and then click **Snipping Tool**. In the **Snipping Tool** dialog box, click the **New arrow**, and then click

Full-screen Snip. Save the snip in your **PowerPoint Chapter 1** folder as a **JPEG file** with the file name **Lastname_Firstname_1B_Slide1_Snip** and then **Close** the Snipping Tool window.

20 On the **Edit tab**, click **Close file**, and then click **OK**.

21 With your picture selected, on the **Home tab**, in the **Share group**, click the **More** button ▼, and then click the **Flickr** button ●●. In the **Sign in to Windows Live** window, type your **Windows Live ID** and **password** and then click **Sign in**. If you have not created a Windows Live ID, refer to Chapter 1, Go! Beyond Word Project 1A.

22 In the **Publish on Flickr** window, click the **Authorize** button, and then sign into Yahoo! with your Yahoo! ID and Password.

23 In the **Flickr window**, in the box on the right with the text *If you arrived at this page because you specifically asked Windows Live Essentials to connect to your Flickr account, click here:* click the **Next** button.

24 Click **OK, I'll Authorize It**, and then **Close** ☒ the Flickr window. In the **Publish on Flickr** dialog box, click **Next**, and then click **Publish**.

25 After the upload completes, in the **Flickr** message box, click **View**.

26 At the bottom of the Flickr window, click **Save**. Start the **Snipping Tool** and create a **New, Full-screen Snip**. **Save** the snip in your **PowerPoint Chapter 1** folder as a **JPEG file** with the file name **Lastname_Firstname_1B_Flickr_Snip** and then click **Save**. Sign out of all accounts and **Close** all open windows, and then submit the two snip files as directed.

Content-Based Assessments

Summary

In this chapter, you created a new PowerPoint presentation and edited an existing presentation by reusing slides from another presentation. You entered, edited, and formatted text in Normal view; worked with slides in Slide Sorter view; and viewed the presentation as a slide show. You also added emphasis to your presentations by inserting pictures, applying font formatting, and modifying layout, alignment, and line spacing.

Key Terms

Matching

Match each term in the second column with its correct definition in the first column by writing the letter of the term on the blank line in front of the correct definition.

_____ 1. The PowerPoint view in which the window is divided into three panes—the Slide pane, the Slides/Outline pane, and the Notes pane.

_____ 2. A presentation page that can contain text, pictures, tables, charts, and other multimedia or graphic objects.

_____ 3. The first slide in a presentation, the purpose of which is to provide an introduction to the presentation topic.

_____ 4. A box on a slide with dotted or dashed borders that holds title and body text or other content such as charts, tables, and pictures.

_____ 5. A set of unified design elements that provides a look for your presentation by applying colors, fonts, and effects.

_____ 6. An outline level in a presentation represented by a bullet symbol and identified in a slide by the indentation and the size of the text.

_____ 7. Small circles and squares that indicate that a picture is selected.

_____ 8. A green circle located above a selected picture with which you can rotate the selected image.

_____ 9. A collection of formatting options that can be applied to a picture, text, or object.

_____ 10. A slide that displays at the end of every slide show to indicate that the presentation is over.

A Black slide

B Formatting

C List level

D Normal view

E Notes page

F Placeholder

G Rotation handle

H Sizing handles

I Slide

J Slide handouts

K Slide transitions

L Style

M Text alignment

N Theme

O Title slide

_____ 11. Printed images of slides on a sheet of paper.

_____ 12. A printout that contains the slide image on the top half of the page and notes that you have created in the Notes pane on the lower half of the page.

_____ 13. The process of changing the appearance of the text, layout, and design of a slide.

_____ 14. The term that refers to the horizontal placement of text within a placeholder.

_____ 15. Motion effects that occur in Slide Show view when you move from one slide to the next during a presentation.

Multiple Choice

Circle the correct answer.

1. In Normal view, the pane that displays a large image of the active slide is the:
   A. Slide pane   B. Slides/Outline pane   C. Notes pane

2. In Normal view, the pane that displays below the Slide pane is the:
   A. Slide Sorter pane   B. Slides/Outline pane   C. Notes pane

3. The buttons in the lower right corner that control the look of the presentation window are the:
   A. Normal buttons   B. View buttons   C. Thumbnails buttons

4. The process of modifying a presentation by adding and deleting slides or by changing the contents of individual slides is referred to as:
   A. Editing   B. Formatting   C. Aligning

5. The arrangement of elements, such as title and subtitle text, lists, pictures, tables, charts, shapes, and movies, on a PowerPoint slide is referred to as:
   A. Theme modification   B. Editing   C. Layout

6. Text that prints at the top of a sheet of slide handouts or notes pages is a:
   A. Header   B. Footer   C. Page number

7. Text that displays at the bottom of every slide or that prints at the bottom of a sheet of slide handouts or notes.
   A. Header   B. Footer   C. Page number

8. The command that locates all occurrences of specific text and replace it with alternative text is:
   A. Replace   B. Find   C. Edit

9. The view in which all of the slides in your presentation display in miniature is:
   A. Slide Sorter view   B. Normal view   C. Reading view

10. A view similar to Slide Show view but that also displays the title bar, status bar, and taskbar is:
    A. Slide Sorter view   B. Normal view   C. Reading view

Content-Based Assessments

Skills Review | Project **1C** Nature Preserve

In the following Skills Review, you will create a new presentation by inserting content and pictures, adding notes and footers, and applying a presentation theme. Your completed presentation will look similar to Figure 1.48.

Project Files

For Project 1C, you will need the following files:

> New blank PowerPoint presentation
> p01C_Bay
> p01C_Snorkel

You will save your presentation as:

> Lastname_Firstname_1C_Nature_Preserve

Project Results

Figure 1.48

(Project 1C Nature Preserve continues on the next page)

Content-Based Assessments

1 **Start** PowerPoint to display a new blank presentation in Normal view.

a. In the **Slide pane**, click in the title placeholder, which contains the text *Click to add title*. Type **Hanauma Bay**

b. Click in the subtitle placeholder, and then type **Oahu's Nature Preserve**

c. In the title, right-click *Hanauma*, and then on the shortcut menu, click **Ignore All**.

d. On the Ribbon, click the **Design tab**. In the **Themes group**, click the **More** button to display the **Themes gallery**. Recall that the themes display alphabetically. Using the ScreenTips, locate and then click **Apothecary** to apply the Apothecary theme to the presentation.

e. On the Quick Access Toolbar, click the **Save** button, navigate to your **PowerPoint Chapter 1** folder, and then **Save** the presentation as **Lastname_Firstname_1C_Nature_Preserve**

2 On the **Home tab**, in the **Slides group**, click the **New Slide button arrow**. In the gallery, click the **Picture with Caption** layout to insert a new slide.

a. In the **Slide pane**, click the text *Click to add title*, and then type **Marine Life Conservation District**

b. Click in the text placeholder below the title, and then type **Founded in 1990**

c. In the picture placeholder, click the **Insert Picture from File** button, and then navigate to your student data files. Click **p01C_Bay**, and then press Enter to insert the picture.

d. With the picture selected, on the **Format tab**, in the **Picture Styles group**, click the **More** button to display the **Picture Styles** gallery. Use the ScreenTips to locate, and then click the style **Drop Shadow Rectangle**.

e. In the **Adjust group**, click the **Artistic Effects** button, and then in the fourth row, click the second effect—**Texturizer**.

3 On the **Home tab**, in the **Slides group**, click the **New Slide button arrow**. In the gallery, click the **Comparison** layout to insert a new slide. In the title placeholder, type **Guest Information**

a. Below the title, on the left side of the slide, click in the small placeholder containing the bolded words *Click to add text*. Type **Hours of Operation**

b. On the right side of the slide, click in the small placeholder containing the bolded words *Click to add text*. Type **Regulations**

c. On the left side of the slide, click in the content placeholder. Type **Winter hours** and then press Enter. Press Tab to increase the list level, and then type **October though March** Press Enter. Type **Open from 6am - 6pm** and then press Enter.

d. On the **Home tab**, in the **Paragraph group**, click the **Decrease List Level** button. Type **Summer hours** and then press Enter. On the **Home tab**, in the **Paragraph group**, click the **Increase List Level** button. Type **April through September** and then press Enter. Type **Open from 6am - 7pm** and then press Enter. On the **Home tab**, in the **Paragraph group**, click the **Decrease List Level** button. Type **Closed every Tuesday**

e. On the right side of the slide, click in the content placeholder. Type **Visitors must watch an educational movie before proceeding to the bay** and then press Enter. Type **Marine life may not be removed or harmed in any way**

f. **Save** your presentation.

4 On the **Home tab**, in the **Slides group**, click the **New Slide button arrow**. In the gallery, click **Title and Content** to insert a new slide. In the title placeholder, type **Explore the Reef!**

a. In the content placeholder, click the **Insert Picture from File** button, and then navigate to your student data files. Click **p01C_Snorkel**, and then press Enter to insert the picture.

b. With the picture selected, on the **Format tab**, in the **Picture Styles group**, click the **More** button to display the **Picture Styles** gallery. Locate and click the **Soft Edge Rectangle** style.

c. Below the slide, click in the **Notes pane**, and then type **Visitors should not step on the reef as it can damage the coral.**

5 Insert a **New Slide** using the **Section Header** layout.

a. In the title placeholder, type **Contact Lehua Hawaiian Adventures** In the text placeholder, type **For Additional Information**

b. Right-click **Lehua**, and then on the shortcut menu, click **Ignore All** to ignore the spelling of *Lehua*.

(Project 1C Nature Preserve continues on the next page)

PowerPoint | Chapter 1

6 On the Ribbon, click the **Slide Show tab**. In the **Start Slide Show group**, click the **From Beginning** button.

a. Click the left mouse button or press `Spacebar` to advance to the second slide. Continue to click or press `Spacebar` until the last slide displays, and then click or press `Spacebar` one more time to display a black slide.

b. With the black slide displayed, click the left mouse button or press `Spacebar` to exit the slide show and return to the presentation.

7 Click the **Insert tab**, and then in the **Text group**, click the **Header & Footer** button to display the **Header and Footer** dialog box.

a. In the **Header and Footer** dialog box, click the **Notes and Handouts tab**. Under **Include on page**, select the **Date and time** check box. If necessary, click the Update automatically option button so that the current date prints on the notes and handouts.

b. If necessary, clear the Header check box to omit this element. Select the **Page number** and **Footer** check boxes. In the **Footer** box, type **Lastname_Firstname_1C_Nature_Preserve** and then click **Apply to All**.

c. Click the **File tab** to display **Backstage** view, and then on the right, click **Properties**. Click **Show Document Panel**, and then in the **Author** box, delete any text and type your firstname and lastname. In the **Subject** box, type your course name and section number, and in the **Keywords** box, type **snorkel, nature Close** the **Document Information Panel**.

d. **Save** your presentation. Submit your presentation electronically or print **Handouts, 6 Slides Horizontal** as directed by your instructor. **Close** the presentation.

End You have completed Project 1C ———————————————————

Content-Based Assessments

Apply **1B** skills from these Objectives:

5 Edit an Existing Presentation
6 Format a Presentation
7 Use Slide Sorter View
8 Apply SlideTransitions

Skills Review | Project **1D** Kauai Beaches

In the following Skills Review, you will edit an existing presentation by inserting slides from another presentation, applying font and slide formatting, and applying slide transitions. Your completed presentation will look similar to Figure 1.49.

Project Files

For Project 1D, you will need the following files:

> p01D_Kauai_Beaches
> p01D_Hawaii_Slides

You will save your presentation as:

> Lastname_Firstname_1D_Kauai_Beaches

Project Results

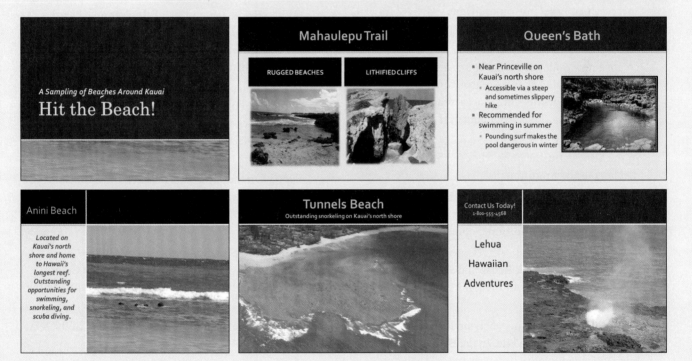

Figure 1.49

(Project 1D Kauai Beaches continues on the next page)

Content-Based Assessments

1 **Start** PowerPoint. From your student files, open **p01D_Kauai_Beaches**. Click the **File tab** to display **Backstage** view, click **Save As**, navigate to your **PowerPoint Chapter 1** folder, and then using your own name, **Save** the file as **Lastname_Firstname_1D_Kauai_Beaches** Take a moment to examine the content of the presentation.

a. In the **Slides/Outline pane**, click the **Outline tab** to display the presentation outline.

b. In the **Outline tab**, in **Slide 2**, click anywhere in the second bullet point, which begins with the text *Accessible via.*

c. On the **Home tab**, in the **Paragraph group**, click the **Increase List Level** button one time.

d. In the **Outline tab**, click at the end of the second bullet point after the word *summer.* Press Enter to create a new bullet point at the same list level as the previous bullet point. On the **Home tab**, in the **Paragraph group**, click the **Increase List Level** button one time. Type **Pounding surf makes the pool dangerous in winter**

e. In the **Slides/Outline pane**, click the **Slides tab** to display the slide thumbnails.

2 Display **Slide 1**. On the **Home tab**, in the **Slides group**, click the **New Slide button arrow** to display the **Slide Layout** gallery and additional options for inserting slides.

a. Below the gallery, click **Reuse Slides** to open the **Reuse Slides** pane on the right side of the PowerPoint window.

b. In the **Reuse Slides** pane, click the **Browse** button, and then click **Browse File**. In the **Browse** dialog box, navigate to your student files, and then double-click **p01D_Hawaii_Slides**.

c. At the bottom of the **Reuse Slides** pane, select the **Keep source formatting** check box.

d. In the **Reuse Slides** pane, click the first slide— *Hawaii Slides*—to insert the slide into the current presentation after **Slide 1**. In the **Reuse Slides** pane, click the second slide—**Anini Beach** to insert it as the third slide in your presentation.

e. In your **1D_Kauai_Beaches** presentation, in the **Slides/Outline pane**, click **Slide 4** to display it in the Slide pane.

f. In the **Reuse Slides** pane, click the fourth slide— *Mahaulepu Trail*—and then click the fifth slide— *Tunnels Beach*—to insert both slides after **Slide 4**. In the **Reuse Slides** pane, click the **Close** button.

3 Display **Slide 1**, and then select the title—*Hit the Beach!*

a. Point to the Mini toolbar, and then click the **Font arrow** to display the available fonts. Click **Century**, and then click the **Font Size arrow**. Click **60** to change the font size.

b. Select the subtitle—*A Sampling of Beaches Around Maui.* Use the Mini toolbar to change the **Font Size** to **28**, and then apply **Bold** and **Italic**.

c. On the **Home tab**, in the **Editing group**, click the **Replace** button. In the **Replace** dialog box, click in the **Find what** box. Type **Maui** and then in the **Replace with** box, type **Kauai**

d. In the **Replace** dialog box, click the **Replace All** button to replace two occurrences of *Maui* with *Kauai.* Click **OK** to close the message box, and then in the **Replace** dialog box, click the **Close** button.

e. Display **Slide 3**, and then select the title—*Anini Beach.* On the Mini toolbar, click the **Font Color button arrow**. Under **Theme Colors**, in the ninth column, click the fourth color—**Green, Accent 5, Lighter 40%**.

f. Display **Slide 4**, and then select the title—*Queen's Bath.* On the Mini toolbar, click the **Font Color button** to apply **Green, Accent 5, Lighter 40%** to the selection.

4 Display **Slide 7**, and then click anywhere in the text **Lehua Hawaiian Adventures**.

a. On the **Home tab**, in the **Paragraph group**, click the **Center** button to center the text within the placeholder.

b. In the **Paragraph group**, click the **Line Spacing** button. In the list, click **1.5** to change from single-spacing between lines to one-and-a-half spacing between lines.

c. Display **Slide 1**. On the **Home tab**, in the **Slides group**, click the **Layout** button to display the **Slide Layout** gallery. At the top of the gallery, under **Module**, click **Title Slide** to change the slide layout.

(Project 1D Kauai Beaches continues on the next page)

Content-Based Assessments

Skills Review | Project **1D** Kauai Beaches (continued)

5 In the lower right corner of the PowerPoint window, in the **View** buttons, click the **Slide Sorter** button to display the slide thumbnails in Slide Sorter view.

a. Click **Slide 2**, and then notice that a thick outline surrounds the slide, indicating that it is selected. Press Delete to delete the slide.

b. Point to **Slide 3**, hold down the mouse button, and then drag to position the vertical move bar to the left of **Slide 2**. Release the mouse button to move the slide.

c. Point to **Slide 4**, hold down the mouse button, and then drag so that the vertical move bar displays to the left of **Slide 2**. Release the mouse button to move the slide.

d. In the **View** buttons, click the **Normal** button to return the presentation to Normal view.

6 Display **Slide 1**. On the **Transitions tab**, in the **Transition to This Slide group**, click the **Wipe** button to apply the Wipe transition to the slide.

a. In the **Transition to This Slide group**, click the **Effect Options** button, and then click **From Top**.

b. In the **Timing group**, click the **Duration** box **up spin arrow** twice to change the **Duration** to *01.50*.

c. In the **Timing group**, under **Advance Slide**, verify that the **On Mouse Click** check box is selected, and select it if necessary.

d. In the **Timing group**, click the **Apply To All** button so that the transition settings are applied to all of the slides in the presentation.

e. Click the **Slide Show tab**. In the **Start Slide Show group**, click the **From Beginning** button, and then view your presentation, clicking the mouse button to advance through the slides. When the black slide displays, click the mouse button one more time to display the presentation in Normal view.

f. On the **Insert tab**, in the **Text group**, click the **Header & Footer** button to display the **Header and Footer** dialog box. Click the **Notes and Handouts tab**. Under **Include on page**, select the **Date and time** check box, and then if necessary, select Update automatically.

g. Clear the **Header** check box if necessary, and then select the **Page number** and **Footer** check boxes. In the **Footer** box, using your own name, type **Lastname_Firstname_1D_Kauai_Beaches** and then click **Apply to All**.

h. Click the **File tab**, and then on the right side of the window, click **Properties**. Click **Show Document Panel**, and then in the **Author** box, delete any text and type your firstname and lastname. In the **Subject** box, type your course name and section number, and in the **Keywords** box, type **Kauai, beaches Close** the **Document Information Panel**.

i. **Save** your presentation. Submit your presentation electronically or print **Handouts, 6 Slides Horizontal** as directed by your instructor. **Close** the presentation.

End You have completed Project 1D

Apply **1A** skills from these Objectives:

1 Create a New Presentation

2 Edit a Presentation in Normal View

3 Add Pictures to a Presentation

4 Print and View a Presentation

Mastering PowerPoint | Project **1E** Big Island

In the following Mastering PowerPoint project, you will create a new presentation that Lehua Hawaiian Adventures will use in their promotional materials to describe features of the Big Island of Hawaii. Your completed presentation will look similar to Figure 1.50.

Project Files

For Project 1E, you will need the following files:

> New blank PowerPoint presentation
> p01E_Waves
> p01E_Lava_Arch
> p01E_Bridge

You will save your presentation as:

> Lastname_Firstname_1E_Big_Island

Project Results

Figure 1.50

(Project 1E Big Island continues on the next page)

Content-Based Assessments

1 **Start** PowerPoint to display a new blank presentation, and then change the **Design** by applying the **Pushpin** theme. As the title of this presentation type **The Big Island of Hawaii** and as the subtitle type **Lehua Hawaiian Adventures** Correct spelling errors on this slide by choosing the **Ignore All** option for the word *Lehua*. Save the presentation in your **PowerPoint Chapter 1** folder as **Lastname_Firstname_1E_Big_Island**

2 Insert a **New Slide** using the **Picture with Caption** layout. In the title placeholder, type **Coastal Contrasts** In the content placeholder on the right side of the slide, from your student files, insert the picture **p01E_Waves**. Format the picture with the **Bevel Rectangle** picture style and the **Paint Brush** artistic effect.

3 In the text placeholder, type **Where Beaches with Black Sand Meet Deep Blue Waters** and then in the **Notes pane**, type **Black sand beaches are formed from ground lava and are primarily located on the southeast side of the island.**

4 Insert a **New Slide** using the **Comparison** layout. In the title placeholder, type **An Island of Opposites** In the placeholder with blue text on the left side of the slide, type **Youngest and Biggest** and then in the place holder with blue text on the right side of the slide, type **Topography and Weather**

5 In the large content placeholder on the left side of the slide, type the following four bullet points, increasing and decreasing the list level as shown below:

    Less than 1 million years old
        Kauai is the oldest at 5 million
    Larger than the other Hawaiian islands
        Still growing

6 In the large content placeholder on the right side of the slide, type the following four bullet points, increasing and decreasing the list level as shown.

    Twelve climate zones
        Summer and Winter seasons
        From rainforests to permafrost
    Lush greenery and stark lava flows

7 Insert a new slide with the **Title and Content** layout. In the title placeholder, type **Where Lava Meets the Sea** and then in the content placeholder, from your student files, insert the picture **p01E_Lava_Arch**. Apply the **Double Frame, Black** picture style.

8 Insert a **New Slide** using the **Picture with Caption** layout. In the title placeholder, type **Explore the Coastline** In the text placeholder, type **Take your time as you meander the over 200 miles of coastline that rings the Big Island. Hike the lava flows, explore the tide pools, and marvel at the deep blue waters that make Hawaii a stunning escape to paradise.**

9 In the placeholder on the right, from your student files, insert the picture **p01E_Bridge**, and then apply the **Bevel Rectangle** picture style.

10 Insert a **Header & Footer** on the **Notes and Handouts**. Include the **Date and time** updated automatically, the **Page number**, and a **Footer**—using your own name—with the text **Lastname_Firstname_1E_Big_Island** and apply to all the slides.

11 Display the **Document Information Panel**. Replace the text in the **Author** box with your own firstname and lastname. In the **Subject** box, type your course name and section number, and in the **Keywords** box, type **Big Island Close** the **Document Information Panel**.

12 **Save** your presentation, and then view the slide show from the beginning. Submit your presentation electronically or print **Handouts, 6 Slides Horizontal** as directed by your instructor. **Close** the presentation.

End **You have completed Project 1E** ——————————————————

Content-Based Assessments

Apply 1B skills from these Objectives:

5 Edit an Existing Presentation

6 Format a Presentation

7 Use Slide Sorter View

8 Apply Slide Transitions

Mastering PowerPoint | Project **1F** Tour

In the following Mastering PowerPoint project, you will edit a presentation describing the land and sea tours offered by Lehua Hawaiian Adventures. Your completed presentation will look similar to Figure 1.51.

Project Files

For Project 1F, you will need the following files:

> p01F_Tour
> p01F_Sample_Slides

You will save your presentation as:

> Lastname_Firstname_1F_Tour

Project Results

Figure 1.51

(Project 1F Tour continues on the next page)

Content-Based Assessments

1 **Start** PowerPoint, and then from your student data files, open the file **p01F_Tour**. In your **PowerPoint Chapter 1** folder, **Save** the file as **Lastname_Firstname_1F_Tour**

2 Display the presentation **Outline**. In the **Outline tab**, in **Slide 2**, click at the end of the first bullet point after the words *1 p.m.* Press Enter, and then increase the list level of the new bullet point. Type **Meet at our LHA office in Kona**

3 In the **Slides/Outline pane**, click the **Slides tab** to display the slide thumbnails, and then display **Slide 1**. Display the **Reuse Slides** pane, and then click the **Browse** button. Click **Browse File**, and then in the **Browse** dialog box, from your student files, open **p01F_Sample_Slides**. Select the **Keep source formatting** check box, and then from this group of slides, insert the second and third slides—*Hamakua Coast and Hilo* and *Akaka Falls*.

4 In the **Slides/Outline pane**, click **Slide 4** to display it in the **Slide pane**, and then from the **Reuse Slides** pane, insert the fifth, sixth, and eighth slides—*Captain Cook's Monument*, *Explore the Reef*, and *Start Your Adventure!* **Close** the **Reuse Slides** pane.

5 Display **Slide 1**, and then change the layout to **Title Slide**. Select the title—*The Big Island Land and Sea Tours*. Change the **Font** to **Constantia**, and the **Font Size** to **48**. Change the **Font Color** to **Black, Background 1**.

6 Display **Slide 3**, and then select the paragraph in the content placeholder. Apply **Bold** and **Italic**, and then **Center** the text. Change the **Line Spacing** to **1.5**.

7 In **Slide Sorter** view, delete **Slide 6**. Then select **Slides 4** and **5** and move both slides so that they are positioned after **Slide 1**. In **Normal** view, display **Slide 1**. Apply the **Split** transition and change the **Effect Options** to **Horizontal Out**. Apply the transition to all of the slides in the presentation. View the slide show from the beginning.

8 **Insert** a **Header & Footer** on the **Notes and Handouts**. Include the **Date and time** updated automatically, the **Page number**, and a **Footer** with the text **Lastname_Firstname_1F_Tour** Apply to all the slides.

9 Check spelling in the presentation. If necessary, select the Ignore All option if proper names are indicated as misspelled.

10 Display the **Document Information Panel**. Replace the text in the **Author** box with your own firstname and lastname. In the **Subject** box, type your course name and section number, and in the **Keywords** box, type **tours, Big Island** **Close** the **Document Information Panel**.

11 **Save** your presentation, and then submit your presentation electronically or print **Handouts, 6 Slides Horizontal** as directed by your instructor. **Close** the presentation.

End **You have completed Project 1F**

Mastering PowerPoint | Project **1G** Volcano Tour

In the following Mastering PowerPoint project, you will edit an existing presentation that describes the tour of Volcanoes National Park offered by Lehua Hawaiian Adventures. Your completed presentation will look similar to Figure 1.52.

Project Files

For Project 1G, you will need the following files:

> p01G_Crater_Information
> p01G_Lava
> p01G_Volcano_Tour

You will save your presentation as:

> Lastname_Firstname_1G_Volcano_Tour

Project Results

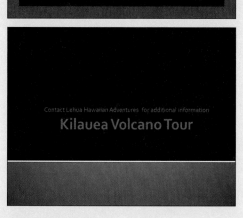

Figure 1.52

(Project 1G Volcano Tour continues on the next page)

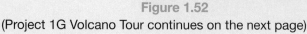

Content-Based Assessments

1 **Start** PowerPoint, and then from your student files, open the file **p01G_Volcano_Tour**. In your **PowerPoint Chapter 1** folder, **Save** the file as **Lastname_Firstname_1G_Volcano_Tour**

2 Replace all occurrences of the text **Diamond Head** with **Kilauea** Display **Slide 3**, open the **Reuse Slides** pane, and then from your student files browse for and display the presentation **p01G_Crater_Information**. If necessary, clear the Keep source formatting check box, and then insert both slides from the **p01G_Crater_Information** file. **Close** the **Reuse Slides** pane.

3 Display the presentation outline, and then in **Slide 3**, increase the list level of the bullet point beginning *You will hike*. In either the **Slide pane** or the **Outline**, click at the end of the last bullet point after the word *flow*, and then insert a new bullet point. Decrease its list level. Type **Tour precautions** and then press [Enter]. Increase the list level, and then type the following two bullet points.

> **Wear sturdy, covered shoes**
>
> **Expect uneven terrain**

4 Display the slide thumbnails. In **Slide 1**, select the subtitle—*The Big Island's Most Majestic Sight*—and then change the **Font Color** to **White, Text 1** and the **Font Size** to **28**. On **Slide 2**, center the caption text located below the slide title and apply **Bold** and **Italic**. Change the **Line Spacing** to **2.0**. Click in the content placeholder on the right, and then from your student files, insert the picture **p01G_Lava**. Format the picture with the **Beveled Oval, Black** picture style and the **Paint Brush** artistic effect.

5 In **Slide Sorter** view, move **Slide 5** between **Slides 3** and **4**. In **Normal** view, on **Slide 5**, change the slide **Layout** to **Title Slide**, and then type the following notes in the **Notes pane: Recent volcanic activity at the national park site may result in changes to the tour itinerary.** Apply the **Uncover** transition and change the **Effect Options** to **From Top**. Change the **Timing** by increasing the **Duration** to **01.50**. Apply the transition effect to all of the slides. View the slide show from the beginning.

6 **Insert** a **Header & Footer** on the **Notes and Handouts**. Include the **Date and time** updated automatically, the **Page number**, and a **Footer**, using your own name, with the text **Lastname_Firstname_1G_Volcano_Tour**

7 Check spelling in the presentation. If necessary, select the Ignore All option if proper names are indicated as misspelled.

8 Display the **Document Information Panel**. Replace the text in the **Author** box with your own firstname and lastname. In the **Subject** box, type your course name and section number, and in the **Keywords** box, type **Kilauea, volcano Close** the Document Information Panel.

9 **Save** your presentation. Submit your presentation electronically or print **Handouts, 6 Slides Horizontal** as directed by your instructor. **Close** the presentation.

End **You have completed Project 1G** _____

GO! Fix It | Project **1H** Hawaii Guide

Project Files

For Project 1H, you will need the following files:

> p01H_Hawaii_Guide
> p01H_Islands

You will save your presentation as:

> Lastname_Firstname_1H_Hawaii_Guide

In this project, you will edit a presentation prepared by Lehua Hawaiian Adventures that describes some of the activities on each of the Hawaiian Islands. From the student files that accompany this textbook, open the file p01H_Hawaii_Guide, and then save the file in your chapter folder as **Lastname_Firstname_1H_Hawaii_Guide**

To complete the project, you should know:

- All of the slides in the p01H_Islands presentation should be reused in this presentation and inserted after Slide 2. Correct two spelling errors and ignore all instances of proper names that are indicated as misspelled.

- The Opulent theme should be applied.

- Slides 3 through 8 should be arranged alphabetically according to the name of the island

- On the Maui and Molokai slides, the list level of the second bullet points should be decreased.

- The Layout for Slide 2 should be Section Header, the slide should be moved to the end of the presentation, and the Flip transition using the Left effect option should be applied to all of the slides in the presentation.

- Document Properties should include your name, course name and section, and the keywords **guide, islands** A Header & Footer should be inserted on the Notes and Handouts that includes the Date and time updated automatically, the Page number, and a Footer with the text **Lastname_Firstname_1H_Hawaii_Guide**

Save your presentation and submit electronically or print Handouts, 4 Slides Horizontal as directed by your instructor. Close the presentation.

End **You have completed Project 1H** ——————————————

Content-Based Assessments

GO! Make It | Project 1I Dolphin Encounter

Project Files

For Project 1I, you will need the following files:

> p01I_Dolphin_Encounters
> p01I_Dolphin

You will save your presentation as:

> Lastname_Firstname_1I_Dolphin_Encounters

From your student files, open p01I_Dolphin_Encounters, and then save it in your PowerPoint Chapter 1 folder as **Lastname_Firstname_1I_Dolphin_Encounters**

By using the skills you practiced in this chapter, create the slide shown in Figure 1.53 by inserting a new Slide 2 with the layout and text shown in the figure. The title font size is 36, and the font color is Black, Background 1. The caption text font is Arial, and the font size is 16 with bold and italic applied. To complete the slide, from your student files, insert the picture p01H_Dolphin. Insert the date and time updated automatically, the file name, and a page number in the Notes and Handouts footer. In the Document Information Panel, add your name and course information and the keyword **dolphin** Save your presentation, and then print or submit electronically as directed by your instructor.

Project Results

Figure 1.53

Dolphin Encounters!

Learn about dolphins during our 30-minute training program. Then join the trainers in our pool as you swim and play with our dolphin friends!

End You have completed Project 1I

Apply a combination of
the **1A** and **1B** skills.

GO! Solve It | Project **1J** Planning Tips

Project Files

For Project 1J, you will need the following file:

p01J_Planning_Tips

You will save your presentation as:

Lastname_Firstname_1J_Planning_Tips

Open the file p01J_Planning_Tips and save it as **Lastname_Firstname_1J_Planning_Tips**
Complete the presentation by applying a theme and by correcting spelling errors. Format the
presentation attractively by applying appropriate font formatting and by changing text alignment
and line spacing. Change the layout of at least one slide to a layout that will accommodate a
picture. Insert a picture that you have taken yourself, or use one of the pictures in your student
data files that you inserted in other projects in this chapter. On the last slide, insert an appropriate
picture, and then apply picture styles to both pictures. Apply slide transitions to all of the slides
in the presentation, and then insert a header and footer that includes the date and time updated
automatically, the file name in the footer, and the page number. Add your name, your course
name and section number, and the keywords **planning, weather** to the Properties area. Save and
print or submit as directed by your instructor.

Performance Elements		Performance Level		
		Exemplary: You consistently applied the relevant skills	**Proficient:** You sometimes, but not always, applied the relevant skills	**Developing:** You rarely or never applied the relevant skills
	Apply a theme	An appropriate theme was applied to the presentation.	A theme was applied but was not appropriate for the presentation.	A theme was not applied.
	Apply font and slide formatting	Font and slide formatting is attractive and appropriate.	Adequately formatted but difficult to read or unattractive.	Inadequate or no formatting.
	Use appropriate pictures and apply styles attractively	Two appropriate pictures are inserted and styles are applied attractively.	Pictures are inserted but styles are not applied or are inappropriately applied.	Pictures are not inserted.

End You have completed Project 1J

Content-Based Assessments

GO! Solve It | Project **1K** Hikes

Project Files

For Project 1K, you will need the following file:

   p01K_Hikes

You will save your presentation as:

   Lastname_Firstname_1K_Hikes

Open the file p01K_Hikes and save it as **Lastname_Firstname_1K_Hikes** Complete the presentation by applying an appropriate theme. Move Slide 2 to the end of the presentation, and then change the layout to one appropriate for the end of the presentation. Format the presentation attractively by applying font formatting and by changing text alignment and line spacing. Review the information on Slide 3, and then increase list levels appropriately on this slide. Apply picture styles to the two pictures in the presentation and an artistic effect to at least one picture. Apply slide transitions to all of the slides. Insert a header and footer that includes the date and time updated automatically, the file name in the footer, and the page number. Add your name, your course name and section number, and the keywords **hiking Akaka Falls, Waimea Canyon** to the Properties area. Save and print or submit as directed by your instructor.

Performance Elements		Performance Level		
		Exemplary: You consistently applied the relevant skills	**Proficient:** You sometimes, but not always, applied the relevant skills	**Developing:** You rarely or never applied the relevant skills
	Apply a theme	An appropriate theme was applied to the presentation.	A theme was applied but was not appropriate for the presentation.	A theme was not applied.
	Apply appropriate formatting	Formatting is attractive and appropriate.	Adequately formatted but difficult to read or unattractive.	Inadequate or no formatting.
	Apply appropriate list levels	List levels are applied appropriately.	Some, but not all, list levels are appropriately applied.	Changes to list levels were not made.

End You have completed Project 1K

Outcomes-Based Assessments

Rubric

The following outcomes-based assessments are *open-ended assessments*. That is, there is no specific correct result; your result will depend on your approach to the information provided. Make *Professional Quality* your goal. Use the following scoring rubric to guide you in *how* to approach the problem, and then to evaluate *how well* your approach solves the problem.

The *criteria*—Software Mastery, Content, Format and Layout, and Process—represent the knowledge and skills you have gained that you can apply to solving the problem. The *levels of performance*—Professional Quality, Approaching Professional Quality, or Needs Quality Improvements—help you and your instructor evaluate your result.

	Your completed project is of Professional Quality if you:	Your completed project is Approaching Professional Quality if you:	Your completed project Needs Quality Improvements if you:
1-Software Mastery	Choose and apply the most appropriate skills, tools, and features and identify efficient methods to solve the problem.	Choose and apply some appropriate skills, tools, and features, but not in the most efficient manner.	Choose inappropriate skills, tools, or features, or are inefficient in solving the problem.
2-Content	Construct a solution that is clear and well organized, contains content that is accurate, appropriate to the audience and purpose, and is complete. Provide a solution that contains no errors in spelling, grammar, or style.	Construct a solution in which some components are unclear, poorly organized, inconsistent, or incomplete. Misjudge the needs of the audience. Have some errors in spelling, grammar, or style, but the errors do not detract from comprehension.	Construct a solution that is unclear, incomplete, or poorly organized; contains some inaccurate or inappropriate content; and contains many errors in spelling, grammar, or style. Do not solve the problem.
3-Format and Layout	Format and arrange all elements to communicate information and ideas, clarify function, illustrate relationships, and indicate relative importance.	Apply appropriate format and layout features to some elements, but not others. Overuse features, causing minor distraction.	Apply format and layout that does not communicate information or ideas clearly. Do not use format and layout features to clarify function, illustrate relationships, or indicate relative importance. Use available features excessively, causing distraction.
4-Process	Use an organized approach that integrates planning, development, self-assessment, revision, and reflection.	Demonstrate an organized approach in some areas, but not others; or, use an insufficient process of organization throughout.	Do not use an organized approach to solve the problem.

Apply a combination of the 1A and 1B skills.

GO! Think | Project 1L Big Island

Project Files

For Project 1L, you will need the following files:

New blank PowerPoint presentation
p01L_Fishing
p01L_Monument

You will save your presentation as:

Lastname_Firstname_1L_Big_Island

Carl Kawaoka, Tour Operations Manager for Lehua Hawaiian Adventures, is developing a presentation describing sea tours on the Big Island of Hawaii to be shown at a travel fair on the mainland. In the presentation, Carl will be showcasing the company's two most popular sea excursions: The Captain Cook Monument Snorkeling Tour and the Kona Deep Sea Fishing Tour.

On the Captain Cook Monument Snorkeling Tour, guests meet at 8:00 a.m. at the Lehua Hawaiian Adventures Kona location and then board a 12-passenger rigid hull inflatable raft. Captained by a U.S. Coast Guard licensed crew, the raft is navigated along the Hawaii coastline, exploring sea caves, lava tubes, and waterfalls. Upon arrival at the Monument, guests snorkel in Hawaii's incredible undersea world of colorful fish, sea turtles, and stingrays. Lehua Hawaiian Adventures provides the lunch, snacks, drinks, and snorkeling equipment and asks that guests bring their own towels, sunscreen, swim suits, and sense of adventure. This tour lasts 5 hours and the fee is $85.

On the Kona Deep Sea Fishing Tour, guests meet at 7:00 a.m. at the Lehua Hawaiian Adventures Kona location and then board a 32-foot Blackfin fishing boat. The boat is captained by a U.S. Coast Guard licensed crew of three. A maximum of six guests are allowed on each trip, which sails, weather permitting, every Wednesday, Friday, and Saturday. For deep sea fishing, there is no better place than the Kona coast. On full-day adventures, it is common for guests to catch marlin, sailfish, ahi, ono, and mahi-mahi. This tour lasts 8 hours and the fee is $385.

Using the preceding information, create a presentation that Carl can show at the travel fair. The presentation should include four to six slides describing the two tours. Apply an appropriate theme and use slide layouts that will effectively present the content. From your student files, insert the pictures p01L_Fishing and p01L_Monument on appropriate slides and apply picture styles or artistic effects to enhance the pictures. Apply font formatting and slide transitions, and modify text alignment and line spacing as necessary. Save the file as **Lastname_Firstname_1L_Big_Island** and then insert a header and footer that include the date and time updated automatically, the file name in the footer, and the page number. Add your name, your course name and section number, and the keywords **sea tours, deep sea fishing, snorkeling tours** to the Properties area. Save and print or submit as directed by your instructor.

End You have completed Project 1L ————————————————

Outcomes-Based Assessments

Apply a combination of the **1A** and **1B** skills.

GO! Think | Project **1M** Beaches

Project Files

For Project 1M, you will need the following files:

New blank PowerPoint presentation
p01M_Black_Sand
p01M_Kite_Surf
p01M_Lithified_Cliffs
p01M_Reef
p01M_Tide_Pools

You will save your presentation as:

Lastname_Firstname_1M_Beaches

Katherine Okubo, President of Lehua Hawaiian Adventures, is making a presentation to groups of tourists at a number of hotels on the Hawaiian Islands. She would like to begin the presentation with an introduction to the beaches of Hawaii before discussing the many ways in which her company can assist tourists with selecting the places they would like to visit. The following paragraphs contain some of the information about the shorelines and beaches that Katherine would like to include in the presentation.

The shorelines of Hawaii vary tremendously, from black sand beaches with pounding surf to beaches of pink and white sand with calm waters perfect for snorkeling. Many of the shorelines provide picturesque hiking, shallow tide pools for exploring, beautiful reef where fish and turtles delight snorkelers, and waves that the most adventurous kite and board surfers enjoy. The terrain and the water make it easy for visitors to find a favorite beach in Hawaii.

The northern shore of Oahu is famous for its surfing beaches, while the southern shores of Kauai provide hikers with amazing views of the lithified cliffs formed by the power of the ocean. Black sand beaches are common on Hawaii, formed by the lava flows that created the islands. The reef that buffers many beaches from the open ocean is home to a wide variety of sea life that can be enjoyed while scuba diving and snorkeling.

Using the preceding information, create the first four to six slides of a presentation that Katherine can show during her discussion. Apply an appropriate theme and use slide layouts that will effectively present the content. Several picture files listed at the beginning of this project have been provided that you can insert in your presentation. Apply font formatting, picture styles, and slide transitions, and modify text alignment and line spacing as necessary. Save the file as **Lastname_Firstname_1M_Beaches** and then insert a header and footer that include the date and time updated automatically, the file name in the footer, and the page number. Add your name, your course name and section number, and the keywords **beaches, Black Sands beach, tide pools, lithified cliffs, scuba, snorkeling** to the Properties area. Save and print or submit as directed by your instructor.

End You have completed Project **1M**

Outcomes-Based Assessments

Apply a combination of the **1A** and **1B** skills.

You and GO! | Project **1N** Travel

Project Files

For Project 1N, you will need the following file:

New blank PowerPoint presentation

You will save your presentation as:

Lastname_Firstname_1N_Travel

Choose a place to which you have traveled or would like to travel. Create a presentation with at least six slides that describes the location, the method of travel, the qualities of the location that make it interesting or fun, the places you can visit, and any cultural activities in which you might like to participate. Choose an appropriate theme, slide layouts, and pictures, and then format the presentation attractively. Save your presentation as **Lastname_Firstname_1N_Travel** and submit as directed.

End You have completed Project 1N ————————————

Apply a combination of the **1A** and **1B** skills.

GO! Collaborate | Project **1O** Bell Orchid Hotels Group Running Case

This project relates to the **Bell Orchid Hotels**. Your instructor may assign this group case project to your class. If your instructor assigns this project, he or she will provide you with information and instructions to work as part of a group. The group will apply the skills gained thus far to help the Bell Orchid Hotels achieve their business goals.

End You have completed Project 1O ————————————

Photos appearing in this chapter supplied by Alicia Vargas and used with permission.

NOTES

Formatting PowerPoint Presentations

OUTCOMES

At the end of this chapter you will be able to:

OBJECTIVES

Mastering these objectives will enable you to:

PROJECT 2A
Format a presentation to add visual interest and clarity.

1. Format Numbered and Bulleted Lists (p. 585)
2. Insert Clip Art (p. 589)
3. Insert Text Boxes and Shapes (p. 594)
4. Format Objects (p. 598)

PROJECT 2B
Enhance a presentation with WordArt and diagrams.

5. Remove Picture Backgrounds and Insert WordArt (p. 609)
6. Create and Format a SmartArt Graphic (p. 614)

karnizz/Shutterstock

In This Chapter

A PowerPoint presentation is a visual aid in which well-designed slides help the audience understand complex information while keeping them focused on the message. Color is an important element that enhances your slides and draws the audience's interest by creating focus. When designing the background and element colors for your presentation, be sure that the colors you use provide contrast so that the text is visible on the background

Fascination Entertainment Group operates 15 regional theme parks across the United States, Mexico, and Canada. Park types include traditional theme parks, water parks, and animal parks. This year the company will launch three of its new "Fascination Parks" where attractions combine fun and the discovery of math and science information, and where teens and adults enjoy the free Friday night concerts.

Project 2A Employee Training Presentation

Project Activities

In Activities 2.01 through 2.14, you will format a presentation for Yuki Hiroko, Director of Operations for Fascination Entertainment Group, that describes important safety guidelines for employees. Your completed presentation will look similar to Figure 2.1.

Project Files

For Project 2A, you will need the following file:

p02A_Safety

You will save your presentation as:

Lastname_Firstname_2A_Safety

Project Results

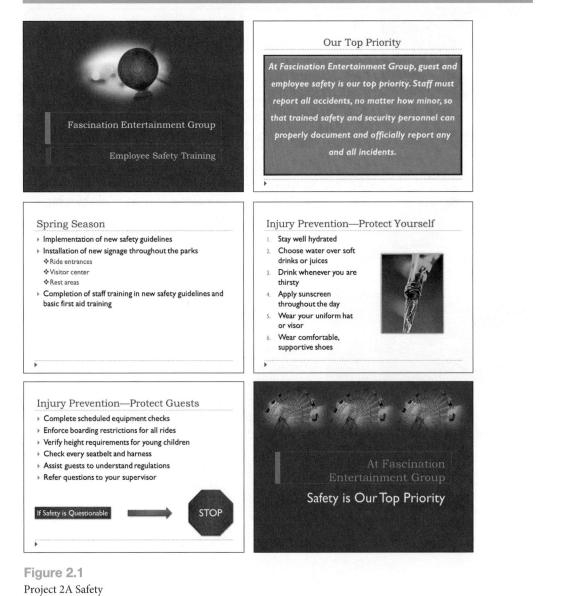

Figure 2.1
Project 2A Safety

Objective 1 | Format Numbered and Bulleted Lists

Recall that formatting is the process of changing the appearance of the text, layout, or design of a slide. You can format slide content by changing the bulleted and numbered list styles and colors.

Activity 2.01 | Selecting Placeholder Text

Recall that a placeholder is a box on a slide with dotted or dashed borders that holds title and body text or other content such as charts, tables, and pictures. You can format placeholder contents by selecting text or by selecting the entire placeholder.

1 **Start** PowerPoint. From the student files that accompany this textbook, locate and open **p02A_Safety**. On the **File tab**, click **Save As**, and then navigate to the location where you are storing your projects for this chapter. Create a new folder named **PowerPoint Chapter 2** and then in the **File name** box and using your own name, type **Lastname_Firstname_2A_Safety** Click **Save** or press Enter. Take a moment to view each slide and become familiar with the contents of this presentation.

2 Display **Slide 2**. Click anywhere in the content placeholder with the single bullet point, and then compare your screen with Figure 2.2.

   A dashed border displays, indicating that you can make editing changes to the placeholder text.

Figure 2.2

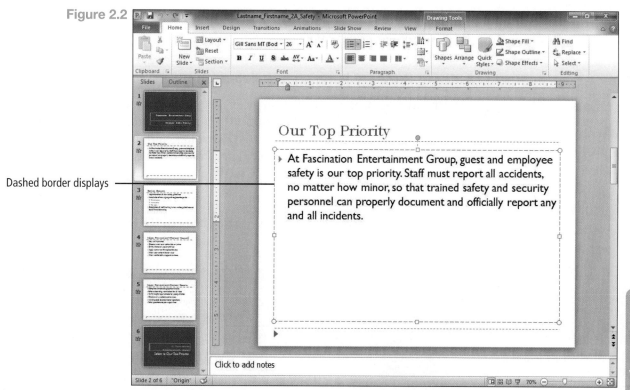

Dashed border displays

3 Point anywhere on the dashed border to display the ⊕ pointer, and then click one time to display the border as a solid line. Compare your screen with Figure 2.3.

> When a placeholder's border displays as a solid line, all of the text in the placeholder is selected, and any formatting changes that you make will be applied to *all* of the text in the placeholder.

Figure 2.3

Solid border indicates that all placeholder text is selected

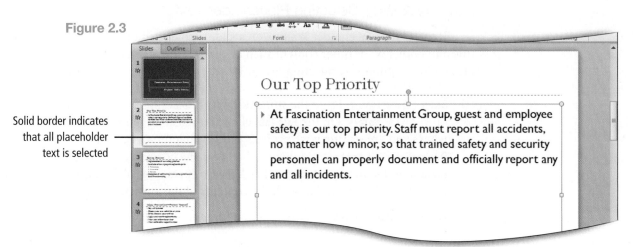

4 With the border of the placeholder displaying as a solid line, click in the **Font Size** box `44 ▾` to select the number, and then type **30** and press Enter. Notice that the font size of *all* of the placeholder text increases.

5 Save 🖫 your presentation.

Activity 2.02 | Changing a Bulleted List to a Numbered List

1 Display **Slide 4**, and then click anywhere in the bulleted list. Point to the blue dashed border (the red dashed lines at the top and bottom are part of the decorative elements of the theme) to display the ⊕ pointer, and then click one time to display the border as a solid line indicating that all of the text is selected.

2 On the **Home tab**, in the **Paragraph group**, click the **Numbering** button `▤ ▾`, and then compare your slide with Figure 2.4.

> All of the bullet symbols are converted to numbers. The color of the numbers is determined by the presentation theme.

Figure 2.4

Numbering button

Solid border surrounds placeholder

Bullet symbols converted to numbers

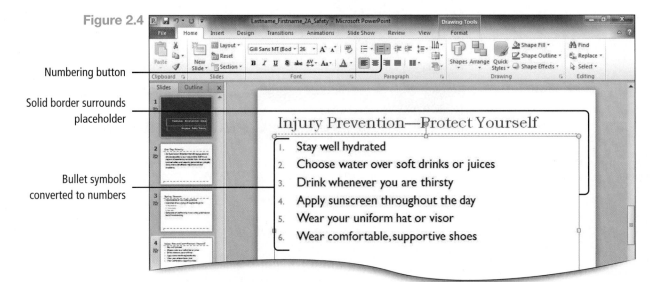

3 **Save** 🖫 your presentation.

Activity 2.03 | Modifying a Bulleted List Style

The presentation theme includes default styles for the bullet points in content placeholders. You can customize a bullet by changing its style, color, and size.

1 Display **Slide 3**, and then select the three second-level bullet points—*Ride entrances, Visitor center,* and *Rest areas.*

2 On the **Home tab**, in the **Paragraph group**, click the **Bullets button arrow** 📇 to display the **Bullets** gallery, and then compare your screen with Figure 2.5.

> The Bullets gallery displays several bullet characters that you can apply to the selection.

Figure 2.5

Bullets button arrow

Bullets gallery

Selected bullet points

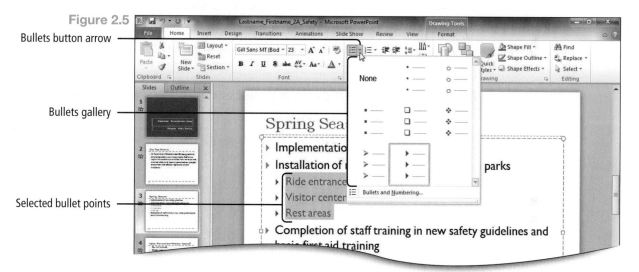

3 At the bottom of the **Bullets** gallery, click **Bullets and Numbering**. In the **Bullets and Numbering** dialog box, point to each bullet style to display its ScreenTip. Then, in the second row, click **Star Bullets**. If the Star Bullets are not available, in the second row of bullets, click the second bullet style, and then click the Reset button.

PowerPoint | Chapter 2

4 Below the gallery, click the **Color** button. Under **Theme Colors**, in the sixth column, click the fifth color—**Red, Accent 2, Darker 25%**. In the **Size** box, select the existing number, type **100** and then compare your dialog box with Figure 2.6.

Figure 2.6

Bullets and Numbering dialog box

Star Bullets selected

Bullet size changed to 100% of text

Bullet color changed

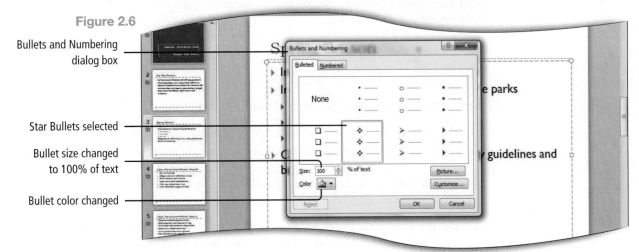

5 Click **OK** to apply the bullet style, and then **Save** 🖫 your presentation.

> **More Knowledge | Using Other Symbols as Bullet Characters**
>
> Many bullets styles are available to insert in your presentation. In the Bullets and Numbering dialog box, click the Customize button to view additional bullet styles.

Activity 2.04 | Removing a Bullet Symbol from a Bullet Point

The Bullet button is a toggle button, enabling you to turn the bullet symbol on and off. A slide that contains a single bullet point can be formatted as a single paragraph *without* a bullet symbol.

1 Display **Slide 2**, and then click in the paragraph. On the **Home tab**, in the **Paragraph group**, click the **Bullets** button 📇. Compare your screen with Figure 2.7.

> The bullet symbol no longer displays, and the bullet button is no longer selected. Additionally, the indentation associated with the list level is removed.

Figure 2.7

Bullets button

Bullet symbol and indentation removed from paragraph

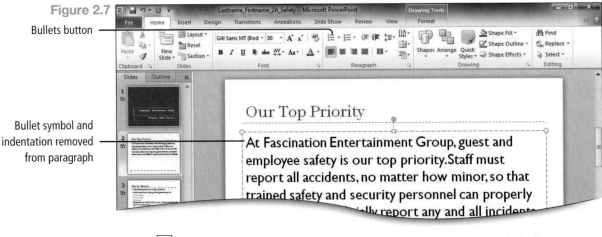

2 **Center** 📄 the paragraph. On the **Home tab**, in the **Paragraph group**, click the **Line Spacing** button 📄, and then click **1.5**.

3 Click the dashed border to display the solid border and to select all of the text in the paragraph, and then apply **Bold** 🅱 and **Italic** 🔘. Click in the slide title, and then click the **Center** button 📄. **Save** 🖫 your presentation.

Objective 2 | Insert Clip Art

There are many sources from which you can insert images into a presentation. One type of image that you can insert is a *clip*—a single media file such as art, sound, animation, or a movie.

Activity 2.05 | Inserting Clip Art

1 Display **Slide 4**, and then on the **Home tab**, in the **Slides group**, click the **Layout** button. Click **Two Content** to change the slide layout.

2 In the placeholder on the right side of the slide, click the **Clip Art** button 🖼 to display the **Clip Art** pane, and then compare your screen with Figure 2.8.

Figure 2.8

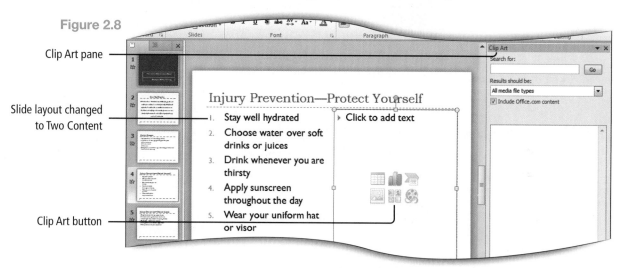

Clip Art pane

Slide layout changed to Two Content

Clip Art button

3 In the **Clip Art** pane, click in the **Search for** box, and then replace any existing text with **bottled water** so that PowerPoint can search for images that contain the keyword *bottled water*.

4 Click the **Results should be arrow**, and then click as necessary to *clear* the **Illustrations**, **Videos**, and **Audio** check boxes and to select only the **Photographs** check box. Compare your screen with Figure 2.9.

> With the Photographs check box selected, PowerPoint will search for images that were created with a digital camera or a scanner.

Figure 2.9

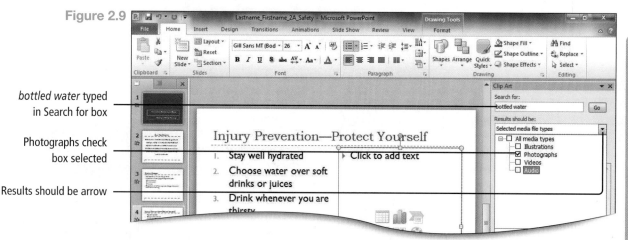

bottled water typed in Search for box

Photographs check box selected

Results should be arrow

PowerPoint | Chapter 2

5 In the **Clip Art** pane, click the **Results should be arrow** to close the list. Then, if necessary, select the **Include Office.com content** check box so that images available on Office.com are included in the search.

6 In the **Clip Art** pane, click **Go** to display clips in the Clip Art pane. Scroll through the clips, and then locate and point to the image of the water pouring from a glass water bottle on a blue background. Compare your screen with Figure 2.10.

When you point to an image in the Clip Art pane, a ScreenTip displays the keywords and information about the size of the image.

Figure 2.10

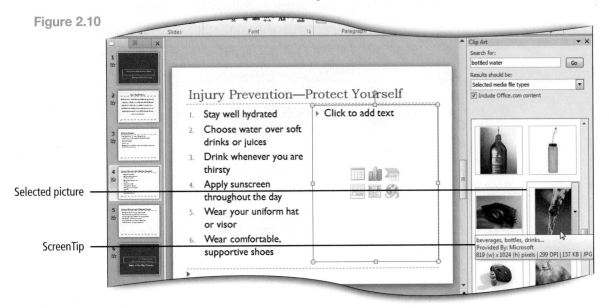

Selected picture

ScreenTip

> **Alert! | Is the Water Bottle Picture Unavailable?**
>
> If you are unable to locate the suggested picture, choose another similar image.

7 Click the water bottle picture to insert it in the content placeholder on the right side of the slide. **Close** ☒ the **Clip Art** pane, and then compare your slide with Figure 2.11.

On the Ribbon, the Picture Tools display, and the water bottle image is surrounded by sizing handles, indicating that it is selected.

Figure 2.11

Picture Tools display

Picture inserted and selected

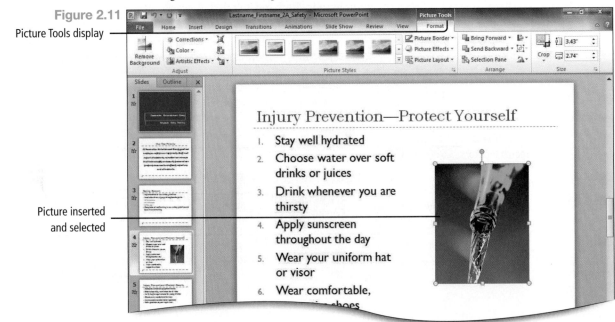

8 Display **Slide 1**. Click the **Insert tab**, and then in the **Images group**, click **Clip Art**.

9 In the **Clip Art** pane, in the **Search for** box, search for **red lights** and then click **Go**. Scroll as necessary to locate the picture of the single red warning light. Point to the picture, and then compare your screen with Figure 2.12.

> If you cannot locate the picture, select another appropriate image.

Figure 2.12

red lights typed in
Search for box

Selected picture

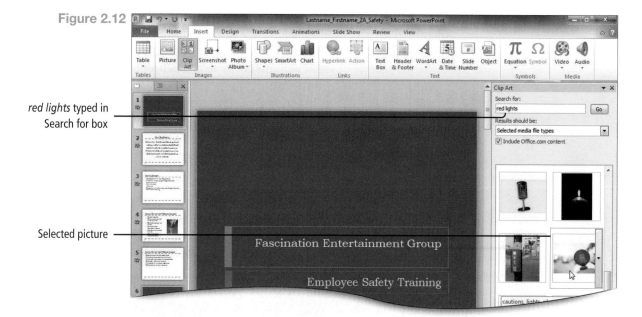

10 Click the **red light** picture to insert it in the center of the slide, and then **Close** ☒ the **Clip Art** pane. **Save** 🖫 your presentation.

> When you use the Clip Art command on the Ribbon instead of the Clip Art button in a content placeholder, PowerPoint inserts the image in the center of the slide.

Activity 2.06 | Moving and Sizing Images

Recall that when an image is selected, it is surrounded by sizing handles that you can drag to resize the image. You can also resize an image using the Shape Height and Shape Width boxes on the Format tab. When you point to the image, rather than pointing to a sizing handle, the move pointer—a four-headed arrow—displays, indicating that you can move the image.

> **Another Way**
>
> Alternatively, drag a corner sizing handle to resize an image proportionately.

1 If necessary, select the picture of the red light. On the **Format tab**, in the **Size group**, click in the **Shape Height** box 🔟, and then replace the selected number with **3.5**

2 Press Enter to resize the image. Notice that the picture is resized proportionately, and the **Width** box displays *5.26*. Compare your screen with Figure 2.13.

> When a picture is resized in this manner, the width adjusts in proportion to the picture height.

Figure 2.13

3.5 typed in
Shape Height box

PowerPoint | Chapter 2

3 Display the **View tab**. In the **Show group**, verify that the **Ruler** check box is selected and if necessary, select it. On the horizontal and vertical rulers, notice that *0* displays in the center.

> Horizontally, the PowerPoint ruler indicates measurements from the center *out* to the left and to the right. Vertically, the PowerPoint ruler indicates measurements from the center up and down.

4 Point to the picture to display the 🔁 pointer. Hold down Shift, and then drag the picture to the right until the left edge of the picture is aligned with the **left half of the horizontal ruler at 3 inches**. If necessary, hold down Ctrl and press an arrow key to move the picture in small increments in any direction for a more precise placement. Compare your screen with Figure 2.14.

> Pressing Shift while dragging an object constrains object movement in a straight line either vertically or horizontally. Here, pressing Shift maintains the vertical placement of the picture.

Figure 2.14

Ruler check box selected

Horizontal ruler

Left edge of picture aligns with left half of horizontal ruler at 3 inches

Vertical ruler

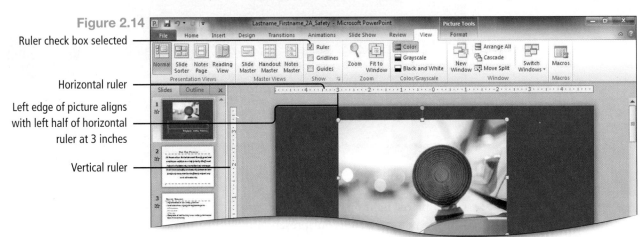

5 Display **Slide 6**. On the **Insert tab**, in the **Images group**, click the **Clip Art** button. In the **Clip Art** pane, search for **amusement park** and then click **Go**. Locate and click the picture of the Ferris wheel with the sky and clouds in the background, and then compare your slide with Figure 2.15.

> If you cannot locate the image, select another appropriate image.

Figure 2.15

Keyword *amusement park* typed in Search for box

Selected picture

Selected picture inserted

6 **Close** ✖ the **Clip Art** pane, and be sure that the picture is still selected. On the **Format tab**, in the **Size group**, click in the **Shape Height** box 🔟. Replace the displayed number with **2.5** and then press Enter to resize the picture. Compare your screen with Figure 2.16.

Figure 2.16

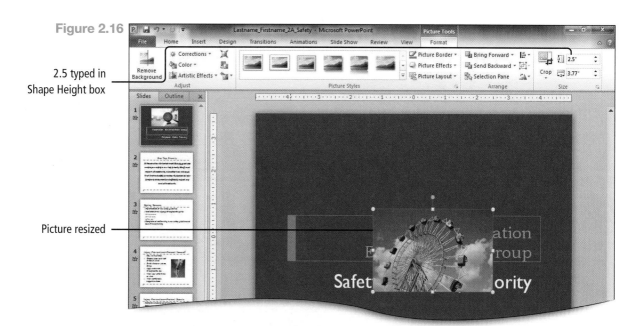

2.5 typed in
Shape Height box

Picture resized

7 **Save** 💾 your presentation.

> **More Knowledge** | **Moving an Object by Using the Arrow Keys**
>
> You can use the directional arrow keys on your keyboard to move a picture, shape, or other object in small increments. Select the object so that its outside border displays as a solid line. Then, on your keyboard, hold down the [Ctrl] key and press the directional arrow keys to move the selected object in precise increments.

Activity 2.07 | Changing the Shape of a Picture

An inserted picture is rectangular in shape; however, you can modify a picture by changing its shape.

1 Display **Slide 1**, and then select the picture.

2 On the **Format tab**, in the **Size group**, *point* to the **Crop button arrow**, and then compare your screen with Figure 2.17.

The Crop button is a split button. The upper section—the Crop button—enables the *crop* feature, which reduces the size of a picture by removing vertical or horizontal edges. The lower section—the Crop arrow—displays cropping options, such as the option to crop a picture to a shape.

Figure 2.17

Crop button arrow

PowerPoint | **Chapter 2**

3 Click the **Crop button arrow**, and then point to **Crop to Shape** to display a gallery of shapes. Compare your screen with Figure 2.18.

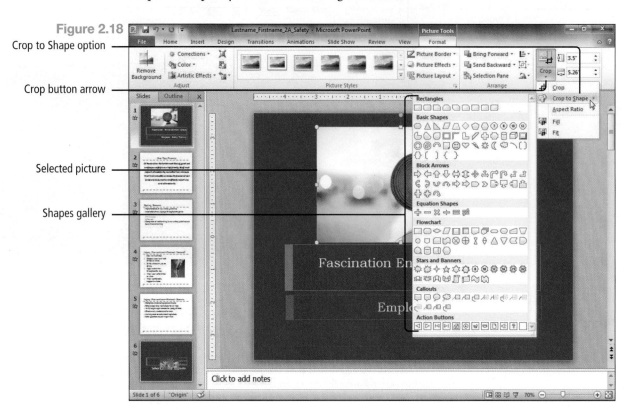

Figure 2.18

Crop to Shape option

Crop button arrow

Selected picture

Shapes gallery

4 Under **Basic Shapes**, in the first row, click the first shape—**Oval**—to change the picture's shape to an oval. **Save** 🖫 your presentation.

Objective 3 | Insert Text Boxes and Shapes

You can use objects, including text boxes and shapes, to draw attention to important information or to serve as containers for slide text. Many shapes, including lines, arrows, ovals, and rectangles, are available to insert and position anywhere on your slides.

Activity 2.08 | Inserting a Text Box

A *text box* is an object with which you can position text anywhere on a slide.

1 Display **Slide 5** and verify that the rulers display. Click the **Insert tab**, and then in the **Text group**, click the **Text Box** button.

2 Move the ⬇ pointer to several different places on the slide, and as you do so, in the horizontal and vertical rulers, notice that *ruler guides*—dotted vertical and horizontal lines that display in the rulers indicating the pointer's position—move also.

Use the ruler guides to help you position objects on a slide.

3 Position the pointer so that the ruler guides are positioned on the **left half of the horizontal ruler at 4.5 inches** and on the **lower half of the vertical ruler at 1.5 inches**, and then compare your screen with Figure 2.19.

Figure 2.19

Horizontal ruler guide
positioned on the left half
of horizontal ruler
at 4.5 inches

Pointer

Vertical ruler guide
positioned on the lower
half of vertical ruler
at 1.5 inches

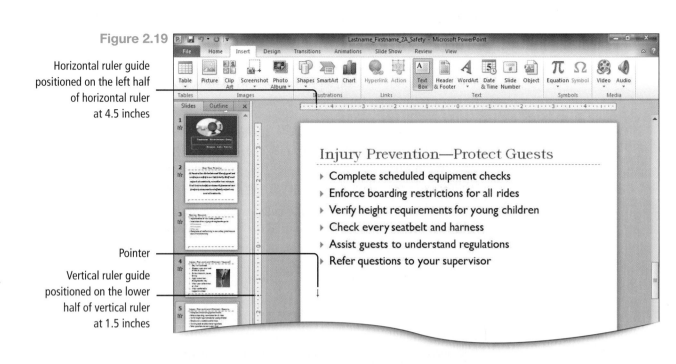

4 Click one time to create a narrow rectangular text box. With the insertion point blinking inside the text box, type **If Safety is Questionable** Notice that as you type, the width of the text box expands to accommodate the text. Compare your screen with Figure 2.20.

> Do not be concerned if your text box is not positioned exactly as shown in Figure 2.20.

Figure 2.20

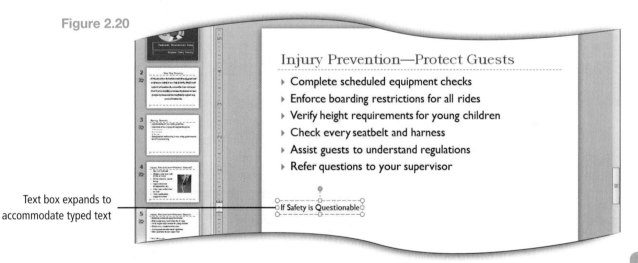

Text box expands to
accommodate typed text

Alert! | Does the Text in the Text Box Display Vertically, One Character at a Time?

If you move the pointer when you click to create the text box, PowerPoint sets the width of the text box and does not widen to accommodate the text. If this happened to you, your text may display vertically instead of horizontally or it may display on two lines. Click Undo, and then repeat the steps again, being sure that you do not move the mouse when you click to insert the text box.

---

5 Select the text that you typed, change the **Font Size** to **24** and then **Save** 🖫 your presentation.

> You can format the text in a text box by using the same techniques that you use to format text in any other placeholder. For example, you can change the font, font style, font size, and font color.

Activity 2.09 | Inserting, Sizing, and Positioning Shapes

Shapes include lines, arrows, stars, banners, ovals, rectangles, and other basic shapes you can use to illustrate an idea, a process, or a workflow. Shapes can be sized and moved using the same techniques that you use to size and move clip art images.

1 With **Slide 5** displayed, click the **Insert tab**, and then in the **Illustrations group**, click the **Shapes** button to display the **Shapes** gallery. Under **Block Arrows**, click the first shape—**Right Arrow**. Move the pointer into the slide until the ⊞ pointer—called the *crosshair pointer*—displays, indicating that you can draw a shape.

2 Move the ⊞ pointer to position the ruler guides at approximately **zero on the horizontal ruler** and on the **lower half of the vertical ruler at 1.5 inches**. Compare your screen with Figure 2.21.

Figure 2.21

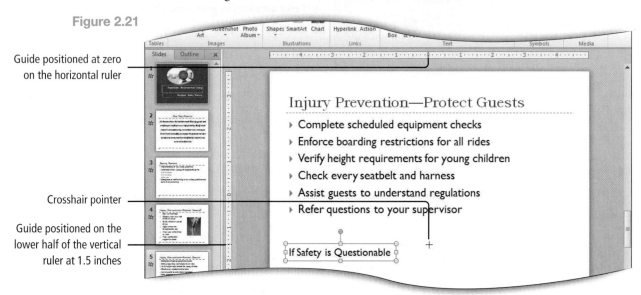

Guide positioned at zero on the horizontal ruler

Crosshair pointer

Guide positioned on the lower half of the vertical ruler at 1.5 inches

3 Click the mouse button to insert the arrow. Click the **Format tab**, and then in the **Size group**, click in the **Shape Height** box ⊞ to select the number. Type **.5** and then click in the **Shape Width** box ⊡. Type **2** and then press `Enter` to resize the arrow. Compare your screen with Figure 2.22.

Figure 2.22

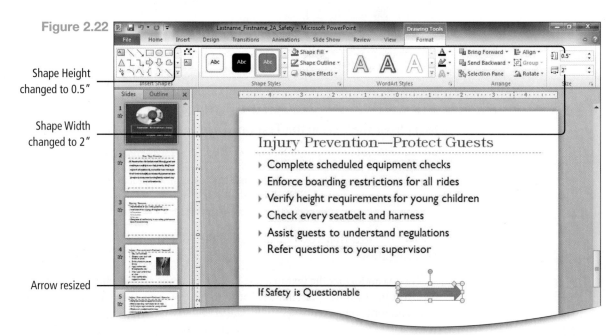

Shape Height changed to 0.5″

Shape Width changed to 2″

Arrow resized

4 On the **Format tab**, in the **Insert Shapes group**, click the **More** button ⊡. In the gallery, under **Basic Shapes**, in the first row, click the second to last shape—**Octagon**.

5 Move the ➕ pointer to position the ruler guides on the **right half of the horizontal ruler at 2.5 inches** and on the **lower half of the vertical ruler at 1 inch**, and then click one time to insert an octagon.

6 On the **Format tab**, in the **Size group**, click in the **Shape Height** box ⬚ to select the number. Type **2** and then click in the **Shape Width** box ⬚. Type **2** and then press Enter to resize the octagon. Compare your slide with Figure 2.23. Do not be concerned if your shapes are not positioned exactly as shown in the figure.

Figure 2.23

Shape Height and Width each changed to 2″

Octagon inserted and sized

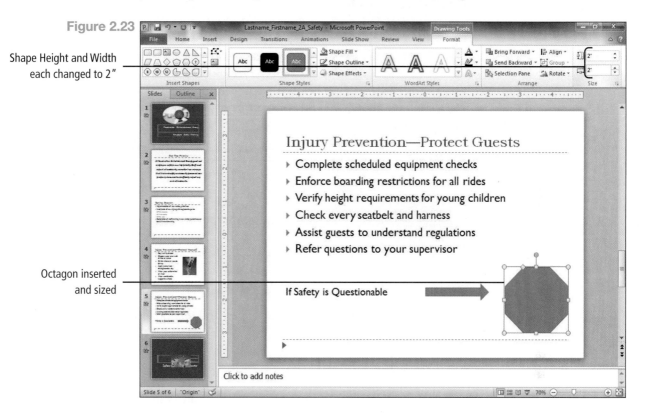

7 **Save** 🖫 your presentation.

Activity 2.10 | Adding Text to Shapes

Shapes can serve as a container for text. After you add text to a shape, you can change the font and font size, apply font styles, and change text alignment.

1 On **Slide 5**, if necessary, click the octagon so that it is selected. Type **STOP** and notice that the text is centered within the octagon.

2 Select the text *STOP*, and then on the Mini toolbar, change the **Font Size** to **32**. Compare your screen with Figure 2.24, and then **Save** 🖫 your presentation.

Figure 2.24

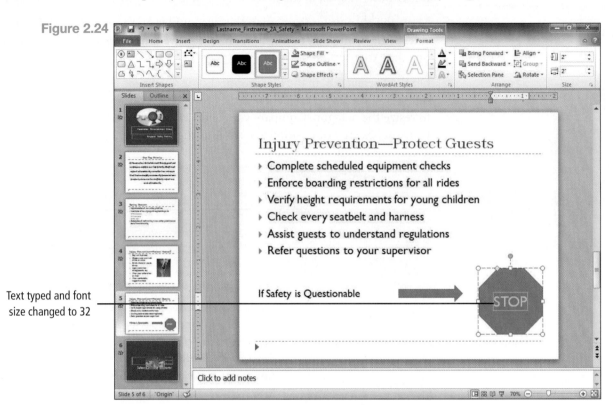

Text typed and font size changed to 32

Objective 4 | Format Objects

Apply styles and effects to clip art, shapes, and text boxes to complement slide backgrounds and colors.

Activity 2.11 | Applying Shape Fills, Outlines, and Styles

Changing the inside ***fill color*** and the outside line color is a distinctive way to format a shape. A fill color is the inside color of text or of an object. Use the Shape Styles gallery to apply predefined combinations of these fill and line colors and also to apply other effects.

1 On **Slide 5**, click anywhere in the text *If Safety is Questionable* to select the text box. On the **Format tab**, in the **Shape Styles group**, click the **More** button ⏷ to display the **Shape Styles** gallery.

2 In the last row, click the third style—**Intense Effect - Red, Accent 2**. Select the **octagon** shape, and then apply the same style you applied to the text box—**Intense Effect - Red, Accent 2**.

3 Select the **arrow**, and then display the **Shape Styles** gallery. In the last row, click the second style—**Intense Effect - Blue, Accent 1**.

4 Click in a blank part of the slide so that no objects are selected, and then compare your screen with Figure 2.25.

Figure 2.25

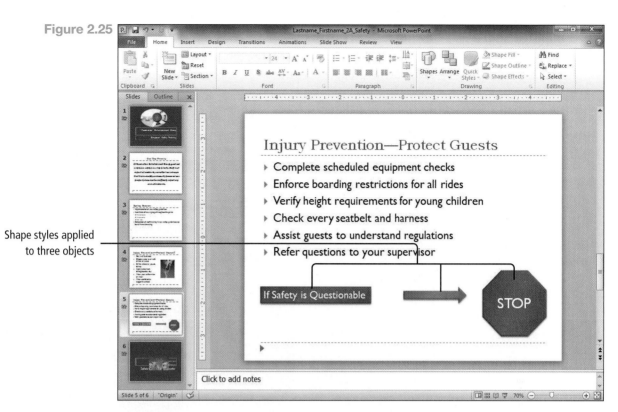

Shape styles applied to three objects

---

5 Display **Slide 2**, and then click anywhere in the paragraph of text to select the content placeholder.

6 On the **Format tab**, in the **Shape Styles group**, click the **Shape Fill** button, and then point to several of the theme colors and watch as Live Preview changes the inside color of the text box. In the fifth column, click the first color—**Blue, Accent 1**.

7 In the **Shape Styles group**, click the **Shape Outline** button. Point to **Weight**, click **3 pt**, and notice that a thick outline surrounds the text placeholder. Click in a blank area of the slide so that nothing is selected, and then compare your slide with Figure 2.26.

> You can use combinations of shape fill, outline colors, and weights to format an object.

Figure 2.26

Shape fill and 3 pt outline applied to text placeholder

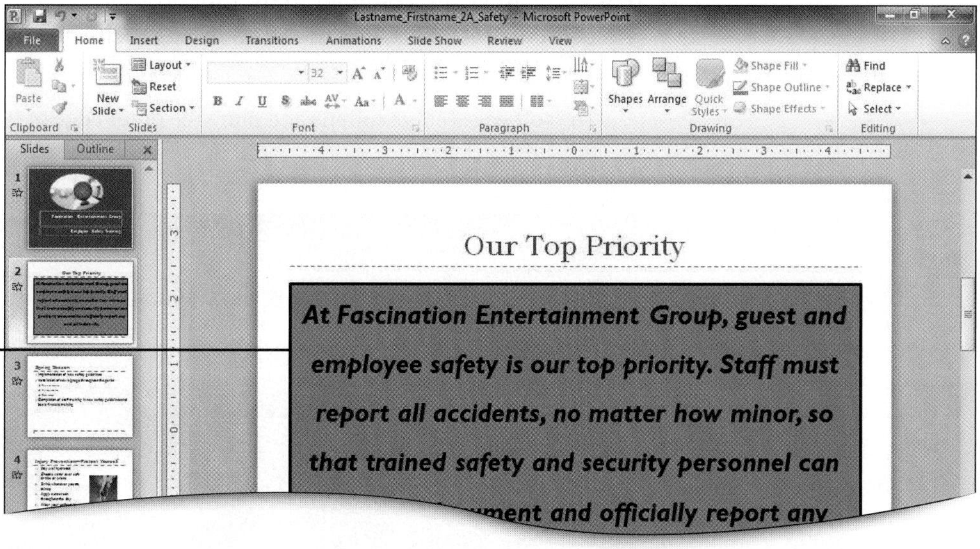

8 Click in the paragraph, and then press Ctrl + A to select all of the paragraph text, right-click in the selection to display the Mini toolbar, and then click the **Font Color button arrow** A ⋅ to display the **Theme Colors** gallery. Click the first color—**White, Background 1**. **Save** 🖫 your presentation.

Activity 2.12 | Applying Shape and Picture Effects

1 On **Slide 2**, if necessary, select the blue content placeholder. On the **Format tab**, in the **Shape Styles group**, click the **Shape Effects** button, and then compare your screen with Figure 2.27.

> A list of effects that you can apply to shapes displays. These effects can also be applied to pictures and text boxes.

Figure 2.27

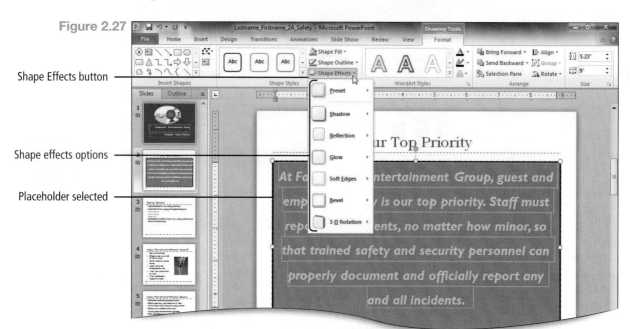

Shape Effects button

Shape effects options

Placeholder selected

2 Point to **Bevel** to display the **Bevel** gallery. Point to each bevel to view its ScreenTip and to use Live Preview to examine the effect of each bevel on the content placeholder. In the last row, click the last bevel—**Art Deco**.

3 Display **Slide 1**, and then select the picture. On the **Format tab**, in the **Picture Styles group**, click the **Picture Effects** button.

4 Point to **Soft Edges**, and then in the **Soft Edges** gallery, point to each style to view its effect on the picture. Click the last **Soft Edges** effect—**50 Point**, and then compare your screen with Figure 2.28.

> The soft edges effect softens and blurs the outer edge of the picture so that it blends into the slide background.

Figure 2.28

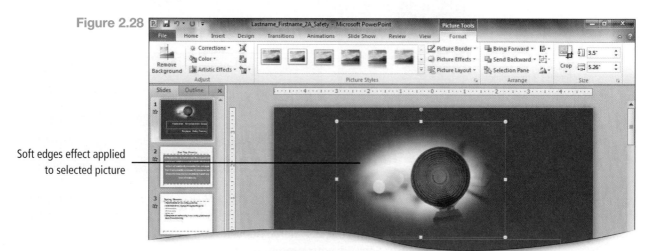

Soft edges effect applied to selected picture

5 Display **Slide 4**, and then select the picture. On the **Format tab**, in the **Picture Styles group**, click the **Picture Effects** button, and then point to **Glow**.

6 Point to several of the effects to view the effect on the picture, and then under **Glow Variations**, in the second row, click the second glow effect—**Red, 8 pt glow, Accent color 2**. Click in a blank area of the slide to deselect the picture. Compare your slide with Figure 2.29, and then **Save** [💾] your presentation.

The glow effect applies a colored, softly blurred outline to the selected object.

Figure 2.29

Glow effect applied to picture

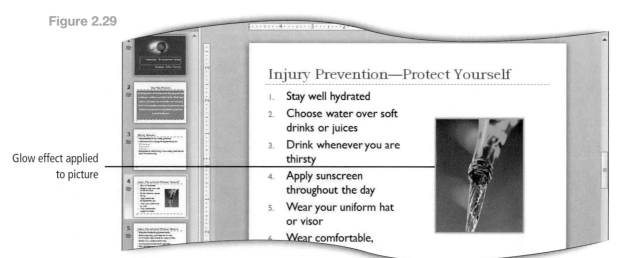

Activity 2.13 | Duplicating Objects

1 Display **Slide 6**, point to the picture to display the [🔧] pointer, and then drag up and to the left so that the upper left corner of the picture aligns with the upper left corner of the slide.

2 Press and hold down Ctrl, and then press D one time. Release Ctrl.

A duplicate of the picture overlaps the original picture and the duplicated image is selected.

3 Point to the duplicated picture to display the [🔧] pointer, and then drag down and to the right approximately 1 inch in both directions so that both pictures are visible. Compare your screen with Figure 2.30. Do not be concerned if your pictures are not positioned exactly as shown in the figure.

Figure 2.30

Original picture moved to upper left corner of slide

Duplicated picture moved so that both pictures are visible

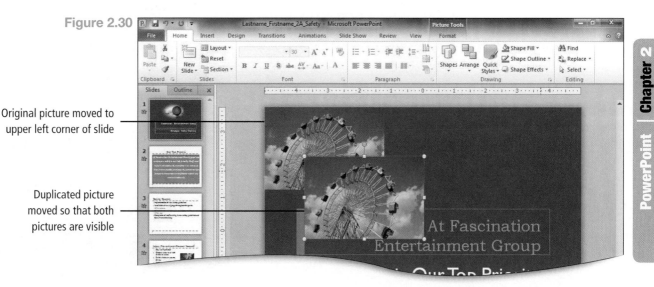

4 With the duplicated image selected, hold down Ctrl, and then press D to insert a third copy of the image.

5 Click anywhere on the slide so that none of the three pictures are selected. **Save** 🖫 your presentation, and then compare your screen with Figure 2.31. Do not be concerned if your pictures are not positioned exactly as shown.

Figure 2.31

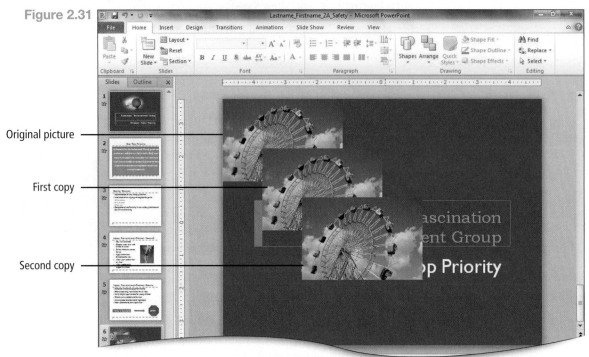

Original picture
First copy
Second copy

Activity 2.14 | Aligning and Distributing Objects

When you insert multiple objects on a slide, you can use commands on the Ribbon to align and distribute the objects precisely.

Another Way
Hold down Shift and click each object that you want to select.

1 With **Slide 6** displayed, position the pointer in the gray area of the Slide pane just outside the upper left corner of the slide to display the ⬉ pointer. Drag down and to the right to draw a transparent blue rectangle that encloses the three pictures. Compare your slide with Figure 2.32.

Figure 2.32

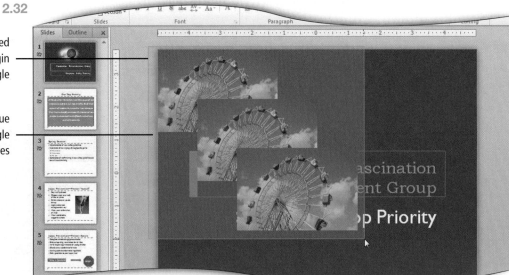

Pointer initially positioned outside of slide to begin selection rectangle

Transparent, blue selection rectangle encloses three pictures

2 Release the mouse button to select the three objects, and then compare your screen with Figure 2.33.

Objects completely enclosed by a selection rectangle are selected when the mouse button is released.

Figure 2.33

Three pictures selected

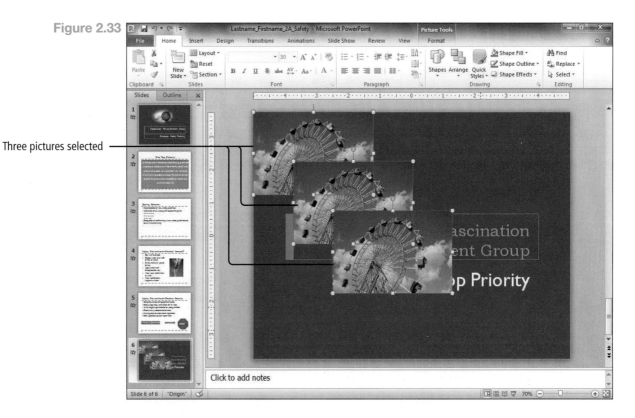

3 Click the **Format tab**, and then in the **Arrange group**, click the **Align** button. Toward the bottom of the menu, click **Align to Slide** to activate this setting.

When you select an alignment option, this setting will cause the objects to align with the edges of the slide.

4 On the **Format tab**, in the **Arrange group**, click the **Align** button again, and then click **Align Top**.

The top of each of the three pictures aligns with the top edge of the slide.

5 Click in a blank area of the slide so that nothing is selected. Then, click the third picture. Point to the picture so that the pointer displays, and then drag to the right so that its upper right corner aligns with the upper right corner of the slide.

6 Hold down Shift and click the remaining two pictures so that all three pictures are selected. On the **Format tab**, in the **Arrange group**, click the **Align** button. Click **Align Selected Objects** to activate this setting.

When you select an alignment option, this setting will cause the objects that you select to align relative to each other.

7 With the three pictures still selected, on the **Format tab**, in the **Arrange group**, click the **Align** button again, and then click **Distribute Horizontally**. Compare your screen with Figure 2.34.

> The three pictures are spaced and distributed evenly across the top of the slide and aligned with the top edge of the slide.

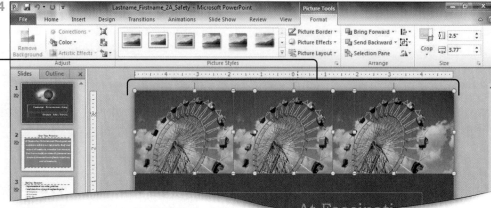

8 With the three pictures selected, on the **Format tab**, in the **Picture Styles group**, click the **Picture Effects** button. Point to **Soft Edges**, and then click **50 Point** to apply the picture effect to all three images.

9 Display **Slide 5**, hold down Shift, and then at the bottom of the slide, click the **text box**, the **arrow**, and the **octagon** to select all three objects.

10 With the three objects selected, on the **Format tab**, in the **Arrange group**, click the **Align** button. Be sure that **Align Selected Objects** is still active—a check mark displays to its left. Then, click **Align Middle**. Click the **Align** button again, and then click **Distribute Horizontally**.

> The midpoint of each object aligns and the three objects are distributed evenly.

11 Click anywhere on the slide so that none of the objects are selected, and then compare your screen with Figure 2.35.

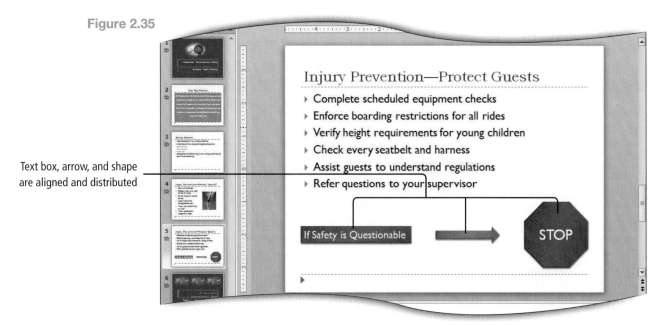

12 On the **Slide Show tab**, in the **Start Slide Show group**, click the **From Beginning** button, and then view the slide show. Press Esc when the black slide displays.

13 On the **Insert tab**, in the **Text group**, click the **Header & Footer** button to display the **Header and Footer** dialog box. Click the **Notes and Handouts tab**. Under **Include on page**, select the **Date and time** check box, and then select **Update automatically**. If necessary, clear the Header check box. Select the **Page number** and **Footer** check boxes. In the **Footer** box, using your own name, type **Lastname_Firstname_2A_Safety** and then click **Apply to All**.

14 Display the **Document Properties**. Replace the text in the **Author** box with your own firstname and lastname, in the **Subject** box, type your course name and section number, and in the **Keywords** box, type **safety, injury prevention Close** the **Document Information Panel**.

15 **Save** your presentation 🖫. Print **Handouts 6 Slides Horizontal**, or submit your presentation electronically as directed by your instructor.

16 **Close** the presentation and exit PowerPoint.

End **You have completed Project 2A** ———————————————

GO! Beyond Office

Objective | Share a Presentation with Others on SkyDrive

Recall that Windows Live SkyDrive is a free file storage and file sharing service provided by Windows Live. Files that you store on your SkyDrive can be shared with other users. When you share a presentation with another Windows Live user, that person can edit the file using the PowerPoint Web App if PowerPoint 2010 is not available. When you share the presentation with a user that does not have a Windows Live account, the presentation can be viewed but it cannot be edited.

> **Alert! | Working with Web-Based Applications and Services**
>
> Computer programs and services on the Web receive continuous updates and improvements. Thus, the steps to complete this Web-based Activity may differ from the ones shown. You can often look at the screens and the information presented to determine how to complete the Activity.

Activity | Sharing a Presentation with Others on SkyDrive

In this Activity, you will save a presentation on your SkyDrive and you will make the file available to another user. You will log in as another user and edit the file in the PowerPoint Web App.

1 If you have a yahoo.com e-mail account or created one in GO! Beyond PowerPoint 1B, skip to Step 2. Otherwise, start your Web browser. In the address bar, type **www.yahoo.com** and then on the left side of the Yahoo! window, click Mail. At the bottom of the Sign in to Yahoo box, click Create New Account and then follow the steps to create a Yahoo! ID. Close your Web browser.

2 Launch your Web browser, navigate to **www.live.com** and then log in to your **Windows Live account**. If you do not have a Windows Live account, refer to Go! Beyond Office Word Project 1A to create the account.

3 At the top of the window, click **SkyDrive**, and then click your **GO! Beyond Office-PowerPoint** folder. If the folder does not exist, at the top of the window, to the right of Create, click the Create folder button ⬇, and then in the Name box, type **GO! Beyond Office-PowerPoint** and then click Next. Click Continue to display the GO! Beyond Office-PowerPoint folder.

Recall that you can share files on your SkyDrive with others. You will save your PowerPoint file for this activity in this folder.

4 Near the top of the window, click **Add files**, and then click **select documents from your computer**. Navigate to the location where you are storing your files, open your **PowerPoint Chapter 2** folder, and then click your **Lastname_Firstname_2A_Safety** file. Click

Open. A progress bar displays as the file uploads to your SkyDrive.

5 Click the **Continue** button to return to your **GO! Beyond Office-PowerPoint** folder.

Your Lastname_Firstname_2A_Safety file displays along with any other files that you have saved in the folder.

6 Point to your **Lastname_Firstname_2A_Safety** file, and notice that to the right of the **Last modified by** column, the **Show information** button ⓘ displays. Click the **Show information** button ⓘ so that on the right, under **Sharing**, the **Send a link** text displays. If **Send a link** does not display, click the **Show information** button ⓘ again. Click **Send a link**.

On the displayed Send a link page, you can enter e-mail addresses for those contacts with whom you'd like to share the folder.

7 In the **To** box, type your complete **Yahoo! e-mail address** for example, Firstname_Lastname@yahoo.com. Verify that the **Require recipients to sign in with Windows Live ID** check box is *cleared*.

When the *Require recipients to sign in with Windows Live ID* check box is cleared, a contact who does *not* have a Windows Live ID can view the files stored on your SkyDrive. When the check box is selected, only contacts with a Windows Live ID may view the SkyDrive files.

8 Click the **Send** button to send the link to your Yahoo! e-mail account, and then sign out of your Windows Live account.

9 Open a new tab in your browser, go to **www.yahoo.com** and log in to your **Yahoo! e-mail** account, and then open your **Inbox**. Click the message from your Windows Live account with the subject that indicates that a document has been shared with you. If the message does not display, you may need to wait a few moments or check your Spam folder.

The message indicates that the folder GO! Beyond Office-PowerPoint has been shared with you on Windows Live, and a View folder button displays so that you can access the folder from this message.

10 If the text *This message contains blocked images* displays, click the Show Images button. Display the **Start** menu 🪟, and then click **All Programs**. On the list of programs, click the **Accessories** folder, and then click **Snipping Tool**. In the **Snipping Tool** dialog box, click the **New arrow**. On the displayed list, click **Full-screen Snip**, and then click the **Save Snip** button 🖫. In the **Save As** dialog box, navigate to and open your **PowerPoint Chapter 2** folder. Be sure the **Save as type** box displays *JPEG file*. In the **File name** box, type **Lastname_Firstname_2A_ Notification_Snip** and then click **Save**. **Close** ❎ the **Snipping Tool** window to return to your Inbox.

11 In the message, click the **View folder** button to display the *GO! Beyond Office-PowerPoint* folder on the Windows Live SkyDrive in a new window. Point to your **Lastname_Firstname_2A_Safety** file to display the 👆 pointer, and then click the file name to display the presentation in Reading view in a new window. Compare your screen with Figure A.

Although the file exists on the SkyDrive that is linked to your Windows Live account, you can view the file from your Yahoo! e-mail account because you were sent a link from Windows Live. You cannot edit the file in the PowerPoint Web App unless you are logged in with a Windows Live account.

12 Above the displayed slide, click **Start Slide Show** to display the full-screen slide show in your browser window.

13 Start the **Snipping Tool**, and then create a **Full-screen Snip**. On the **Snipping Tool** markup window toolbar, click the **Save Snip** button 🖫. In the **Save As** dialog box, navigate to your **PowerPoint Chapter 2** folder. Be sure the **Save as type** box displays **JPEG file**. In the **File name** box, type **Lastname_Firstname_2A_ Safety_SkyDrive_Snip** and then click **Save**.

14 **Close** the slide show window, sign out of all accounts, **Close** all open windows, and then submit your two snip files as directed.

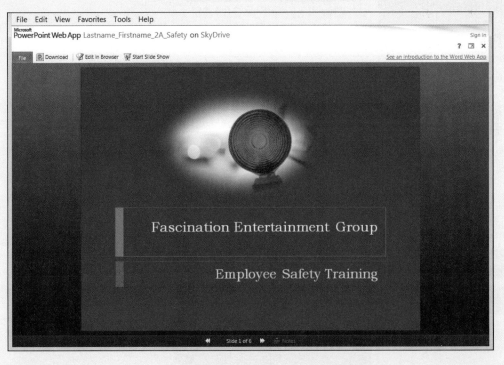

Figure A

Project 2B Event Announcement

myitlab
Project 2B Training

Project Activities

In Activities 2.15 through 2.24, you will format slides in a presentation for the Fascination Entertainment Group Marketing Director that informs employees about upcoming events at the company's amusement parks. You will enhance the presentation using SmartArt and WordArt graphics. Your completed presentation will look similar to Figure 2.36.

Project Files

For Project 2B, you will need the following files:

> p02B_Celebrations
> p02B_Canada_Contact
> p02B_Mexico_Contact
> p02B_US_Contact

You will save your presentation as:

> Lastname_Firstname_2B_Celebrations

Project Results

Figure 2.36
Project 2B Celebrations

Objective 5 | Remove Picture Backgrounds and Insert WordArt

To avoid the boxy look that results when you insert an image into a presentation, use **Background Removal** to flow a picture into the content of the presentation. Background Removal removes unwanted portions of a picture so that the picture does not appear as a self-contained rectangle.

WordArt is a gallery of text styles with which you can create decorative effects, such as shadowed or mirrored text. You can choose from the gallery of WordArt styles to insert a new WordArt object or you can customize existing text by applying WordArt formatting.

Activity 2.15 | Removing the Background from a Picture and Applying Soft Edge Options

1 **Start** PowerPoint. From your student files, open **p02B_Celebrations**. On the **View tab**, in the **Show group**, if necessary, select the Ruler check box. In your **PowerPoint Chapter 2** folder, save the file as **Lastname_Firstname_2B_Celebrations**

2 Display **Slide 6**. Notice how the picture is a self-contained rectangle and that it has a much darker black background than the presentation. Click the picture to select it, and then on the **Format tab**, in the **Adjust group**, click the **Remove Background** button. Compare your screen with Figure 2.37.

PowerPoint determines what portion of the picture is the foreground—the portion to keep—and which portion is the background—the portion to remove. The background is overlaid in magenta, leaving the remaining portion of the picture as it will look when the background removal is complete. A rectangular selection area displays that can be moved and sized to select additional areas of the picture. The Background Removal options display in the Refine group on the Ribbon.

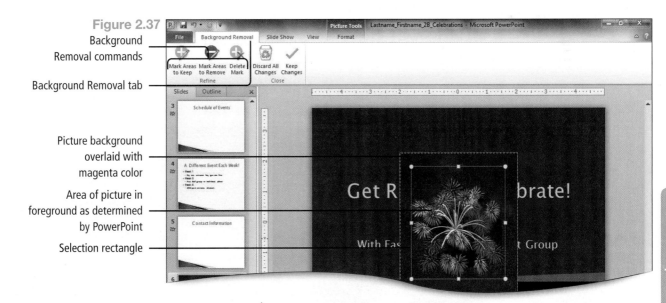

Figure 2.37

Background Removal commands

Background Removal tab

Picture background overlaid with magenta color

Area of picture in foreground as determined by PowerPoint

Selection rectangle

PowerPoint | Chapter 2

3 On the **selection rectangle**, point to the left center sizing handle to display the ⟷ pointer, and then drag to the left so that the left edge of the selection area aligns with the dashed border surrounding the picture. Compare your screen with Figure 2.38.

> When you move or size the selection area, the areas outside the selection are treated as background and are removed. Thus, you have control over which portions of the picture that you keep. Here, by resizing the selection area on the left, a larger area of each *flower* in the fireworks is included in the foreground of the picture. On the right side of the fireworks picture, some dark red shadowing is visible as part of the picture.

Figure 2.38

Additional portion of fireworks display as foreground

Selection rectangle aligns with dashed border

Another Way

In the status bar, use the Zoom Slider options to increase the Zoom to 100%.

4 On the **View tab**, in the **Zoom group**, click the **Zoom** button. In the **Zoom** dialog box, select **100%**, and then click **OK** to increase the size of the slide in the Slide pane. Notice on the right side of the fireworks picture the dark red shadowing in a triangular shape that is visible between some of the outer flowers of the fireworks display. Compare your slide with Figure 2.39.

Figure 2.39

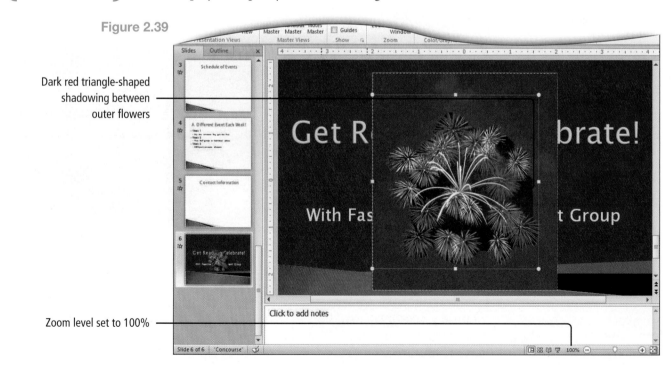

Dark red triangle-shaped shadowing between outer flowers

Zoom level set to 100%

5 On the **Background Removal tab**, in the **Refine group**, click the **Mark Areas to Remove** button, and then position the pencil pointer so that the ruler guides align on the **right half of the horizontal ruler at 1 inch** and on the **lower half of the vertical ruler at 0.5 inch**. Click one time to insert a deletion mark, and then compare your screen with Figure 2.40. If your mark is not positioned as shown in the figure, click Undo and begin again.

> You can surround irregular-shaped areas that you want to remove with deletion marks. Here, you can begin to surround the dark red shadow by placing a deletion mark in one corner of the red triangular area.

Figure 2.40

Mark Areas to Remove button

Deletion mark

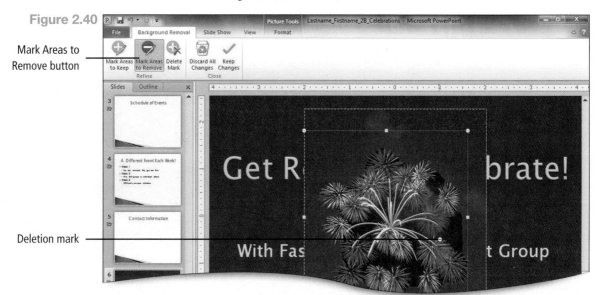

6 With the pencil pointer still active, position the pointer to align the ruler guides on the **right half of the horizontal ruler at approximately 1.5 inches** and on the **lower half of the vertical ruler to 0.75 inch** so that the pointer is aligned on the right edge of the dark red triangle. Click one time to insert another mark. Compare your screen with Figure 2.41.

> The two inserted marks provide PowerPoint sufficient information to remove the triangular-shaped red and black shadowed area. If the area is not removed as shown in the figure, insert additional deletion marks as necessary.

Figure 2.41

Background area removed from picture

Additional deletion mark inserted

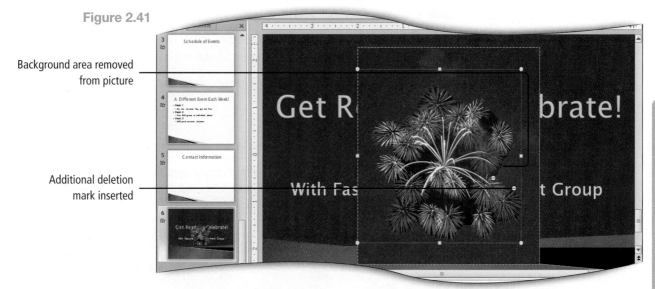

7 On the **Background Removal tab**, in the **Close group**, click the **Keep Changes** button to remove the background. On the far right edge of the status bar, click the **Fit slide to current window** button 🔲.

8 With the picture selected, on the **Format tab**, in the **Picture Styles group**, click the **Picture Effects** button, point to **Soft Edges**, and then click **50 Point**. In the **Adjust group**, click the **Artistic Effects** button, and then in the fourth row, click the third effect—**Crisscross Etching**.

9 In the **Size group**, click in the **Shape Height** box ⬚, replace the number with **3.5** and then press ⏎. In the **Arrange group**, click the **Align** button ⬚, and then click **Align Center**. Click the **Align** button ⬚ again, and then click **Align Middle**. Compare your slide with Figure 2.42, and then **Save** ⬚ your presentation.

Figure 2.42

Picture sized, moved, and formatted

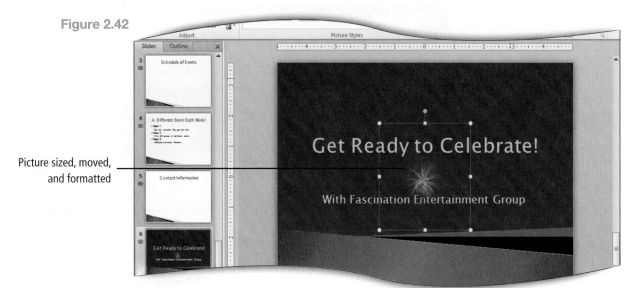

Activity 2.16 | Applying WordArt Styles to Existing Text

1 On **Slide 6**, click anywhere in the word *Get* to activate the title placeholder, and then select the title—*Get Ready to Celebrate*. Click the **Format tab**, and then in the **WordArt Styles group**, click the **More** button ⬚.

The WordArt Styles gallery displays in two sections. If you choose a WordArt style in the Applies to Selected Text section, you must first select all of the text to which you want to apply the WordArt. If you choose a WordArt style in the Applies to All Text in the Shape section, the WordArt style is applied to all of the text in the placeholder or shape.

2 Under **Applies to Selected Text**, in the first row, click the fourth style—**Fill – White, Outline – Accent 1**, and then compare your screen with Figure 2.43.

Figure 2.43

WordArt style is applied to selected text

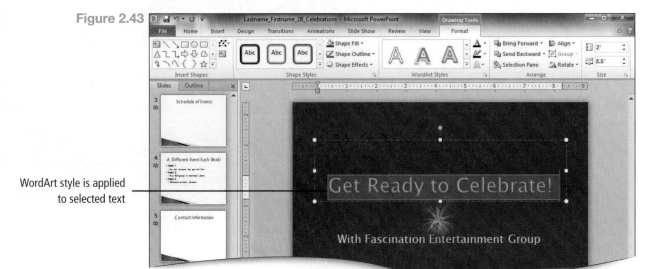

3 With the text still selected, in the **WordArt Styles group**, click the **Text Fill button arrow** ![A]. Under **Theme Colors**, in the sixth column, click the fourth color—**Dark Red, Accent 2, Lighter 40%**, and then compare your screen with Figure 2.44.

Figure 2.44

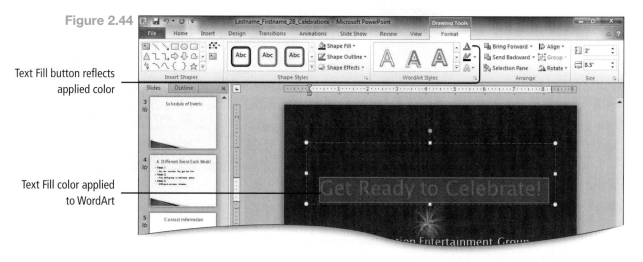

Text Fill button reflects applied color

Text Fill color applied to WordArt

4 Display **Slide 1**, and then click anywhere in the title—*Fascination Entertainment Group*.

5 Click the **Format tab**, and then in the **WordArt Styles group**, click the **More** button ![down] to display the **WordArt Styles** gallery. Under **Applies to All Text in the Shape**, in the first row, click the third style—**Fill – Dark Red, Accent 2, Warm Matte Bevel**, and then compare your screen with Figure 2.45.

Figure 2.45

WordArt style applied to title

6 Save ![save] your presentation.

Activity 2.17 | Inserting a WordArt Object

In addition to formatting existing text using WordArt, you can insert a new WordArt object anywhere on a slide.

1 Display **Slide 2**. Click the **Insert tab**, and then in the **Text group**, click the **WordArt** button. In the gallery, in the last row, click the third WordArt style—**Fill – Dark Red, Accent 2, Matte Bevel**.

> In the center of your slide, a WordArt placeholder displays *Your text here*. Text that you type will replace this text and the placeholder will expand to accommodate the text. The WordArt is surrounded by sizing handles with which you can adjust its size.

2 Type **Get Ready for 2014!** to replace the WordArt placeholder text. Compare your screen with Figure 2.46.

Figure 2.46

WordArt inserted in the center of slide

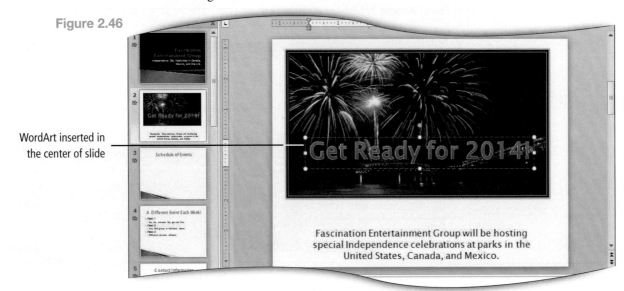

3 Point to the WordArt border to display the � pointer. Hold down Shift, and then drag down to position the WordArt between the picture and the text at the bottom of the slide and centered between the left and right edge of the slide. Use Ctrl + any of the arrow keys to move the WordArt in small increments. Compare your slide with Figure 2.47 and move the WordArt again if necessary.

Recall that holding down Shift when dragging an object constrains the horizontal and vertical movement so that the object is moved in a straight line.

Figure 2.47

WordArt dragged to new location

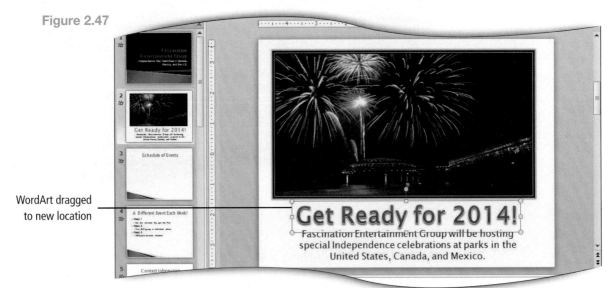

4 **Save** 🖫 your presentation.

Objective 6 | Create and Format a SmartArt Graphic

A **SmartArt graphic** is a visual representation of information that you create by choosing from among various layouts to communicate your message or ideas effectively. SmartArt graphics can illustrate processes, hierarchies, cycles, lists, and relationships. You can include text and pictures in a SmartArt graphic, and you can apply colors, effects, and styles that coordinate with the presentation theme.

Activity 2.18 | Creating a SmartArt Graphic from Bulleted Points

You can convert an existing bulleted list into a SmartArt graphic. When you create a SmartArt graphic, consider the message that you are trying to convey, and then choose an appropriate layout. The table in Figure 2.48 describes types of SmartArt layouts and suggested purposes.

Microsoft PowerPoint SmartArt Graphic Types	
Graphic Type	**Purpose of Graphic**
List	Shows non-sequential information
Process	Shows steps in a process or timeline
Cycle	Shows a continual process
Hierarchy	Shows a decision tree or displays an organization chart
Relationship	Illustrates connections
Matrix	Shows how parts relate to a whole
Pyramid	Shows proportional relationships with the largest component on the top or bottom
Picture	Includes pictures in the layout to communicate messages and ideas

Figure 2.48

Another Way

Right-click on a bulleted list to display the shortcut menu, and then click **Convert to SmartArt**.

---→ **1** Display **Slide 4**, and then click anywhere in the bulleted list placeholder. On the **Home tab**, in the **Paragraph group**, click the **Convert to SmartArt** button. Below the gallery, click **More SmartArt Graphics**.

Three sections comprise the Choose a SmartArt Graphic dialog box. The left section lists the SmartArt graphic types. The center section displays the SmartArt graphics according to type. The third section displays the selected SmartArt graphic, its name, and a description of its purpose.

2 On the left side of the **Choose a SmartArt Graphic** dialog box, click **List**. Use the ScreenTips to locate and then click **Vertical Bullet List**. Compare your screen with Figure 2.49.

Figure 2.49

Vertical Bullet List selected

List type selected

SmartArt graphic types

Gallery of SmartArt graphics within each type

Preview, name, and description of selected SmartArt graphic—Vertical Bullet List—displays

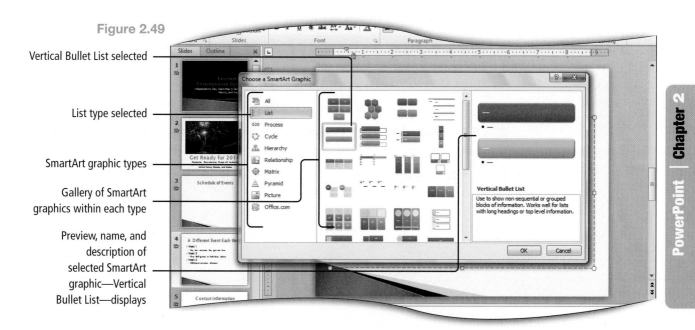

PowerPoint | Chapter 2

3 In the **Choose a SmartArt Graphic** dialog box, click **OK**. If the Text Pane displays to the right of the SmartArt graphic, click its Close button ⊠. Compare your screen with Figure 2.50, and then **Save** 🖫 your presentation.

It is not necessary to select all of the text in the list. By clicking in the list, PowerPoint converts all of the bullet points to the selected SmartArt graphic. On the Ribbon, the SmartArt contextual tools display two tabs—Design and Format. The thick border surrounding the SmartArt graphic indicates that it is selected and displays the area that the object will cover on the slide.

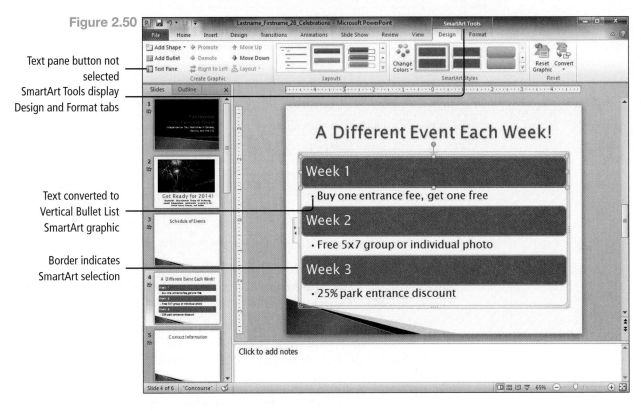

Figure 2.50

Text pane button not selected
SmartArt Tools display Design and Format tabs

Text converted to Vertical Bullet List SmartArt graphic

Border indicates SmartArt selection

Activity 2.19 | Adding Shapes in a SmartArt Graphic

If a SmartArt graphic does not have enough shapes to illustrate a concept or display the relationships, you can add more shapes.

Another Way
Right-click the shape, point to **Add Shape**, and then click **Add Shape After**.

- - → **1** Click in the shape that contains the text *Week 3*. In the **SmartArt Tools**, click the **Design tab**. In the **Create Graphic group**, click the **Add Shape arrow**, and then click **Add Shape After** to insert a shape at the same level. Type **Week 4**

The text in each of the SmartArt shapes resizes to accommodate the added shape.

2 On the **Design tab**, in the **Create Graphic group**, click the **Add Bullet** button to add a bullet below the *Week 4* shape.

3 Type **25% discount on food and beverages** Compare your slide with Figure 2.51, and then **Save** 🖫 your presentation.

Figure 2.51

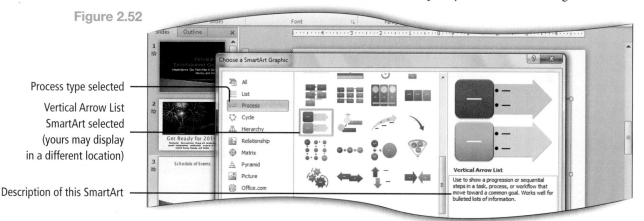

Shape added and text typed

Bullet added and text typed

Activity 2.20 | Creating a SmartArt Graphic Using a Content Layout

1 Display **Slide 3**. In the center of the content placeholder, click the **Insert SmartArt Graphic** button to open the **Choose a SmartArt Graphic** dialog box.

2 On the left, click **Process**, and then scroll as necessary and use the ScreenTips to locate **Vertical Arrow List**. Click **Vertical Arrow List**. Compare your screen with Figure 2.52.

Figure 2.52

Process type selected

Vertical Arrow List SmartArt selected (yours may display in a different location)

Description of this SmartArt

3 Click **OK** to insert the SmartArt graphic.

The SmartArt graphic displays with two rounded rectangle shapes and two arrow shapes. You can type text directly into the shapes or you can type text in the Text Pane, which may display to the left of your SmartArt graphic. You can display the Text Pane by clicking the Text Pane tab on the left side of the SmartArt graphic border, or by clicking the Text Pane button in the Create Graphic group. Depending on your software settings, the Text Pane may display.

4 In the SmartArt graphic, click in the first orange rectangle, and then type **Canada** In the arrow shape to the immediate right, click in the first bullet point. Type **July 2014** and then press Del to remove the second bullet point in the arrow shape.

5 Click in the second orange rectangle, and then type **U.S.** In the arrow shape to the immediate right, click in the first bullet point. Type **July 2014** and then press Del. Compare your slide with Figure 2.53.

Figure 2.53

Text Pane button not selected

Text typed in SmartArt Graphic

6   Click in the *U.S.* rectangle. On the **Design tab**, in the **Create Graphic group**, click the **Add Shape arrow**. Click **Add Shape After** to insert a new rectangle and arrow. Type **Mexico** and then in the arrow shape to the right, type **September 2014**

7   Display **Slide 5**. In the center of the content placeholder, click the **Insert SmartArt Graphic** button [icon]. In the **Choose a SmartArt Graphic** dialog box, click **Picture**, and then scroll as necessary to locate **Vertical Picture Accent List**. Click **Vertical Picture Accent List**, and then click **OK** to insert the graphic.

8   In the SmartArt graphic, in the top rectangle shape, type **Rachel Lewis** and then press Enter. Type **United States** and then click in the middle rectangle shape. Type **Javier Perez** and then press Enter. Type **Mexico** and then click in the last rectangle shape, type **Annette Johnson** and then press Enter. Type **Canada**

9   In the top circle shape, click the **Insert Picture from File** button [icon]. Navigate to your student files, click **p02B_US_Contact**, and then press Enter to insert the picture. Using the technique you just practiced, in the middle circle shape, insert **p02B_Mexico_Contact**. In the last circle shape, insert **p02B_Canada_Contact**. Compare your screen with Figure 2.54, and then **Save** [icon] your presentation.

Figure 2.54

Vertical Picture Accent List SmartArt graphic inserted

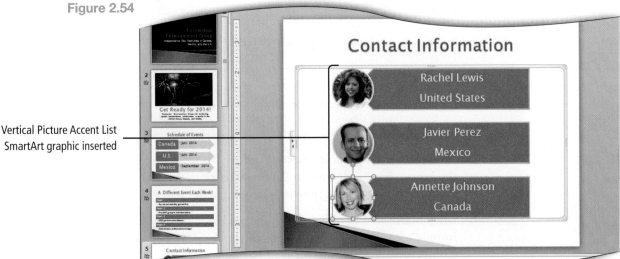

Activity 2.21 | Changing the SmartArt Layout

1 Display **Slide 3**, and then click anywhere in the SmartArt graphic. In the **SmartArt Tools**, click the **Design tab**. In the **Layouts group**, click the **More** button ⊽, and then click **More Layouts**. In the **Choose a SmartArt Graphic** dialog box, click **Hierarchy**. Locate and click **Hierarchy List**, and then click **OK**.

2 Compare your slide with Figure 2.55, and then **Save** 🖫 the presentation.

Figure 2.55

Hierarchy List
layout applied

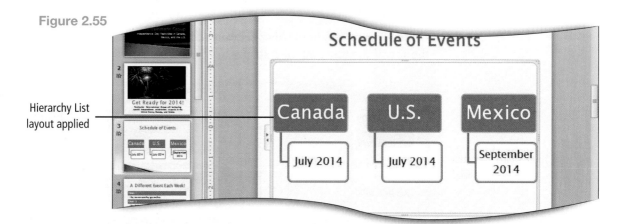

Activity 2.22 | Changing the Color and Style of a SmartArt Graphic

SmartArt Styles are combinations of formatting effects that you can apply to SmartArt graphics.

1 With **Slide 3** displayed and the SmartArt graphic selected, on the **Design tab**, in the **SmartArt Styles group**, click the **Change Colors** button. In the color gallery, under **Colorful**, click the first style—**Colorful - Accent Colors**—to change the color.

2 On the **Design tab**, in the **SmartArt Styles group**, click the **More** button ⊽ to display the **SmartArt Styles gallery**. Under **3-D**, click the second style, **Inset**. Compare your slide with Figure 2.56.

Figure 2.56

Color changed and style
applied to SmartArt

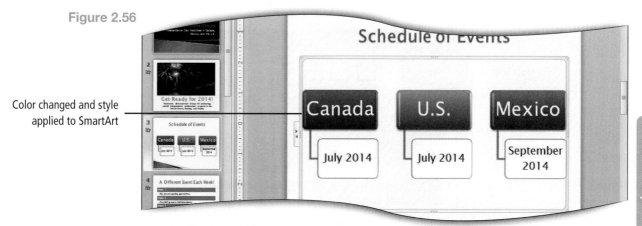

3 Display **Slide 5**, and select the SmartArt. On the **Design tab**, in the **SmartArt Styles group**, click the **Change Colors** button. Under **Accent 2**, click the second style—**Colored Fill - Accent 2**. On the **Design tab**, in the **SmartArt Styles group**, click the **More** button ⊽. Under **Best Match for Document**, click the last style, **Intense Effect**. **Save** 🖫 the presentation.

Activity 2.23 | Customizing the Size and Shape of a SmartArt Graphic

You can select individual or groups of shapes in a SmartArt graphic and make them larger or smaller, and you can change selected shapes to another type of shape.

1 With **Slide 5** displayed, click in the upper red shape that contains the text *Rachel Lewis*. Hold down Shift, and then click in each of the two remaining red shapes containing the text *Javier Perez* and *Annette Johnson* so that all three text shapes are selected.

2 On the **Format tab**, in the **Shapes group**, click the **Larger** button two times to increase the size of the three selected shapes. Compare your screen with Figure 2.57.

Figure 2.57

Three shapes selected and resized

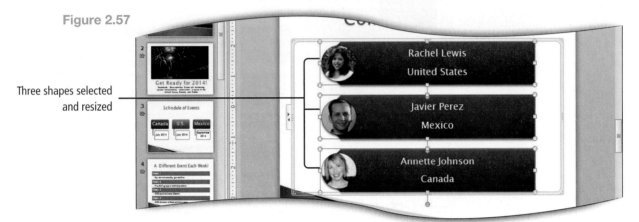

3 With the three shapes selected, on the **Home tab**, in the **Font group**, increase the **Font Size** to **28**.

4 Select the first circle picture, and then hold down Shift and click the remaining two circles so that all three circles are selected. In the **SmartArt Tools**, on the **Format tab**, in the **Shapes group**, click the **Change Shape** button. Under **Rectangles**, click the first shape—**Rectangle**—to change the circles to rectangles. With the three shapes selected, in the **Shapes group**, click the **Larger** button two times. Compare your screen with Figure 2.58, and then **Save** the presentation.

Figure 2.58

Larger button

Change Shape button

Three shapes changed to rectangles and resized

Activity 2.24 | Converting a SmartArt to Text

1 Display **Slide 4**, and then click anywhere in the SmartArt graphic. On the **Design tab**, in the **Reset group**, click the **Convert** button, and then click **Convert to Text** to convert the SmartArt graphic to a bulleted list. Compare your screen with Figure 2.59.

Figure 2.59

SmartArt graphic converted to text

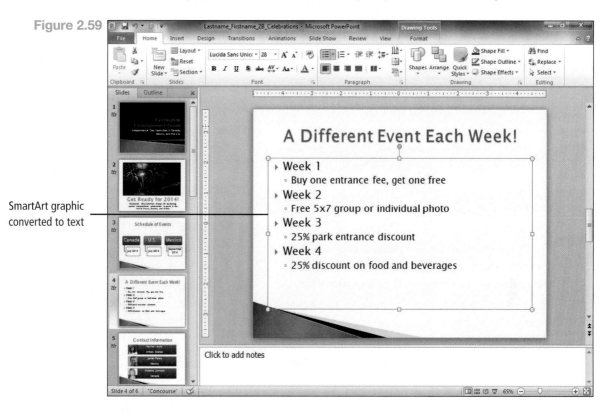

2 Display the **Document Properties**. Replace the text in the **Author** box with your own firstname and lastname, in the **Subject** box, type your course name and section number, and in the **Keywords** box, type **Independence day, celebrations Close** the **Document Information Panel**.

3 Insert a **Header & Footer** on the **Notes and Handouts**. Include the **Date and time updated automatically**, the **Page number**, and a **Footer** with the text **Lastname_Firstname_2B_Celebrations** Apply to all the slides. View the presentation from the beginning, and then make any necessary adjustments.

4 **Save** 🖫 your presentation. Print **Handouts 6 Slides Horizontal**, or submit your presentation electronically as directed by your instructor.

5 **Close** the presentation.

End **You have completed Project 2B**

PowerPoint | Chapter 2

GO! Beyond Office

Objective | Save Your Presentation Slides as Pictures and Create a Movie Using Windows Live Movie Maker

Windows Live Movie Maker is a Windows Live Essentials program used to make your photos and videos into movies. You can add special effects, transitions, sounds, and captions, and you can share your movies online.

> **Alert!** | **Working with Web-Based Applications and Services**
>
> Computer programs and services on the Web receive continuous updates and improvements. Thus, the steps to complete this Web-based Activity may differ from the ones shown. You can often look at the screens and the information presented to determine how to complete the Activity.

Activity | Saving Presentation Slides as Pictures and Creating a Movie Using Windows Live Movie Maker

In this Activity, you will save all the slides in a presentation as pictures in the JPEG file format. Then, you will create a video from the slides using Windows Live Movie Maker.

1 **Start** PowerPoint. On the **File tab**, click **Open**, navigate to your **PowerPoint Chapter 2** folder, and then open your **Lastname_Firstname_2B_Celebrations** file.

2 Click the **File tab**, and then click **Save As**. Click the **Save as type arrow** to display a list of file types. Click **JPEG File Interchange Format**, and then click **Save**.

3 In the displayed message box, click the **Every Slide** button to save every slide in the presentation as a picture with the .jpg extension. In the **Microsoft PowerPoint** message box, click **OK**, and then **Exit** PowerPoint.

Within your PowerPoint Chapter 2 folder, PowerPoint creates a folder with the same name as the file name. In the new folder, each slide is saved as a picture with the file names Slide1, Slide2, Slide3, and so on.

4 From the **Start** menu , click **All Programs**, and then click **Windows Live Movie Maker**.

On the left, the ***Preview monitor*** displays. When you add videos and photos, the Preview monitor displays the movie. On the right, the pictures and videos that you add to your movie display in the ***storyboard***.

5 At the right side of the Windows Live Movie Maker window, click the text *Click here to browse for videos and photos*. In the **Add Videos and Photos** dialog box, navigate to your **PowerPoint Chapter 2 folder**, and then **Open** your **Lastname_Firstname_2B_Celebrations** folder.

Six files display—one for each of the six slides in your PowerPoint presentation file.

6 In the **Add Videos and Photos** dialog box, press Ctrl + A to select all six pictures, and then click **Open** to import the pictures into Windows Live Movie Maker and display them in the storyboard. Compare your screen with Figure A.

The six imported slides display in the storyboard, and the first picture in the movie displays in the Preview monitor.

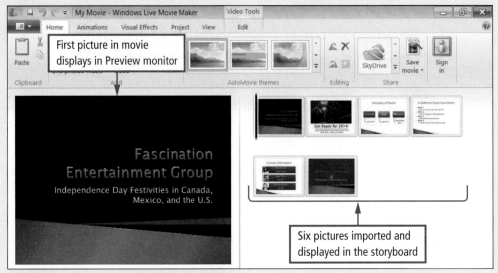

Figure A

GO! Beyond Office

7 Under the **Preview monitor**, click the **Play** button ▶ to view the movie. Notice that each picture displays for seven seconds and that in the storyboard, a black bar—the *playback indicator*—moves across the slides indicating the progress of the movie.

The numbers that display below the Preview monitor indicate the time that has elapsed while the movie is playing followed by the overall length of the movie—in this case, 42 seconds.

8 On the **Home tab**, in the **AutoMovie themes group**, click the **More** button ▽, and then click the second theme—**Contemporary**. In the **Windows Live Movie Maker** message box, click **No** because you will not be adding music to this video.

When you apply a theme to the movie, additional pictures are added so that you can enter titles and captions. The transitions applied to each picture and the additional four pictures increase the length of the movie to 59.50 seconds.

9 Below the first picture, double-click the text *My Movie* and notice that in the Preview monitor, a text box displays. Select the text in the text box—*My Movie*—and then type your own first and last names. Click the **Play** button ▶ and notice that your name displays when the first picture displays. View the entire movie.

10 In the storyboard, select and delete the last three pictures—**Directed**, **Starring**, and **Filmed On Location**.

Seven pictures comprise your movie, and its length is reduced to 40 seconds.

11 Press ⌃Ctrl + A to select all seven pictures. On the **Edit tab**, click the **Duration arrow**, and then click **4.00** to change the length of time that each picture displays

during the movie from seven seconds to four seconds. Click the **Play** button ▶ and notice the timing change.

12 Click the first picture to select it. Start the **Snipping Tool** and create a **New**, **Full-screen Snip**. Save the snip in your **PowerPoint Chapter 2** folder as a **JPEG file** with the file name **Lastname_Firstname_2B_Movie_Snip** and then click **Save**. **Close** the **Snipping Tool** window to return to Windows Live Movie Maker.

13 On the **Home tab**, in the **Share group**, click **SkyDrive**. In the **Windows Live Movie Maker** dialog box, click the smallest resolution size, and then enter your **Windows Live ID** and **Password**. **Sign in** to Windows Live. In the **Publish on Windows Live SkyDrive** dialog box, with the insertion point blinking, type **PowerPoint 2B Movie** to create an album on your SkyDrive in which the movie will be stored. Click the **Everyone (public) arrow**, and then click **Me**. Click **Publish**.

After a few moments, a message box displays indicating that your Movie has been published.

14 Click the **Watch online** button. If necessary, sign in, or in the **sign in window**, under your account, click the **Continue** button. Compare your screen with Figure B.

Your movie displays on your SkyDrive in the PowerPoint 2B Movie folder.

15 Start the **Snipping Tool** and create a **New**, **Full-screen Snip**. Save the snip in your **PowerPoint Chapter 2** folder as a **JPEG file** with the file name **Lastname_Firstname_2B_Movie_SkyDrive_Snip** and then click **Save**. Sign out of your account, and then **Close** all open windows. When prompted to save your movie, click **No**. Submit your two snip files as directed.

Figure B

Content-Based Assessments

Summary

In this chapter, you formatted a presentation by changing the bullet style and by applying WordArt styles to text. You enhanced your presentations by inserting, sizing, and formatting shapes, pictures, and SmartArt graphics, resulting in a professional-looking presentation.

Key Terms

Matching

Match each term in the second column with its correct definition in the first column by writing the letter of the term on the blank line in front of the correct definition.

_____ 1. The line style in which a placeholder border displays, indicating that all of the text in the placeholder is selected.

_____ 2. A common format for a slide that contains a single point without a bullet symbol.

_____ 3. A single media file, for example art, sound, animation, or a movie.

_____ 4. A four-headed arrow-shaped pointer that indicates that you can reposition an object or image.

_____ 5. An object within which you can position text anywhere on the slide.

_____ 6. Vertical and horizontal lines that display in the rulers to provide a visual indication of the pointer position so that you can draw a shape.

_____ 7. Lines, arrows, stars, banners, ovals, or rectangles used to illustrate an idea, a process, or a workflow.

_____ 8. The pointer that indicates that you can draw a shape.

_____ 9. The inside color of text or an object.

_____ 10. A style gallery displaying predefined combinations of shape fill and line colors.

_____ 11. A setting used to align selected objects.

_____ 12. The command that reduces the size of a picture by removing vertical or horizontal edges.

_____ 13. A gallery of text styles from which you can create shadowed or mirrored text.

_____ 14. A visual representation of information that you create by choosing from among layouts to communicate your message or ideas.

_____ 15. Combinations of formatting effects that are applied to SmartArt graphics.

A Align to Slide

B Clip

C Crop

D Crosshair pointer

E Fill color

F Move pointer

G Paragraph

H Ruler guides

I Shapes

J Shape Styles

K SmartArt graphic

L SmartArt Styles

M Solid

N Text box

O WordArt

Content-Based Assessments

Multiple Choice

Circle the correct answer.

1. The color of the numbers or bullet symbols in a list is determined by the:
   A. Slide layout   B. Presentation theme   C. Gallery

2. When you point to an image in the Clip Art pane, the screen element that displays the keywords and information about the size of the image is the:
   A. ScreenTip   B. Navigation bar   C. Menu

3. To horizontally or vertically position selected objects on a slide relative to each other, use the:
   A. Align tools   B. Distribute tools   C. Crop tools

4. The command that removes unwanted portions of a picture so that the picture does not appear as a self-contained rectangle is:
   A. Shape height   B. Picture adjust   C. Background removal

5. The SmartArt type that shows steps in a process or timeline is:
   A. Radial   B. Process   C. List

6. The SmartArt type that shows a continual process is:
   A. Hierarchy   B. Radial   C. Cycle

7. The SmartArt type with which you can show a decision tree or create an organization chart is:
   A. Matrix   B. Pyramid   C. Hierarchy

8. The SmartArt type that illustrates connections is:
   A. Picture   B. Radial   C. Relationship

9. The SmartArt type that shows how parts relate to a whole is:
   A. Matrix   B. Pyramid   C. Radial

10. The SmartArt type that shows proportional relationships with the largest component on the top or bottom is:
    A. Matrix   B. Pyramid   C. Relationship

Skills Review | Project **2C** 10K Run

In the following Skills Review, you will create a presentation that describes the annual 10K Run sponsored by Fascination Entertainment Group at the Santa Clara Park location. Your completed presentation will look similar to Figure 2.60.

Project Files

For Project 2C, you will need the following file:

p02C_10K_Run

You will save your presentation as:

Lastname_Firstname_2C_10K_Run

Project Results

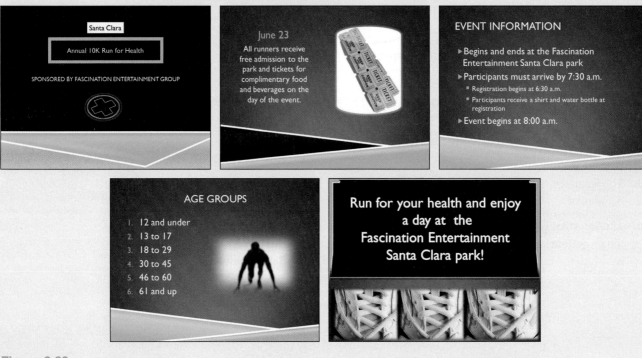

Figure 2.60

(Project 2C 10K Run continues on the next page)

Content-Based Assessments

1 **Start** PowerPoint. From the student files that accompany this textbook, locate and open **p02C_10K_Run**. **Save** the presentation in your **PowerPoint Chapter 2** folder as **Lastname_Firstname_2C_10K_Run**

a. If necessary, display the Rulers. With **Slide 1** displayed, on the **Insert tab**, in the **Illustrations group**, click the **Shapes** button, and then under **Basic Shapes**, in the second row, click the fifth shape—**Frame**.

b. Move the pointer to align the ruler guides with the **left half of the horizontal ruler at 3 inches** and with the **upper half of the vertical ruler at 2.5 inches**, and then click to insert the Frame.

c. On the **Format tab**, in the **Size group**, click in the **Shape Height** box to select the number, and then type **1.2** Click in the **Shape Width** box. Replace the selected number with **5.5** and then press Enter to resize the shape.

d. With the frame selected, type **Annual 10K Run for Health** and then change the **Font Size** to **24**. On the **Format tab**, in the **Shape Styles group**, click the **Shape Fill** button, and then under **Theme Colors**, in the seventh column, click the first color—**Gold, Accent 3**.

2 Select the picture of the cross inside the circle. On the **Format tab**, in the **Picture Styles group**, click the **Picture Effects** button. Click **Glow**, and then in the first column, click the second effect—**Green, 8 pt glow, Accent color 1**.

a. On the **Insert tab**, in the **Text group**, click the **Text Box** button. Move the pointer to position the ruler guides on the **horizontal ruler at 0 inches** and on the **upper half of the vertical ruler at 3 inches**, and then click to insert the text box.

b. Type **Santa Clara** and then change the **Font Size** to **24**. On the **Format tab**, in the **Shape Styles group**, click the **More** button. In the first row, click the fourth style—**Colored Outline - Gold, Accent 3**.

c. With the text box selected, hold down Shift, and then click the frame shape, the title placeholder, and the picture so that all four objects are selected. Under **Drawing Tools**, on the **Format tab**, in the **Arrange group**, click the **Align** button, and then click **Align to Slide**. Click the **Align** button again, and then click **Align Center**.

d. With the four objects still selected, click the **Align** button, and then click **Align Selected Objects**. Click the **Align** button again, and then click **Distribute Vertically**. **Save** the presentation.

3 Display **Slide 2**, and then click in the title placeholder containing the text *June 23*.

a. On the **Home tab**, in the **Paragraph group**, click the **Bullets** button to remove the bullet symbol from the title. Change the **Font Size** to **36** and then **Center** the text.

b. On the right side of the slide, in the content placeholder, click the **Clip Art** button. In the **Clip Art pane**, in the **Search for** box, type **keep this coupon** and then set the results to **Photographs**. Select the **Include Office.com content** button, and then click **Go**. Insert the picture of the light yellow tickets. Close the **Clip Art pane**.

c. With the picture selected, on the **Format tab**, in the **Size group**, click the **Crop button arrow**, and then click **Crop to Shape**. Under **Basic Shapes**, in the second row, click **Can** to change the shape of the white area surrounding the tickets.

d. On the **Format tab**, in the **Picture Styles group**, click the **Picture Effects** button, point to **Glow**, and then in the first column, click the third effect—**Green, 11 pt glow, Accent color 1**.

4 Display **Slide 3**, and then select the third and fourth bullet points—the two, second-level bullet points.

a. On the **Home tab**, in the **Paragraph group**, click the **Bullets button arrow**, and then click **Bullets and Numbering**. In the first row of bullets, click the last style—**Filled Square Bullets**. Replace the number in the **Size** box with **125** and then click the **Color** button. In the seventh column, click the first color—**Gold, Accent 3**—and then click **OK** to change the bullet style.

b. Display **Slide 4**, and then click the bulleted list placeholder. Click the dashed border so that it displays as a solid line, and then on the **Home tab**, in the **Paragraph group**, click the **Numbering button** to change the bullets to numbers.

5 Display **Slide 5**, and then select the picture of the shoe. On the Format tab, in the Size group, change the **Height** to **2.5**

(Project 2C 10K Run continues on the next page)

PowerPoint | Chapter 2

Skills Review | Project **2C** 10K Run (continued)

a. With the picture selected, on the **Format tab**, in the **Picture Styles group**, click **Picture Effects**, and then point to **Soft Edges**. Click **10 Point**.

b. With the picture selected, hold down Ctrl, and then press D to create a duplicate of the picture. Drag the duplicated picture to the right about 1 inch, and then hold down Ctrl, and press D to create another duplicate.

c. Hold down Shift, and then click the first two shoe pictures so that all three pictures are selected. On the **Format tab**, in the **Arrange group**, click the **Align** button, and then click **Align to Slide**. Click the **Align** button again, and then click **Align Bottom**. Click the **Align** button again, and then click **Distribute Horizontally**.

d. **Insert** a **Header & Footer** on the **Notes and Handouts**. Include the **Date and time updated automatically**, the **Page number**, and a **Footer** with the text **Lastname_Firstname_2C_10K_Run** Click **Apply to All**.

e. Display the **Document Properties**. Replace the text in the **Author** box with your own firstname and lastname, in the **Subject** box, type your course name and section number, and in the **Keywords** box, type **10K, health Close** the **Document Information Panel**.

f. View your slide show from the beginning, and then **Save** your presentation. Submit your presentation electronically or print **Handouts 6 Slides Horizontal** as directed by your instructor. **Close** the presentation and exit PowerPoint.

End **You have completed Project 2C**

Content-Based Assessments

Apply 2B skills from these Objectives:

5 Remove Picture Backgrounds and Insert WordArt

6 Create and Format a SmartArt Graphic

Skills Review | Project **2D** Wave Rider

In the following Skills Review, you will format a presentation by inserting and formatting WordArt and SmartArt graphics. Your completed presentation will look similar to Figure 2.61.

Project Files

For Project 2D, you will need the following file:

p02D_Wave_Rider

You will save your presentation as:

Lastname_Firstname_2D_Wave_Rider

Project Results

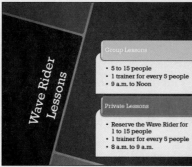 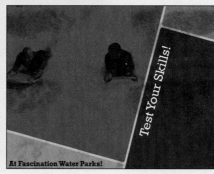

Figure 2.61

(Project 2D Wave Rider continues on the next page)

Skills Review | Project **2D** Wave Rider (continued)

1 **Start** PowerPoint. From the student files that accompany this textbook, locate and open **p02D_Wave_Rider**. **Save** the presentation in your **PowerPoint Chapter 2** folder as **Lastname_Firstname_2D_Wave_Rider**

a. With **Slide 1** displayed, select the title—*Catch A Wave*. On the **Format tab**, in the **WordArt Styles group**, click the **More** button. Under **Applies to All Text in the Shape**, click the last style—**Fill - Light Blue, Accent 1, Metal Bevel, Reflection**.

b. Display **Slide 2**. On the **Insert tab**, in the **Text group**, click the **WordArt** button. In the **WordArt gallery**, in the second row, click the fourth style—**Fill - Light Blue, Accent 1, Inner Shadow - Accent 1**. With the text *Your text here* selected, type **Surf's Up!**

c. With the WordArt selected, on the **Format tab**, in the **Arrange group**, click the **Align** button, and then click **Align Top**. Click the **Align** button again, and then click **Align Left** so that the WordArt is positioned in the upper left corner of the slide. **Save** the presentation.

2 Display **Slide 3**. In the center of the content placeholder, click the **Insert SmartArt Graphic** button to open the **Choose a SmartArt Graphic** dialog box. On the left, click **Process**, and then scroll as necessary and locate and click **Circle Arrow Process**. Click **OK**.

a. In the SmartArt graphic, the first instance of *Text* is selected. Type **Skill** and then in the middle circle arrow, replace *Text* with **Balance** In the last circle arrow, replace *Text* with **Practice**

b. On the **SmartArt Tools Design tab**, in the **Create Graphic group**, click the **Add Shape arrow**. Click **Add Shape After** to insert a circle arrow. Type **Fun**

c. On the **SmartArt Tools Design tab**, in the **SmartArt Styles group**, click the **Change Colors** button, and then under **Colorful**, click the last style **Colorful Range - Accent Colors 5 to 6**. In the **SmartArt Styles group**, click the **More** button, and then under **Best Match for Document**, click the last style—**Intense Effect**.

3 Display **Slide 4**. In the content placeholder, right-click anywhere in the bulleted list. On the shortcut menu, point to **Convert to SmartArt**, and at the bottom of the gallery, click **More SmartArt Graphics**. On the left side of the **Choose a SmartArt Graphic** dialog box, click **List**. Locate and click **Lined List**, and then click **OK** to convert the list to a SmartArt graphic.

a. On the **SmartArt Tools Design tab**, in the **SmartArt Styles group**, click the **Change Colors** button. In the **Color** gallery, under **Colorful**, click the last style—**Colorful Range - Accent Colors 5 to 6**.

b. On the **Design tab**, in the **SmartArt Styles group**, click the **More** button to display the **SmartArt Styles gallery**. Under **3-D**, in the first row, click the third style—**Cartoon**.

c. With the SmartArt selected, on the **SmartArt Tools Design tab**, in the **Layouts group**, click the **More** button, and then click **More Layouts**. On the left side of the dialog box, click **List**, and then locate and click **Vertical Box List**. Click **OK**.

d. In the SmartArt, click the upper large rectangle containing the bulleted list. Hold down Shift, and then click the rectangle containing the second bulleted list so that both bulleted list rectangles are selected. On the **Format tab**, in the **Shapes group**, click the **Change Shape** button, and then under **Rectangles**, click the last shape—**Round Diagonal Corner Rectangle**.

e. Select the green shape containing the text *Group Lessons*. Hold down Shift, and then click the shape containing the text *Private Lessons*. With both shapes still selected, on the **Format tab**, in the **Shapes group**, click the **Larger** button three times to increase the size of the two selected shapes.

4 Display **Slide 5**. On the **Insert tab**, in the **Text group**, click the **WordArt** button. In the **WordArt** gallery, in the fifth row, click the second style—**Fill - Black, Background 1, Metal Bevel**. With the text *Your text here* selected, type **At Fascination Water Parks!**

a. Change the WordArt **Font Size** to **24**. With the WordArt selected, on the **Format tab**, in the **Arrange group**, click the **Align** button, and then click **Align Bottom**. Click the **Align** button again, and then click **Align Left** so that the WordArt is positioned in the lower left corner of the slide.

b. **Insert** a **Header & Footer** on the **Notes and Handouts**. Include the **Date and time updated automatically**, the **Page number**, and a **Footer** with the text **Lastname_Firstname_2D_Wave_Rider** and **Apply to All**.

c. Display the **Document Properties**. Replace the text in the **Author** box with your own firstname and

(Project 2D Wave Rider continues on the next page)

lastname, in the **Subject** box, type your course name and section number, and in the **Keywords** box, type **water parks, wave rider Close** the **Document Information Panel**. View the presentation from the beginning.

d. **Save** your presentation. Submit your presentation electronically or print **Handouts 6 Slides Horizontal** as directed by your instructor. **Close** the presentation and exit PowerPoint.

End **You have completed Project 2D** ——————————————————

Content-Based Assessments

Mastering PowerPoint | Project 2E Job Fair

In the following Mastering PowerPoint project, you will format a presentation describing employment opportunities at the Fascination Entertainment Group theme parks. Your completed presentation will look similar to Figure 2.62.

Project Files

For Project 2E, you will need the following file:

p02E_Job_Fair

You will save your presentation as:

Lastname_Firstname_2E_Job_Fair

Project Results

Figure 2.62

(Project 2E Job Fair continues on the next page)

Content-Based Assessments

1 **Start** PowerPoint. From the student files that accompany this textbook, locate and open **p02E_Job_Fair**. In your **PowerPoint Chapter 2** folder, **Save** the file as **Lastname_Firstname_2E_Job_Fair**

2 On **Slide 2**, remove the bullet symbol from the paragraph. **Center** the paragraph, apply **Bold** and **Italic** to the text, and then set the **Line Spacing** to **1.5**. With the content placeholder selected, display the **Shape Styles** gallery, and then in the second row, apply the last style—**Colored Fill - Red, Accent 6**.

3 On **Slide 3**, apply **Numbering** to the first-level bullet points—*Competitive pay and benefits, Flexible schedules,* and *Perks*. Under each of the numbered items, change all of the circle bullet symbols to **Checkmark Bullets**, and then change the bullet color to the last color in the last row—**Red, Accent 6, Darker 50%**.

4 In the content placeholder on the right side of the slide, insert a **Clip Art** photograph by searching for **ferris wheel lights** and then insert the ferris wheel on the red background as shown in Figure 2.62 at the beginning of this project. Change the picture **Height** to **3** and then **Crop** the picture shape to **Rounded Rectangle**. Modify the **Picture Effect** by applying the first **Glow** style in the second row—**Gold, 8 pt glow, Accent color 1**.

5 Display **Slide 4**. From the **Shapes** gallery, under **Basic Shapes**, insert a **Bevel** aligned with the **left half of the horizontal ruler at 1 inch** and the **upper half of the vertical ruler at 0.5 inches**. Change the **Shape Height** to **1** and the **Shape Width** to **4** In the bevel, type **1-800-555-7854** and then change the **Font Size** to **28**.

6 Insert a **Text Box** aligned with the **left half of the horizontal ruler at 2 inches** and with the **upper half of the vertical ruler at 2 inches**. In the text box, type **Be a part of our team!** On the **Format tab**, from the **Shape Styles** gallery, in the second row, apply the first style—**Colored Fill - Black, Dark 1**. Change the **Font Size** to **28**.

7 Select the bevel and the text box, and then, using the **Align Selected Objects** option, apply **Align Center** alignment. Select the bevel, the text box, and the *Contact Human Resources Today!* placeholder, and then, using the **Align Selected Objects** option, **Distribute Vertically**. Apply the **Box** transition to all of the slides in the presentation, and then view the slide show from the beginning.

8 **Insert** a **Header & Footer** on the **Notes and Handouts**. Include the **Date and time updated automatically**, the **Page number**, and a **Footer** with the text **Lastname_Firstname_2E_Job_Fair** Apply to all.

9 Display the **Document Properties**. Replace the text in the **Author** box with your own firstname and lastname, in the **Subject** box, type your course name and section number, and in the **Keywords** box, type **employment** **Close** the **Document Information Panel**.

10 **Save** your presentation. Submit your presentation electronically or print **Handouts 4 Slides Horizontal** as directed by your instructor. **Close** the presentation and exit PowerPoint.

End **You have completed Project 2E**

Apply **2B** skills from these Objectives:

5 Remove Picture Backgrounds and Insert WordArt

6 Create and Format a SmartArt Graphic

Mastering PowerPoint | Project **2F** Attractions

In the following Mastering PowerPoint project, you will format a presentation describing new attractions at several of the Fascination Entertainment Group parks. Your completed presentation will look similar to Figure 2.63.

Project Files

For Project 2F, you will need the following file:

> p02F_Attractions

You will save your presentation as:

> Lastname_Firstname_2F_Attractions

Project Results

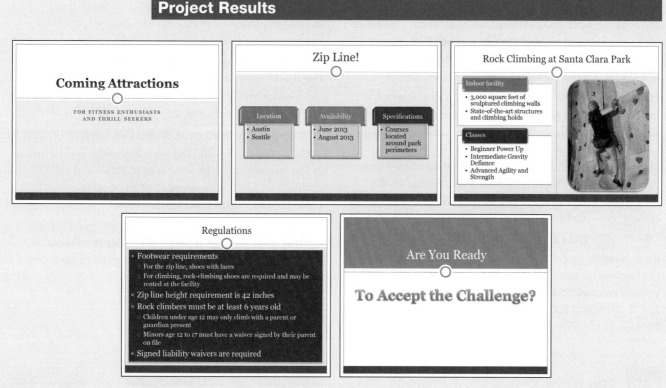

Figure 2.63

(Project 2F Attractions continues on the next page)

Content-Based Assessments

1 Start PowerPoint. From the student files that accompany this textbook, open **p02F_Attractions**, and then **Save** the file in your **PowerPoint Chapter 2** folder as **Lastname_Firstname_2F_Attractions**

2 On **Slide 1**, select the title and display the **WordArt** gallery. Under **Applies to Selected Text**, in the last row, apply the second WordArt style—**Gradient Fill - Dark Red, Accent 6, Inner Shadow**.

3 On **Slide 2**, in the content placeholder, insert a **List** type **SmartArt** graphic—**Horizontal Bullet List**. In the top-left rectangle, type **Location** and then in the two bullet points below *Location*, type **Austin** and **Seattle** In the top-center rectangle, type **Availability** and then in the rectangle below *Availability*, type **June 2013** and **August 2013** In the top-right rectangle, type **Specifications** and in the lower rectangle type **Courses located around park perimeters** Delete the extra bullet point.

4 Change the SmartArt color to **Colorful Range - Accent Colors 5 to 6**, and then apply the **3-D Inset** style. Select the three upper rectangle shapes—*Location*, *Availability*, and *Specifications*—and then change the shapes to the **Snip Same Side Corner Rectangle** shape. On the **Format tab**, in the **Shapes group**, click the **Larger** button two times to increase the size of the snipped rectangle shapes.

5 On **Slide 3**, convert the bulleted list to a **SmartArt** graphic by applying the **Vertical Box List** graphic. Change

the SmartArt color to **Colorful Range - Accent Colors 5 to 6**, and then apply the **Polished 3-D** style.

6 On **Slide 4**, select the content placeholder, and then from the **Shape Styles** gallery, in the third row, apply the last style—**Light 1 Outline, Colored Fill - Dark Red, Accent 6**.

7 On **Slide 5**, insert a **WordArt**—the third style in the fifth row—**Fill - Brown, Accent 2, Warm Matte Bevel**. Replace the WordArt text with **To Accept the Challenge?** Change the **Font Size** to **48**.

8 Insert a **Header & Footer** on the **Notes and Handouts**. Include the **Date and time updated automatically**, the **Page number**, and a **Footer** with the text **Lastname_Firstname_2F_Attractions**

9 Display the **Document Properties**. Replace the text in the **Author** box with your own firstname and lastname, in the **Subject** box, type your course name and section number, and in the **Keywords** box, type **zip line, rock wall Close** the **Document Information Panel**.

10 Save your presentation, and then view the slide show from the beginning. Submit your presentation electronically or print **Handouts 6 Slides Horizontal** as directed by your instructor. **Close** the presentation and exit PowerPoint.

End You have completed Project 2F —————————————

Apply **2A** and **2B** skills
from these Objectives:

1 Format Numbered
and Bulleted Lists

2 Insert Clip Art

3 Insert Text Boxes and
Shapes

4 Format Objects

5 Remove Picture
Backgrounds and
Insert WordArt

6 Create and Format a
SmartArt Graphic

Mastering PowerPoint | Project **2G** Orientation

In the following Mastering PowerPoint project, you will edit an existing presentation that is shown to Fascination Entertainment Group employees on their first day of a three-day orientation. Your completed presentation will look similar to Figure 2.64.

Project Files

For Project 2G, you will need the following files:

p02G_Orientation
p02G_Maya_Ruiz
p02G_David_Jensen
p02G_Ken_Lee

You will save your presentation as:

Lastname_Firstname_2G_Orientation

Project Results

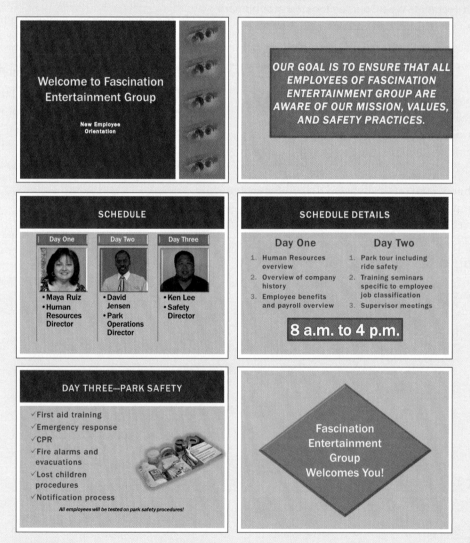

Figure 2.64

(Project 2G Orientation continues on the next page)

1 **Start** PowerPoint, and then from your student data files, open the file **p02G_Orientation**. In your **PowerPoint Chapter 2** folder, **Save** the file as Lastname_Firstname_2G_Orientation

2 On **Slide 1**, format the title as a **WordArt** using the fourth style in the first row—**Fill - White, Outline - Accent 1**. Select the five pictures, and then using the **Align to Slide** option, align the pictures using the **Distribute Vertically** and **Align Right** commands. On **Slide 2**, change the **Shape Style** of the content placeholder to the second style in the last row—**Intense Effect - Tan, Accent 1**.

3 On **Slide 3**, convert the bulleted list to the **Picture** type **SmartArt** graphic—**Title Picture Lineup**. Change the color to **Colorful Range - Accent Colors 5 to 6**, and then apply the **3-D Inset** style. In the three picture placeholders, from your student files insert the following pictures: **p02G_Maya_Ruiz**, **p02G_David_Jensen**, and **p02G_Ken_Lee**.

4 On **Slide 4**, change the two bulleted lists to **Numbering**. Then, insert a **WordArt** using the **Fill - White, Drop Shadow** style with the text **8 a.m. to 4 p.m.** and position the WordArt centered below the two content placeholders. Apply a **Shape Style** to the WordArt using **Intense Effect - Tan, Accent 1**.

5 On **Slide 5**, change the bullet symbols to **Checkmark Bullets**, and then in the placeholder on the right, insert a **Clip Art** photograph by searching for **first aid kit** Insert the picture of the opened first aid box, and then remove the background from the picture so that only the items in the kit display. Mark areas to keep and remove as necessary. Change the **Shape Height** to **3.25** and then apply the **Brown, 18 pt glow, Accent color 4** picture effect.

6 On **Slide 5**, insert a **Text Box** aligned with the **left half of the horizontal ruler at 4 inches** and with the **lower half of the vertical ruler at 2.5 inches**. In the text box, type **All employees will be tested on park safety procedures!** Apply **Italic**, and then **Align Center** the text box using the **Align to Slide** option.

7 Insert a **New Slide** with the **Blank** layout. From the **Shapes** gallery, under **Basic Shapes**, insert a **Diamond** of any size anywhere on the slide. Then, resize the diamond so that its **Shape Height** is **6** and its **Shape Width** is **8** Using the **Align to Slide** option, apply the **Align Center**, and **Align Middle** alignment commands. Apply the **Moderate Effect - Tan, Accent 1** shape style to the diamond, and then in the diamond, type **Fascination Entertainment Group Welcomes You!** Change the **Font Size** to **40**, and then apply the **Art Deco Bevel** effect to the diamond shape.

8 **Insert** a **Header & Footer** on the **Notes and Handouts**. Include the **Date and time updated automatically**, the **Page number**, and a **Footer** with the text **Lastname_Firstname_2G_Orientation** Apply to all.

9 Display the **Document Properties**. Replace the text in the **Author** box with your own firstname and lastname, in the **Subject** box, type your course name and section number, and in the **Keywords** box, type **orientation, employee training Close** the **Document Information Panel**.

10 **Save** your presentation, and then view the slide show from the beginning. Submit your presentation electronically or print **Handouts 6 Slides Horizontal** as directed by your instructor. **Close** the presentation and exit PowerPoint.

End **You have completed Project 2G**

Content-Based Assessments

GO! Fix It | Project 2H Summer Jobs

Project Files

For Project 2H, you will need the following file:

p02H_Summer_Jobs

You will save your presentation as:

Lastname_Firstname_2H_Summer_Jobs

In this project, you will edit several slides from a presentation prepared by the Human Resources Department at Fascination Entertainment Group regarding summer employment opportunities. From the student files that accompany this textbook, open the file p02H_Summer_Jobs, and then save the file in your chapter folder as **Lastname_Firstname_2H_Summer_Jobs**

To complete the project you should know:

- The Theme should be changed to Module and two spelling errors should be corrected.
- On Slide 1, the pictures should be aligned with the top of the slide and distributed horizontally.
- On Slide 2, the bulleted list should be converted to a Vertical Box List SmartArt and an attractive style should be applied. The colors should be changed to Colorful Range - Accent Colors 5 to 6.
- On Slide 3, the bulleted list should be formatted as a numbered list.
- On Slide 4, insert a Fill - White, Drop Shadow WordArt with the text **Apply Today!** and position the WordArt centered approximately 1 inch below the title placeholder.
- Document Properties should include your name, course name and section, and the keywords **summer jobs, recruitment** A Header & Footer should be inserted on the Notes and Handouts that includes the Date and time updated automatically, the Page number, and a Footer with the text **Lastname_Firstname_2H_Summer_Jobs**

Save and submit your presentation electronically or print Handouts 4 Slides Horizontal as directed by your instructor. Close the presentation.

End **You have completed Project 2H** _____

Content-Based Assessments

GO! Make It | Project 2I Renovation Plans

Project Files

For Project 2I, you will need the following file:

New blank PowerPoint presentation

You will save your presentation as:

Lastname_Firstname_2I_Renovation_Plans

By using the skills you practiced in this chapter, create the first two slides of the presentation shown in Figure 2.65. Start PowerPoint to begin a new blank presentation, and apply the Urban theme and the Aspect color theme. Type the title and subtitle shown in Figure 2.65, and then change the background style to Style 12 and the title font size to 40. Apply the Fill - Black, Background 1, Metal Bevel WordArt style to the title. Save the file in your PowerPoint Chapter 2 folder as **Lastname_Firstname_2I_Renovation_Plans**

To locate the picture on Slide 1, search for a clip art photograph with the keyword **carnival rides** Resize the picture Height to **2** and then apply soft edges, duplicate, align, and distribute the images as shown in the figure.

Insert a new Slide 2 using the Content with Caption layout. Insert the Basic Matrix SmartArt layout shown in Figure 2.65 and change the color and style as shown. Type the title and caption text, changing the title Font Size to 28 and the caption text Font Size to 18. Modify line spacing and apply formatting to the caption text as shown in Figure 2.65. Insert the date, file name, and page number in the Notes and Handouts footer. In the Document Information Panel, add your name and course information and the keywords **renovation, goals** Save, and then print or submit electronically as directed by your instructor.

Project Results

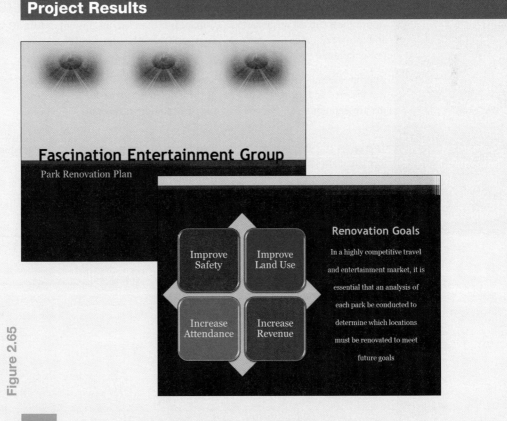

Figure 2.65

End You have completed Project 2I

Content-Based Assessments

GO! Solve It | Project **2J** Business Summary

Project Files

For Project 2J, you will need the following file:

p02J_Business_Summary

You will save your presentation as:

Lastname_Firstname_2J_Business_Summary

Open the file p02J_Business_Summary and save it in your chapter folder as **Lastname_Firstname_2J_Business_Summary** Format the presentation attractively by applying appropriate font formatting and by changing text alignment and line spacing. Insert at least one clip art image and change the picture shape and effect. On Slide 2, align and format the text box and shape attractively and insert a clip art image that can be duplicated, aligned, and distributed across the bottom edge of the slide. On Slide 3, insert an appropriate photo on the right. On Slide 4, convert the bulleted list to an appropriate SmartArt graphic and format the graphic appropriately. Apply slide transitions to all of the slides in the presentation and insert a header and footer that includes the date and time updated automatically, the file name in the footer, and the page number. Add your name, your course name and section number, and the keywords **business summary, revenue** to the Properties area. Save, and then print or submit electronically as directed by your instructor.

	Performance Level		
	Exemplary: You consistently applied the relevant skills	**Proficient:** You sometimes, but not always, applied the relevant skills	**Developing:** You rarely or never applied the relevant skills
Insert and format appropriate clip art	Appropriate clip art was inserted and formatted in the presentation.	Clip art was inserted but was not appropriate for the presentation or was not formatted.	Clip art was not inserted.
Insert and format appropriate SmartArt graphic	Appropriate SmartArt graphic was inserted and formatted in the presentation.	SmartArt graphic was inserted but was not appropriate for the presentation or was not formatted.	SmartArt graphic was not inserted.
Format text boxes and shapes attractively	Text boxes and shapes were formatted attractively.	Text boxes and shapes were formatted but the formatting was inappropriately applied.	Inadequate or no formatting.
Insert transitions	Appropriate transitions were applied to all slides.	Transitions were applied to some, but not all slides.	Transitions were not applied.

Performance Elements (vertical label)

End **You have completed Project 2J**

Content-Based Assessments

Apply a combination of
the **2A** and **2B** skills.

GO! Solve It | Project **2K** Hotel

Project Files

For Project 2K, you will need the following file:

    p02K_Hotel

You will save your presentation as:

    Lastname_Firstname_2K_Hotel

Open the file p02K_Hotel and save it as **Lastname_Firstname_2K_Hotel** Complete the presentation by inserting a clip art image on the first slide and applying appropriate picture effects. On Slide 2, format the bullet point as a single paragraph, and then on Slide 3, convert the bulleted list to an appropriate SmartArt graphic. Change the SmartArt color and apply a style. On Slide 4, insert and attractively position a WordArt with the text **Save the Date!** Apply slide transitions to all of the slides. Insert a header and footer that includes the date and time updated automatically, the file name in the footer, and the page number. Add your name, your course name and section number, and the keywords **hotel, accommodations** to the Properties area. Save your presentation. Print or submit as directed by your instructor.

	Performance Level		
	Exemplary: You consistently applied the relevant skills	**Proficient:** You sometimes, but not always, applied the relevant skills	**Developing:** You rarely or never applied the relevant skills
Insert and format appropriate clip art	Appropriate clip art was inserted and formatted in the presentation.	Clip art was inserted but was not appropriate for the presentation or was not formatted.	Clip art was not inserted.
Insert and format appropriate SmartArt graphic	Appropriate SmartArt graphic was inserted and formatted in the presentation.	SmartArt graphic was inserted but was not appropriate for the presentation or was not formatted.	SmartArt graphic was not inserted.
Insert and format appropriate WordArt	Appropriate WordArt was inserted and formatted in the presentation.	WordArt was inserted but was not appropriate for the presentation or was not formatted.	WordArt was not inserted.
Insert transitions	Appropriate transitions were applied to all slides.	Transitions were applied to some, but not all slides.	Transitions were not applied.

(Performance Elements)

 End You have completed Project 2K

PowerPoint | Chapter 2

NOTES

Enhancing a Presentation with Animation, Video, Tables, and Charts

OUTCOMES

At the end of this chapter you will be able to:

OBJECTIVES

Mastering these objectives will enable you to:

PROJECT 3A
Customize a presentation with animation and video.

1. Customize Slide Backgrounds and Themes (p. 645)
2. Animate a Slide Show (p. 652)
3. Insert a Video (p. 659)

PROJECT 3B
Create a presentation that includes data in tables and charts.

4. Create and Modify Tables (p. 671)
5. Create and Modify Charts (p. 676)

megumi ito/Shutterstock

In This Chapter

Recall that a presentation theme applies a consistent look to a presentation. You can customize a presentation by modifying the theme and by applying animation to slide elements, and you can enhance your presentations by creating tables and charts that help your audience understand numeric data and trends just as pictures and diagrams help illustrate a concept. The data that you present should determine whether a table or a chart would most appropriately display your information. Styles applied to your tables and charts unify these slide elements by complementing your presentation theme.

The projects in this chapter relate to **Golden Grove**, a growing city located between Los Angeles and San Diego. Just 10 years ago the population was under 100,000; today it has grown to almost 300,000. Community leaders have always focused on quality and economic development in decisions on housing, open space, education, and infrastructure, making the city a model for other communities its size around the United States. The city provides many recreational and cultural opportunities with a large park system, thriving arts, and a friendly business atmosphere.

Project 3A Informational Presentation

Project Activities

In Activities 3.01 through 3.11, you will edit and format a presentation that Mindy Walker, Director of Golden Grove Parks and Recreation, has created to inform residents about the benefits of using the city's parks and trails. Your completed presentation will look similar to Figure 3.1.

Project Files

For Project 3A, you will need the following files:

p03A_Park
p03A_Pets
p03A_Trails
p03A_Walking_Trails
p03A_Trails_Video

You will save your presentation as:

Lastname_Firstname_3A_Walking_Trails

Project Results

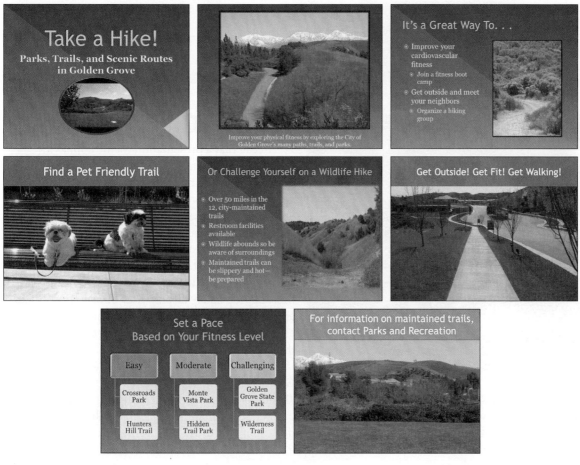

Figure 3.1
Project 3A Walking Trails

Objective 1 | Customize Slide Backgrounds and Themes

You have practiced customizing presentations by applying themes with unified design elements, backgrounds, and colors that provide a consistent look in your presentation. Additional ways to customize a slide include changing theme fonts and colors, applying a background style, modifying the background color, or inserting a picture on the slide background.

Activity 3.01 | Changing the Theme Colors and Theme Fonts

Recall that the presentation theme is a coordinated, predefined set of colors, fonts, lines, and fill effects. In this activity, you will open a presentation in which the Verve theme is applied, and then you will change the *theme colors*—a set of coordinating colors that are applied to the backgrounds, objects, and text in a presentation.

In addition to theme colors, every presentation theme includes *theme fonts* that determine the font to apply to two types of slide text—headings and body. The *Headings font* is applied to slide titles and the *Body font* is applied to all other text. When you apply a new theme font to the presentation, the text on every slide is updated with the new heading and body fonts.

1 From the student files that accompany this textbook, locate and open **p03A_Walking_Trails**. Display **Backstage** view, click **Save As**, and then navigate to the location where you are storing your projects for this chapter. Create a new folder named **PowerPoint Chapter 3** and then in the **File name** box and using your own name, type **Lastname_Firstname_3A_Walking_Trails** Click **Save** or press Enter.

2 Click the **Design tab**, and then in the **Themes group**, click the **Colors** button to display the list of theme colors. Point to several themes and notice the color changes on **Slide 1**. Scroll the **Theme Colors** list, and then click **Metro** to change the theme colors.

Changing the theme colors does not change the overall design of the presentation. In this presentation, the *Verve* presentation theme is still applied to the presentation. By modifying the theme colors, you retain the design of the *Verve* theme. The colors of the *Metro* theme, which coordinate with the pictures in the presentation, are available as text, accent, and background colors.

3 With **Slide 1** displayed, click anywhere in the title placeholder. Click the **Home tab**, and then in the **Font group**, click the **Font button arrow**. Notice that at the top of the **Font** list, under **Theme Fonts**, Century Gothic (Headings) and Century Gothic (Body) display. Compare your screen with Figure 3.2.

Figure 3.2

Theme fonts

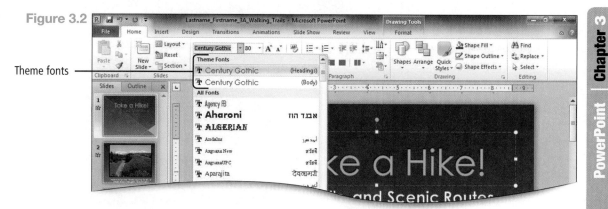

PowerPoint | Chapter 3

4   Click anywhere on the slide to close the Font list. Click the **Design tab**, and then in the **Themes group**, click the **Fonts** button.

> This list displays the name of each theme and the pair of fonts in the theme. The first and larger font in each pair is the Headings font and the second and smaller font in each pair is the Body font.

5   Point to several of the themes and watch as Live Preview changes the title and subtitle text. Then, scroll to the bottom of the **Theme Fonts** list and click **Urban**. Compare your screen with Figure 3.3, and then **Save** your presentation.

Figure 3.3

Theme Fonts applied to presentation

Theme Colors applied to presentation

Activity 3.02 | Applying a Background Style

1   With **Slide 1** displayed, on the **Design tab**, in the **Background group**, click the **Background Styles** button. Compare your screen with Figure 3.4.

> A *background style* is a slide background fill variation that combines theme colors in different intensities or patterns.

Figure 3.4

Background Styles button

Background Styles gallery

2 Point to each of the background styles to view the style on **Slide 1**. Then, in the first row, *right-click* **Style 2** to display the shortcut menu. Click **Apply to Selected Slides** and then compare your screen with Figure 3.5.

> The background style is applied only to Slide 1.

3 **Save** ⊞ your presentation.

Figure 3.5

Background style applied to slide

More Knowledge | Applying Background Styles to All Slides in a Presentation

To change the background style for all of the slides in the presentation, click the background style that you want to apply and the style will be applied to every slide.

Activity 3.03 | Hiding Background Graphics

Many of the PowerPoint 2010 themes contain graphic elements that display on the slide background. In the Verve theme applied to this presentation, the background includes a triangle and lines that intersect near the lower right corner of the slide. Sometimes the background graphics interfere with the slide content. When this happens, you can hide the background graphics.

1 Display **Slide 6**, and notice that on this slide, you can clearly see the triangle and lines on the slide background.

> You cannot delete these objects because they are a part of the slide background; however, you can hide them.

2 Display **Slide 5**, and notice that the background graphics distract from the connecting lines on the diagram. On the **Design tab**, in the **Background group**, select the **Hide Background Graphics** check box, and then compare your slide with Figure 3.6.

> The background objects no longer display behind the SmartArt diagram.

Figure 3.6

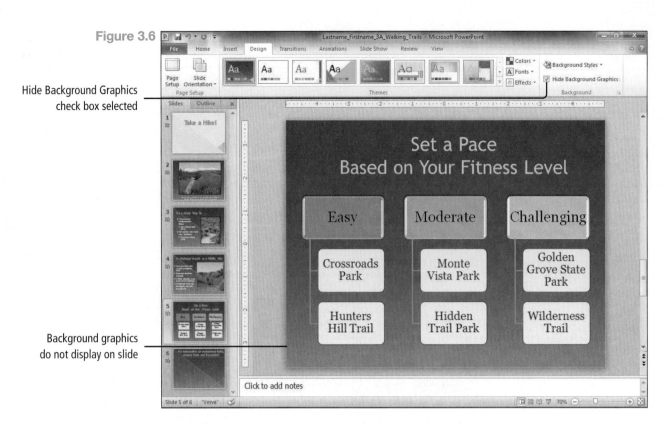

Hide Background Graphics
check box selected

Background graphics
do not display on slide

3 **Save** 🖫 the presentation.

Activity 3.04 | Formatting a Slide Background with a Picture

You can insert a picture on a slide background so the image fills the entire slide.

1 Display **Slide 3**, and then click the **Home tab**. In the **Slides group**, click the **New Slide arrow**, and then click the **Title Only** layout to insert a new slide with the Title Only layout.

2 With the new **Slide 4** displayed, click the **Design tab**. In the **Background group**, select the **Hide Background Graphics** check box, and then click the **Background Styles** button. Below the displayed gallery, click **Format Background**.

> In the Format Background dialog box, you can customize a slide background by changing the formatting options.

3 If necessary, on the left side of the dialog box, click Fill. On the right side of the dialog box, under **Fill**, click the **Picture or texture fill** option button, and then notice that on the slide background, a textured fill displays. Compare your screen with Figure 3.7.

Figure 3.7

Format Background
dialog box

Fill selected

Picture or texture fill
option button selected

Textured fill displays
on slide background

Hide Background Graphics
check box selected

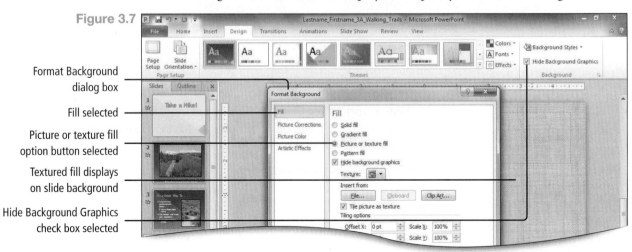

4 Under **Insert from**, click the **File** button to display the **Insert Picture** dialog box. Navigate to your student files, and then click **p03A_Pets**. Click **Insert**, and then at the bottom of the **Format Background** dialog box, click **Close**. Compare your slide with Figure 3.8 and notice that the picture displays as the background of Slide 4.

> When a picture is applied to a slide background using the Format Background option, the picture is not treated as an object. The picture fills the background and you cannot move it or size it.

Figure 3.8

Picture inserted on slide background

5 Click in the title placeholder, type **Find a Pet Friendly Trail** and then notice that the background picture does not provide sufficient contrast with the text to display the title effectively.

6 With your insertion point still in the title placeholder, click the **Format tab**. In the **Shape Styles group**, click the **Shape Fill button arrow**. In the fifth column, click the last color—**Green, Accent 1, Darker 50%**. Select the title text, and then on the **Format tab**, in the **WordArt Styles group**, in the first row, click the third style—**Fill - White, Drop Shadow**. **Center** ≡ the text.

> The green fill color and the white WordArt style provide good contrast against the slide background so that the text is readable.

7 Point to the outer edge of the title placeholder to display the ⬚ pointer, and then drag the placeholder up and to the left so that its upper left corner aligns with the upper left corner of the slide. Point to the center right sizing handle and drag to the right so that the placeholder extends to the right edge of the slide. Click outside of the placeholder, and then compare your slide with Figure 3.9.

Figure 3.9

Title placeholder moved
and sized, fill color applied

Text centered and
WordArt style applied

Find a Pet Friendly Trail

8 Display **Slide 5**, and then insert a **New Slide** with the **Title Only** layout. On the **Design tab**, in the **Background group**, select the **Hide Background Graphics** check box, and then click the **Background Styles** button. Click **Format Background**.

9 Under **Fill**, click the **Picture or texture fill** option button. Under **Insert from**, click **File**. Navigate to your student files, click **p03A_Trails**, click **Insert**, and then **Close** the dialog box. In the title placeholder, type **Get Outside! Get Fit! Get Walking!** and then **Center** ≡ the text.

10 Select the text, and then change the **Font Size** to **36**. Then, apply the same **Shape Fill** color and **WordArt** style to the title placeholder that you applied to the title on **Slide 4**. Size the placeholder so that it extends from the left edge of the slide to the right edge of the slide, and then drag the placeholder up so that its upper edge aligns with the upper edge of the slide. Click outside of the title so that it is not selected. Compare your slide with Figure 3.10.

The green fill color and white text provide good contrast with the slide background and complement the green color of the grass on the slide.

Figure 3.10

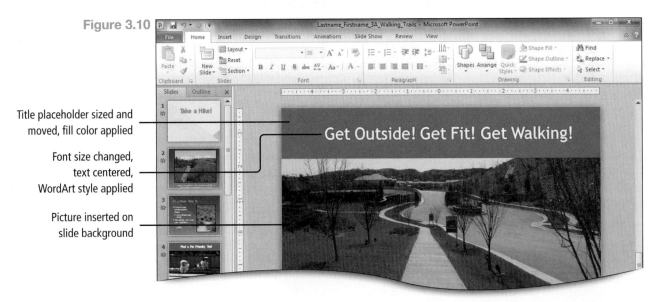

Title placeholder sized and
moved, fill color applied

Font size changed,
text centered,
WordArt style applied

Picture inserted on
slide background

Get Outside! Get Fit! Get Walking!

11 Display **Slide 8**, and then format the slide background with a picture from your student files—**p03A_Park**. On the **Design tab**, in the **Background group**, select the **Hide Background Graphics** check box.

12 Select the title placeholder. On the **Format tab**. In the **Shape Styles group**, click the **More** button ⯆. In the **Shape Styles** gallery, in the second row, click the sixth style—**Colored Fill – Periwinkle, Accent 5**.

13 Select the text, and then on the **Format tab**, in the **WordArt Styles group**, click the third style—**Fill - White, Drop Shadow**. Click outside of the placeholder, and then compare your slide with Figure 3.11. **Save** 🖫 the presentation.

Figure 3.11

Title formatted, shape style applied

Picture inserted on slide background

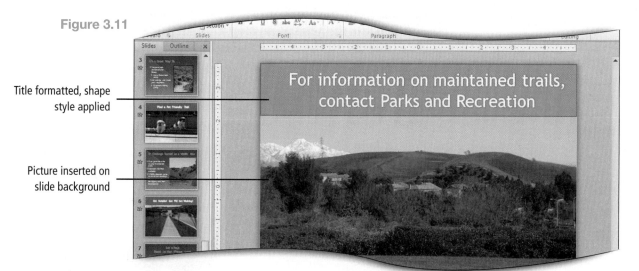

Activity 3.05 | Applying a Background Fill Color and Resetting a Slide Background

1 Display **Slide 1**, and then click the **Design tab**. In the **Background group**, click the **Background Styles** button, and then click **Format Background**.

2 In the **Format Background** dialog box, if necessary, click the Solid fill option button. Under **Fill Color**, click the **Color** button 🎨. Under **Theme Colors**, in the first column, click the last color—**White, Background 1, Darker 50%**. Click **Close**.

> The solid fill color is applied to the slide background.

3 On the **Design tab**, in the **Background group**, click the **Background Styles** button. Below the gallery, click **Reset Slide Background**, and then **Save** 🖫 the presentation.

> After making many changes to a slide background, you may decide that the original theme formatting is the best choice for displaying the text and graphics on a slide. The Reset Slide Background feature restores the original theme and color theme formatting to a slide.

Objective 2 | Animate a Slide Show

Animation is a visual or sound effect added to an object or text on a slide. Animation can focus the audience's attention, providing the speaker with an opportunity to emphasize important points using the slide element as an effective visual aid.

Activity 3.06 | Applying Animation Entrance Effects and Effect Options

Entrance effects are animations that bring a slide element onto the screen. You can modify an entrance effect by using the animation Effect Options command.

1 Display **Slide 3**, and then click anywhere in the bulleted list placeholder. On the **Animations tab**, in the **Animation group**, click the **More** button ⊡. If necessary, scroll slightly so that the word *Entrance* displays at the top of the Animation gallery, and then compare your screen with Figure 3.12.

Recall that an entrance effect is animation that brings an object or text onto the screen. An *emphasis effect* is animation that emphasizes an object or text that is already displayed. An *exit effect* is animation that moves an object or text off the screen.

Figure 3.12

Entrance effects

Animation gallery

Emphasis effects

Exit effects

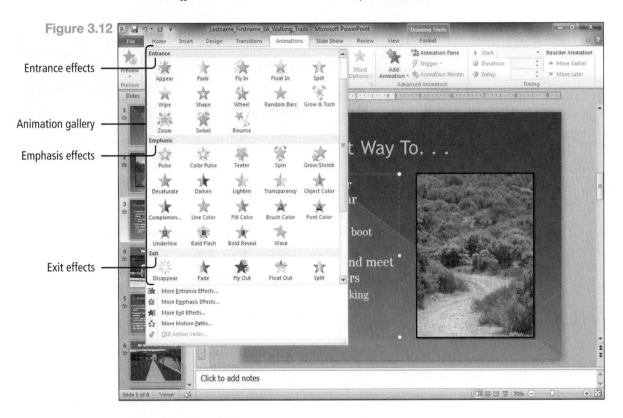

2 Under **Entrance**, click **Split**, and then notice the animation applied to the list. Compare your screen with Figure 3.13.

The numbers *1* and *2* display to the left of the bulleted list placeholder, indicating the order in which the bullet points will be animated during the slide show. For example, the first bullet point and its subordinate bullet are both numbered *1*. Thus, both will display at the same time.

Figure 3.13

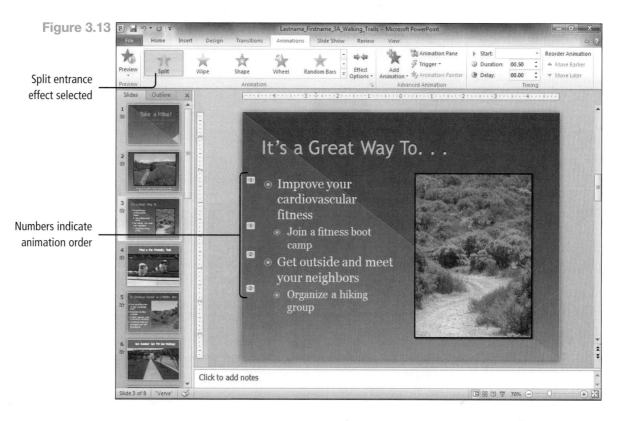

Split entrance effect selected

Numbers indicate animation order

3 Select the bulleted text placeholder. In the **Animation group**, click the **Effect Options** button, and then compare your screen with Figure 3.14.

The Effect Options control the direction and sequence in which the animation displays. Additional options may be available with other entrance effects.

Figure 3.14

Effect Options button

Selected placeholder

4　Click **Vertical Out** and notice the direction from which the animation is applied.

5　Select the picture. In the **Animation group**, click the **More** button ⬇, and then below the gallery, click **More Entrance Effects**. Compare your screen with Figure 3.15.

　　The Change Entrance Effect dialog box displays additional entrance effects grouped in four categories: Basic, Subtle, Moderate, and Exciting.

Figure 3.15

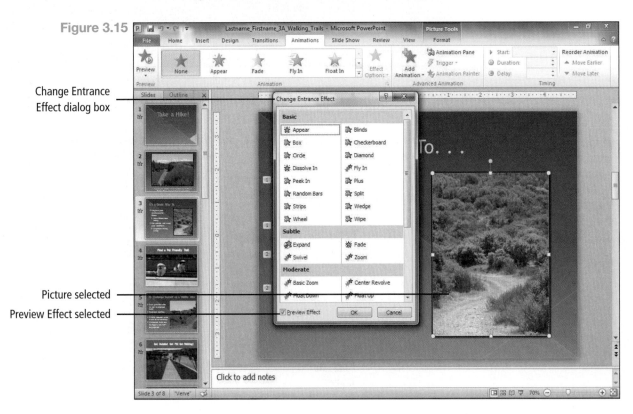

Change Entrance Effect dialog box

Picture selected

Preview Effect selected

6 In the lower right corner of the **Change Entrance Effect** dialog box, verify that the **Preview Effect** check box is selected. Under **Basic**, click **Dissolve In**, and then watch as Live Preview displays the selected entrance effect. Click **OK**.

> The number *3* displays next to the picture, indicating that it is third in the slide animation sequence.

7 Select the title. On the **Animations tab**, in the **Animation group**, click the **More** button ⊽, and then under **Entrance**, click **Split** to apply the animation to the title.

> The number *4* displays next to the title, indicating that it is fourth in the slide animation sequence.

8 Save 🖫 the presentation.

Activity 3.07 | Setting Animation Timing Options

Timing options control when animated items display in the animation sequence.

1 With **Slide 3** displayed, on the **Animations tab**, in the **Preview group**, click the **Preview** button.

> The list displays first, followed by the picture, and then the title. The order in which animation is applied is the order in which objects display during the slide show.

2 Select the title. On the **Animations tab**, in the **Timing group**, under **Reorder Animation**, click the **Move Earlier** button two times, and then compare your screen with Figure 3.16.

> To the left of the title placeholder, the number *1* displays. You can use the Reorder Animation buttons to change the order in which text and objects are animated during the slide show.

Figure 3.16

Reorder Animation options

Animation reordered so that title displays first

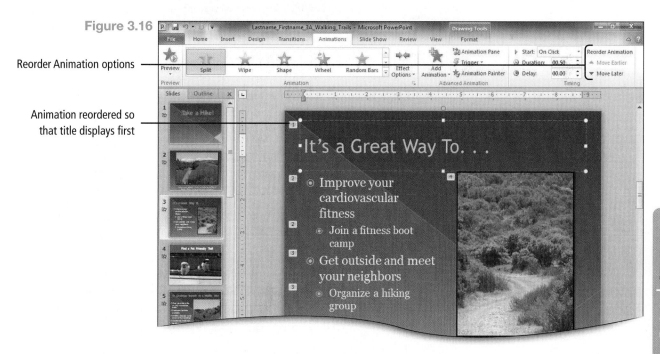

PowerPoint | Chapter 3

3 With the title selected, on the **Animations tab**, in the **Timing group**, click the **Start button arrow** to display three options—*On Click, With Previous,* and *After Previous.* Compare your screen with Figure 3.17.

> The ***On Click*** option begins the animation sequence for the selected slide element when the mouse button is clicked or the ⌴Spacebar⌴ is pressed. The ***With Previous*** option begins the animation sequence at the same time as the previous animation or slide transition. The ***After Previous*** option begins the animation sequence for the selected slide element immediately after the completion of the previous animation or slide transition.

Figure 3.17

Start button arrow —

Start options —

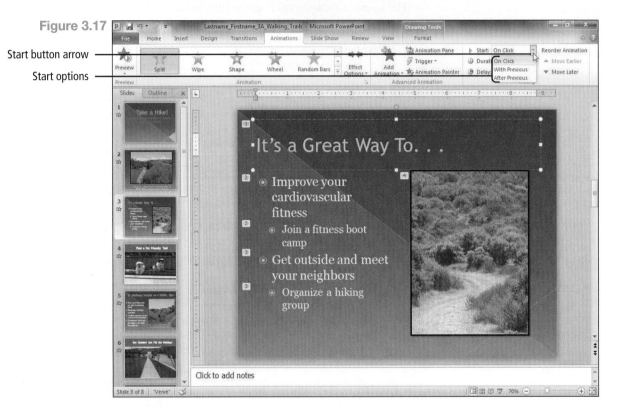

4 Click **After Previous**, and then notice that the number *1* is changed to *0*, indicating that the animation will begin immediately after the slide transition; the presenter does not need to click the mouse button or press ⌴Spacebar⌴ to display the title.

5 Select the picture, and then in the **Timing group**, click the **Start arrow**. Click **With Previous** and notice that the number is changed to *2*, indicating that the animation will begin at the same time as the second set of bullet points in the bulleted list.

6 On the **Animations tab**, in the **Preview group**, click the **Preview** button and notice that the title displays first, and that the picture displays at the same time as the second set of bullet points.

7 Display **Slide 1**, and then click in the title placeholder. On the **Animations tab**, in the **Animation group**, click the **Entrance** effect **Fly In**, and then click the **Effect Options** button. Click **From Top**. In the **Timing group**, click the **Start arrow**, and then click **After Previous**.

> The number *0* displays to the left of the title indicating that the animation will begin immediately after the slide transition.

8 With the title selected, in the **Timing group**, click the **Duration** down arrow so that *00.25* displays in the **Duration** box. Compare your screen with Figure 3.18.

Duration controls the speed of the animation. You can set the duration of an animation by typing a value in the Duration box, or you can use the spin box arrows to increase and decrease the duration in 0.25-second increments. When you decrease the duration, the animation speed increases. When you increase the duration, the animation is slowed.

Figure 3.18

Duration set to *00.25*

Fly In animation applied to title

Zero displays to the left of title placeholder

Duration down arrow

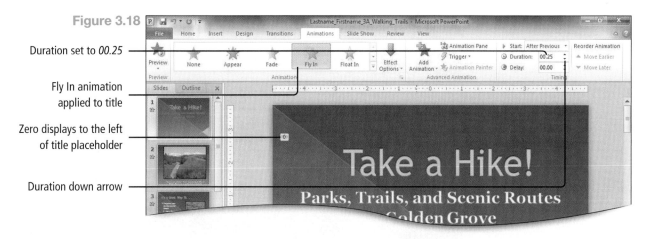

9 Select the subtitle, and then in the **Animation group**, apply the **Fly In** entrance effect. In the **Timing group**, click the **Start arrow**, and then click **After Previous**. In the **Timing group**, select the value in the **Delay** box, type **00.50** and then press Enter. Compare your screen with Figure 3.19.

You can use Delay to begin a selected animation after a specified amount of time has elapsed. Here, the animation is delayed by one-half of a second after the completion of the previous animation—the title animation. You can type a value in the Delay or Duration boxes, or you can use the up and down arrows to change the timing.

Figure 3.19

Fly In animation applied to subtitle

Delay set to *00.50*

10 View the slide show from the beginning and notice the animation on Slides 1 and 3. When the black slide displays, press Esc to return to Normal view, and then **Save** 🖫 the presentation.

Activity 3.08 | Using Animation Painter and Removing Animation

Animation Painter is a feature that copies animation settings from one object to another.

1 Display **Slide 3**, and then click anywhere in the bulleted list. On the **Animations tab**, in the **Advanced Animation group**, click the **Animation Painter** button. Display **Slide 5**, and then point anywhere in the bulleted list placeholder to display the Animation Painter pointer ⬚. Compare your screen with Figure 3.20.

Figure 3.20

Animation Painter button

Animation Painter pointer

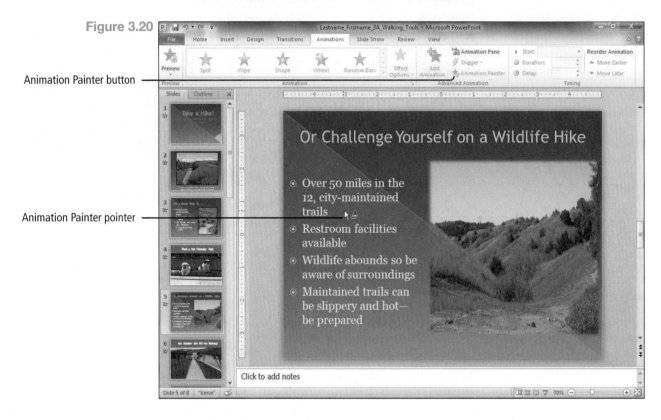

2 Click the bulleted list to copy the animation settings from the list on **Slide 3** to the list on **Slide 5**.

3 Display **Slide 3**, and then select the picture. Using the technique that you just practiced, use **Animation Painter** to copy the animation from the picture on **Slide 3** to the picture on **Slide 5**. With **Slide 5** displayed, compare your screen with Figure 3.21.

The numbers displayed to the left of the bulleted list and the picture indicate that animation is applied to the objects.

Figure 3.21

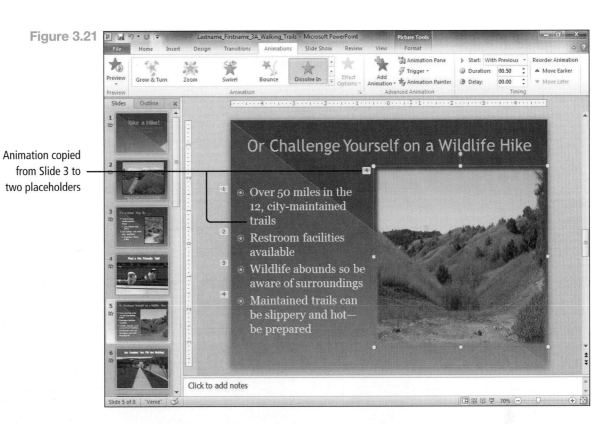

Animation copied from Slide 3 to two placeholders

4 Display **Slide 3**, and then click in the title placeholder. On the **Animations tab**, in the **Animation group**, click the **More** button. At the top of the gallery, click **None** to remove the animation from the title placeholder. Compare your screen with Figure 3.22, and then **Save** the presentation.

Figure 3.22

Animation set to None

Animation removed from title

Objective 3 | Insert a Video

You can insert, size, and move videos in a PowerPoint presentation, and you can format videos by applying styles and effects. Video editing features in PowerPoint 2010 enable you to trim parts of a video and to fade the video in and out during a presentation.

Activity 3.09 | Inserting a Video

1 Display **Slide 1**. On the **Insert tab**, in the **Media group**, click the upper part of the **Video** button. In the **Insert Video** dialog box, navigate to your student files, and then click **p03A_Trails_Video**. Click **Insert**, and then compare your screen with Figure 3.23.

> The video displays in the center of the slide, and playback and volume controls display in the control panel below the video. Video formatting and editing tools display on the Ribbon.

Figure 3.23

Video Tools display

Video inserted

Control panel

2 Below the video, on the control panel, click the **Play/Pause** button ▶ to view the video and notice that as the video plays, the control panel displays the time that has elapsed since the start of the video.

3 On the **Format tab**, in the **Size group**, click in the **Video Height** box. Type **3** and then press Enter. Notice that the video width adjusts proportionately.

4 Point to the video to display the pointer, and then drag the video down so that the top of the video is aligned at **zero on the vertical ruler**. On the **Format tab**, in the **Arrange group**, click the **Align** button, and then click **Align Center** to center the video horizontally on the slide. Compare your screen with Figure 3.24.

Figure 3.24

Video height and
width changed

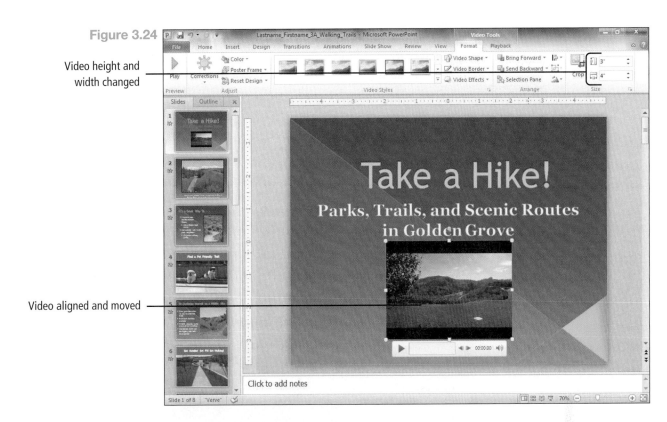

Video aligned and moved

5 In the lower right corner of the PowerPoint window, in the **View** buttons, click the **Slide Show** button to display **Slide 1** in the slide show.

6 Point to the video to display the pointer, and then compare your screen with Figure 3.25.

When you point to the video during the slide show, the control panel displays.

Figure 3.25

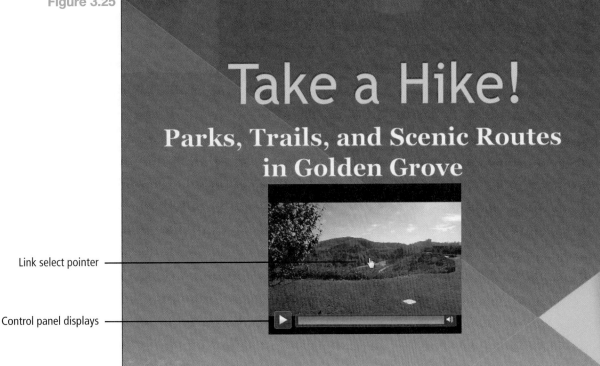

Link select pointer

Control panel displays

7 With the  pointer displayed, click the mouse button to view the video. Move the pointer away from the video and notice that the control panel no longer displays. When the video is finished, press Esc to exit the slide show.

8 **Save** 🖫 the presentation.

Activity 3.10 | Formatting a Video

You can apply styles and effects to a video and change the video shape and border. You can also recolor a video so that it coordinates with the presentation theme.

1 With **Slide 1** displayed, select the video. On the **Format tab**, in the **Video Styles group**, click the **More** button 🔽 to display the **Video Styles** gallery.

2 Using the ScreenTips to view the style name, under **Moderate**, click the first style—**Compound Frame, Black**. Compare your screen with Figure 3.26.

Figure 3.26

Compound Frame, Black style applied to video

3 In the **Video Styles group**, click the **Video Shape** button, and then under **Basic Shapes**, click the first shape—**Oval**. In the **Video Styles group**, click the **Video Border** button, and then in the third column, click the fifth color—**Blue-Gray, Background 2, Darker 25%**. In the **Video Styles group**, click the **Video Effects** button, point to **Bevel**, and then click the last bevel—**Art Deco**. Compare your screen with Figure 3.27.

You can format a video with any combination of styles and effects.

Figure 3.27

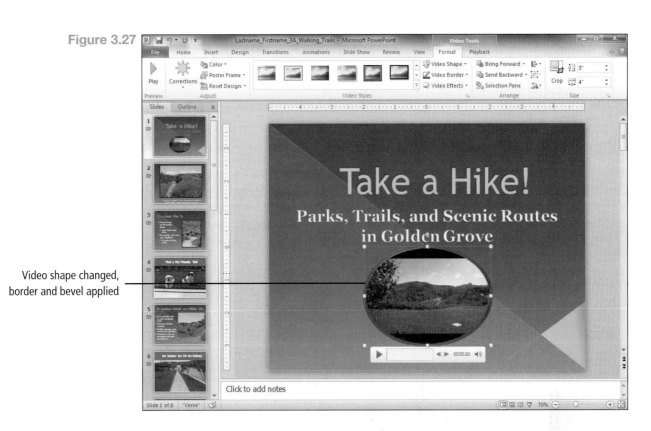

Video shape changed, border and bevel applied

4 If necessary, select the video. On the **Format tab**, in the **Adjust group**, click the **Color** button to display the **Recolor** gallery.

> The first row of the Recolor gallery displays options to recolor the video in grayscale, sepia, washout, or black and white variations. The remaining rows in the gallery display options to recolor the video in the theme colors.

5 In the **Recolor** gallery, in the second row, point to the first style—**Light Blue, Text color 2 Dark** and notice that Live Preview displays the video in the selected color. Compare your screen with Figure 3.28.

Figure 3.28

Color button

Recolor gallery

Selected color

Live Preview displays the video in the selected color

6   Click **Light Blue, Text color 2 Dark** to change the color of the video.

7   In the **Adjust group**, click the **Color** button to display the Recolor gallery. In the first row, click the first color—**No Recolor**, and then **Save** 🖫 the presentation.

>   The No Recolor option restores the video to its original color.

Activity 3.11 │ Editing and Compressing a Video

You can *trim*—delete parts of a video to make it shorter—and you can compress a video file to reduce the file size of your PowerPoint presentation.

1   If necessary, select the video. On the **Playback tab**, in the **Editing group**, click the **Trim Video** button, and then compare your screen with Figure 3.29.

>   At the top of the displayed Trim Video dialog box, the file name and the video duration display. Below the video, a timeline displays with start and end markers indicating the video start and end time. Start Time and End Time boxes display the current start and end of the video. The Previous Frame and Next Frame buttons move the video forward and backward one frame at a time.

Figure 3.29

Duration of video
Video file name
Timeline end marker
End Time box
Timeline start marker
Start Time box

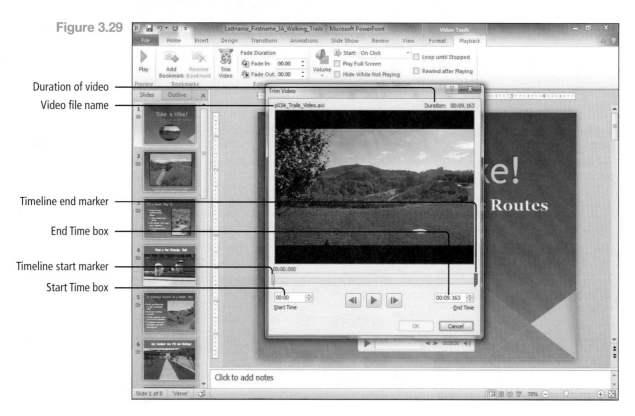

Another Way

Drag the red ending marking until its ScreenTip displays the ending time that you want; or type in the box.

2 Click in the **End Time** box, and then use the spin box arrows to set the End Time to **0:07.040**. Compare your screen with Figure 3.30.

The blue section of the timeline indicates the portion of the video that will play during the slide show. The gray section indicates the portion of the video that is trimmed.

Figure 3.30

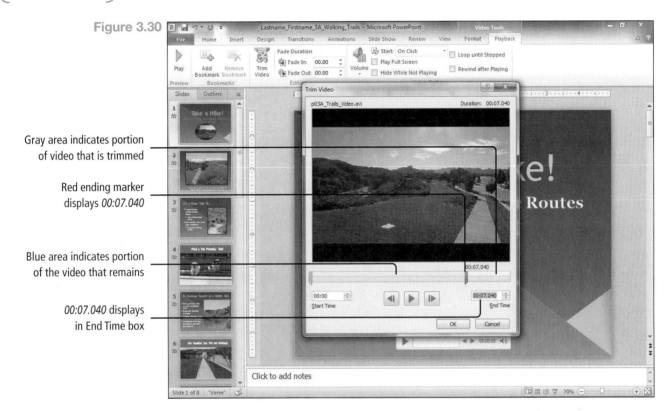

Gray area indicates portion of video that is trimmed

Red ending marker displays *00:07.040*

Blue area indicates portion of the video that remains

00:07.040 displays in End Time box

3 Click **OK** to apply the trim settings.

4 Display **Backstage** view, and then on the **Info tab**, click the **Compress Media** button. Read the description of each video quality option, and then click **Low Quality.** Compare your screen with Figure 3.31.

The Compress Media dialog box displays the slide number on which the selected video is inserted, the video file name, the original size of the video file, and when compression is complete, the amount that the file size was reduced.

Figure 3.31

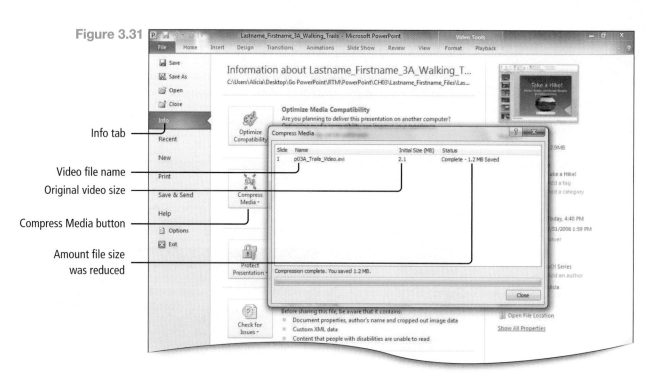

Info tab

Video file name

Original video size

Compress Media button

Amount file size
was reduced

5 In the **Compress Media** dialog box, click **Close**, and then click the **Home tab** to return to **Slide 1**.

6 If necessary, select the video. On the **Playback tab**, in the **Video Options group**, click the **Start arrow**, and then click **Automatically** so that during the slide show, the video will begin automatically. Compare your screen with Figure 3.32.

Figure 3.32

Start option set to
Automatically

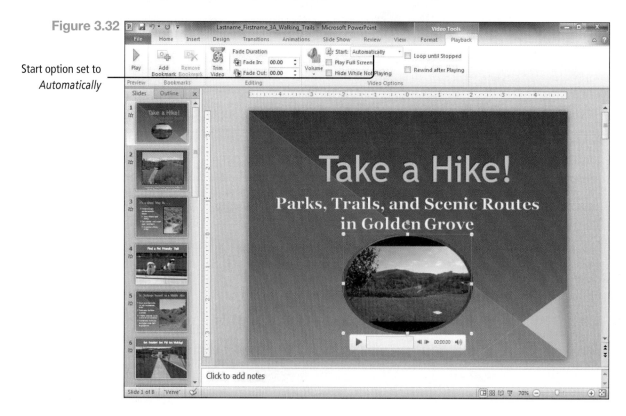

7 Click the **Slide Show tab**, in the **Start Slide Show group**, click the **From Beginning** button, and then view the slide show. Press ⎋ when the black slide displays.

Note | Your Video May Look Blurry

On playback, a compressed video may look slightly blurry. If you are certain that your presentation file will not be transmitted over the Internet, for example, in an e-mail message or in your learning management system, it is not necessary to compress the video.

---

8 On the **Insert tab**, in the **Text group**, click the **Header & Footer** button to display the **Header and Footer** dialog box. Click the **Notes and Handouts tab**. Under **Include on page**, select the **Date and time** check box, and then select **Update automatically**. If necessary, clear the **Header** check box, and then select the **Page number** and **Footer** check boxes. In the **Footer** box, using your own name, type **Lastname_Firstname_3A_ Walking_Trails** and then click **Apply to All**.

9 Show the **Document Panel**. Replace the text in the **Author** box with your own firstname and lastname. In the **Subject** box, type your course name and section number, and in the **Keywords** box, type **trails, hiking Close** the **Document Information Panel**.

10 **Save** 💾 your presentation. Print **Handouts 4 Slides Horizontal**, or submit your presentation electronically as directed by your instructor.

11 **Close** the presentation and exit PowerPoint.

End **You have completed Project 3A** ————————————

GO! Beyond Office

Objective | Create a Link in the OneNote Web App to a Presentation Stored on a SkyDrive

OneNote is a Microsoft application with which you can create a digital notebook that gives you a single location where you can gather and organize information in the form of notes. The OneNote Web App enables you to share your OneNote notebooks on the Web.

> **Alert! | Working with Web-Based Applications and Services**
>
> Computer programs and services on the Web receive continuous updates and improvements. Thus, the steps to complete this Web-based Activity may differ from the ones shown. You can often look at the screens and the information presented to determine how to complete the Activity.

Activity | Creating a Link in the OneNote Web App to a Presentation Stored on a SkyDrive

In this Activity, you will upload a presentation to your SkyDrive, and then create a link to it in a OneNote Web App notebook. Then you will add notes regarding the presentation to your notebook.

1 **Start** PowerPoint, and then open your **Lastname_Firstname_3A_Walking_Trails** presentation.

2 On the **File tab**, click **Save & Send**, and then click **Save to Web**. On the right, click the **Sign In** button, and then if necessary, sign in to your Windows Live account. If you do not have a Windows Live account, refer to Go! Beyond Word Project 1A to create the account, and create a folder in that account named GO! Beyond Office-PowerPoint.

3 Under **Windows Live SkyDrive Shared Folders**, click **GO! Beyond Office-PowerPoint**, click the **Save As** button, and then wait a moment for the **Save As** dialog box to display. Click **Save**.

In the PowerPoint status bar, a progress bar and message indicate that the file is being uploaded to the server. This file is a large file containing a video and may take several minutes to upload.

4 When the file upload is complete, **Close** PowerPoint.

5 Launch your Web browser, navigate to **www.live.com**, and then log in to your **Windows Live account**.

6 At the top of the screen, click **SkyDrive**, and then click your **GO! Beyond Office-PowerPoint** folder.

In the folder, your Lastname_Firstname_3A_Walking_Trails file displays along with any other files you have uploaded to this location.

7 Start the **Snipping Tool**, and then create a **Full-screen Snip**. On the **Snipping Tool** markup window toolbar, click the **Save Snip** button. In the **Save As** dialog box, navigate to your **PowerPoint Chapter 3** folder. Be sure the **Save as type** box displays **JPEG file**. In the **File**

name box, type **Lastname_Firstname_3A_SkyDrive_Snip** and then click **Save**. **Close** the **Snipping Tool** window.

8 Near the top of the window, to the right of **Create**, click the **OneNote notebook** icon. In the **Name** box, with the text *Notebook1* selected, using your own name, type **Lastname_Firstname_3A_Notebook** and then click **Save**.

The OneNote Web App displays a new notebook stored on the SkyDrive. A *notebook* is a collection of files organized by major divisions called *sections*. Each section contains pages where notes are inserted. On the left, the Navigation pane indicates that this notebook has one Untitled Section and Page.

9 In the Navigation pane, point to **Untitled Section**, and then right-click. On the shortcut menu, click **Rename**. In the **Enter a section name** box, type **PowerPoint** and then click **OK** to rename the section.

10 With the insertion point blinking in the blank **Untitled Page** box, type **Walking Trails Presentation** to rename the Untitled Page.

Below the page title, the date and time display to keep track of when you create the notes.

11 Click approximately one inch below the time that displays on your page, and then type **Information for Residents**

12 On the **Home tab**, in the **Styles group**, click the **Heading 1** style to apply the style to the text that you typed.

13 Press [Enter] and then type **This presentation will inform residents about some of the opportunities for exploring the city while maintaining a fitness program.** Press [Enter].

GO! Beyond Office

14 At the top of the OneNote Web App window, following your notebook name, click the text *SkyDrive*, which is an active link, and notice that your OneNote notebook and your PowerPoint presentation display in your **GO! Beyond Office-PowerPoint** folder.

15 Point to the file name of your **Lastname_Firstname_3A_Walking_Trails** presentation to display the 🖑 pointer, and then click to display the presentation in your browser window.

> Above the presentation, a yellow warning bar indicates that the PowerPoint Web App cannot display the video in the presentation.

16 In your Web browser address bar, click one time to select the Web address of your presentation. On your keyboard, press Ctrl + C to copy the address.

17 At the top of the PowerPoint Web App window, click the text *SkyDrive*, and then click **Lastname_Firstname_3A_Notebook** to open your OneNote notebook. Notice that the text you typed and the formatting you applied display, even though you did not save the notebook.

> OneNote saves your work as it is entered. You do not need to save your work.

18 Click below the sentence that you typed on the page. On the **Insert tab**, in the **Links group**, click **Link**. In the displayed **Link** dialog box, with the insertion point blinking in the **Address** box, press Ctrl + V to paste the link to your presentation in the **Address** box.

19 Click in the **Display text** box, type **Walking Trails Information Presentation** and then click the **Insert** button. Compare your screen with Figure A.

> The text you typed displays in blue, underlined text, indicating that the text is a link.

20 Start the **Snipping Tool**, and then create a **Full-screen Snip**. On the **Snipping Tool** markup window toolbar, click the **Save Snip** button 💾. In the **Save As** dialog box, navigate to your **PowerPoint Chapter 3** folder. Be sure the **Save as type** box displays **JPEG file**. In the **File name** box, type **Lastname_Firstname_3A_OneNote_Snip** and then click **Save**. **Close** the **Snipping Tool** window.

21 Point to the link that you inserted, hold down Ctrl, and then click to open the presentation slide show. Click the mouse button to advance the slides. When the last slide displays, close the window, sign out of your Windows Live account, and then close all windows. Submit your two snip files as directed.

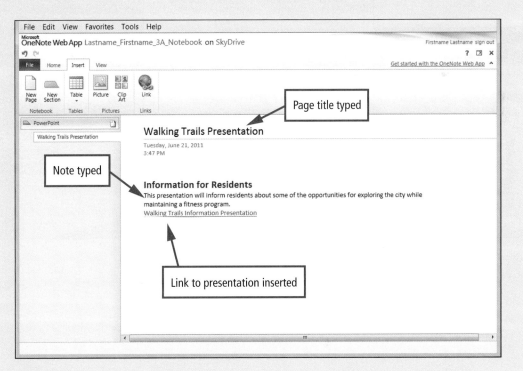

Figure A

Project 3B Summary and Analysis Presentation

Project Activities

In Activities 3.12 through 3.17, you will add a table and two charts to a presentation that Mindy Walker, Director of Parks and Recreation, is creating to inform the City Council about enrollment trends in Golden Grove recreation programs. Your completed presentation will look similar to Figure 3.33.

Project Files

For Project 3B, you will need the following file:

p03B_Recreation_Enrollment

You will save your presentation as:

Lastname_Firstname_3B_Recreation_Enrollment

Project Results

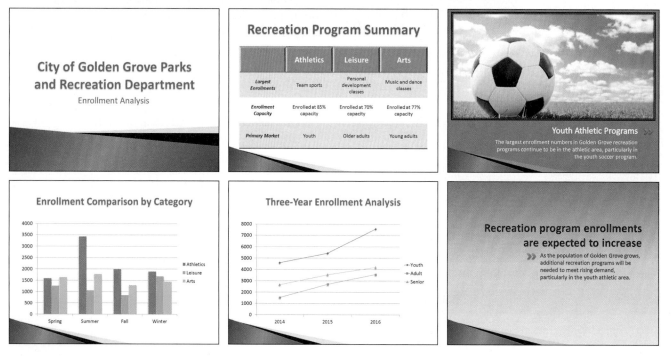

Figure 3.33
Project 3B Recreation Enrollment

Objective 4 | Create and Modify Tables

A *table* is a format for information that organizes and presents text and data in columns and rows. The intersection of a column and row is referred to as a *cell* and is the location in which you type text in a table.

Activity 3.12 | Creating a Table

There are several ways to insert a table in a PowerPoint slide. For example, you can use the Draw Table pointer, which is useful when the rows and columns contain cells of different sizes. Another way is to insert a slide with a Content Layout and then click the Insert Table button. Or, click the Insert tab and then click Table. In this activity, you will use a Content Layout to create a table.

1 **Start** PowerPoint. From your student files, open **p03B_Recreation_Enrollment**, and then **Save** the presentation in your **PowerPoint Chapter 3** folder as **Lastname_Firstname_3B_Recreation_Enrollment**

2 With **Slide 1** displayed, on the **Home tab**, in the **Slides group**, click the **New Slide** button to insert a slide with the **Title and Content** layout. In the title placeholder, type **Recreation Program Summary** and then **Center** ≣ the title.

3 In the content placeholder, click the **Insert Table** button ▦ to display the **Insert Table** dialog box. In the **Number of columns** box, type **3** and then press Tab. In the **Number of rows** box, type **2** and then compare your screen with Figure 3.34.

Here you enter the number of columns and rows that you want the table to contain.

Figure 3.34

Table set for 3 columns and 2 rows

Insert Table button

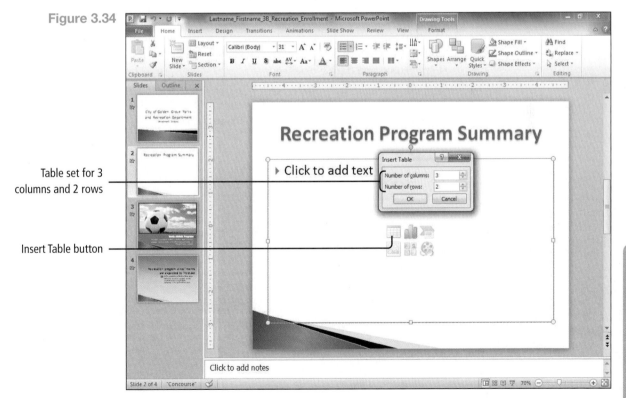

4 Click **OK** to create a table with three columns and two rows. Notice that the insertion point is blinking in the upper left cell of the table.

The table extends from the left side of the content placeholder to the right side, and the three columns are equal in width. By default, a style is applied to the table.

PowerPoint | Chapter 3

5 With the insertion point positioned in the first cell of the table, type **Athletics** and then press ⎄Tab⎄.

> Pressing ⎄Tab⎄ moves the insertion point to the next cell in the same row. If the insertion point is positioned in the last cell of a row, pressing ⎄Tab⎄ moves the insertion point to the first cell of the next row.

Alert! | Did You Press ⎄Enter⎄ Instead of ⎄Tab⎄?

In a table, pressing ⎄Enter⎄ creates another line in the same cell. If you press ⎄Enter⎄ by mistake, you can remove the extra line by pressing ⎄Backspace⎄.

---

6 With the insertion point positioned in the second cell of the first row, type **Leisure** and then press ⎄Tab⎄. Type **Arts** and then press ⎄Tab⎄ to move the insertion point to the first cell in the second row. Compare your table with Figure 3.35.

Figure 3.35

Text typed in first row

Insertion point positioned in second row

7 With the insertion point positioned in the first cell of the second row, type **Team sports** and then press ⎄Tab⎄. Type **Personal development classes** and then press ⎄Tab⎄. Type **Music and dance classes**

8 Press ⎄Tab⎄ to insert a new blank row.

> When the insertion point is positioned in the last cell of a table, pressing ⎄Tab⎄ inserts a new blank row at the bottom of the table.

9 In the first cell of the third row, type **Youth** and then press ⎄Tab⎄. Type **Older adults** and then press ⎄Tab⎄. Type **Young adults** and then compare your table with Figure 3.36. **Save** 🖫 your presentation.

Figure 3.36

Text typed in third row

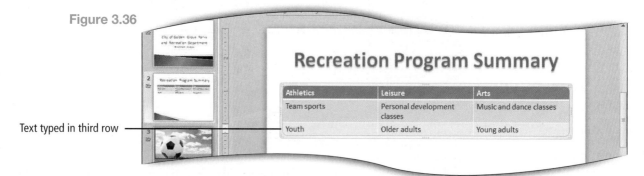

Alert! | Did You Add an Extra Row to the Table?

Recall that when the insertion point is positioned in the last cell of the table, pressing ⎄Tab⎄ inserts a new blank row. If you inadvertently inserted a blank row in the table, on the Quick Access Toolbar, click Undo.

Activity 3.13 | Modifying the Layout of a Table

You can modify the layout of a table by inserting or deleting rows and columns, changing the alignment of the text in a cell, adjusting the height and width of the entire table or selected rows and columns, and by merging multiple cells into one cell.

1 Click in any cell in the first column, and then click the **Layout tab**. In the **Rows & Columns group**, click the **Insert Left** button.

> A new first column is inserted and the width of the columns is adjusted so that all four columns are the same width.

2 In the *second* row, click in the first cell, and then type **Largest Enrollments**

3 In the third row, click in the first cell, and then type **Primary Market** Compare your table with Figure 3.37.

Figure 3.37

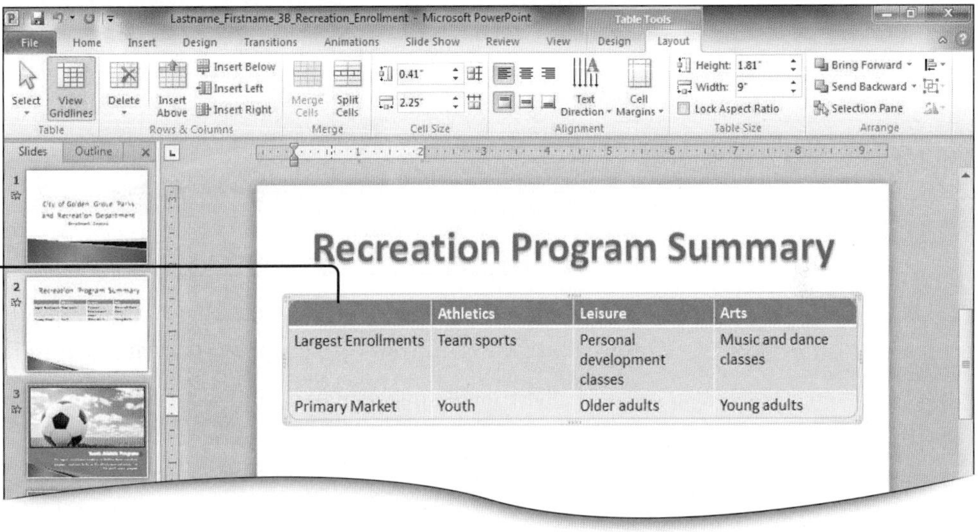

Column inserted and text typed

4 With the insertion point positioned in the third row, on the **Layout tab**, in the **Rows & Columns group**, click the **Insert Above** button to insert a new third row. In the first cell, type **Enrollment Capacity** and then press ⇥. Type the remaining three entries, pressing ⇥ to move from cell to cell: **Enrolled at 85% capacity** and **Enrolled at 70% capacity** and **Enrolled at 77% capacity**

5 At the center of the lower border surrounding the table, point to the cluster of four dots—the sizing handle—to display the ⬍ pointer. Compare your screen with Figure 3.38.

Figure 3.38

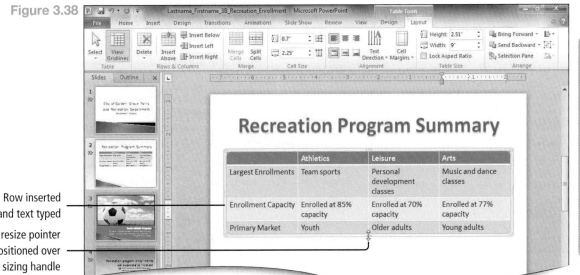

Row inserted and text typed

Vertical resize pointer positioned over sizing handle

6 Drag down to resize the table until the lower left corner of the table outline is just above the graphic in the lower left corner of the slide. Compare your screen with Figure 3.39.

Figure 3.39

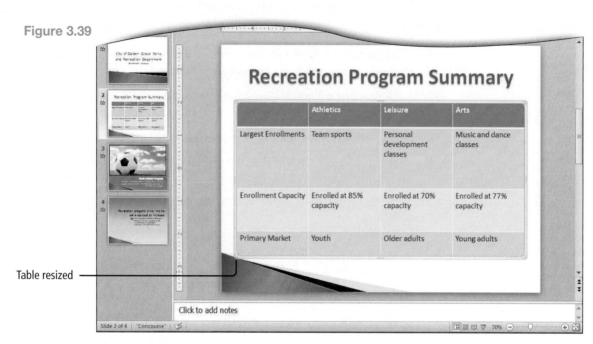

Table resized

7 Click in the first cell of the table. On the **Layout tab**, in the **Cell Size group**, click the **Distribute Rows** button. Compare your table with Figure 3.40.

The Distribute Rows command adjusts the height of the rows in the table so that they are equal.

Figure 3.40

Distribute Rows button

Table rows equal in height

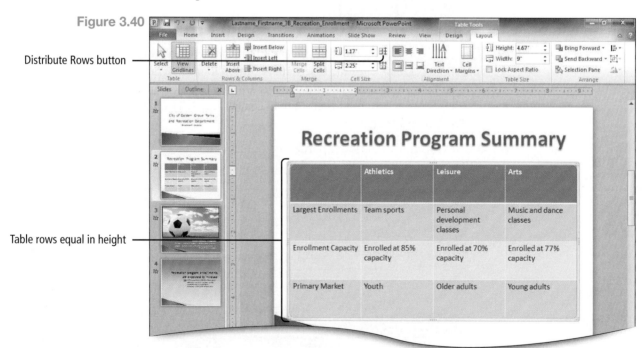

8 On the **Layout tab**, in the **Table group**, click **Select**, and then click **Select Table**. In the **Alignment group**, click the **Center** button, and then click the **Center Vertically** button.

All of the text in the table is centered horizontally and vertically within the cells.

9 **Save** your presentation.

> **More Knowledge** | Deleting Rows and Columns
>
> To delete a row or column from a table, click in the row or column that you want to delete. Click the Layout tab, and then in the Rows & Columns group, click Delete. In the displayed list, click Delete Columns or Delete Rows.

Activity 3.14 | Modifying a Table Design

You can modify the design of a table by applying a *table style*. A table style formats the entire table so that it is consistent with the presentation theme. There are color categories within the table styles—Best Match for Document, Light, Medium, and Dark.

1 Click in any cell in the table. In the **Table Tools**, click the **Design tab**, and then in the **Table Styles group**, click the **More** button ⏷. In the displayed **Table Styles** gallery, point to several of the styles to view the Live Preview of the style.

2 Under **Medium**, scroll as necessary, and then in the third row, click the third button—**Medium Style 3 – Accent 2**—to apply the style to the table.

3 On the **Design tab**, in the **Table Style Options group**, clear the **Banded Rows** check box. Notice that each row except the header row displays in the same color.

> The check boxes in the Table Style Options group control where Table Style formatting is applied.

4 Select the **Banded Rows** check box.

5 Move the pointer outside of the table so that it is positioned to the left of the first row in the table to display the ➡ pointer, as shown in Figure 3.41.

Figure 3.41

Select row pointer ⟶

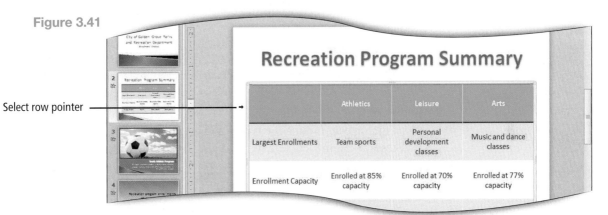

6 With the ➡ pointer pointing to the first row in the table, click the mouse button to select the entire row so that you can apply formatting to the selection. Move the pointer into the selected row, and then right-click to display the Mini toolbar and shortcut menu. On the Mini toolbar, change the **Font Size** to **28**.

7 With the first row still selected, in the **Table Tools**, on the **Design tab**, in the **Table Styles group**, click the **Effects** button ▨. Point to **Cell Bevel**, and then under **Bevel**, click the first bevel—**Circle**.

8 Position the pointer above the first column to display the ⬇ pointer, and then right-click to select the first column and display the shortcut menu. Click **Bold** **B** and **Italic** *I*.

9 Click in a blank area of the slide, and then compare your slide with Figure 3.42. **Save** 🖫 the presentation.

Figure 3.42

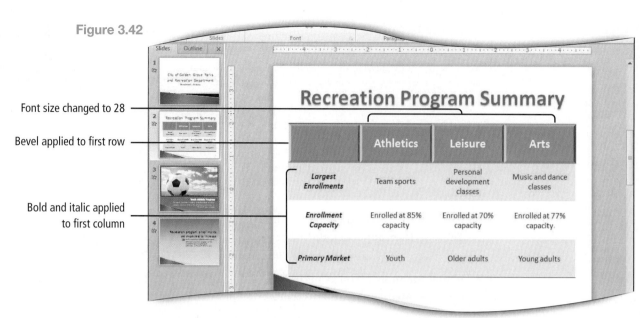

Font size changed to 28

Bevel applied to first row

Bold and italic applied to first column

Objective 5 | Create and Modify Charts

A *chart* is a graphic representation of numeric data. Commonly used chart types include bar and column charts, pie charts, and line charts. A chart that you create in PowerPoint is stored in an Excel worksheet that is incorporated into the PowerPoint file.

Activity 3.15 | Creating a Column Chart and Applying a Chart Style

A *column chart* is useful for illustrating comparisons among related numbers. In this activity, you will create a column chart that compares enrollment in each category of recreation activities by season.

1 Display **Slide 3**, and then add a **New Slide** with the **Title and Content** layout. In the title placeholder, type **Enrollment Comparison by Category** and then **Center** ≡ the title and change the **Font Size** to **36**.

2 In the content placeholder, click the **Insert Chart** button 📊 to display the **Insert Chart** dialog box. Notice the types of charts that you can insert in your presentation. If necessary, on the left side of the dialog box, click Column.

3 Point to the first chart to display the ScreenTip *Clustered Column*. Compare your screen with Figure 3.43.

Figure 3.43

Clustered Column chart

Chart types

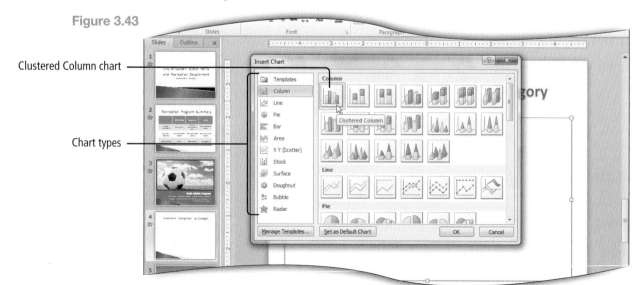

4 Click **Clustered Column**. Click **OK**, and then compare your screen with Figure 3.44.

The PowerPoint window displays a column chart on one side of your screen. On the other side of your screen, an Excel worksheet displays columns and rows. A cell is identified by the intersecting column letter and row number, forming the *cell reference*.

The worksheet contains sample data in a data range outlined in blue, from which the chart in the PowerPoint window is generated. The column headings—*Series 1*, *Series 2*, and *Series 3* display in the chart *legend* and the row headings—*Category 1*, *Category 2*, *Category 3*, and *Category 4*—display as *category labels*. The legend identifies the patterns or colors that are assigned to the data series in the chart. The category labels display along the bottom of the chart to identify the categories of data.

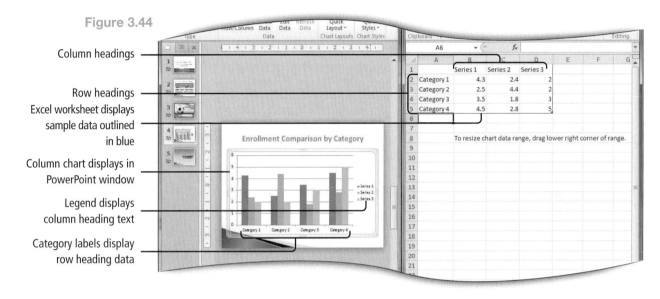

Figure 3.44

Column headings

Row headings

Excel worksheet displays sample data outlined in blue

Column chart displays in PowerPoint window

Legend displays column heading text

Category labels display row heading data

5 In the Excel window, click in cell **B1**, which contains the text *Series 1*. Type **Athletics** and then press Tab to move to cell **C1**.

The chart legend is updated to reflect the change in the Excel worksheet.

6 In cell **C1**, which contains the text *Series 2*, type **Leisure** and then press Tab to move to cell **D1**. Type **Arts** and then press Tab. Notice that cell **A2**, which contains the text *Category 1*, is selected. Compare your screen with Figure 3.45.

The blue box outlining the range of cells defines the area in which you are entering data. When you press Tab in the rightmost cell, the first cell in the next row becomes active.

Figure 3.45

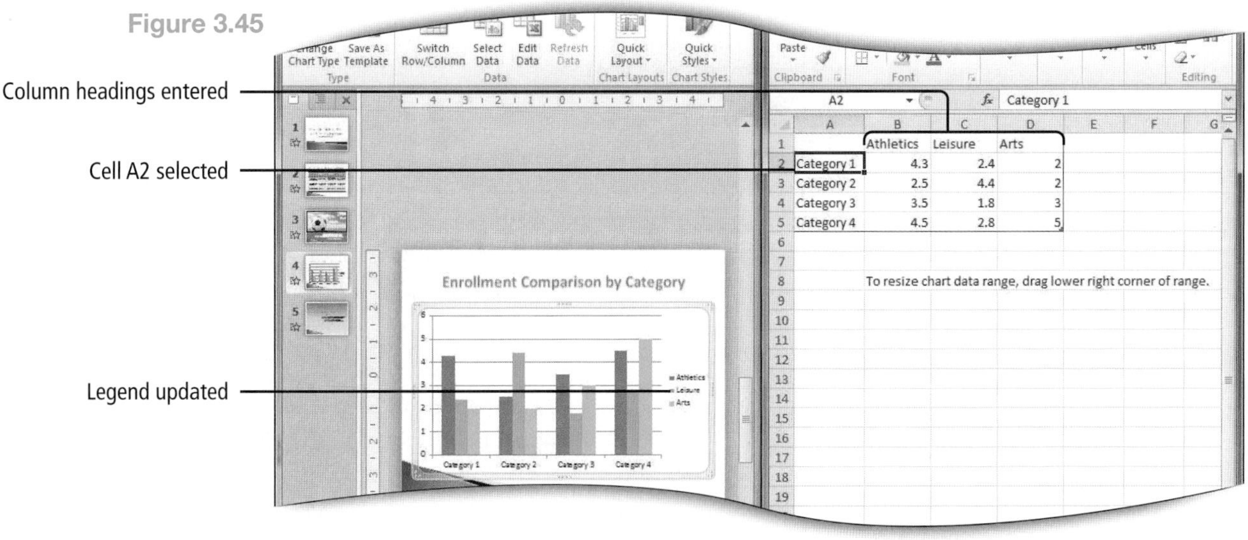

Column headings entered

Cell A2 selected

Legend updated

7 Beginning in cell **A2**, type the following data, pressing ⎯Tab⎯ to move from cell to cell.

	Athletics	Leisure	Arts
Spring	1588	1263	1639
Summer	3422	1058	1782
Fall	1987	852	1293
Winter	1889	1674	

8 In cell **D5**, which contains the value *5*, type **1453** and then press ⎯Enter⎯.

Pressing ⎯Enter⎯ in the last cell of the blue outlined area maintains the existing data range.

Alert! | Did You Press ⎯Tab⎯ After the Last Entry?

If you pressed ⎯Tab⎯ after entering the data in cell D5, you expanded the chart range. In the Excel window, click Undo.

---

9 Compare your worksheet and your chart with Figure 3.46. Correct any typing errors by clicking in the cell that you want to change, and then retype the data.

Each of the 12 cells containing the numeric data that you entered is a *data point*—a value that originates in a worksheet cell. Each data point is represented in the chart by a *data marker*—a column, bar, area, dot, pie slice, or other symbol in a chart that represents a single data point. Related data points form a *data series*; for example, there is a data series for *Athletics*, *Leisure*, and *Arts*. Each data series has a unique color or pattern represented in the chart legend.

Figure 3.46

Worksheet data entered

Chart data markers reflect data in Excel worksheet

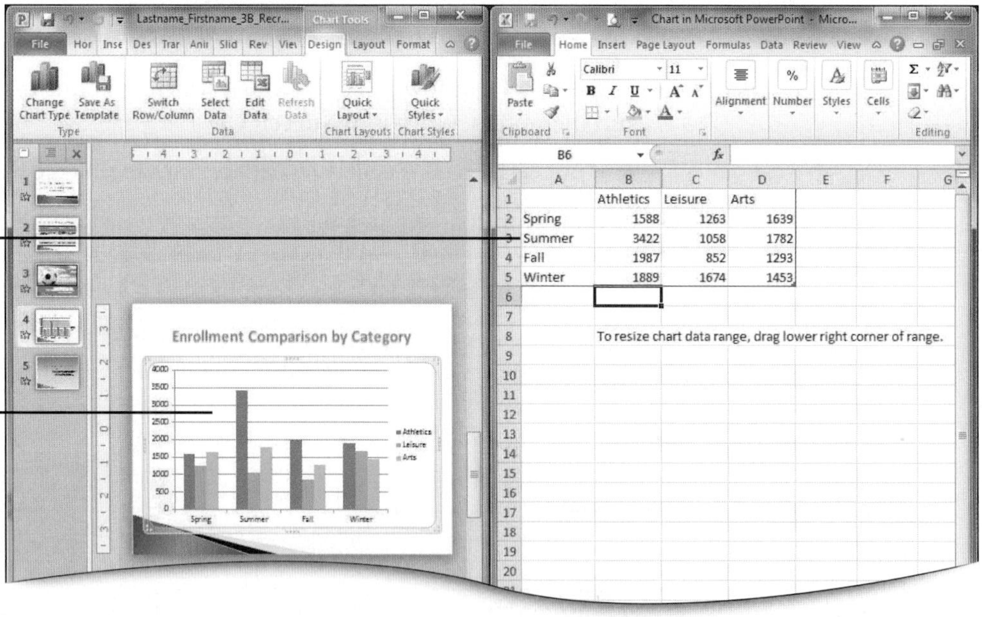

10 In the Excel window, click the **File tab**, and then click **Close**.

You are not prompted to save the Excel worksheet because the worksheet data is a part of the PowerPoint presentation. When you save the presentation, the Excel data is saved with it.

11 Be sure the chart is selected; click the outer edge of the chart if necessary to select it. In the **Chart Tools**, click the **Design tab**, and then in the **Chart Styles group**, click the **More** button ⎯▼⎯.

12 In the **Chart Styles** gallery, the chart styles are numbered sequentially. Use ScreenTips to display the style numbers. Click **Style 10** to apply the style to the chart.

13 Save 🖫 your presentation.

More Knowledge | **Editing the Chart Data After Closing Excel**

You can redisplay the Excel worksheet and make changes to the data after you have closed Excel. To do so, in PowerPoint, click the chart to select it, and then on the Design tab in the Data group, click Edit Data.

Activity 3.16 | Creating a Line Chart and Deleting Chart Data

To analyze and compare annual data over a three-year period, the presentation requires an additional chart. Recall that there are a number of different types of charts that you can insert in a PowerPoint presentation. In this activity, you will create a *line chart*, which is commonly used to illustrate trends over time.

1 With **Slide 4** displayed, add a **New Slide** with the **Title and Content** layout. In the title placeholder, type **Three-Year Enrollment Analysis** and then **Center** 🖹 the title and change the **Font Size** to **36**.

2 In the content placeholder, click the **Insert Chart** button 📊. On the left side of the displayed **Insert Chart** dialog box, click **Line**, and then on the right, under **Line**, click the fourth chart—**Line with Markers**. Click **OK**.

3 In the Excel worksheet, click in cell **B1**, which contains the text *Series 1*. Type **Youth** and then press ⌜Tab⌟. Type **Adult** and then press ⌜Tab⌟. Type **Senior** and then press ⌜Tab⌟.

4 Beginning in cell **A2**, type the following data, pressing ⌜Tab⌟ to move from cell to cell. If you make any typing errors, click in the cell that you want to change, and then retype the data.

	Youth	Adult	Senior
2014	4586	1534	2661
2015	5422	2699	3542
2016	7565	3572	4183

5 In the Excel window, position the pointer over **row heading 5** so that the 🠖 pointer displays. Compare your screen with Figure 3.47.

Figure 3.47

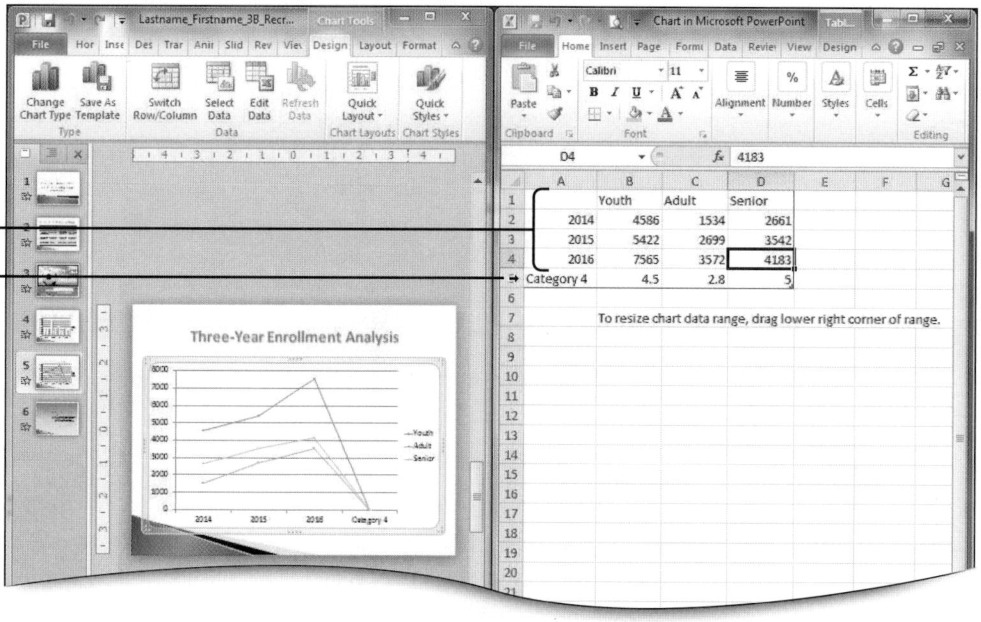

Data entered in worksheet

Row select pointer

PowerPoint | Chapter 3

6 With the ➡ pointer displayed, *right-click* to select the row and display the shortcut menu. On the shortcut menu, click **Delete** to delete the extra row from the worksheet, and then compare your screen with Figure 3.48.

The data in the worksheet contains four columns and four rows, and the blue outline defining the chart data range is resized. You must delete columns and rows that you do not want to include in the chart. You can add additional rows and columns by typing column and row headings and then entering additional data. When data is typed in cells adjacent to the chart range, the range is resized to include the new data.

Figure 3.48

Row with sample data deleted

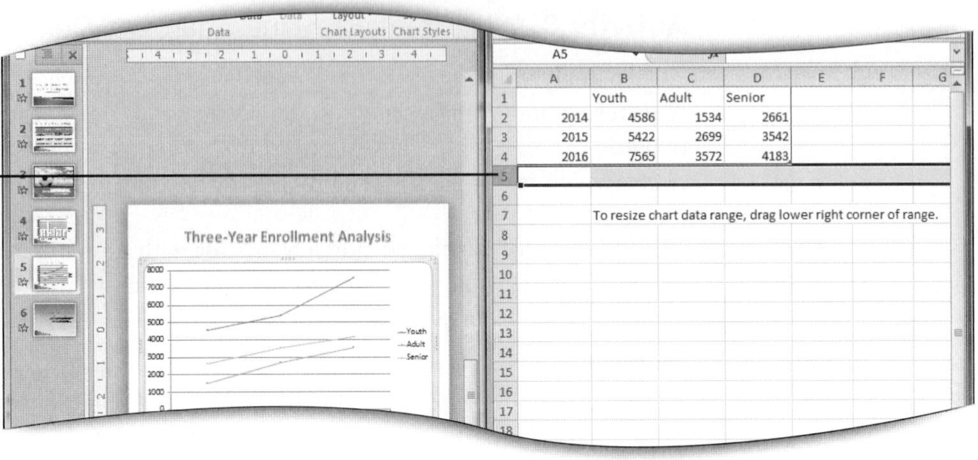

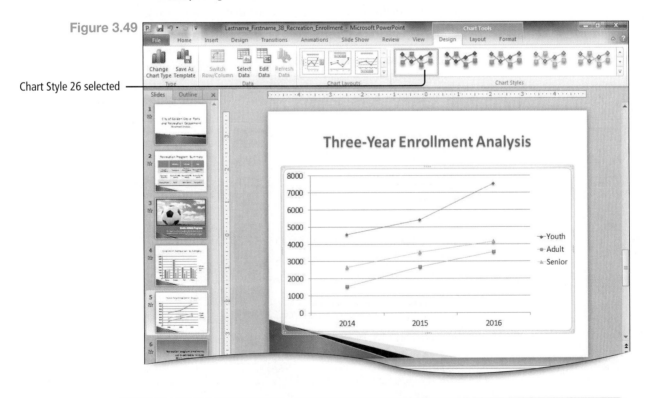

7 **Close** ✖ the Excel window. In the **Chart Styles group**, click the **More** button ▾. In the **Chart Styles** gallery, click **Style 26**, and then compare your slide with Figure 3.49. **Save** 💾 your presentation.

Figure 3.49

Chart Style 26 selected

More Knowledge | **Deleting Columns**

To delete a worksheet column, position the pointer over the column letter that you want to select so that the ⬇ pointer displays. Right-click to select the column and display the shortcut menu. Click Delete.

Activity 3.17 | Animating a Chart

1 Display **Slide 4**, and then click the column chart to select it. On the **Animations tab**, in the **Animation group**, click the **More** button ⏷, and then under **Entrance,** click **Split**.

2 In the **Animation group**, click the **Effect Options** button, and then under **Sequence**, click **By Series**. Compare your screen with Figure 3.50.

> The By Series option displays the chart one data series at a time, and the numbers 1, 2, 3, and 4 to the left of the chart indicate the four parts of the chart animation sequence. The chart animation sequence includes the background, followed by the Athletics data series for each season, and then the Leisure series, and then the Arts series.

Figure 3.50

Split animation applied to chart

Numbers indicate animation sequence

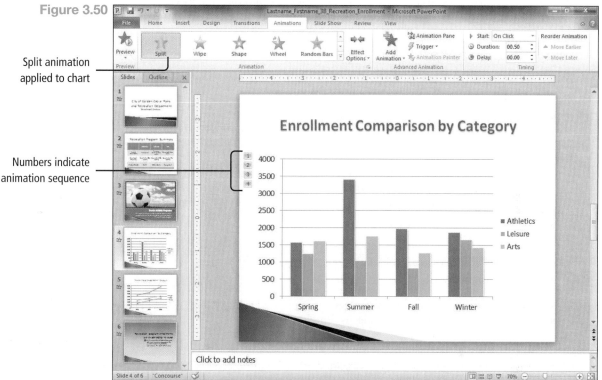

3 Click the **Slide Show tab**. In the **Start Slide Show group**, click **From Current Slide** to view the animation on **Slide 4**. Press Spacebar to display the legend and labels. Press Spacebar again to display the *Athletics* data.

4 Continue to press Spacebar to advance through the remaining animation effects. After the animations for Slide 4 are complete, press Esc to end the slide show and return to the presentation.

5 Insert a **Header & Footer** for the **Notes and Handouts**. Include the **Date and time updated automatically**, the **Page number**, and a **Footer** with the file name **Lastname_ Firstname_3B_Recreation_Enrollment**

6 Show the **Document Panel**. Replace the text in the **Author** box with your own firstname and lastname. In the **Subject** box, type your course name and section number, and in the **Keywords** box, type **enrollment, recreation Close** the **Document Information Panel**.

7 **Save** 🖫 your presentation. Print **Handouts 6 Slides Horizontal**, or submit your presentation electronically as directed by your instructor. **Close** the presentation and exit PowerPoint.

End You have completed Project 3B

GO! Beyond Office

Objective | Save a Presentation as a Movie and Upload the Movie to YouTube

YouTube is a Web site on which you can upload and view videos. You can create a video from a PowerPoint presentation and then share the video by uploading it to YouTube.

Alert! | Working with Web-Based Applications and Services

Computer programs and services on the Web receive continuous updates and improvements. Thus, the steps to complete this Web-based Activity may differ from the ones shown. You can often look at the screens and the information presented to determine how to complete the Activity.

Activity | Saving a Presentation as a Movie and Uploading the Movie to YouTube

When you save a presentation as a video, the transitions, animations, sounds, and timings are included in the video.

1 **Start** PowerPoint and then open your **Lastname_Firstname_3B_Recreation_Enrollment** file. On the **File tab**, click **Save & Send**, and then in the center panel, under **File Types**, click **Create a Video**.

2 On the right, click the **Computer & HD Displays arrow**, and then click **Internet & DVD** to select a resolution that will display well on YouTube.

3 Change the value in the **Seconds to spend on each slide** to **03.00**, and then click **Create Video**. Navigate to your **PowerPoint Chapter 3** folder, and then click **Save**.

In the status bar, a green progress bar displays; when the progress bar no longer displays, the video is complete.

You can work on other tasks while the video is being created.

4 **Close** PowerPoint, and then click **Start**. Click **Computer**, navigate to the location where your **PowerPoint Chapter 3** folder is stored, and then open the folder. Notice that a movie icon displays to the left of the file name and the file type indicates that the file is a Windows Media Audio/Video file. Compare your screen with Figure A.

Your folder may display additional files. Additionally, information about your file may not display depending upon your folder view.

Figure A

---

5 **Close** the Windows Explorer window, and then launch your Web browser. In the address bar, type **http://youtube.com**

6 If you have a YouTube account, sign in to the account and then skip to Step 8. Otherwise, in the YouTube window, click **Create Account** and then in the **Your current email address** box, type your Windows Live e-mail address. In the **Username** box, type a user name and then click **Check Availability** to see if the username is available. If it is not, type another username and continue to check availability until you have entered a username that is available.

7 Complete the remainder of the form, and then click the **I accept. Create my account.** button. Notice that to use YouTube, you must have a Google account. If you have a Google account, type the **Password**, and then click **Link accounts**. If you do not have an account, follow the instructions to create a Google Account.

8 At the top of the **YouTube** window, locate and click **Upload**. In the **Upload Video Files** page, click **Select files from your computer**. Navigate to the location where you stored your movie, select the movie, and then in the lower right corner of the dialog box, click **Open**.

After the file is uploaded, a message displays indicating that the upload is complete and that the video is being processed. When processing is complete, a link to the video displays. Depending upon the size of the file, this may take several minutes.

9 Below the video, in the **Description** box, type **GO! Beyond Office-PowerPoint**

10 Under **Privacy**, select **Unlisted** so that only those people with whom you share a link can view your video. Click **Save changes**.

11 Start the **Snipping Tool**, and then create a **Full-screen Snip**. On the **Snipping Tool** markup window toolbar, click the **Save Snip** button. In the **Save As** dialog box, navigate to your **PowerPoint Chapter 3** folder. Be sure the **Save as type** box displays **JPEG file**. In the **File name** box, type **Lastname_Firstname_3B_YouTube_Snip** and then click **Save**. **Close** the **Snipping Tool** window.

12 To the right of the filename, click the **Watch** button to view your movie.

Your video, including slide animations and transitions, displays.

13 To delete your video, in the upper right corner of the YouTube window, click your **username** to display your account. Click **My Videos**. To the left of your video, click the **check box** to select it. Above your video, click the **Actions** button, and then click **Delete** to display a message indicating that this is a permanent deletion. Click **Continue**.

Your video is deleted from YouTube.

14 Sign out of your YouTube account, **Close** all open windows, and then submit your snip file as directed.

Content-Based Assessments

Summary

In this chapter, you formatted a presentation by applying background styles, inserting pictures on slide backgrounds, and changing the theme fonts. You enhanced your presentation by inserting video, applying animation effects, and by changing effect and timing options. You practiced creating tables to present information in an organized manner, and you used charts to visually represent data.

Key Terms

After Previous 656	**Data point** 678	**Section** 668
Animation 652	**Data series** 678	**Table** 671
Animation Painter 658	**Emphasis effect** 652	**Table style** 675
Background style 646	**Entrance effect** 652	**Theme colors** 645
Body font 645	**Exit effect** 652	**Theme font** 645
Category label 677	**Headings font** 645	**Timing options** 655
Cell 671	**Legend** 677	**Trim** 664
Cell reference 677	**Line chart** 679	**With Previous** 656
Chart 676	**Notebook** 668	**YouTube** 682
Column chart 676	**On Click** 656	
Data marker 678	**OneNote** 668	

Matching

Match each term in the second column with its correct definition in the first column by writing the letter of the term on the blank line in front of the correct definition.

_____ 1. A slide background fill variation that combines theme colors in different intensities.

_____ 2. A theme that determines the font applied to two types of slide text—headings and body.

_____ 3. Of the two types of fonts in the theme font, the type that is applied to slide titles.

_____ 4. Of the two types of fonts in the theme font, the type that is applied to all slide text except titles.

_____ 5. A visual or sound effect added to an object or text on a slide.

_____ 6. Animations that bring a slide element onto the screen.

_____ 7. Animation that emphasizes an object or text that is already displayed.

_____ 8. Animation that moves an object or text off the screen.

_____ 9. A format for information that organizes and presents text and data in columns and rows.

_____ 10. The intersection of a column and row.

_____ 11. Formatting applied to an entire table so that it is consistent with the presentation theme.

_____ 12. A graphic representation of numeric data.

_____ 13. A type of chart used to compare data.

_____ 14. A combination of the column letter and row number identifying a cell.

_____ 15. A chart element that identifies the patterns or colors that are assigned to the each data series in the chart.

A Animation

B Background style

C Body font

D Cell

E Cell reference

F Chart

G Column chart

H Emphasis effect

I Entrance effect

J Exit effect

K Headings font

L Legend

M Table

N Table style

O Theme font

Multiple Choice

Circle the correct answer.

1. The set of coordinating colors applied to the backgrounds, objects, and text in a presentation is called:

   A. theme colors　　　　　**B.** colors set　　　　　**C.** coordinating colors

2. The command that is used to prevent background graphics from displaying on a slide is:

   A. Hide Background Styles　　**B.** Cover Background Graphics　　**C.** Hide Background Graphics

3. Animation options that control when animated items display in the animation sequence are called:

   A. timing options　　　　　**B.** effect options　　　　　**C.** sequence options

4. A feature that copies animation settings from one object to another is:

   A. copy　　　　　**B.** format painter　　　　　**C.** animation painter

5. The action of deleting parts of a video to make it shorter is referred to as:

   A. edit　　　　　**B.** trim　　　　　**C.** crop

6. A chart element that identifies categories of data is a:

   A. data marker　　　　　**B.** category label　　　　　**C.** category marker

7. A column, bar, area, dot, pie slice, or other symbol in a chart that represents a single data point is a:

   A. data marker　　　　　**B.** data point　　　　　**C.** data series

8. A chart value that originates in a worksheet cell is a:

   A. data marker　　　　　**B.** data point　　　　　**C.** data series

9. A group of related data points is called a:

   A. data marker　　　　　**B.** data point　　　　　**C.** data series

10. A type of chart that shows trends over time is a:

    A. pie chart　　　　　**B.** column chart　　　　　**C.** line chart

Apply 3A skills from these Objectives:

1 Customize Slide Backgrounds and Themes
2 Animate a Slide Show
3 Insert a Video

Skills Review | Project **3C** Park

In the following Skills Review, you will format a presentation by applying slide background styles, colors, pictures, and animation. Your completed presentation will look similar to Figure 3.51.

Project Files

For Project 3C, you will need the following files:

p03C_Park
p03C_Park_Scenery
p03C_Park_Video

You will save your presentation as:

Lastname_Firstname_3C_Park

Project Results

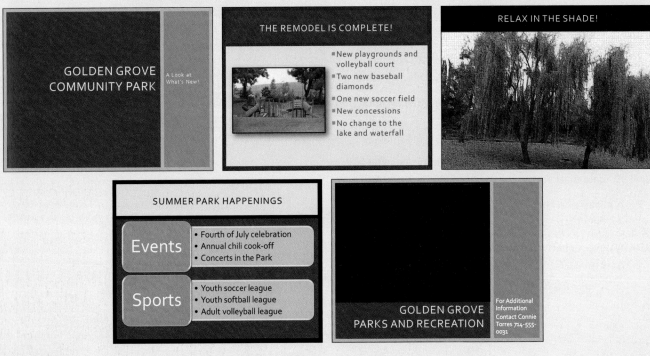

Figure 3.51

(Project 3C Park continues on the next page)

1 **Start** PowerPoint, from your student files open **p03C_Park**, and then **Save** the presentation in your **PowerPoint Chapter 3** folder as **Lastname_Firstname_ 3C_Park**

a. On the **Design tab**, in the **Themes group**, click the **Colors** button, and then click **Apothecary** to change the theme colors. On the **Design tab**, in the **Themes group**, click the **Fonts** button, and then click **Module** to change the theme fonts.

b. Display **Slide 2**, and then on the **Home tab**, in the **Slides group**, click the **New Slide arrow**. Click **Title Only** to insert a new slide with the Title Only layout. Click in the title placeholder. On the **Format tab**, in the **Shape Styles group**, click the **More** button, and then in the last row, click the first style—**Intense Effect - Black, Dark 1**. In the title placeholder, type **Relax in the Shade!**

c. On the **Design tab**, in the **Background group**, select the **Hide Background Graphics** check box.

d. On the **Design tab**, in the **Background group**, click the **Background Styles** button. Below the gallery, click **Format Background**, and then in the **Format Background** dialog box, verify that on the left side, **Fill** is selected. On the right side of the dialog box, under **Fill**, click the **Picture or texture fill** option button. Under **Insert from**, click the **File** button, and then navigate to your student data files. Click **p03C_ Park_Scenery**, and then click **Insert**. In the **Format Background** dialog box, click **Close** to format the slide background with the picture.

e. Point to the outer edge of the title placeholder to display the [↖] pointer, and then drag the placeholder up and to the left so that its top left corner aligns with the top left corner of the slide. Point to the center right sizing handle and drag to the right so that the placeholder extends to the right edge of the slide.

2 Display **Slide 4**. On the **Design tab**, in the **Background group**, click the **Background Styles** button. In the first row, point to the last button—**Style 4**. *Right-click* to display the shortcut menu, and then click **Apply to Selected Slides** to apply the black background to Slide 4.

a. Display **Slide 2**. On the **Design tab**, in the **Background group**, click the **Background Styles** button. Below the gallery, click **Format Background**.

b. In the **Format Background** dialog box, verify that on the left side, **Fill** is selected. On the right side, under **Fill**, click the **Solid Fill** option button, and then under **Fill Color**, click the **Color** button. In the eighth column, click the last color—**Brown, Accent 4, Darker 50%** and then click **Close** to apply the background fill color to the slide.

3 Display **Slide 5**, and then on the **Insert tab**, in the **Media group**, click the **Video** button. Navigate to your student files, and then click **p03_Park_Video**. Click **Insert** to insert the video.

a. With the video selected, on the **Format tab**, in the **Size group**, replace the value in the **Video Height** box with **5.5** and then press [Enter].

b. Point to the video, and then drag up and to the left so that its upper left corner aligns with the upper left corner of the dark brown rectangle.

c. With the video selected, on the **Format tab**, in the **Video Styles** group, click the **Video Effects** button, point to **Bevel**, and then click the last style—**Art Deco**.

d. With the video selected, on the **Playback tab**, in the **Video Options group**, click the **Start arrow**, and then click **Automatically**.

4 Display **Slide 2**, and then click anywhere in the bulleted list placeholder. On the **Animations tab**, in the **Animation group**, click the **More** button, and then under **Entrance**, click **Split**.

a. In the **Animation group**, click the **Effect Options** button, and then click **Vertical Out**.

b. In the **Timing group**, click the **Start arrow**, and then click **After Previous** so that the list displays after the slide transition.

c. In the **Timing group**, click the **Duration up arrow** two times so that *01.00* displays in the **Duration** box. Click the **Delay up arrow** one time so that *00.25* displays in the **Delay** box.

5 Display **Slide 3**, and then click in the title placeholder. On the **Animations tab**, in the **Animation group**, click the **More** button, and then under **Entrance**, click **Wipe**. In the **Timing group**, click the **Start arrow**, and then click **After Previous**.

a. Select the title, and then in the **Advanced Animation group**, click the **Animation Painter** button. Click

(Project 3C Park continues on the next page)

Skills Review | Project **3C** Park (continued)

Slide 1, and then click the subtitle to apply the animation effect to the subtitle.

b. On **Slide 1**, select the title. On the **Animations tab**, in the **Animation group**, click the More button, and then click **None** to remove the animation from the title.

c. On the **Slide Show tab**, in the **Start Slide Show group**, click **From Beginning**, and then view your presentation, clicking the mouse button to advance through the slides.

d. Insert a **Header & Footer** for the **Notes and Handouts**. Include the **Date and time updated**

automatically, the **Page number**, and a **Footer** with the file name **Lastname_Firstname_3C_Park** Click **Apply to All**.

e. Show the **Document Panel**. Replace the text in the **Author** box with your own first and last name. In the **Subject** box, type your course name and section number, and in the **Keywords** box, type **park, summer Close** the **Document Information Panel**.

f. **Save** your presentation. Print **Handouts 6 Slides Horizontal**, or submit your presentation electronically as directed by your instructor. **Close** the presentation.

End You have completed Project 3C _____

Content-Based Assessments

Apply **3B** skills from these Objectives:

4 Create and Modify Tables

5 Create and Modify Charts

Skills Review | Project **3D** Technology Budget

In the following Skills Review, you will format a presentation by inserting and formatting a table, column chart, and line chart. Your completed presentation will look similar to Figure 3.52.

Project Files

For Project 3D, you will need the following file:

p03D_Technology_Budget

You will save your presentation as:

Lastname_Firstname_3D_Technology_Budget

Project Results

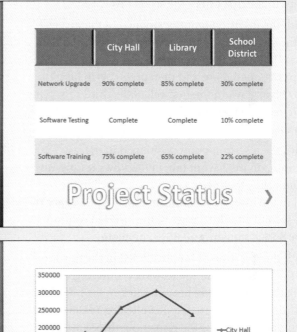

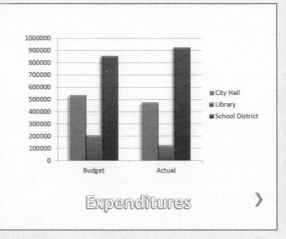

Figure 3.52

(Project 3D Technology Budget continues on the next page)

PowerPoint | Chapter 3

Content-Based Assessments

1 **Start** PowerPoint, from your student files open **p03D_Technology_Budget**, and then **Save** the presentation in your **PowerPoint Chapter 3** folder as **Lastname_Firstname_3D_Technology_Budget**

a. Display **Slide 2**. In the content placeholder, click the **Insert Table** button to display the **Insert Table** dialog box. In the **Number of columns box**, type **3** and then press Tab. In the **Number of rows** box, type **2** and then click **OK** to create the table.

b. In the first row of the table, click in the second cell. Type **City Hall** and then press Tab. Type **School District** and then press Tab to move the insertion point to the first cell in the second row.

c. With the insertion point positioned in the first cell of the second row, type **Network Upgrade** and then press Tab. Type **90% complete** and then press Tab. Type **30% complete** and then press Tab to insert a new blank row. In the first cell of the third row, type **Software Training** and then press Tab. Type **75% complete** and then press Tab. Type **22% complete**

d. With the insertion point positioned in the last column, on the **Layout tab**, in the **Rows & Columns group**, click the **Insert Left** button. Click in the top cell of the inserted column, and then type **Library** In the second and third rows of the inserted column, type **85% complete** and **65% complete**

e. With the insertion point positioned in the third row, on the **Layout tab**, in the **Rows & Columns group**, click the **Insert Above** button. Click in the first cell of the row you inserted, type **Software Testing** and then press Tab. Type the remaining three entries in the row as follows: **Complete** and **Complete** and **10% complete**

2 At the center of the lower border surrounding the table, point to the cluster of four dots—the sizing handle—and make the table larger by dragging down until the lower edge of the table aligns at **2 inches on the lower half of the vertical ruler**.

a. Click in the first cell of the table. On the **Layout tab**, in the **Cell Size group**, click the **Distribute Rows** button.

b. On the **Layout tab**, in the **Table group**, click **Select**, and then click **Select Table**. In the **Alignment group**, click the **Center** button, and then click the **Center Vertically** button.

c. Click in any cell in the table. In the **Table Tools**, click the **Design tab**, and then in the **Table Styles group**, click the **More** button. Under **Medium**, in the third row, click the second style—**Medium Style 3 – Accent 1**—to apply the style to the table.

d. Move the pointer outside of the table so that is positioned to the left of the first row in the table to display the ➡ pointer, click one time to select the entire row. Click the **Design tab**, and then in the **Table Styles group**, click the **Effects** button. Point to **Cell Bevel**, and then under **Bevel**, click the first bevel—**Circle**. Change the **Font Size** of the text in the first row to **24**.

3 Display **Slide 3**. In the content placeholder, click the **Insert Chart** button to display the **Insert Chart** dialog box. Click the first chart—*Clustered Column*—and then click OK.

a. In the Excel window, click in cell **B1**, which contains the text *Series 1*. Type **City Hall** and then press Tab to move to cell **C1**.

b. In cell **C1**, which contains the text *Series 2*, type **Library** and then press Tab to move to cell **D1**, which contains the text *Series 3*. Type **School District** and then press Tab.

c. Beginning in cell **A2**, type the following data, pressing Tab to move from cell to cell.

	City Hall	Library	School District
Budget	535650	210000	856350
Actual	475895	125760	925785

d. In the Excel window, position the pointer over **row heading 4** so that the ➡ pointer displays. Then, drag down to select both **rows 4** and **5**. *Right-click* in one of the selected the rows and display the shortcut menu. On the shortcut menu, click **Delete**. **Close** the Excel window.

e. If necessary, click the edge of the chart so that it is selected. In the **Chart Tools**, click the **Design tab**, and then in the **Chart Styles group**, click the **More** button. In the **Chart Styles** gallery, click **Style 26** to apply the style to the chart.

f. With the chart selected, click the **Animations tab**, and then in the **Animation group**, click the **More** button. Under **Entrance**, click **Split**. In the

(Project 3D Technology Budget continues on the next page)

Animation group, click the **Effect Options** button, and then under **Sequence**, click **By Series**.

4 Display **Slide 4**. In the content placeholder, click the **Insert Chart** button. On the left side of the displayed **Insert Chart** dialog box, click **Line**, and then under **Line**, click the fourth chart—**Line with Markers**. Click **OK**.

a. In the Excel worksheet, click in cell **B1**, which contains the text *Series 1*. Type **City Hall** and then press [Tab]. Type **Library** and then press [Tab]. Type **School District** and then press [Tab].

b. Beginning in cell **A2**, type the following data, pressing [Tab] to move from cell to cell.

	City Hall	Library	School District
Quarter 1	186575	10265	125685
Quarter 2	139670	38675	256830
Quarter 3	83620	42730	305760
Quarter 4	66030	34090	237510

c. **Close** the Excel window.

d. On the **Chart Tools Design tab**, in the **Chart Styles group**, click the **More** button. In the **Chart Styles** gallery, click **Style 34**.

e. Insert a **Header & Footer** for the **Notes and Handouts**. Include the **Date and time updated automatically**, the **Page number**, and a **Footer** with the file name **Lastname_Firstname_3D_Technology_Budget** Click **Apply to All**.

f. Show the **Document Panel**. Replace the text in the **Author** box with your own first and last name. In the **Subject** box, type your course name and section number, and in the **Keywords** box, type **technology, budget Close** the **Document Information Panel**.

g. View the slide show from the beginning, and then **Save** your presentation. Print **Handouts 4 Slides Horizontal**, or submit your presentation electronically as directed by your instructor. **Close** the presentation and exit PowerPoint.

End You have completed Project 3D ——————————————

Apply **3A** skills from these Objectives:

1 Customize Slide Backgrounds and Themes
2 Animate a Slide Show
3 Insert a Video

Mastering PowerPoint | Project **3E** Arboretum

In the following Mastering PowerPoint project, you will format a presentation created by the Golden Grove Public Relations department that describes the City of Golden Grove Arboretum. Your completed presentation will look similar to Figure 3.53.

Project Files

For Project 3E, you will need the following files:

p03E_Arboretum
p03E_Arboretum_Flower
p03E_Arboretum_Video

You will save your presentation as:

Lastname_Firstname_3E_Arboretum

Project Results

Figure 3.53

(Project 3E Arboretum continues on the next page)

Content-Based Assessments

1 **Start** PowerPoint. From the student files that accompany this textbook, locate and open **p03E_ Arboretum**. Change the **Theme Colors** for the presentation to **Opulent**, and the **Theme Fonts** to **Clarity**. Save the presentation in your **PowerPoint Chapter 3** folder as **Lastname_Firstname_3E_ Arboretum**

2 On **Slide 1**, format the background with a picture from your student files—**p03E_Arboretum_Flower**.

3 On **Slide 2**, display the **Background Styles** gallery, right-click **Background Style 10**, and then apply the style to this slide only. Select the paragraph on the left side of the slide, and then apply the **Split** entrance effect. Change the **Effect Options** to **Horizontal Out**. Change the **Start** setting to **After Previous**, and then change the **Duration** to **01.00**.

4 On **Slide 3**, format the **Background Style** by applying a **Solid fill—Pink, Accent 1, Darker 50%**. **Center** the title, and then remove the entrance effect from the title.

5 On **Slide 4**, hide the background graphics, and then apply background **Style 10**. From your student files, insert the video **p03E_Arboretum_Video**. Change the **Video Height** to **4.5** and then using the **Align to Slide** option, apply the **Align Center** and **Align Middle** options. Format

the video by applying, from the **Video Styles** gallery, a **Moderate** style—**Rotated, Gradient**. Change the **Start** setting to **Automatically**.

6 **Insert** a **WordArt** using the third style in the fourth row—**Gradient Fill - Black, Outline - White, Outer Shadow**. Type **Visit the Arboretum!** Drag the WordArt so that its lower left corner aligns with the lower left corner of the slide.

7 Display **Slide 2**, and then use **Animation Painter** to apply the animation from the paragraph on the left side of the slide to the bulleted list on **Slide 3**.

8 **Insert** a **Header & Footer** on the **Notes and Handouts**. Include the **Date and time updated automatically**, the **Page number**, and a **Footer** with the text **Lastname_Firstname_3E_Arboretum**

9 Update the **Document Properties** with your name, course name and section number, and the **Keywords arboretum information Close** the **Document Information Panel**.

10 **Save** your presentation, and then view the slide show from the beginning. Submit your presentation electronically, or print **Handouts 4 Slides Horizontal** as directed by your instructor. **Close** the presentation.

End **You have completed Project 3E** —————————————————

Content-Based Assessments

Mastering PowerPoint | Project **3F** Budget

In the following Mastering PowerPoint project, you will format several of the slides in a presentation that the City Manager is developing for an upcoming City Council meeting. Your completed presentation will look similar to Figure 3.54.

Project Files

For Project 3F, you will need the following file:

   p03F_Budget

You will save your presentation as:

   Lastname_Firstname_3F_Budget

Project Results

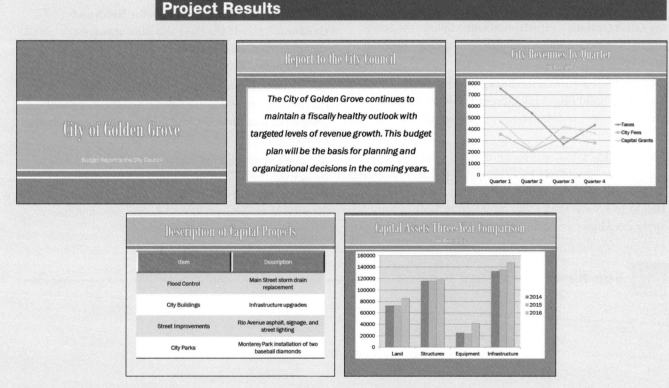

Figure 3.54

(Project 3F Budget continues on the next page)

Content-Based Assessments

Mastering PowerPoint | Project **3F** Budget (continued)

1 **Start** PowerPoint. From your student files open **p03F_Budget**, and then **Save** the presentation in your **PowerPoint Chapter 3** folder as **Lastname_Firstname_3F_Budget**

2 On **Slide 3**, in the content placeholder, insert a **Line with Markers** chart. In the Excel worksheet, in cell **B1**, type **Taxes** and then enter the following data:

	Taxes	City Fees	Capital Grants
Quarter 1	7550	3550	4650
Quarter 2	5380	2095	2185
Quarter 3	2695	3260	4220
Quarter 4	4360	2790	3670

3 **Close** the Excel window. Apply **Chart Style 37** to the chart, and then apply the **Wipe** entrance effect to the chart.

4 On **Slide 4**, in the content placeholder, insert a **Table** with **2 columns** and **5 rows**, and then type the text in **Table 1** at the bottom of the page.

5 Resize the table so that its lower edge extends to **3 inches on the lower half of the vertical ruler**, and then distribute the table rows. Align the table text so that it is centered horizontally and vertically within the cells. Apply table style **Medium Style 3 - Accent 4**, and then apply a **Circle Bevel** to the first row. Change the table text **Font Size** to **20**.

6 On **Slide 5**, in the content placeholder, insert a **Clustered Column** chart. In the Excel worksheet, in cell **B1**, type **2014** and then enter the following data:

	2014	2015	2016
Land	72627	73823	85685
Structures	115746	115920	117812
Equipment	25002	23485	41762
Infrastructure	132586	135860	147873

7 **Close** the Excel window. Apply **Chart Style 34** to the chart, and then apply the **Wipe** entrance effect to the chart. Change the **Effect Options** so that the animation is applied **By Series**. Change the **Timing** so that the animation starts **After Previous**.

8 Insert a **Header & Footer** for the **Notes and Handouts**. Include the **Date and time updated automatically**, the **Page number**, and a **Footer** with the file name **Lastname_Firstname_3F_Budget** Update the **Document Properties** with your name, course name and section number, and the **Keywords budget, revenue, capital Close** the **Document Information Panel**.

9 View the slide show from the beginning, and then **Save** your presentation. Print **Handouts 6 Slides Horizontal**, or submit your presentation electronically as directed by your instructor. **Close** the presentation.

Table 1

Item	Description
Flood Control	Main Street storm drain replacement
City Buildings	Infrastructure upgrades
Street Improvements	Rio Avenue asphalt, signage, and street lighting
City Parks	Monterey Park installation of two baseball diamonds

--- ▶ (Return to Step 5)

End **You have completed Project 3F** _____

Content-Based Assessments

Apply **3A** and **3B** skills from these Objectives:

1 Customize Slide Backgrounds and Themes
2 Animate a Slide Show
3 Insert a Video
4 Create and Modify Tables
5 Create and Modify Charts

Mastering PowerPoint | Project **3G** Restaurants

In the following Mastering PowerPoint project, you will format a presentation that the Golden Grove Public Relations Director will show at a meeting of the National Restaurant Owners Association to encourage new restaurant and catering business in the city. Your completed presentation will look similar to Figure 3.55.

Project Files

For Project 3G, you will need the following files:

> p03G_Restaurants
> p03G_Town_Center
> p03G_Catering

You will save your presentation as:

> Lastname_Firstname_3G_Restaurants

Project Results

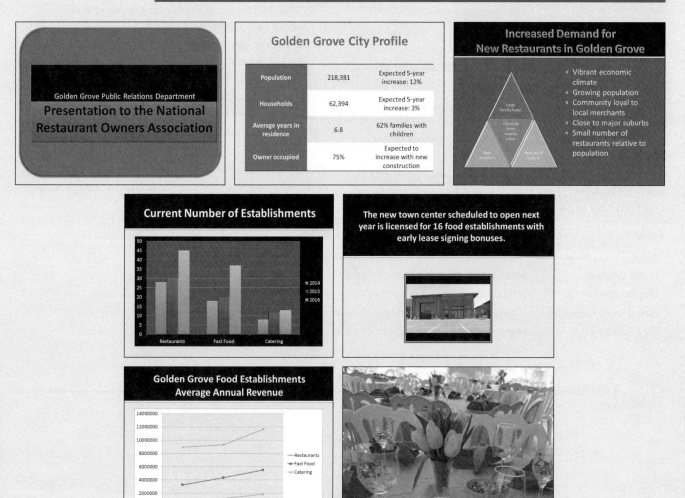

Figure 3.55

(Project 3G Restaurants continues on the next page)

1 Start PowerPoint. From the student files that accompany this textbook, locate and open **p03G_Restaurants**. Change the **Theme Colors** for the presentation to **Apothecary**, and the **Theme Fonts** to **Composite**. **Save** the presentation in your **PowerPoint Chapter 3** folder as Lastname_Firstname_3G_Restaurants

2 On **Slide 2**, insert a **Table** with **3 columns** and **4 rows**. Apply table style **Medium Style 3 - Accent 2**, and then type the information in **Table 1**, shown at the bottom of this page, into the inserted table.

3 On the **Design tab**, in the **Table Style Options group**, select *only* the **First Column** and **Banded Rows** check boxes. Resize the table so that its lower edge extends to **3 inches on the lower half of the vertical ruler**, and then distribute the table rows. Align the table text so that it is centered horizontally and vertically within the cells, and then change the **Font Size** of all of the table text to **24**.

4 On **Slide 3**, display the **Background Styles** gallery, right-click **Background Style 3**, and then apply the style to this slide only. Animate the **SmartArt** graphic using the **Wipe** entrance effect starting **After Previous**. Apply the **Split** entrance effect to the bulleted list placeholder, and then change the **Effect Options** to **Vertical Out**.

5 On **Slide 4**, insert a **Clustered Column** chart. In the Excel worksheet, in cell **B1** type **2014** and then enter the following data:

	2014	2015	2016
Restaurants	28	30	45
Fast Food	18	20	37
Catering	8	12	13

6 In the Excel window, delete **row 5**, and then **Close** the Excel window. Apply **Chart Style 42** to the chart, and then apply the **Wipe** entrance effect to the chart.

7 On **Slide 5**, from your student files, insert the video **p03G_Town_Center**. Change the **Video Height** to **3** and then drag the video down so that its top edge aligns at **zero on the vertical ruler**. Apply the **Align Center**

alignment option, display the **Video Styles** gallery, and then apply the first **Moderate** style—**Compound Frame, Black**. Change the **Video Border** to **Gray-50%, Accent 1, Darker 50%**—in the fifth column, the last color.

8 On the **Playback tab**, change the **Video Options** to **Start** the video **Automatically**. **Trim** the video so that the **End Time** is 00:05.560

9 On **Slide 6**, in the content placeholder, insert a **Line with Markers** chart. In the Excel worksheet, in cell **B1**, type **Restaurants** and then enter the following data:

	Restaurants	Fast Food	Catering
2014	8956231	3284680	856700
2015	9326852	4369571	1235640
2016	11689730	5526895	1894325

10 In the Excel window, delete **row 5**, and then **Close** the Excel window. Apply **Chart Style 34** to the chart, and then use **Animation Painter** to copy the animation from the column chart on **Slide 4** to the line chart on **Slide 6**.

11 On **Slide 7**, hide the background graphics. Format the slide background by inserting a picture from your student files—**p03G_Catering**. Change the title placeholder **Shape Fill** color to **Black, Text 1**, and then change the **Font Color** to **Red, Accent 2**. Size the placeholder so that it extends from the left edge of the slide to the right edge of the slide, and then position it so that its lower edge aligns with the lower edge of the slide. **Center** the text.

12 Insert a **Header & Footer** for the **Notes and Handouts**. Include the **Date and time updated automatically**, the **Page number**, and a **Footer** with the file name Lastname_Firstname_3G_Restaurants Update the **Properties** with your name, course name and section number, and the **Keywords catering, restaurants Close** the **Document Information Panel**.

13 View the slide show from the beginning, and then **Save** your presentation. Print **Handouts 4 Slides Horizontal**, or submit your presentation electronically as directed by your instructor. **Close** the presentation.

Table 1

Population	218,381	Expected 5-year increase: 12%
Households	62,394	Expected 5-year increase: 3%
Average years in residence	6.8	62% families with children
Owner occupied	75%	Expected to increase with new construction

- - → (Return to Step 3)

End You have completed Project 3G

Content-Based Assessments

GO! Fix It | Project 3H Housing Developments

Project Files

For Project 3H, you will need the following file:

p03H_Housing_Developments

You will save your presentation as:

Lastname_Firstname_3H_Housing_Developments

In this project, you will edit several slides from a presentation prepared by the Golden Grove Planning Department regarding real estate developments in the city. From the student files that accompany this textbook, open the file p03H_Housing_Developments, and then save the file in your chapter folder as **Lastname_Firstname_3H_Housing_Developments**

To complete the project, you should know:

- The Theme Colors should be changed to Module and the Theme Fonts should be changed to Apex.

- The titles on Slides 2 and 3 should be centered.

- On Slide 2, the table style Light Style 2 - Accent 2 should be applied and a column should be added to right of the last column in the table. In the inserted column, the following text should be entered in the three cells: **Bering** and **37%** and **August 2016**

- On Slides 3 and 4, the charts should be animated with the Wipe entrance effect.

- Document Properties should include your name, course name and section, and the keywords **property tax, housing** A Header & Footer should be inserted on the Notes and Handouts that includes the Date and time updated automatically, the Page number and a Footer with the text **Lastname_Firstname_3H_Housing_Developments**

Save and submit your presentation electronically or print Handouts 4 Slides Horizontal as directed by your instructor. Close the presentation.

End **You have completed Project 3H** ———————————————

Content-Based Assessments

Apply a combination of the 3A and 3B skills.

GO! Make It | Project 3I Arboretum

Project Files

For Project 3I, you will need the following files:

New blank PowerPoint presentation
p03I_Flowers

You will save your presentation as:

Lastname_Firstname_3I_Arboretum

Start PowerPoint to begin a new blank presentation, and apply the Opulent theme. Save the file in your PowerPoint Chapter 3 folder as **Lastname_Firstname_3I_Arboretum**

By using the skills you practiced in this chapter, create the first two slides of the presentation shown in Figure 3.56. The layout for Slide 1 is Title Only, and the background is formatted with the picture from your student data files—p03I_Flowers. The title Shape Fill color is Purple, Accent 2, Darker 50%. On Slide 2, insert and format the table as shown. Change the Font Size of the text in the first row to 32. Insert the file name, date, and page number in the Notes and Handouts footer. In the Document Information Panel, add your name and course information and the keywords **arboretum, events** Save, and then print or submit electronically as directed by your instructor.

Project Results

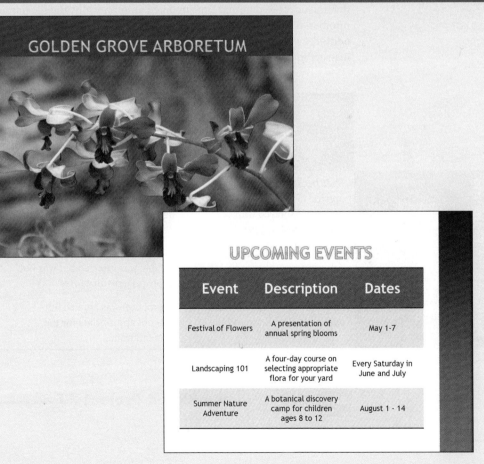

Figure 3.56

End **You have completed Project 3I**

Content-Based Assessments

GO! Solve It | Project 3J Aquatic Center

Project Files

For Project 3J, you will need the following file:

p03J_Aquatic_Center

You will save your presentation as:

Lastname_Firstname_3J_Aquatic_Center

Open the file p03J_Aquatic_Center and save it as **Lastname_Firstname_3J_Aquatic_Center** Complete the presentation by changing the Theme Fonts and then formatting the slide background of at least one of the slides using a Background Style or Solid Fill color. On Slide 4, insert and format a table with the following information regarding the fee schedule for swim passes.

Membership	Monthly	Seasonal
Youth	$10	$25
Adult	$25	$50
Senior	$15	$30

Apply appropriate animation and slide transitions to the slides. Insert a header and footer that includes the date and time updated automatically, the file name in the footer, and the page number. Add your name, your course name and section number, and the keywords **aquatic center, swim program** to the Properties area. Save and then print, or submit it as directed by your instructor.

		Performance Level		
		Exemplary: You consistently applied the relevant skills	**Proficient:** You sometimes, but not always, applied the relevant skills	**Developing:** You rarely or never applied the relevant skills
Performance Elements	Format slide with a background style	Slide background style was applied to at least one slide and text displayed with good contrast against the background.	Slide background was formatted but text did not display well against the chosen background.	Slide background was not formatted with a background style.
	Insert and format appropriate table	Appropriate table was inserted and formatted.	A table was inserted but was not appropriately formatted.	Table was not inserted.
	Apply appropriate animation	Appropriate animation was applied to the presentation.	Animation was applied but was not appropriate for the presentation.	Animation was not applied.

End You have completed Project 3J

Content-Based Assessments

GO! Solve It | Project **3K** Power

Project Files

For Project 3K, you will need the following files:

p03K_Power
p03K_Tower

You will save your presentation as:

Lastname_Firstname_3K_Power

Open the file p03K_Power and save it as **Lastname_Firstname_3K_Power** Complete the presentation by applying a theme and then formatting the slide background of one of the slides with the picture found in your student files—p03K_Tower. Adjust the size, position, fill color, and font color of the slide titles as necessary so that the title text displays attractively against the background picture. Format the background of at least one other slide using a Background Style or Solid Fill color. Insert a new Slide 3 that includes an appropriate title and a table with the following information regarding the power sources that the City uses.

Power Sources	Percent Used by City
Natural gas	32%
Hydroelectric	17%
Renewables	18%
Coal	23%
Nuclear	10%

On Slide 4, insert and format an appropriate chart to demonstrate the revenue collected from residential power sales over the past three years. Revenue in 2014 was 35.5 million dollars, in 2015 revenue was 42.6 million dollars, and in 2016 revenue was 48.2 million dollars. Apply appropriate animation and slide transitions to the slides. Insert a header and footer that includes the date and time updated automatically, the file name in the footer, and the page number. Add your name, your course name and section number, and the keywords **power sources, revenue** to the Properties area. Save and then print or submit the presentation as directed by your instructor.

Performance Level			
	Exemplary: You consistently applied the relevant skills	**Proficient:** You sometimes, but not always, applied the relevant skills	**Developing:** You rarely or never applied the relevant skills
Format two slide backgrounds with pictures and styles	Two slide backgrounds were formatted attractively and text displayed with good contrast against backgrounds.	Slide backgrounds were formatted but text did not display well against the chosen background, or only one slide background was formatted.	Slide backgrounds were not formatted with pictures or styles.
Insert and format appropriate table and chart	Appropriate table and chart were inserted and formatted and the entered data was accurate.	A table and a chart were inserted but were not appropriate for the presentation or either a table or a chart was omitted.	Table and chart were not inserted.
Apply appropriate animation	Appropriate animation was applied to the presentation.	Animation was applied but was not appropriate for the presentation.	Animation was not applied.

(left side label) Performance Elements

 End You have completed Project 3K

(right margin) PowerPoint | Chapter 3

Index

Excel Web App and, 338–339
OneNote Web App link, 356–357
spell checker, 341–343
spreadsheets as, 141, 147, 313
text in, 316–317
values (constant values)
    defined, 316
    displayed, 321
    editing, 349–350
    text, 316–317
    underlying, 321
WordArt in, 403
wrapping text, 352–355

Workspace, SharePoint, 141, 152
Wrap Text button, 190, 295, 352
wrapping text
    around pictures, 189–190, 295
    in worksheets, 352–355
Writer, 220–223. *See also* **Windows Live Essentials**
writer's identification, 248
writer's signature block, 248

X

x-axis, 329, 423
XPS. *See* **PDF**

Y

Yahoo! e-mail account, 472–473, 558–559, 606–607
y-axis, 329, 423
YouTube, presentations on, 682–683

Z

Zoom, 167–168
    defined, 152, 167
    dialog box, 610
    Print Preview and, 152–153, 198
    slider, 167